IMAGES of America

AROUND SHINNSTON

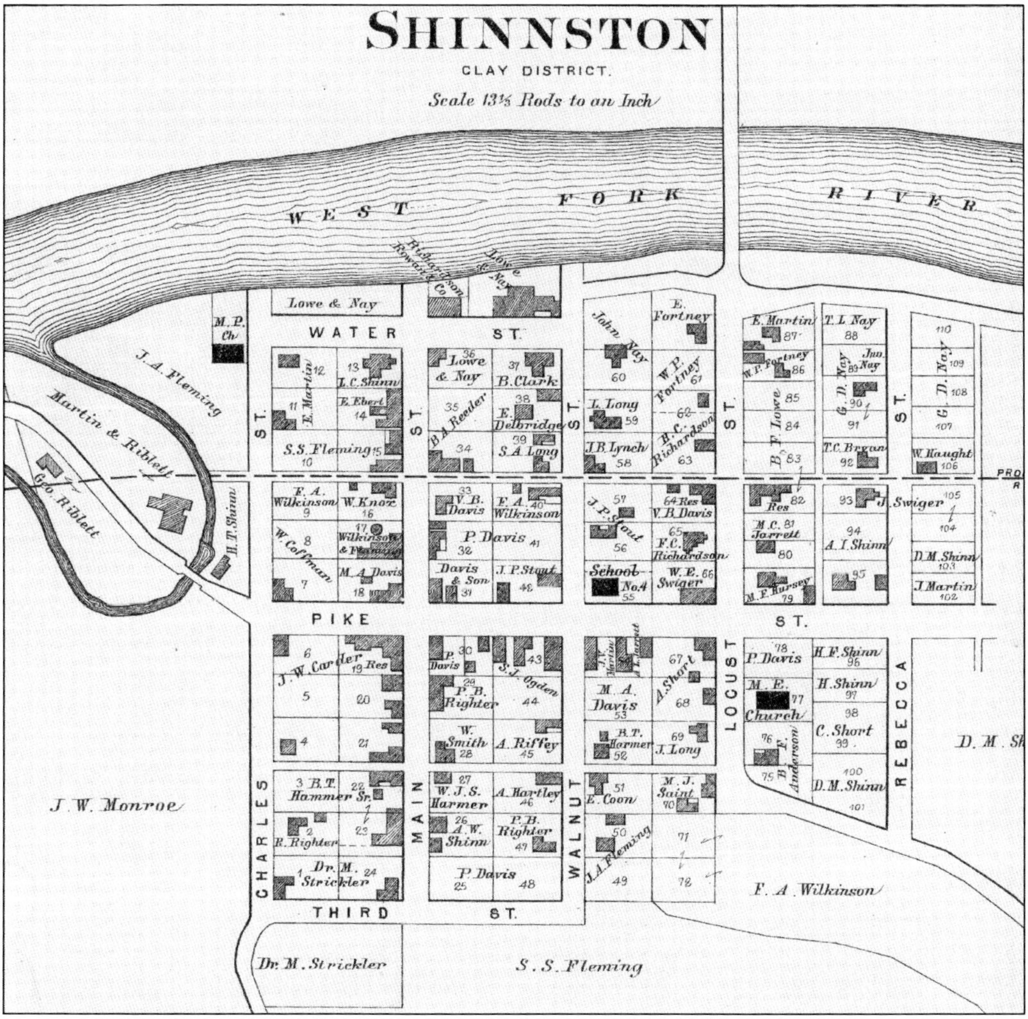

This map of Shinnston was taken from a Harrison County atlas published by D.J. Lake and Company in 1886. Note that this map was made before the railroad came through Shinnston in 1890. The original area laid out for the railroad was changed and moved closer to the river; therefore, leaving a long strip of vacant land that is known today as Davis Court. (Author's collection.)

ON THE COVER: Formerly known as "Koon's Corner," this two-story building at the southwest corner of Pike and Bridge Streets had a store in it as early as the 1870s, when Elmore Koon operated one. The building faced Bridge Street to capture potential customers coming into town from the bridge. Salem Joseph came from Beirut, Lebanon, and operated the store shown here around 1910. Salem Joseph & Brothers was a ladies' and gentlemen's furnishings store. The two-story building was demolished in 1915 to make way for the construction of the three-story structure currently standing. (Author's collection.)

IMAGES
of America

AROUND SHINNSTON

Robert P. Bice III

ARCADIA
PUBLISHING

ISBN 978-1-4671-2372-3

Published by Arcadia Publishing
Charleston, South Carolina

Printed in the United States of America

Library of Congress Control Number: 2014959586

For all general information, please contact Arcadia Publishing:
Telephone 843-853-2070
Fax 843-853-0044
E-mail sales@arcadiapublishing.com
For customer service and orders:
Toll-Free 1-888-313-2665

Visit us on the Internet at www.arcadiapublishing.com

To my parents and grandparents, who had a huge part in my historical interests and also to my silver lab, Walker J., who gave up a lot of play time so I could complete this book

Contents

Acknowledgments

So many people in my past and present have been a part of my continued interest in not only the oral and written histories of our communities, but also our photographic history. I began collecting photographs several years ago, and with each addition to my collection, my interest only grows. Many people are responsible for that growth.

With many fond memories, I would like to extend a posthumous thank-you to the people who always encouraged my interest in history and shared their knowledge of so many community happenings. If I could write an epitaph for these people, it would contain the words *listen*, *remember*, and *share*. These people include family members Bob and Betty Bice, Vic and Patty Andrick, Shirla Richardson, and Grace Scarcella as well as friends Ann Spadafore, Jim Morris, Jim and Theda Tichenor, and Judith Feaster. History can only be appreciated by someone who is willing to listen, and I learned so much from listening to all of these wonderful people.

In addition to those who allowed me to capture a piece of their family's histories in this book, I would also like to thank individuals who contributed images from businesses or who provided information for historical accuracy. These individuals include Deborah Starkey of Lowe Public Library, Jeffrey Loar of Shinnston Masonic Cemetery, Jay Harmer and Pat Kovalck of Harmer Funeral Home, "Skip" and Judy Tichenor, Ken and Patty Ashcraft, Lindsey and Viola Blare, Julie Male, Nancy Loretta, Nancy Sandy, Carolyn Ayers, Jeff Osbourn, John and Mary Rice, Debra Herndon, Les Carpenter, and Harlan "Butch" Janes.

The members of the Shinnston Historical Association were also invaluable in sharing their knowledge of business locations and histories. Many of these people have claimed home to north-central West Virginia since birth and can recount far more than could ever be found in a textbook. These individuals include Deloris Minor, Helen Jones, Wanda Ashcraft, Jackson L. Anderson, Beverly Paushel, Millie Gemondo, Bill and Karen Morgan, Sue and Virginia Livingston, Karleen Price, Chuck and Glenna Barnes, Bob and Beth Bice, Jim Feaster, Paula Harrison, and Judy Asel.

I am thankful to be a small part of these heritages.

INTRODUCTION

Four Shinn brothers settled the area now known as Shinnston in the 1770s: Levi, Clement, Jonathan, and David. The latter left and settled in Hampshire County, while the three remaining brothers each built a home in this area. Clement's home was in the vicinity commonly referred to as East Shinnston. Jonathan's home was located in the area we know as upper Station Street in downtown. Levi's home, located along Route 19, is the only still-standing structure that defines the original settlement.

In 1815, two of Jonathan Shinn's sons, Asa and (Elder) Levi Shinn, marked off streets for a town to be called Shinn's Town. Both brothers had their homes on what is now known as lower Walnut Street. The city would be called Shinnston under the 1877 charter. A 1915 charter adopted a mayor-council form of government. Since 1998, Shinnston has operated under the manager plan.

Shinnston has a well-kept record of many of its firsts. They include a gristmill (established in 1785), church (1786), store (1810), school (1813), post office (1818), fraternal lodge (1848), mayor (1852), band (1850s), bridge (1876), telephone (1886), kerosene streetlights (1886), theater (1889), railroad (1890), newspaper (1897), natural gas (1899), bank (1899), paved road (1902), waterline supply (1902), streetcar (1906), football team (1908), and electric streetlights (1918).

Streets within the downtown section of Shinnston have been given names according to the purpose that particular street served. Main Street was once populated with a school, hotels, stores, and homes. Before a bridge was built connecting the east and west sides of the West Fork River, ferries were operated; one being at this street. When getting off the ferry and coming into Shinnston, one was on the "main" street. Pike Street was the road that was known as the Fairmont-Clarksburg Pike. Walnut Street carried a tree grove of its name but was formerly named Ferry Street, recognizing another ferry operation at the riverside. Locust Street was named for the trees contained at its head, yet appropriately renamed Bridge Street when the 1876 iron structure was built. The northern end of Pike Street was David Mahlon Shinn's land and contains names of his family: Clement (father), Mahlon (David's middle name), and Rebecca (wife and mother). Station Street received its name from the railroad stop at the tracks.

Education has always been encouraged by the many buildings erected for such purpose. Some of these schools were erected by mining companies that established communities, whereas others were built by a district board of education using tax money and public funding. Many of these schools have been razed for the purpose of using the land for other things, while other buildings have simply been replaced by newer structures.

At the start of the European war in 1914, industries all over the nation were affected by the business depression. The oil and gas industries were no exception. The South Penn Oil Company was a large employer of men in the areas around Shinnston and reduced their work force to one-third time. Just a few years later, Spanish influenza was so rampant that schools shut down, churches cancelled services, sports programs were put on hiatus, and businesses temporarily closed. In addition, no Halloween celebrations occurred in the Shinnston area.

The year 1944 proved to be disastrous for many families. The turmoil of World War II was still a threat. Telegrams were arriving weekly at the telegraph office to let families know of beloved soldiers who were killed or missing in action. Then, too, the threat of mine accidents or disasters has always been a worry to the communities. Men have gotten hurt, and sometimes killed, while using equipment. Sixteen men were killed in March 1944 in an explosion at the Katherine Mine. A few months later, the disaster that came to be known as the Shinnston Tornado struck the area, killing 72 of the area citizens and injuring hundreds more. Homes, livestock, and pets were also not invisible to the path of destruction. The quick response of volunteers saved countless lives.

The images selected to be contained in this book capture some of what is considered to be the greatest building bricks of history in the Shinnston area. Bricks have been used for street paving, structure foundations, and building exteriors, but when these images themselves become bricks and are pieced together, it is then that we realize we have built our wall of life within these communities.

One

Churches and Schools

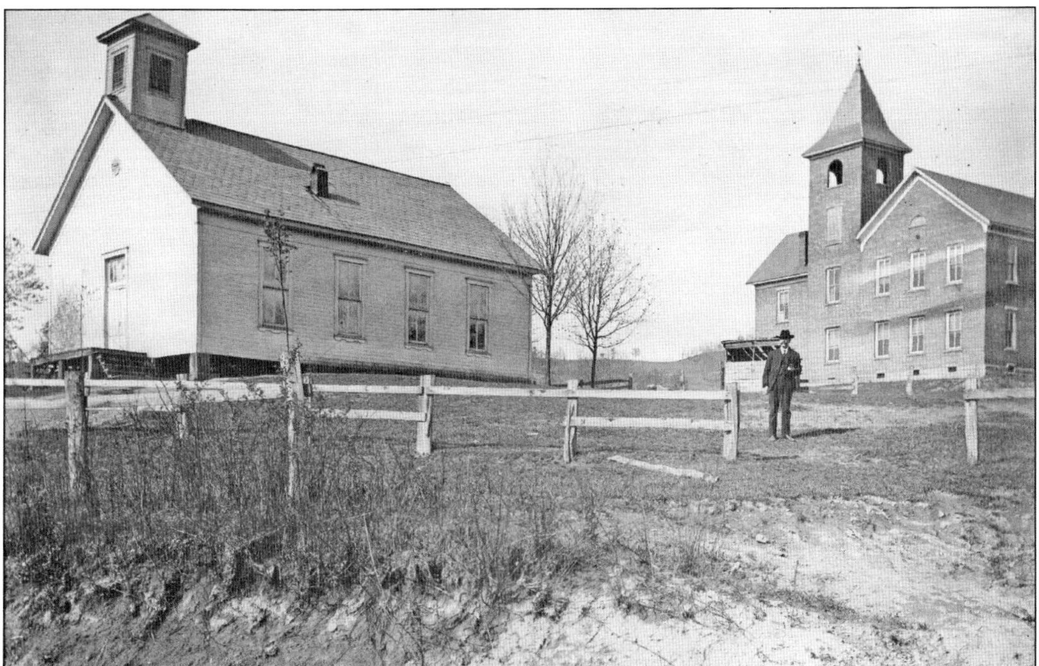

Shown here are both the grade school and Methodist Episcopal Church in Enterprise. Both buildings had bell towers. Due to consolidation in the early 1990s, the school was sold to the church trustees and is now a vacant lot of land; however, the residents of Enterprise can still hear the church bell ringing before services begin. (Courtesy of Harmer Funeral Home.)

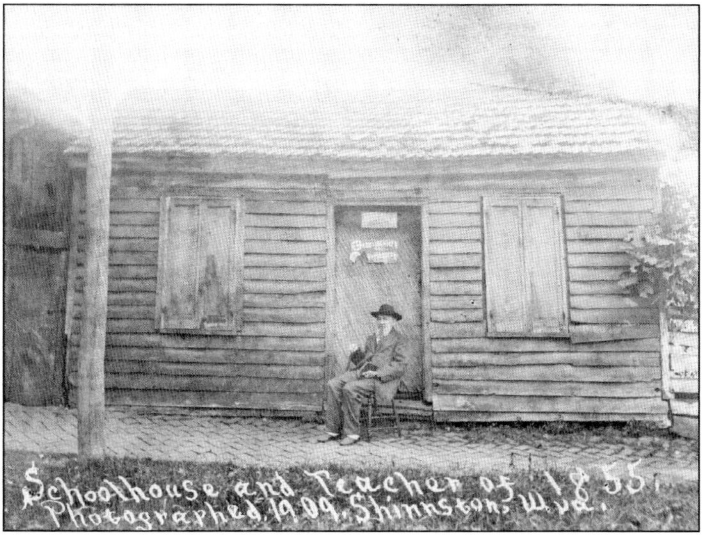

In 1909, Emory Strickler sat for this photograph in front of the schoolhouse he taught at in 1855. Born in 1823, Strickler was Harrison County's first county superintendent of public schools and later became a medical doctor. He died in 1912 at the age of 89. The signs on the schoolhouse door read "Four Fold Liniment" and "Arm & Hammer Soda." Located on upper Main Street, this school building is now a residential site. (Author's collection.)

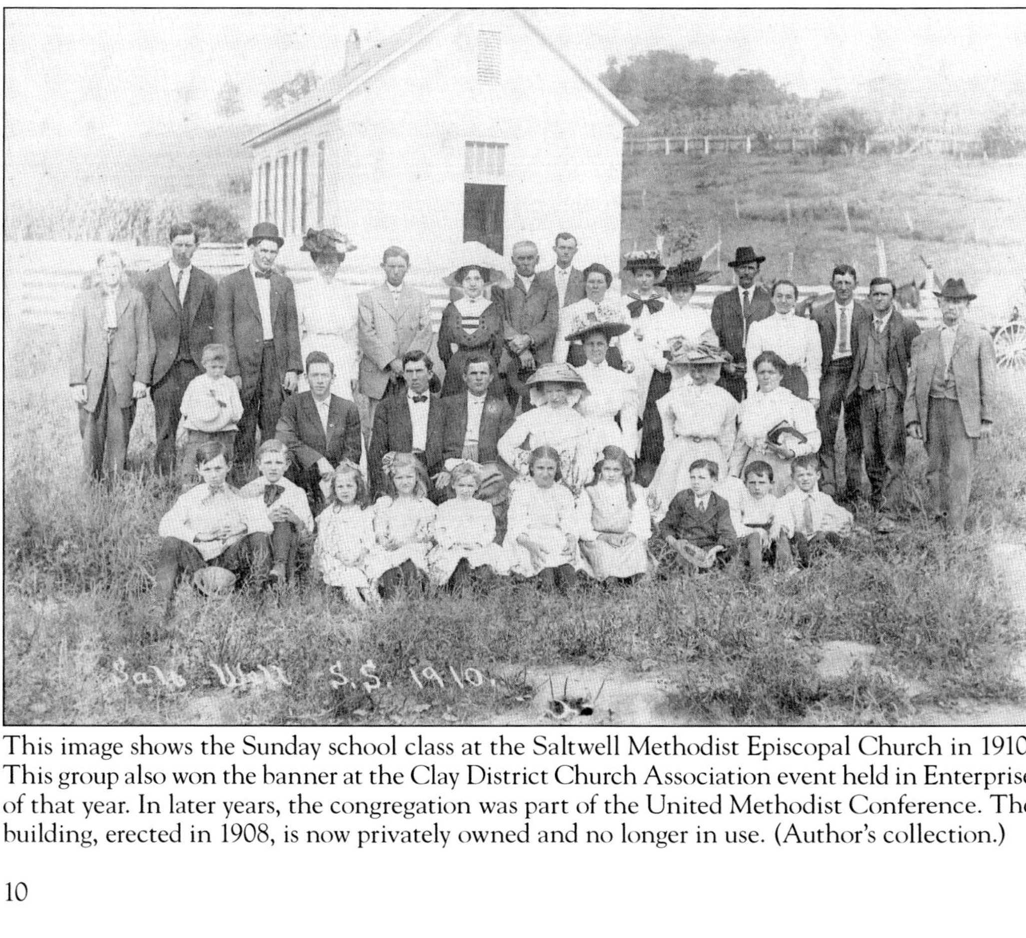

This image shows the Sunday school class at the Saltwell Methodist Episcopal Church in 1910. This group also won the banner at the Clay District Church Association event held in Enterprise of that year. In later years, the congregation was part of the United Methodist Conference. The building, erected in 1908, is now privately owned and no longer in use. (Author's collection.)

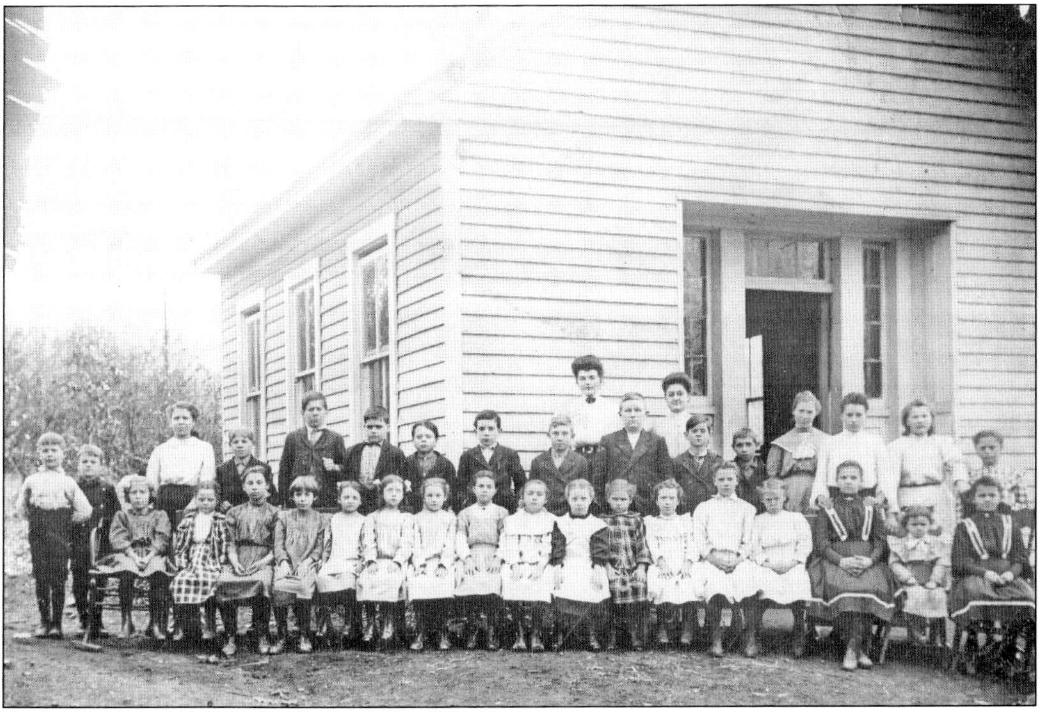

This image of the Viropa School was taken prior to 1913. Originally named Sturm School, then Briar Academy, it simply became Viropa School. The school building was sold to E.J. Sturm in 1913 and replaced by a two-room structure. There was never a brick school at Viropa. (Courtesy of Leslie "Skip" and Judy Tichenor.)

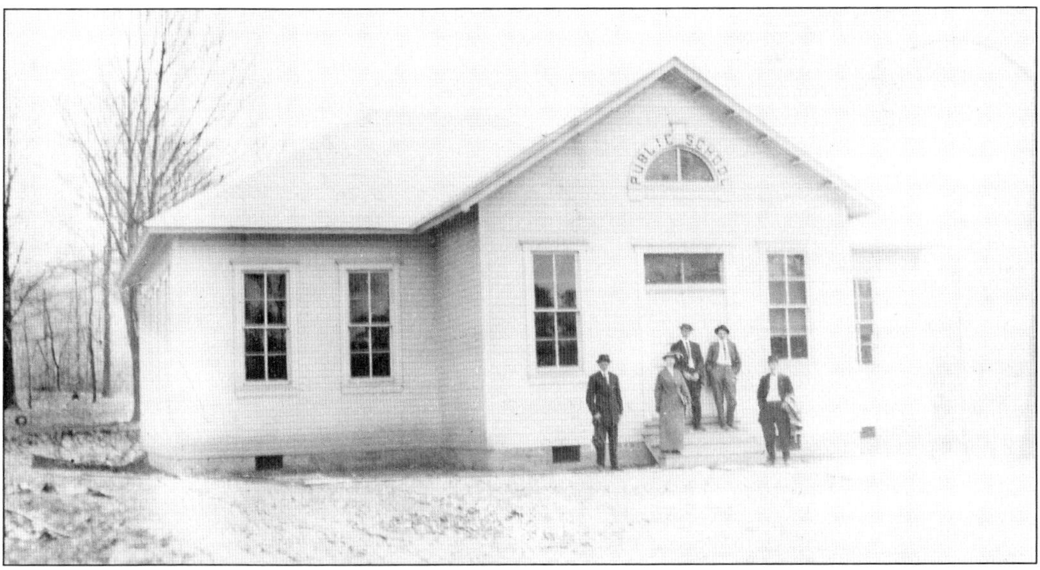

This image, captured prior to 1920, shows the new Viropa Public School. It was a two-room structure built to replace the smaller structure previously located there. The barracks at the Viropa Mine also once housed a black school. In later years, the structure became the residence of William "Tootie" and Susan (Hursey) Oliver. It was later burned, and the property was purchased by Lawrence Costelac. (Courtesy of Leslie "Skip" and Judy Tichenor.)

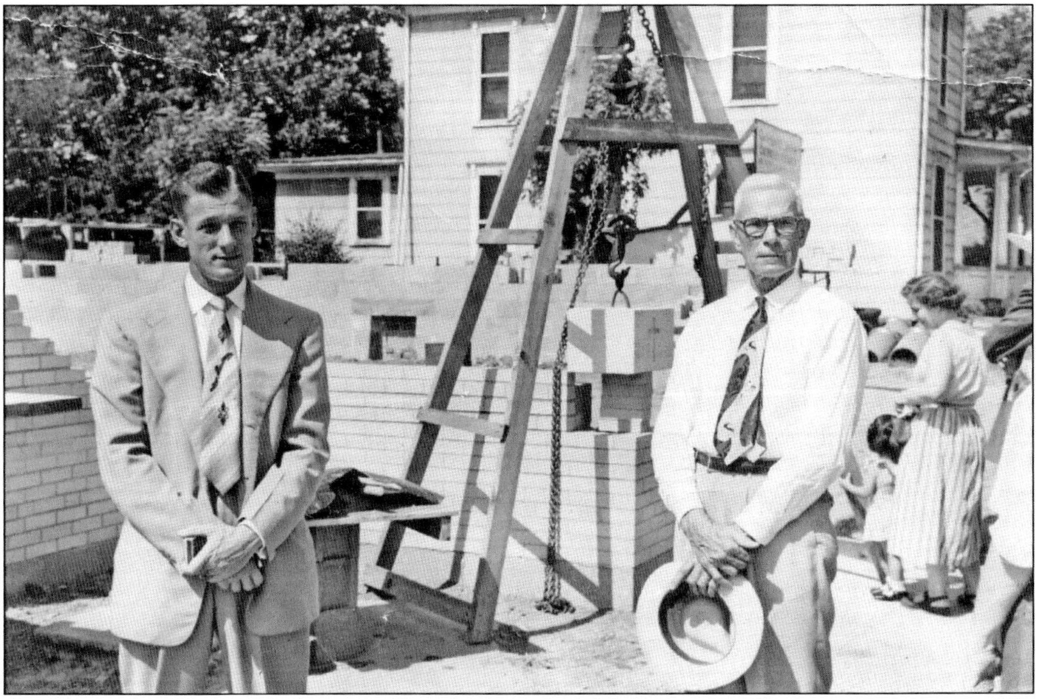

Catholic masses have had a home in Shinnston since 1923. For nearly 30 years, parishioners of St. Ann's gathered in an old harness shop that had been converted into a church building. Construction for a new building began in 1952. Pictured here are Robert and Carnel Lee Richardson, owners of Richardson Lumber & Construction Company, during the laying of the cornerstone for the present church building. (Courtesy of Bob Bice II.)

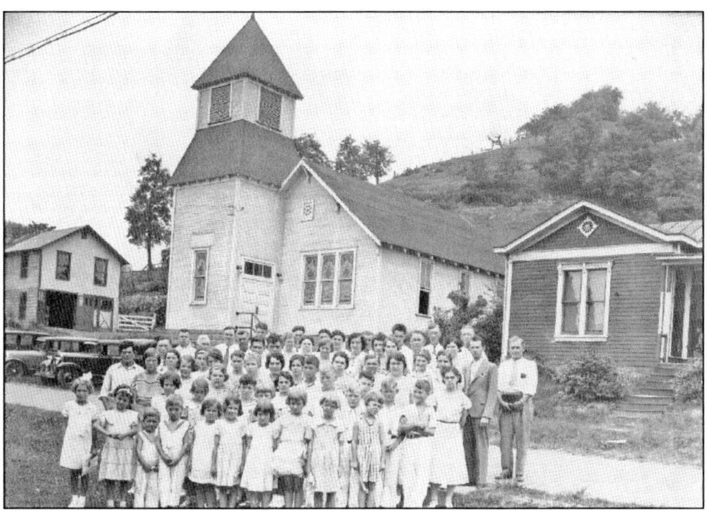

Shinnston's Evangelical United Brethren Church was started on West Side in 1923 in a one-room structure supported by locust posts. In 1932, a basement was constructed under the church containing a kitchen, bathrooms, and classrooms. Gathered here for a 10-year anniversary photograph, the congregation is now known as the Otterbein United Methodist Church. (Courtesy of Beth Andrick Bice.)

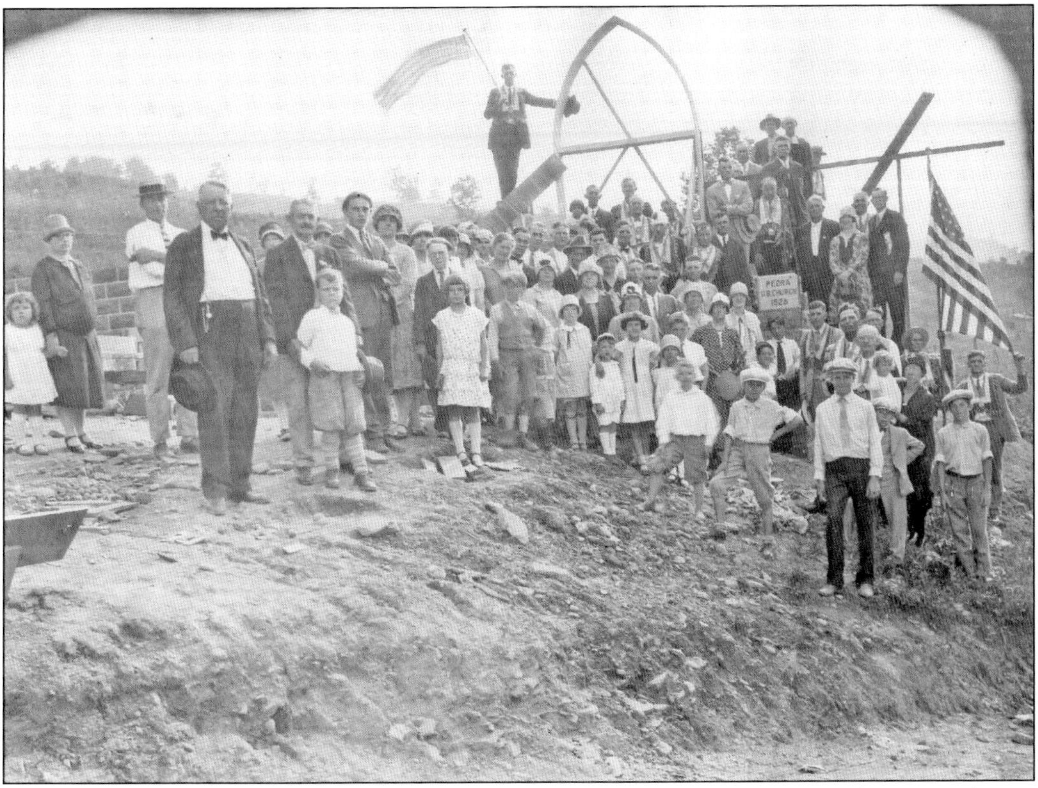

Many church members gathered together near the cornerstone for a photograph in 1928 during the construction of the Peora United Brethren Church. Some of the families pictured include the Cunninghams, Richardsons, Sturms, and Zirkles. Carnel Lee "C.L." Richardson is shown holding the American flag. The building and congregation are now known as the Peora United Methodist Church. (Author's collection.)

West Virginia secretary of state A. James Manchin, fourth from left, was present on Sunday, November 5, 1978, for the 50th anniversary of the Peora United Methodist Church. Some of the families pictured include the Asels, Blares, Carpenters, Cunninghams, Salernos, and Thompsons. (Courtesy of Mary Rose and Ina Jean Carpenter.)

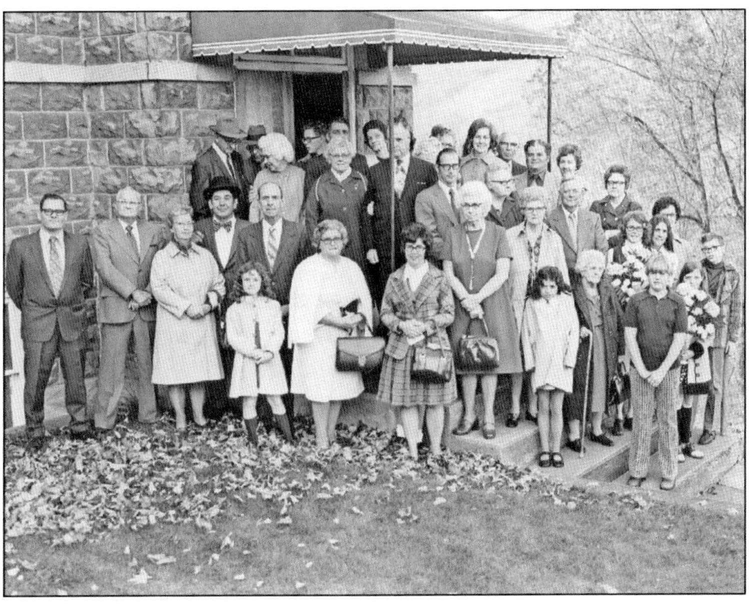

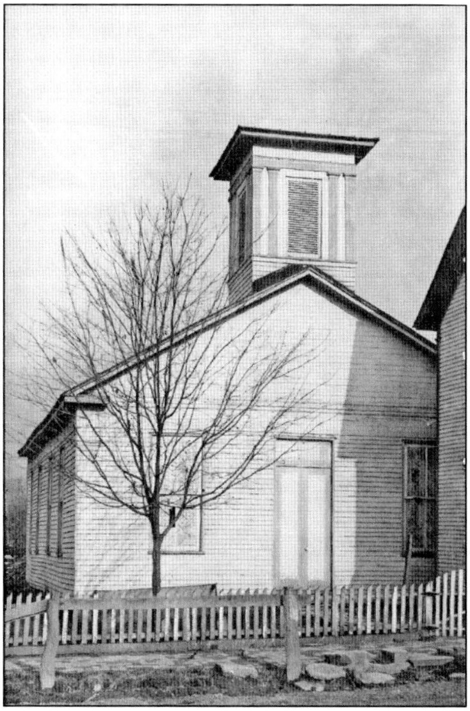

The building pictured here was constructed by John Nay and Bart Clark in 1854 and located on upper Bridge Street in Shinnston. This was the second home to the Methodist Episcopal Church, but the congregation moved to a new building at the northeast corner of Pike and Rebecca Streets in 1912. This structure was torn down in 1914 by Benjamin Anderson, then-owner of the building and lot on which it stood. (Author's collection.)

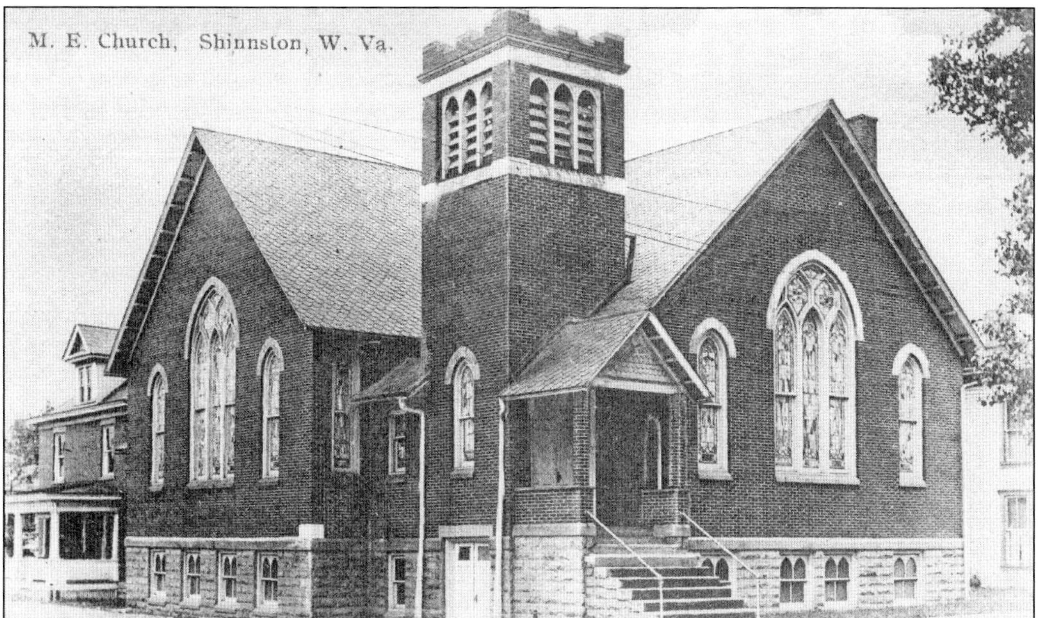

The First United Methodist Church congregation is the oldest Methodist congregation in Harrison County. This structure was erected during the 1911–1912 year at the northeast corner of Pike and Rebecca Streets. During the 1944 tornado, the church served as a relief station along with a temporary morgue in the basement. In October 1972, the church building was demolished. The current one was built in 1976. During the interim period, members of the church gathered in the nearby Epworth Center for services and worship. (Author's collection.)

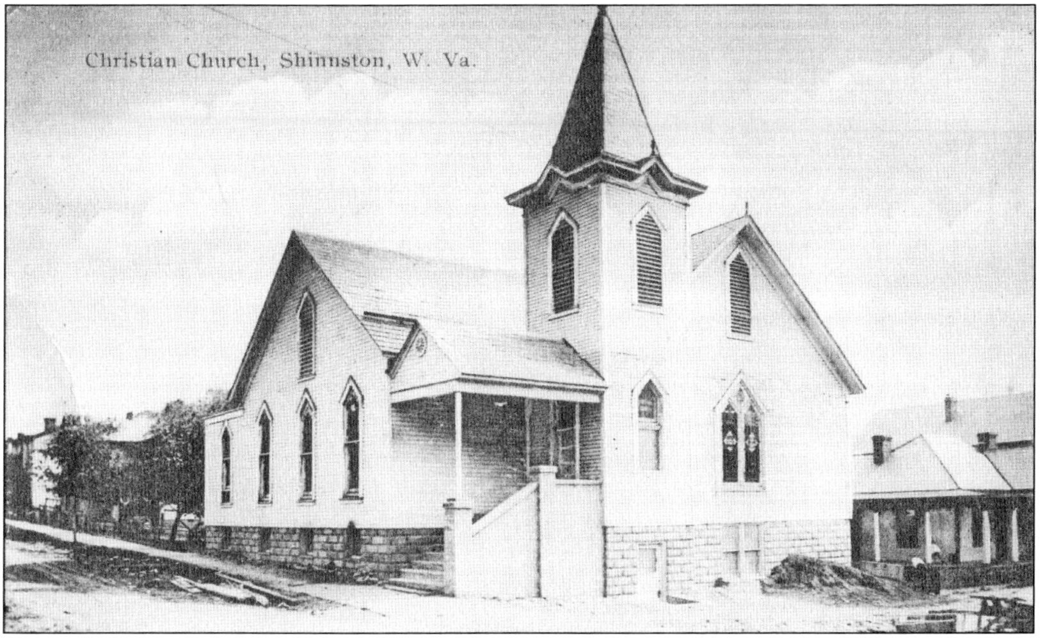

The Christian Church of Shinnston was formed in 1905, and a building at the corner of Charles, Pike, and Monroe Streets was dedicated July 8, 1906. This postcard image, taken shortly after the 1920 addition of a basement and classrooms, shows a pile of fresh dirt just under the basement's double windows. A rare and beautiful trait to its interior is the curved dual stairway that leads to a balcony overlooking the sanctuary. (Courtesy of Glenda Toth.)

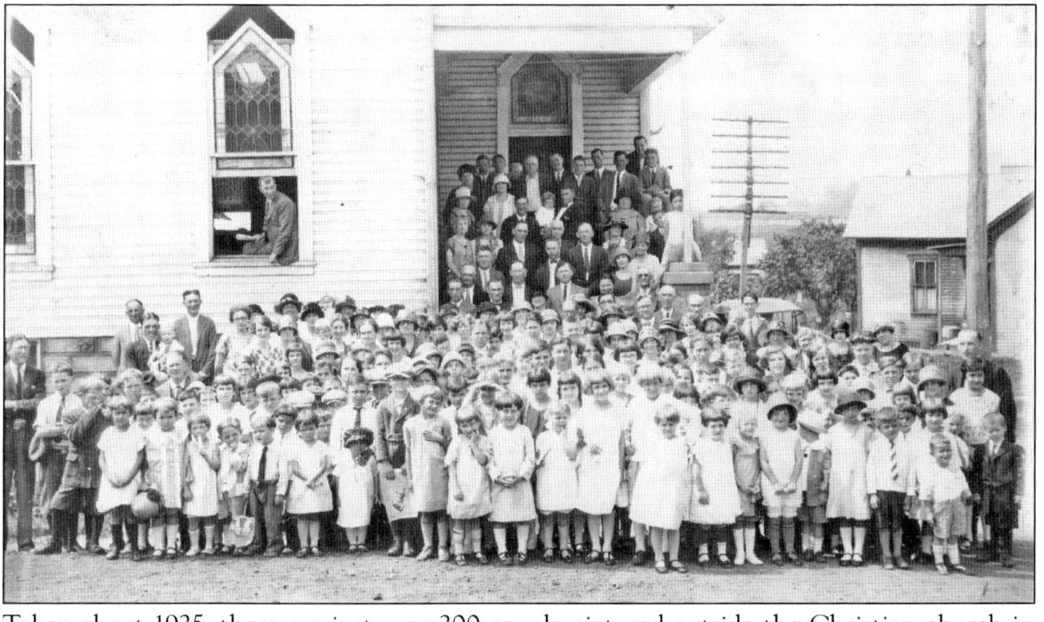

Taken about 1925, there are just over 200 people pictured outside the Christian church in Shinnston, now known as the Charles Street Christian Church. Many stand on Charles Street/Saltwell Road, as there is not enough room on the sidewalk. Note the window, which has one pane raised from the bottom to let cool air in, while the other is lowered from the top to let the rising warm air escape. (Courtesy of Karen Drain.)

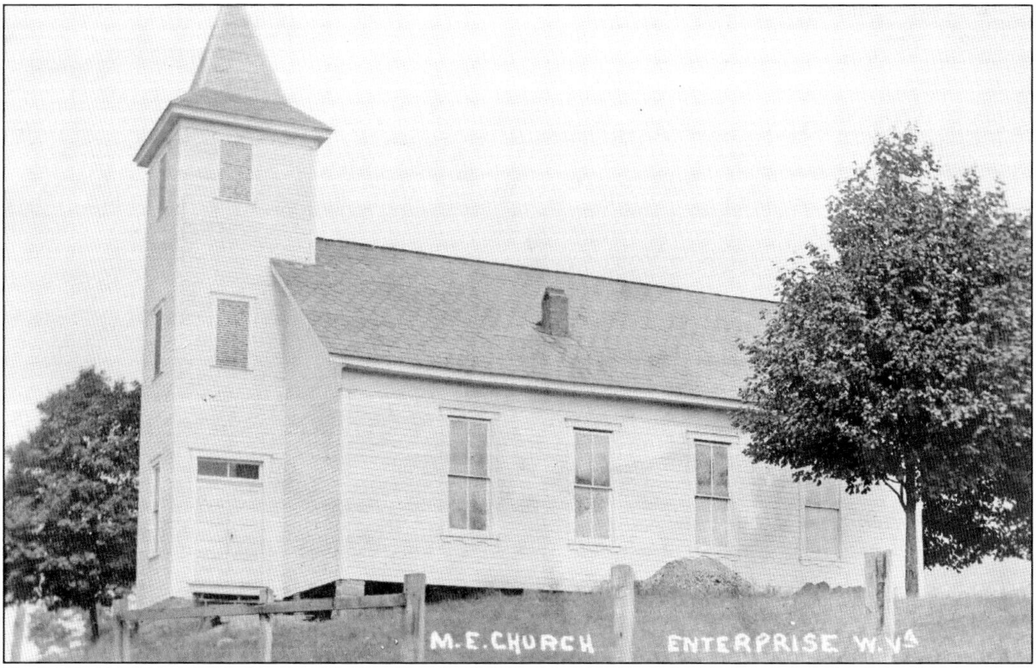

The Methodist Episcopal Church at Enterprise was built in 1897. Taken before a basement was added to the building, stone pillars for structure support can be seen in the photograph. The windows of the church were painted white and marked with lines to give the appearance of frosted glass. The large coal pile under the third window was used to burn in the stoves for heat. The church is now part of the United Methodist Conference. (Author's collection.)

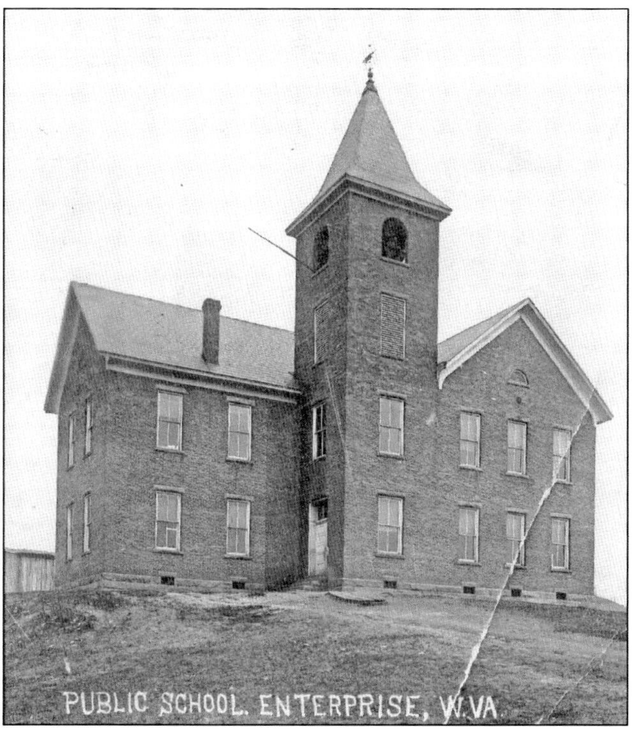

The Enterprise Public School, originally a six-room structure, was completed in 1899. The foundation was made of cut stone, its brick walls were 20 inches thick, and the roof was slate. Each room had two coal stoves for heat. More rooms were later added to the structure, and a multipurpose building was also joined to the property. Due to school consolidation, the doors closed for good in 1990. (Author's collection.)

This church building was the old home of the Baptist congregation of the Shinnston area. Built in 1891, this structure was located on upper Rebecca Street and was in use until the new yellow brick building was constructed in 1915. (Courtesy of Harmer Funeral Home.)

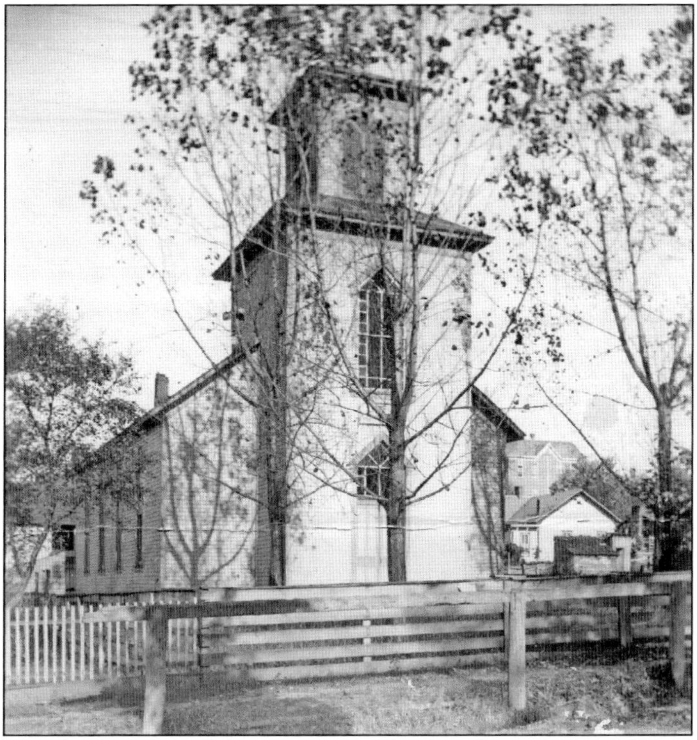

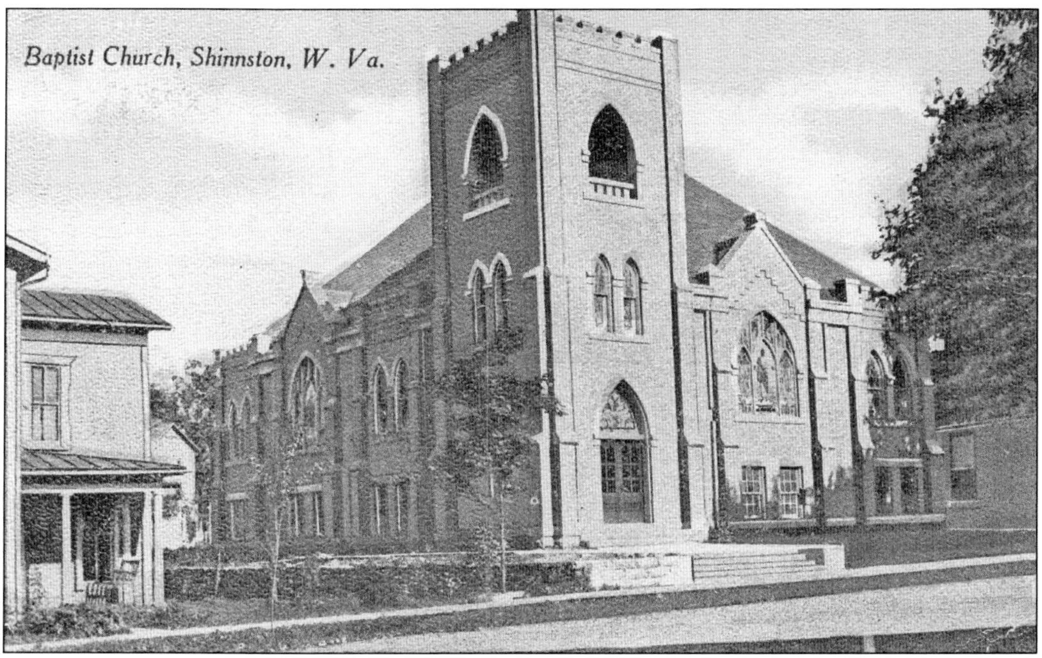

The First Baptist Church of Shinnston moved into this new building on January 10, 1916. Rare for most churches, the steps to the sanctuary, which is on the second level, are enclosed within the building. The interior contains some of the area's finest examples of stained-glass windows. The church's remarkable Moeller organ was originally purchased in 1920 and continues to be in use today. (Author's collection.)

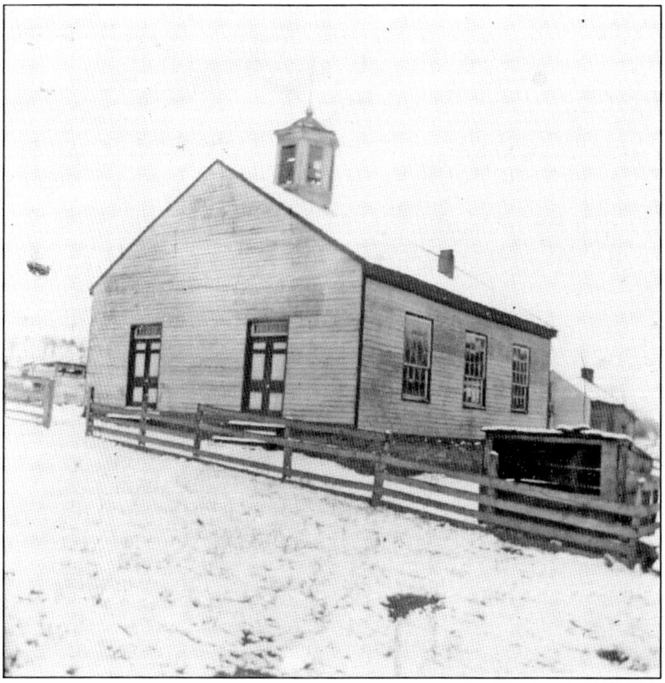

The first house of worship for the Methodist Protestant Church in Shinnston was located along the riverbank on the south side of lower Charles Street. The congregation had been organized in 1841 by Rev. Asa Shinn. This building was constructed in 1852 and was in use until the new building was dedicated on Main Street in 1898. (Courtesy of Harmer Funeral Home.)

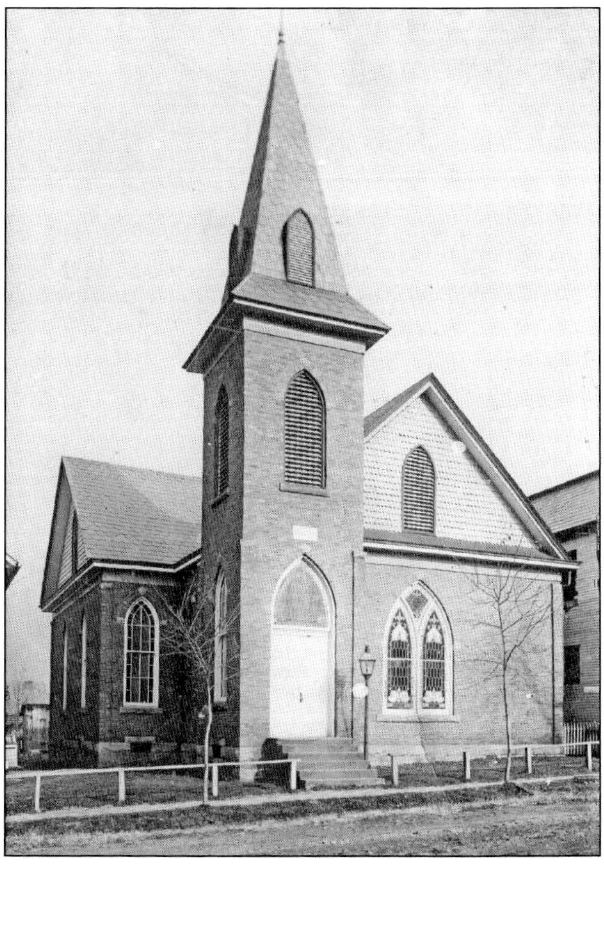

The Methodist Protestant Church on Main Street was constructed in 1897–1898 on land that had been donated by Peter B. Righter to replace the previous structure on lower Charles Street. The building contains very fine stained-glass windows, most of which have "In Memory Of" inscriptions to accompany them. The congregation is today known as the Christ Church United Methodist. (Author's collection.)

This image, taken in 1906, shows the public school on Mahlon Street in Shinnston. All grade levels attended this school, since no separate high school building existed for the 30 enrolled students. There were two faculty members. Built in 1895, the building had two major additions over the years. (Author's collection.)

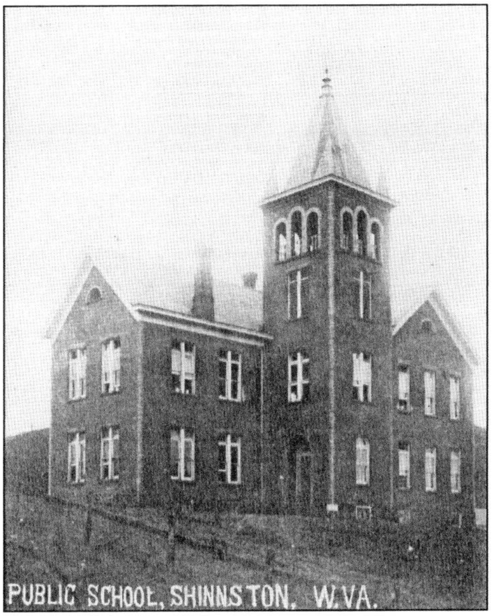

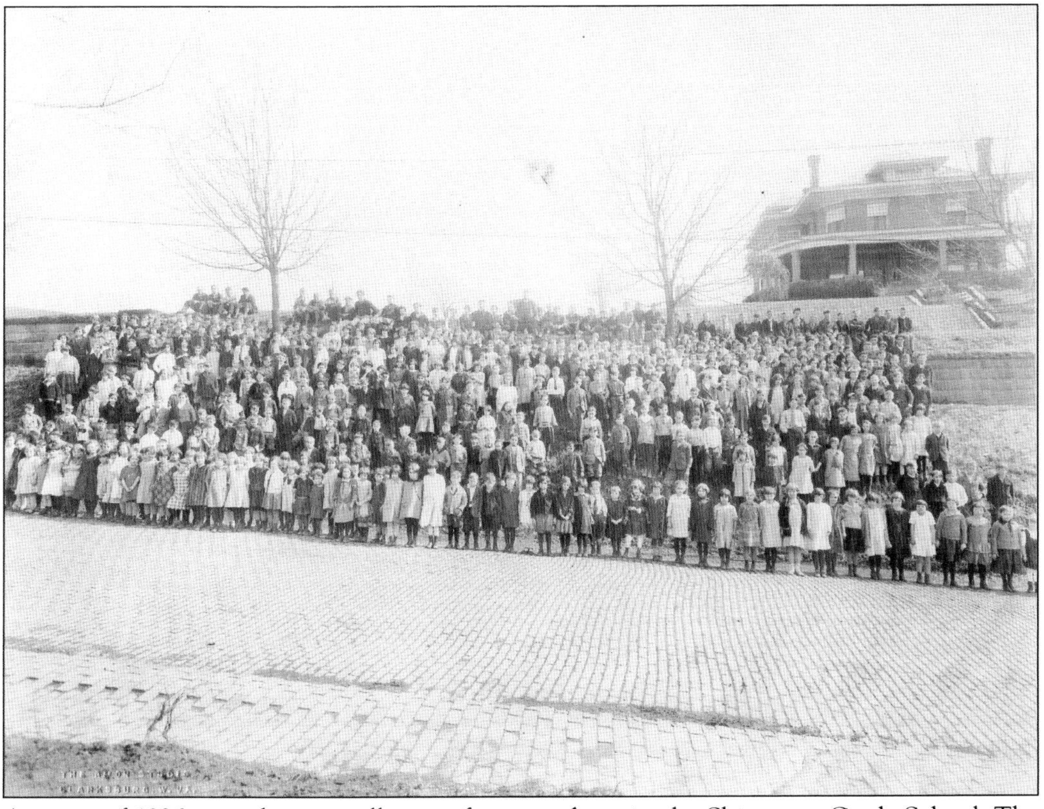

Autumn of 1926 saw a huge enrollment of area students in the Shinnston Grade School. The students are gathered in lines on the hillside between the brick constructed East Avenue and the Orville L. Lowe home, overlooking the school. Lowe was a liveryman and had his buggies, surries, and wagons kept on upper Bridge Street, where the Moose is currently located. The construction of the stone wall surrounding the residence was started in March 1915. (Author's collection.)

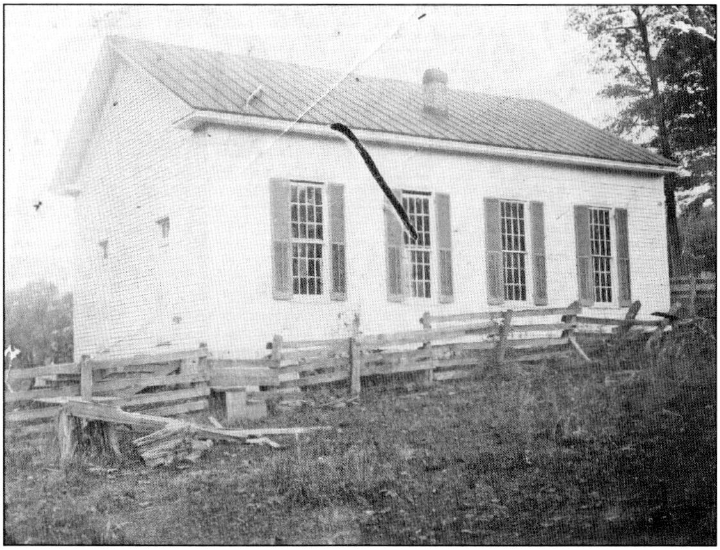

This image of the Shinn's Run Church was taken by Rose Smith. The church was first organized in 1873 with 10 charter members. The membership grew greatly entering the 20th century under the leadership of Rev. W.N. Davis. A graveyard is located adjacent to the church. The building today is a much larger structure and has been known as Shinn's Run Baptist Church for many years. (Courtesy of William Smith Righter.)

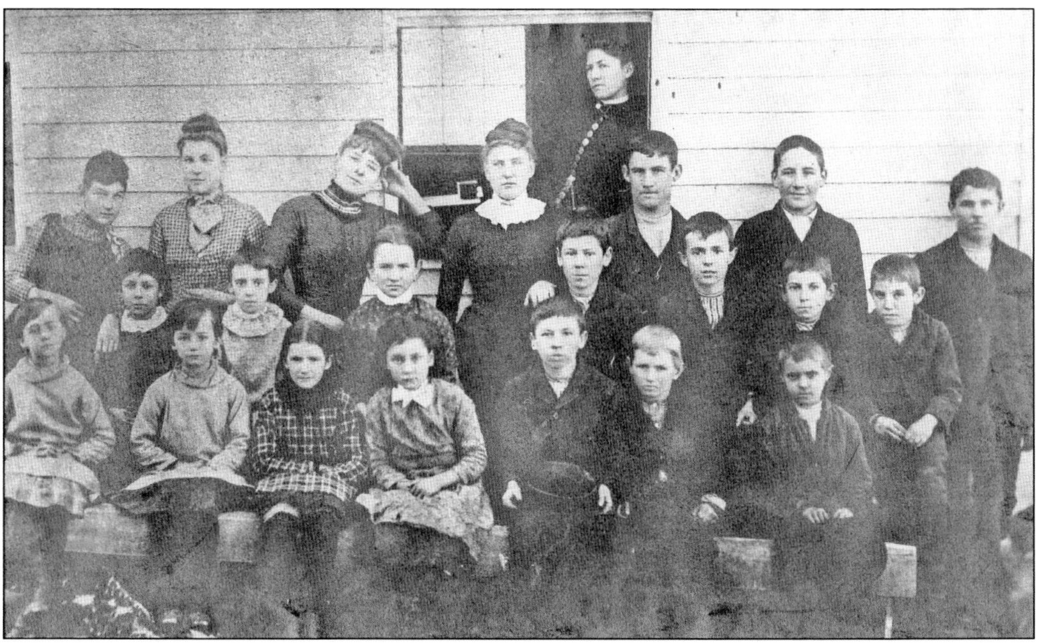

Rose Lee Smith was the teacher (pictured in the window) when this photograph of the one-room Shinn's Run School was taken in the very early 1900s. The building was remodeled in May 1921 and was purchased in 1965 by the members of the Shinn's Run Extension Homemakers to use for club meetings. Since 2005, it has been owned by the Shinn's Run Baptist Church. (Courtesy of William Smith Righter.)

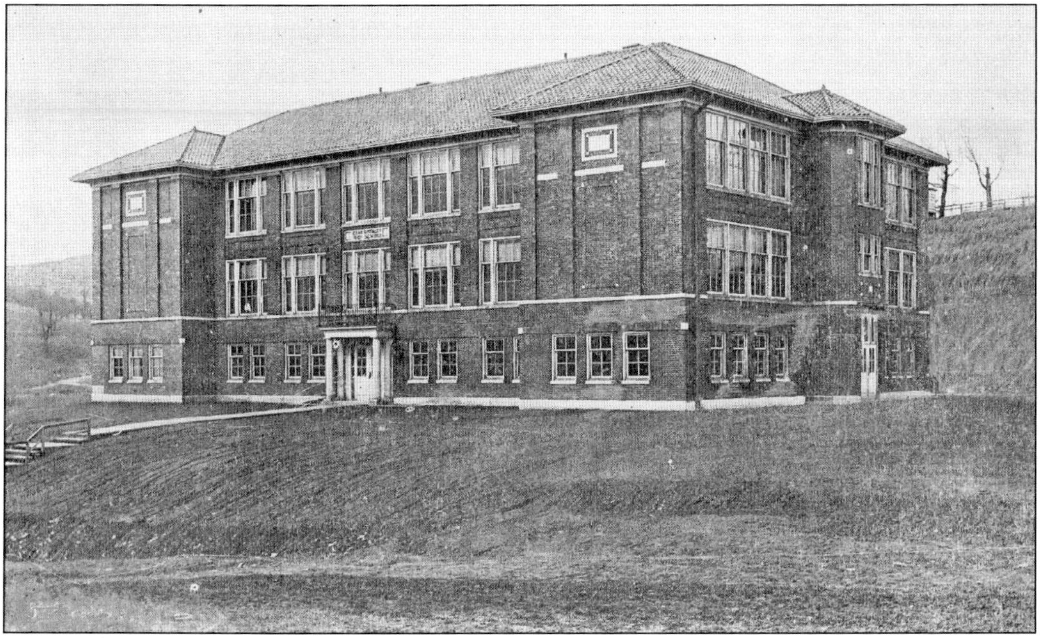

The cornerstone for Shinnston High School was laid on August 23, 1913, by the Masonic Lodge. Frank Packard was the architect, and Charles Short was the awarded contractor. Each district had its own board of education, instead of the county-wide system used today. Consolidated into a new building with Lumberport High School in the fall of 1978, the structure was later used for middle and intermediate schools, as well as Rife's Medical Arts Building. (Author's collection.)

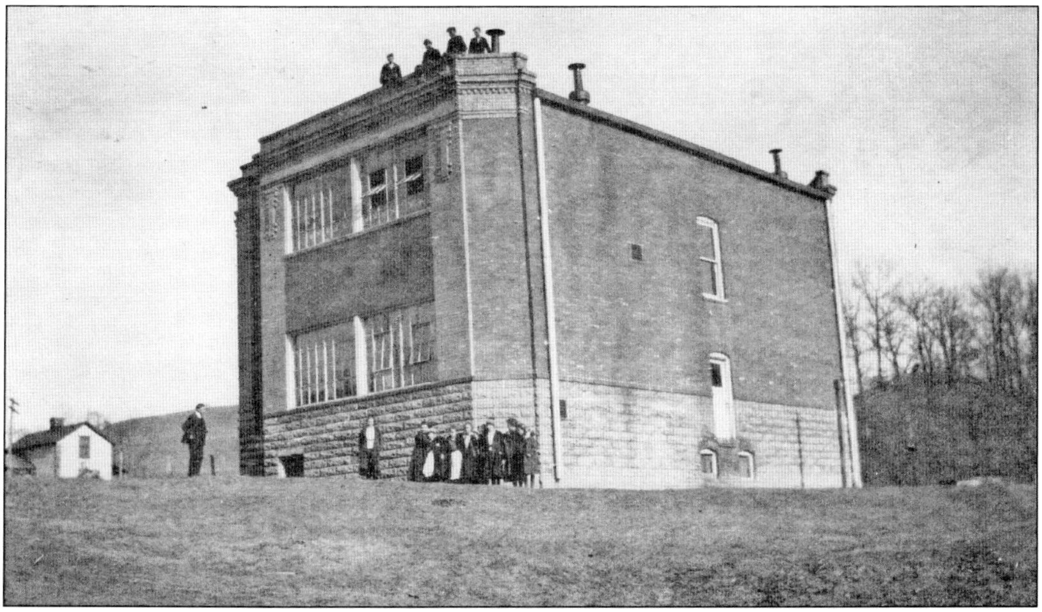

When the Fairmont Coal Company opened up their mine at Gypsy, they developed the community into one that would attract miners with families to come and live. The tradition of a company store and houses were constructed, along with a church and a school building. Shown here is the back side of the two-story Gypsy School about 1915. Once located along the east side of Route 19, the school was razed many years ago. (Author's collection.)

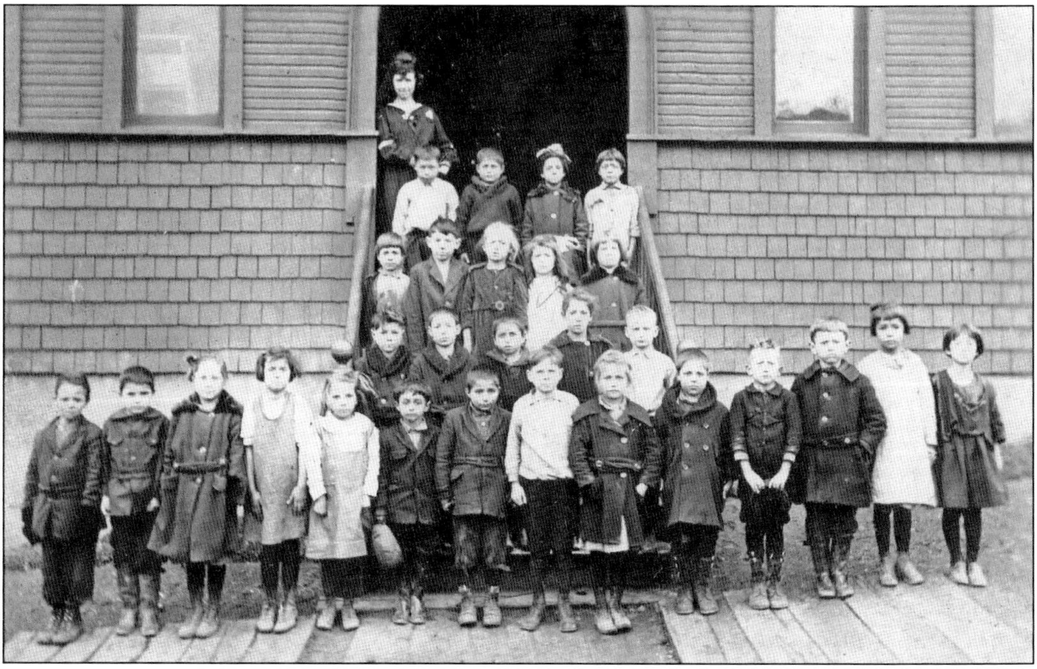

Children from the communities of Owings and Willard attended school here when this photograph was taken at the Owings School on December 13, 1922. Teacher Miss Martin is pictured in the doorway. The two-room building was located on a lot adjacent to the church at Owings and was erected by the board of education in 1911. (Author's collection.)

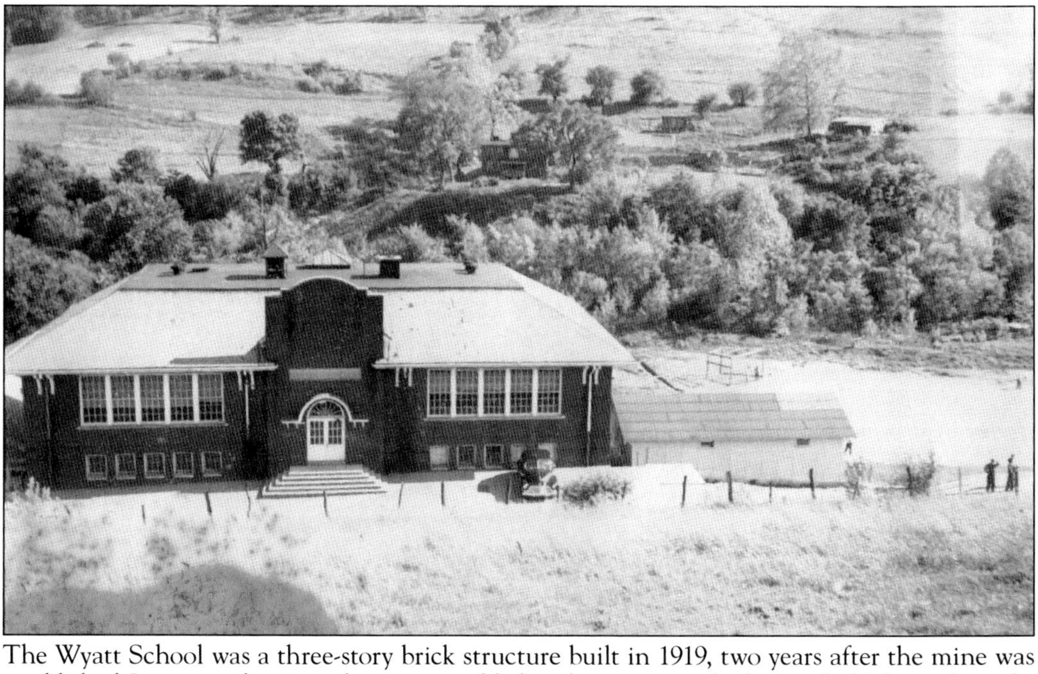

The Wyatt School was a three-story brick structure built in 1919, two years after the mine was established. Later, a cafeteria and gym were added to the property, the latter of which was brought in by rail from the 1928 Chicago Expo, where it was part of the West Virginia display. An arson fire destroyed the school in January 2014. (Courtesy of Tom Moore.)

Two

Sports

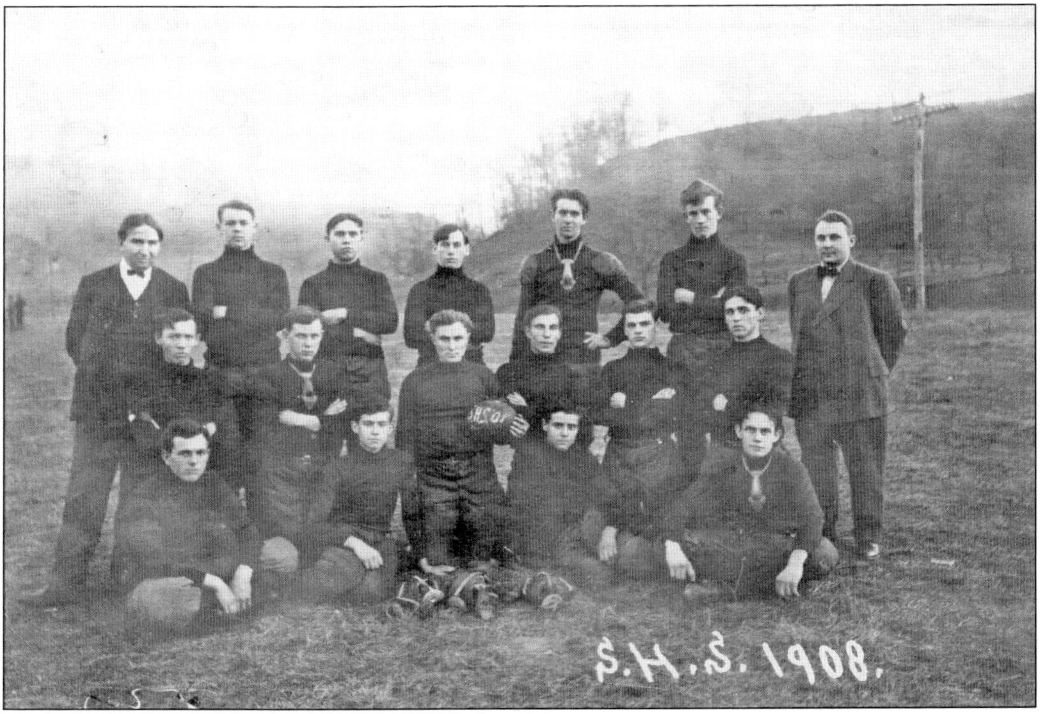

In 1908, all grade levels attended the public school on Mahlon Street, as no separate high school building existed for the 30 students enrolled. This photograph shows the first football team. The team travelled for their second game to Fairmont via streetcar and caught a train to Morgantown. One player was put in the hospital with a broken collar bone, one had a dislocated knee, and yet another had an injured wrist. Morgantown defeated Shinnston, 67-0. (Author's collection.)

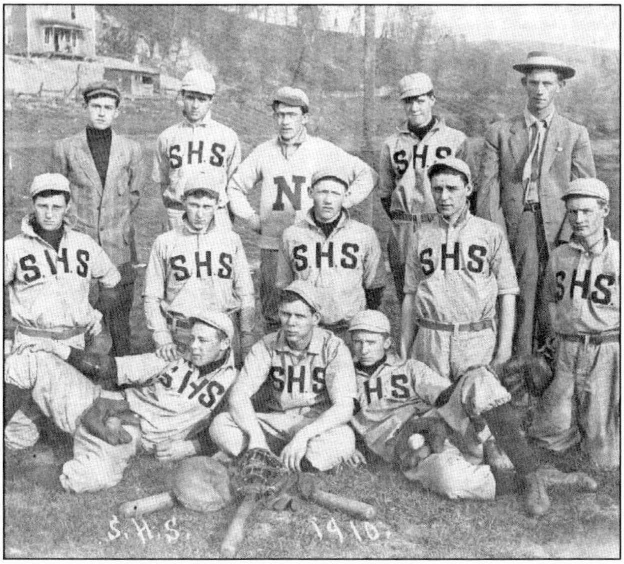

In its earliest years, Shinnston High School (SHS) sports were part of the Monongahela Valley High School League. For four consecutive years, the baseball team at SHS was the league champion. Shown here is the undefeated 1910 team on the Monroe Street field currently used by the Little League. Pictured from left to right are (first row) Clark Pigott, Henson Woofter, and Dude McGee; (second row) Lawrence Sandy, Leslie Wyatt, John Lowe, Edgar Harmer, and Jimmy Barnes; (third row) Camden Conaway, Harold Jarrett, Coach McCarthy, William Finlayson, and Harvey Ferguson. (Author's collection.)

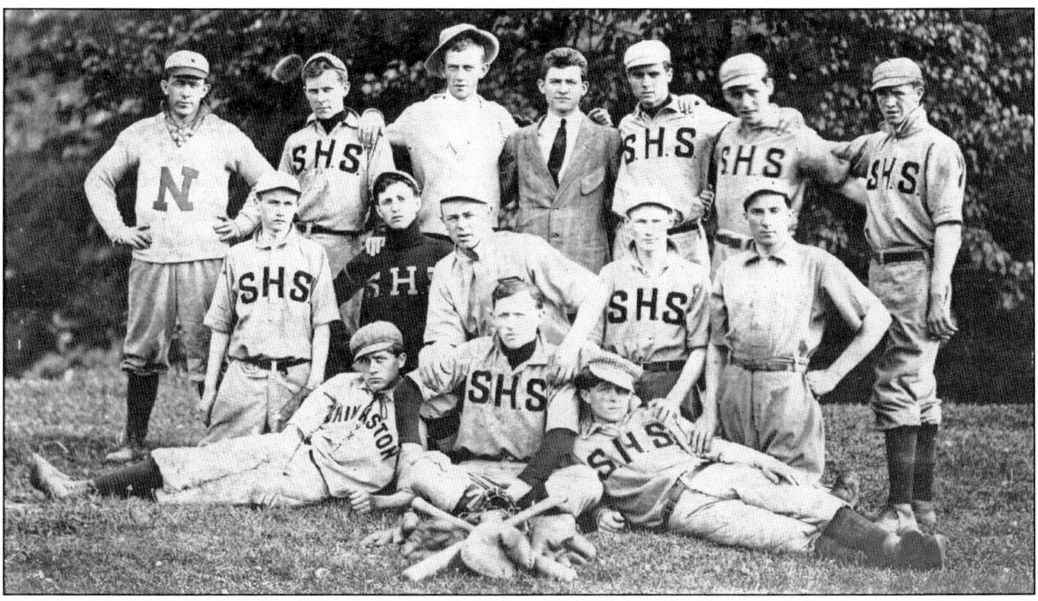

Only one game was lost for Shinnston High School's 1911 baseball team. Members pictured here from left to right are (first row) pitcher Earl Johnson, catcher Okey Shreve, and pitcher Dale Johnson; (second row) unidentified, Lawrence Sandy, John Lowe, Jimmy Barnes, and Russell Jaynes; (third row) coach W.E. "Mac" McCarthy, Leslie Wyatt, assistant manager Harvey Ferguson, manager Camden Conoway, Harold Jarrett, Edgar Harmer, and Bill Finlayson. Earl Johnson pitched against the Cincinnati Reds when they came to Clarksburg for an exhibition game in 1917. (Author's collection.)

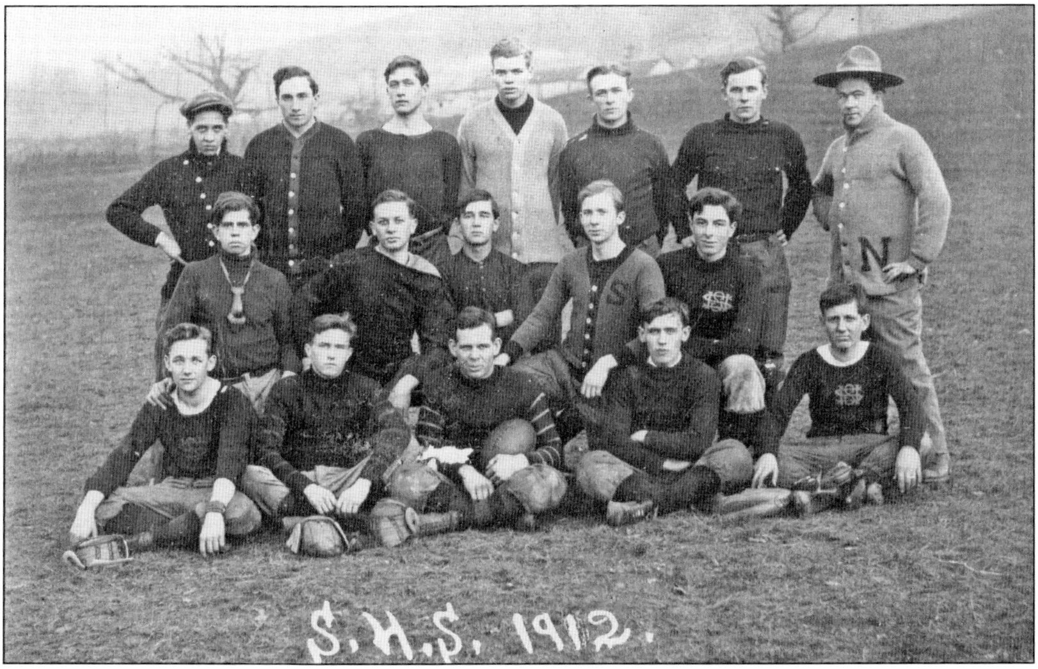

Shinnston High School's football team is shown here in 1912. Pictured from left to right are (first row) Edwin Watkins, James Finlayson, Henson Woofter, Paul Lowe, and Walter Burnett; (second row) Lester Shreve, Paul Pigott, Loy Griffin, Robert McGee, and Allen Startzman; (third row) Harold Sturm, Russell Jaynes, Earl Johnson, Lynn Robey, Dale Johnson, Leslie Wyatt, and Coach William McCarthy. (Author's collection.)

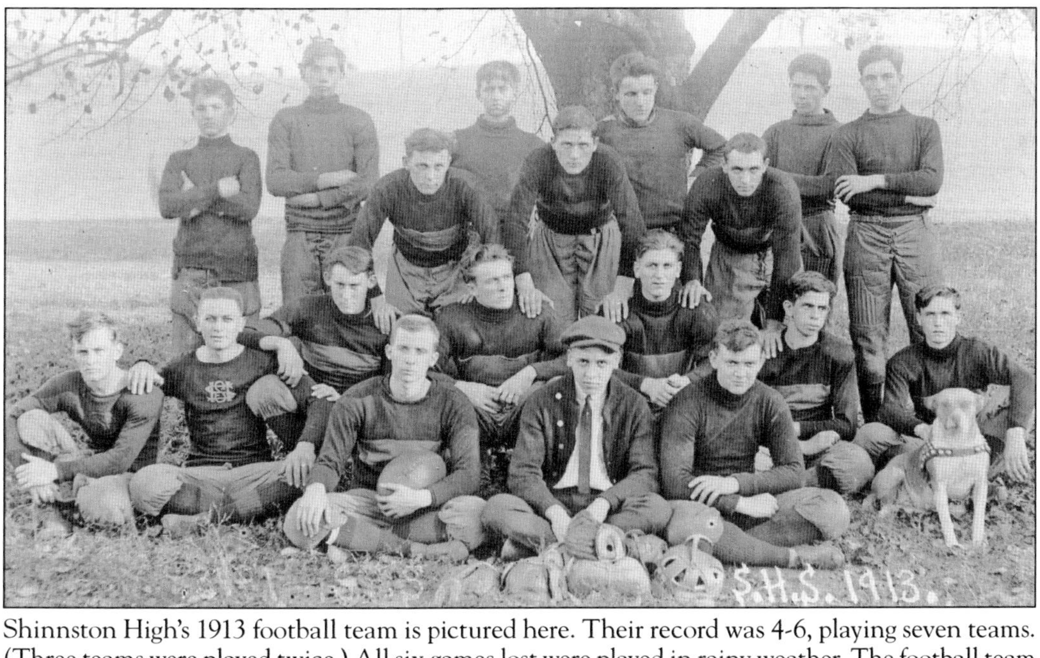

Shinnston High's 1913 football team is pictured here. Their record was 4-6, playing seven teams. (Three teams were played twice.) All six games lost were played in rainy weather. The football team grew in number each year as more boys became interested in the game. Many members of this team were in their senior year of high school when this image was captured. (Author's collection.)

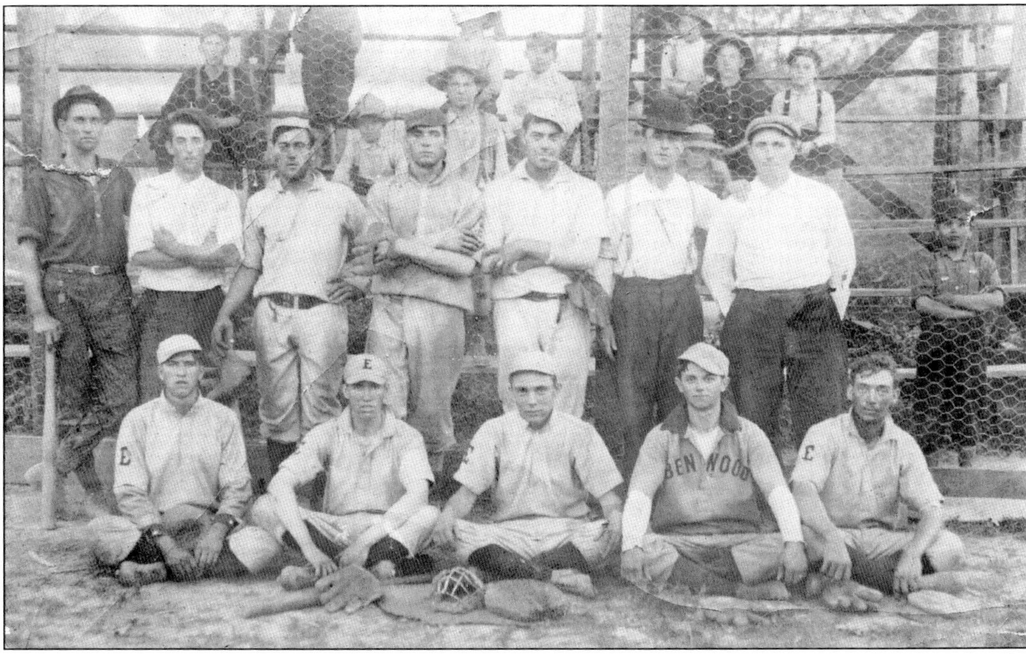

The Enterprise Mine baseball team is shown here around 1908. Several of the players have the letter "E" on their arm. Some miners were on teams at mines they previously worked, as evident with the Benwood jersey. The baseball diamond in Enterprise was located directly across the ravine from the Enterprise Public School. This area has now been coal stripped. (Author's collection.)

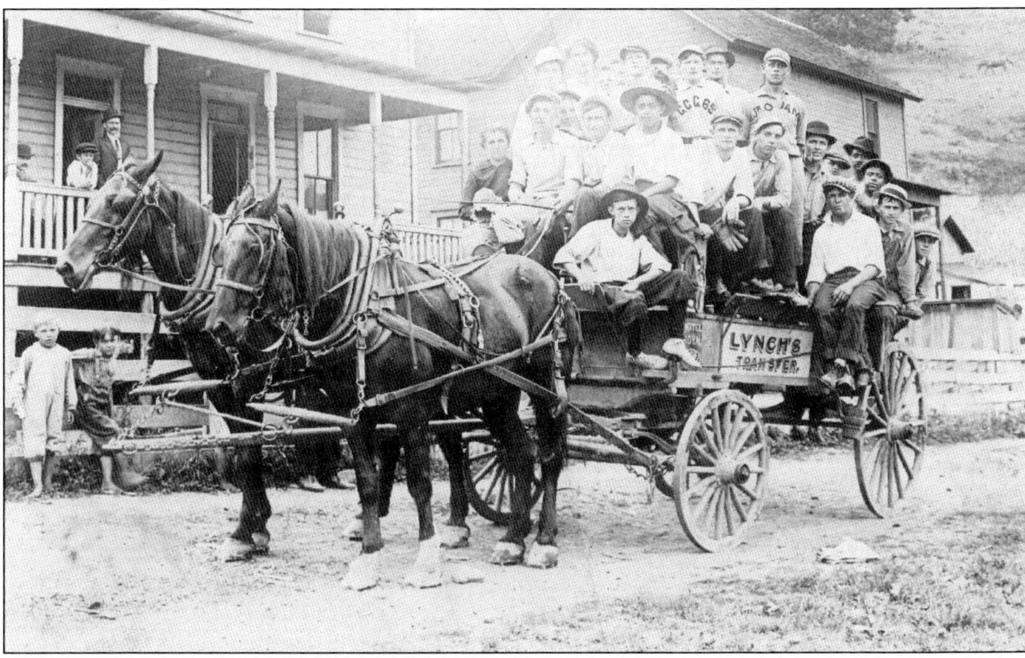

The Lynch's Transfer wagon and team were used to haul the baseball team from Consolidation Coal Company's Solon Mine. Twenty-four people are on the wagon, including one woman and at least two boys. Note the Hotel Royal sign also posted on the wagon for advertisement. Most mining baseball team games were played on Sunday afternoons. (Author's collection.)

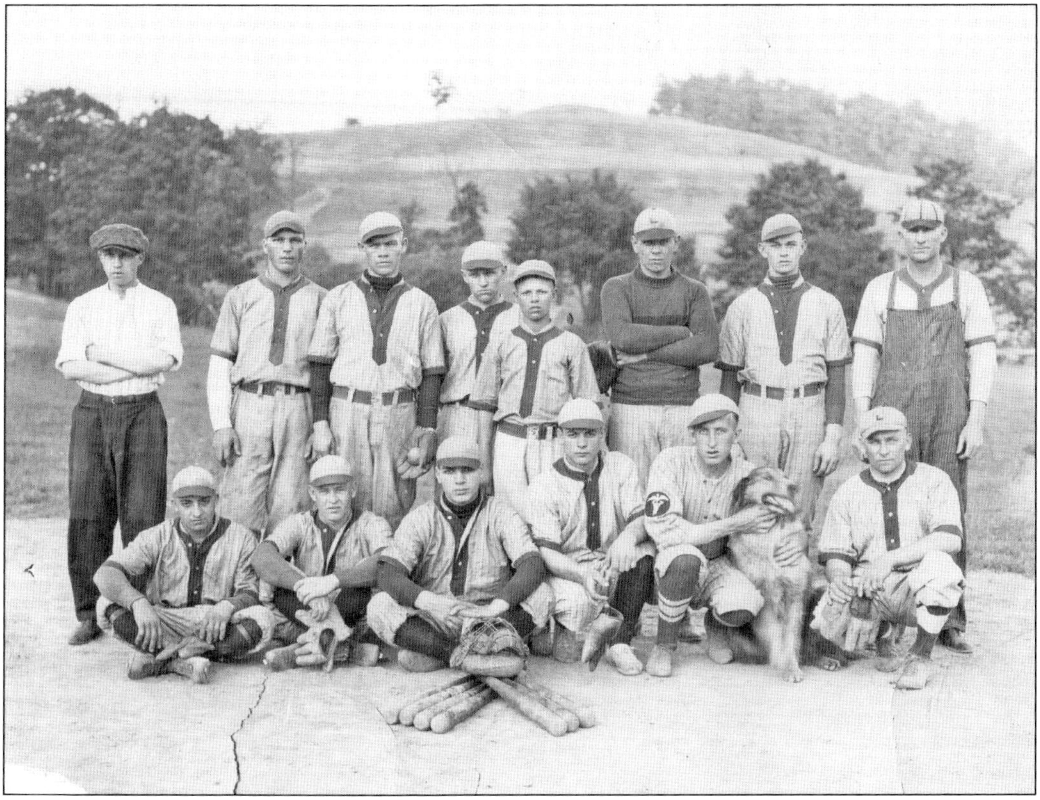

Many mining communities formed baseball teams among the miners, which enabled playtime with other mining communities. Oftentimes, miners tried to be hired at the mines where the best ballplayers were working. This image shows the 1918 baseball team formed at the Gypsy Mine. John Hogue is at far right in the first row. Note the child standing center, an example of how sons worked in the mines to provide more income to the household. (Author's collection.)

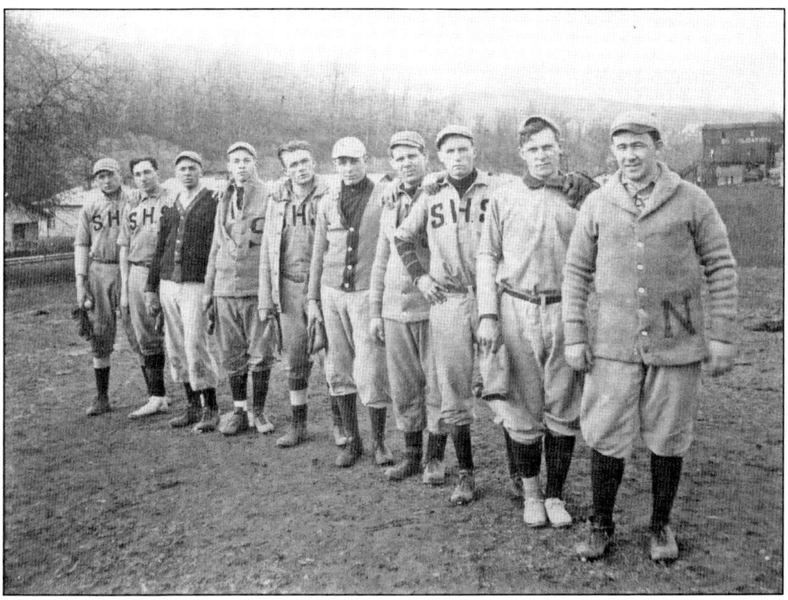

The 1913 Shinnston High School baseball team is shown on their practice field near what is Vincent Lumber today. The Ehlen Mine Tipple can be seen in the background. Six games were played that season: three home and three away. Coach William Edward McCarthy is shown at far right. (Author's collection.)

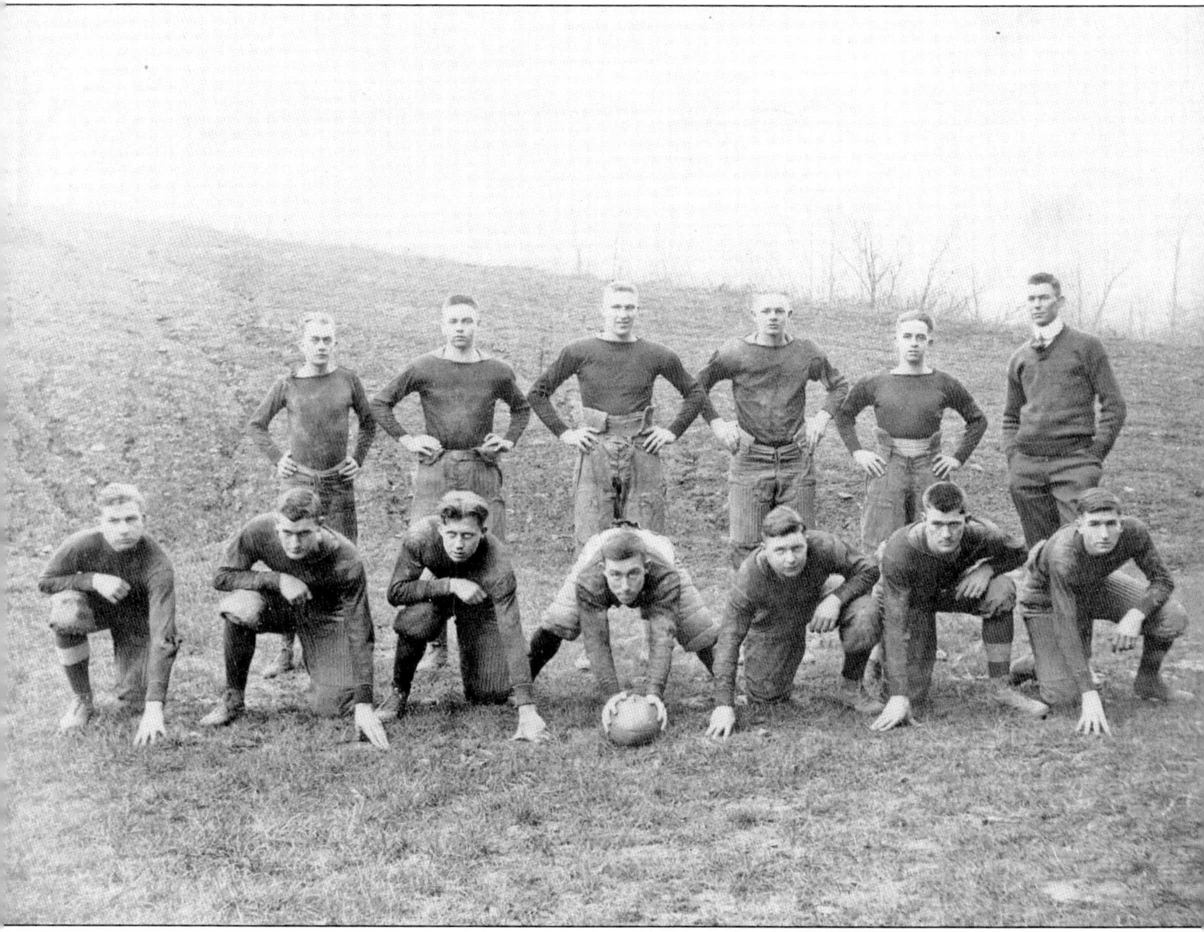

Clay District High School 1917 football team is pictured here with their coach, Eli Camden "Cam" Henderson. Eight games were played that season; three in eight days with no substitution. No player was removed due to injuries, and games were played on the Long farm in East Shinnston. Coach Henderson later served as the head football coach at Davis & Elkins College, as well as Marshall College, where he also excelled in basketball. The arena at Marshall University is named in his memory. (Author's collection.)

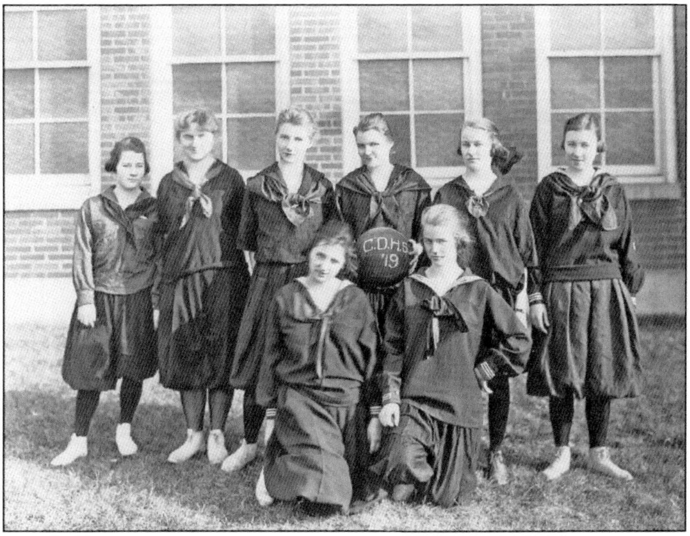

The girls' basketball team of Clay District High School is pictured here during the 1918–1919 school year. The flu epidemic that swept the country that year had reached the Shinnston area by the fall of 1918 and prevented some games from being played. The girls ended the season with a 5-2 record. Their coach was Claude Tetrick, a West Virginia University graduate who taught mathematics and was in charge of athletics and military training. (Author's collection.)

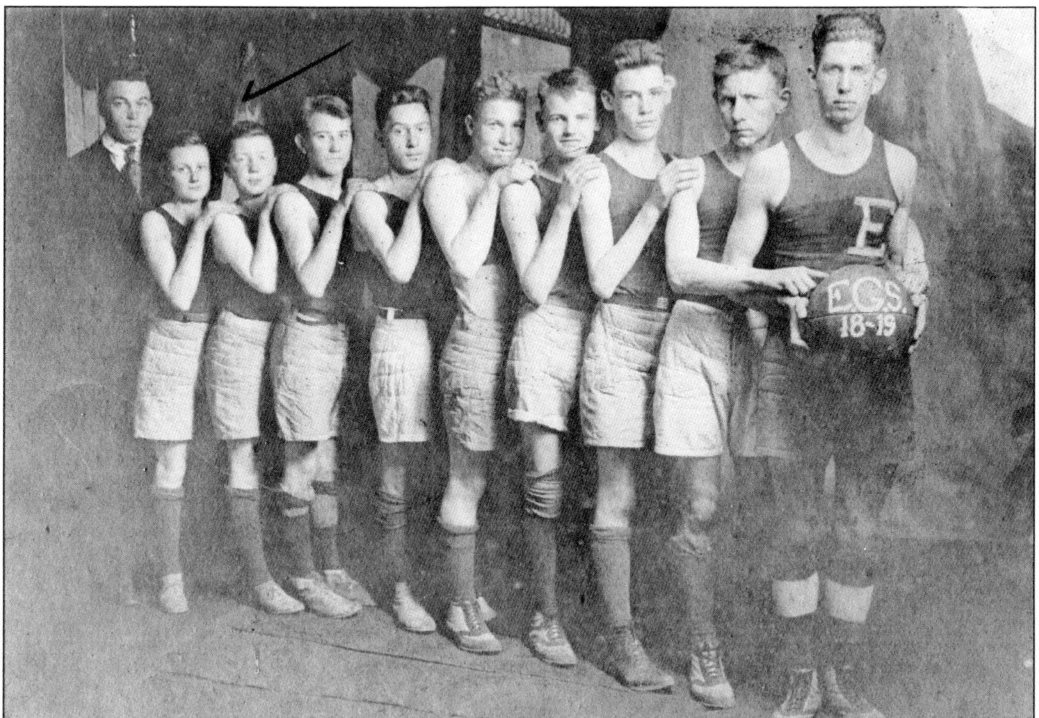

The Enterprise Grade School boys' basketball team is shown here for the 1918–1919 school year. Coach McNutt is shown at far left. The team was comprised of, from left to right, Ed Nay, James Stewart, two unidentified boys, Bernard Tetrick, Darrell "Botchie" Hildreth, Phil Sturm, Leo Collins, and Garnet Morris (holding the ball). (Author's collection.)

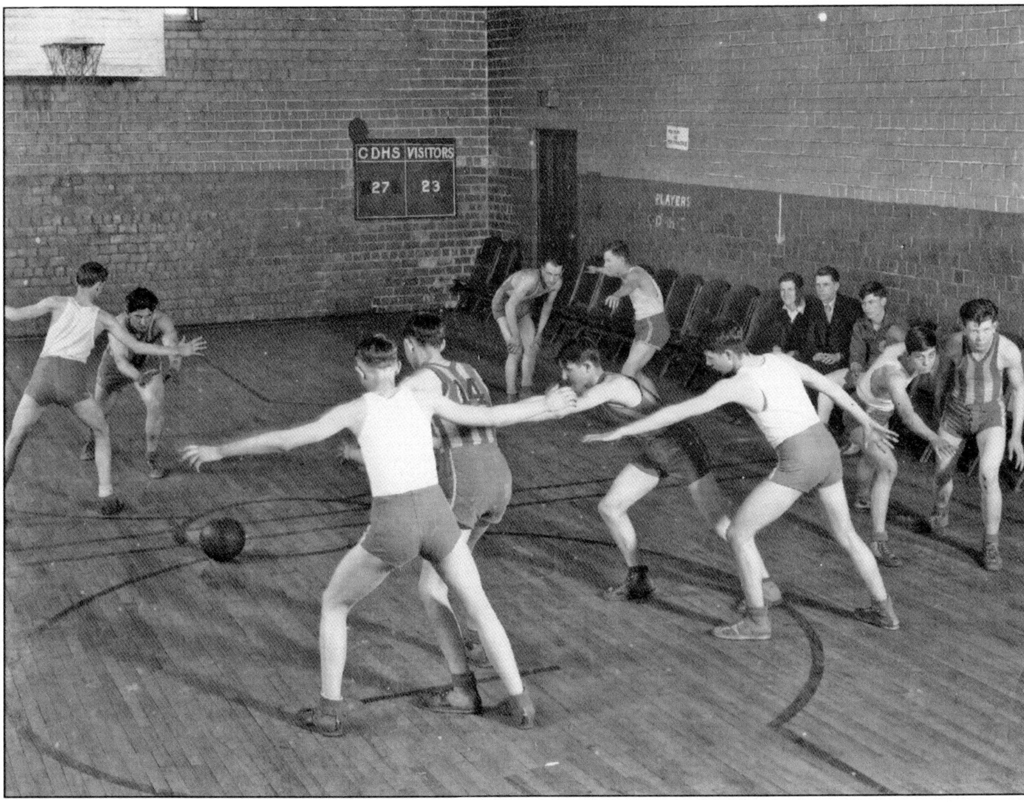

The gymnasium of Clay District High School, later Shinnston High School, suffered cuts in construction costs, leaving no appropriate room for a basketball court. Many games were played in other gyms. In this photograph, members of the 1930s boys' basketball team are in the middle of a game—or are they? Note that the ball is not moving, and each boy is carefully posed on court. (Author's collection.)

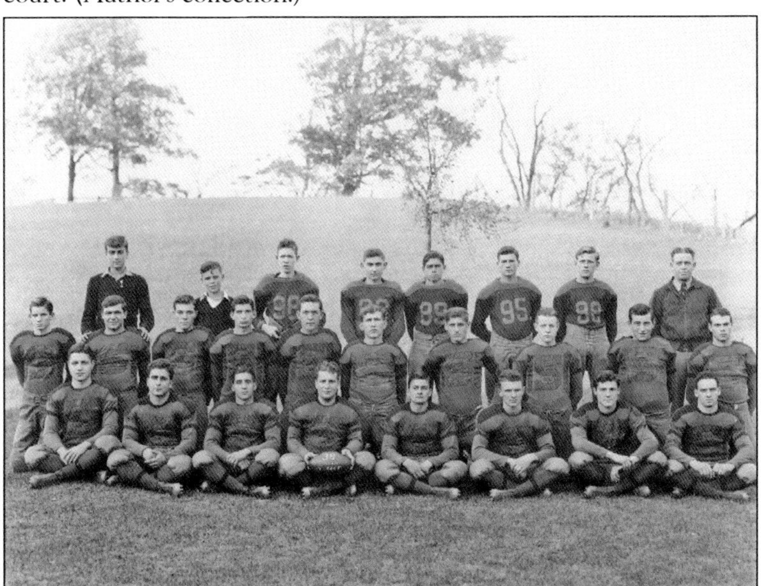

The 1936 Shinnston High School football team was comprised of many young athletic men. Shown far right in the third row is coach Theodore "Ted" Leader. This would be one of the last teams he coached before being killed in a plane crash on April 8, 1939, in Boone County. (Author's collection.)

Pictured here is a mid-1940s girls' basketball team sponsored by the Shinnston Moose Lodge. Players include, from left to right (first row) Wanda (Strader) Emmel, Carol Wilson, Margaret Smith, Ladoris "Tee" (Casto) Roberts, and Martha Endress; (second row) Margaret Emmel, Patty (Andrick) Ashcraft, and Mildred Peterson, with coach Jimmy Metz. (Author's collection.)

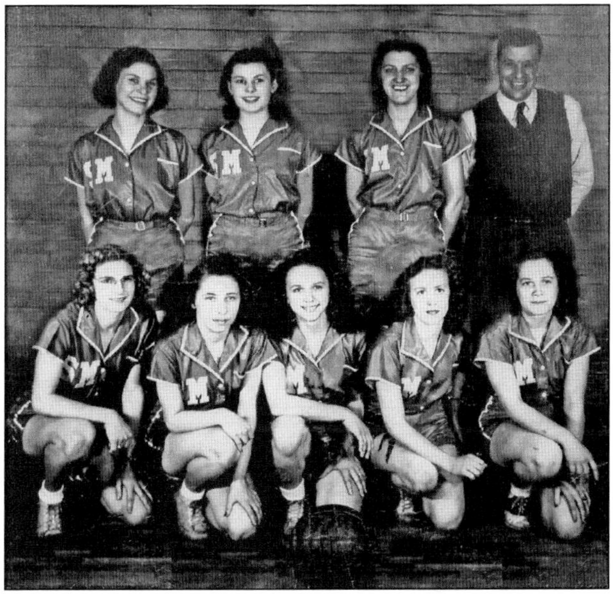

EMERGENCY DOCTOR LIST

R. S. COFFINDAFFER, MEMORIAL CLINIC
Phones: Office 163 Res. 264

S. W. JABAUT, Consol. Coal Co.
Phones: Office 123 Res. 455

N. B. COX, PHONE 190

C. G. STROUD, Phone, Office 371 Res. 371

DRS. L. S. WORNAL AND R. B. NUTTER
IN MILITARY SERVICE

LUMBERPORT
JAMES C. REPASS, Baby Specialist
Phones: Office 2531 Res. 2271
CHILDREN'S DAY, SHINNSTON, THURS. MORNING
AT DR. COFFINDAFFERS

D. P. CRUIKSHANK, Katherine Coal Co.
Phones: Office 2501 Res. 2191

JAMES M. BARR, Worthington, Phone 1312

Dentists
B. A. STARCHER, Phone 137
C. L. PRICE, Phone 122
W. O. KOON, Phone 242
H. V. FLANAGAN, Phone 454

Optometrist, FRED W. BURNETT
Phone 127

RICE-REXALL DRUG STORE
GEO RICE, PROP., SHINNSTON, W. VA.
Phone 227 Emergency Night Phone 349

On the back of the 1945–1946 Shinnston High School basketball schedule appeared this emergency physician contact list. One optometrist and four dentists were working in the area, along with several medical doctors. The schedule was wallet-size, making these numbers easily accessible. (Author's collection.)

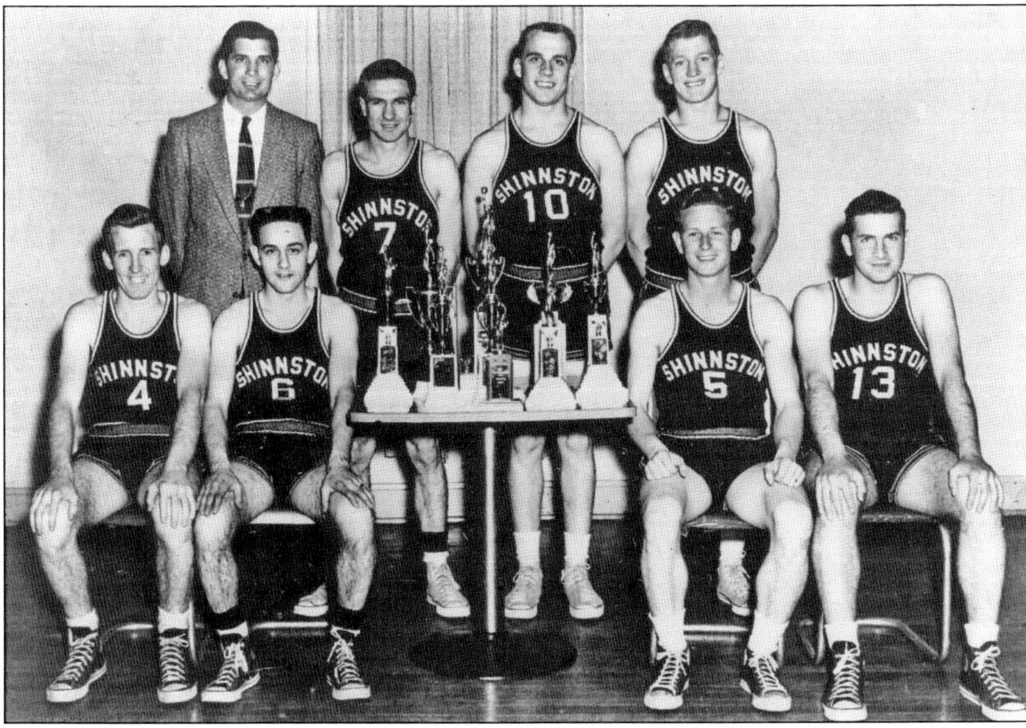

This independent basketball team was sponsored by the Shinnston Moose in 1956. The young men pictured were from Shinnston, and the team's record was 33 wins and 1 loss, which was by one point. From left to right are (first row) Don Springston, Tom Romeo, Junior Southern, and Dave Simon; (second row) coach John Ashcraft, Frank Spadafore, Roger Tetrick, and Francis "Whitey" McDougal. (Author's collection.)

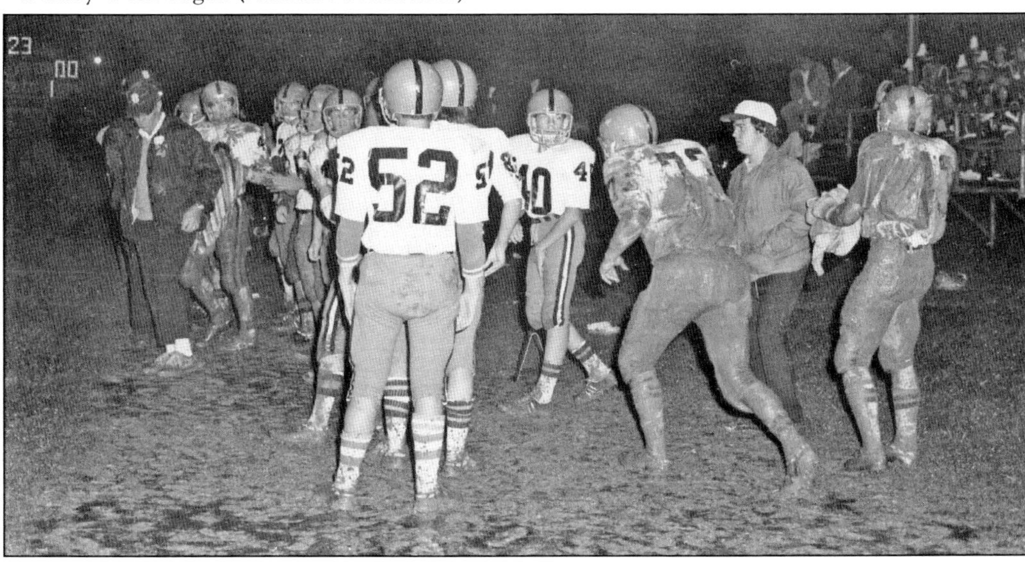

It was a very muddy game during this 1975 football season for Shinnston High School, but the rain did not dampen the spirit of the class of 1976. The Spartans played many good games, but finished the season with a 2-6-2 record. Coaching staff this year consisted of Tom Harvey, Bill Stoneking, and Robert Beto. (Courtesy of Bob Bice II.)

Three

Coal Mining and Railroad

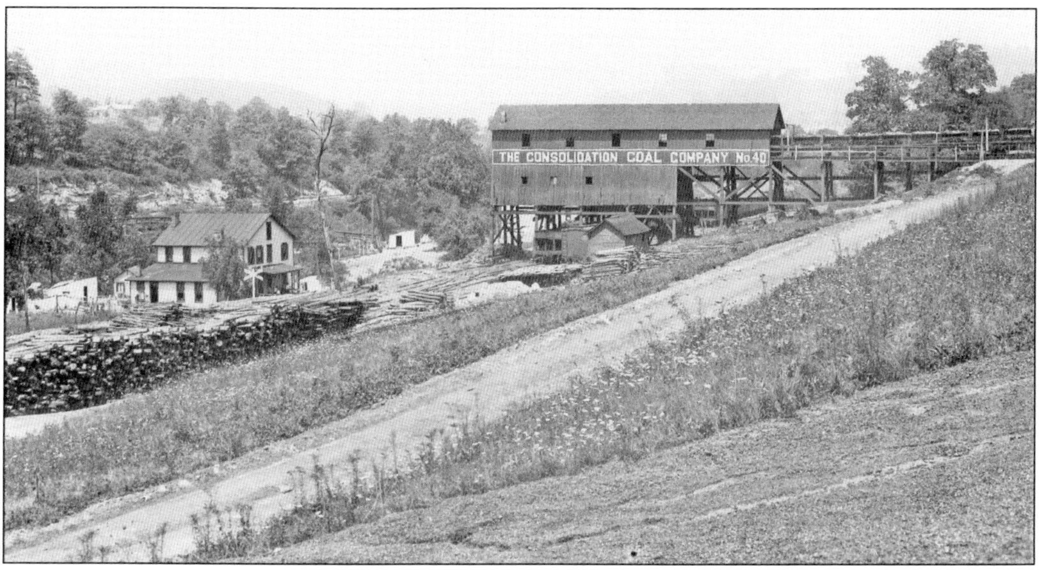

The Viropa Mine was established by the Fairmont Coal Company during the 1899–1902 period. Named for three states—Virginia, Ohio, and Pennsylvania—it was once a thriving mining community with a tipple, large company store, several single- and two-story company houses, and a swinging bridge, which crossed the West Fork River and connected the east and west sides of the community. The east side contained the mine, company store, railroad, and housing. The west side had a schoolhouse, several more houses, barracks, and a community park, as well as the streetcar. The Consolidation Coal Company purchased the Viropa Mine from the Fairmont Coal Company in October 1910. This image was taken in 1911. (Courtesy of Bob Bice II.)

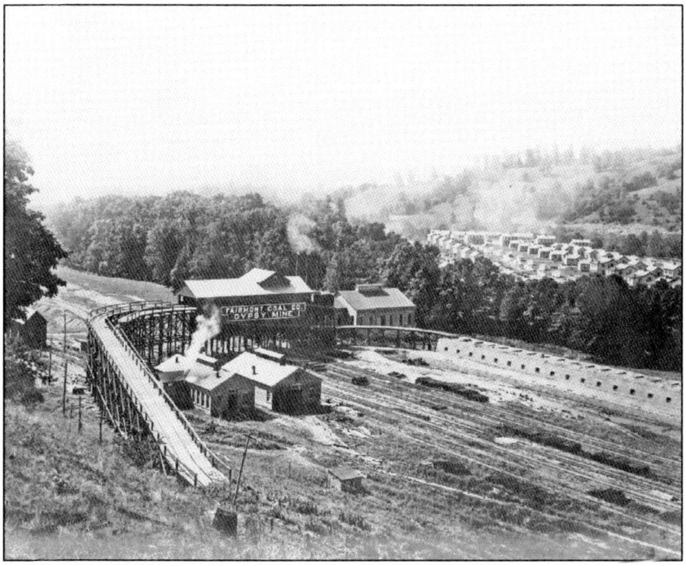

Taken before 1910 when Consolidation Coal Company bought Fairmont Coal Company, this photograph shows the Gypsy Mine in operation. The area, which was named Gypsy Grove back to Civil War times, simply became Gypsy, as Gypsy (Fleming) Ward was both a daughter of former West Virginia governor A.B. Fleming and granddaughter of coal pioneer James Otis Watson. The coal camp is pictured in the background. Also note the many coke ovens. (Author's collection.)

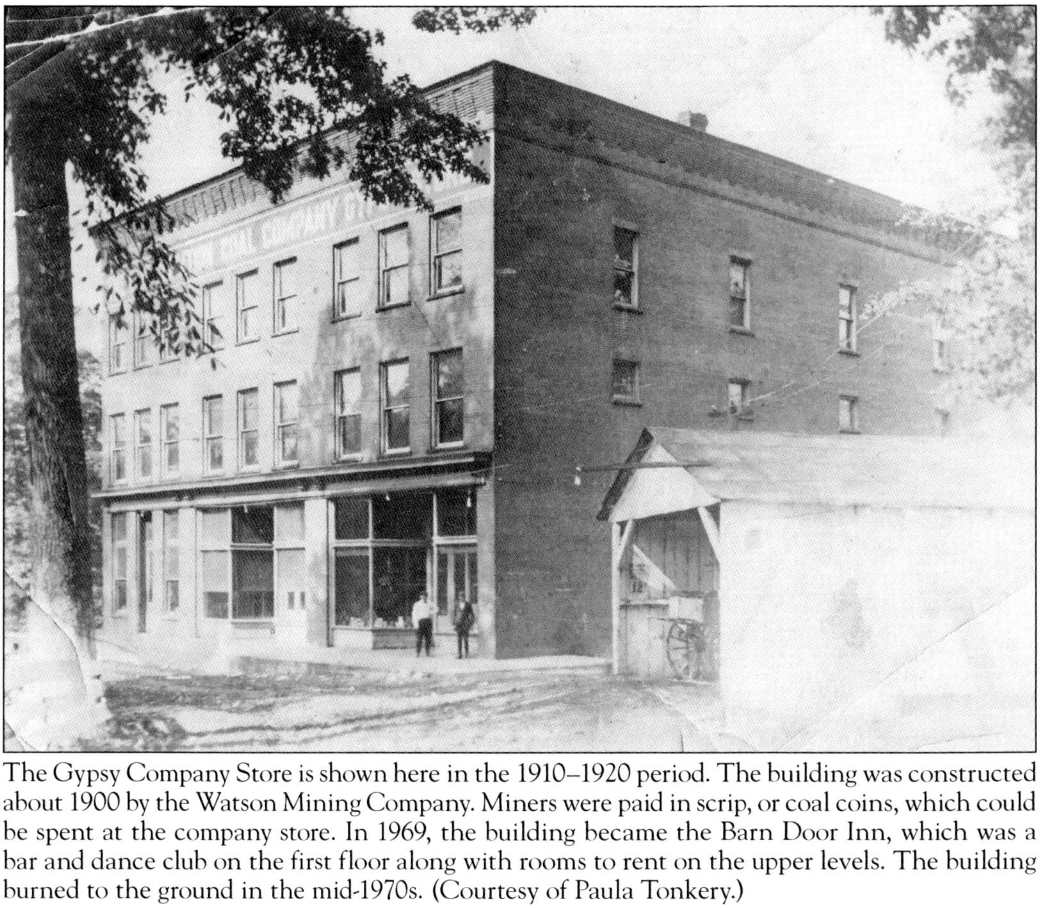

The Gypsy Company Store is shown here in the 1910–1920 period. The building was constructed about 1900 by the Watson Mining Company. Miners were paid in scrip, or coal coins, which could be spent at the company store. In 1969, the building became the Barn Door Inn, which was a bar and dance club on the first floor along with rooms to rent on the upper levels. The building burned to the ground in the mid-1970s. (Courtesy of Paula Tonkery.)

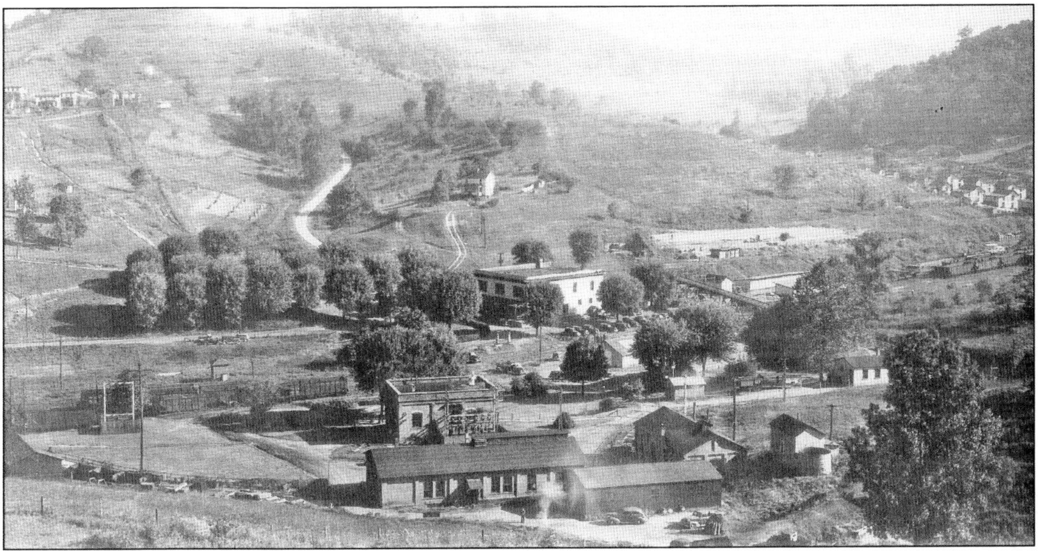

Owings was established as a coal mining community in 1909–1910 by the Watson family and was named for Minnie (Owings) Watson. Like most mining communities, the "Mine on Mudlick" was home to all the amenities needed to make a living. In addition to the workload at the mine, there was a company store (pictured center), church building, and schoolhouse, and 101 houses were constructed. (Courtesy of Lowe Public Library.)

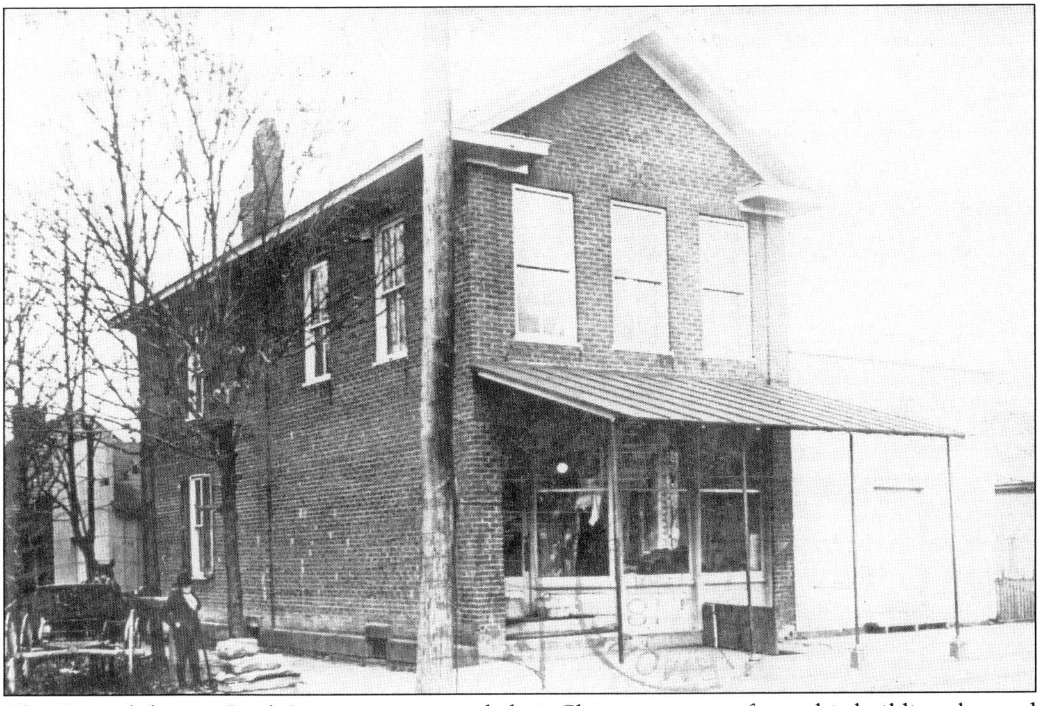

The Consolidation Coal Company operated their Shinnston store from this building, located at the northwest corner of Pike and Main Streets. They sold practically everything from shoes and clothes to fresh vegetables and groceries. Later, the building was used as the mayor's office. Its last occupant was Shinnston Plumbing Company before being razed for the future city office building. (Author's collection.)

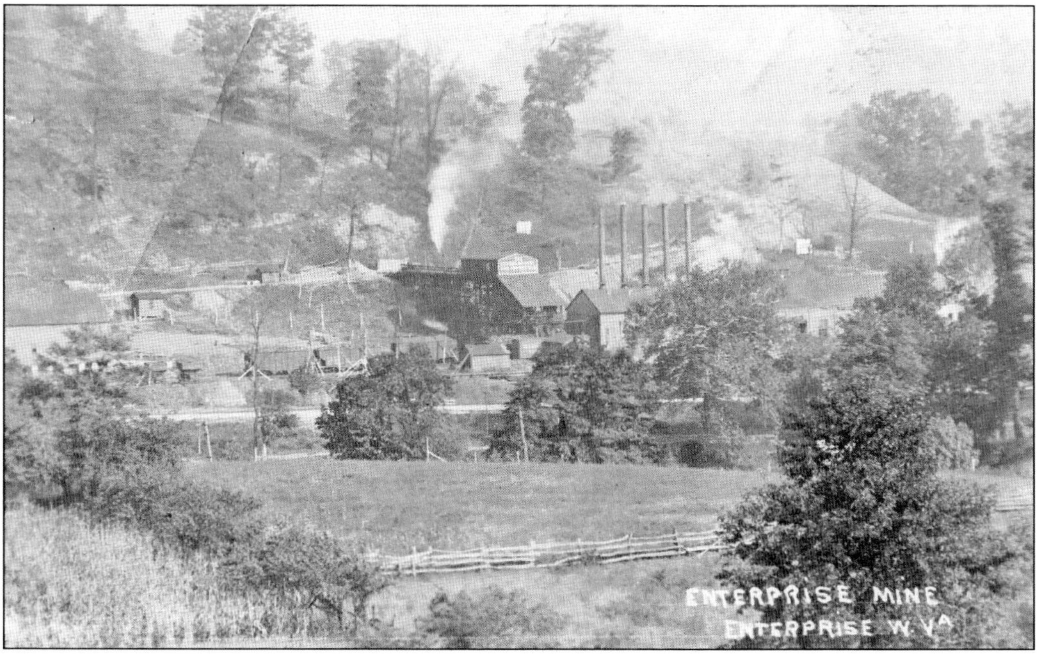

Enterprise Mine is shown here in 1911 during full operation. According to the late James V. Morris, the mine blew up on December 16, 1911. One man was killed. The mining community was one of the few which had houses below the railroad tracks, close to the river. These houses accessed a community boardwalk, which led to the company store and mine. The mine closed in the early 1930s. The coke ovens are still very visible near the old mine. (Author's collection.)

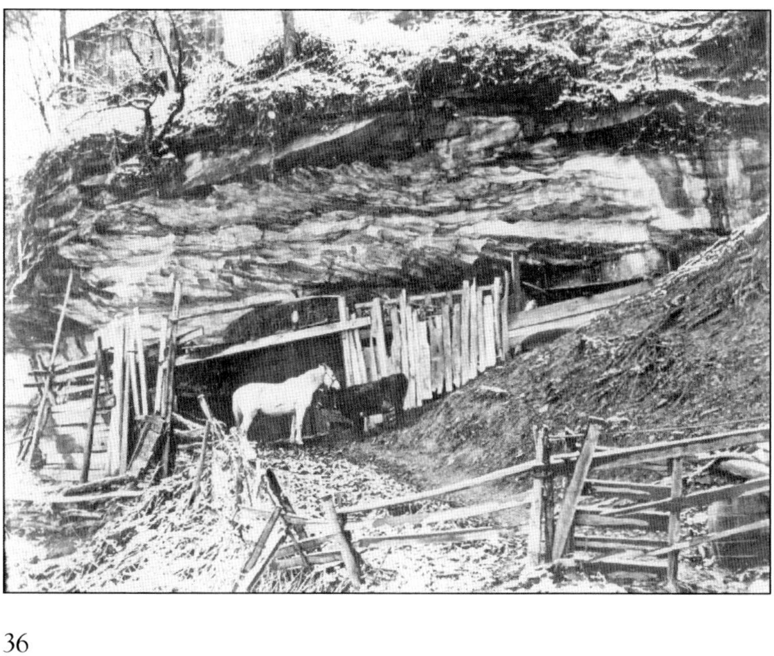

Oftentimes, mules and horses were used for work inside the mine, as well as for hauling machinery outside the mine. These animals were kept tied near the Enterprise Mine opening and were referred to as "cliff dwellers." The image was taken about 1910 and sold on a postcard. (Author's collection.)

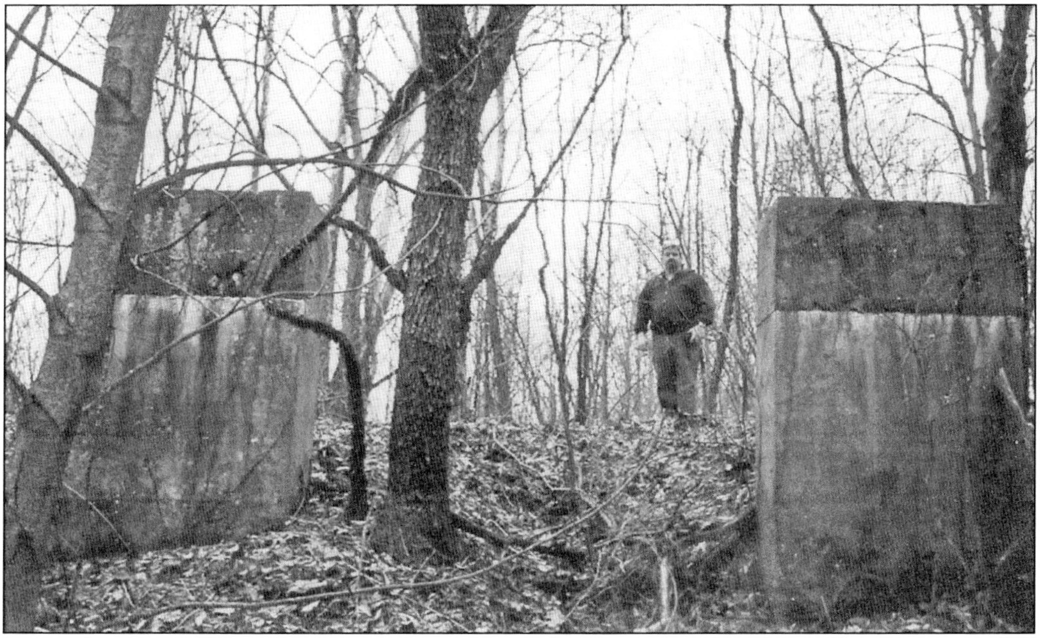

Robert Bice II, father of the author, is shown here in 2005 beside the pillars that once held the support for the swinging bridge near the Viropa Mine. The bridge provided access from the mine, housing, and railroad on the east side to the school, park, and streetcar on the west side. (Author's collection.)

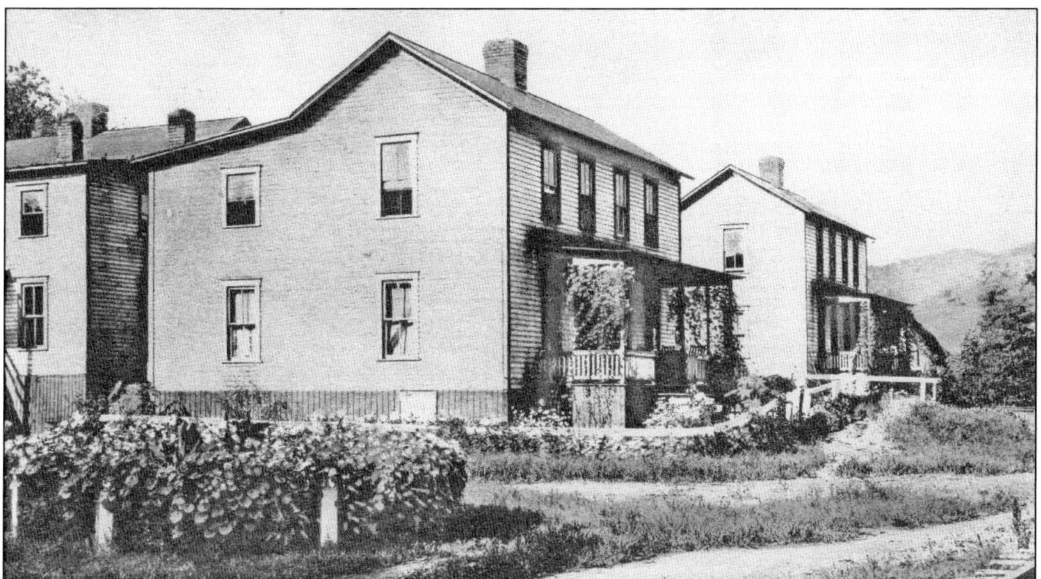

This 1917 postcard image shows the traditional multifamily company houses at Riverdale. The houses were divided into halves, with each mirroring the other in layout. These homes were built for miners' families to live in and were well kept by the families, as well as the mining company. These postcards were printed in color to entice others to work and live at the mining camp. Located just north of Shinnston on the east side of the West Fork River, this land is now part of the Riverdale Estates development. (Author's collection.)

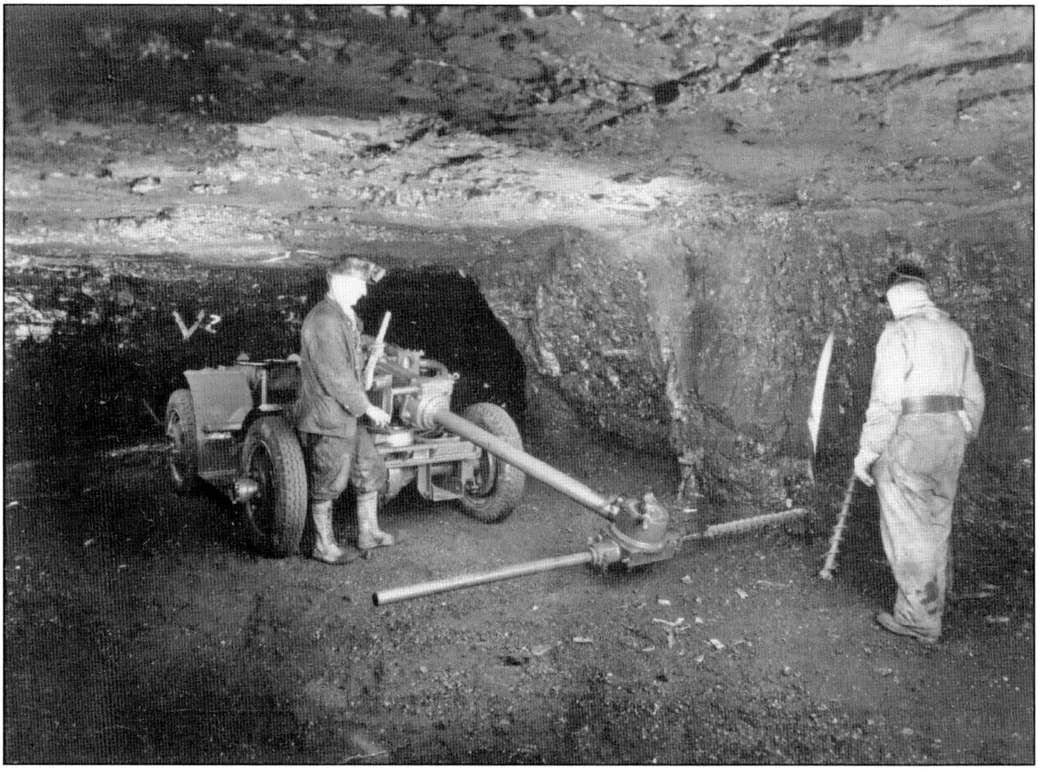

This image was taken inside one of the Katherine Coal Company's mines along Wyatt Road near Shinnston in the 1940s. The men shown here were working under Supt. John Hogue and are running a piece of machinery to help break out the coal. The men are wearing headlamps, but other mine lighting was used when the photograph was taken. (Courtesy of Bob Bice II.)

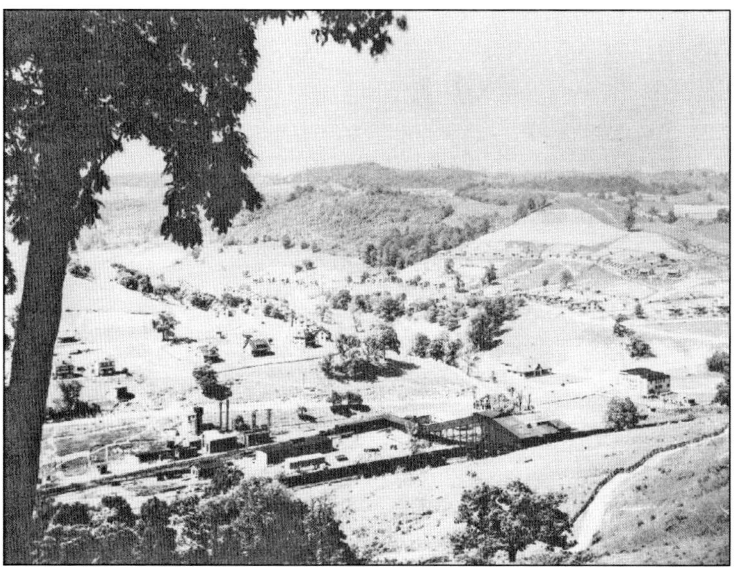

Wyatt is pictured here in an aerial view from the road to Cunningham Run. Both "Bosses' Row" and the miners' homes are seen. Originally settled in 1865 by Eli Sharp, the town was simply named Goosetown since Sharp raised geese for a living. It was renamed Wyatt in honor of Dr. Zachariah Wyatt for his efforts treating residents during a diphtheria epidemic. (Courtesy of Tom Moore.)

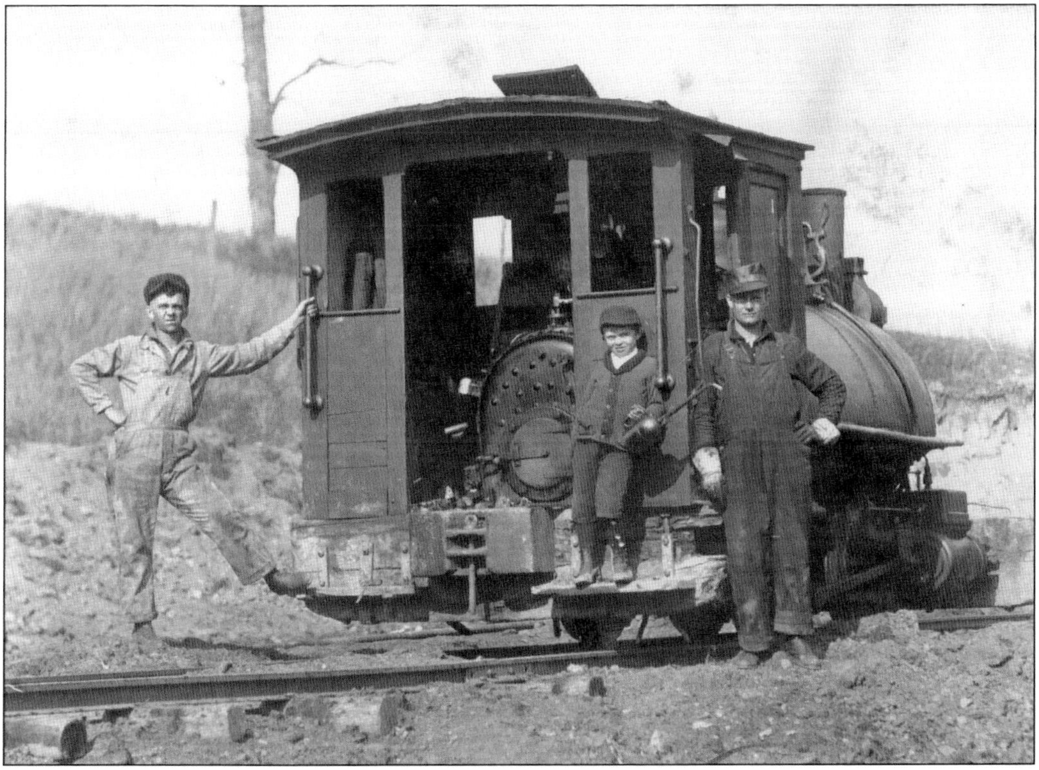

This locomotive is on the track headed to the Wyatt Mines. The mines were established by the Consolidation Coal Company and in operation from 1917 to 1928. The mine was very productive in its earliest years, adding a school, bank, homes, and several small businesses to the town. (Courtesy of Tom Moore.)

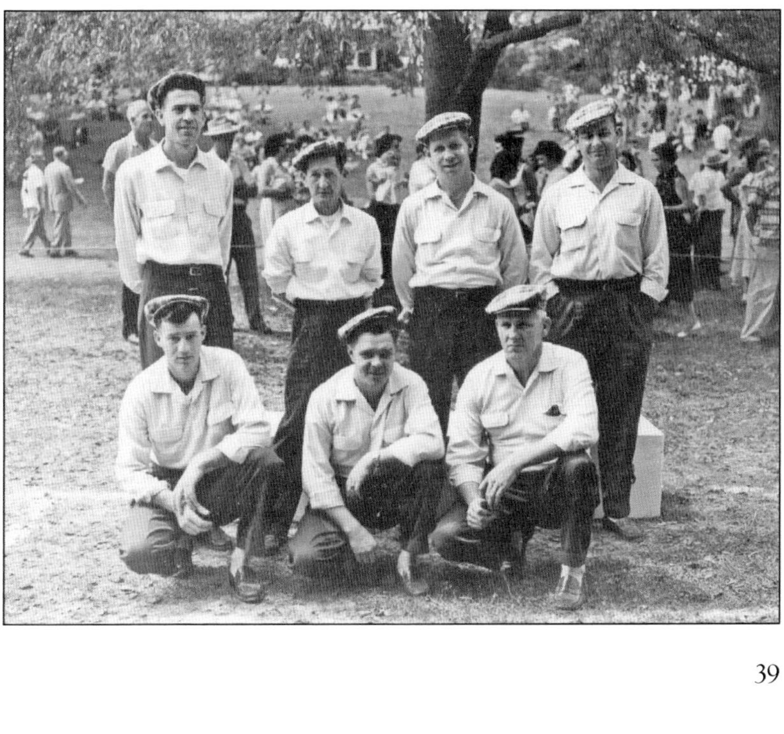

The Williams Mine No. 98 First Aid Team is pictured here in the 1950s. From left to right are (first row) John Matheny, Earl O'Dell, and Paul Slokey; (second row) Howard Rutter, Earl Pigott, Clyde "Snuffy" Smith Jr., and Victor Miller. The Williams Mine closed in 1979. (Author's collection.)

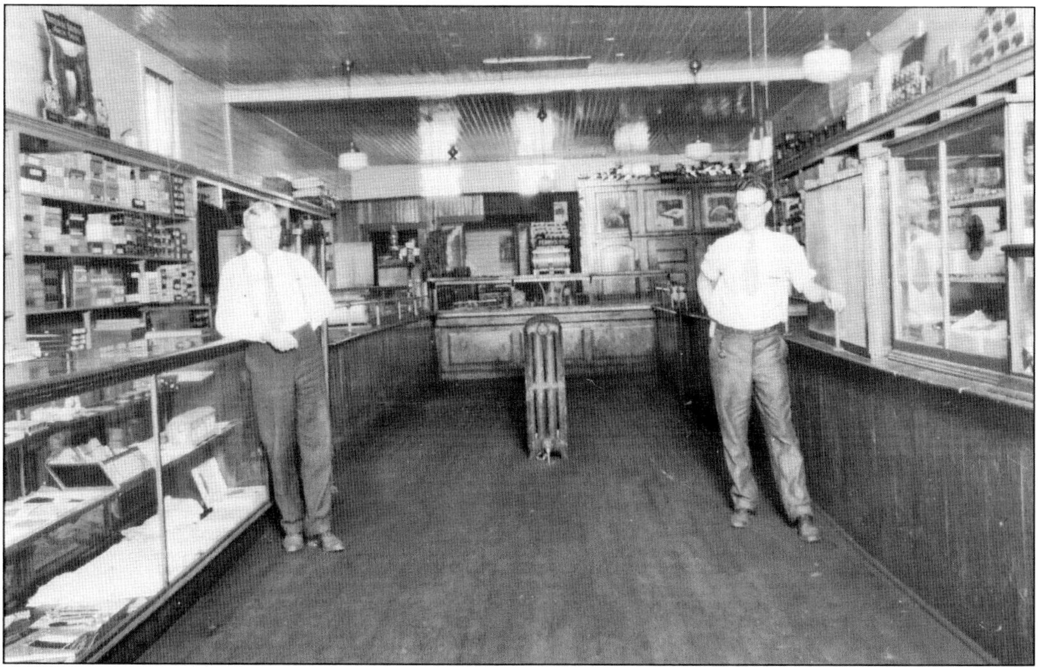

Mining companies operated company store buildings to provide necessary supplies to sell to the local miners. These two men worked at the McCandish Mine Company Store at Meadowbrook. Manager John Herbert McGee is pictured at left with store clerk Bill Orr on the right. Note the large steam heater in the middle of the room. (Author's collection.)

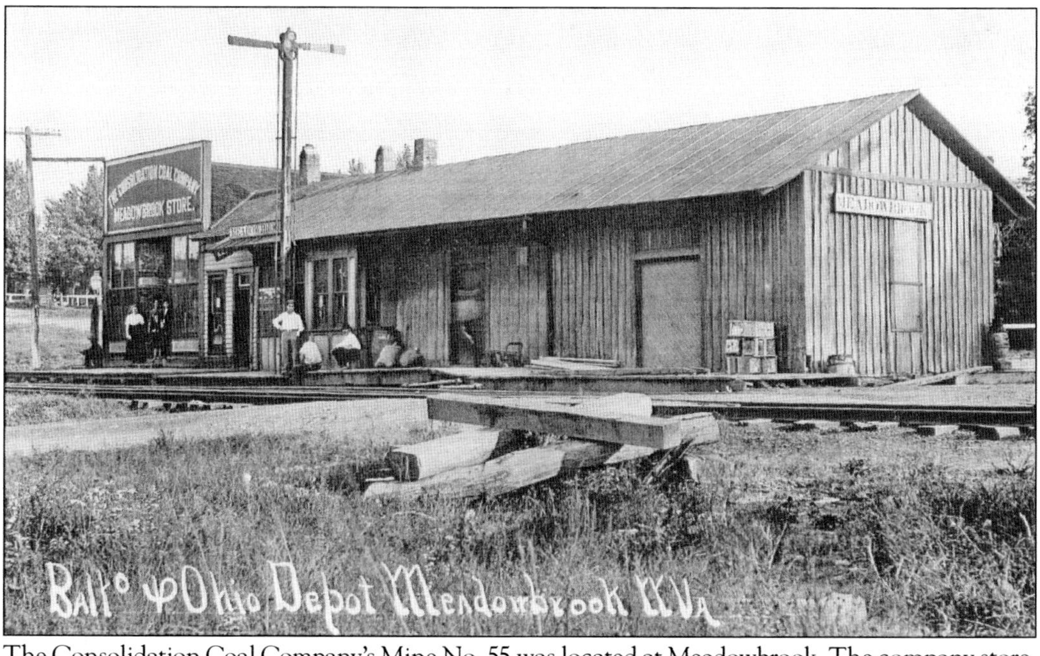

The Consolidation Coal Company's Mine No. 55 was located at Meadowbrook. The company store, pictured here adjacent to the railroad depot, was a smaller store due to the fact that Meadowbrook had other mining companies operating mines that also provided company store buildings. This image was taken about 1910. (Author's collection.)

Four

Oil and Gas

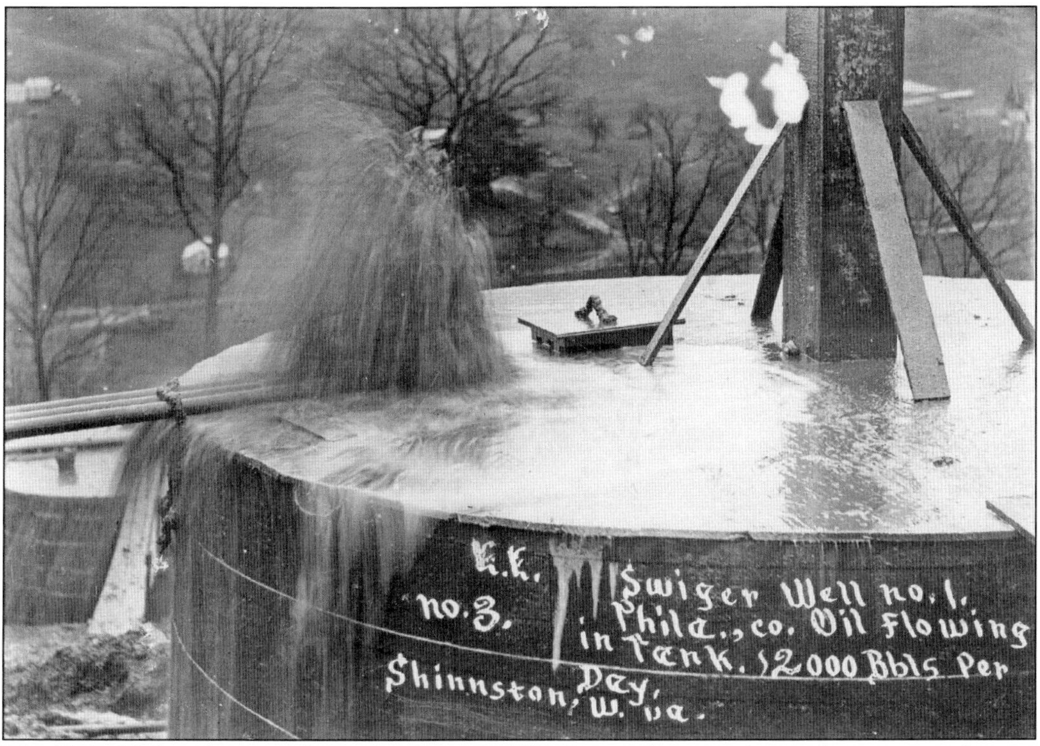

The Philadelphia Company's no. 1 well on the E.E. Swiger farm was located approximately one-half mile northwest of Adamsville in what is known as Francis Mines. Initially, it had the largest oil production of any well drilled in the state of West Virginia. Flowing so fast and freely, much of its initial production was wasted oil until dams and ponds were hurriedly made to hold it. It was estimated that this well produced approximately 450 barrels an hour. Once under control and flowing through four two-inch lead lines, the flow tests proved its production to be over 4,000 barrels in 24 hours. (Author's collection.)

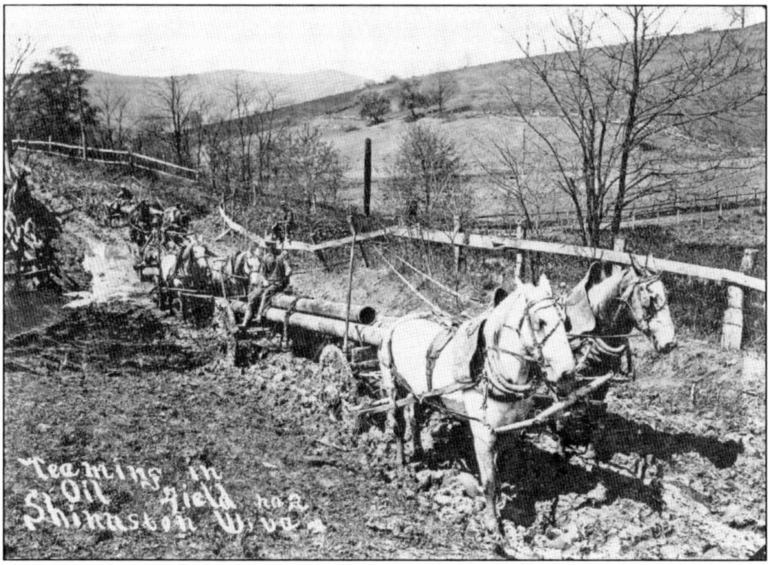

Teaming in oil fields was a costly job. Teams were mostly comprised of horses or oxen to get through the muddy trenches and over the hillsides, transporting everything from the pipeline to the engines, as well as the drilling equipment. Three teams of horses are shown here transporting pipeline. (Author's collection.)

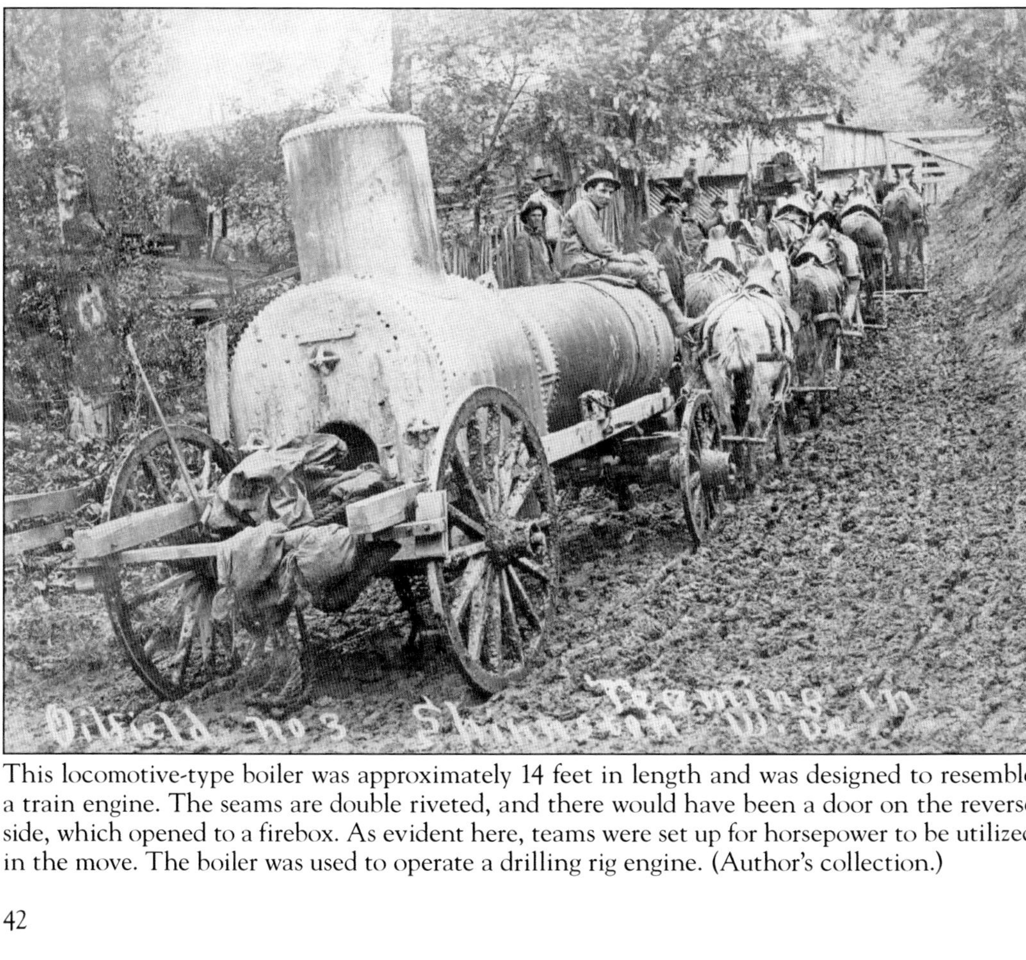

This locomotive-type boiler was approximately 14 feet in length and was designed to resemble a train engine. The seams are double riveted, and there would have been a door on the reverse side, which opened to a firebox. As evident here, teams were set up for horsepower to be utilized in the move. The boiler was used to operate a drilling rig engine. (Author's collection.)

Teams of horses were responsible for hauling the equipment and supplies to the oil fields, but it was the labor of mankind that built the derricks. Shown here are five men in a field near Shinnston, working on a derrick before it is moved to an oil well site. The equipment they are using is from Beaver Falls, Pennsylvania. (Courtesy of Mary Rose and Ina Jean Carpenter.)

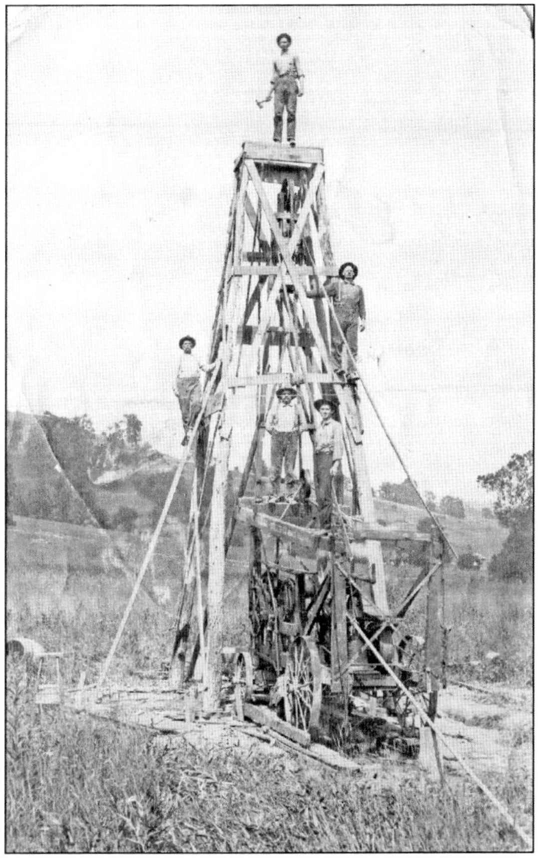

The first oil well drilled in Shinnston happened in December 1908 on the R.R. Hardesty farm. It was located along Mudlick Run between Shinnston and Adamsville. The initial primary intent of the well was for it to be a gas well; therefore, no data was obtained of its original oil production amount. Shown here is one of the wells on the Hardesty farm. (Courtesy of Lowe Public Library.)

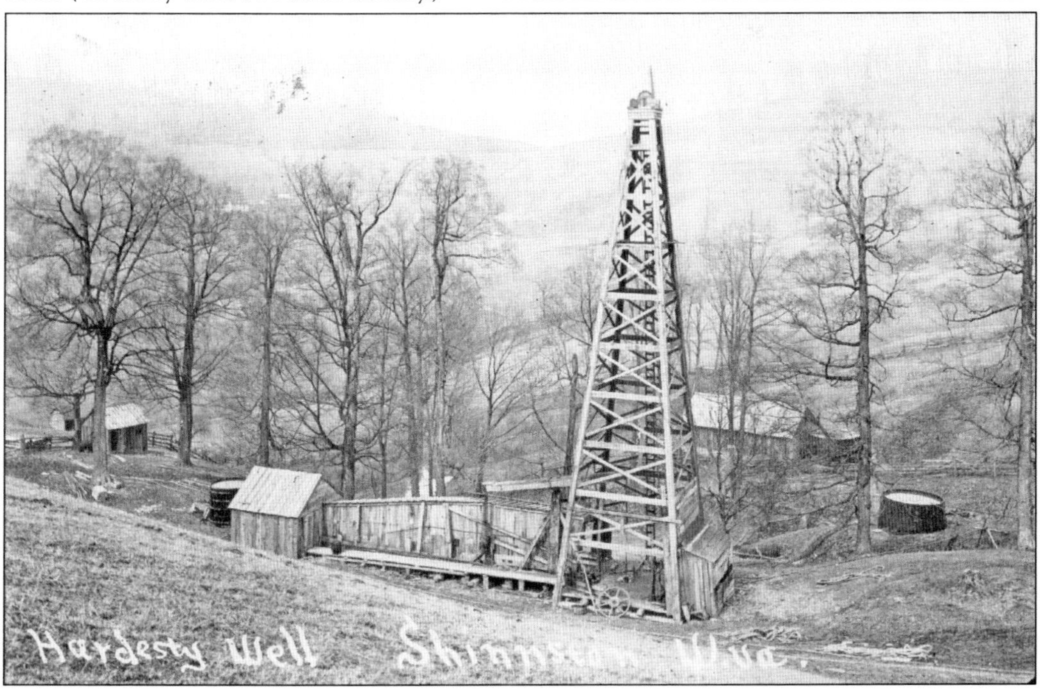

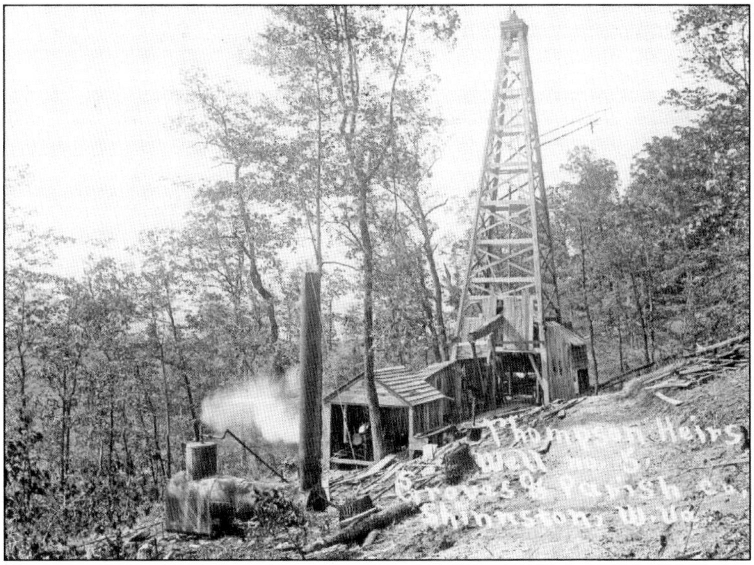

The discovery of oil in the Coon's Run area and other areas near Shinnston developed into an oil boom, which proved to be exciting for many landowners. The Thompson heirs benefitted from the royalties of this well, erected on their undeveloped land by the Groves and Parish Company. Any possible space available to drill was used. (Courtesy of Lowe Public Library.)

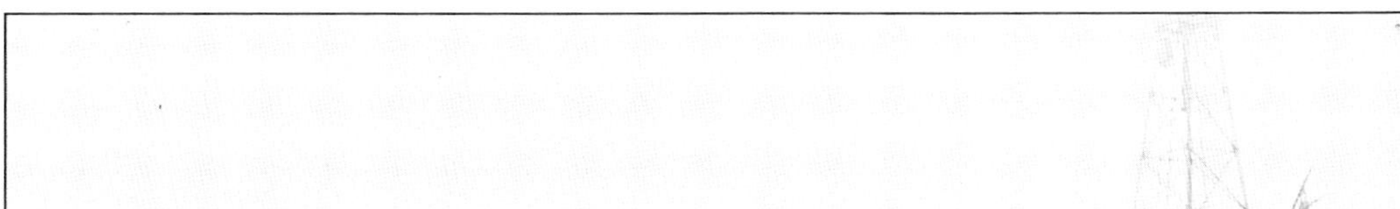

During the 1909–1911 years, the T.B. Martin Well No. 1 had a steady decline in oil production, the gauge showing less than 900 barrels in a 24-hour period. At the same time, other wells on the Martin farm were beginning to increase production; thus, the reason for multiple wells. (Courtesy of Lowe Public Library.)

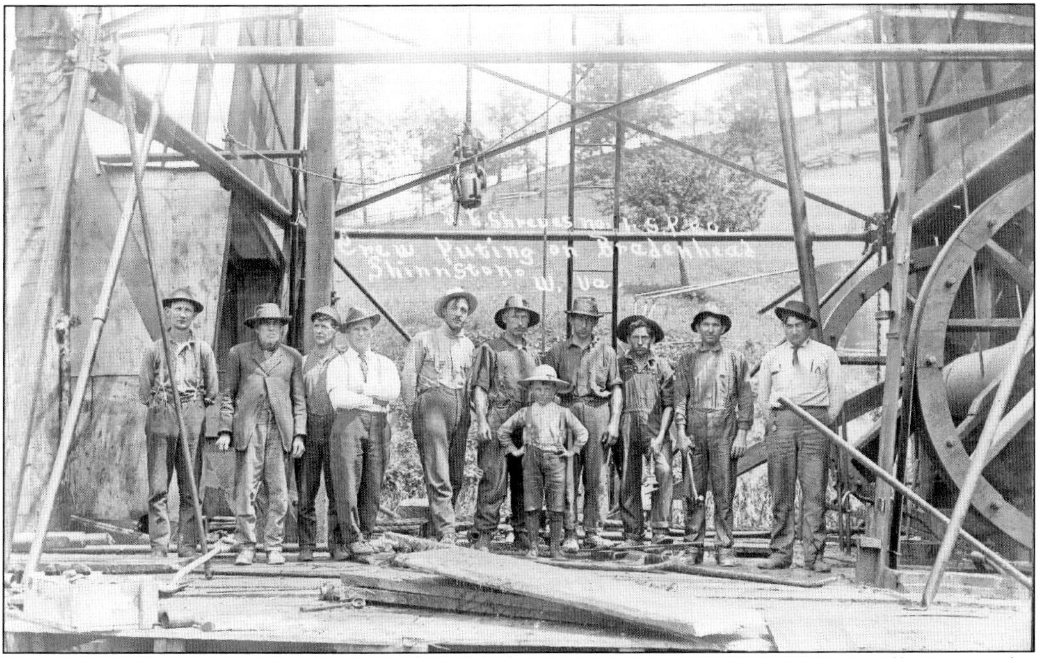

Shown here are employees of the South Penn Company putting a Bradenhead on well no. 1 on the Shreves farm. All wells had to be equipped with a Bradenhead, which was a casing head having a stuffing box packed to make a gastight connection. Pressure meant a leak and gave cause for a new oil string to be run. Note the child present. (Courtesy of Lowe Public Library.)

Oil Roustabouts for the Philadelphia Company are shown here in the Mudlick Oil Field near Shinnston. Roustabout was the term given to men who maintained everything in the oil fields from setting up the oil well heads, drilling, maintaining the well, and keeping clear the fields and roads surrounding them. There was no job they wouldn't do, and often they were put in difficult and dangerous jobs. Working long term for the oil companies classified the men as roughnecks. (Courtesy of Lowe Public Library.)

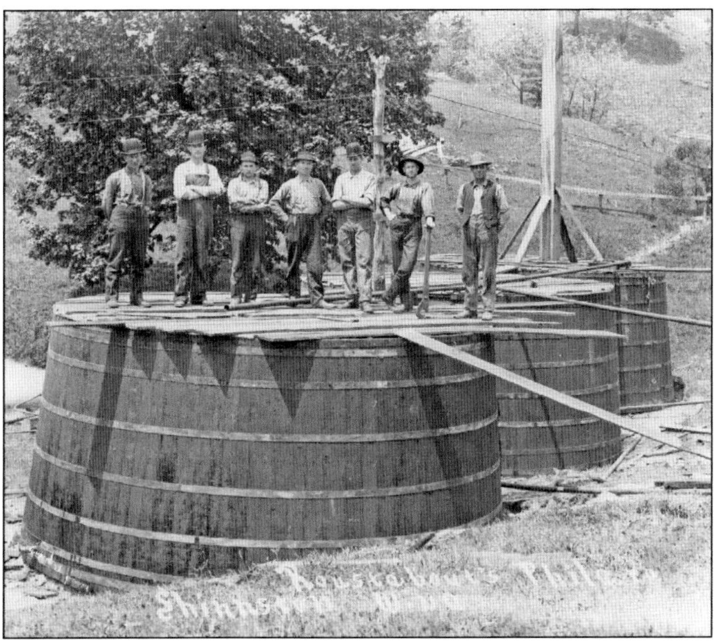

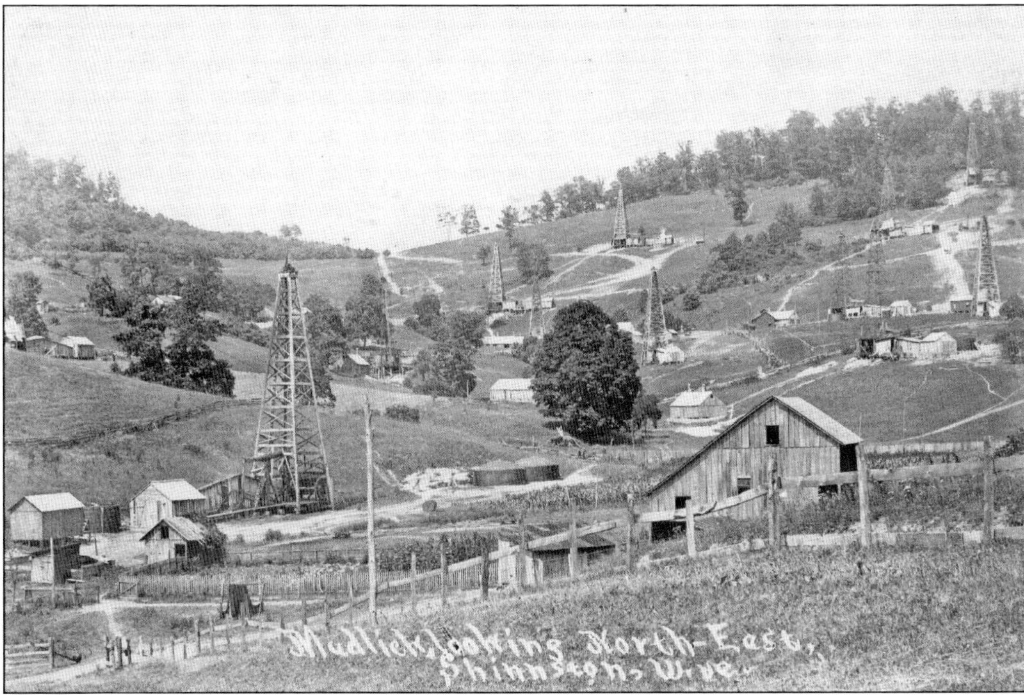

This image shows many oil derricks at Mudlick, between Shinnston and Adamsville along Janes Hill. Many families owned farms in this section and benefitted from the oil under the land. Such families with wells shown here include those of the Andersons, Coons, Hardestys, Longs, and Nays. (Author's collection.)

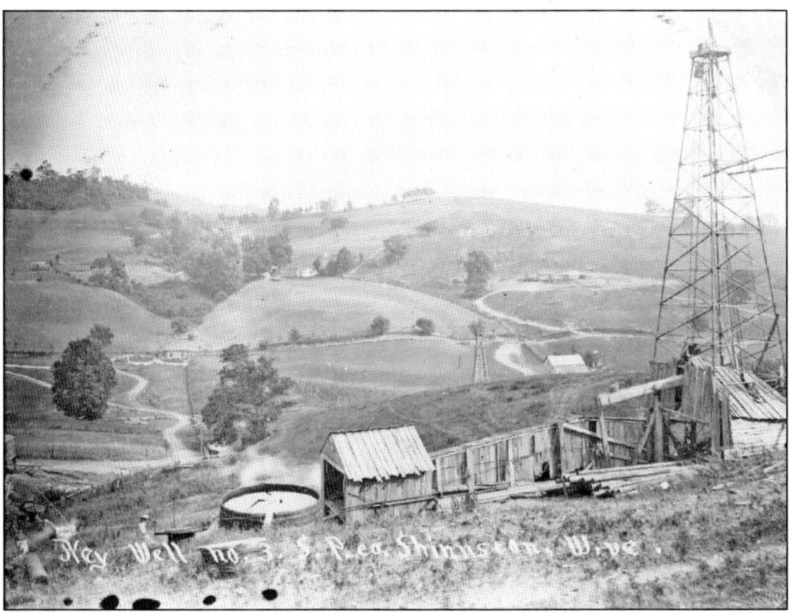

The South Penn Oil Company's gas and oil well no. 3 was located on the Fred Nay farm at Mudlick, between Shinnston and Adamsville. The Nay farm consisted of over 52 acres and became an oil field along with a farm in the early 1900s. Two other wells are shown here; one of which was also owned by the Nay family. (Courtesy of Lowe Public Library.)

The George F. Tetrick well was located close to the Laurel Run section of Shinnston area's oil pool. In February 1910, Tetrick granted the South Penn Oil Company permission to lay, maintain, and operate two-inch pipeline to an oil well shown here. The photograph was taken by Shinnston jeweler and photographer Muta Swiger. (Courtesy of Lowe Public Library.)

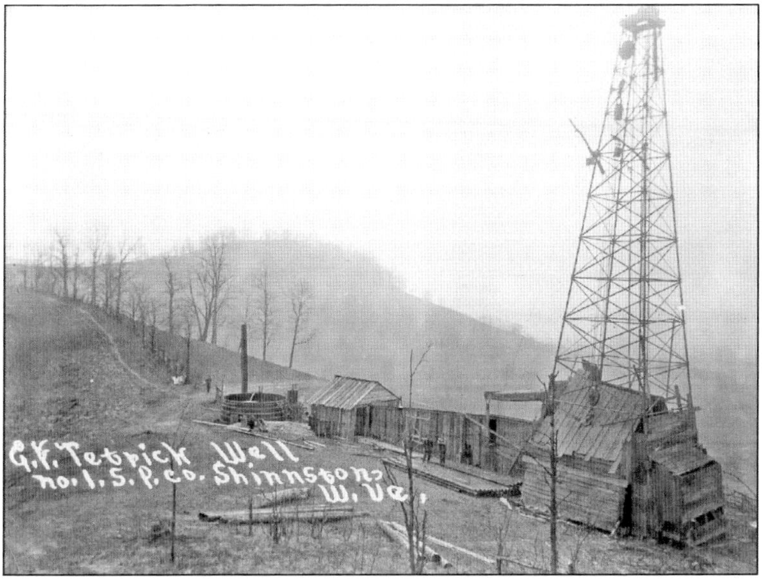

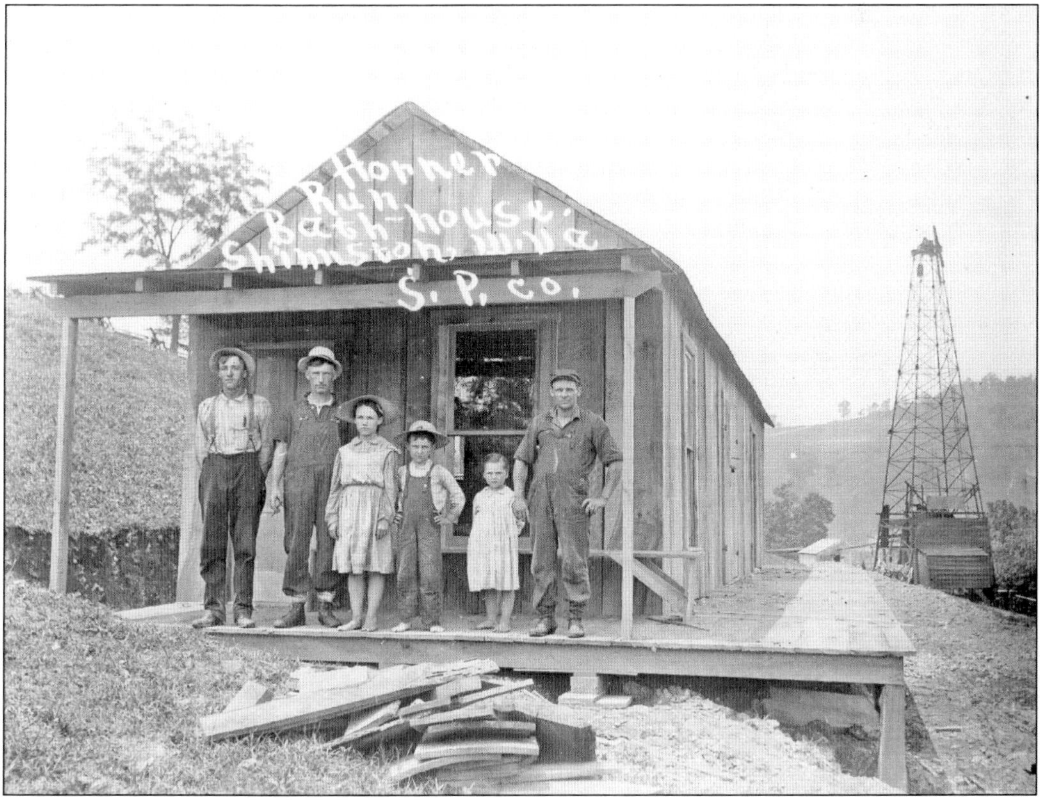

Working in the oil fields was a dirty job that left the worker's skin stained for most of the day. At the day's end, local bathhouses provided a way for these men to clean up in preparation for dinner. This bathhouse was located on Horner's Run, near Adamsville, and was used by the men working for the South Penn Oil Company. This company later became Pennzoil, which is now part of Shell. (Courtesy of Lowe Public Library.)

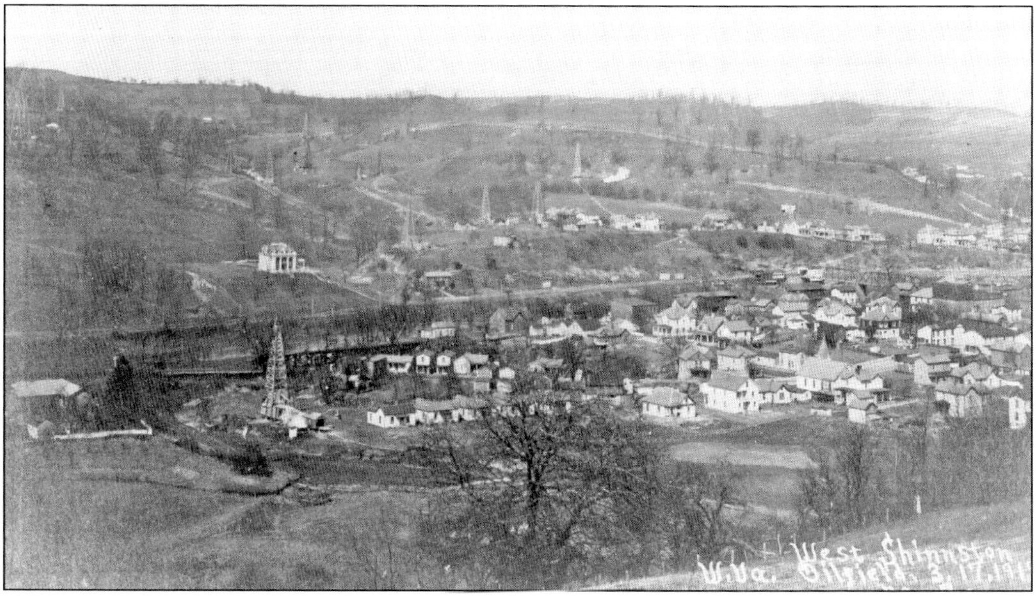

During the oil boom of the early 1900s, there was a large focus on Shinnston's west side, as pictured here. Many of these derricks were located within the neighborhood, just a short distance from houses. Muta Swiger took this photograph on March 17, 1913. (Courtesy of Lowe Public Library.)

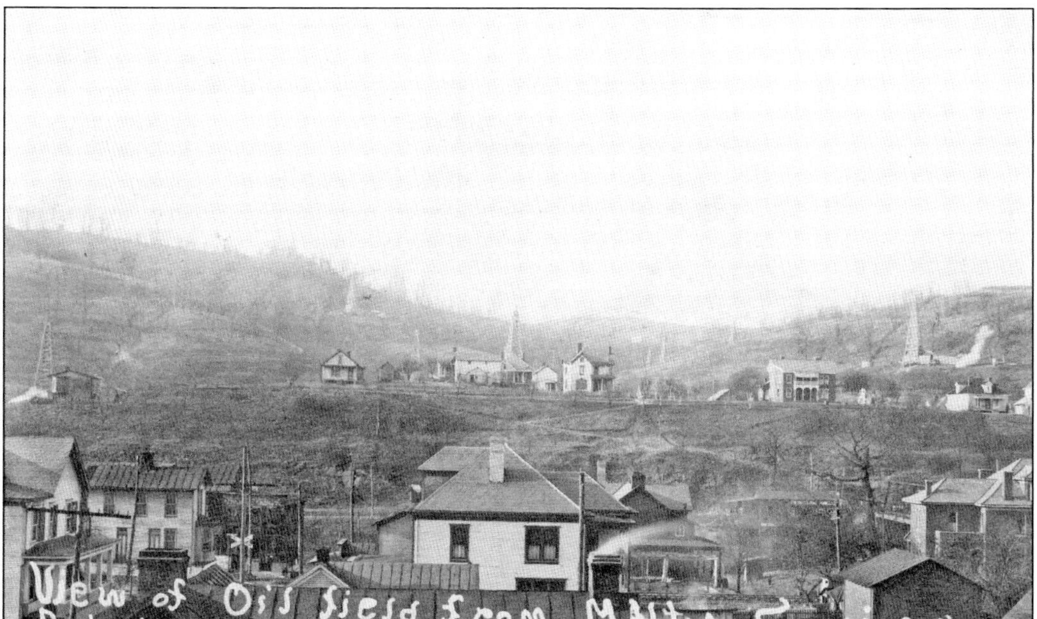

This image was taken during the 1912–1913 winter from atop what is currently part of Harmer Funeral Home. The house at the left edge is now operated as the Gillum House Bed and Breakfast. The early population of west side's oil fields is visible among many of the homes still standing there. (Author's collection.)

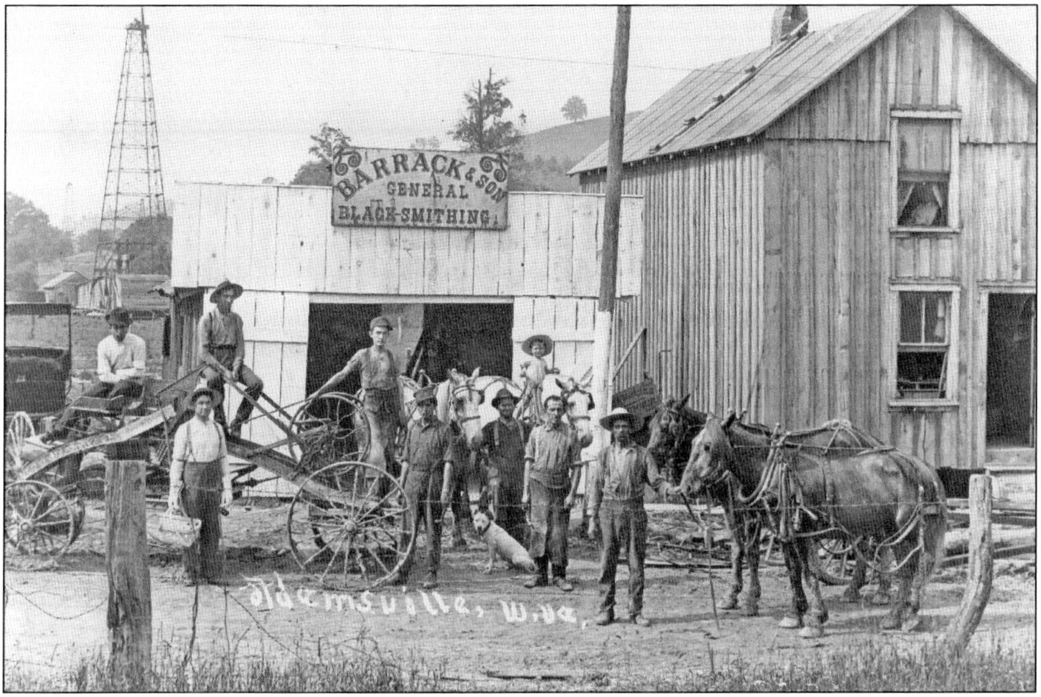

Teaming in oil fields involved using horses. A blacksmith was needed to keep horseshoes available and make needed tools. Barrack and Son was a blacksmithing operation located at Adamsville. In addition to tools used on the oil rigs, this establishment also produced items used for horses, as well as gates and agricultural equipment used on the many farms in Adamsville. (Courtesy of Lowe Public Library.)

In addition to barracks for temporary housing, many landowners opened up their own homes or built cheap housing designed specifically to house renters. Nestled in the middle of the oil fields, the Tennant family used their home as a boardinghouse to provide sleeping and eating accommodations for the workers. (Courtesy of Lowe Public Library.)

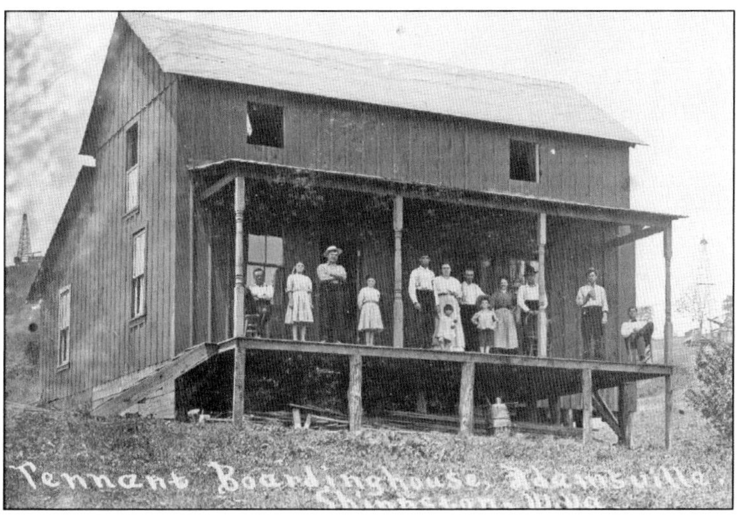

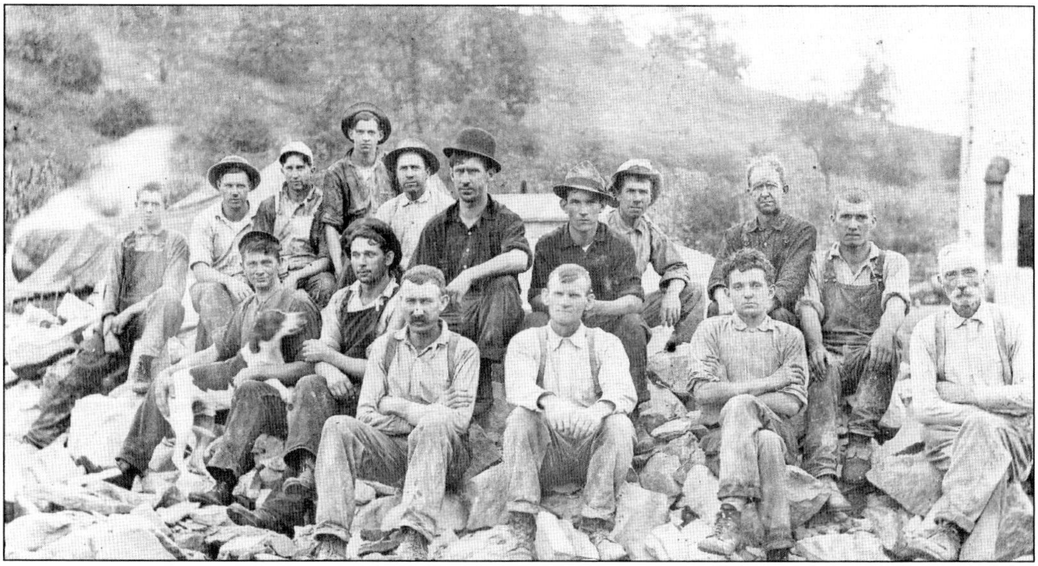

This image shows the group of men who built the gas pumping station at Peora sitting on rock outside the plant. The older man on the right is Isaac Arthur Carpenter, who was on site everyday watching construction, so he was included in the photograph. Equipment was hauled on wagon into Peora by horses, referred to as teams. Note the dog present. (Courtesy of Mary Rose and Ina Jean Carpenter.)

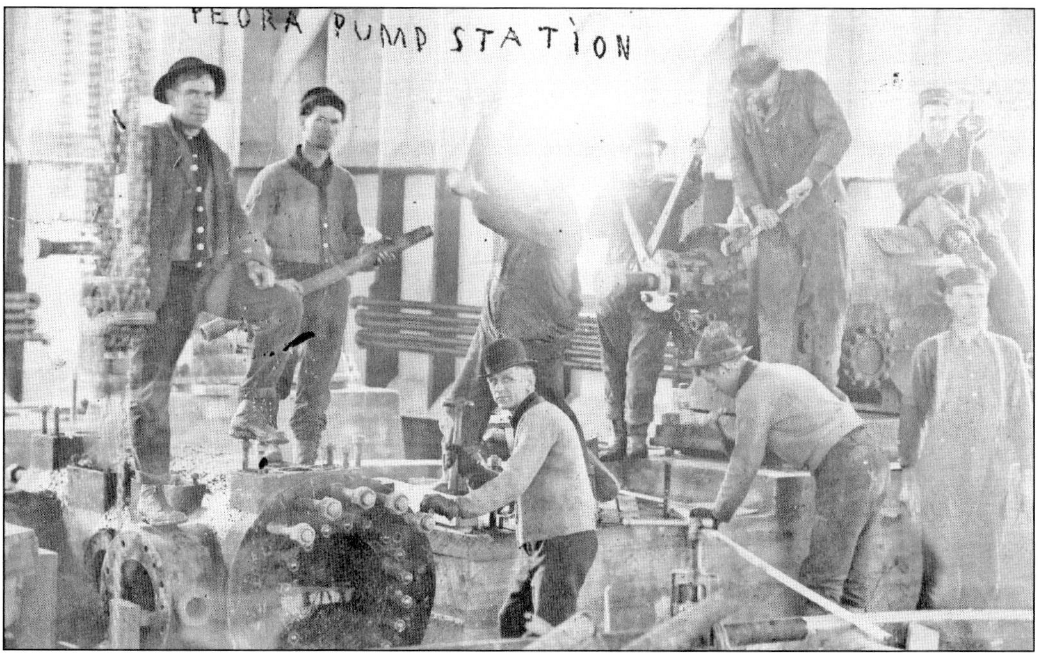

Every man had his own responsibility for keeping the Hope Natural Gas Pump Station at Peora in routine. These nine men were inside workers that grabbed their tools and got together for this photograph when they were installing equipment. The equipment was brought in by teams of horses. (Courtesy of Mary Rose and Ina Jean Carpenter.)

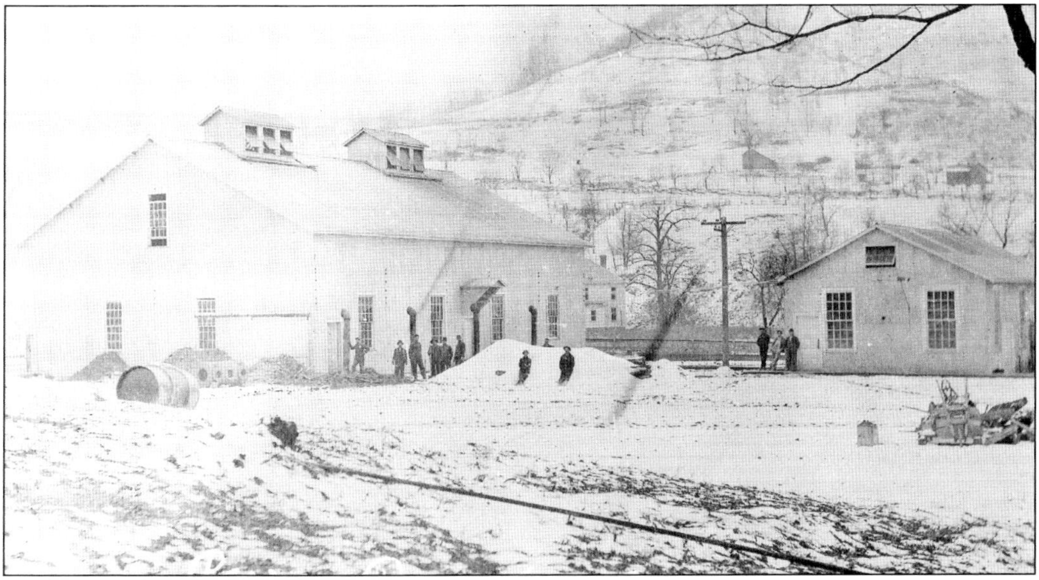

The Peora Pump Station is shown here around 1920. The building was a gas-pressure station erected by the Hope Natural Gas Company on land owned by the Ogden family. The building on the left is no longer standing, and the one on the right was purchased by the Peora Farm Women's Club in 1952. Later, it was known as the Peora Community Center. (Courtesy of Mary Rose and Ina Jean Carpenter.)

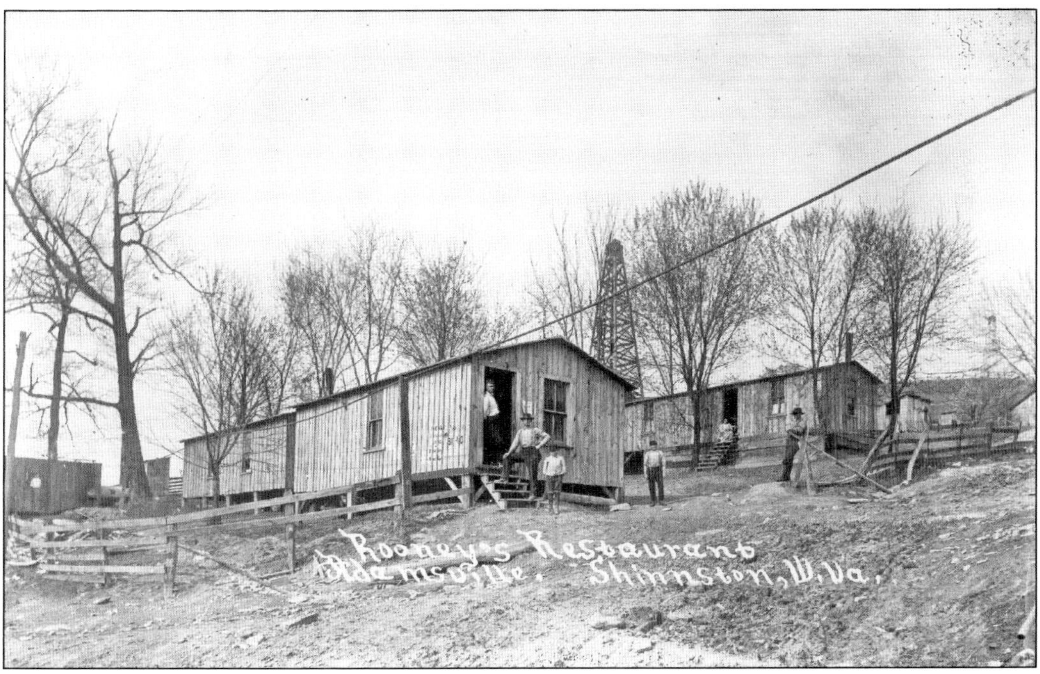

Rooney's Restaurant at Adamsville was located in a barrack-type dwelling on a hillside. Families lived out of most of these dwellings while the men worked the fields. Oftentimes, the landowners operated a space to gain additional income from the workers and even hired the wives of these men to cook. (Courtesy of Lowe Public Library.)

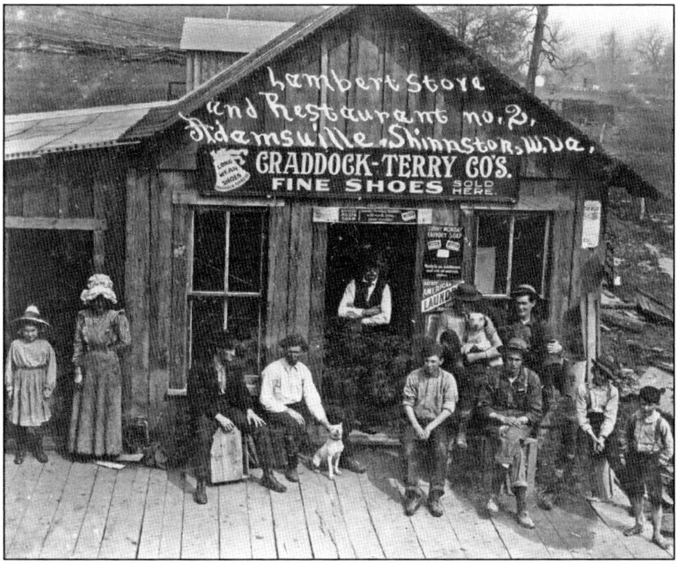

Working in the oil fields wore out shoes quickly. General mercantile stores, such as the one pictured here, were opened as a means to provide basic necessities. To double the accommodations, as well as provide more income to the operator, the Lambert brothers offered meals at a small charge for men coming in off the oil fields. The business was also an agent for laundry cleaning. The sign above the doorway reads, "Sunny Monday Bubbles will wash away your troubles." (Courtesy of Lowe Public Library.)

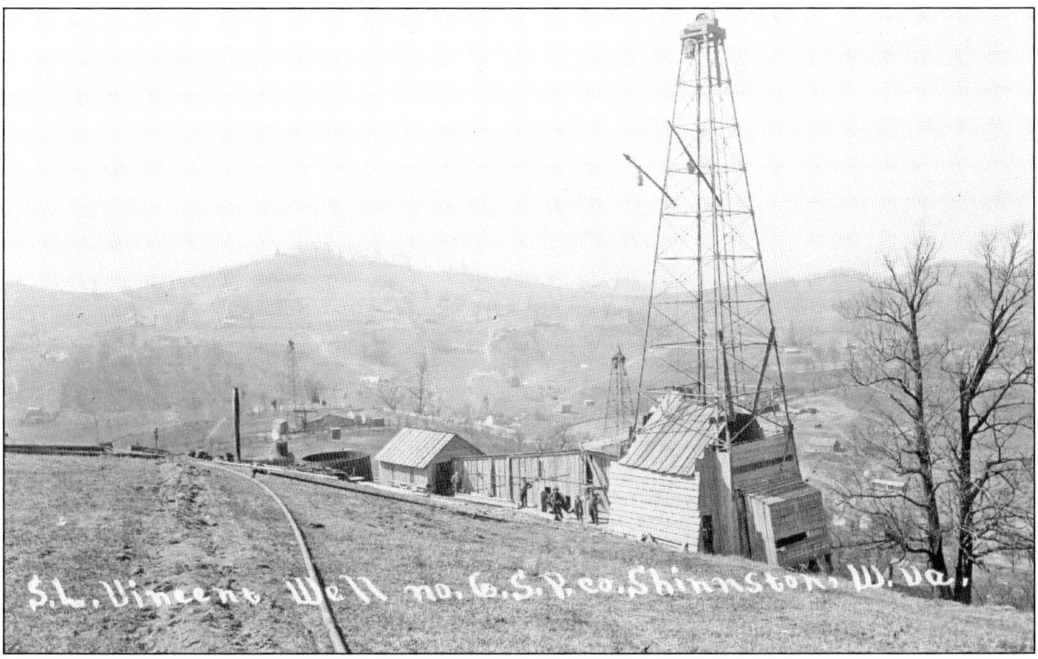

Located one-quarter mile south of Adamsville, the South Penn Oil Company erected this well on the Stephen L. Vincent farm. The well started almost flush with the Pittsburgh coal seam. The Vincent family had many oil wells on their land, this being the sixth. (Courtesy of Lowe Public Library.)

Five

Communities

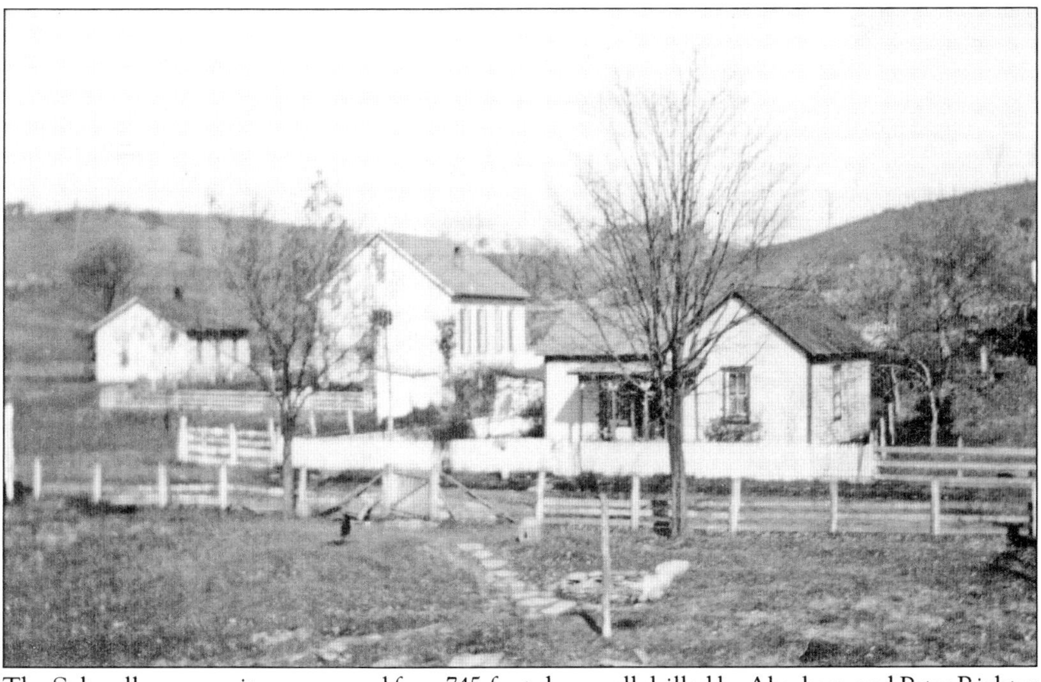

The Saltwell community was named for a 745-foot-deep well drilled by Abraham and Peter Righter in 1835. It attracted large crowds to come and light a match over the natural gas from the well, which stayed lit. The well is shown here in the foreground with the school (now remodeled into a home), a church, and a farmhouse, which was replaced by a two-story structure in 1945. The most recent longtime owner of the Saltwell Farm was the Herbert Andrick family, who owned it from 1955 to 2005. (Author's collection.)

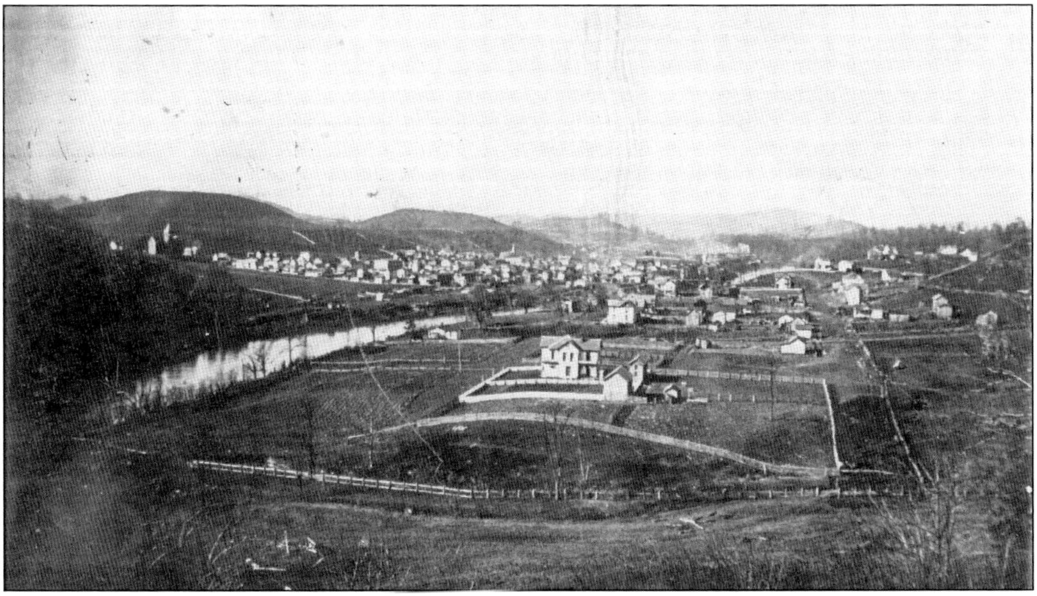

This 1906 image depicts the entrance into Shinnston from the north along present-day Route 19. In the early 1930s, the house in the foreground was known as Smith's Tourist Home, operated by Clyde and Buna Smith; it burned down many years ago. The dirt street on the right side of the photograph is currently known as Clark Street, which leads to Drain Hill. (Author's collection.)

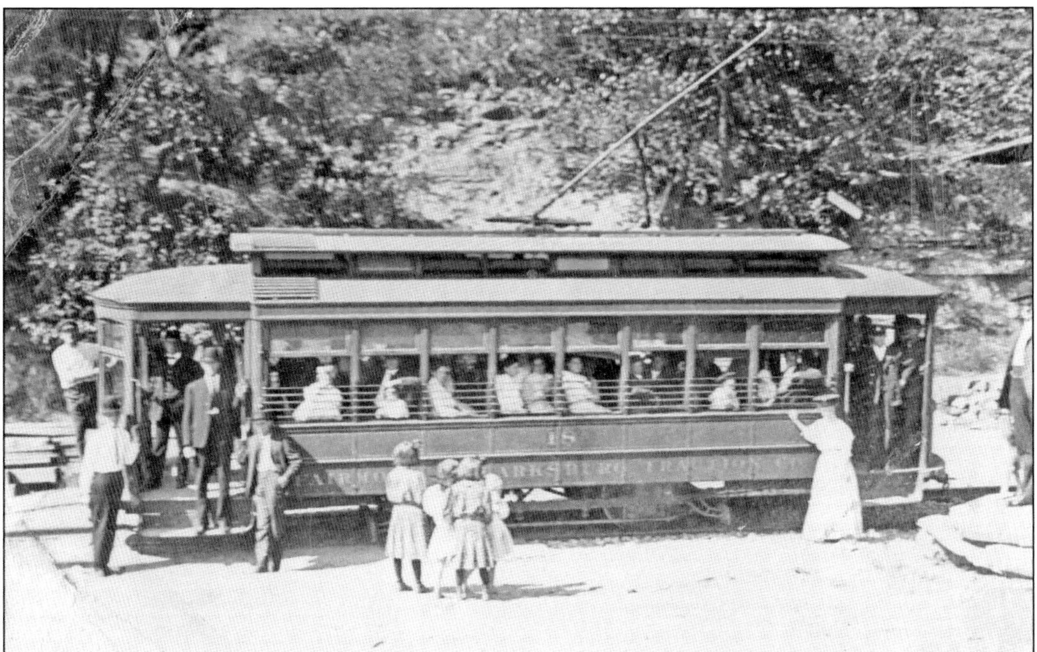

The first streetcar to come into Shinnston was worthy of this photograph, which was taken on September 1, 1906. Streetcars were a very easy and popular mode of transportation until the end of the Great Depression and World War II, when automobile use continued to rise. The last streetcar to run through Shinnston was on April 27, 1947. (Courtesy of Lowe Public Library.)

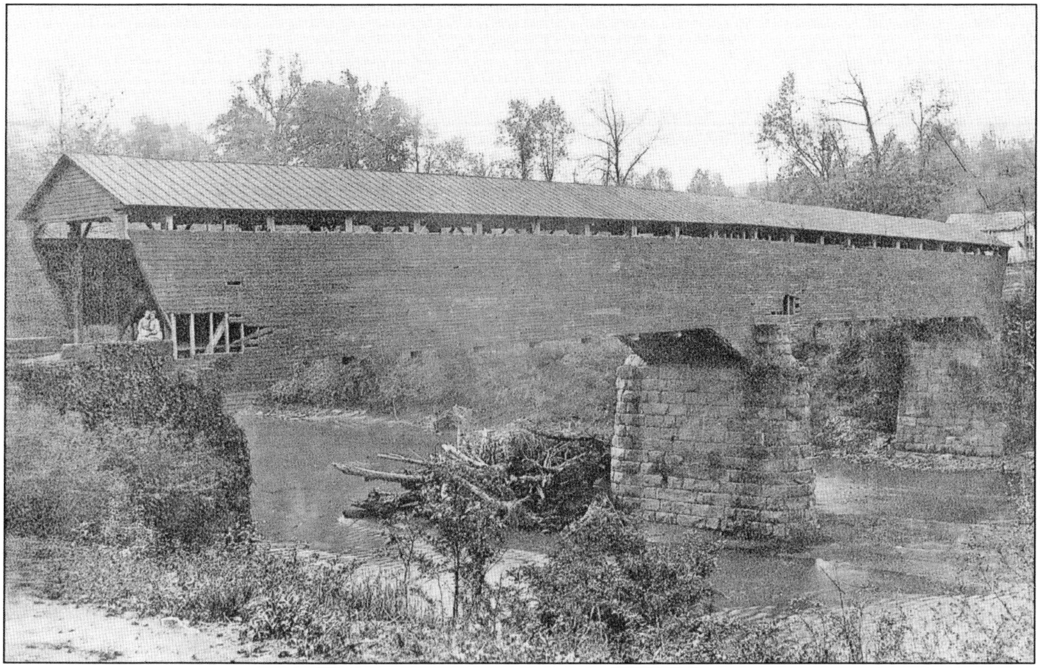

The Maulsby Bridge was built by Elmore Hart in 1855. About 100 yards long, it spanned the West Fork River near present-day Gypsy. When Gen. William Jones's celebrated raid came through on April 30, 1863, a skirmish occurred near the bridge. The bridge was abandoned in 1926 and was dismantled shortly thereafter. The center pier, built of large stones, is still visible today. (Author's collection.)

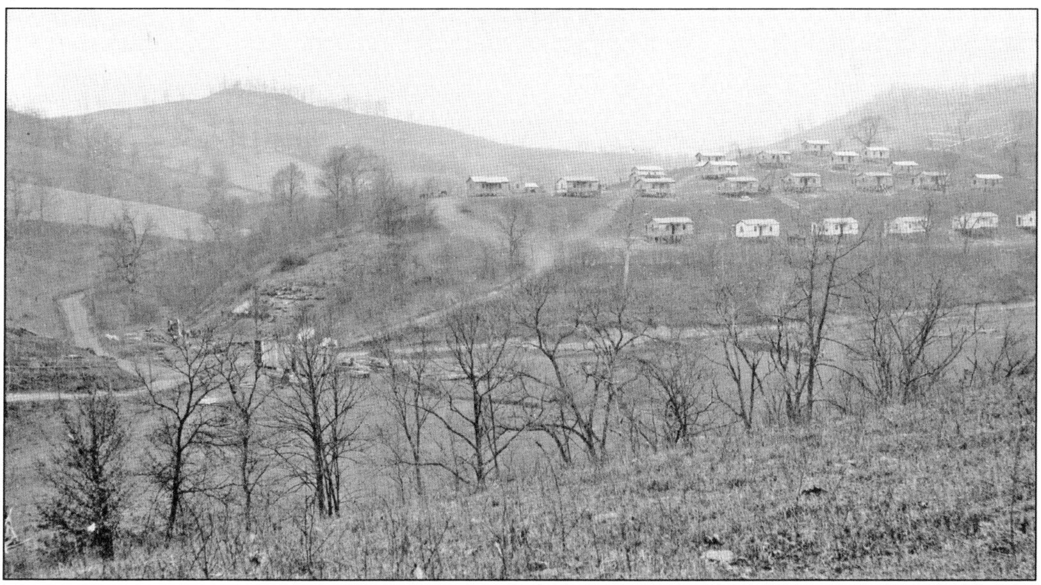

In 1917, the Shinnston Planing Mill Company received a contract for building a large company store and 110 company-type dwelling houses at Wyatt. The houses had solid stone foundations laid by stonemason George Ice of Barrackville. The Mill had previously moved several houses from Robinson Run to Wyatt. The first row homes were painted and nearing completion. The upper levels rows are still being worked on. (Author's collection.)

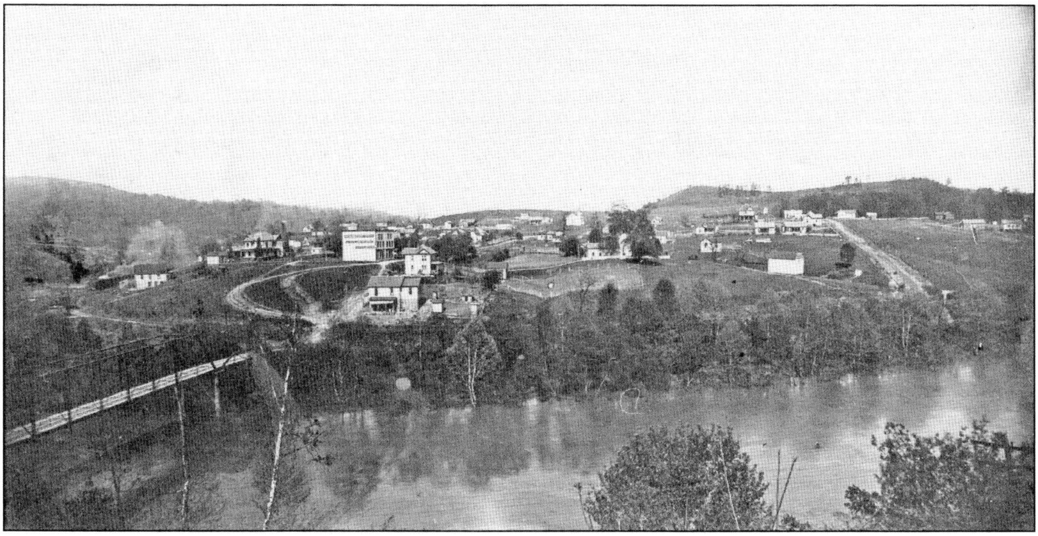

This image of Haywood was taken from the Lumberport side of the West Fork River in 1906. Photography was becoming more of an interest as people began buying the images and mailing them as postcards. This postcard was mailed to Trafford City, Pennsylvania. (Author's collection.)

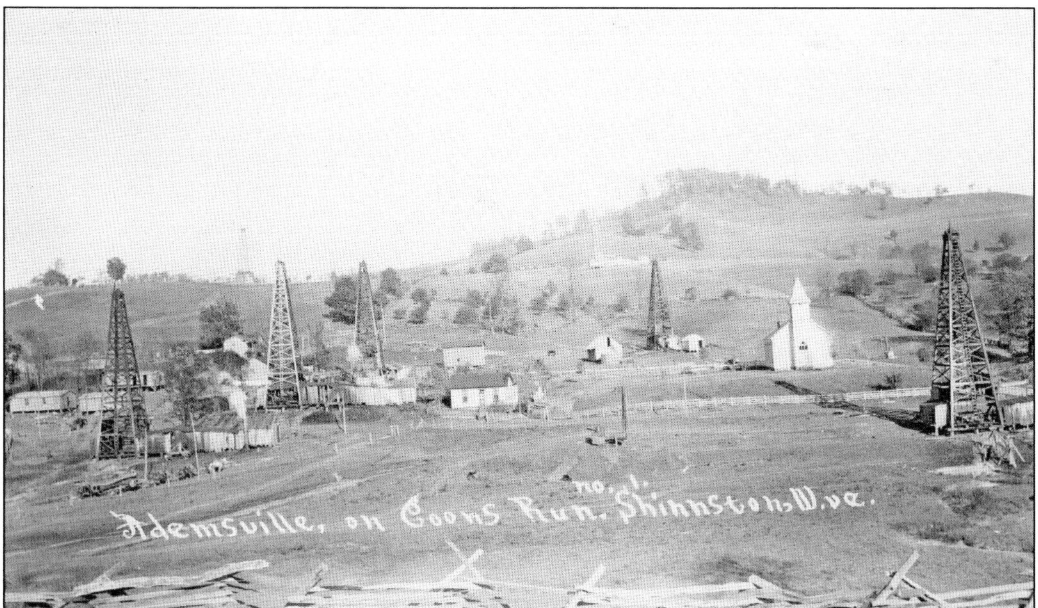

This early 1910s view of the community of Adamsville shows several oil derricks erected upon many acres of farmland. A few homes and barracks are also visible. The Coon's Run Baptist Church, seen at right, was built in 1899. (Courtesy of Lowe Public Library.)

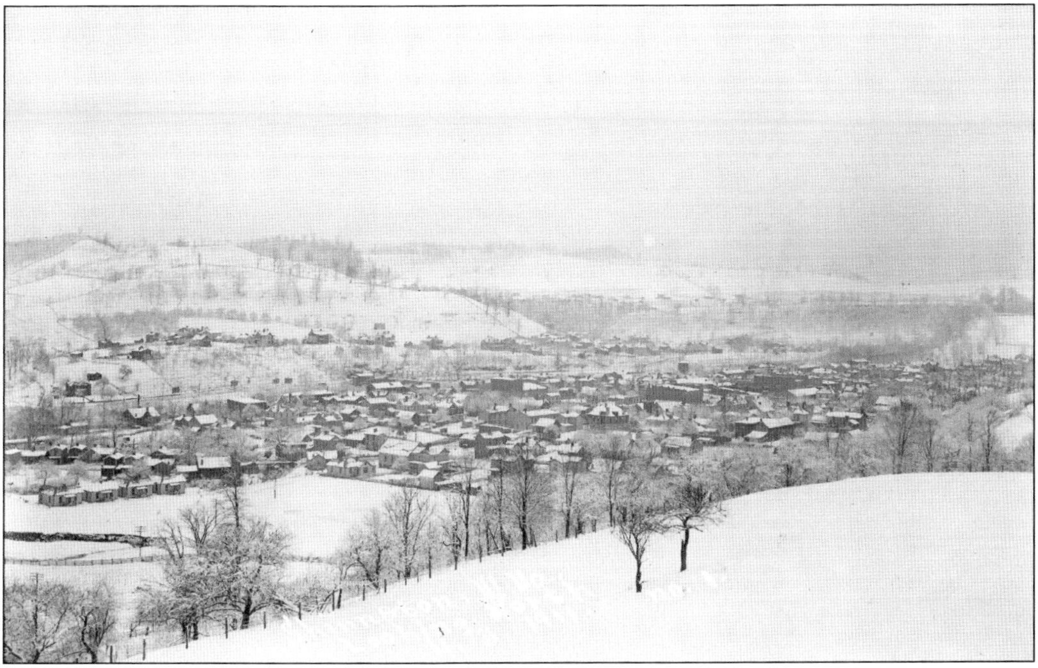

It was a cold spring morning when Muta Swiger snapped this image of Shinnston from Monroe Hill on April 3, 1911. Most of downtown is visible, with west side and north Shinnston in the distance. Less than two years after this image was captured, west side would be populated with oil derricks. (Courtesy of Lowe Public Library.)

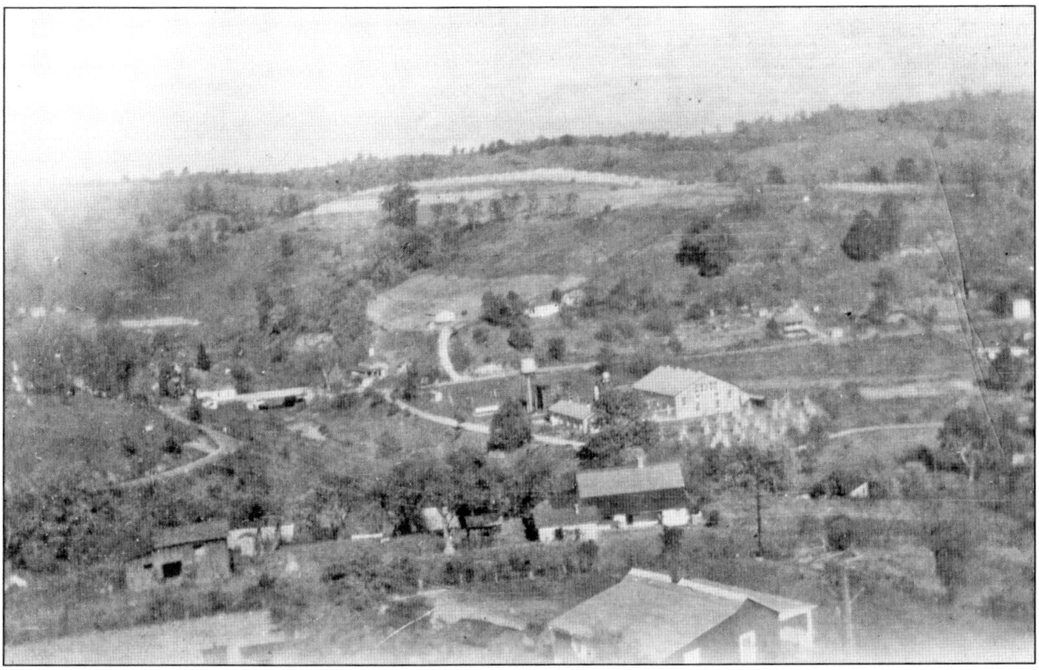

Located three miles northwest of Shinnston is the community of Peora. In this early 1930s image, many farms are visible surrounding the Peora Pump Station. Cunningham Run can be seen starting in the far left of the image. (Courtesy of Mary Rose and Ina Jean Carpenter.)

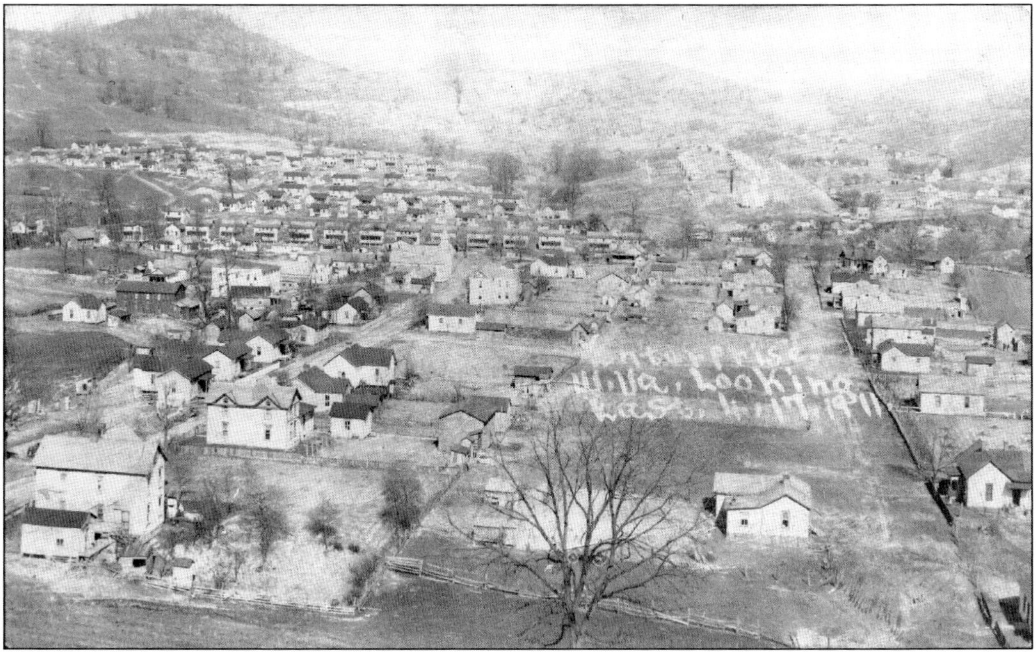

Enterprise is the northernmost community along State Route 19 in Harrison County. Settled in 1773 by the McIntire family, it was considered Indian Territory for many years after its founding. The early settlers sought refuge in building forts, such as blockhouses. One of many area stories is that of John and Rachel Rose McIntire, who were scalped and killed by Indians in May 1791. (Author's collection.)

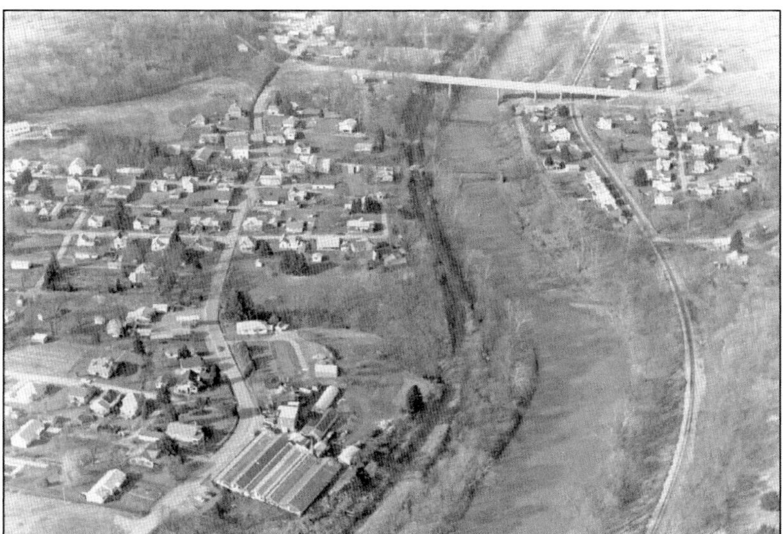

This aerial view of Enterprise was taken in 1987. Route 19 is seen on the left with Bice's Greenhouses in the foreground. The railroad tracks are easily visible on the east side of the West Fork River. Several company houses are seen in the photograph, as are the old and new bridges. (Courtesy of Bob Bice II.)

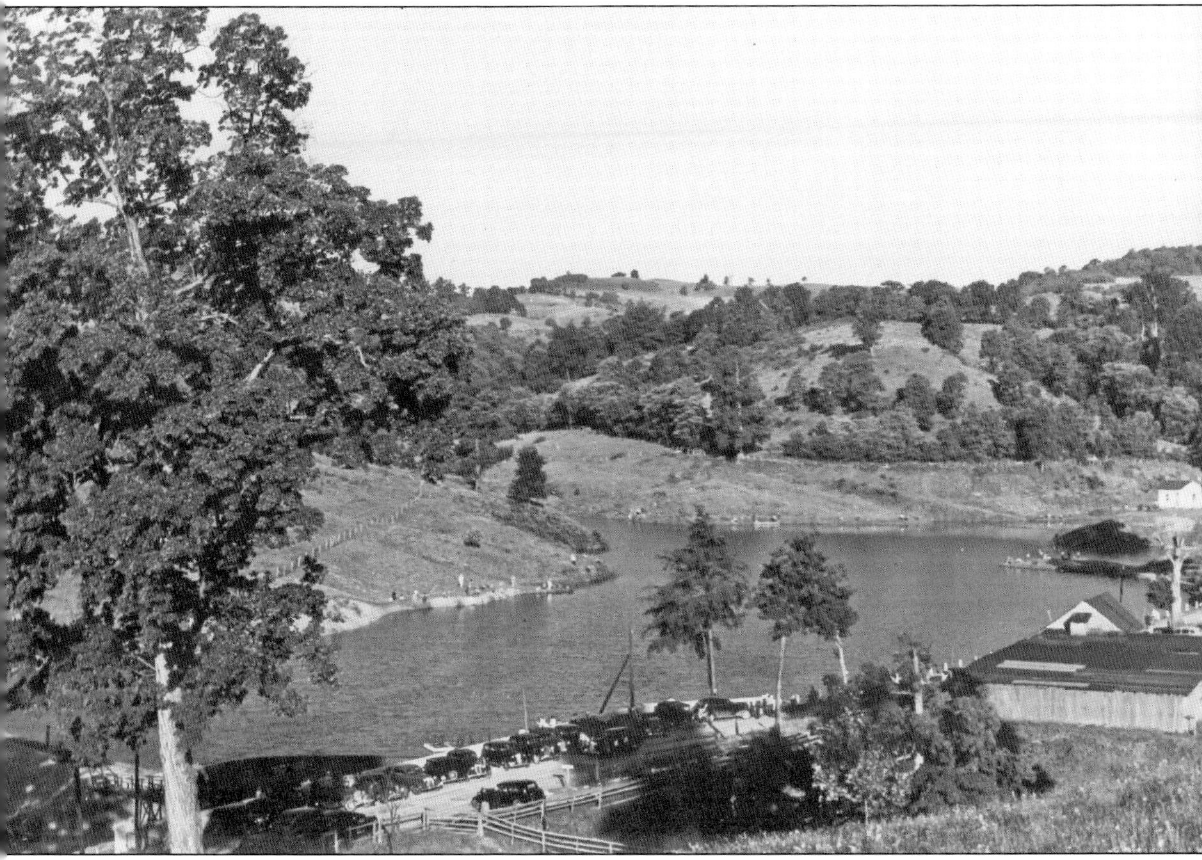

This c. 1940 image of the water reservoir of Shinnston near Robinson Run was taken at a time when picnics and fishing were enjoyed there. The reservoir held approximately 25 million gallons of water at capacity. Tests were run in the early 1940s, revealing contamination with sulphur. The sealing of a Katherine Mine opening on the Amos Robinson farm proved to nearly eliminate the contamination, but other problems later developed, and the reservoir was abandoned. Salerno Brothers later filled the reservoir in. (Courtesy of Lowe Public Library.)

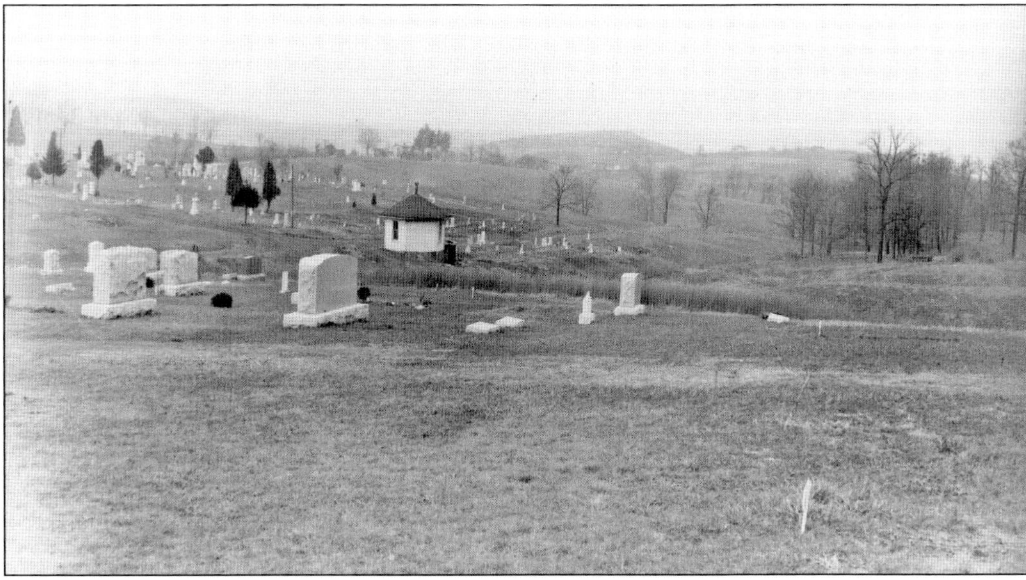

The Shinnston Masonic Cemetery was first established as a cemetery after the lodge purchased two acres of land in 1883. The first person buried in it was the infant daughter of Benjamin Franklin Lowe. Some graves have since been moved into the cemetery; some of the stones are older than the cemetery itself. (Courtesy of Shinnston Masonic Cemetery.)

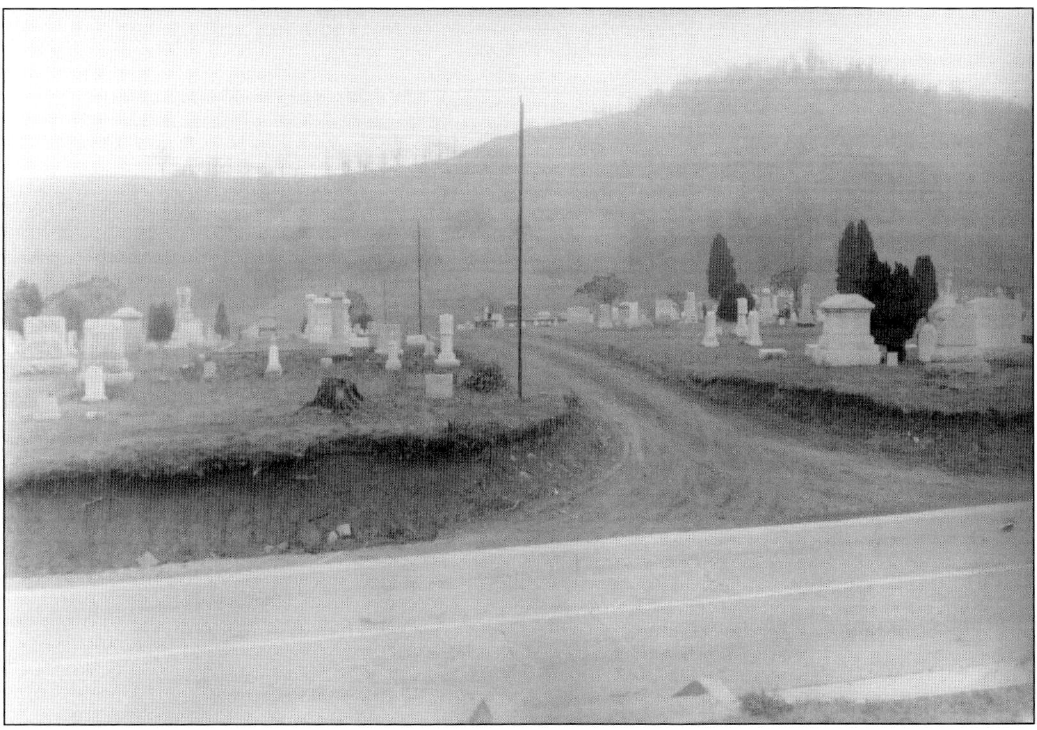

The Shinnston Masonic Cemetery is the largest cemetery in the areas surrounding Shinnston. The road in front of the cemetery was first paved in 1914. This image was taken before the wall was built between the cemetery and the highway. Note that the driveway is a dirt road. (Courtesy of Shinnston Masonic Cemetery.)

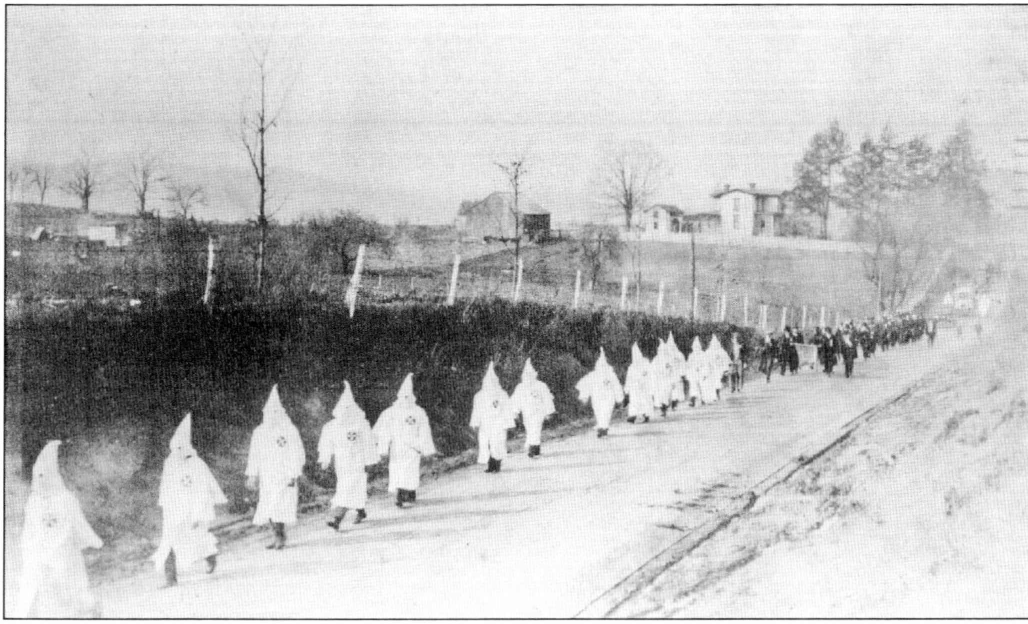

Ku Klux Klan members are shown leading the funeral procession for Samuel Wable in 1924. Klan chapters in West Virginia organized shortly after the Civil War but remained silent until the 1920s. Largely referring to a secret racist society, many Klansmen around Shinnston also enforced a strict moral adherence to all races. Many members were leading businessmen of the area. The house in the background still stands across from the Levi Shinn log house. (Courtesy of Shinnston Masonic Cemetery.)

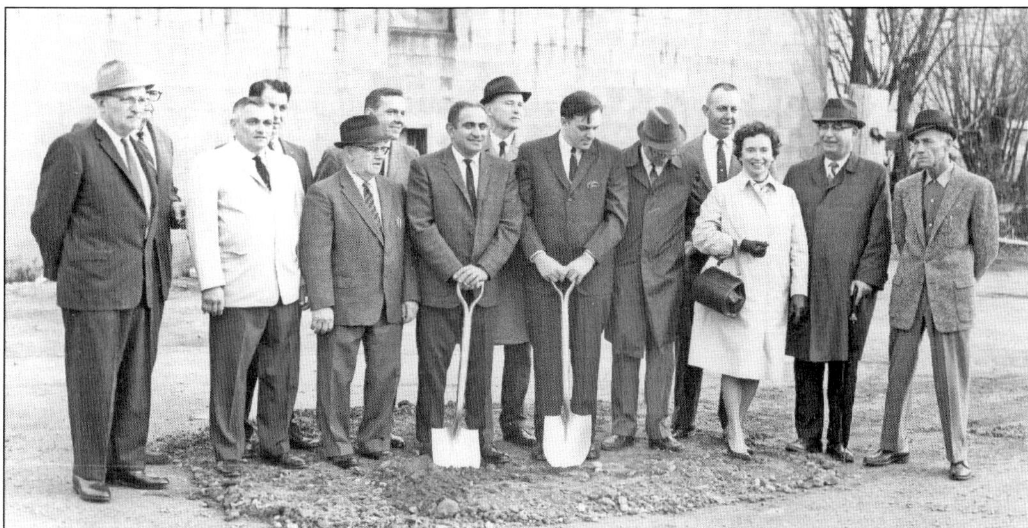

Leaders of the City of Shinnston gather for a ground-breaking ceremony in March 1968 for a new city building on lower Bridge Street. Pictured from left to right are Councilmen Ed Royal, Warren Hursey, Patsy Alessio, Paul Tate, John Morgan, and John W. Currey; Mayor George Simon (with shovel); Councilman Jerry Harbert; recorder Robert Toth (also with shovel); Thad Meredith, publisher of the *Shinnston News*; Supt. Walter P. Hudkins; City Clerk Lena Poling; City Attorney David Abruzzino; and Robert Riley of L&R Construction Company. (Author's collection.)

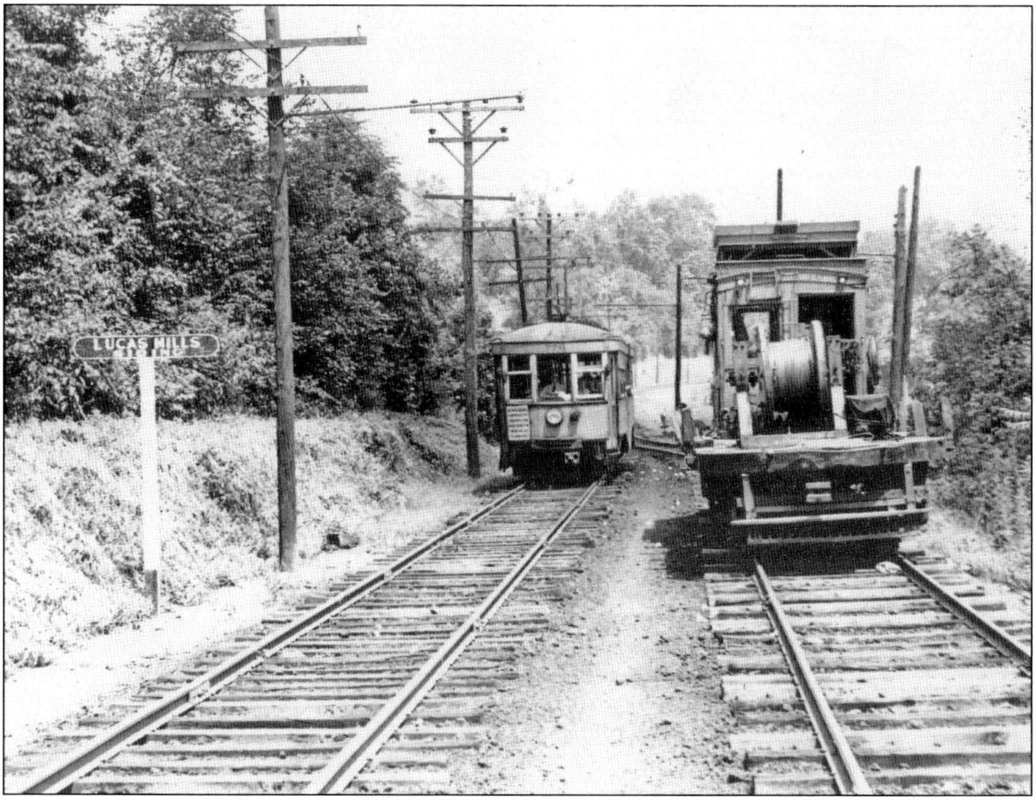

This streetcar is shown approaching the community of Lucas Mills, the first stop in Shinnston heading north. Once located across the West Fork River from Pleasant Hill and along the Wyatt Road, Lucas Mills derived its name from a steam sawmill that two Lucas brothers operated. The electrified vehicles were once a very popular mode of transportation. (Author's collection.)

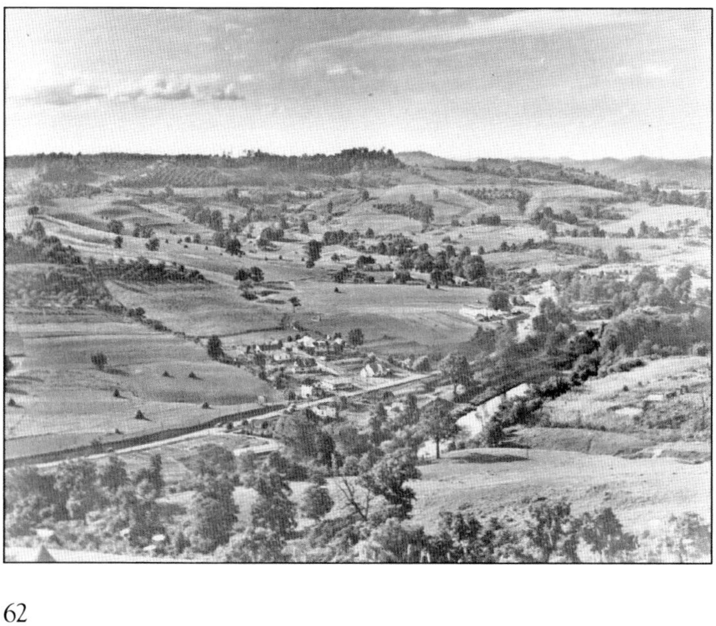

The midway point between Shinnston and Enterprise is appropriately named Midway, visible in the center of the photograph. Worth and Jim Tetrick's greenhouses are seen in the foreground with Felix Sturm's greenhouses visible at center, right. Viropa is seen on the right side of the photograph with some of the foundations from the company houses seen at the image's right edge. (Courtesy of Shinnston Historical Association.)

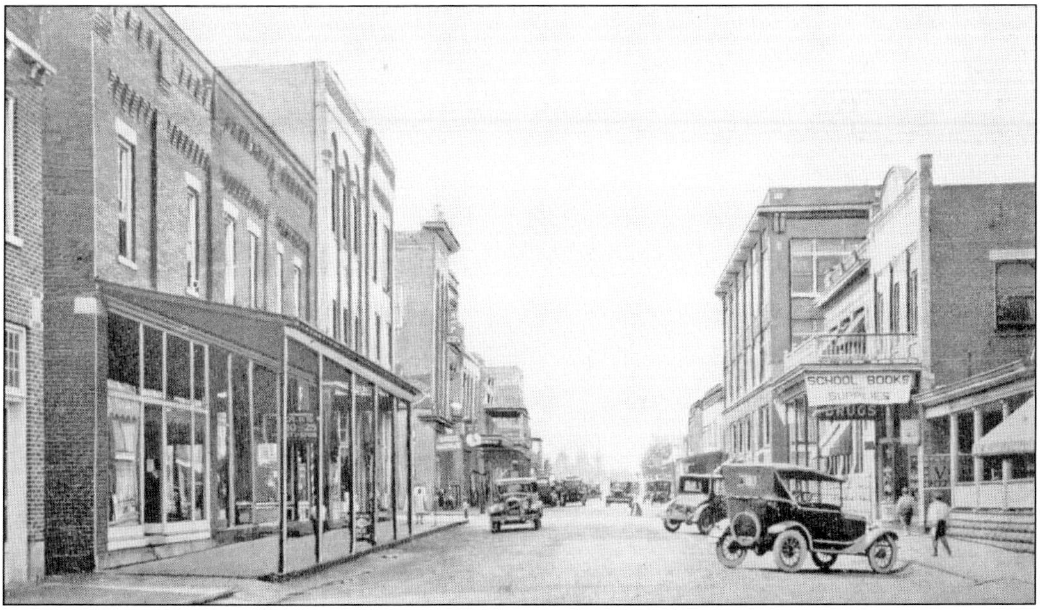

This postcard image shows an early view of Pike Street populated with both business and travel. Before motor vehicles became the primary mode of travel, automobile owners could park in any direction along Pike Street. In the background, vehicles can be seen swerving around one another to avoid collisions. Note the businesses with covered walkways. (Author's collection.)

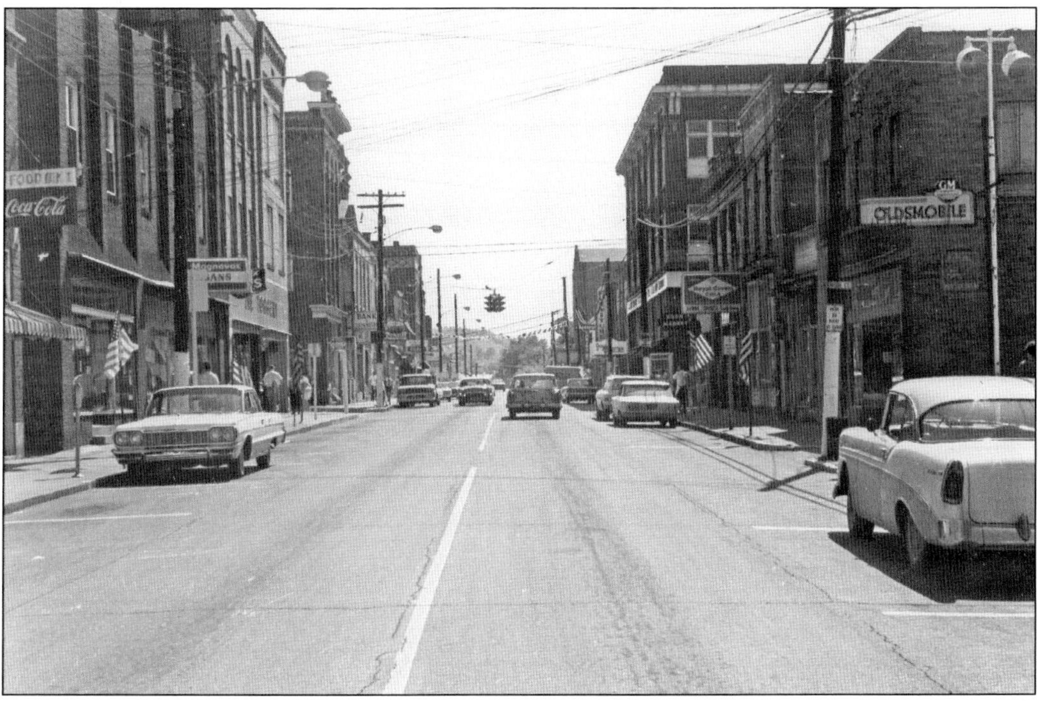

In the 1960s, Shinnston was a flood of businesses along Pike Street. Seen in this photograph are the Oldsmobile garage, Louie Tate's Confectionary, State Food Store, G.C. Murphy, Joyce Furniture Co., Anderson Chevrolet, A&P store, Rice Theatre, the Toggery, Hawker Hardware, Bank of Shinnston, Rice-Rexall, and Simon's Confectionary. (Author's collection.)

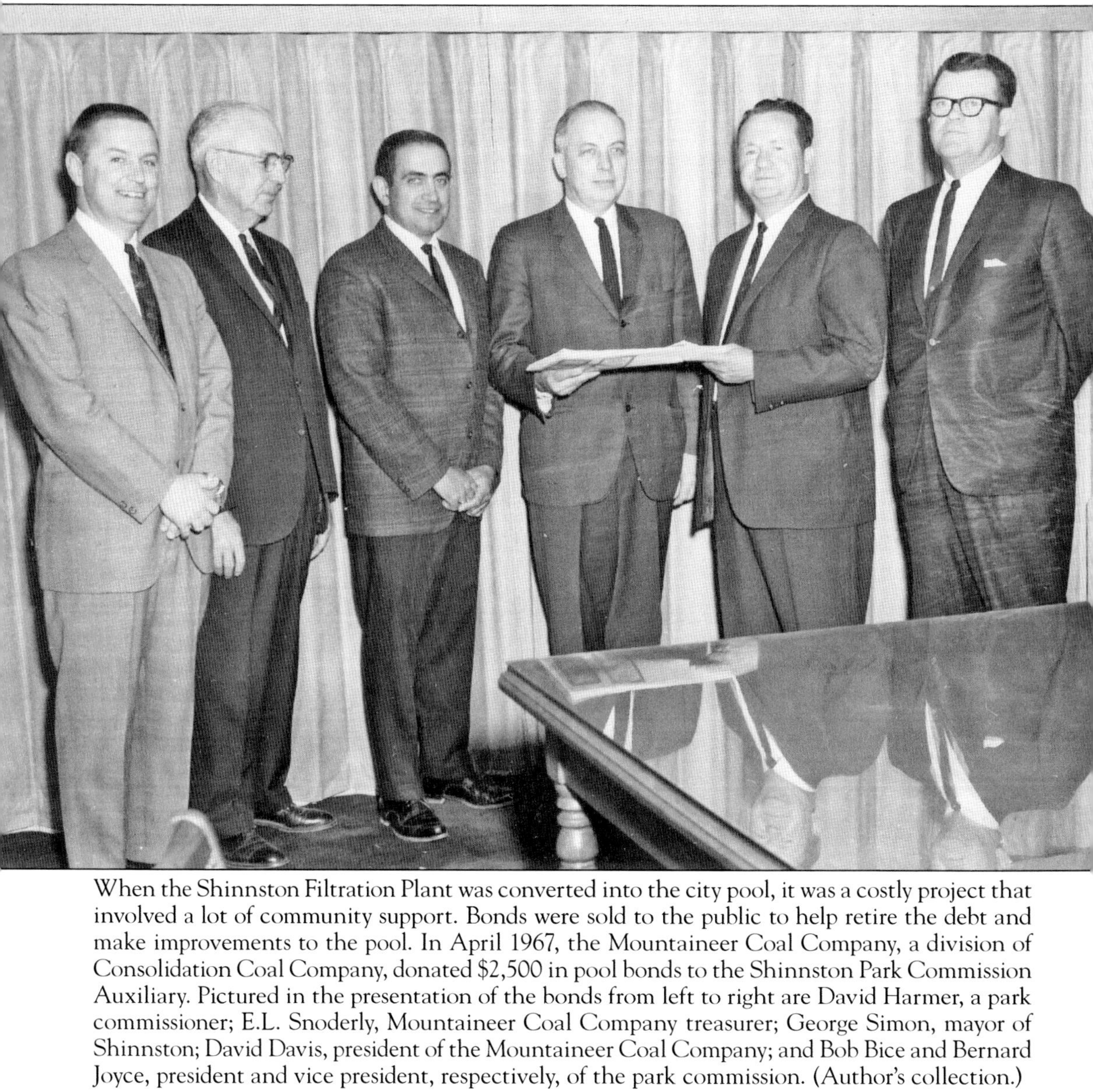

When the Shinnston Filtration Plant was converted into the city pool, it was a costly project that involved a lot of community support. Bonds were sold to the public to help retire the debt and make improvements to the pool. In April 1967, the Mountaineer Coal Company, a division of Consolidation Coal Company, donated $2,500 in pool bonds to the Shinnston Park Commission Auxiliary. Pictured in the presentation of the bonds from left to right are David Harmer, a park commissioner; E.L. Snoderly, Mountaineer Coal Company treasurer; George Simon, mayor of Shinnston; David Davis, president of the Mountaineer Coal Company; and Bob Bice and Bernard Joyce, president and vice president, respectively, of the park commission. (Author's collection.)

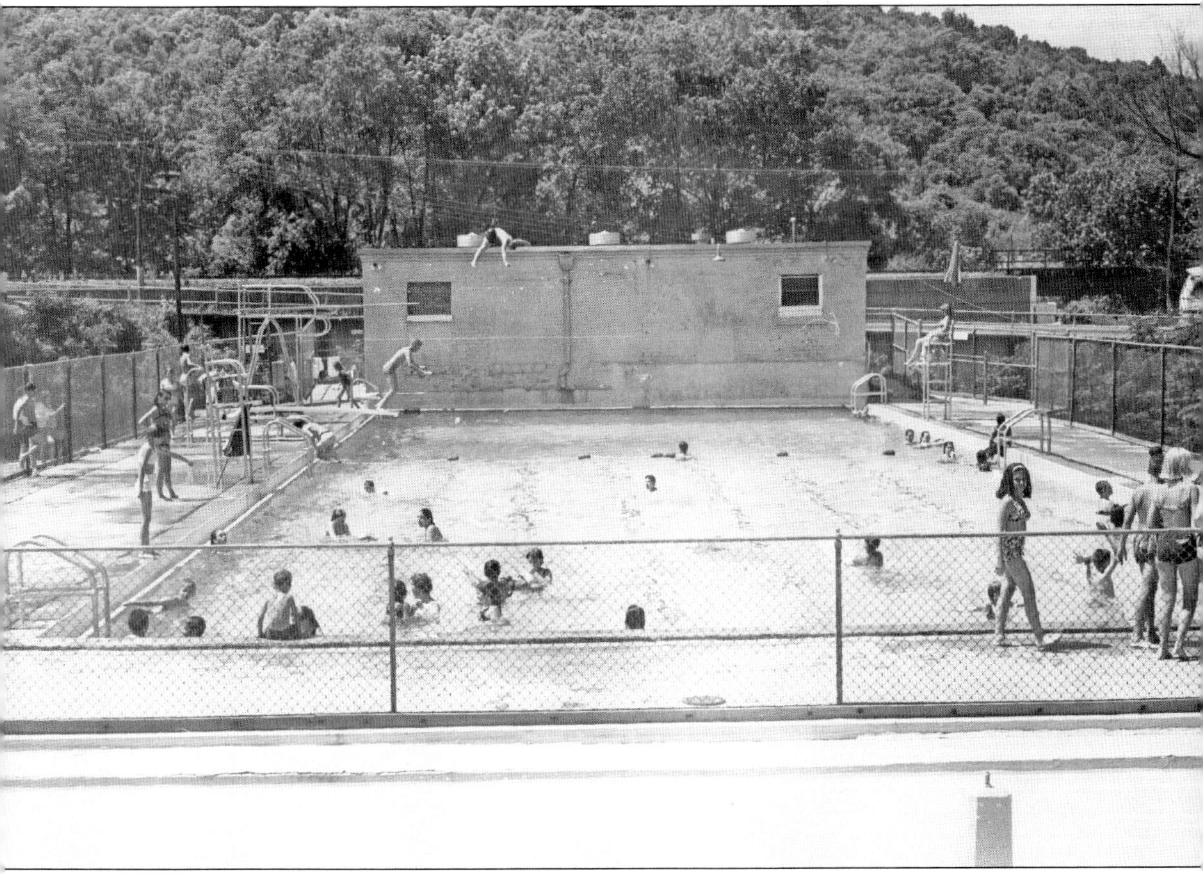

This image of the old Shinnston pool was taken from the Monroe Street side, looking toward Pike Street and the West Fork River. Note the diver steadying himself on the board, as well as the one caught midair off the high dive. There are approximately 40 people using the pool, with a lifeguard station on each side. The building was previously the site of the old water filtration plant, which was built in 1921 and shut down in 1948. The pool was constructed in 1956 and closed in 1991. Area residents now use the more modern facility, located at Shinnston City Park in East Shinnston. (Author's collection.)

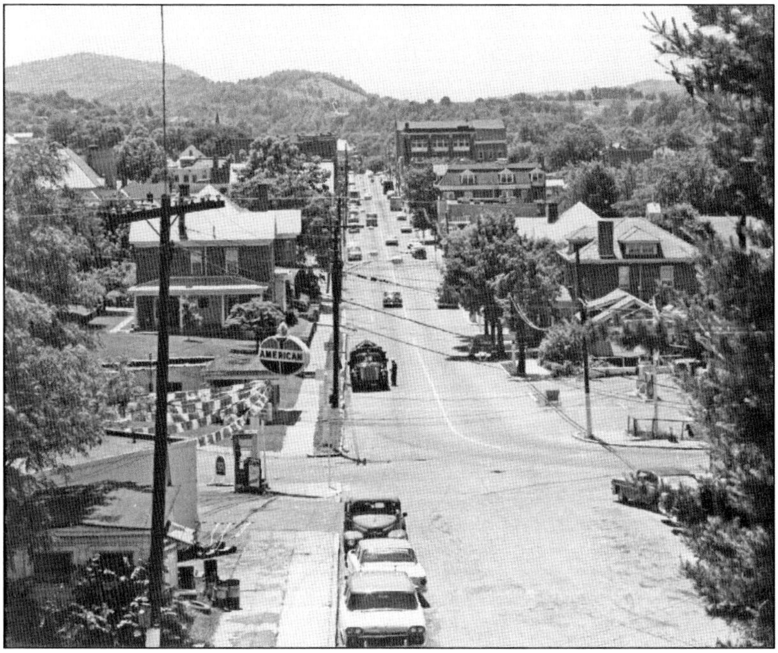

Three gas stations can easily be seen in this photograph of Pike Street from the old high school hill. At one time, there were seven gas stations between the high school and the Saltwell Road intersection. No gas stations are located along this stretch of road today. (Author's collection.)

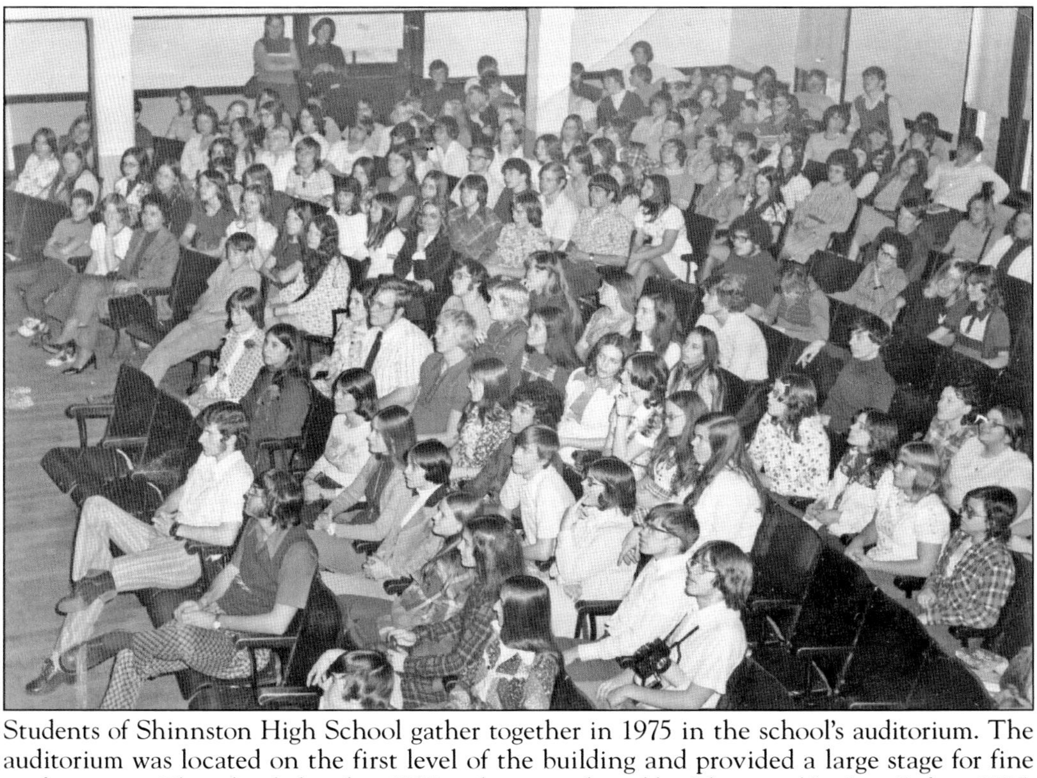

Students of Shinnston High School gather together in 1975 in the school's auditorium. The auditorium was located on the first level of the building and provided a large stage for fine performances. The school closed in 1993 and was purchased by Glenn and Jo Ann Rife in 1995. In the early 2000s, the auditorium was used for auctions. (Courtesy of Beth Andrick Bice.)

Six

Businesses

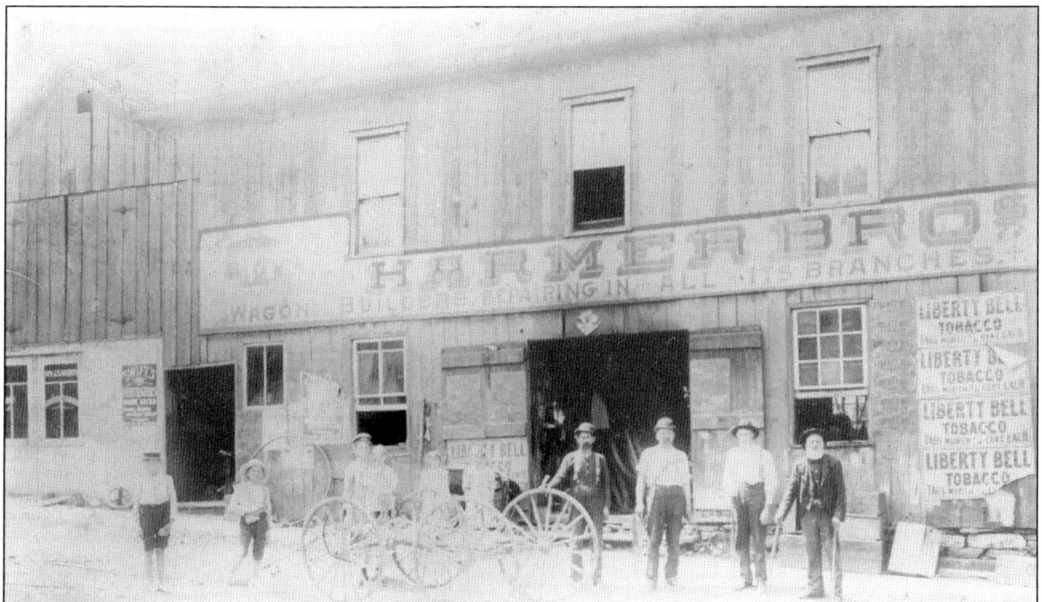

In 1852, Winchester native Benjamin Tyson Harmer Sr. was working as a wagon apprentice in Front Royal, Virginia, where he answered a telegram to come work in Shinnston. He built his shop and residence on the south side of upper Main Street. Being a skilled artisan, he was also often called upon to make coffins. As wagons became nonessential in daily life, the undertaking business expanded. Today, Harmer Funeral Home is under the ownership of Jay D. Harmer, great-great grandson of B. Tyson Harmer Sr. (Courtesy of Harmer Funeral Home.)

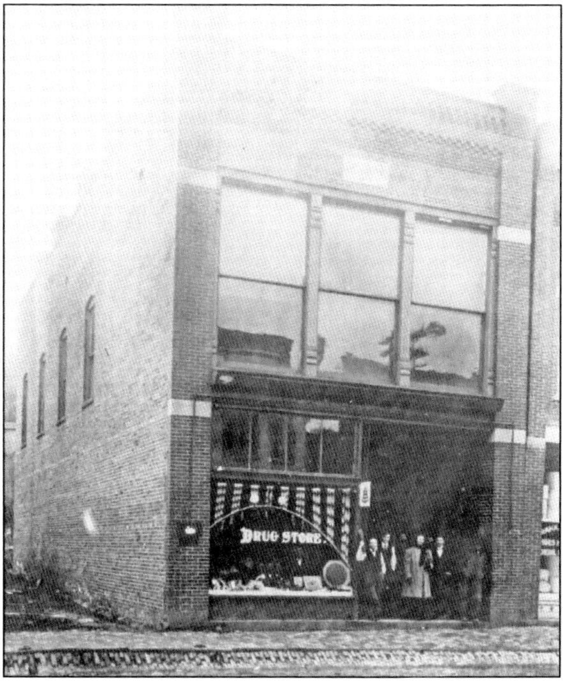

The building pictured here was originally constructed in 1903 as the Shinnston Pharmacy building. W.D. Bryan was the first proprietor, and in 1911 Ralph Johnson took over. George and Jean Rice bought the business in 1942, renaming it Rice-Rexall. Six people are standing in the entrance. At the right edge of the photograph, the Frank Abruzzino general merchandise store can be seen. (Courtesy of Lowe Public Library.)

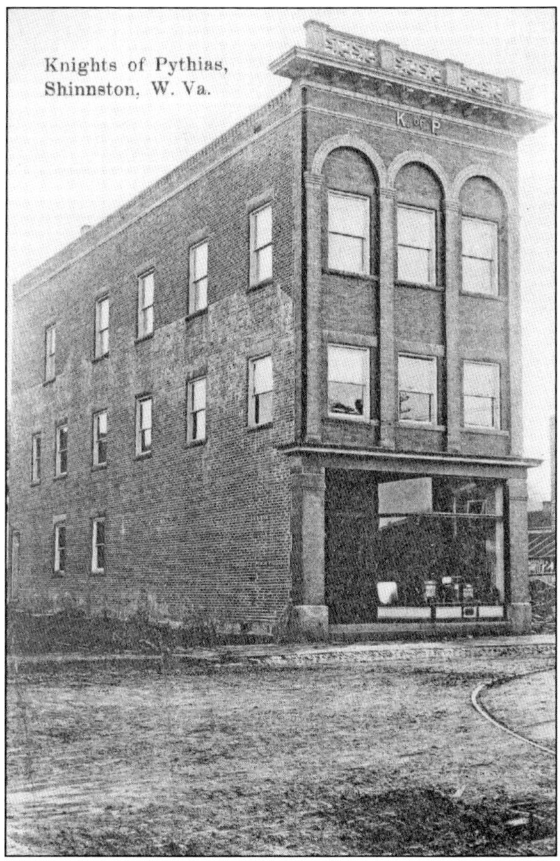

This building, located at the southeast corner of Pike and Bridge Streets, was erected in the very early 1900s. The Knights of Pythias held their meetings on the third floor. Thomas Hawker purchased C.C. Hamilton's hardware store and renamed it Leslie Hawker and Company Hardware Store, eventually locating here. Leslie's sons Wayne and Marlin later joined the family business. This is now part of the WesBanco complex. (Author's collection.)

The Farmers Bank opened in June 1899 as Shinnston's first bank at the southeast corner of Pike and Walnut Streets. DeWitt Ayers was nearly killed during the excavation for the building when he was accidentally buried beneath ground. The building housed the bank, the IOOF Lodge, an insurance office, barbershop, and bathroom, as well as the Shinnston Union Telephone Company. (Author's collection.)

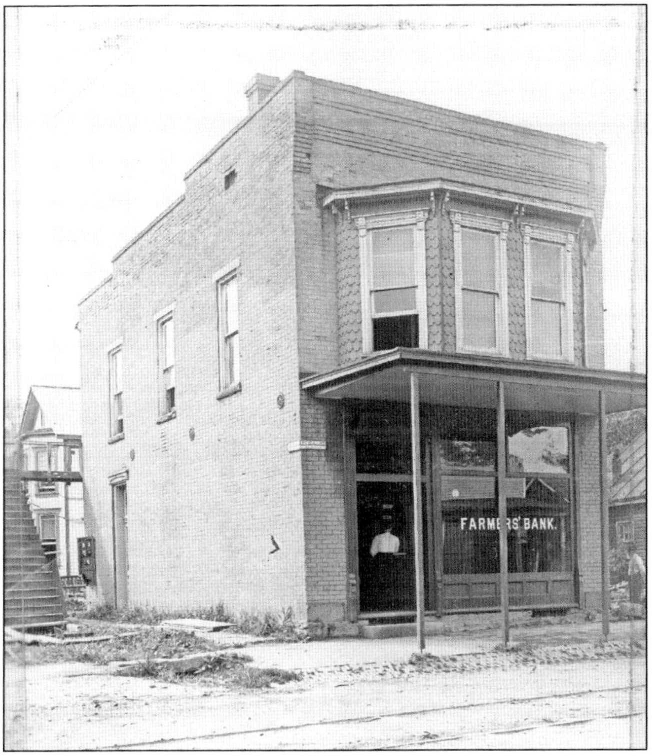

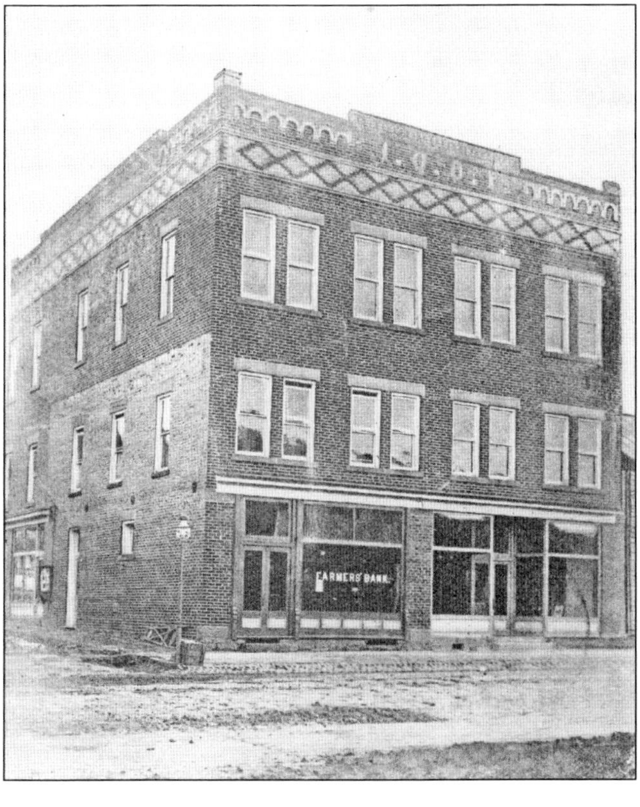

Visible in this 1911 photograph, the IOOF building was once a two-story structure that housed the Farmers Bank. The third story was added by the lodge, and meetings were held there. For many years, the mayor's office was located in the back of the building with an entrance on Walnut Street. (Author's collection.)

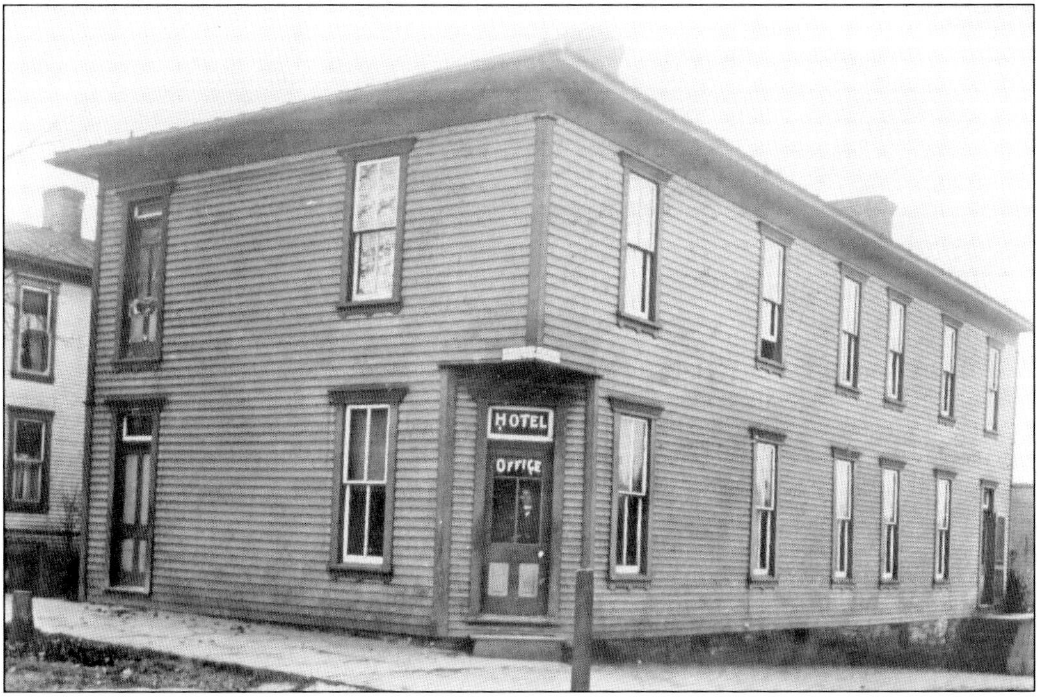

The Oak Hotel, located at the southeast corner of Pike and Main Streets, was a two-story structure that replaced the building that previously housed the Red Lion Tavern. John and Sarah Carder bought the Red Lion Tavern and renamed it Carder House. This structure was built about 1892 and eventually passed through several owners before being razed in 1926. The proprietor of the hotel can be seen inside the doorway. (Courtesy of Lowe Public Library.)

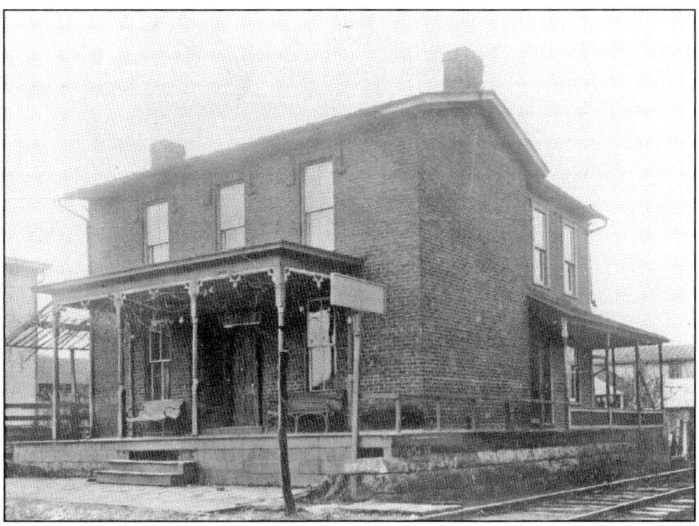

The Robey Boarding House was located at the south corner of Bridge and Railroad Streets. It was established in the 1890s and ran successfully into the very early 1900s by Elizabeth (Randall) Robey, who also sold meals to non-boarders. It was later operated by the Saunders and Alley families. This photograph was taken when the Leeson family was operating Leeson Hotel. (James M. Currey collection, courtesy of Leigh C. Merrifield.)

The lower-level brickwork was nearing completion in this 1909 view of the First National Bank building. Located at the northwest corner of Pike and Bridge Streets, the bank was in operation for nearly eight months when they moved into this building on April 19, 1910. In 1919, the Peoples Bank of Shinnston merged with First National Bank, doubling their capital stock. (Author's collection.)

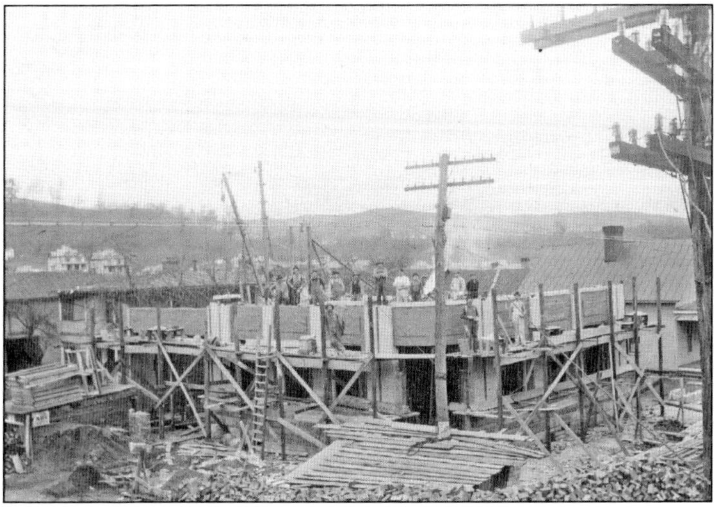

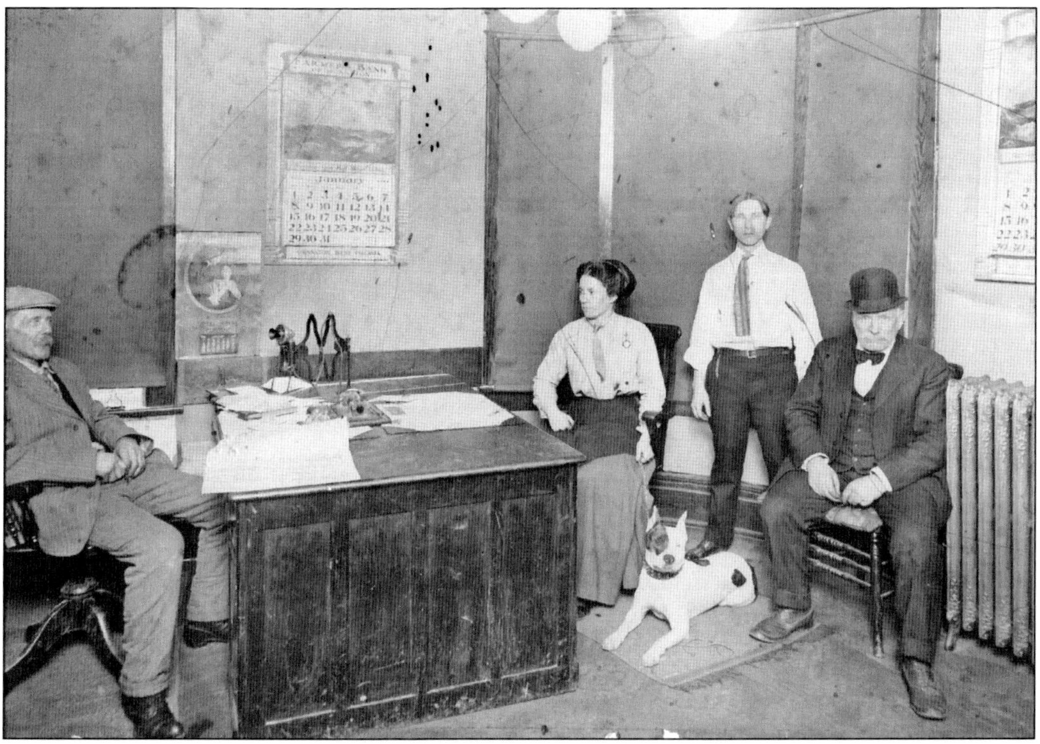

First National Bank was one of two banks in Shinnston when this photograph was taken on its second level in January 1911. The oil and gas boom brought many transactions, this being with the Pittsburgh and West Virginia Gas Company. T.B. Peddicord is seated opposite Vera Jamison while Wiley Villers (standing) and Jefferson Peddicord look at the camera. The calendars on the wall advertise the Farmers Bank and Hotel Royal. (Author's collection.)

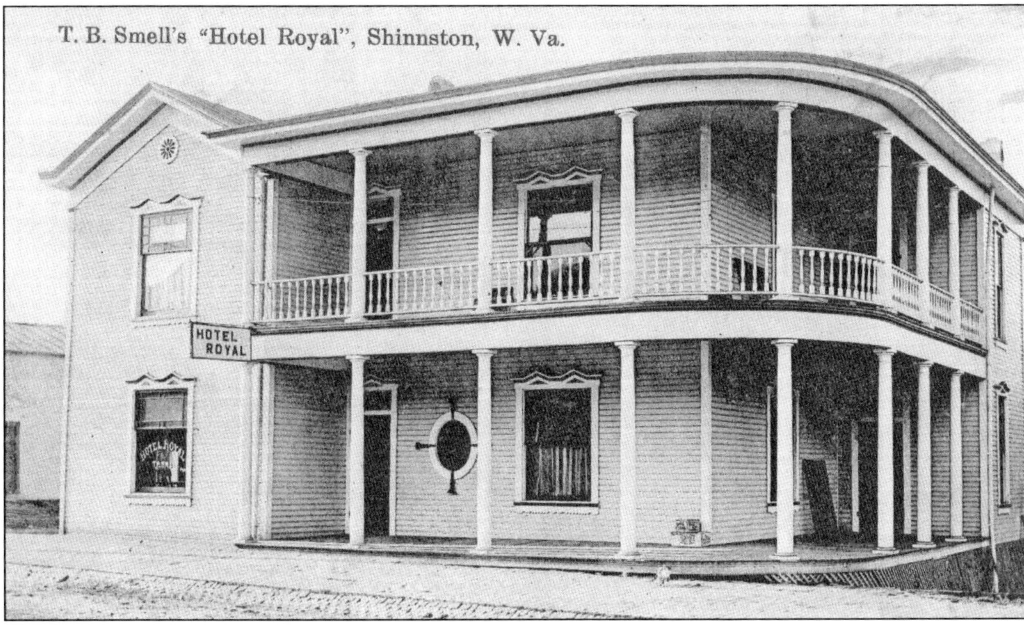

Thomas Smell bought this building at the northwest corner of Pike and Rebecca Streets in the early 1900s and operated Hotel Royal. In addition to sleeping rooms, lunch to the public was sold. Occupants included Dell Fuller, George Baldwin, Frank Williams, and O.L. Reed. Hotel Royal later became Chalfant's Tea Room. After extensive remodeling, Noel Riley turned it into Riley's Funeral Home in 1934. The building was razed in 1976 and is now a vacant lot. (Author's collection.)

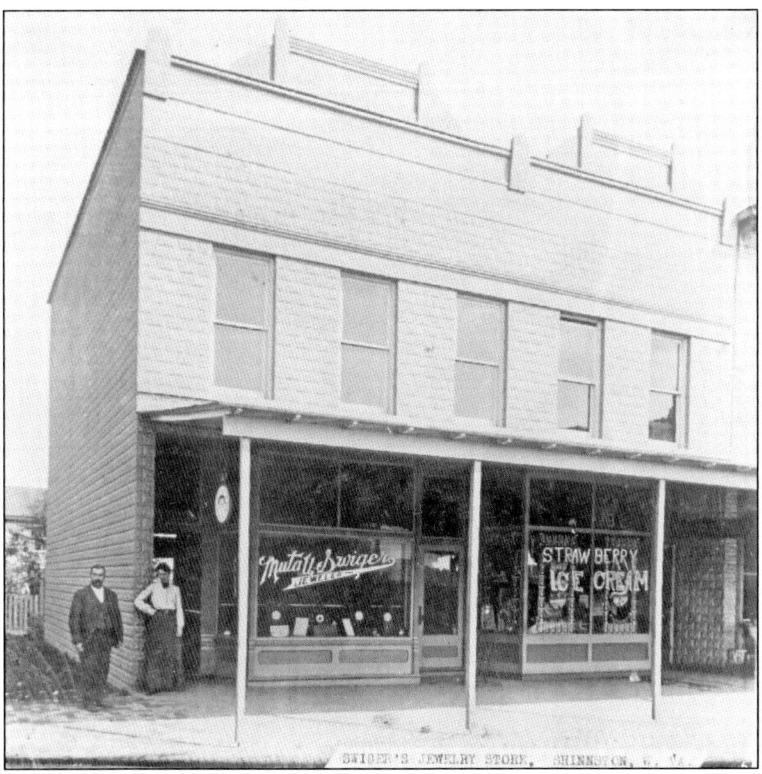

Muta Swiger established his jewelry store at the northwest corner of Pike and Walnut Streets in the 1890s. In addition to fine watches and jewelry, he sold cut glass, china, clocks, records, school books, and photographs. He is responsible for capturing many of the photographs in this book. After Swiger died in 1952, the business was continued by his assistant, Florida Haggerty, until around 1962. (Courtesy of Harmer Funeral Home.)

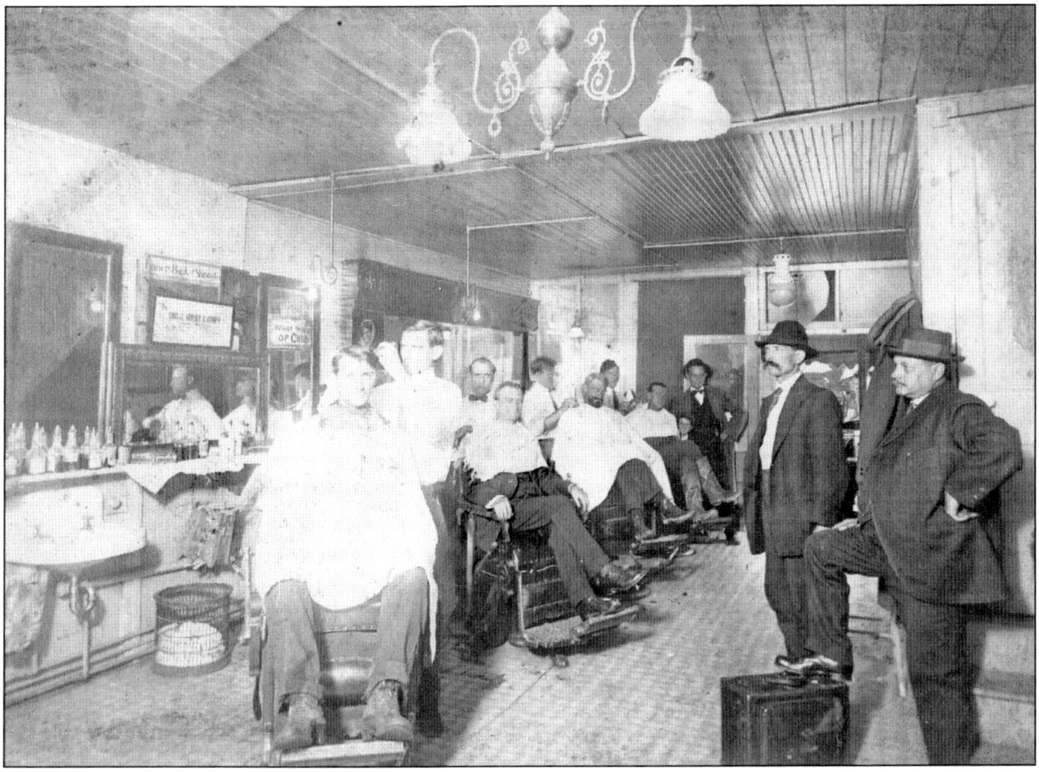

This photograph demonstrates the importance of wanting to look your best. Four barbers, each busy at a chair, turn their customers toward the cameraman while three others wait for service. This barbershop was located on the west side of the 200 block of Pike Street. (Author's collection.)

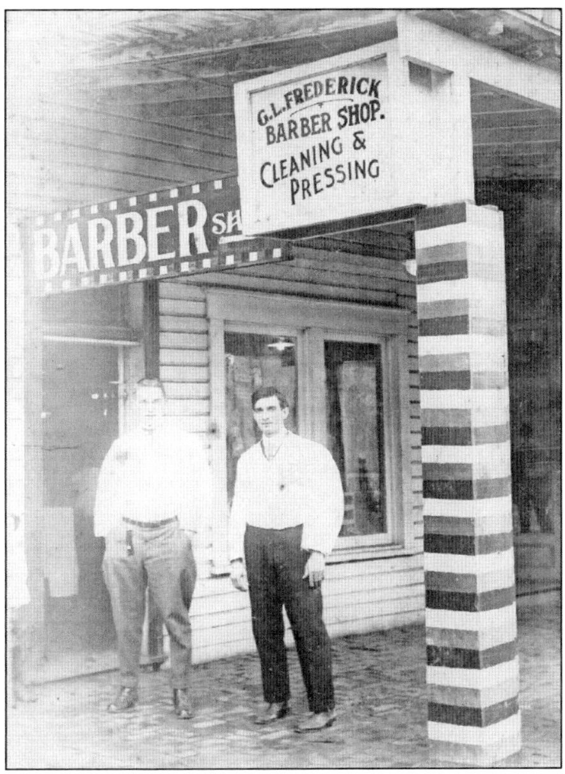

George Frederick's barbershop was located in the 300 block on the east side of Pike Street when this photograph was taken about 1915. Jay Riggs and Ruble Marsh later purchased his cleaning and pressing business, which they added to their joint venture, the Toggery. In 1916, Frederick relocated his barbershop to the basement of the Shinnston Furniture and Undertaking building for one year, with an entrance on Bridge Street. (Author's collection.)

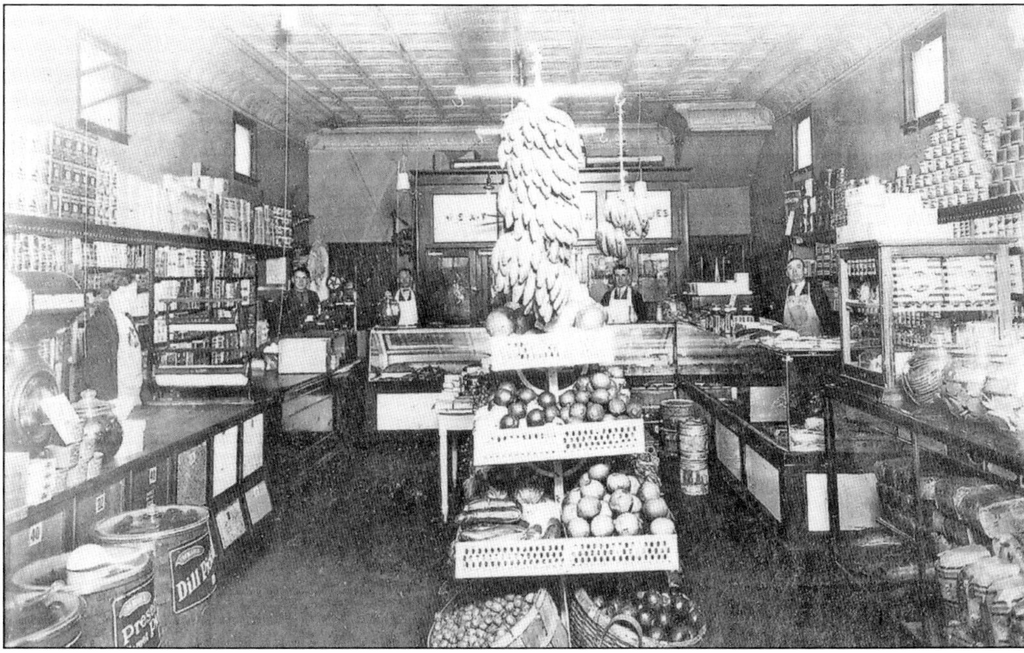

The interior of the Hurst Brothers Store is shown here. They sold groceries and were well known for their fine cut meats. Glen, Howard, and Albert Hurst were the proprietors. The store was located on upper Bridge Street in the vicinity of the current American Legion building and was in operation during the mid- to late 1920s. (Author's collection.)

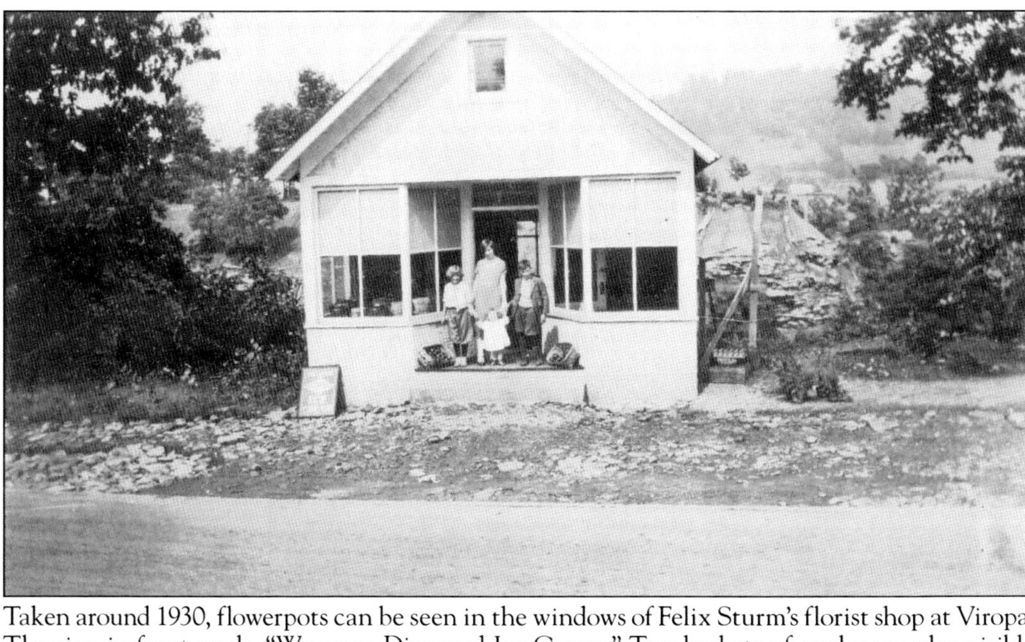

Taken around 1930, flowerpots can be seen in the windows of Felix Sturm's florist shop at Viropa. The sign in front reads, "We serve Diamond Ice Cream." Two baskets of apples are also visible in front. The flower shop was located on the lot where D&J Auto now parks cars. (Courtesy of Leslie "Skip" and Judy Tichenor.)

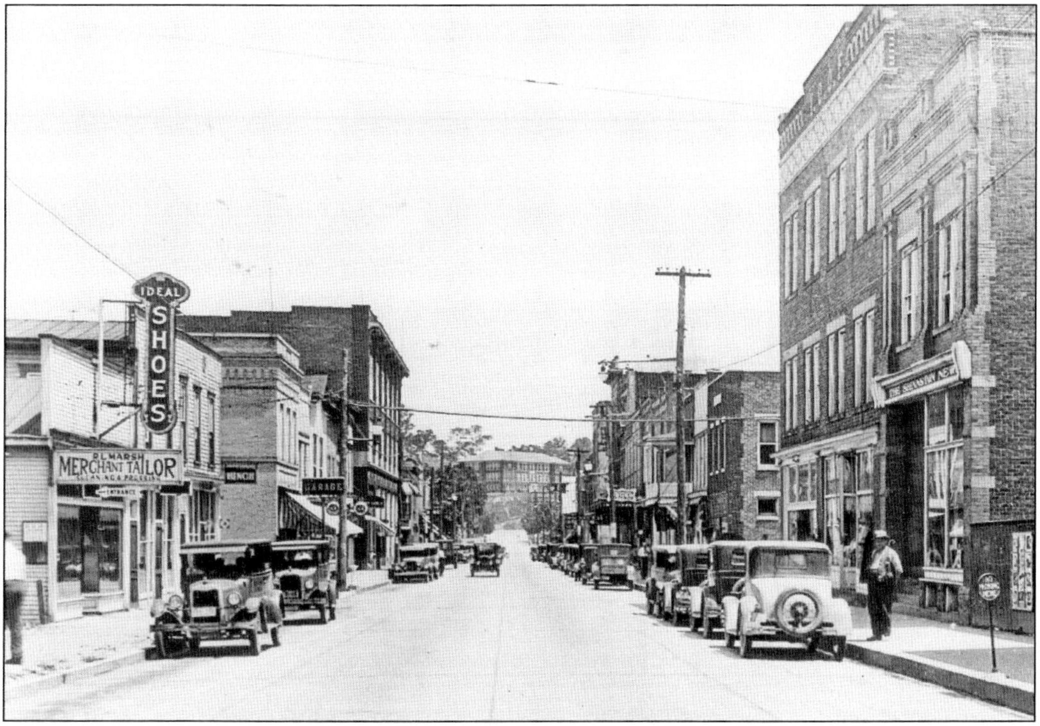

This 1930s image of Pike Street in Shinnston shows a clean town built with pride. Ruble Marsh's cleaning business is seen at the left edge. The largest building in town, seen at left, housed the G.C. Murphy Company for many years. The *Shinnston News* office at right is still operating from this same location. In the distance, Shinnston High School can be seen, overlooking the city. (Author's collection.)

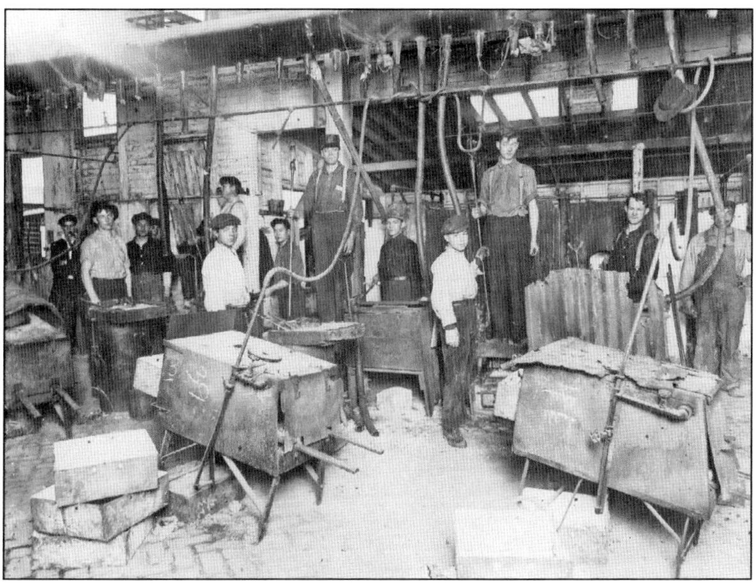

In addition to the stemware factory, located on Robinson Court, Shinnston was home to two glass factories. The Marion Glass Company was located at the end of Rebecca Street along the West Fork River. This factory, Paquet Glass Company, was chartered in 1919 and located in the field behind present Vincent Lumber. At least 13 people are in the photograph. (Author's collection.)

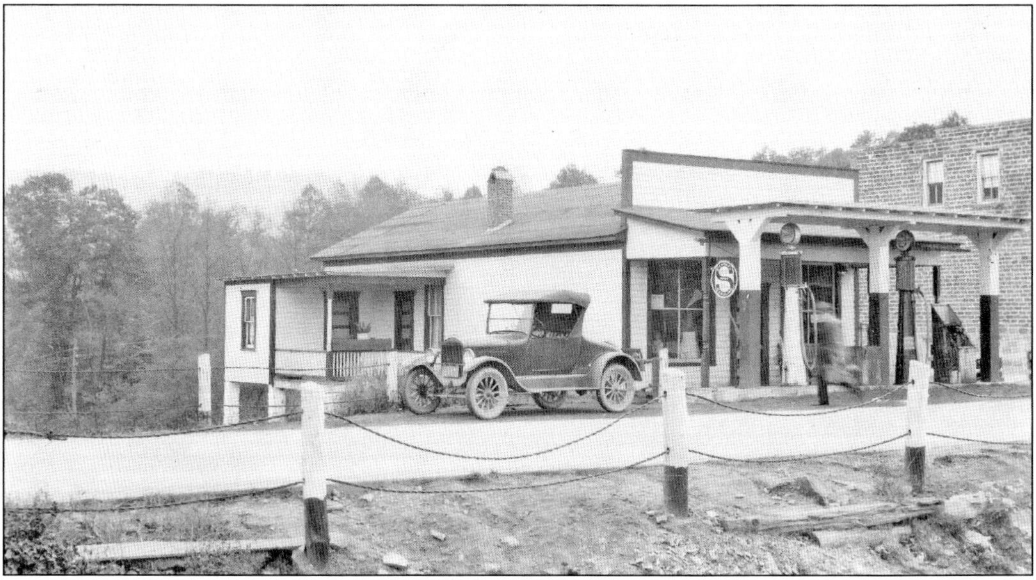

Hogue's Store and Filling Station is shown here about 1925. Located at the southern end of the Gypsy Bridge, John and Clara (Cunningham) Hogue operated the store out of a section of their home. Note the man running near the first gas pump. Razed in 2011, the home was last occupied by Sam and Tressie Male. (Author's collection.)

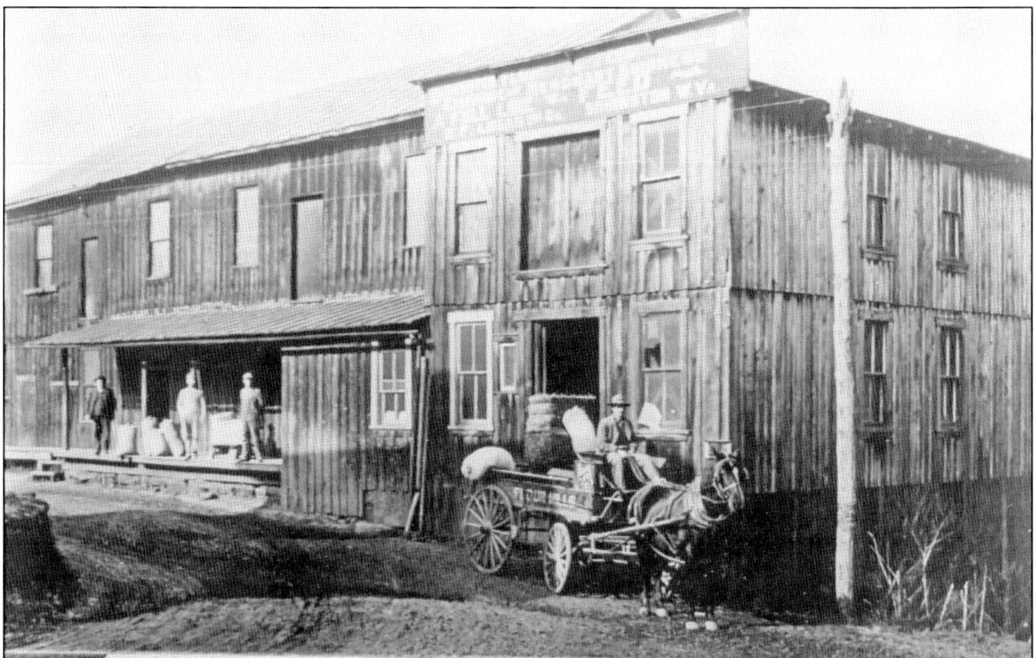

Shinnston Flour and Feed Mill, located along the riverbank between Walnut and Main Streets, was a milling establishment converted from a saw and planing mill by John Nay and B.F. Lowe in the late 1800s. Grain was brought in and crushed using the roller mill to produce flour. The business also operated as wholesale merchandise and sold groceries. Sold several times before going out of operation in 1935, the last owner was Charles F. Lucas. (Courtesy of Lowe Public Library.)

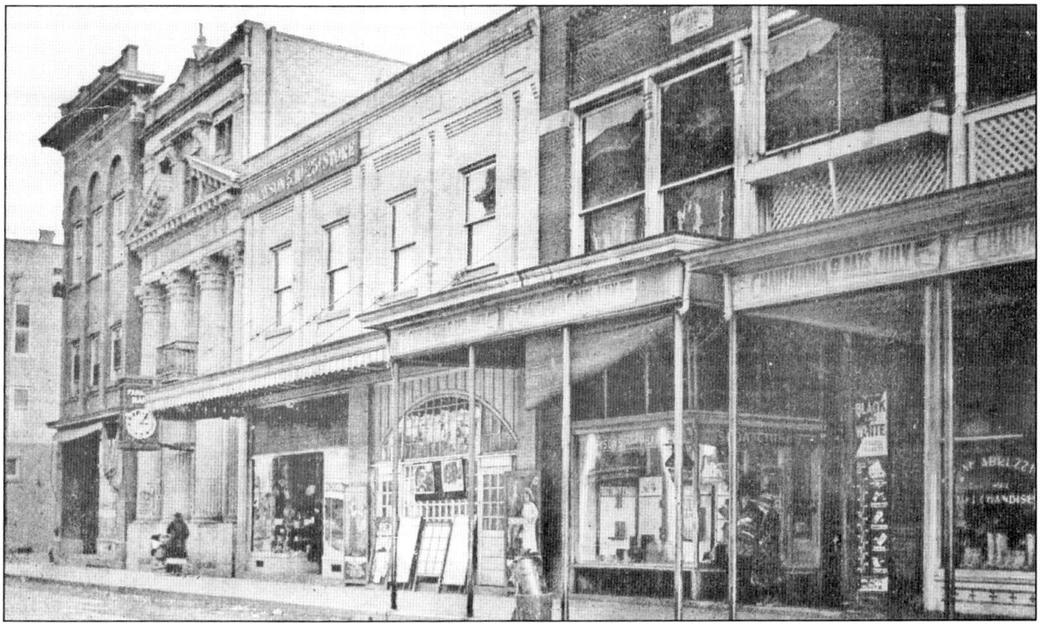

Businesses seen along Pike Street pre-1925 are, from left to right, Hawker's Hardware, Farmers Bank, Finlayson's 5&10, Princess-Rex Theatre, Johnson's Pharmacy, and Frank Abruzzino's general merchandise store. For silent films at the theater, Esta Cunningham and Lois (Hurst) Beattie played piano, using appropriate scores for different scenes. Note the clock in front of Farmers Bank, installed on December 9, 1914. (James M. Currey Collection, Courtesy of Leigh C. Merrifield.)

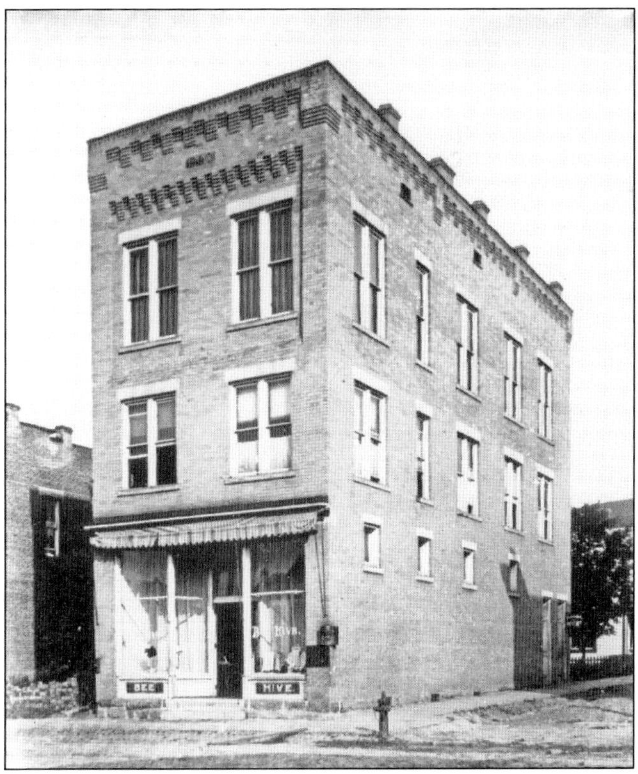

The Masonic Lodge constructed this building at the northeast corner of Pike and Bridge Streets in 1902. It was the second three-story building to be erected in Shinnston; the third floor was used as the Lodge Hall. The Bee Hive, pictured here, was a department store operated by Willa Lowe. Since 1992, Dr. Robert Powelson and his wife, Beth, both of Shinnston Family Eyecare, have owned this building. (Courtesy of Bob Bice II.)

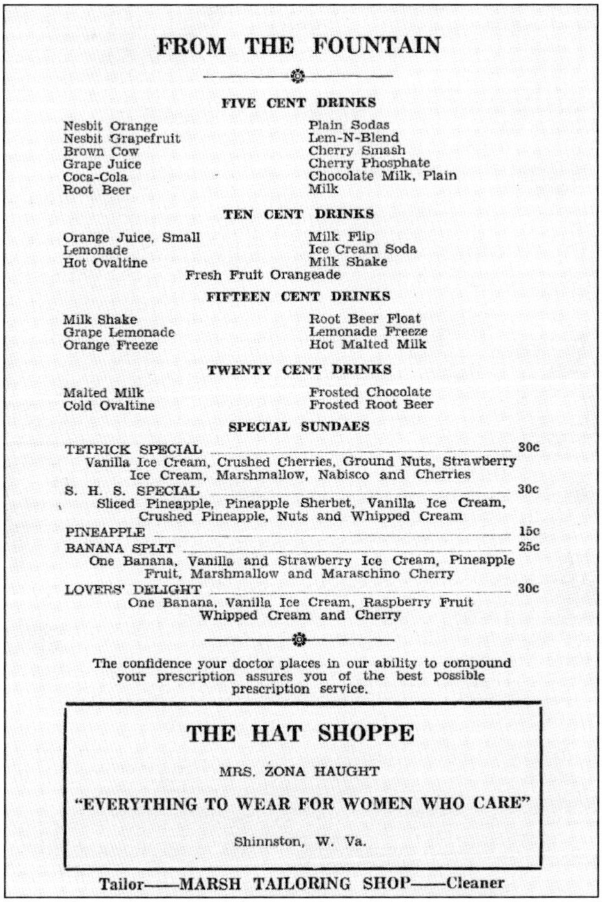

FROM THE FOUNTAIN

FIVE CENT DRINKS

Nesbit Orange	Plain Sodas
Nesbit Grapefruit	Lem-N-Blend
Brown Cow	Cherry Smash
Grape Juice	Cherry Phosphate
Coca-Cola	Chocolate Milk, Plain
Root Beer	Milk

TEN CENT DRINKS

Orange Juice, Small	Milk Flip
Lemonade	Ice Cream Soda
Hot Ovaltine	Milk Shake

Fresh Fruit Orangeade

FIFTEEN CENT DRINKS

Milk Shake	Root Beer Float
Grape Lemonade	Lemonade Freeze
Orange Freeze	Hot Malted Milk

TWENTY CENT DRINKS

Malted Milk	Frosted Chocolate
Cold Ovaltine	Frosted Root Beer

SPECIAL SUNDAES

TETRICK SPECIAL 30c
Vanilla Ice Cream, Crushed Cherries, Ground Nuts, Strawberry Ice Cream, Marshmallow, Nabisco and Cherries

S. H. S. SPECIAL 30c
Sliced Pineapple, Pineapple Sherbet, Vanilla Ice Cream, Crushed Pineapple, Nuts and Whipped Cream

PINEAPPLE 15c

BANANA SPLIT 25c
One Banana, Vanilla and Strawberry Ice Cream, Pineapple Fruit, Marshmallow and Maraschino Cherry

LOVERS' DELIGHT 30c
One Banana, Vanilla Ice Cream, Raspberry Fruit Whipped Cream and Cherry

The confidence your doctor places in our ability to compound your prescription assures you of the best possible prescription service.

THE HAT SHOPPE

MRS. ZONA HAUGHT

"EVERYTHING TO WEAR FOR WOMEN WHO CARE"

Shinnston, W. Va.

Tailor——MARSH TAILORING SHOP——Cleaner

When Arch Tetrick operated the Tetrick Drug Company on Pike Street, it was common for drugstores to also operate soda fountains. This page of the fountain menu lists his three most expensive items: Tetrick Special, Shinnston High School Special, and Lover's Delight—all at 30¢ each! (Author's collection.)

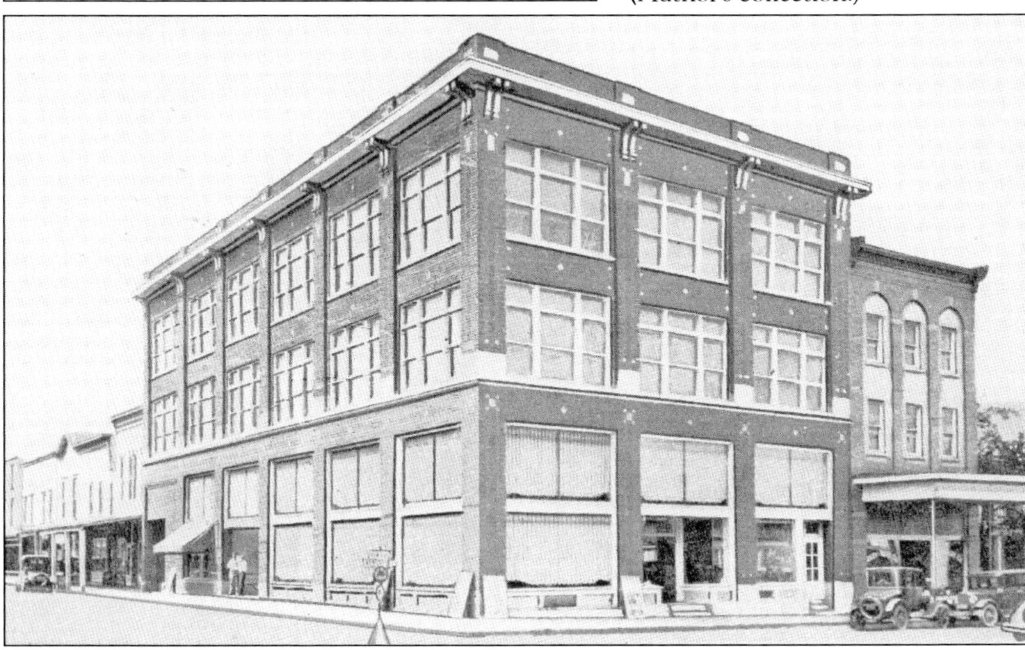

Ground was broken for this three-story brick building at the southwest corner of Pike and Bridge Streets on August 16, 1915. Shinnston Furniture and Undertaking Company moved into this building on May 1, 1916, with 20,000 feet of floor space. Paul Tetrick and Charles Hursey were two of the early undertakers. In addition to furniture and caskets, the company also sold interior designs, such as wallpaper. (Author's collection.)

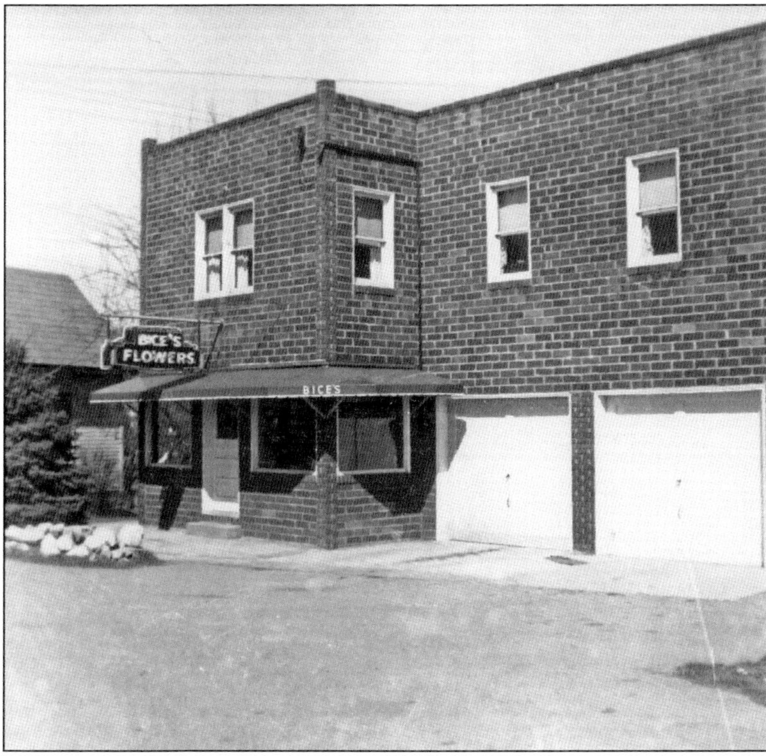

During the 1930s, flower arrangements began being made and sold from Bice's greenhouse. First made in the home and then in the greenhouses, the need for a florist shop was increasing. In 1947, a two-story building was added to accommodate the need. Operated successfully for over 65 years, the flower shop closed on December 31, 2014. The greenhouses remain in operation. (Author's collection.)

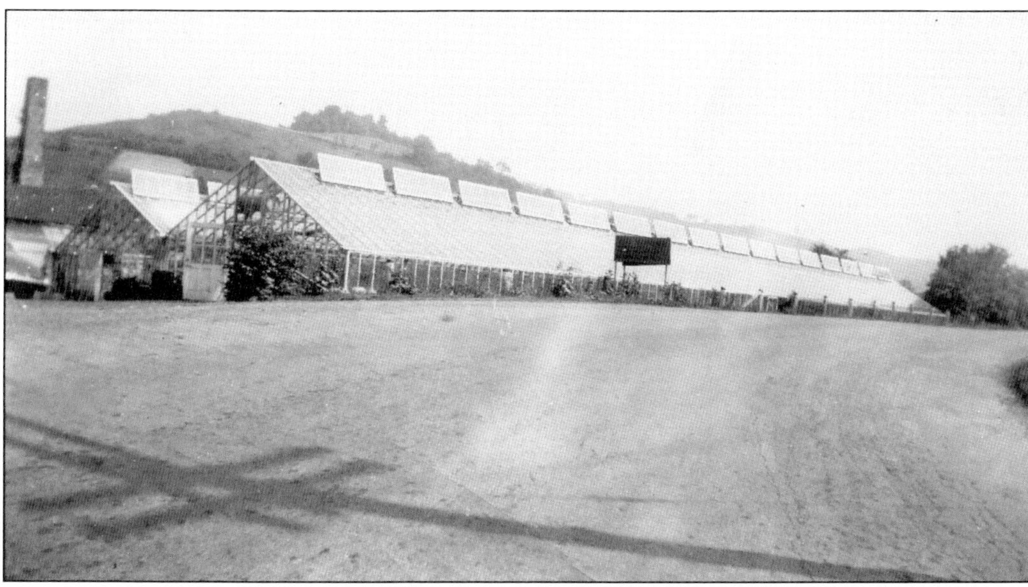

Walter Bice built his first greenhouse in the summer of 1925. He had been growing and selling plants 15 years prior to this. The establishment grew to include eight greenhouses and over 30,000 square feet under glass. This image was taken in June 1944. Note the raised ventilators to let the excessive heat escape. Today, the establishment is run by Walter's grandson and his wife, Bob and Beth (Andrick) Bice. (Author's collection.)

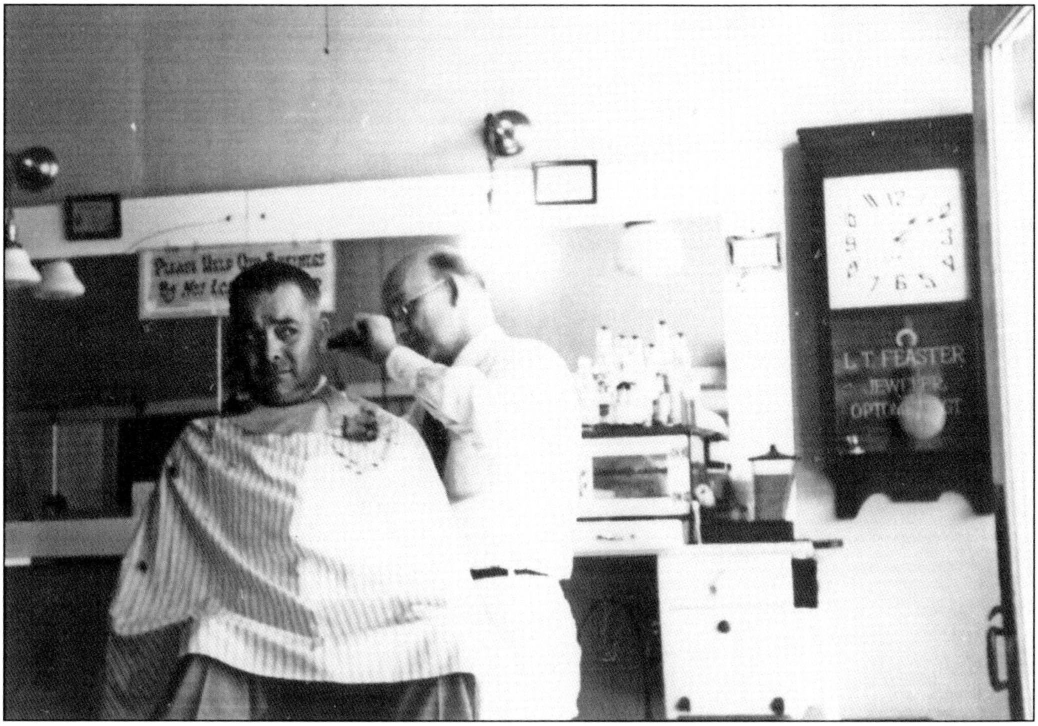

The interior of Jack High's barbershop is shown here in the 1940s. Note the advertisement on the clock: "L.T. Feaster, Jeweler, Optometrist." Other barbers that worked there over time have included Percy Bock, Frank Talerico, George Frederick, and Jack Maxwell. The business was located in a building on the west side of Pike Street between Bridge Street and Robinson Court; there is now a parking lot where the structure once stood. (Courtesy of Nancy Price Biggs.)

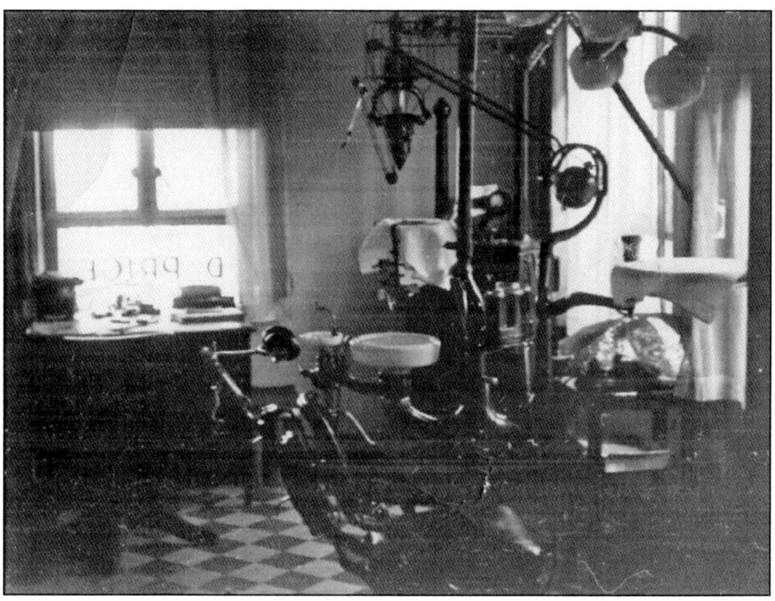

Pictured here about 1940 is the interior of Charles L. Price's dental office, located in the upstairs of the building at the southwest corner of Pike Street and Robinson Court. Dr. Price began his dental practice on September 1, 1929, and purchased the equipment seen here from Dr. Dwight Grimm. A Chinese restaurant is in this building today. (Courtesy of Nancy Price Biggs.)

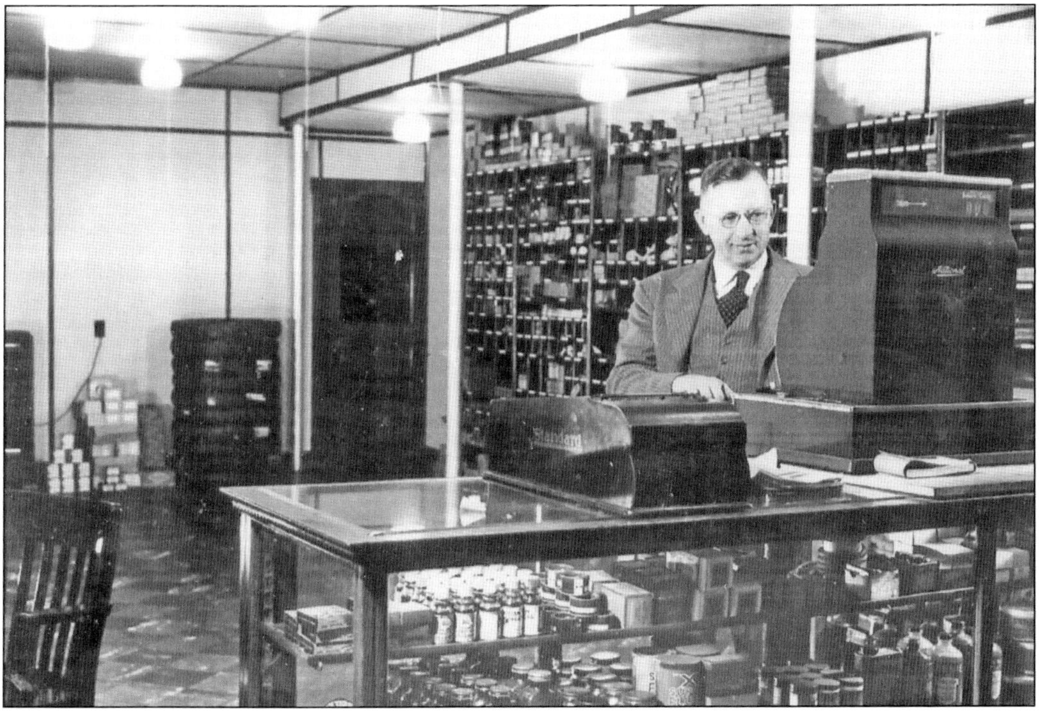

This image depicts the interior of the Anderson Garage Company on the south side of lower Walnut Street in Shinnston. Owner Ben Anderson's son Albert "Pete" Anderson is seen at the register, which is resting on a very large oak store display counter. Note the shelves in the background with auto mechanic parts. The company was later operated by Pete's son Ralph Anderson. (Courtesy of Cindy Anderson Scott.)

FOR ______________________________

____

____

FROM

BIG ELM FRUIT FARM

ROAD SIDE MARKET AND EVERGREEN NURSERY

HOOD BROS., PROPRIETORS C. & P. PHONE

SHINNSTON, W. VA.

The Big Elm Fruit Market was a roadside market stand operated by Charles and Harry Hood, the brothers who owned the Big Elm Farm. In addition to fruit, they also sold dairy products and evergreens. The stand was built by Charles J. McIntire of Enterprise and stood for many years after the brothers' deaths. It burned down in 1978. (Courtesy of Leslie "Skip" and Judy Tichenor.)

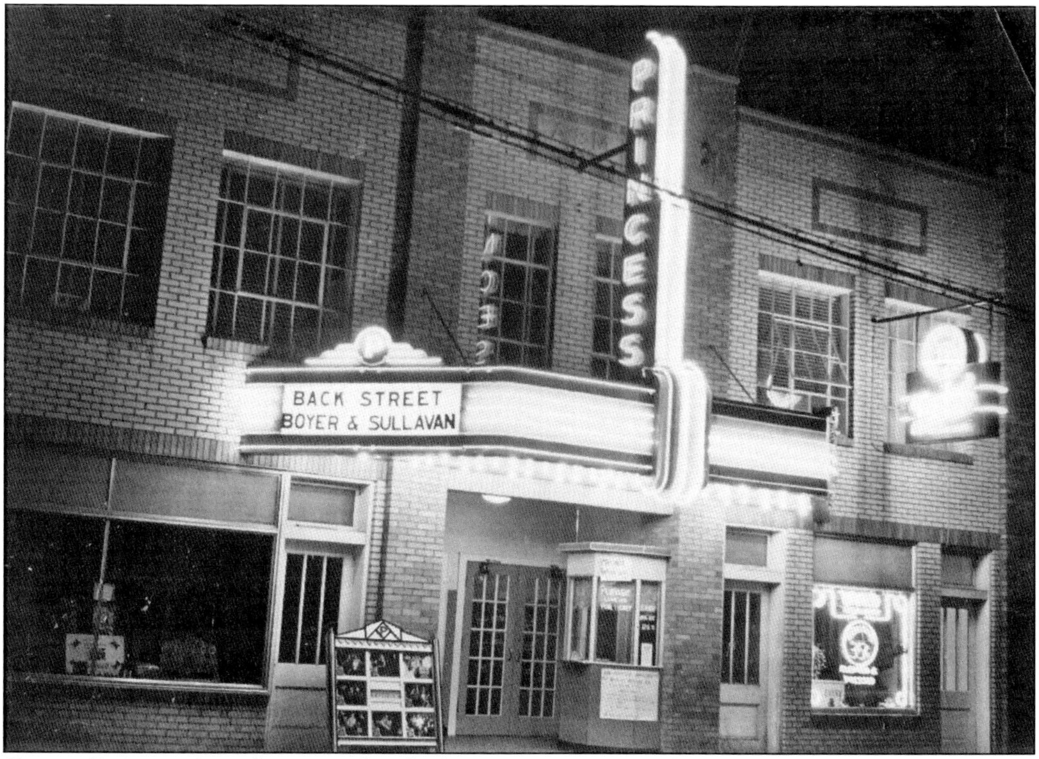

Originally located on the east side of Pike Street, Princess Theatre moved to this building in 1940. Built by Abruzzino & Mazzei, the theater had a balcony section for blacks. Linnie Monroe ran the theater, and Nellie Shinn was a cashier, while Glenn Willis and Marchie Gerod ran the projector. Two businesses operated out of the side storefronts: Feaster's Jewelers on the left and United Dry Cleaners on the right. The right side was later occupied by James Abruzzino's Quality Pastry Shoppe. (Courtesy of Lowe Public Library.)

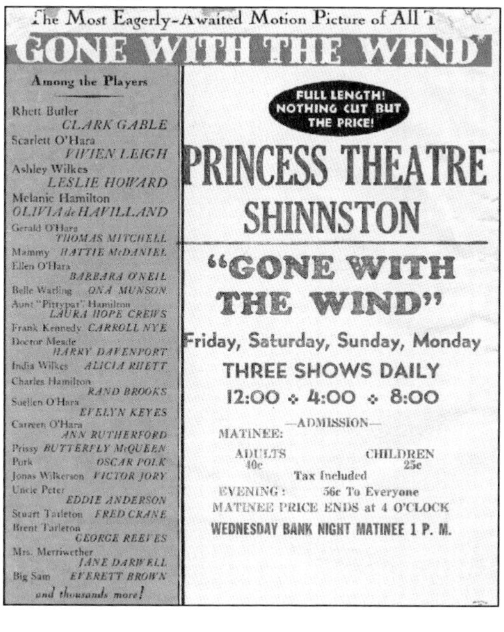

The Most Eagerly-Awaited Motion Picture of All T

GONE WITH THE WIND

Among the Players

Rhett Butler CLARK GABLE
Scarlett O'Hara VIVIEN LEIGH
Ashley Wilkes LESLIE HOWARD
Melanie Hamilton OLIVIA de HAVILLAND
Gerald O'Hara THOMAS MITCHELL
Mammy HATTIE McDANIEL
Ellen O'Hara BARBARA O'NEIL
Belle Watling ONA MUNSON
Aunt "Pittypat" Hamilton LAURA HOPE CREWS
Frank Kennedy CARROLL NYE
Doctor Meade HARRY DAVENPORT
India Wilkes ALICIA RHETT
Charles Hamilton RAND BROOKS
Suellen O'Hara EVELYN KEYES
Carreen O'Hara ANN RUTHERFORD
Prissy BUTTERFLY McQUEEN
Pork OSCAR POLK
Jonas Wilkerson VICTOR JORY
Uncle Peter EDDIE ANDERSON
Stuart Tarleton FRED CRANE
Brent Tarleton GEORGE REEVES
Mrs. Merriwether JANE DARWELL
Big Sam EVERETT BROWN
and thousands more!

FULL LENGTH! NOTHING CUT BUT THE PRICE!

PRINCESS THEATRE
SHINNSTON

"GONE WITH THE WIND"

Friday, Saturday, Sunday, Monday
THREE SHOWS DAILY
12:00 ⋄ 4:00 ⋄ 8:00

—ADMISSION—
MATINEE:
ADULTS 40c CHILDREN 25c
Tax Included
EVENING: 56c To Everyone
MATINEE PRICE ENDS at 4 O'CLOCK
WEDNESDAY BANK NIGHT MATINEE 1 P. M.

Shown here is the back of a program advertising the movie *Gone With the Wind*. It was a supplement to the *Shinnston News*. The Princess Theatre was not a first-run theater, and when the movie finally came to Shinnston, it was a great success. A family of five could watch the matinee for less than $2 or catch the evening show for less than $3. (Author's collection.)

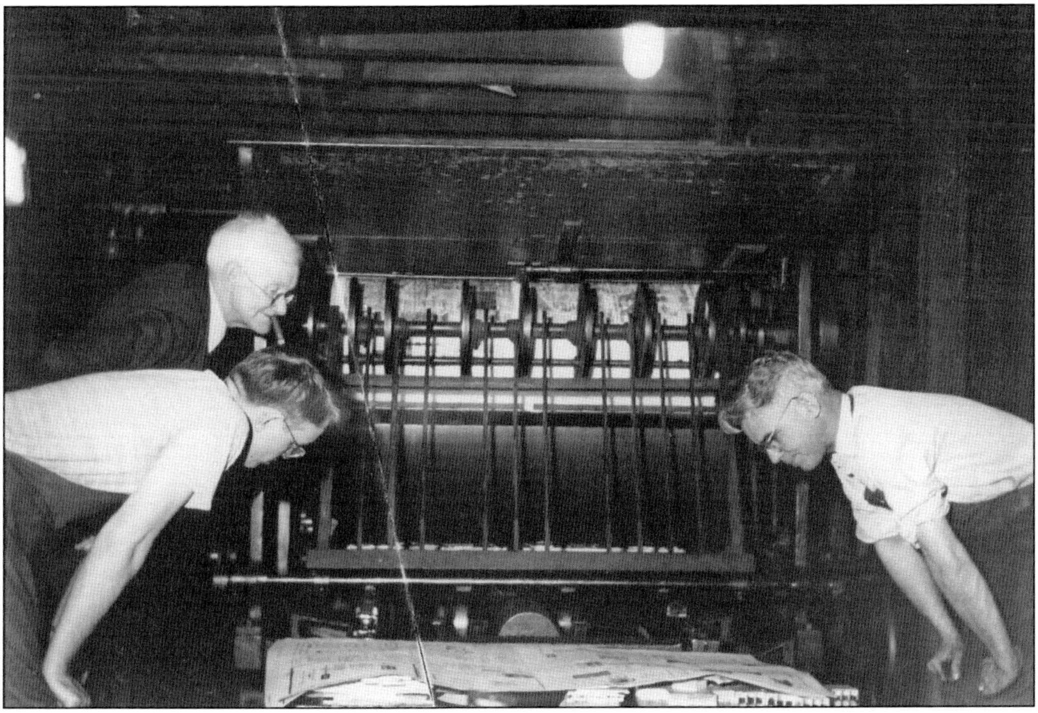

Pictured from left to right are William A. Meredith, his grandson James Meredith Currey, and his son Thaddeus Meredith hovering over a 1950s Christmas edition of the *Shinnston News* as it comes off the press. That original Babcock press, which to this day remains in the basement of the building at 223 Pike Street, was purchased in 1913 and was brought into town by horse and wagon. (James M. Currey Collection, Courtesy of Leigh C. Merrifield.)

The *Shinnston News* has called 223 Pike Street in Shinnston its home since 1909. Printing equipment was housed in the basement, production preparation offices were located on the first floor, and the second floor was comprised of eight rooms that through the years served as a temporary home for many members of the Meredith family. (James M. Currey Collection, Courtesy of Leigh C. Merrifield.)

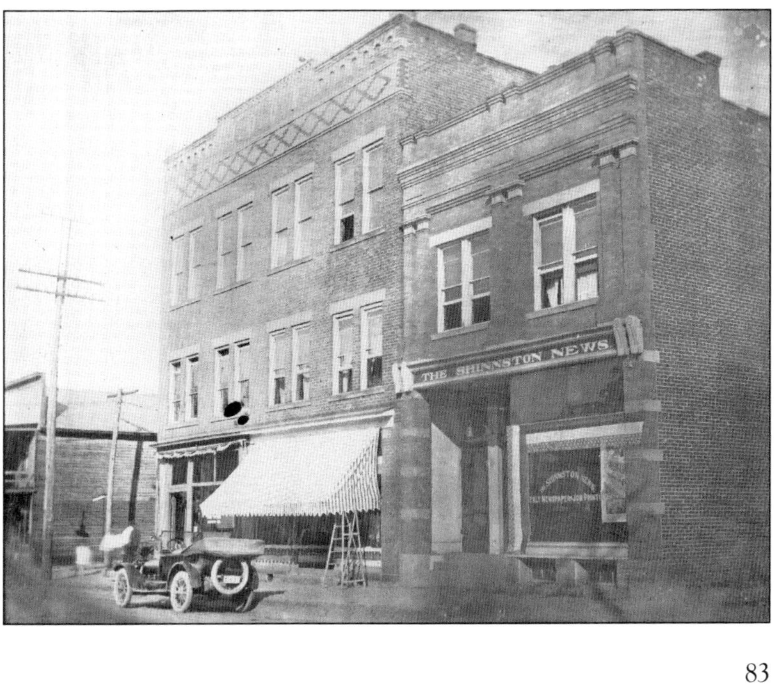

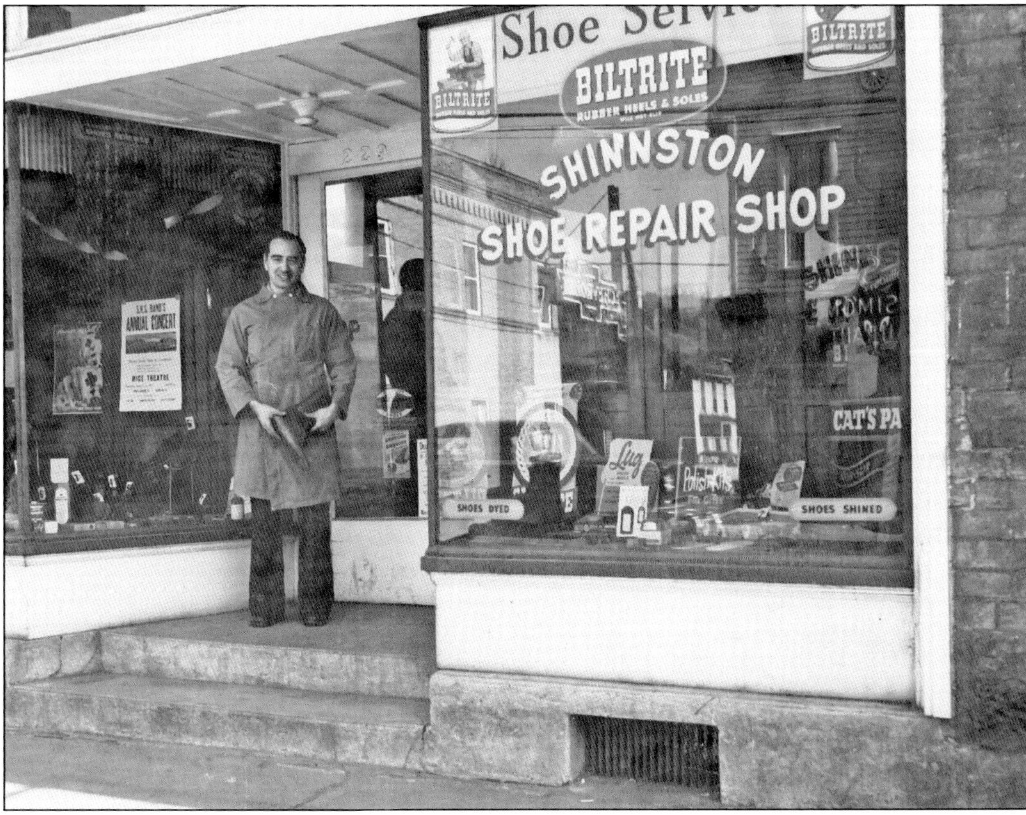

This March 1953 photograph shows Thomas Greco at his shoe repair shop at the southeast corner of Pike and Walnut Streets. Greco began working as an apprentice at a shoe shop in Clarksburg shortly after high school graduation. He opened the shop shown here in 1935 and was in business for nearly 60 years, retiring in August 1994. (Courtesy of Patricia Greco Post.)

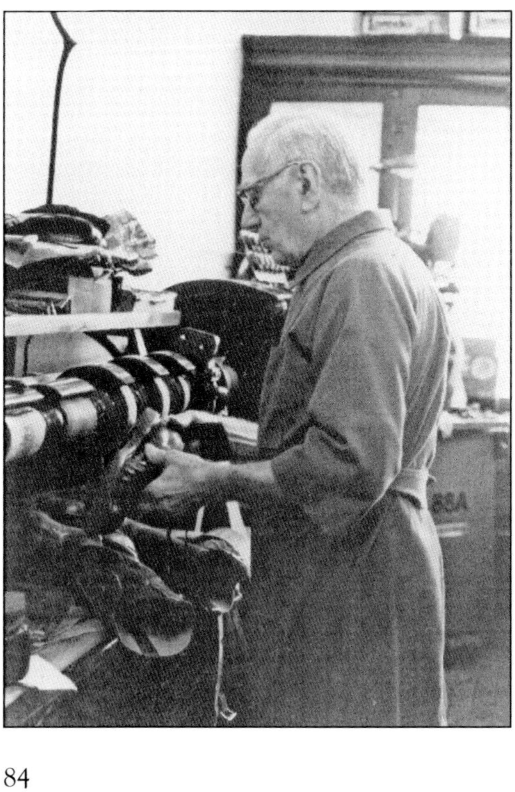

Shinnston shoemaker Thomas Greco is shown here using his well-maintained machines—stitchers, buffers, and finishers—on a customer's shoe. Greco believed in using quality materials to produce fine workmanship. In addition to repairs and polishing, Greco also sold shoes and shoe products. (Courtesy of Patricia Greco Post.)

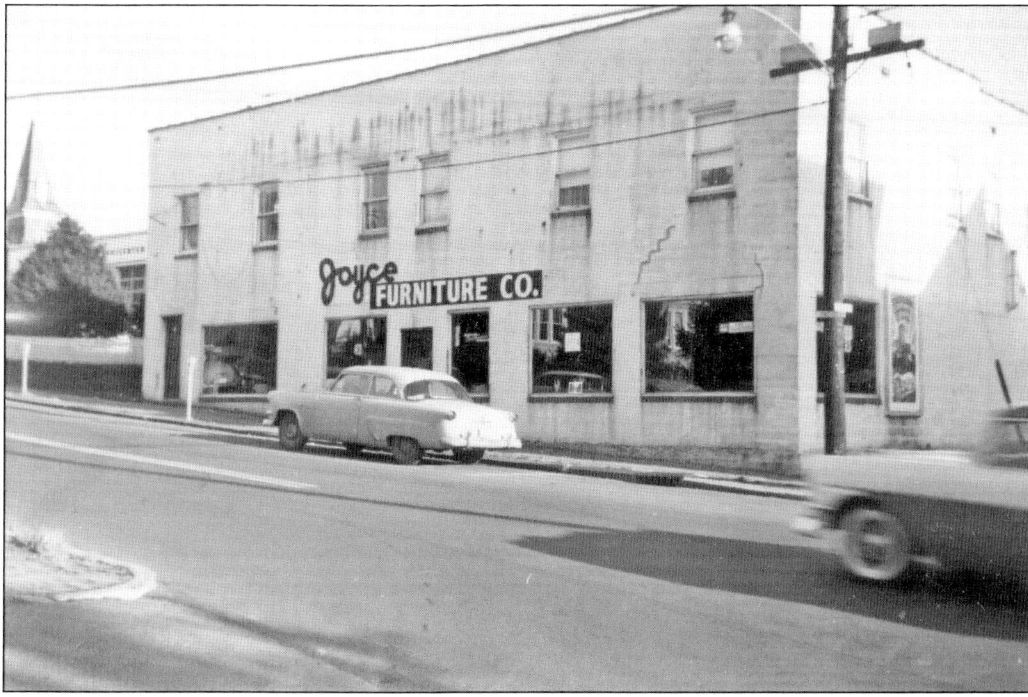

Bernard Joyce opened Joyce Furniture Company in Shinnston in 1957 in the block building once located at the northeast corner of Pike and Charles Streets. By 1964, Joyce Furniture Company had moved into the old Princess Theatre building on Pike Street, where it operated successfully for many years. This building at the corner of Pike and Charles Streets was later used by Walls Auto Parts. (Courtesy of Ann Joyce Riley.)

Bernard and Cile Joyce are shown here during the 1960s in their "uptown" furniture store, located in the old Princess Theatre building on the west side of Pike Street. The business sold everything for the home, including lamps, furniture, wall hangings, and appliances. Gameday Restaurant moved into this building in 2012. (Courtesy of Ann Joyce Riley.)

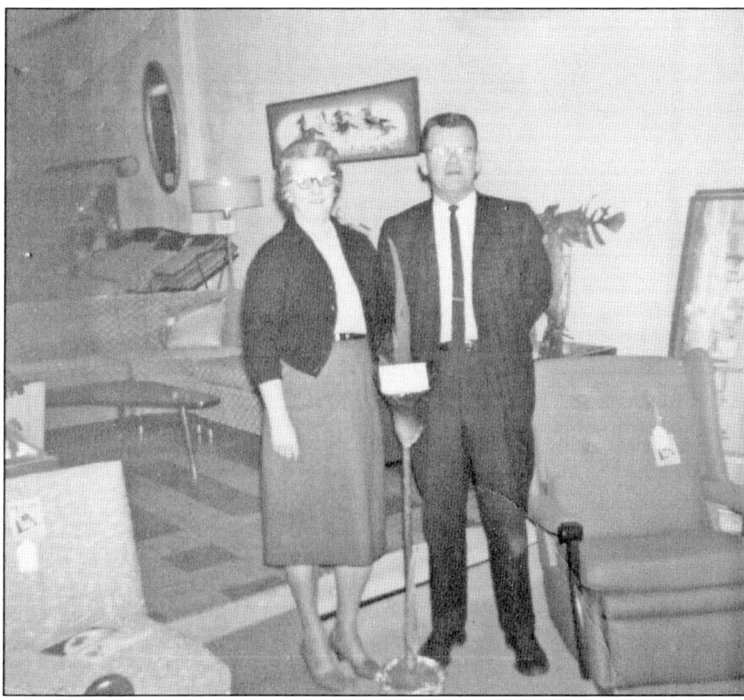

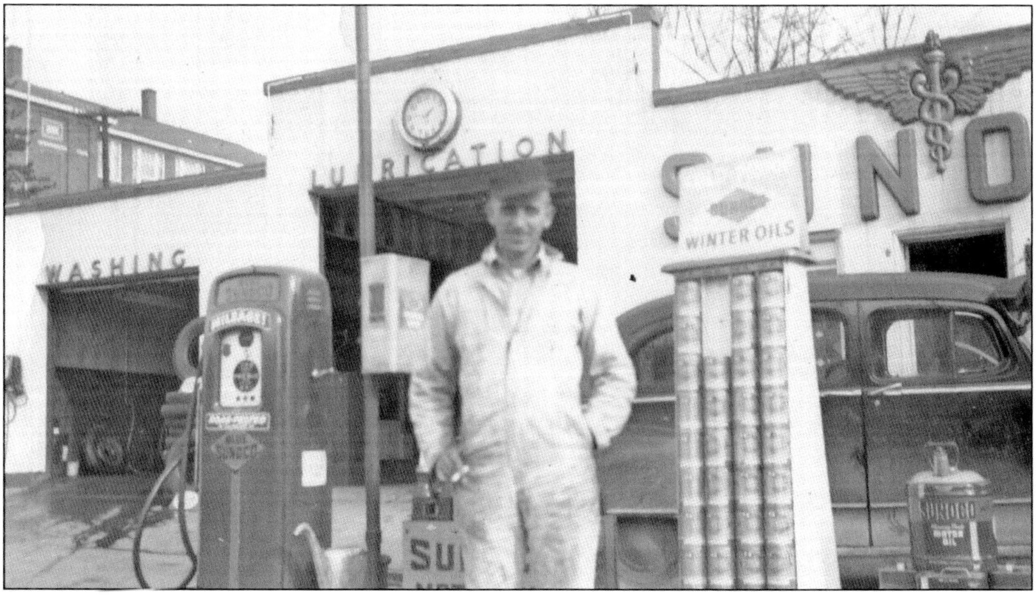

Pictured about 1950, Warren Osbourn stands in front of the Sunoco station at the northeast corner of Pike and Clement Streets. Osbourn operated the station until 1954, when he left the business to open a feed store on Bridge Street. Note the clock on the front of the building. Shinnston High School is visible in the background. (Courtesy of Pauline Osbourn Hammon.)

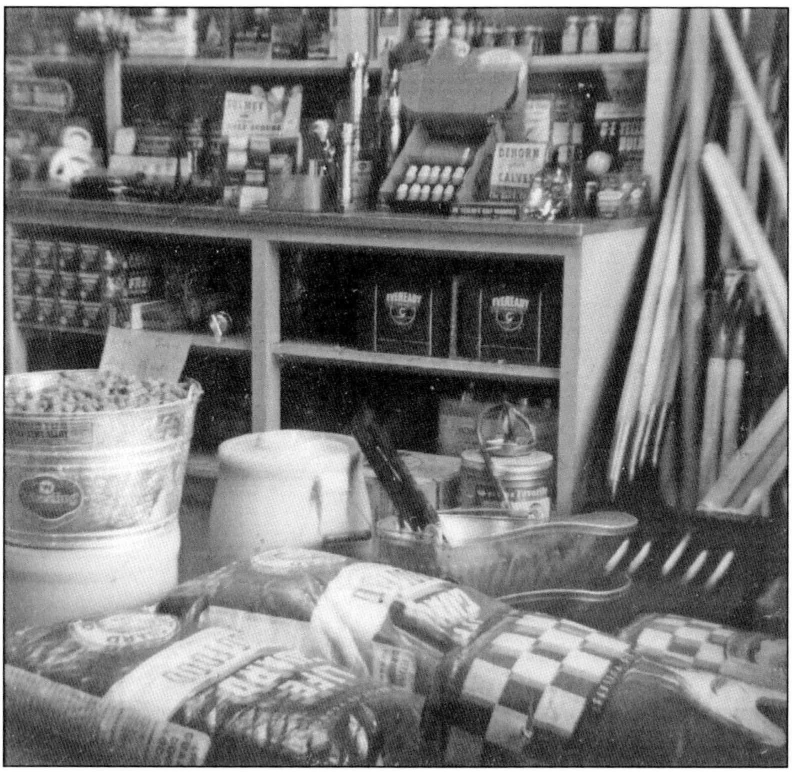

The interior of the P&W Feed Store is shown here in this c. 1960 image. Warren Osbourn opened the feed store in 1954, and he and his wife, Pauline, operated it until 1968. The business was located on the north side of upper Bridge Street in Shinnston, but the building no longer stands; the area is now a parking lot for Shinnston Family Eyecare. (Courtesy of Pauline Osbourn Hammon.)

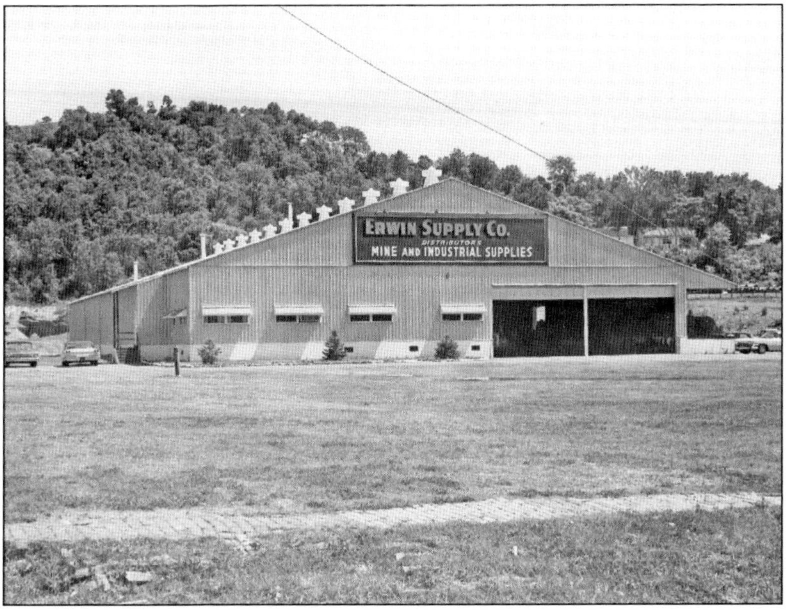

Erwin Supply and Hardware Company located a distribution center in Shinnston in the late 1950s. The land was part of the old Monroe tract of land. In December 1993, United Central Industrial Supply Company purchased Erwin. It is today still a distributor of mining supplies. (Author's collection.)

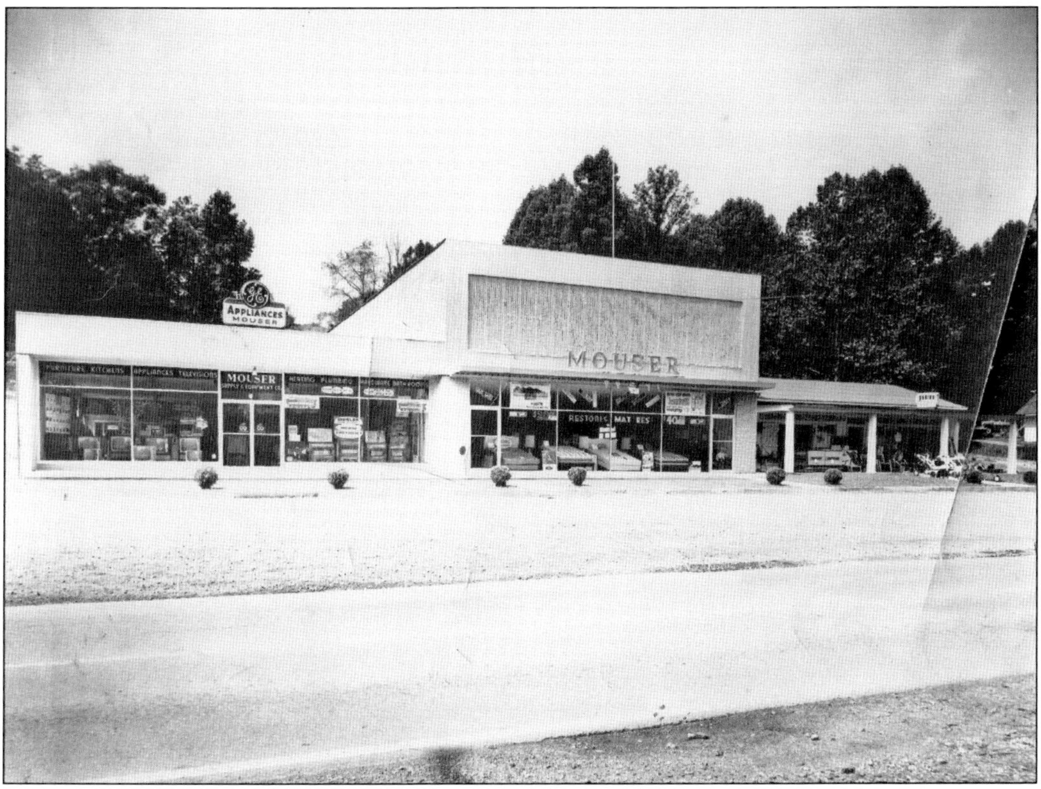

Mouser Supply and Equipment Company sold household furniture, lawn equipment, garden tools, heaters, roofing, paint, and other homeowner items. Established in May 1952 in a small building close to the dip in Enterprise, Bob and Keith Mouser moved their business to the Enterprise straight in 1956. These buildings were constructed in three phases over a six-year period. The company had an attractive glass front and provided over 15,000 feet of floor space. (Author's collection.)

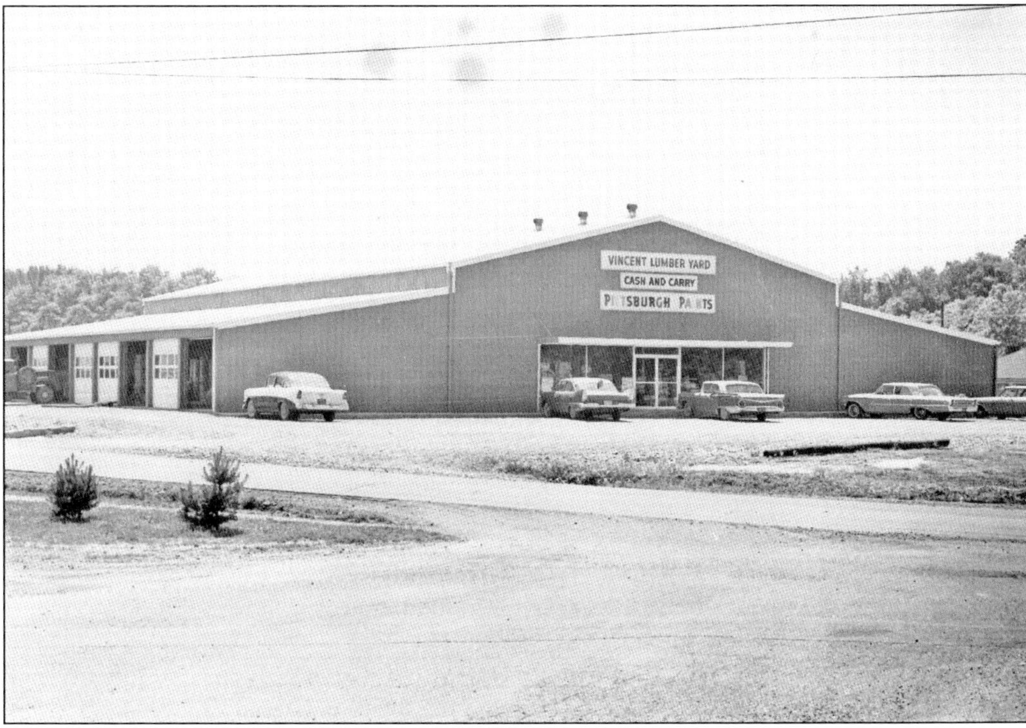

Originally located at 34 Station Street under the name of A.L. Vincent and Son, the Vincent Lumber building, shown here at 347 South Pike Street, was constructed in 1963. Bob Vincent ran the business successfully for many years. The operation is now owned by Vincent's daughter and son-in-law, Diane and Louis Smith. (Author's collection.)

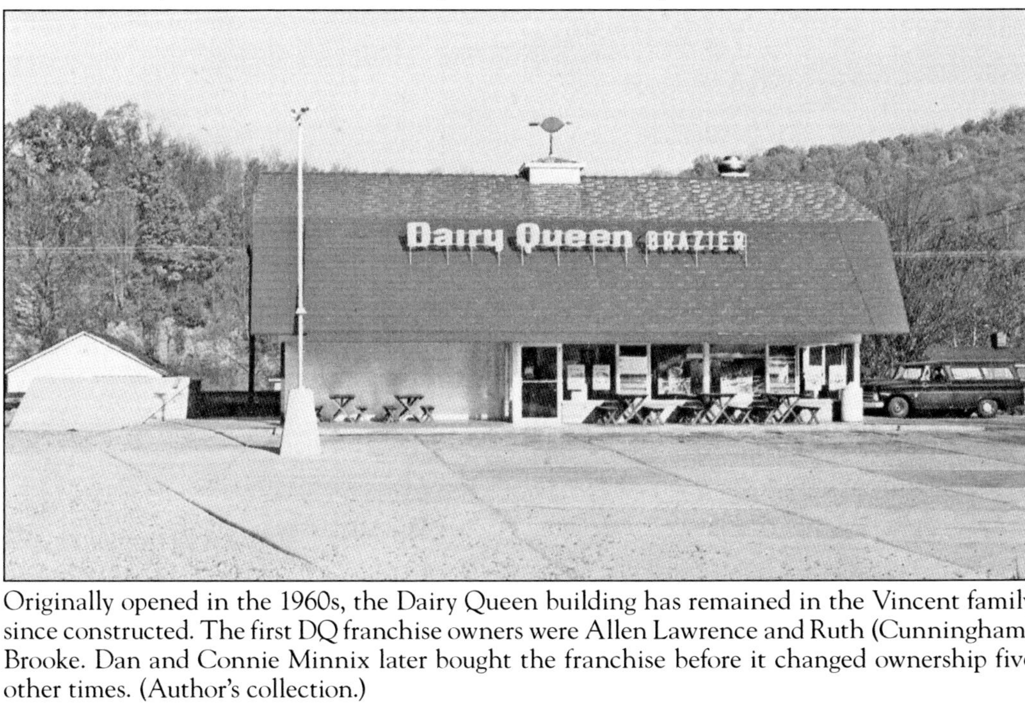

Originally opened in the 1960s, the Dairy Queen building has remained in the Vincent family since constructed. The first DQ franchise owners were Allen Lawrence and Ruth (Cunningham) Brooke. Dan and Connie Minnix later bought the franchise before it changed ownership five other times. (Author's collection.)

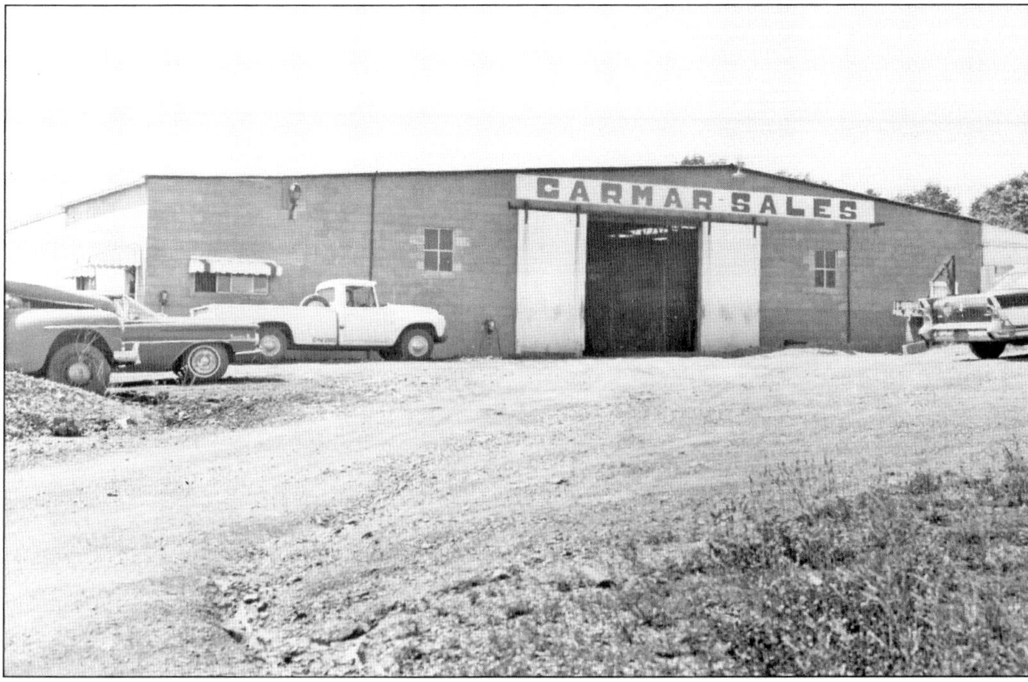

CarMar Sales Company was a modern machine shop and fabricating plant owned by Charles "Bud" and Marion Carpenter. The business was established in Fairmont prior to 1966, with Bill Martz being an original partner. The building, now dilapidated, is located behind Lincoln High School's softball field. (Author's collection.)

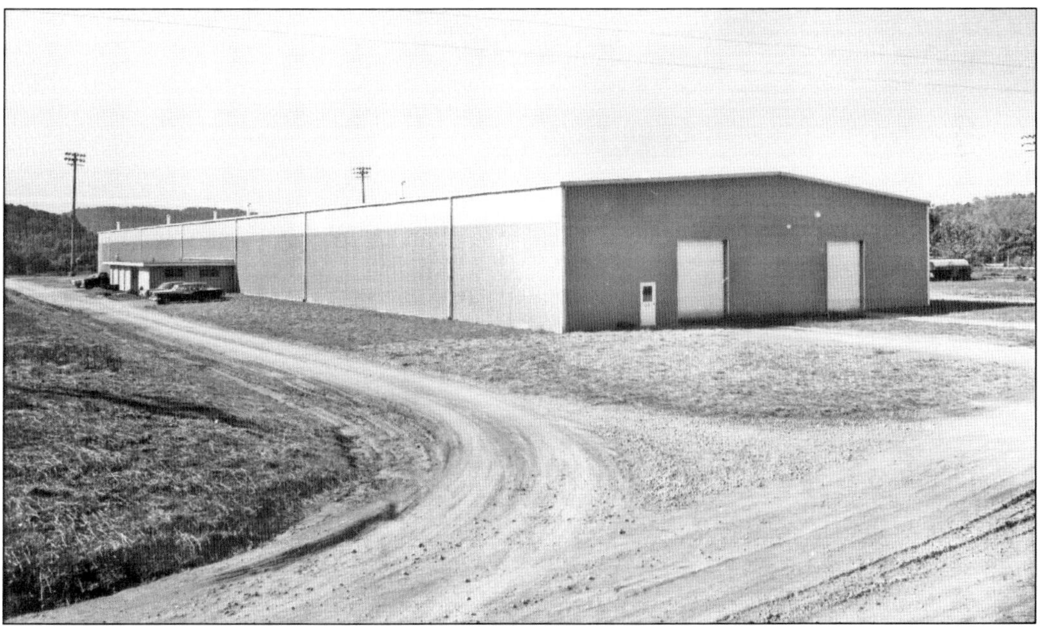

The Carmet Company was a mine tool corporation that came to Shinnston in the late 1960s. Carmet sold the building and property to Commercial Hydraulic Industries Inc. in 1977. The building still stands behind present-day Lincoln High School, opposite the softball field, and is used by Repair King, Inc. (Author's collection.)

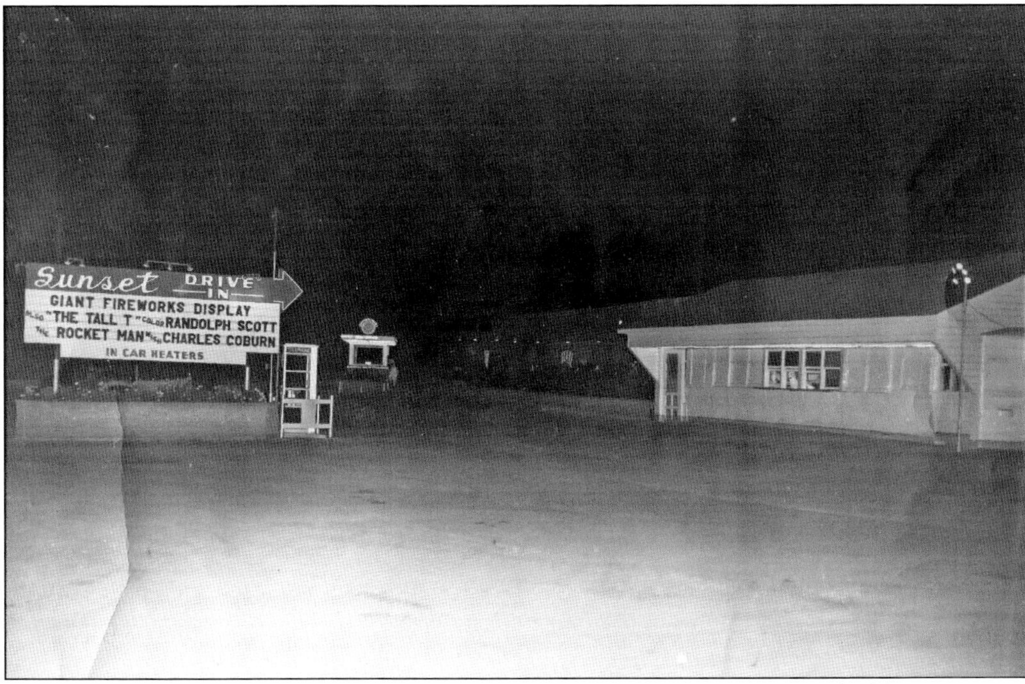

When John Ellis bought the drive-in movie stand at Meadowbrook in 1955, it had been operated out of an old streetcar that began business in 1947. In 1960, the building was remodeled to become a full-time restaurant as well as concession for the drive-in. In 1978, a flea market was also established on site. Today, Ellis Restaurant is owned and operated by Anthony Ellis (the son of John and Jean Ellis) and his wife, Sue. (Courtesy of Anthony Ellis.)

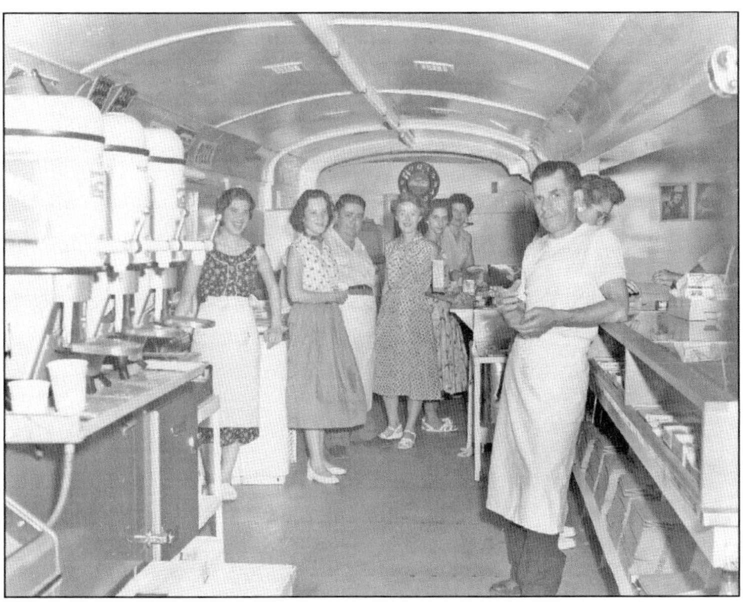

This kitchen staff of Sunset Drive-In, operated by John Ellis, is shown in this image from 1955. From left to right, Mary Katherine Marra, Mary Katherine McConlogue, owner John Ellis, Helen Feeney, Jean Spino, Helen Perez (Simon's wife), Jean Ellis (John's wife), and Simon Perez are all seen preparing food. While the drive-in is still in operation on site, this kitchen is now part of Ellis Restaurant. (Courtesy of Anthony Ellis.)

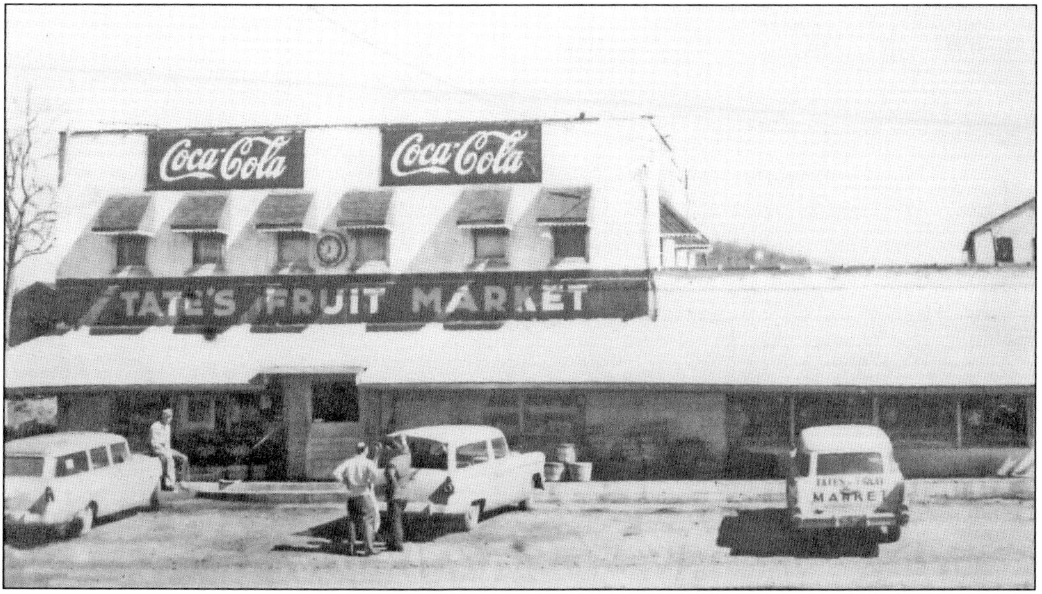

Tate's Fruit Market has been a staple in the area for many years. Located just south of Shinnston at Meadowbrook, the business was operated by John Tate Sr. Now remodeled and enlarged, the building still stands and provides a large residence on the second level. (Author's collection.)

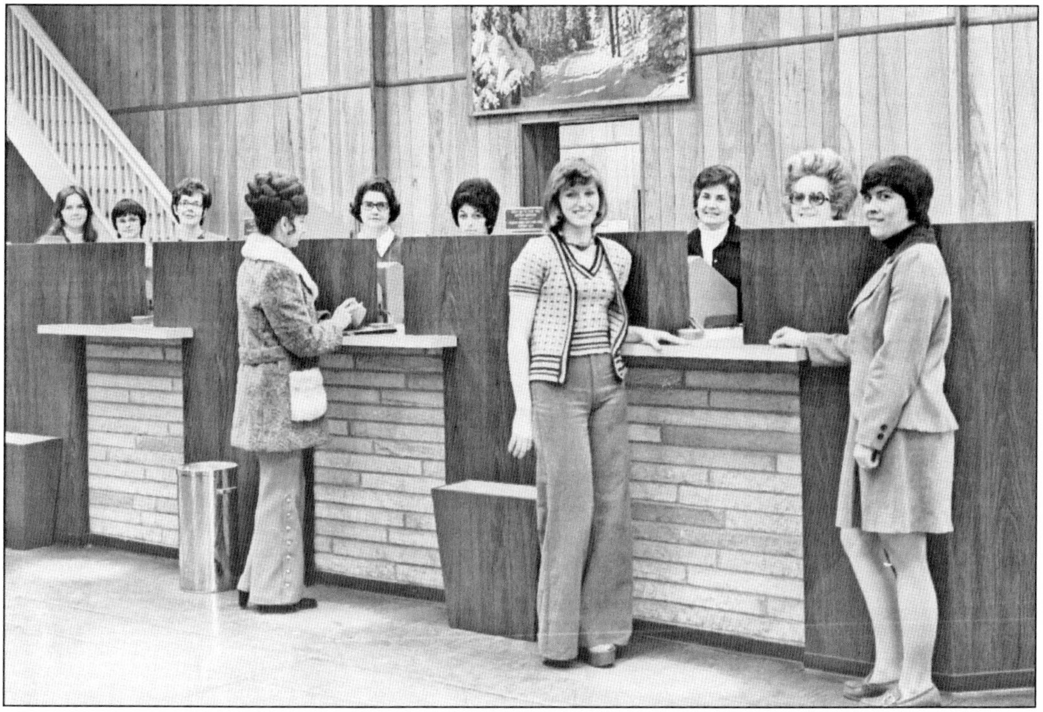

The interior of the Bank of Shinnston has undergone many renovations over the years. This photograph from the 1970s shows the teller desk opposite of where it is today in WesBanco. Pictured from left to right are Julie Male, Becky Moore, Doris Cowan, unidentified customer, Betty Deems, Francie Wagner, Janet Post, Mary Fazalare, Patty Andrick, and Carolyn Corrigan. (Courtesy of Beth Andrick Bice.)

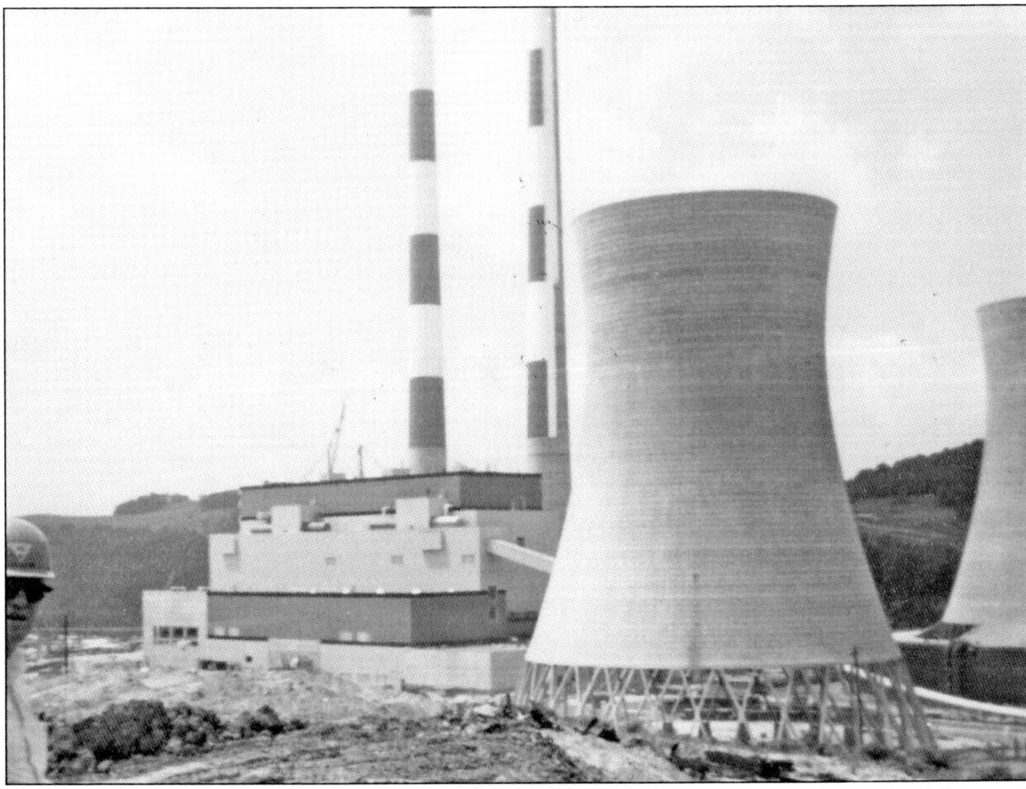

The Harrison Power Station is a coal-fired, electricity-generated power plant located at Haywood. Construction on the plant began in 1958 and finished in 1973. This photograph was taken in July 1972 and shows the cooling towers and generating plant. (Courtesy of Bob Bice II.)

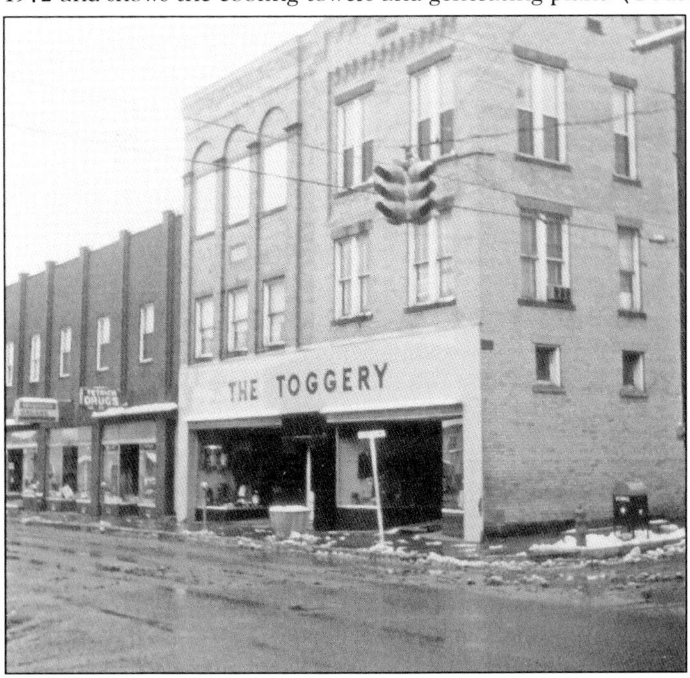

In 1917, Jay Riggs and Ruble Marsh opened the Toggery, a gentleman's store, and jointly operated it with Riggs's former cleaning company. Harold Jarrett later managed the Toggery until 1973 when a Clarksburg Company purchased it. Jarrett was then 80 years old. Originally located in the John Lowe building, this photograph was captured when it was located at the northeast corner of Pike and Bridge Streets. (Author's collection.)

The City of Shinnston building and mayor's office are shown next to the Shinnston Plumbing Company building in this c. 1970 photograph. Shinnston Plumbing was started in 1896 by Howard Harmer and has had many owners over the years. Police chief Buzzy Book is shown at the left edge of the photograph. All of the buildings seen in this photograph have been razed to make clearance for a new city office complex to soon be built. (Author's collection.)

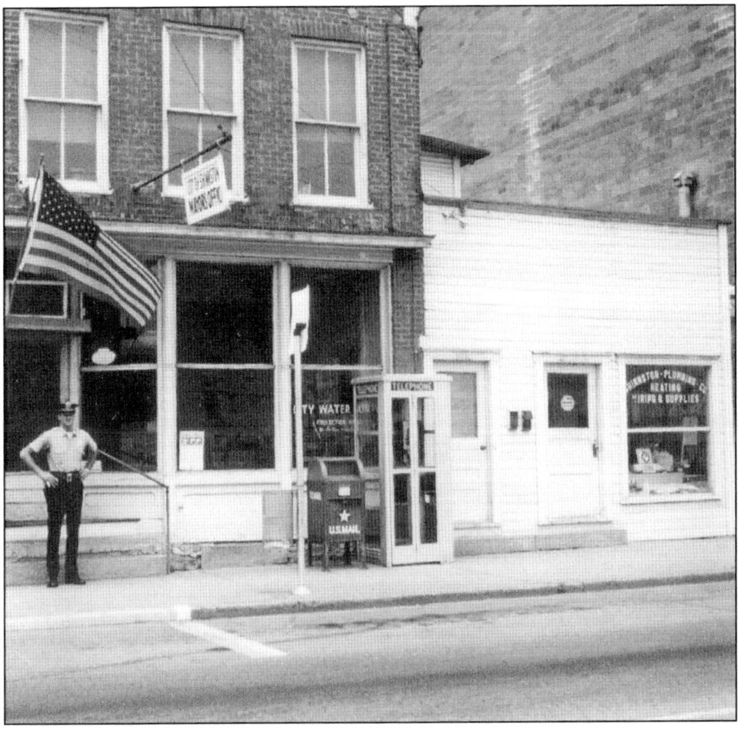

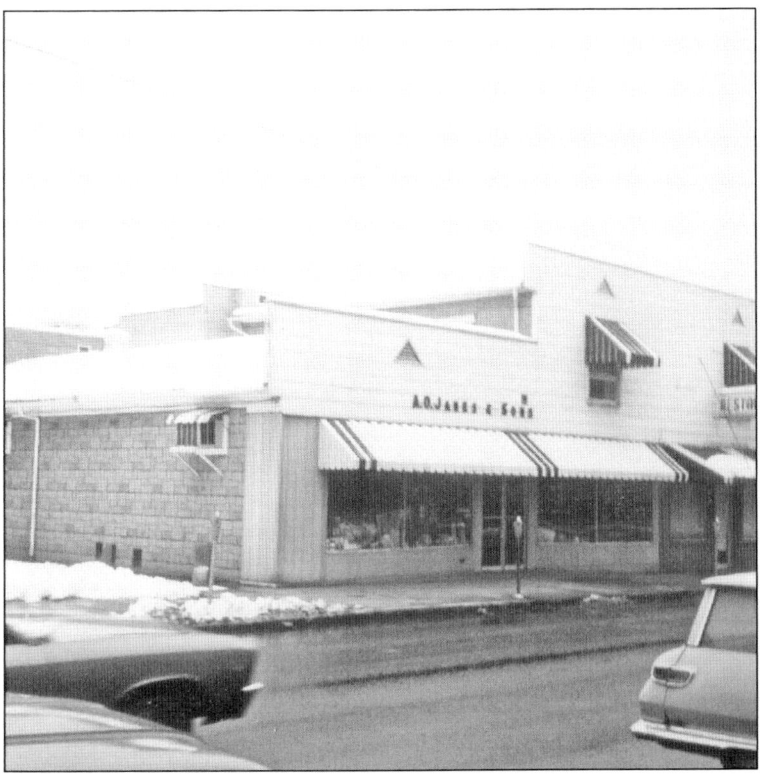

Arthur Otis Janes established a store in partnership with his brother-in-law at Francis Mine. After selling to Abruzzino & Mazzei, he opened a retail grocery store on lower Bridge Street and then another along Pike Street. Just before World War II, A.O. and sons Warren and Harlan bought this location, combining the previous stores. Often remembered for their meat counter and ham salad, A.O. Janes & Sons ran successfully for many years. This photograph was taken around 1970. (Author's collection.)

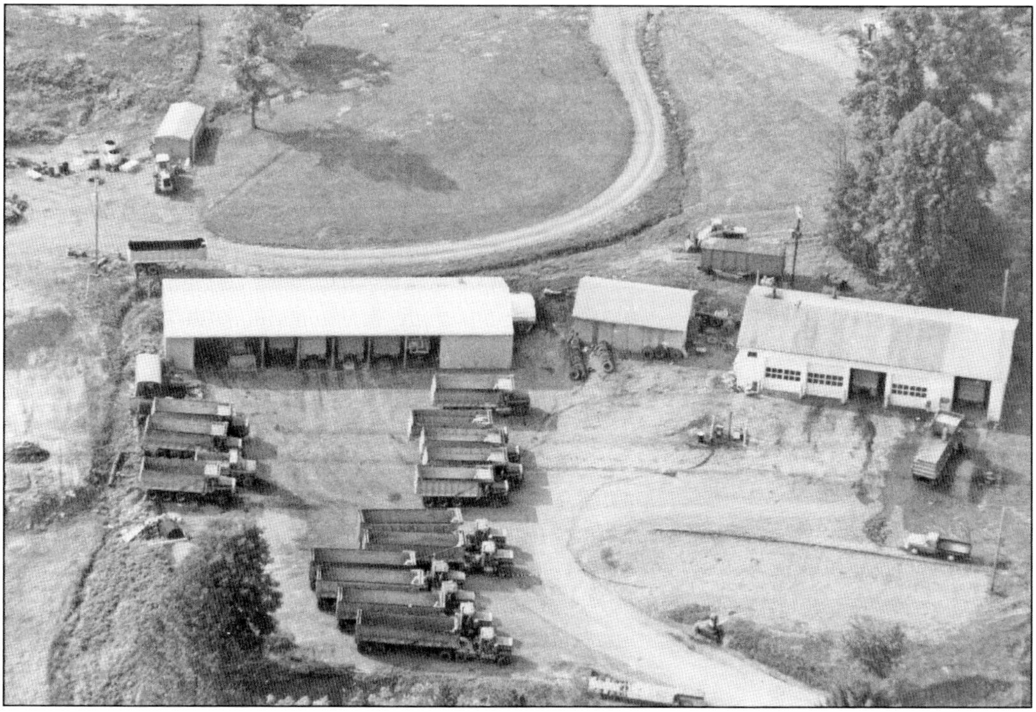

Carl Nuzum Jr. got his start in the trucking business while working at Williams Mine. He bought one truck and on May 12, 1948, Nuzum Trucking Company was established at the Francis Mine community. In 1957, he constructed a building close to his home where he operated the business for 12 years. He relocated to Bethlehem in 1969, where he stayed until his retirement in 2000. Shown here is an aerial view of the operation at Bethlehem. (Courtesy of Carl Nuzum Jr.)

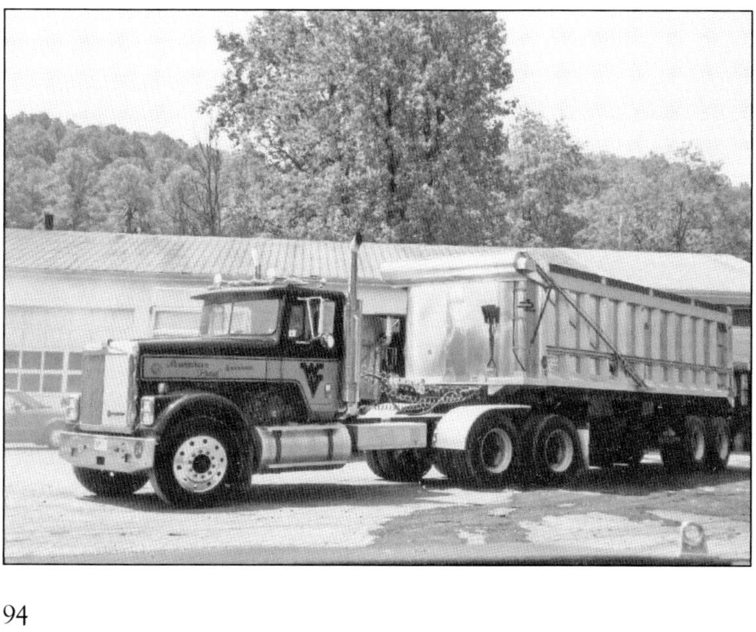

Around 1980, the trucks at Nuzum Trucking Company started having West Virginia University's logo, the flying WV, displayed on them. Shortly after, owner Jr. Nuzum began having the trucks painted blue and old gold before they arrived on site. The company is now owned by Nuzum's son Roger Nuzum and is located along Wyatt Road. (Courtesy of Carl Nuzum Jr.)

Seven

DISASTERS AND TRAGEDIES

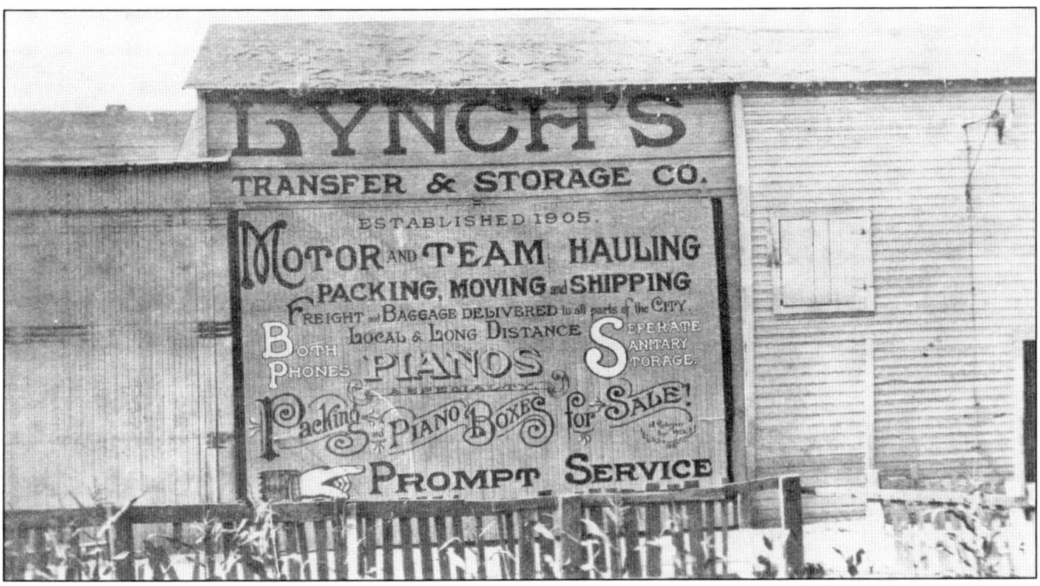

Lynch's Transfer and Storage Company was a moving company owned by father John Lynch and son Russell Lynch. Horses were used for a lot of the transferring and were kept in the stables shown here. The main structure was erected in 1905, with the addition being built in 1922. On November 22, 1937, at about 3:00 p.m., a fire started in the Rex Theatre building, adjacent to the stables. Hugh Cox, an employee of Lynch's, went into the stables to try to get the horses out, but the horses froze, and he could not move them. The roof caught fire, the building burned to the ground, and the horses died. Nearby, Taufig Simon went into his department store and brought boxes of gloves to the firemen on scene. The fire was ruled arson. (Author's collection.)

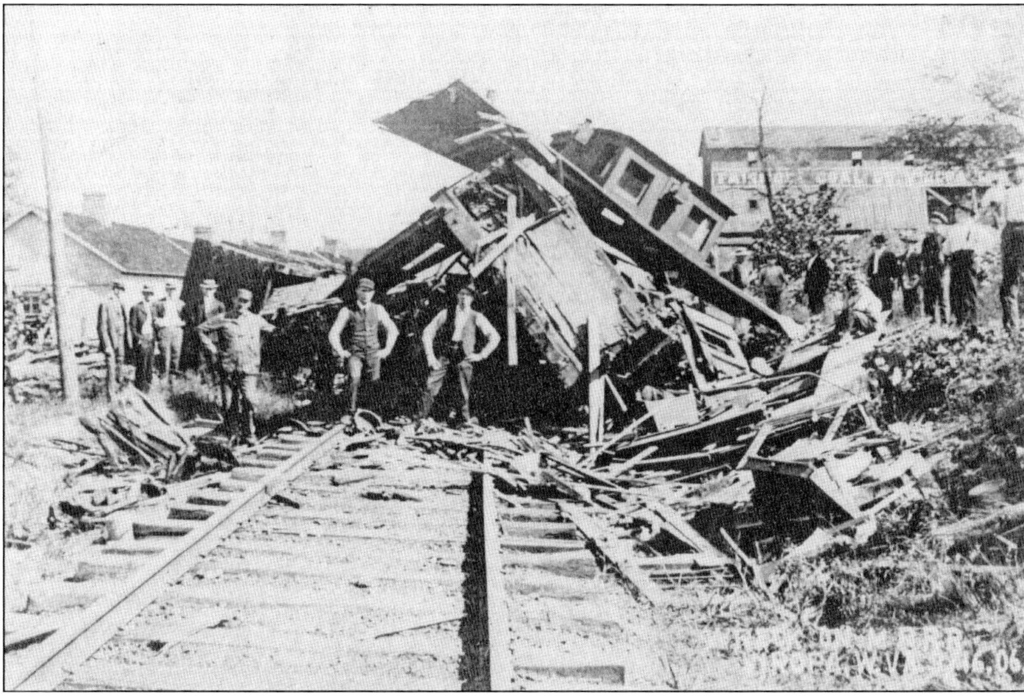

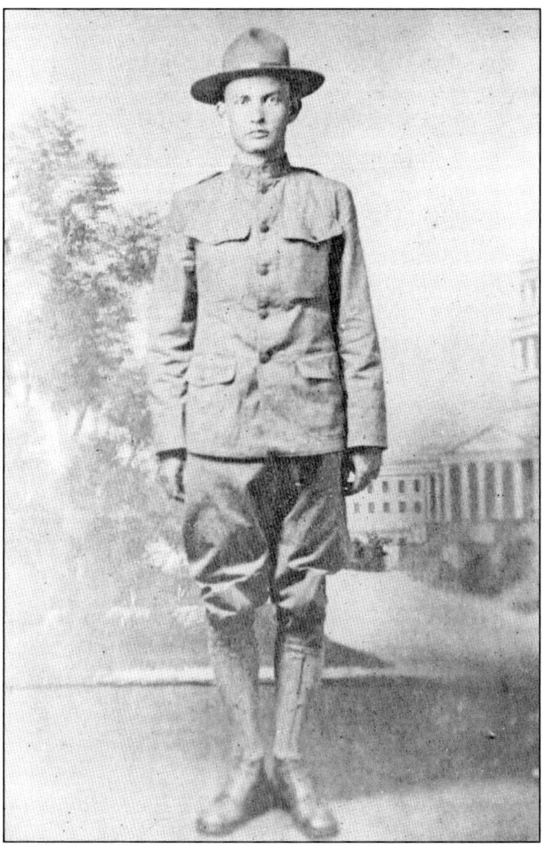

This train wreck occurred at Viropa on the Monongahela River Railroad on September 16, 1906. Sixteen men can be seen in the photograph, including one boy. The coal tipple is visible in the background, indicating the Fairmont Coal Company. Consolidation Coal Company purchased the Viropa Mine in 1910. E.W. Kochler, a contemporary of Muta Swiger, took the photograph. (Author's collection.)

Charles Harrison Hite was born in 1894, the son of Jim and Margaret (Taylor) Hite. He was a graduate of Shinnston High School, class of 1916, and went on to serve our country during World War I. During the 1918 Spanish Influenza Epidemic, he contracted the dreaded illness and died at camp on October 4, 1918. He is buried along with many other victims of the epidemic, in the Enterprise Cemetery. (Author's collection.)

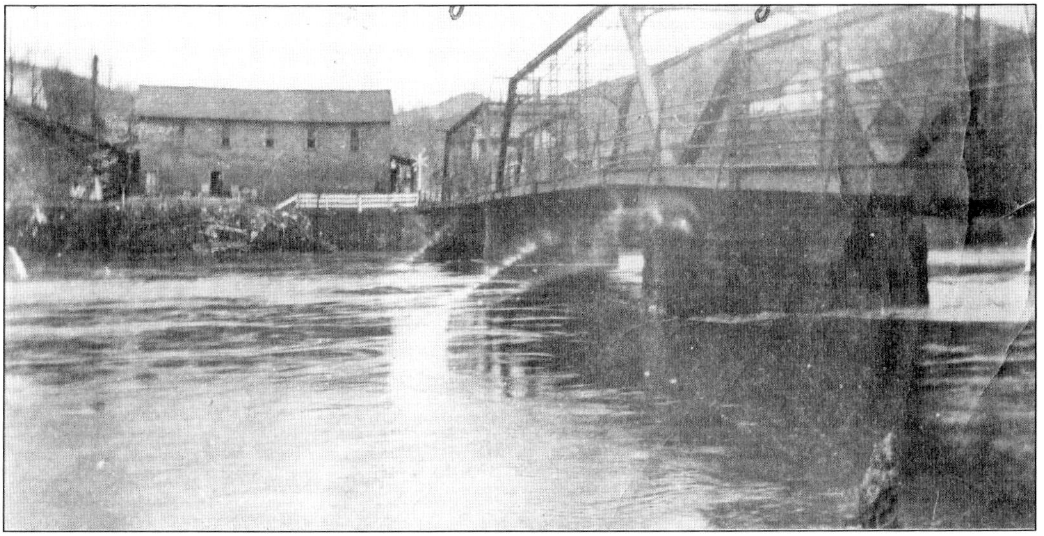

On Sunday morning, January 21, 1917, large amounts of rain began to fall on the Shinnston area. There had been a heavy snowfall in the days before, which began to melt when the temperatures increased. The already saturated ground left the river and its tributaries overflowing, producing floodwaters near the 1888-year level. Streetcar tracks were covered. This image shows the Enterprise Bridge. (Author's collection.)

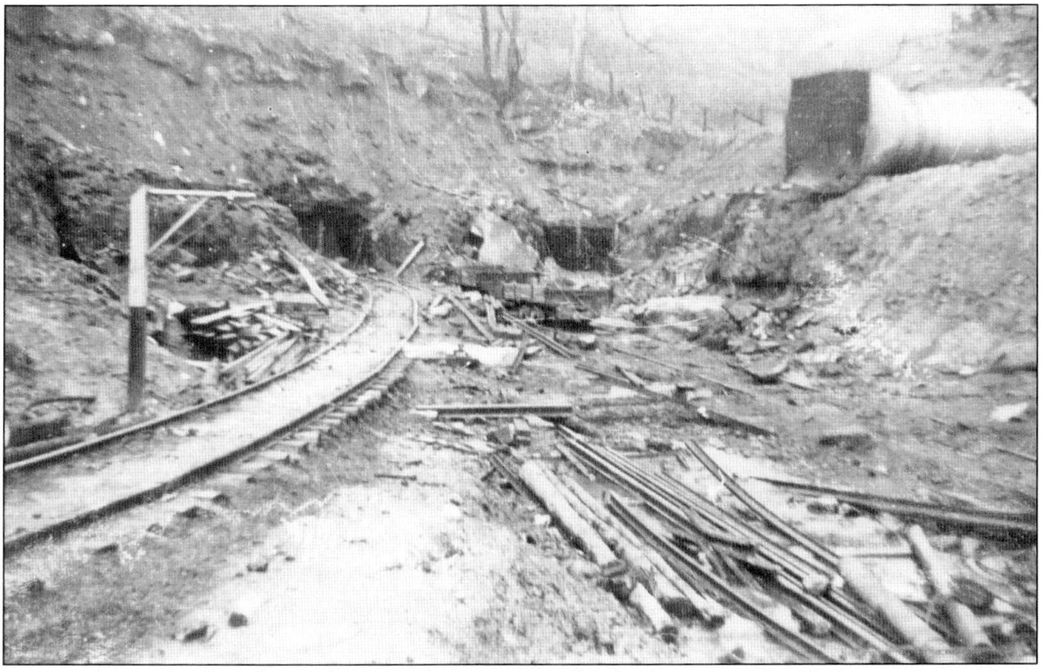

During the night shift for Friday, March 24, 1944, a fire broke out in the Katherine Mine along Wyatt Road. Miners on duty headed out of the mine to reach safety as other men headed in to battle the blaze. Highly explosive fumes filled the tunnels and in the early morning hours of March 25, 1944; a massive explosion took the lives of 16 men inside the mine. (Author's collection.)

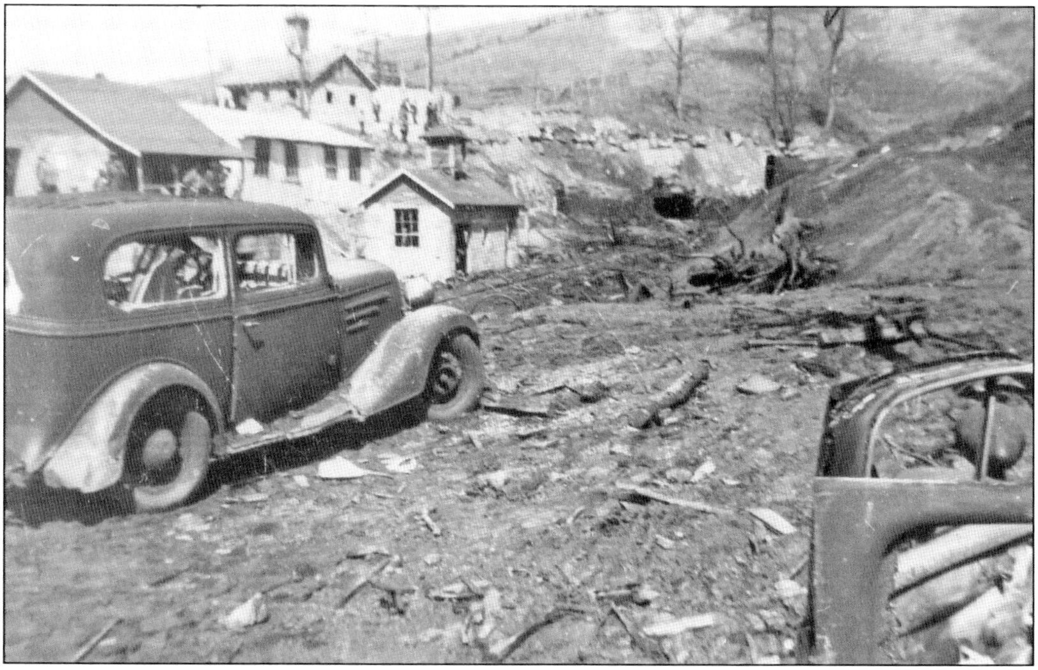

The Katherine Mine was located approximately two miles out of Shinnston along the Wyatt Road. This image shows the mine entrance after its 1944 explosion. John Hogue was the mine superintendent at the time. He escaped death by returning to his vehicle for a forgotten tool. This image by Paul Tennant shows the destruction from the blast. (Courtesy of Barbara Tennant Heldreth.)

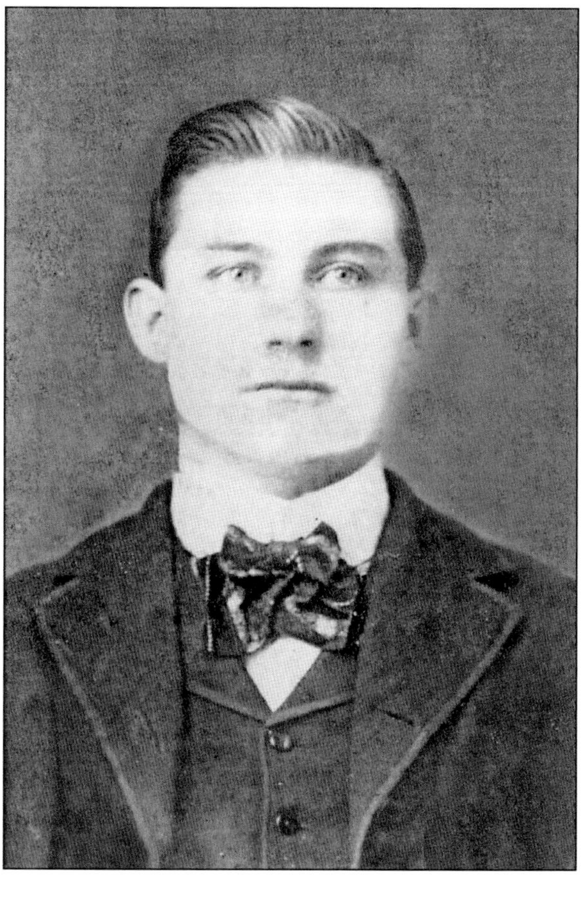

John Henry Comer was born August 10, 1881. He was a coal miner working at Katherine Mine No. 4 when the explosion occurred in March 1944. Entombed with 15 other men after the mine was sealed, his body was recovered on August 1, about 3,000 feet from the mine opening. Having only been working at the mine for one week, he left behind a widow, a sister, six children, and three grandchildren. (Courtesy of Linda Comer.)

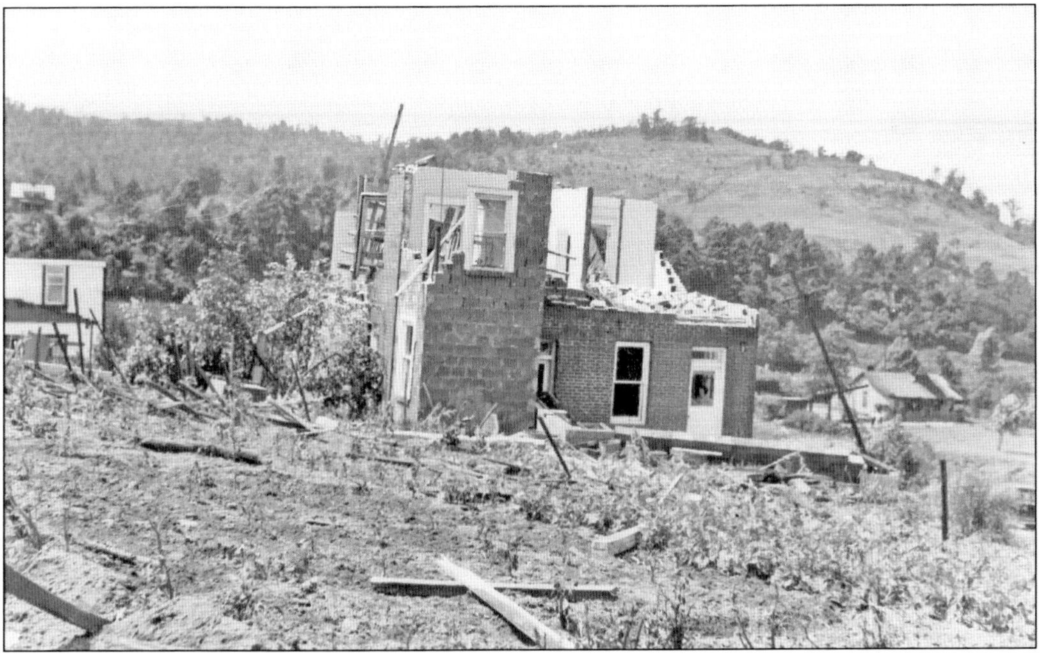

The remains of the large brick Shilley home and apartments after the tornado can be seen here at the intersection of Howard and Vernon Streets in the Pleasant Hill section of Shinnston. Dominick Parrott was one of the occupants at the time. No one was injured. Dr. Karl Clarkson's chiropractic office now fills this site. (Author's collection.)

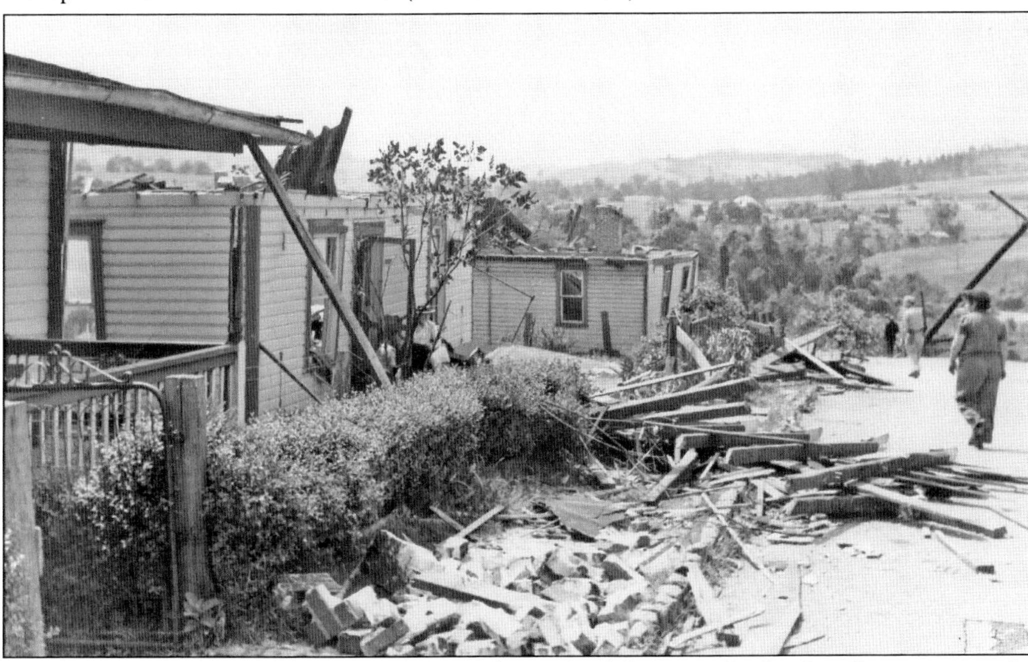

Second Street on Pleasant Hill was right in the path of the tornado that hit Shinnston on the evening of June 23, 1944. Shown here is the front porch of the Pillo home, along with the remains of the Andrick and Storage homes. Note Olive Andrick sitting on her porch, with her second story gone. (Author's collection.)

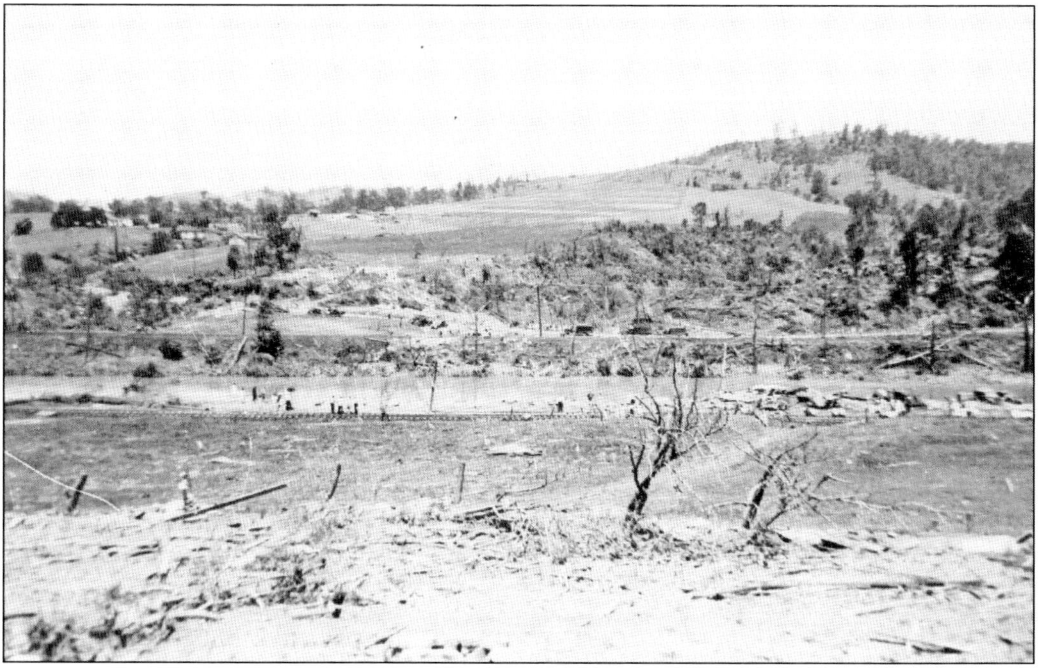

Solon was a small mining community located along the West Fork River in the vicinity below where Vincent Lumber is today. Many of the homes located there were destroyed by the 1944 Shinnston tornado. In this image, taken by Paul Tennant, the river can be seen behind the rubble, with west side in the distance. A swinging pedestrian bridge that crossed the West Fork River was also destroyed. (Courtesy of Barbara Tennant Heldreth.)

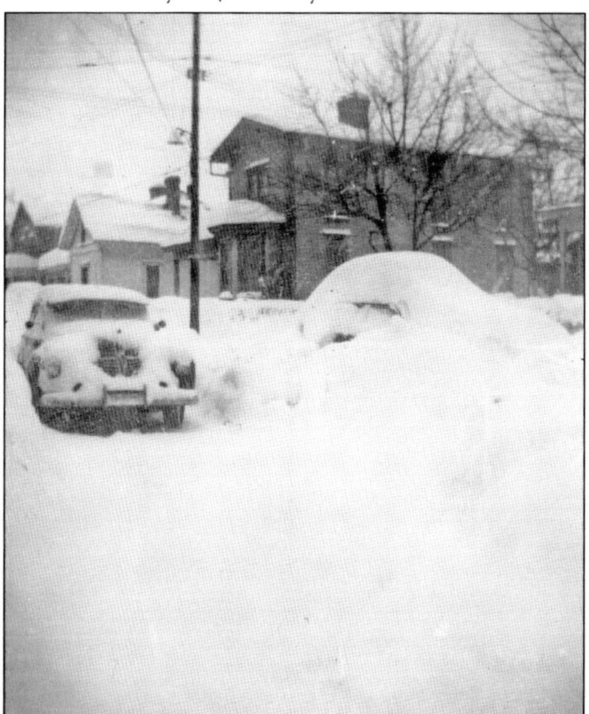

This image was taken from lower Rebecca Street, looking toward Pike Street in November 1950. Measurements differed, but reports of nearly 50 inches were documented in the Shinnston area. Several cars are seen buried beneath nature's wintry gift. As evident here, many streets provided no place for the snow to be shoveled, leaving only one manageable lane of travel. (Author's collection.)

The floodwaters were high for this aerial view of Shinnston from March 7, 1967. Richardson Lumber building is at foreground. The company houses at the former mining community of Ehlen can be seen in the distance, now the site of Shop 'n Save. All but one of the houses pictured center were razed in 2013. (Author's collection.)

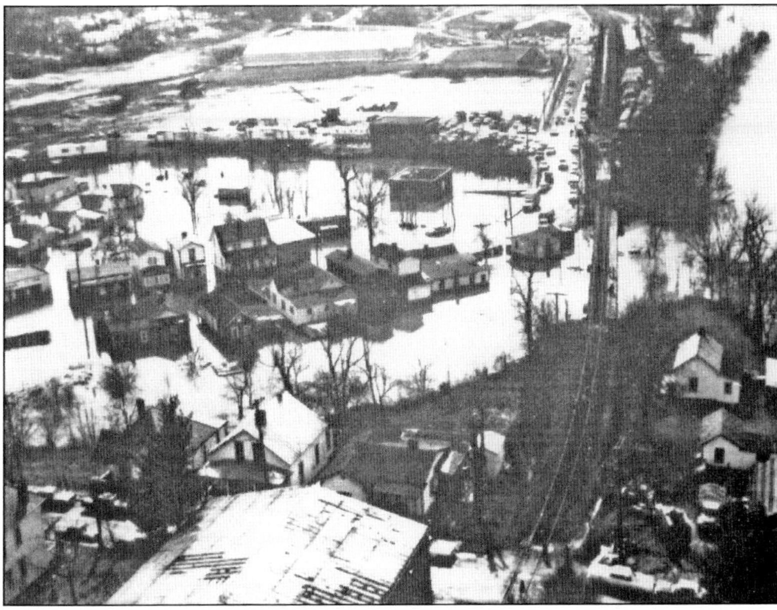

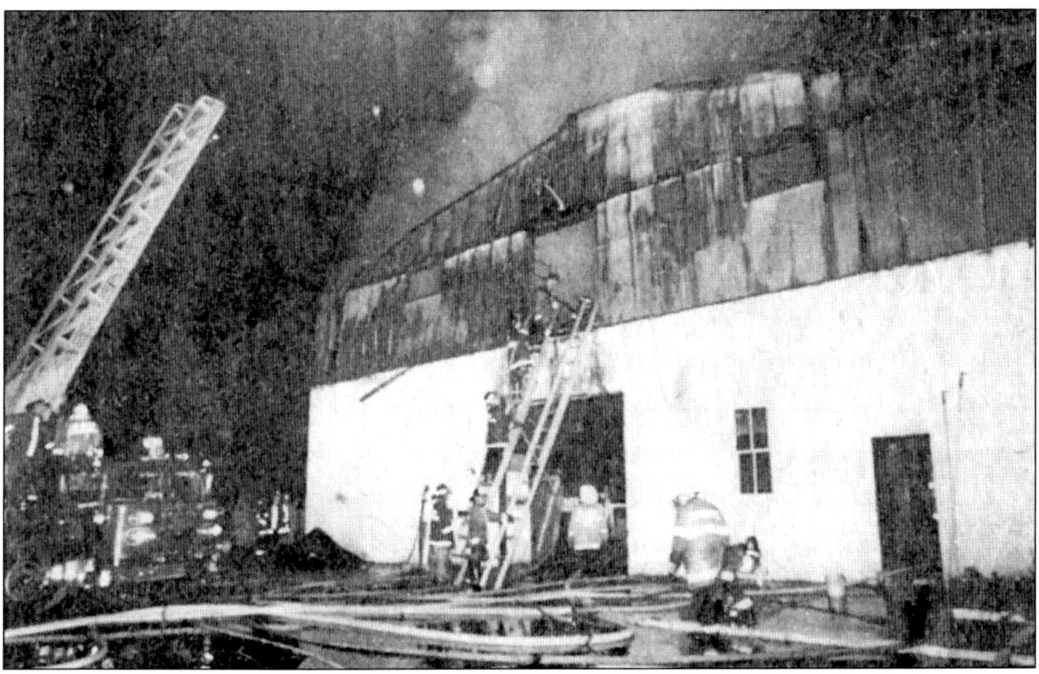

Shinnston's largest fire occurred on May 9, 1981, when Richardson Lumber Company on lower Charles Street burned to the ground. The arson fire started around 11:30 p.m. and quickly swept from one pile of lumber to the next, making the blaze one of the hottest and the brightest ever seen; the glow could be seen from miles away. Seven area fire departments responded, along with young volunteers from nearby Lincoln High School's prom. (Author's collection.)

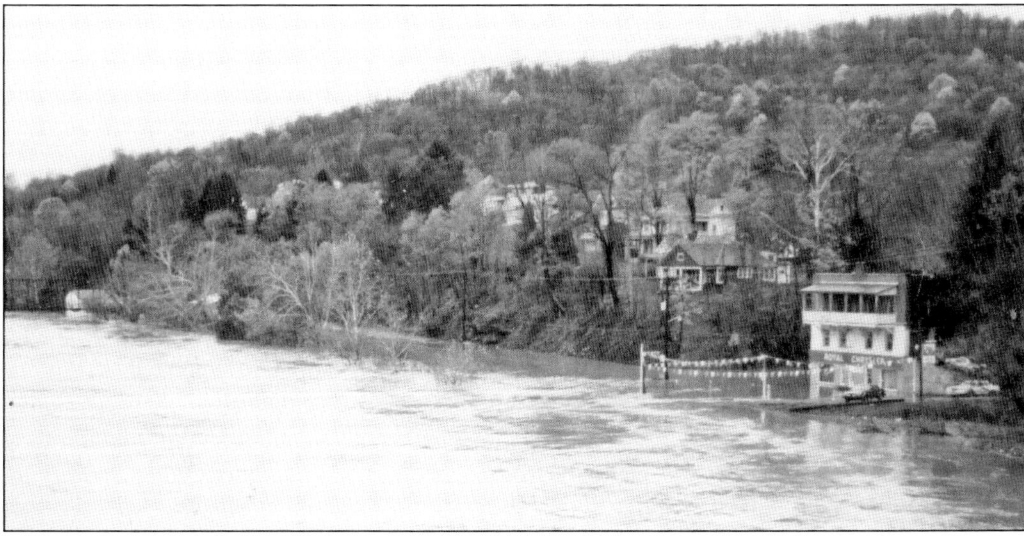

Hood Avenue on Shinnston's west side was not immune to the floodwaters of 1985. This image shows the Royal Chrysler building where Aubrey Nuzum operated Nuzum-Stewart Motor Company, a Dodge and Plymouth dealership. Initially in business with Walter and Luther Stewart, Nuzum later operated it with Paul Gaydos. Matheny's Used Cars later occupied the site. (Author's collection.)

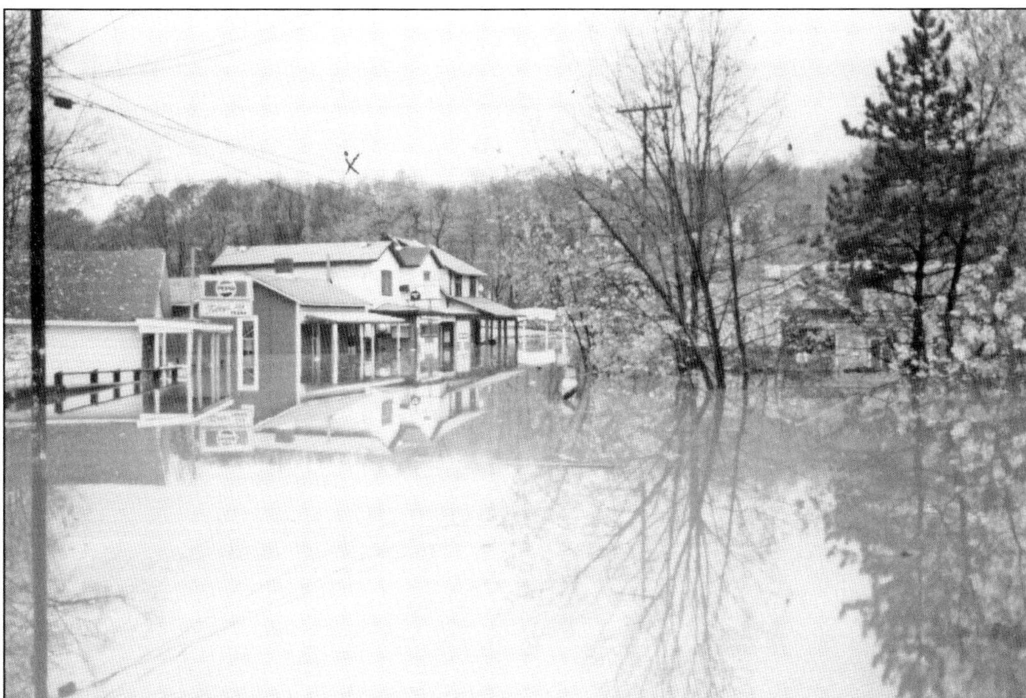

Much of West Virginia was severely damaged by flood waters during early November 1985. The areas around Shinnston were no exception. Big Elm and the bottom of Saltwell Road were both flooded, making the only way out of Shinnston by use of the old Enterprise-Bethlehem Road. This image shows Pike Street, looking south, from the Charles Street Christian Church. (Author's collection.)

Eight

Homes and People

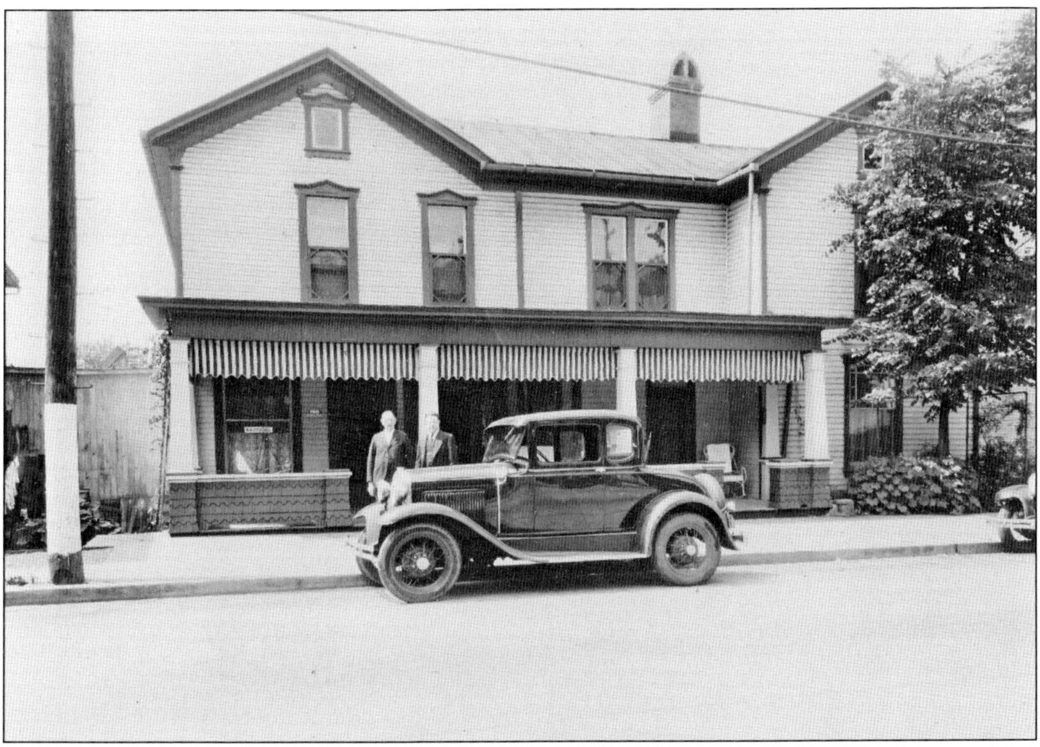

Dr. Napoleon Brock Cox moved into this home at 508 Pike Street about 1910. In 1913, he added onto this house, increasing his office space, which was located on the left side of the house. He practiced medicine here until the age of 91. This is currently the Matheny home, and Dr. Cox's office is now Shinnston Glass and Mirror. (Courtesy of Jim Hess.)

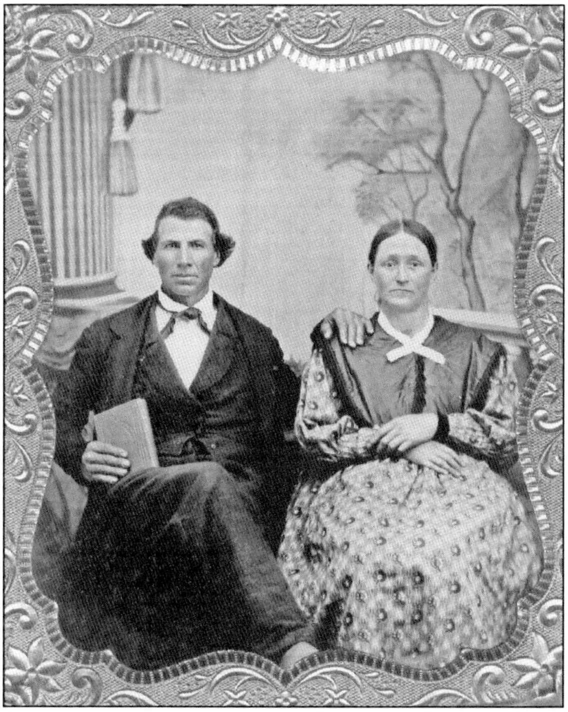

Isaiah and Nancy (Robey) Shinn are shown in this studio portrait. Isaiah was the youngest child of Levi Shinn. He and his family lived at Pine Bluff in a home owned in more recent years by the late Julian Matheny. This is the only photograph known to exist of a member of the first Shinn family to have lived in the old log house. (Courtesy of Shinnston Historical Association.)

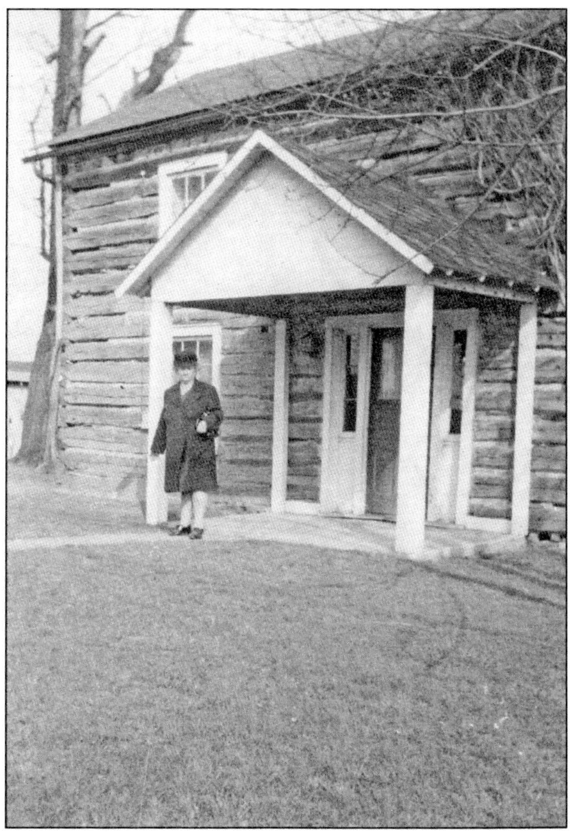

Minnie (Martin) Shingleton is shown in 1940 in front of the Levi Shinn house, where she was born in 1887. Built in 1778, the house is the oldest structure in this part of West Virginia. Containing four large original rooms with a very large central chimney, the logs were squared, and the structure has survived both the 1944 tornado and the 2011 earthquake vibrations felt from Mineral, Virginia. (Courtesy of Shinnston Historical Association.)

One of Shinnston's leading businessmen in the early 1900s was Benjamin Anderson. In the late 1910s, he was one of the vice presidents of the People's Bank of Shinnston. During the Great Depression, he was an organizer and one of the first directors of the Bank of Shinnston. His business, Anderson Garage Company, was incorporated in 1917. (Courtesy of Cindy Anderson Scott.)

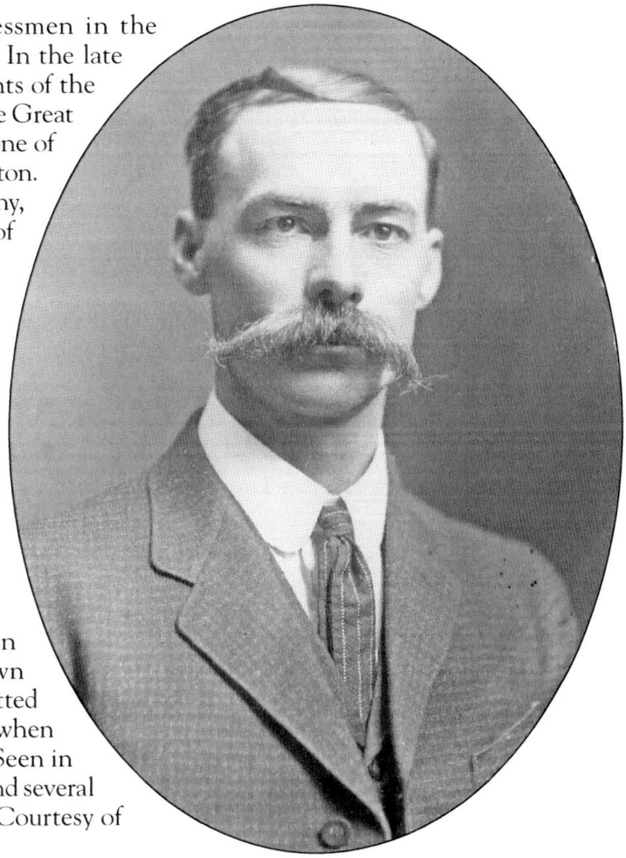

The Benjamin Anderson farm on Anderson's Hollow near Mudlick is shown here around 1910. Many families benefitted from their underlying mineral rights when the oil boom hit the Shinnston area. Seen in this image are at least five oil derricks and several outbuildings. The home still stands. (Courtesy of Cindy Anderson Scott.)

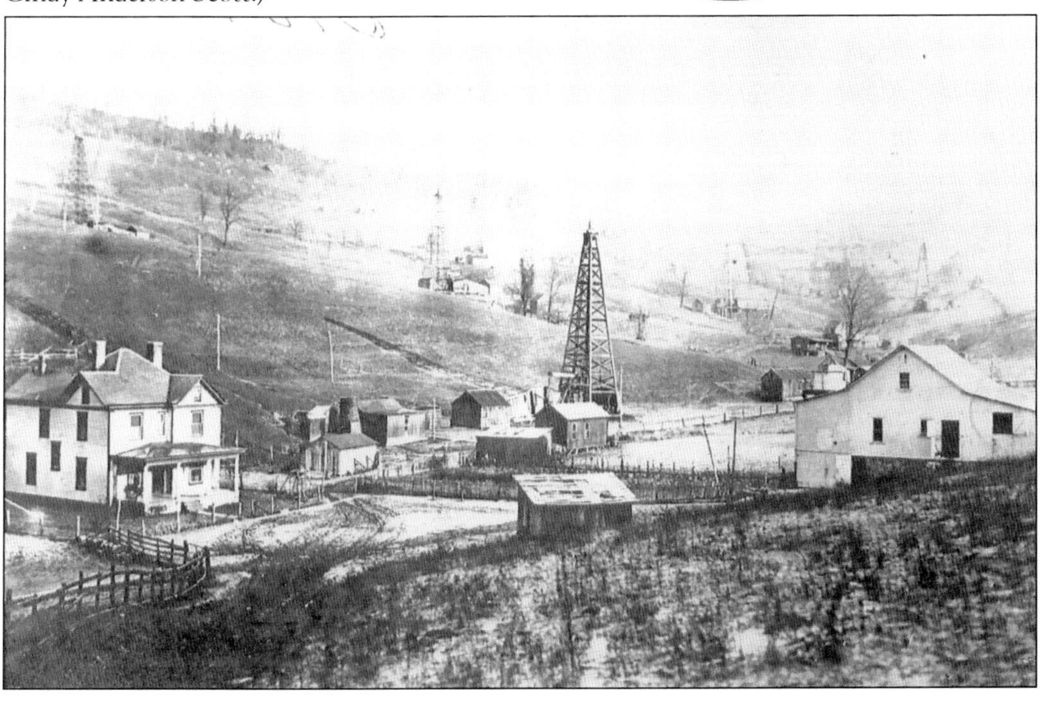

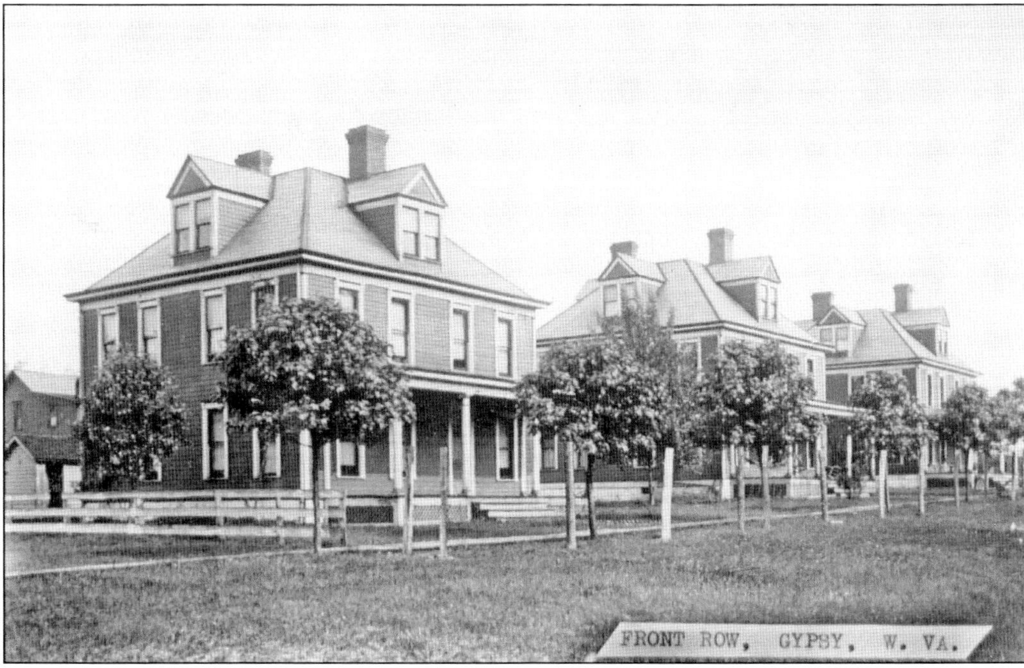

These houses located on the front row at Gypsy are now actually located on the back row. The caption on the postcard was defined using the railroad as a starting point. They were the only three-story company houses built in Gypsy. The middle one burned down many years ago, but the other two remain standing. (Author's collection.)

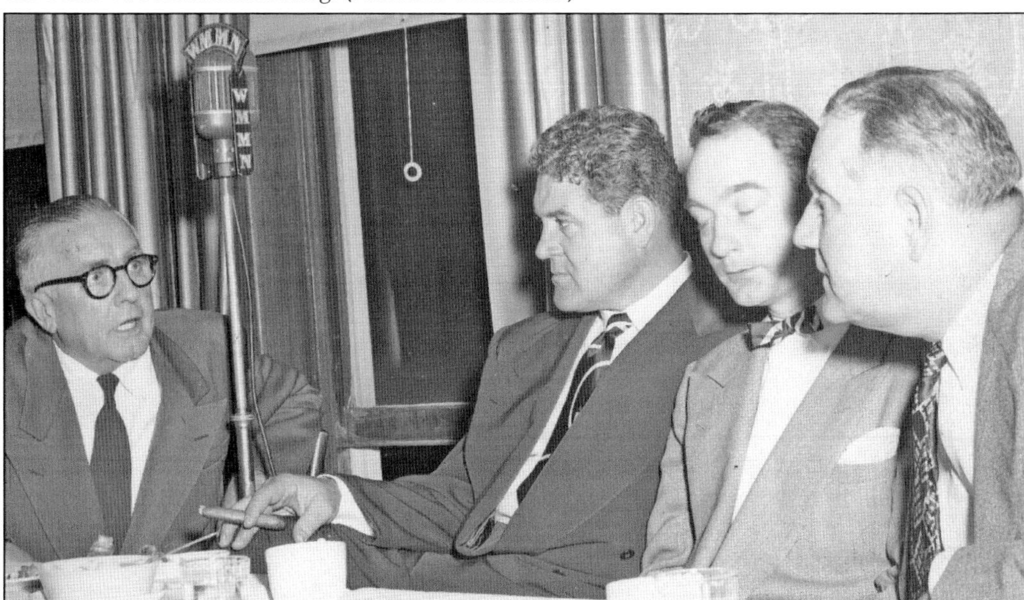

This image was taken in the IOOF building in Shinnston during a dinner when former Los Angeles Rams coach Joe Stydahar was guest speaker. A 1931 Shinnston High School graduate, Stydahar was the first player drafted by the Chicago Bears in the first ever NFL draft. Lincoln High School's Stydahar Field is named in his memory. Pictured from left to right are Warren "Tubby" Hursey, Joe Stydahar, Hayes Webb, and Hardin Harmer. (Courtesy of Bob Bice II.)

Pictured are William Perry Fortney and daughters Mary Ellen Tetrick (left) and Rocina Hess-Robinson (right). In addition to being a preacher in the Christian Church, Perry was also a doctor of medicine, tailor by trade (which he studied in New York City), brick mason, builder, and merchant. He could doctor the sick, baptize them, make their coffin, preach at their funeral, and bury them. His father, Jacob Fortney, was also an early Shinnston pioneer physician. (Author's collection.)

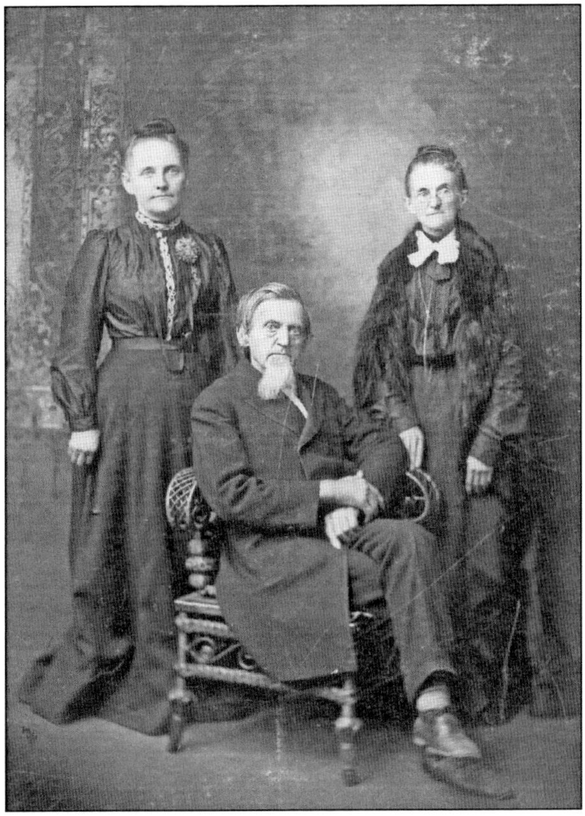

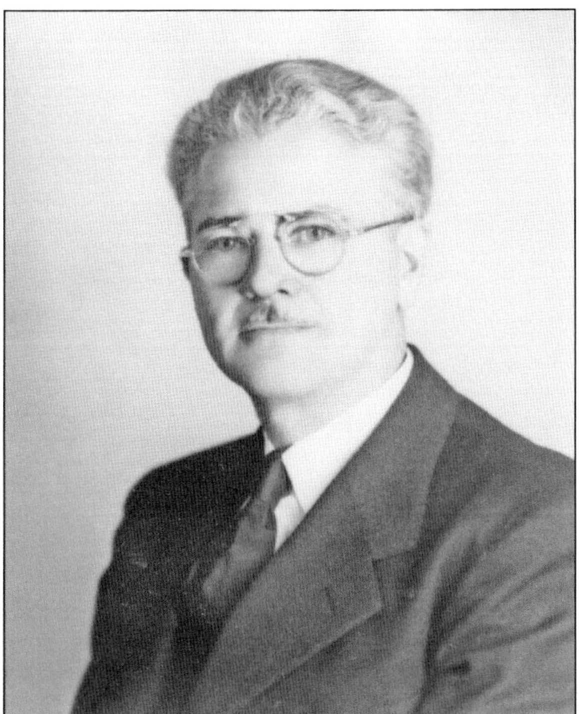

Wayne O. Koon started his dental practice in Monongah. He moved to Shinnston in the 1920s and had his office located first along Pike Street, close to where A.O. Janes & Son was. Later, he purchased his home at 808 Hood Avenue and used part of the home for his dental office. (Courtesy of Kathleen Ellen Hurst.)

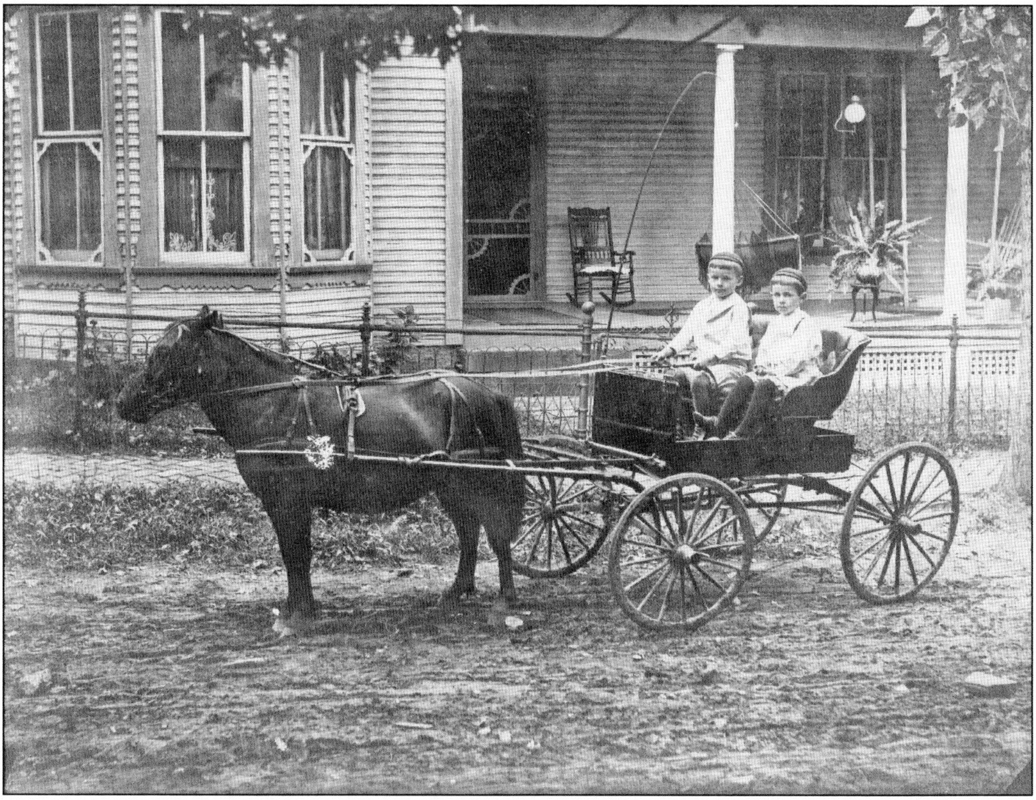

The sons of Leslie Hawker enjoy a pony ride on Station Street in 1909. Wayne, age six and Marlin, age four, were grandsons of the Farmers Bank president Thomas Hawker. Both children grew up to be local businessmen. (Courtesy of Harmer Funeral Home.)

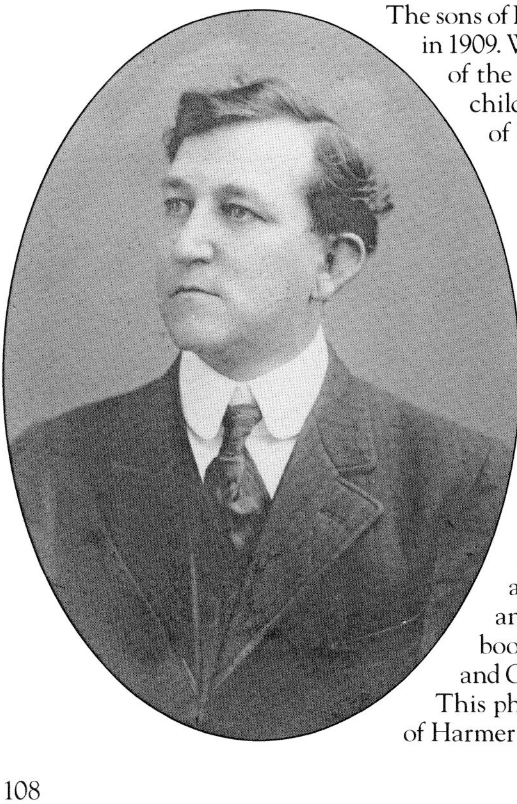

Harvey W. Harmer, the son of Benjamin Tyson Harmer Sr., practiced law in Clarksburg until the age of 92, dying four years later. As a preservationist and historian, he was the author of several local books, including *Old Grist Mills of Harrison County* and *Covered Bridges of Harrison County, West Virginia.* This photograph was taken on June 1, 1909. (Courtesy of Harmer Funeral Home.)

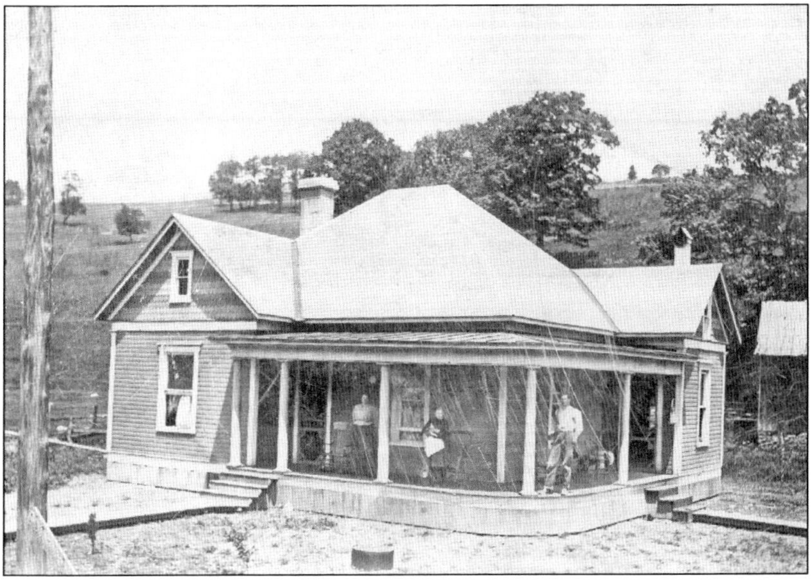

The Lloyd Finley "Finn" Ashcraft home is shown here shortly after completion. It is located at the bottom of Peora Hill, opposite the intersection of Cunningham Run. Shown on the front porch are Finn, his wife Pearl, and their daughter Nell. (Courtesy of Mary Rose and Ina Jean Carpenter.)

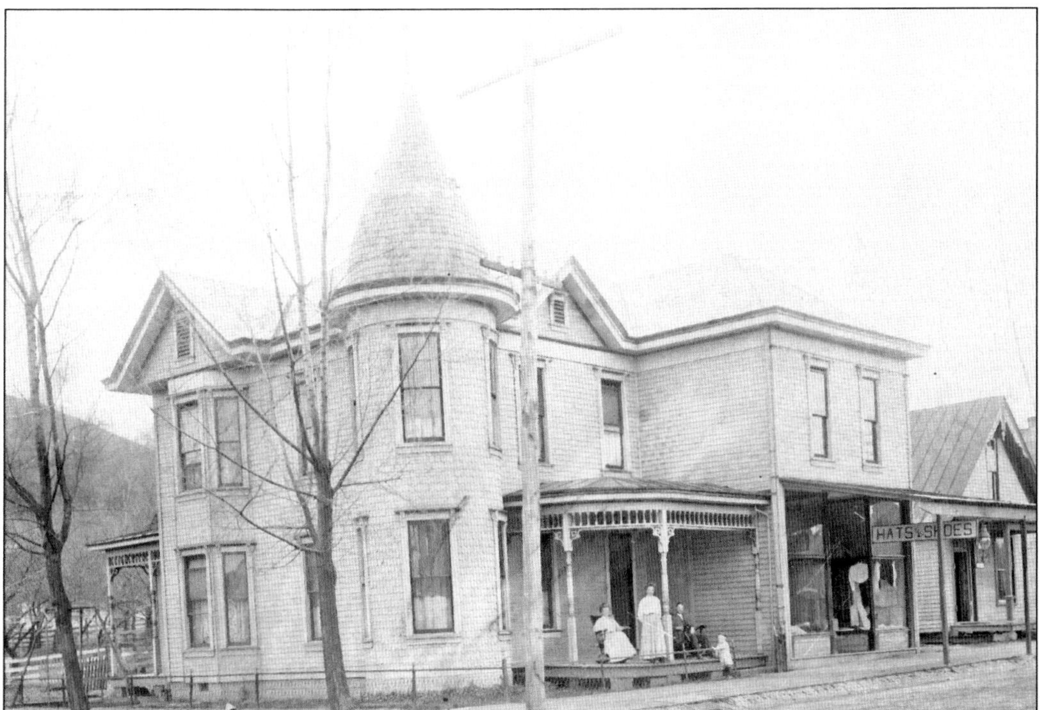

In 1909, Chester Cunningham moved to the southeast corner of Pike and Rebecca Streets, where he lived in the Victorian half and operated a men's store in the other half. In 1920, F.L. Meek ran a plumbing store here. Later, the building was a hotel and then a grocery store before the Pulice family purchased it for use as a Ford dealership. Harrison County EMS has a structure here today. (Author's collection.)

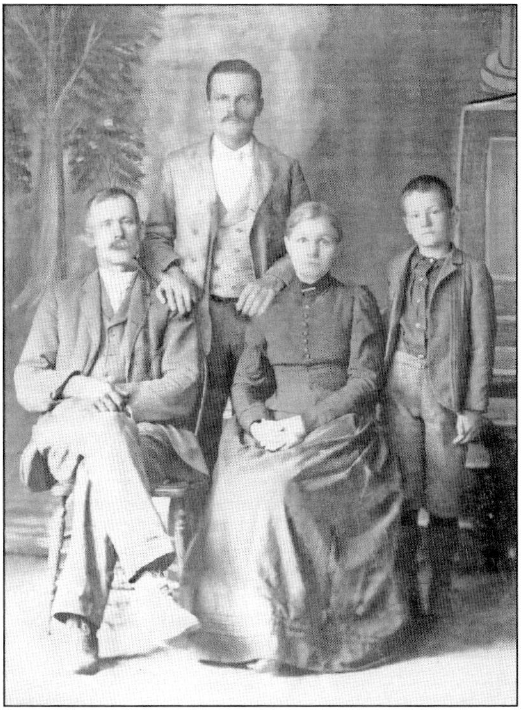

Granville and Angie Nora (Long) Nay are shown here with sons Fred (standing, center) and Lawrence in about 1895. Granville was once proprietor of the Red Lion Tavern (called "Blue Boar Inn" in Granville Davisson Hall's novel *Daughter of the Elm*). Fred operated his own transfer business, which he sold to Lynch's Transfer in 1917 to go into the coal business. A partner in Nay & Hardesty, the firm that owned Anganora Mine (named for Fred's mother) in East Shinnston, he suffered blood poisoning when his miner's lamp caught fire and burned his face and shoulders. He died in June 1918. (Author's collection.)

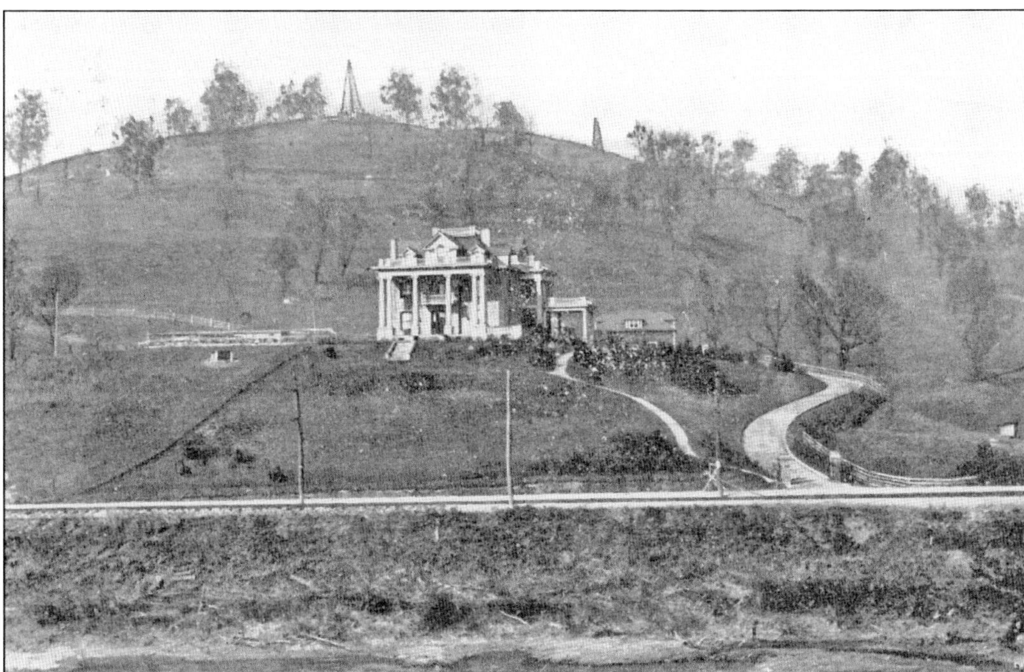

The Lucas mansion in Shinnston has long been a place of grandeur. Basil Harold Lucas built the home for his wife, Mayme. She thought the house was too big and did not care to live in it, so they moved into town, and Mr. and Mrs. Charles Fletcher Lucas purchased the home. It was later occupied by James Edward Lucas. The residence was used in the filming of the 1972 Italian film *1931: Once Upon a Time in New York*. (Author's collection.)

Beatrice Jarrett was a child of Lemuel and Sarah Elizabeth (Bryan) Jarrett. Her father operated a grocery and china store, though he was blind for much of his adulthood. "Auntie Bea," as she was known by many, moved to Fairmont and worked for the Consolidation Coal Company. She later returned to Rebecca Street in Shinnston to care for her parents while working for the Shinnston Bank as a bookkeeper. She never married. (Author's collection.)

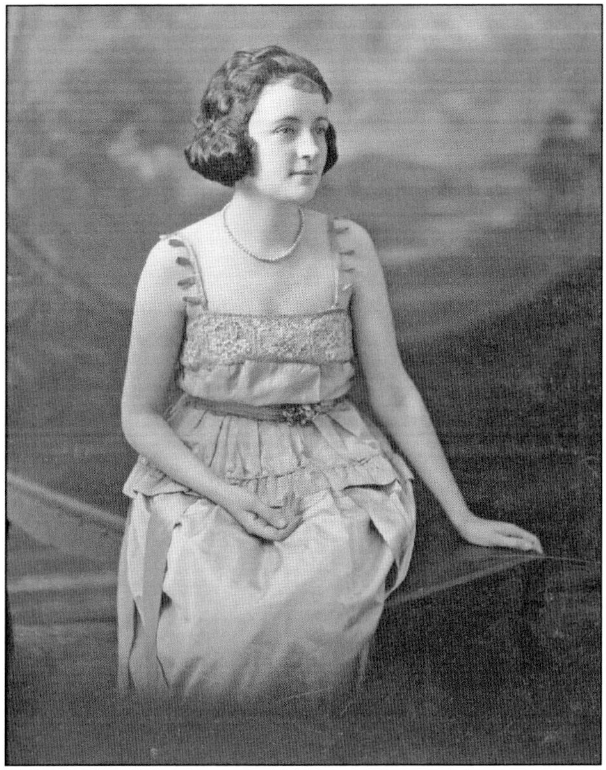

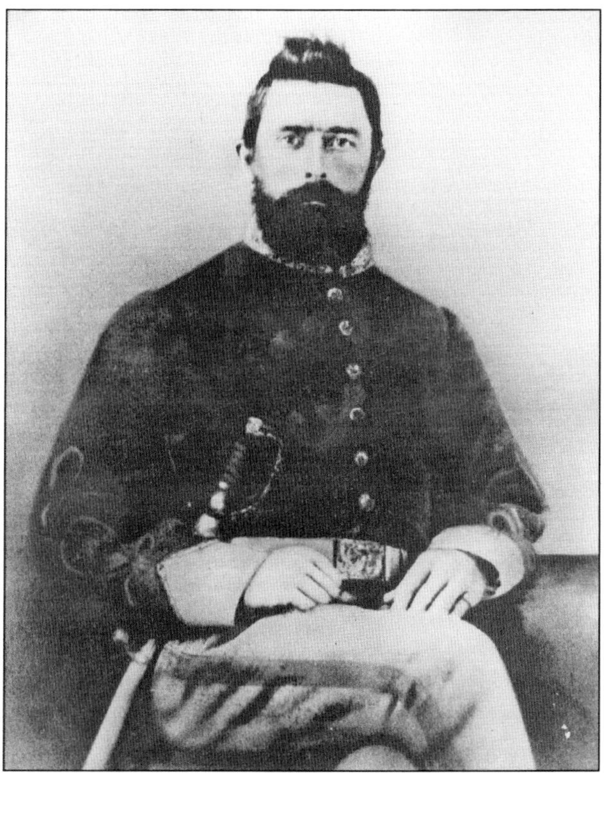

John Righter, born in 1829, was the son of Peter B. Righter, whose home was burned to the ground by federal troops in June 1861. John enlisted for the Confederate cause and was captain for the No. 4 Virginia State Rangers of Marion, Harrison, and Taylor Counties. He was recruited as captain into the Confederate army in March 1863. Captured in Harrison County, West Virginia, on April 3, 1864, he was sent to a military prison in Wheeling. Captain Righter died in 1911. (Courtesy of William Smith Righter.)

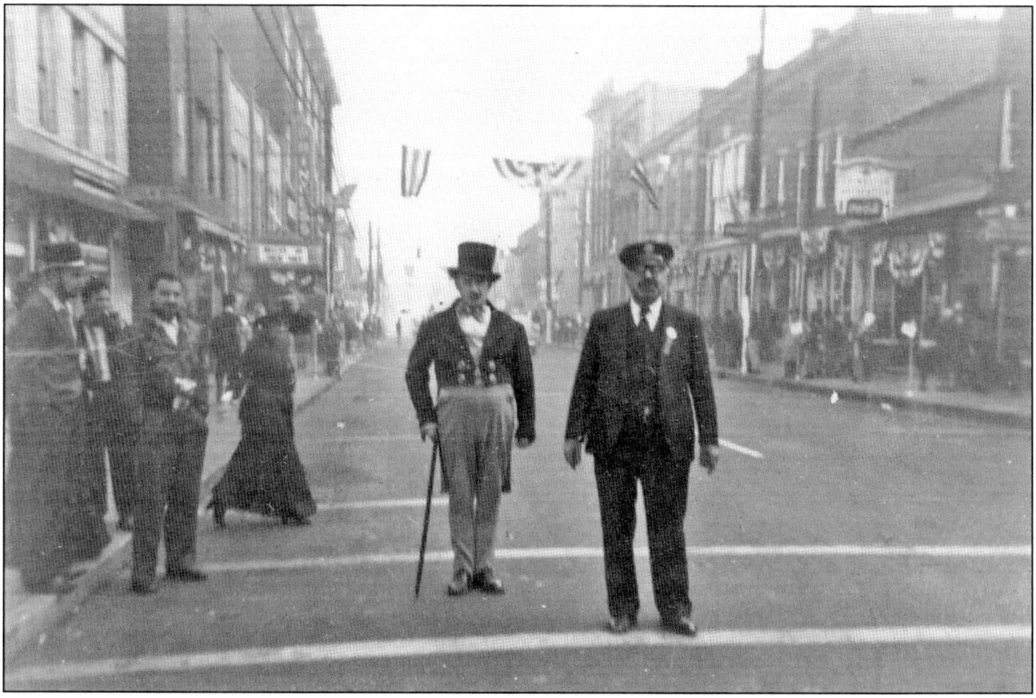

Former Shinnston mayor George Dorsey is shown with Taufig "Tofake" Simon during the 1952 centennial celebration. Tofake was a dry-goods merchant in Shinnston, where he also sold Mexican jumping beans. His store took up two floors and was located in what is now part of the WesBanco complex. He was well known for walking the street with a fez, cigar, and leather slippers. Tofake's step-great-grandson is famous singer-songwriter-actor Justin Timberlake. (Author's collection.)

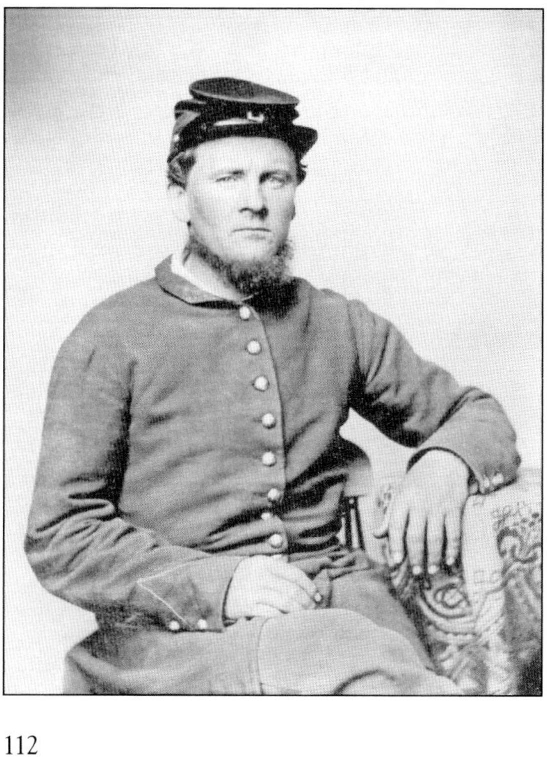

This photograph from a tintype shows Oliver Nay, a Union solider in the First Battle of Bull Run. He later became farrier but was captured in June 1864 and spent several months at the Andersonville Prison in Georgia, where he contracted disease. He was transferred to a Union hospital in Maryland, and died on December 19, 1864. He was brought back to Clarksburg by train and then taken into Shinnston by horse and buggy and buried. (Author's collection.)

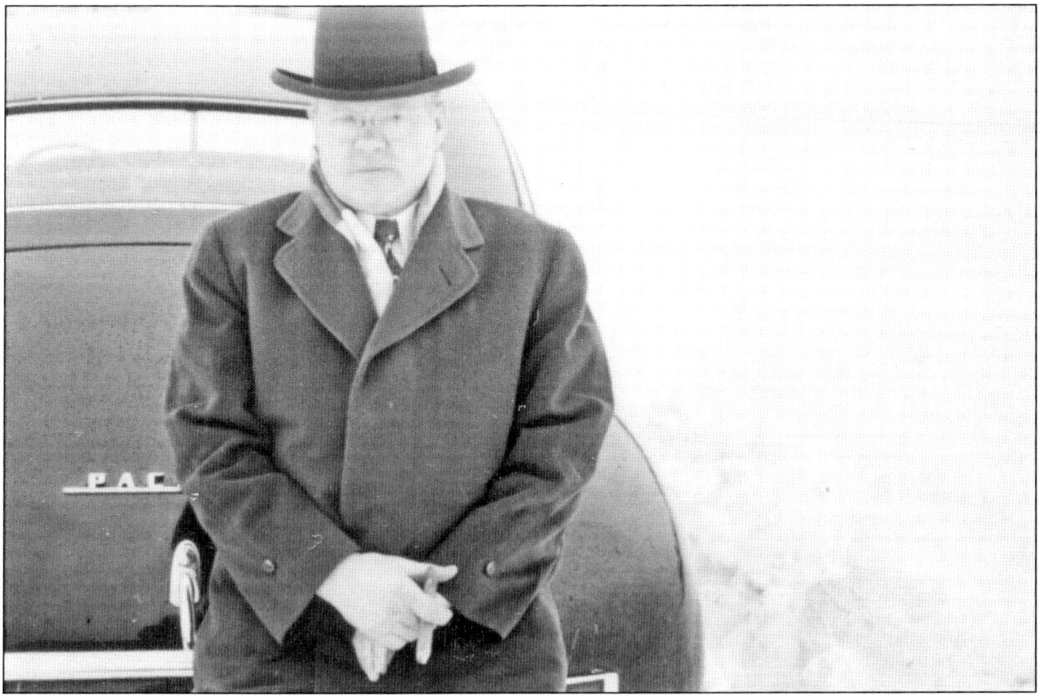

Three Coffindaffer brothers practiced medicine in Shinnston. First, Dorsey arrived in 1909 and established an office over the First National Bank. Killed by a train while on route to aid a child struck by an electrical mining wire, his brother Clyde came to Shinnston and took over his patients from 1920 to 1927. In 1929, Russell Smith Coffindaffer, pictured here, moved to Shinnston, eventually establishing Coffindaffer Memorial Clinic on Main Street. R.S. Coffindaffer's office expanded to the streets in the aftermath of the 1944 tornado. (Courtesy of Bob Bice II.)

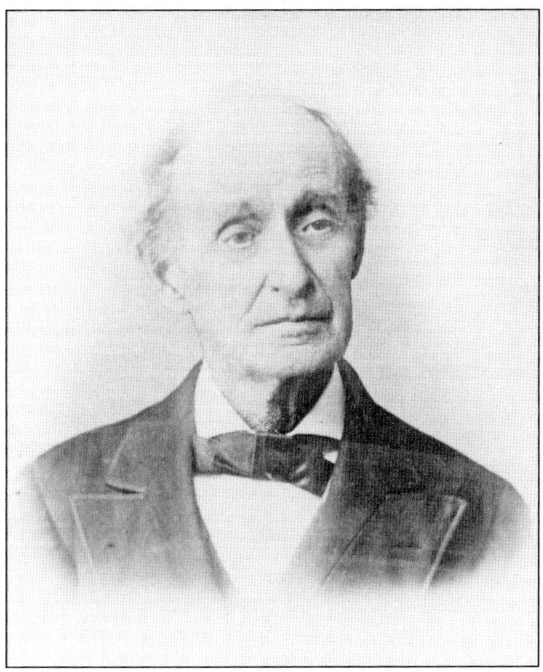

Solomon Stevenson Fleming was elected first mayor of Shinnston in 1852. He lived in a house at the southwest corner of Main Street and Davis Court and had a store in the first level of his home, which was raided by the Confederates during the infamous Jones-Imboden Raid of 1863. He later became a member of the West Virginia House of Delegates. (Courtesy of the City of Shinnston.)

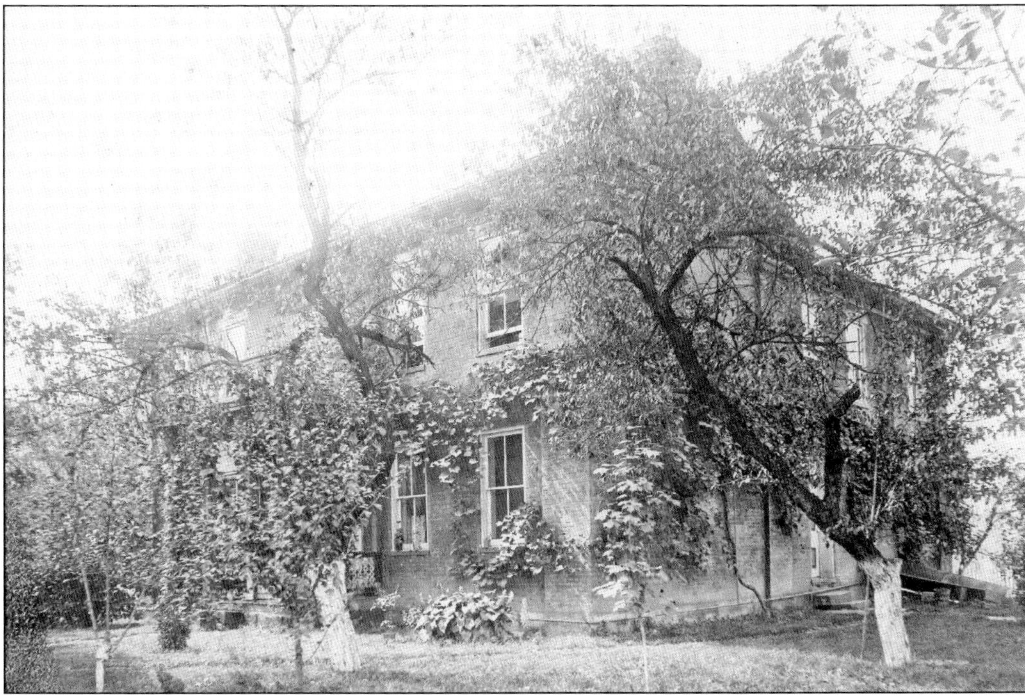

The Monroe home in Shinnston was one of Shinnston's grand brick homes. It sat on a knoll in the vicinity of the current mobile home court behind Rite Aid. Built in 1852 by Seth Shinn, it later became the home of his only daughter, Mary Martha (Shinn) Monroe, and her family. It was razed in 1961. (Courtesy of Tish Brookover Harbert.)

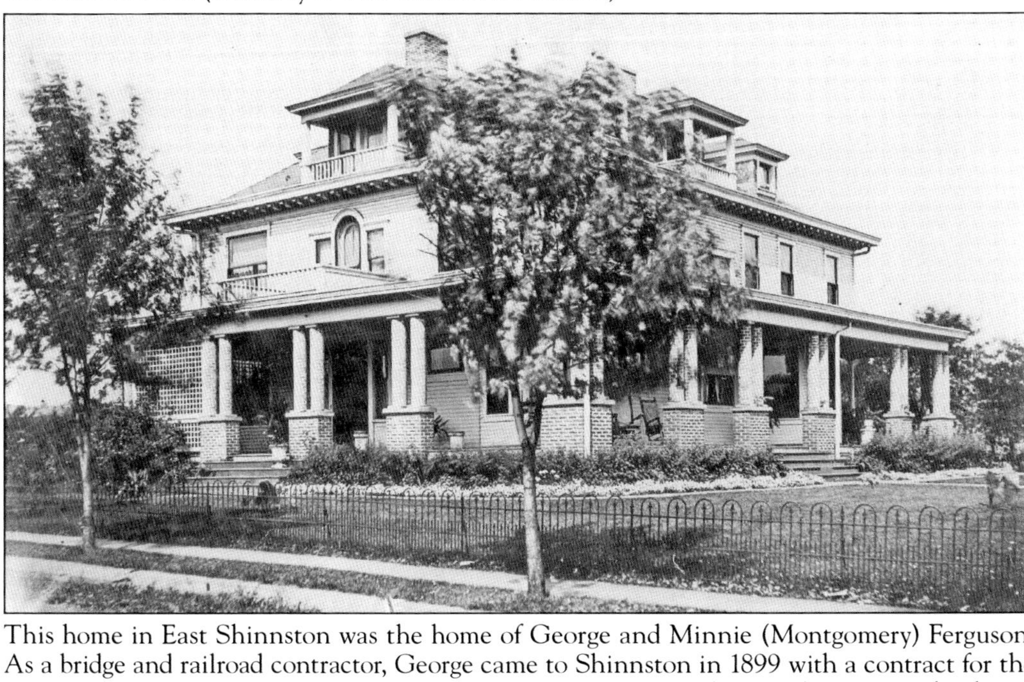

This home in East Shinnston was the home of George and Minnie (Montgomery) Ferguson. As a bridge and railroad contractor, George came to Shinnston in 1899 with a contract for the West Virginia Short Line. Located at the corner of Ferguson and East Pike Streets, this home still stands. (Author's collection.)

Hannah Hood was the only child of Charles and Pleasant (McCord) Hood. Never having married, Hannah inherited the historic Big Elm Farm from her parents and her Uncle Harry Hood, who never married. She lived in the large brick house at the farm on which she was raised. Big Elm Elementary School now sits on part of the Hood Farm. (Author's collection.)

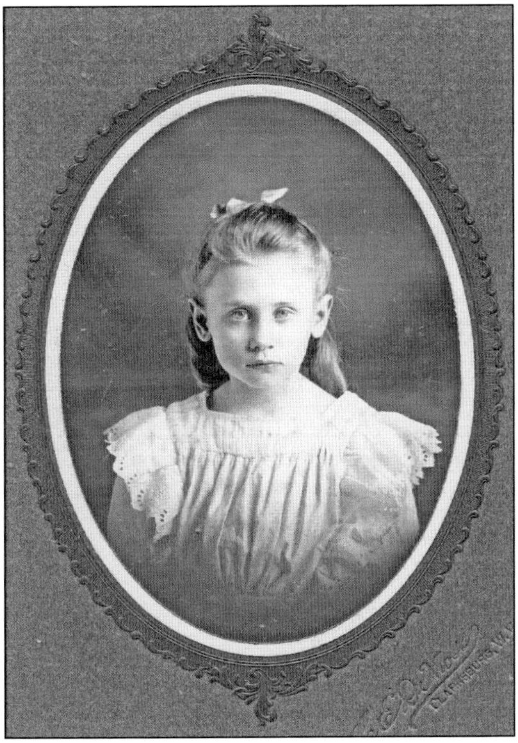

In January 1880, a group of local children got together to establish a Keystone Club. On January 7, 1940, this group of men, then calling themselves members of the Silver Keystone Lodge No.1, got together for a reunion. A few of the men pictured here were charter members, Lemuel Jarrett being one. While he was working as a carpenter, a piece of steel struck his eye, causing blindness. However, he successfully operated a store at the corner of Pike and Walnut Streets. (Courtesy of Harmer Funeral Home.)

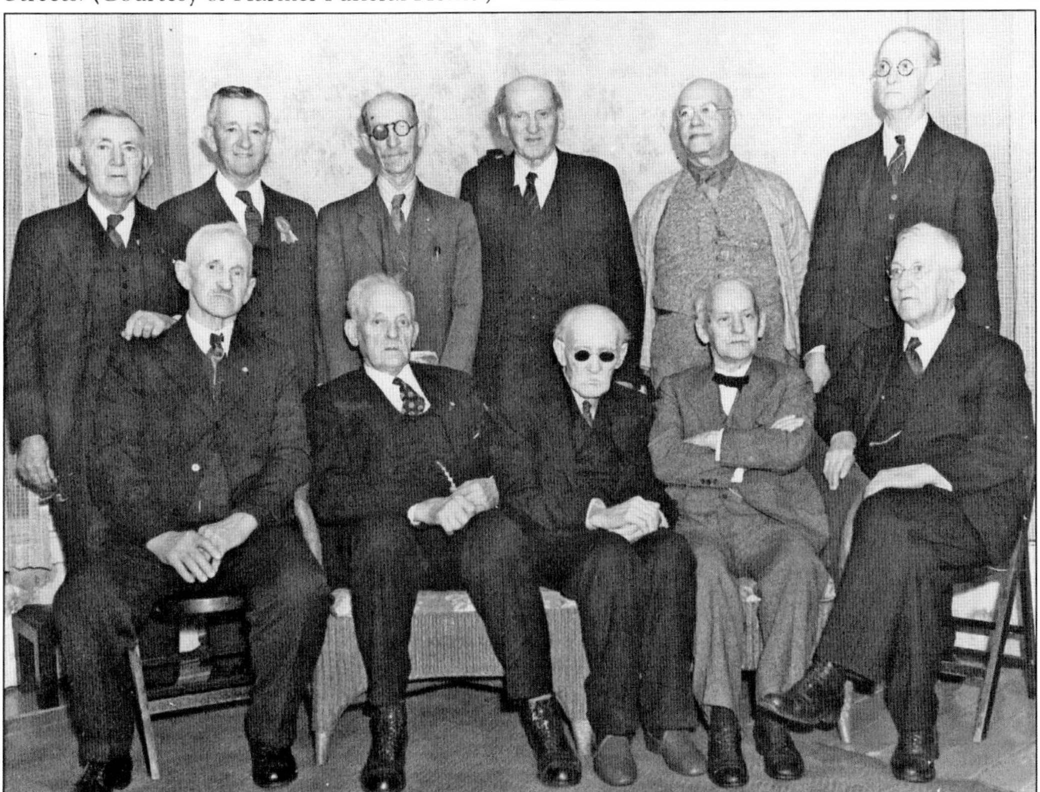

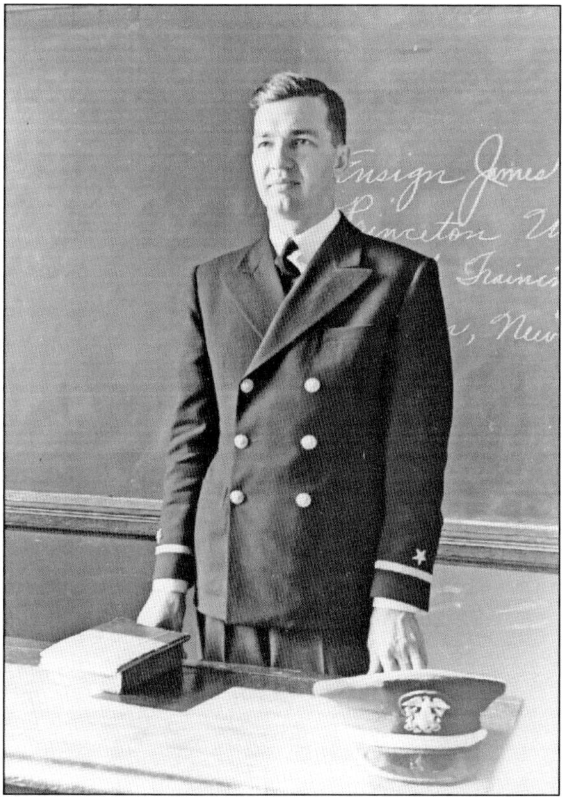

James Victor Morris was an educator at Shinnston High School when Joseph Wharton, school librarian, snapped this photograph on December 8, 1942, Morris's last day before reporting for active duty. At sea for nearly 27 months, he served as lieutenant in top-secret communications on Adm. Cato Glover's staff. He stood on deck and watched Manila fall, with hundreds of dead soldiers floating down the river to the Manila Bay. He was also in New York City when Armistice Day was celebrated on November 11, 1945. (Author's collection.)

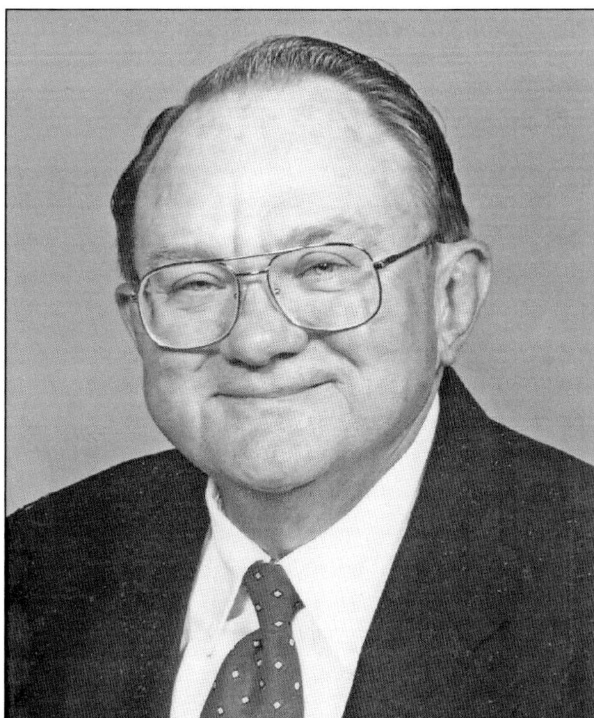

Dr. David V. Haning started practicing dentistry in Shinnston in 1969. He was first established in the Kalaycioglu building on lower Main Street with Dr. Mehmet V. Kalaycioglu. In 1982, he and his wife, Priscilla (Nuzum) Haning, purchased a building along Howard Street where he continued his practice. He retired in 1999. (Courtesy of Priscilla [Nuzum] Haning.)

Nine

Community Pride

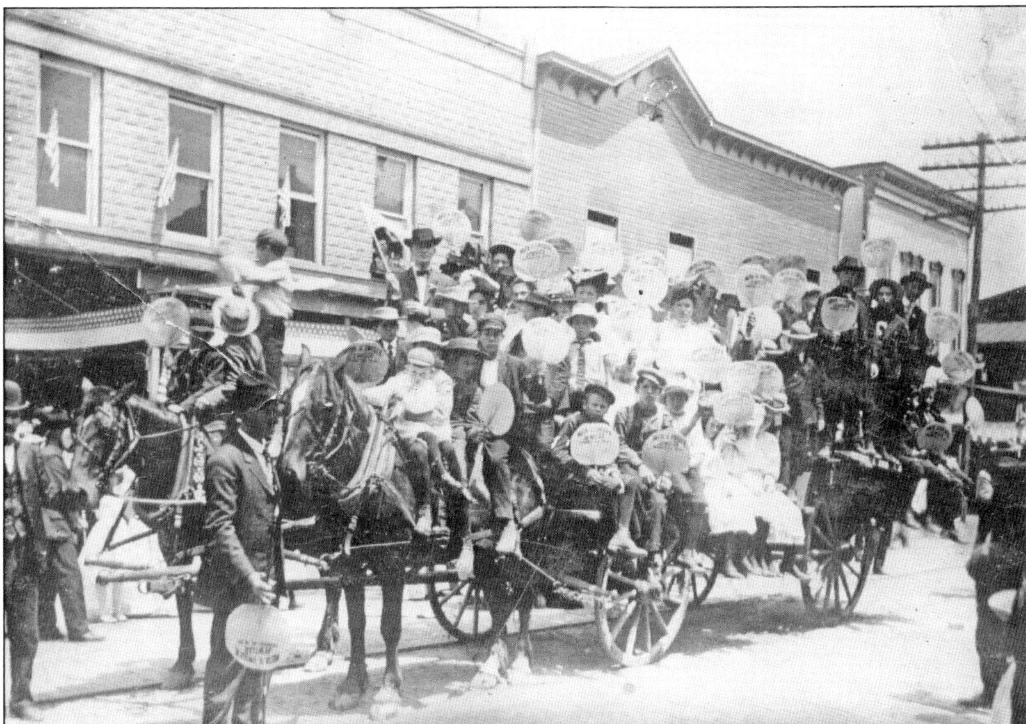

A total of 94 people were being pulled on wagon by this team of horses from Enterprise's Lucius Riley Sturm farm on July 4, 1907. The photograph was taken in front of Muta Swiger's jewelry store, situated near the corner of Pike and Walnut Streets, during a parade. Several people are holding a fan with the words "Muta U. Swiger, Jeweler, Shinnston, W.Va." This team won as "Parade Winner" for having the most people. (Author's collection.)

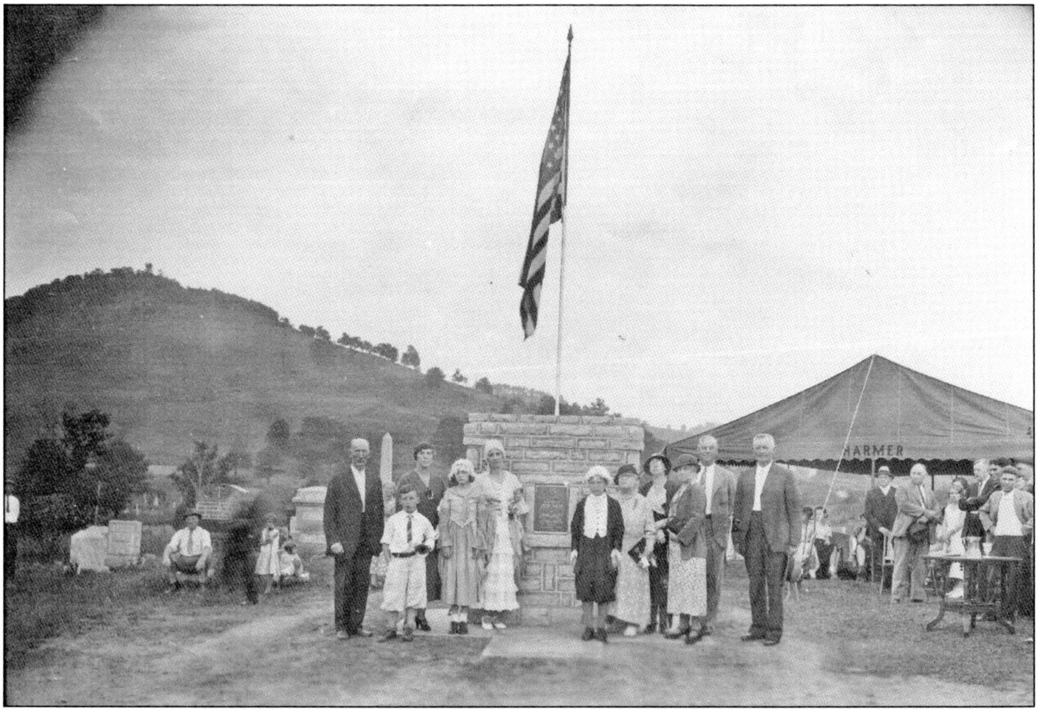

Settled at the time of the American Revolution, Enterprise was home to two Revolutionary War soldiers: Jacob Bigler and Elisha Griffith. In 1933, the Daughters of the American Revolution of Clarksburg dedicated a monument to these men in the Enterprise IOOF Cemetery. A shovel full of earth was taken from what was believed to have been the graves of the two men and placed at the memorial site. (Author's collection.)

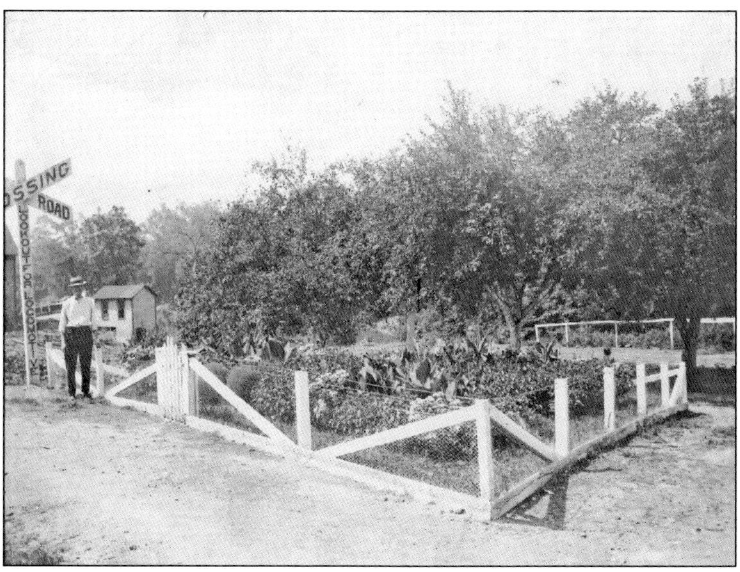

Walter O. Bice is seen standing beside of a flower bed near the Viropa Company Store building about 1917. The flower bed had been a cinder pile, and Bice, the company store manager, who sold flowers and plants on the side, converted it into a flower bed to be more attractive. The image was printed onto a postcard and hand colored to attract foreign miners into the coalfields. (Courtesy of Bob Bice II.)

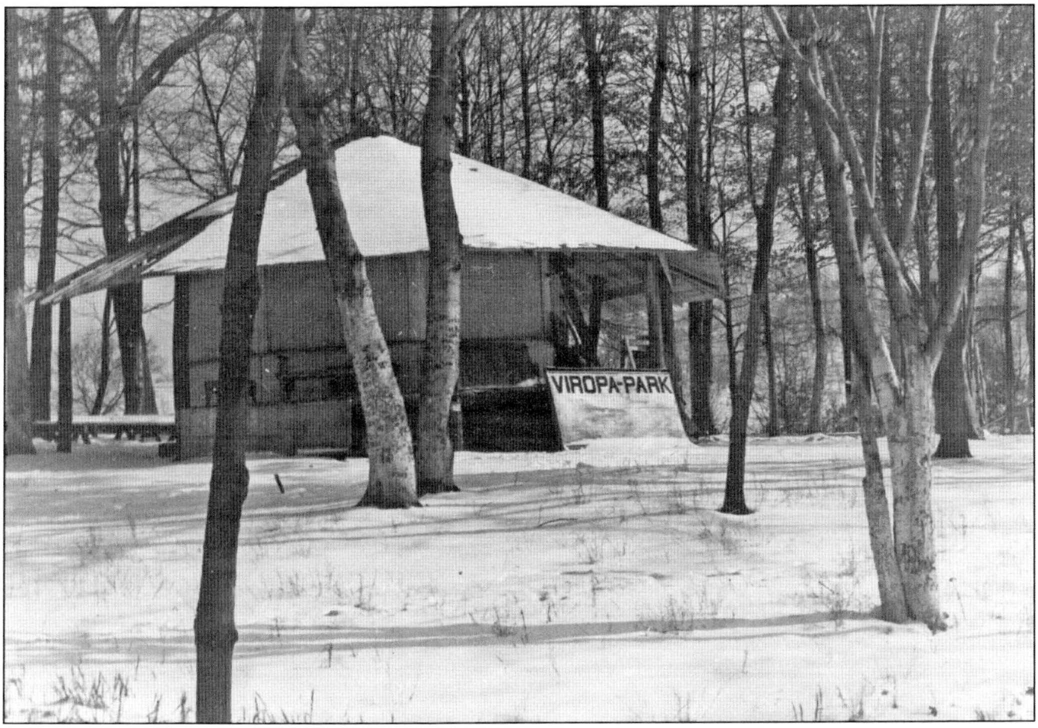

Viropa Park Company was established in 1925. Oftentimes, local country-and-western musical events were held here. The land had been used for many years as a gathering place for Sunday picnics and family reunions, which many attendees reached by way of the streetcar. In early days, the black community held tent revivals there as well. (Courtesy of Lowe Public Library.)

The Shinnston Garden Club was first organized in 1929. In its early years, the women of the club gathered to discuss gardening and lawn improvements and often participated in contests. This image shows the women of the club at the home of Blanche Martin (wife of John Martin) for a Rose Breakfast club meeting on July 3, 1940. (Author's collection.)

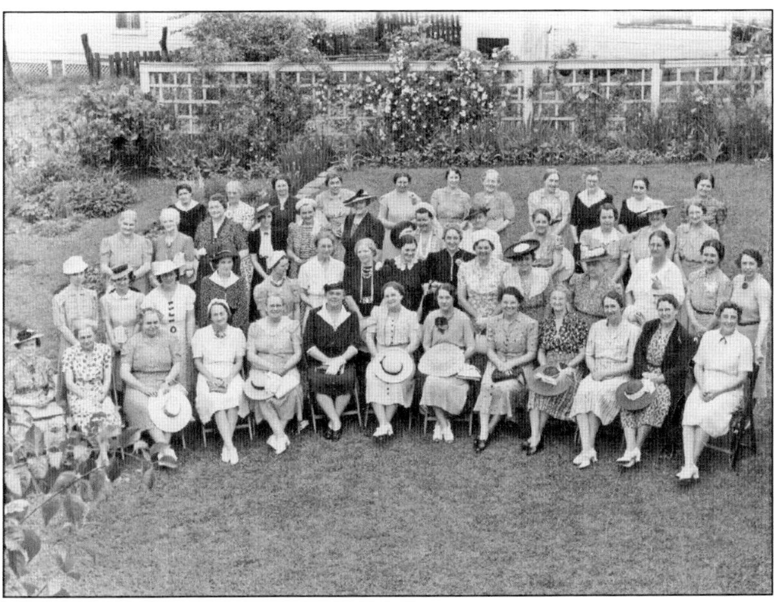

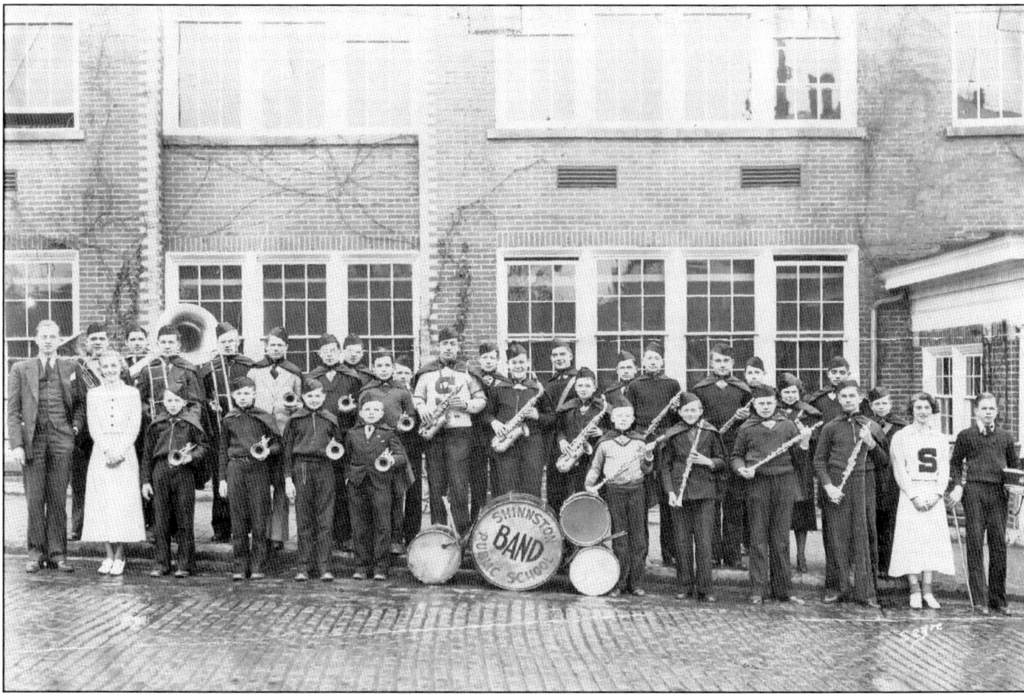

It was "all brick" with the 1933 band standing on the street and sidewalk in front of the grade school building on Mahlon Street. Each band member wears a cape as they proudly display their instruments under the direction of Henry Mayer, at far left. The streets in Shinnston were first paved with brick in 1902. (Author's collection.)

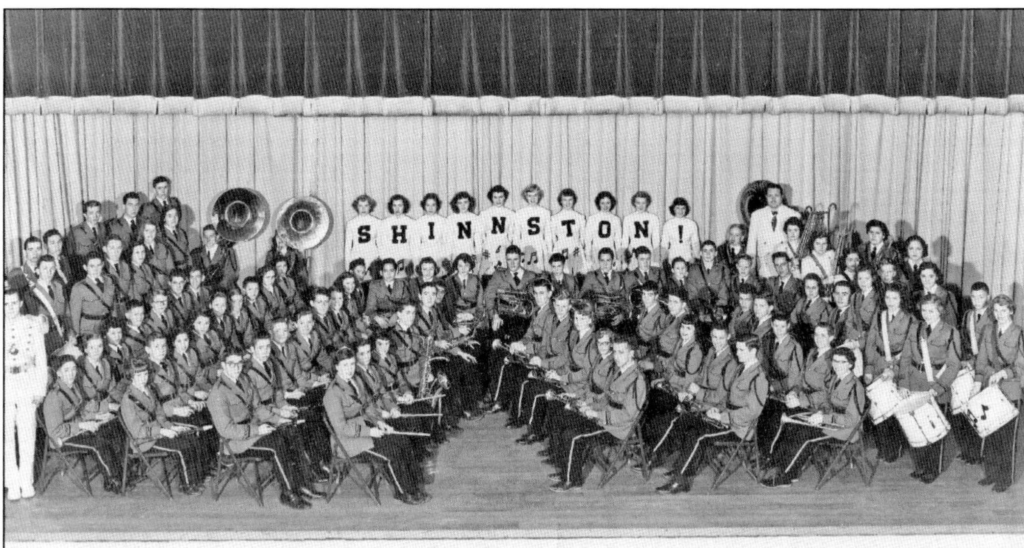

Shown here is the 1951–1952 Shinnston High School band along with the "SHINNSTON!" sponsors. Dick Jones wrote many of the compositions for band director Frank "Buck" Shaffer. The band often performed at the Rice Theatre, won many state titles, and recorded an album. In 1953, Shaffer left SHS and took a job in Porterville, California, where his bands performed in Los Angeles Rams' halftime shows, as well as the Tournament of Roses Parade. (Author's collection.)

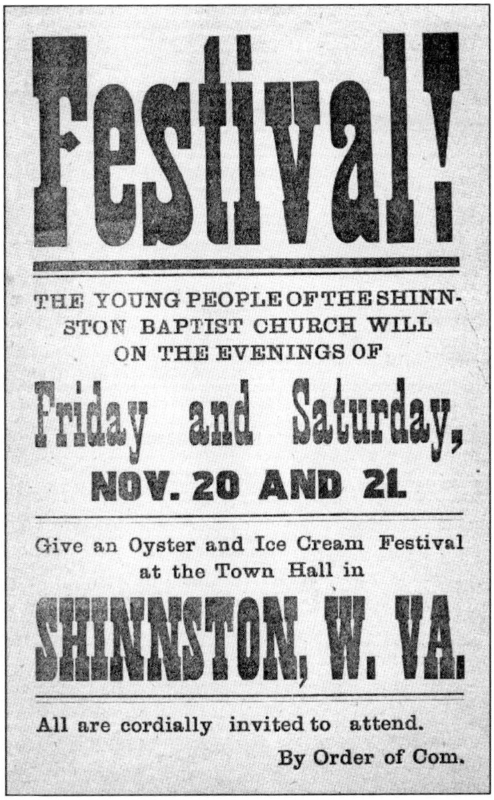

Oftentimes, civic and church organizations held festivals within the community in order to have fellowship amongst themselves. This poster advertises an Oyster and Ice Cream Festival, which was sponsored by the young people of the Shinnston Baptist Church. (Author's collection.)

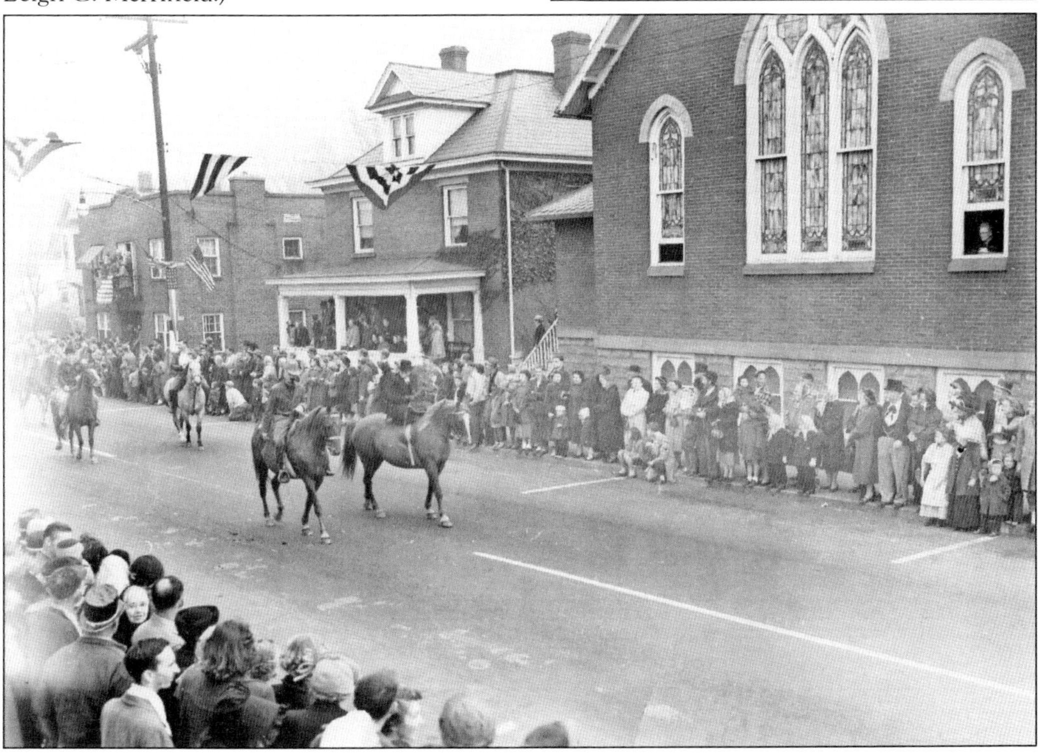

Every available space was taken to be able to catch a view of Shinnston's centennial parade in 1952. The old Methodist church on the corner of Rebecca Street is shown with its windows raised to allow a view of the street. Next door, the church parsonage and the Radabaugh Apartments building each have standing room only on their porches. (James M. Currey collection, courtesy of Leigh C. Merrifield.)

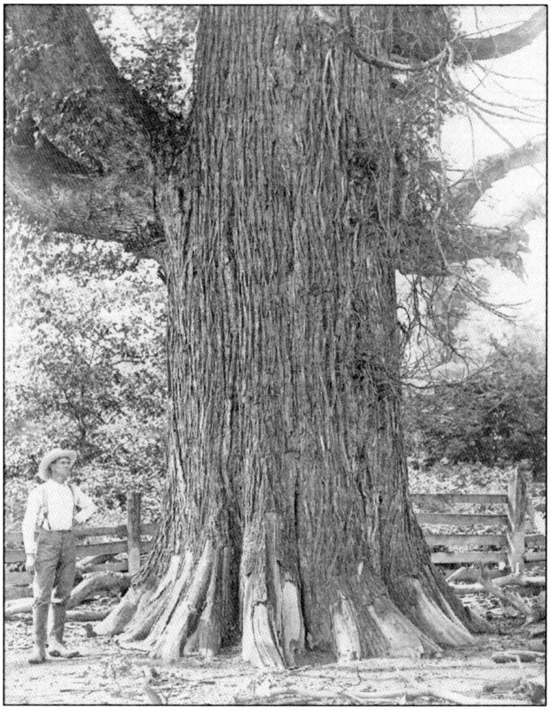

Charles Hood is shown here next to the largest water elm on record. The community, now known as Big Elm, carried the roots of this tree, which won first prize at the Centennial International Exposition of Philadelphia in 1876. Measuring a circumference of more than 30 feet at its base, the tree captured the attention of readers in Granville Davisson Hall's novel, *Daughter of the Elm*, first published in December 1899. Partially based on a true story, the author changed character names slightly to avoid hurt feelings. (Author's collection.)

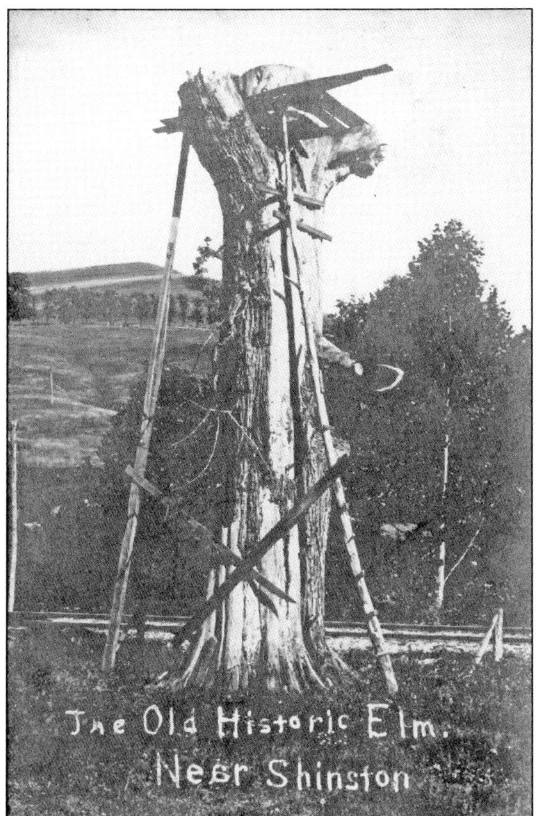

The old historic elm tree is shown here in 1917 while it was being cut down. The tree had been nothing more than a skeleton for more than 10 years when the new road was coming through and forced the tree to be removed. The Hood family, owners of the land on which the tree stood, kept many chips and blocks of the tree to pass out to interested passersby inquiring of its disappearance. Today, there are many novelty items made from the old elm. (Author's collection.)

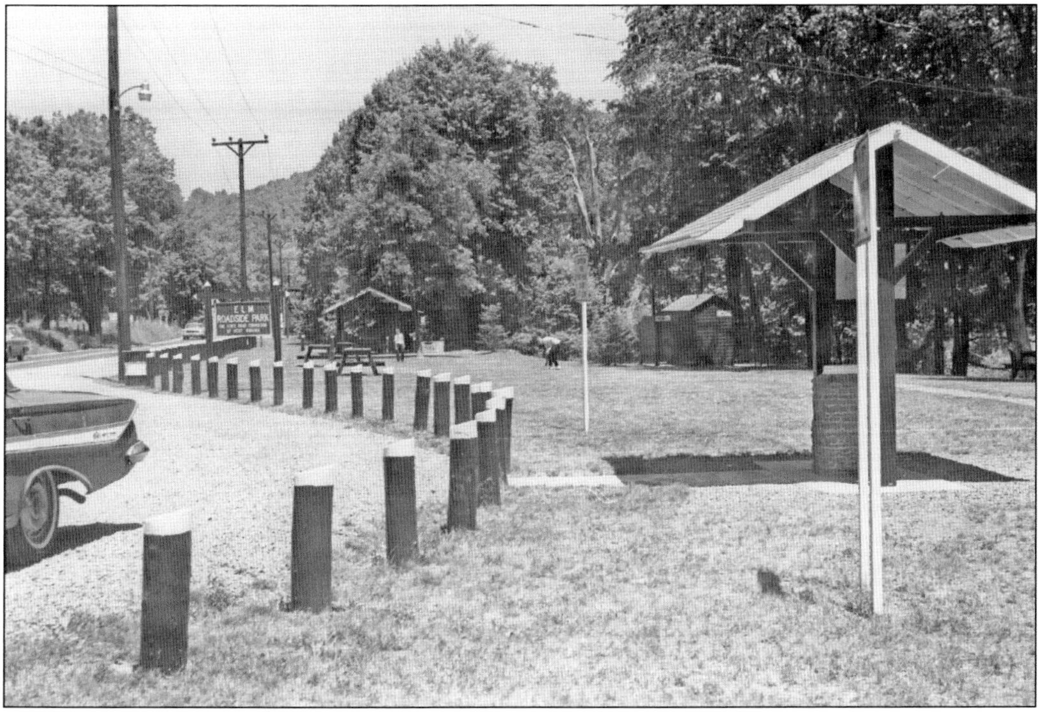

Many families enjoyed picnics and playtime at the Elm Roadside Park, located a short distance north of Shinnston at the community of Big Elm. Well maintained and in use for many years, the park has since been abandoned and is now a pull-off location for travelers. (Author's collection.)

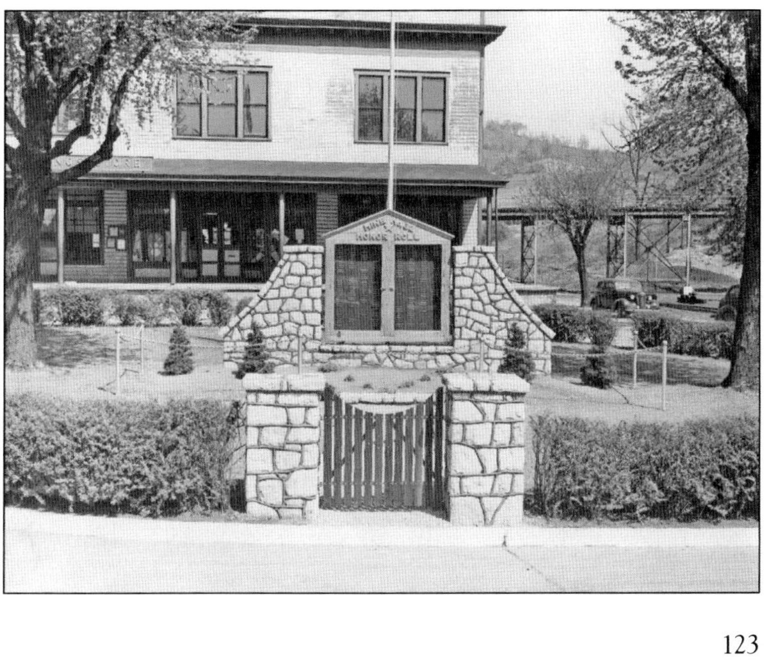

The honor roll for men in service during World War II is shown here in front of the company store at Consolidation Coal Company's Owings Mine No. 32. Over 780 men were employed during this period, many of whom were called to war. Once the honor roll was in place, additional names were added to the larger sign in Shinnston. (Author's collection.)

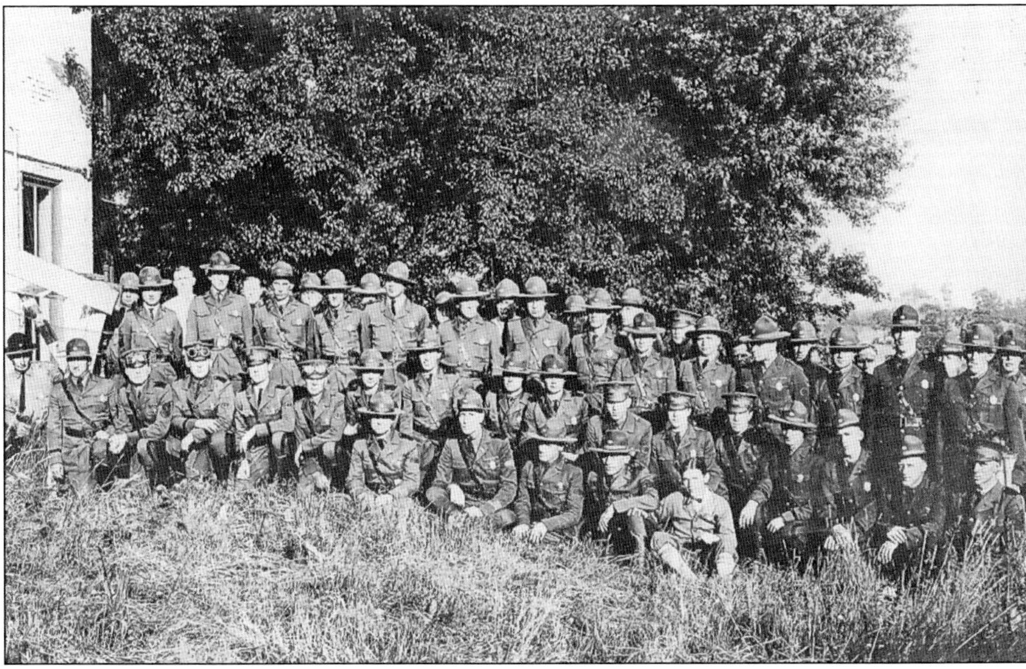

West Virginia State Police, Company A headquarters, located at Haywood Junction on approximately 70 acres of land shortly after the Department of Public Safety became effective in 1919. Barracks, stables, a barn, and garage provided all of the necessities for the detachment, which was situated at a point adjacent to traction and railroad lines. This image was taken there on June 26, 1924. (Author's collection.)

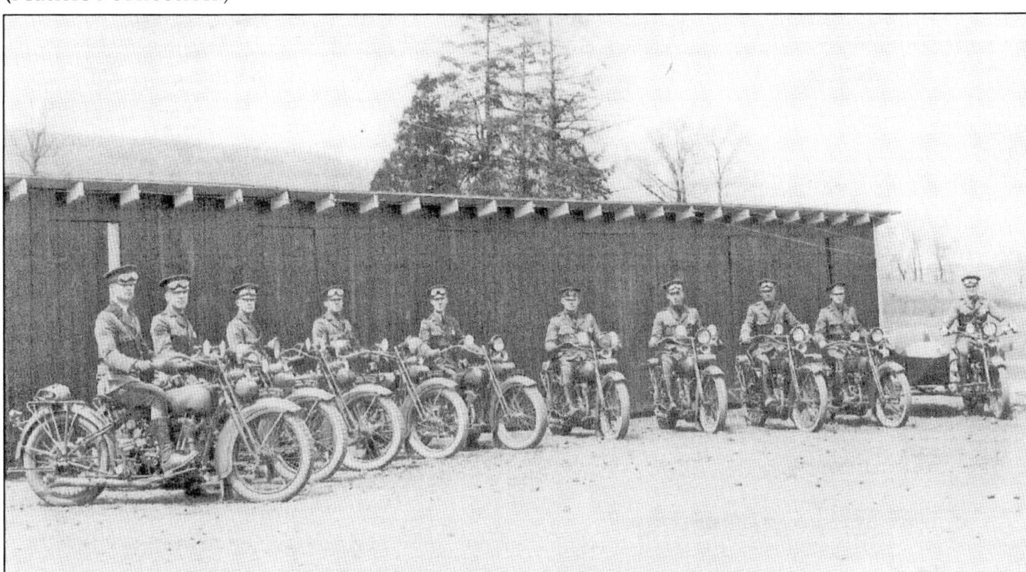

In the early years of the West Virginia State Police, motorcycles and horses were used as a mounted transport patrol along both paved and dirt roads. This image shows patrolmen at the detachment at Haywood during the 1920s. The only man identified is Clyde Smith, sixth from left. In 1927, he was injured in a motorcycle accident, which forced him to take permanent medical leave. (Author's collection.)

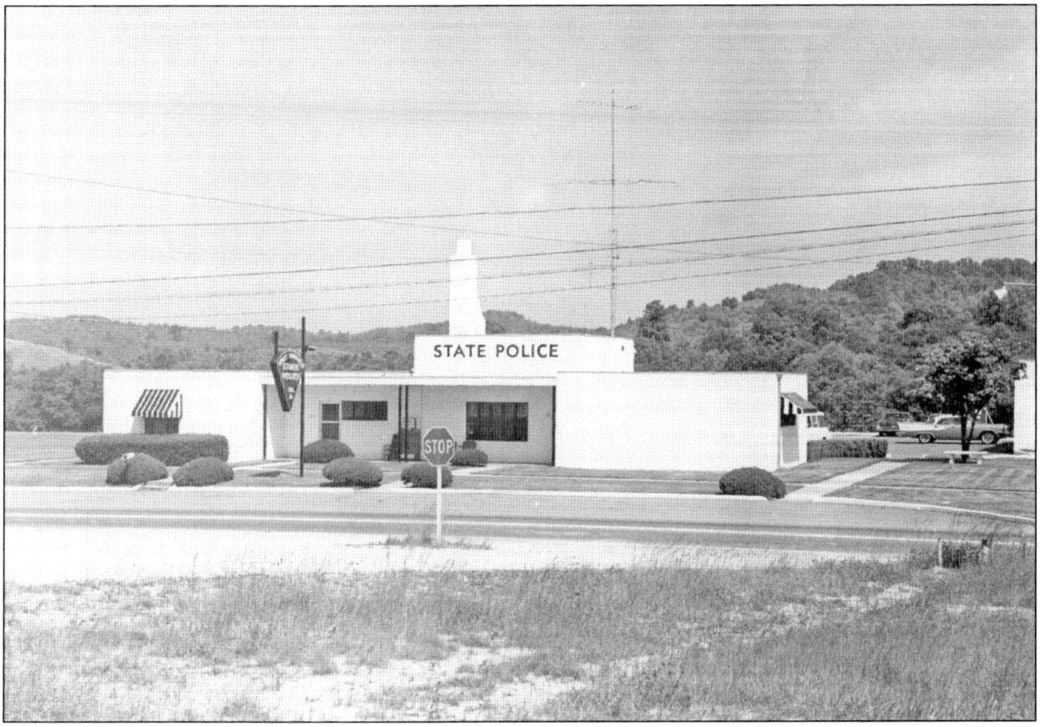

Company A headquarters of the West Virginia State Police is shown here in 1956. Located at Haywood Junction until 1933, the detachment moved to Fairmont until this building was constructed in 1939. This location, across from Lincoln's Stydahar Field, provided officer barracks, garages, and a firing range that serviced 18 detachments. (Author's collection.)

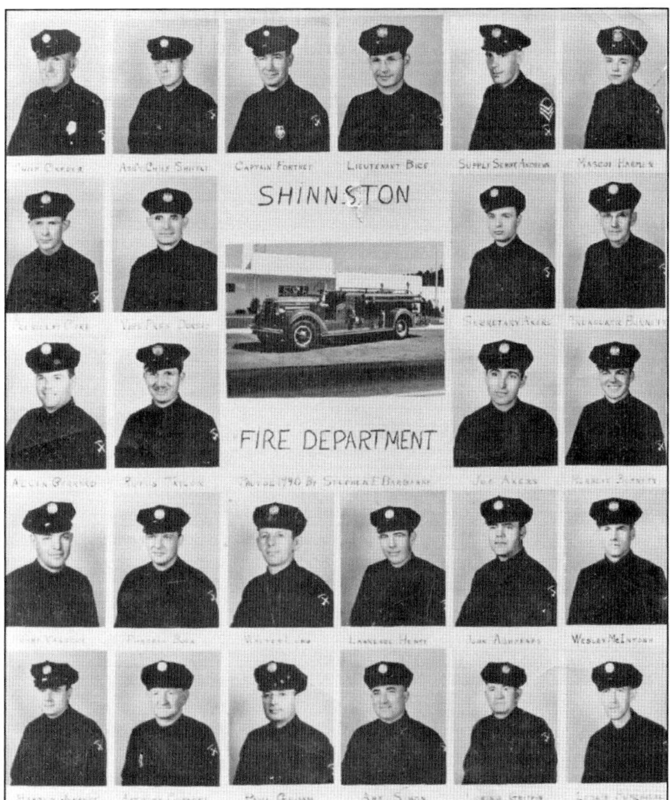

Members of the Shinnston Volunteer Fire Department (SVFD) are shown here in 1940. Several of the firemen pictured were leading businessmen of the Shinnston area while serving their civic duty. The SVFD Company 10 is now located on the south end of lower Bridge Street. (Courtesy of Harmer Funeral Home.)

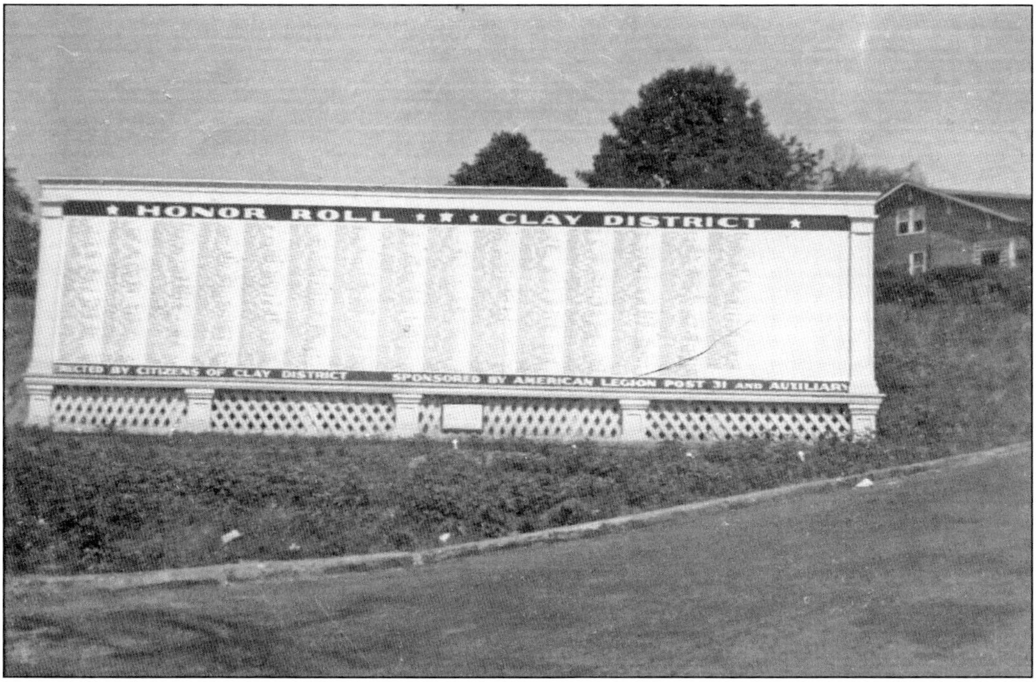

During World War II, many communities erected signs to honor men and women in the service. This was Shinnston's second honor roll board; the original was smaller. As the war progressed and more people became servicemen, additional space was needed. Wood construction and painted names could not withstand nature's constant weather pattern, and the remains were eventually dismantled. Located at the northeast corner of Pike and Clement Streets, this lot is now home to the Clay District Veterans Memorial. (Author's collection.)

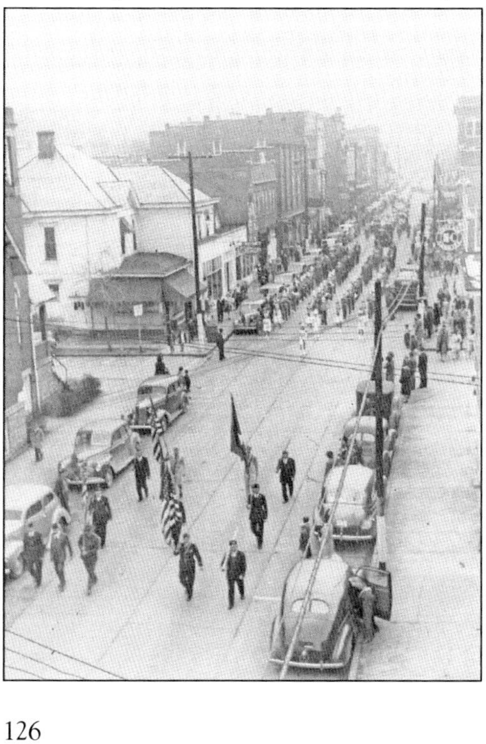

On November 8, 1942, a parade was held in Shinnston to dedicate the Clay District Honor Roll Board, once located at the northeast corner of Pike and Clement Streets. This image shows the parade at the Rebecca Street intersection where George Hall's Shinnston Motor Company, a Ford dealership, can be seen on the left. It burned on March 31, 1975. (James M. Currey Collection, Courtesy of Leigh C. Merrifield.)

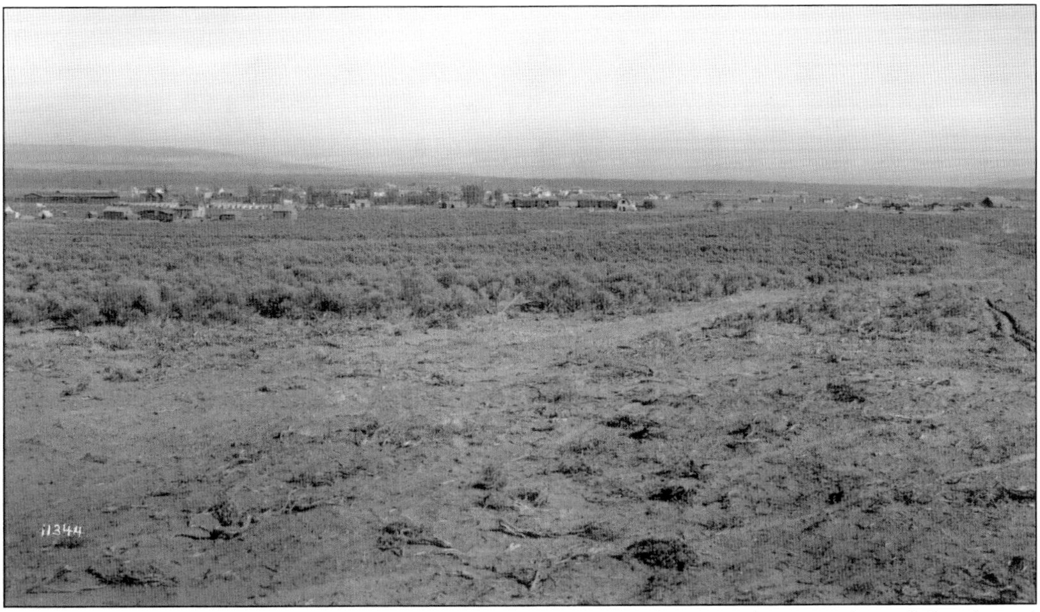

A 1912 railroad brochure stated, "Soil of the district is volcanic ash. It is of good depth and easily cultivated. It has lain for ages in its unbleached condition." Flood sediment left behind by ancient Lake Lewis also adds to the fertility of Grandview's soil. Rattlesnake Mountain, seen in the distance in this photograph from October 1908, was a small island when the lake, part of the glacial Lake Missoula, flooded, filling the Yakima Valley. (Photograph by Asahel Curtis; courtesy of GHC.)

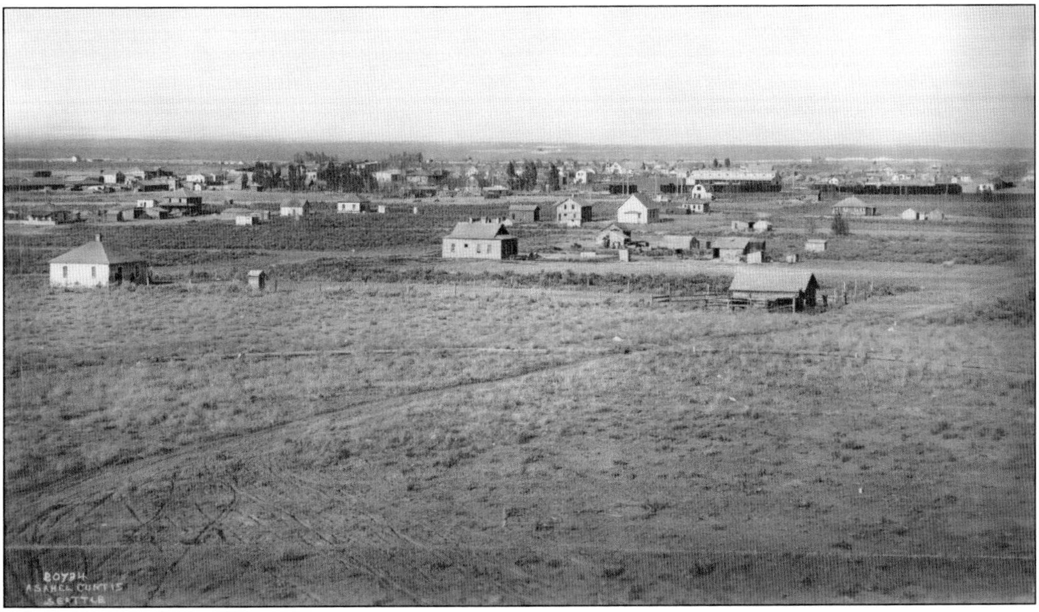

By 1911, Grandview was a scattering of homes and farms. The brochure mentioned above also stated, "The mean summer temperature is 77 degrees and the mean winter temperature 21 degrees above zero. There are times when the mercury reaches 100 degrees in July but the heat is not oppressive. The air is dry. The warmest days are followed by cool nights . . . 300 days of sunshine." (Photograph by Asahel Curtis; courtesy of GHC.)

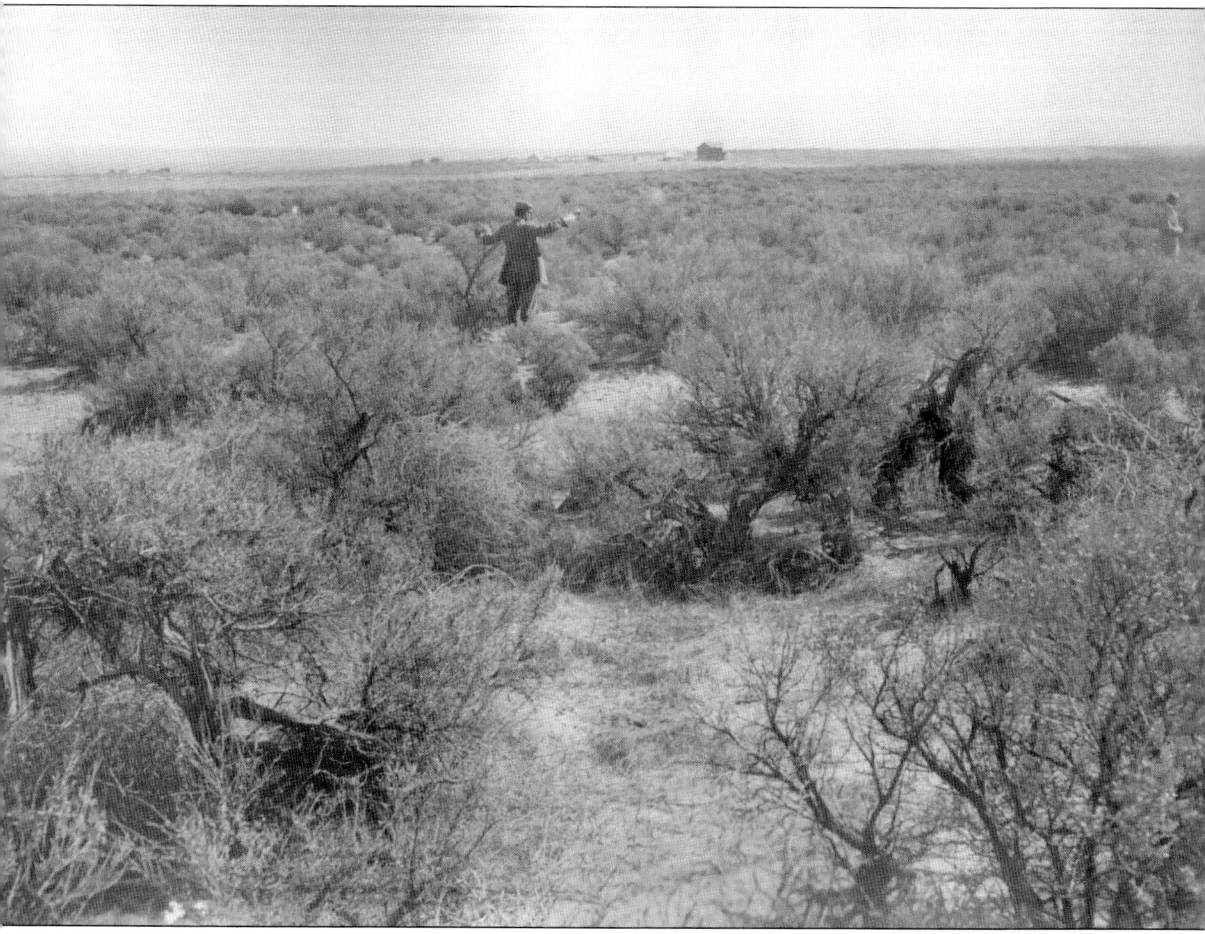

The region was trying its hardest to attract visitors and residents. One 1912 feature story in *Sunset* magazine, the monthly publication of the Southern Pacific Railroad Company, raved about the fertile land, the irrigation systems, and Grandview's distinct advantage over much cheaper Canadian land. Author John Scott Mills wrote, "I do not mean to be uncharitable concerning the country across the line, but having seen both localities it is mystifying to me why a good American citizen will swear allegiance to the English government to take up a homestead in Canada when he can make a better living on a ten-acre tract in the Yakima valley and enjoy some of the comforts of life as he goes through the seasons."

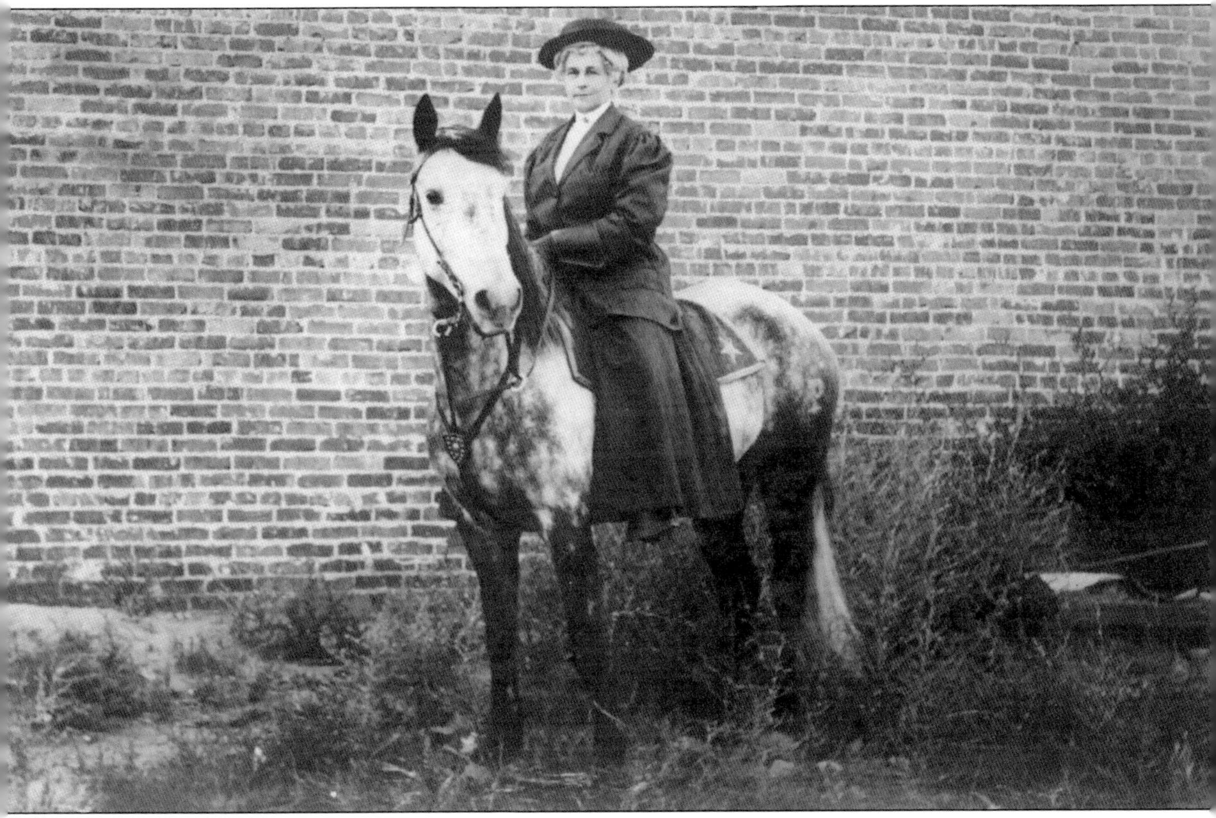

At the direction of Ann E. Sykes, shown here in 1906, the first permanent structure in Grandview was built. That same year, she was named the town's first postmistress, and a ground-floor room in the front part of the home she shared with her mother became the first post office. For the first two years, Sykes carried the mail on horseback to and from Mabton without any expense to the post office. Her income was a share of the receipts, which in the first quarter amounted to $2.42. It took five years before she received an actual salary. In order to supplement her income in those early years, she rented spare rooms to lodgers. By 1922, her salary had grown to $2,400 yearly, but ill health required her resignation. She died in Seattle on January 22, 1931, and was buried in the Grandview Cemetery. Grandview residents began receiving home delivery of mail in April 1949.

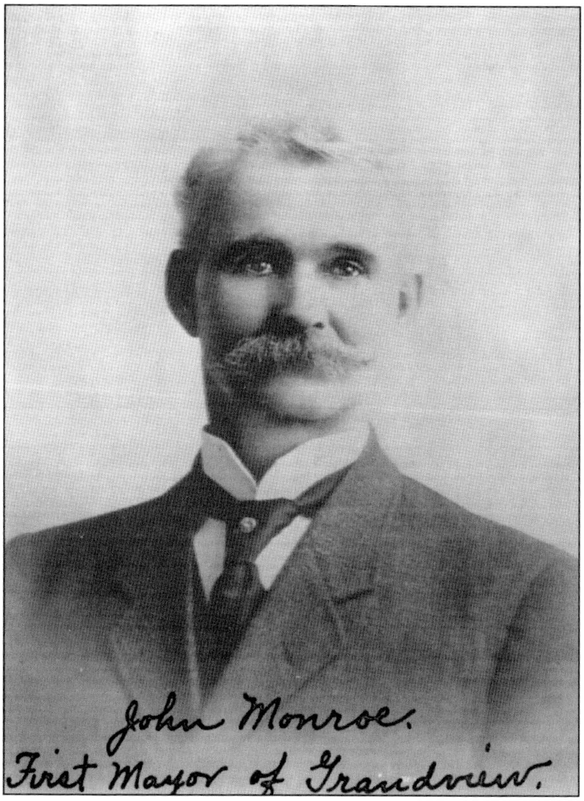

John G. Monroe, Grandview's first mayor (1910–1911), is seen below driving a four-wheeled buggy pulled by a matched pair of horses on Walnut Drive in the Orchard Tracts. The fields on either side of the road are fenced, and one side contains a young orchard. It was one of the last towns incorporated in the lower Yakima Valley, but, beginning with Monroe's administration, Grandview had the largest percentage of growth and improvement during those early years. In 1918, W.D. Lyman wrote, "It has a more completely diversified line of productions than most any of its neighbors. Fruit of all kinds, potatoes, corn, alfalfa, sugar beets, fine grain—everything in fact to be produced in this climate . . . It has one of the most sightly locations, on a slightly elevated and gently rolling surface, from which a view of miles and miles of the greatest expanse of the valley is visible." (Both photographs by Asahel Curtis; courtesy of GHC.)

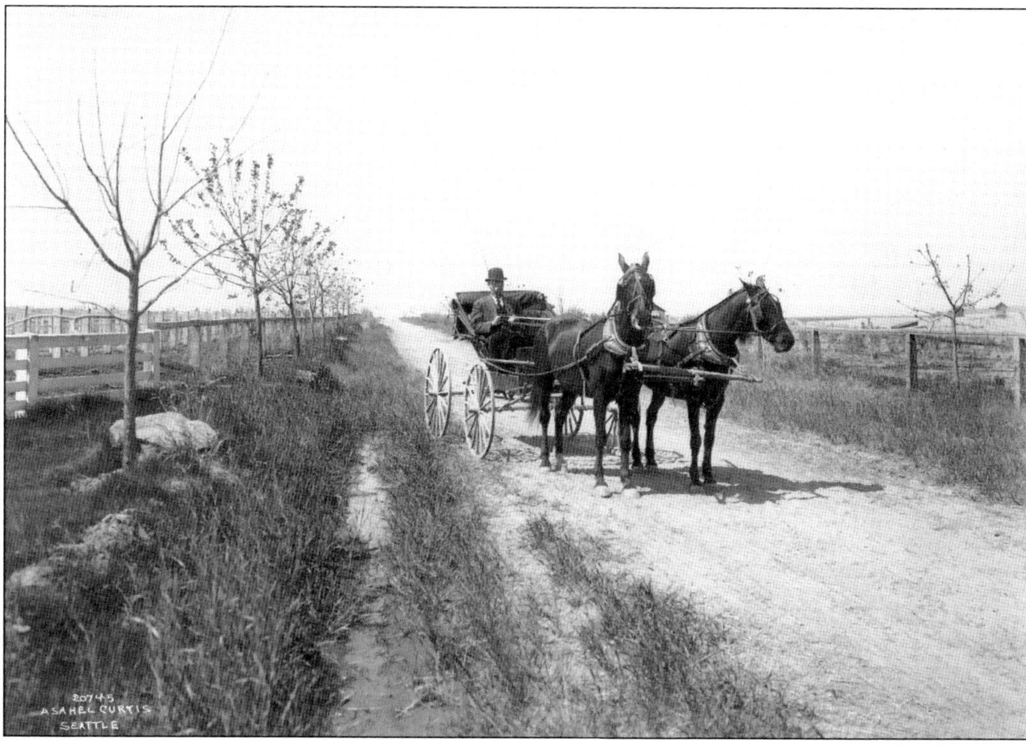

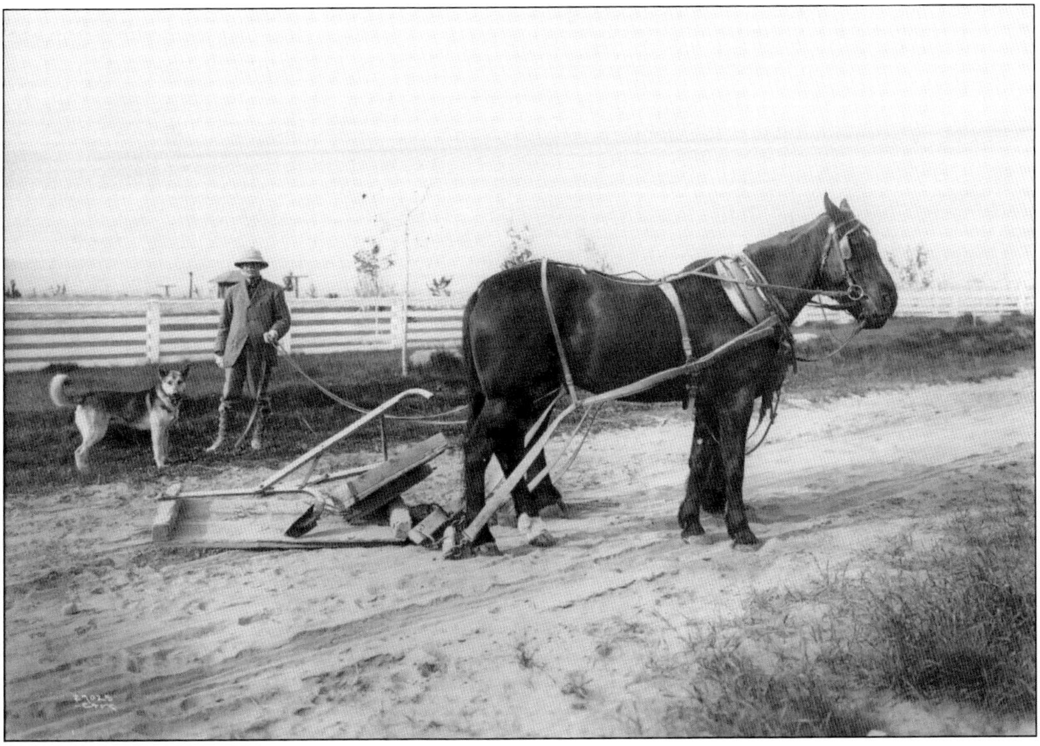

E.F. Blaine, general manager of the Washington Irrigation Company, is seen here at his Grandview ranch on Walnut Drive. Blaine, known as the "Father of Yakima Valley Irrigation," died on January 16, 1942. (Photograph by Asahel Curtis; courtesy of GHC.)

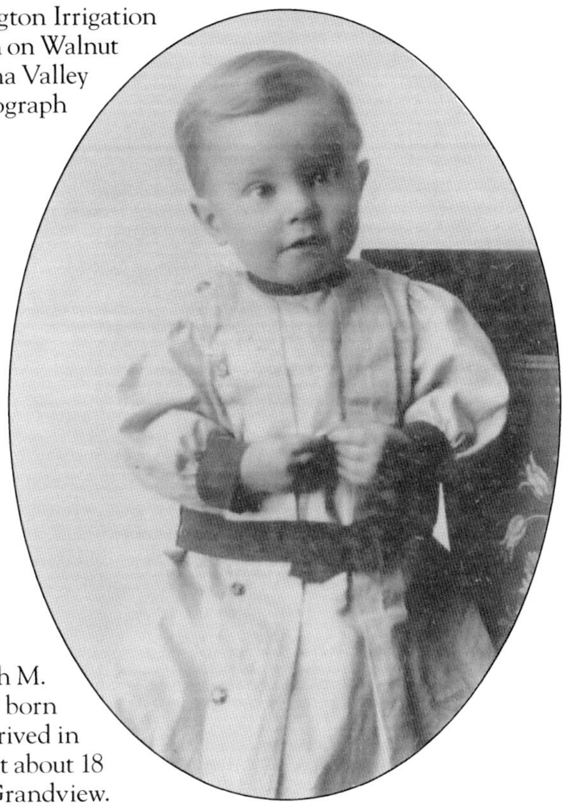

Ralph Morse Fleming, the oldest son of Joseph M. Fleming and Ethel E. (Morse) Fleming, was born on March 24, 1907. His newlywed parents arrived in Grandview in 1906, and Ralph, shown here at about 18 months of age, was the first child born in Grandview.

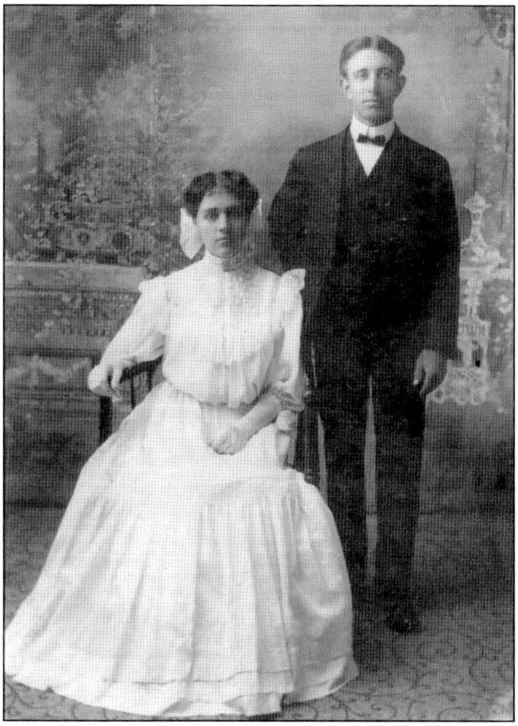

Lulu Pearl Elser, the daughter of Frank and Minnie Elser, and Charles Reese, of Sunnyside, were the first couple married in Grandview, in the spring of 1907. Rev. S.J. Harrison, also of Sunnyside, officiated at the ceremony, which took place at the bride's home in Grandview. Lulu and Charles had four daughters: Evelin, Helen, Irene, and Ines.

Below, William "Frank" Elser (left), his daughters Theo and Ruth, and his wife, Minnie Myrtle (Dean), are pictured in front of their home at 210 West Avenue A. The house was originally part of the McGrath farm, which was on the land chosen by the Oregon-Washington Railroad & Navigation Co. to become the location for the Grandview town site. The enterprising Minnie Elser would eventually turn her home into a hotel.

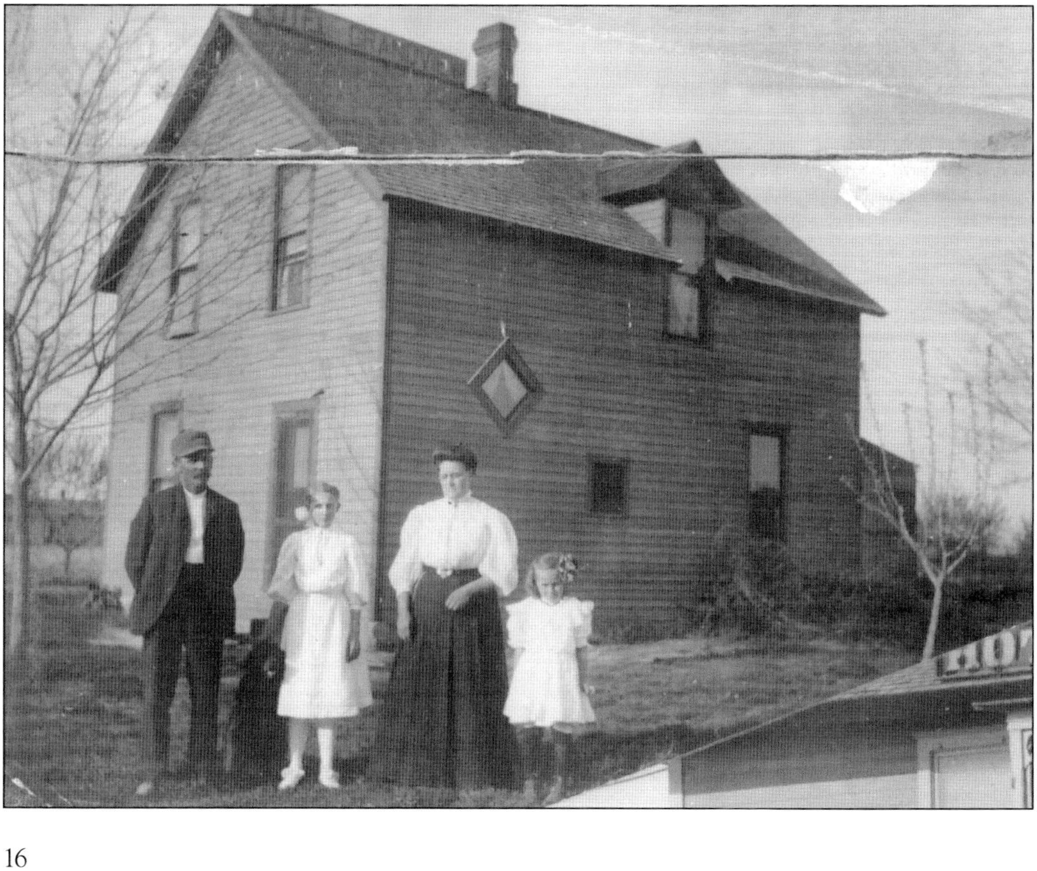

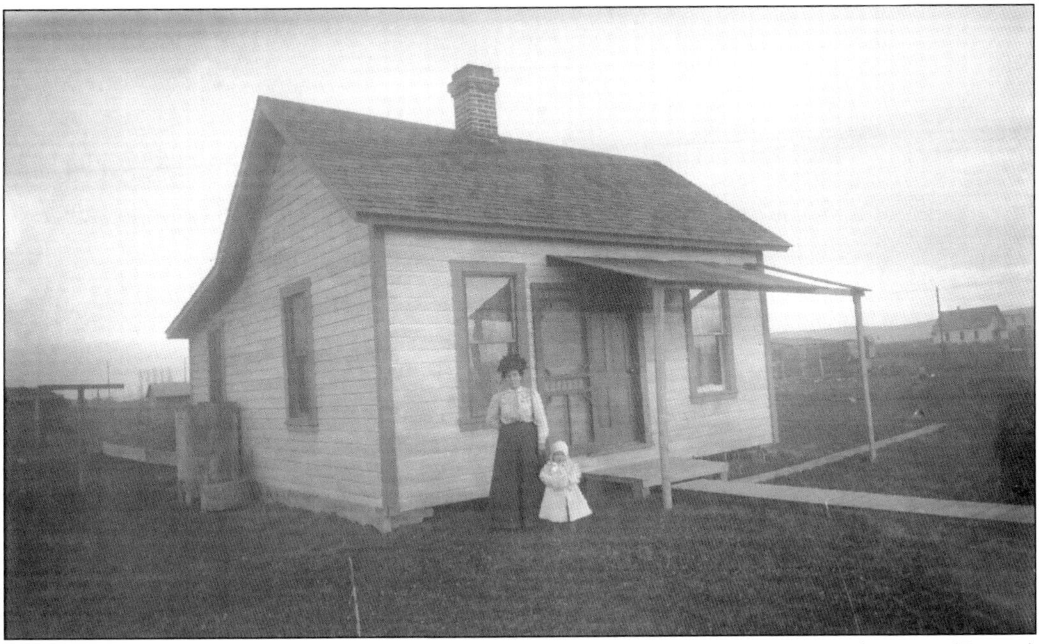

Minnie Mae Morrow was born on June 13, 1907, to Charles David Morrow and May P. (Dyson) Morrow. She was the second child and the first girl born in Grandview. Minnie and her mother are seen here in front of their home at 211 Avenue E. Minnie died on November 18, 1992, in Huntington Beach, California.

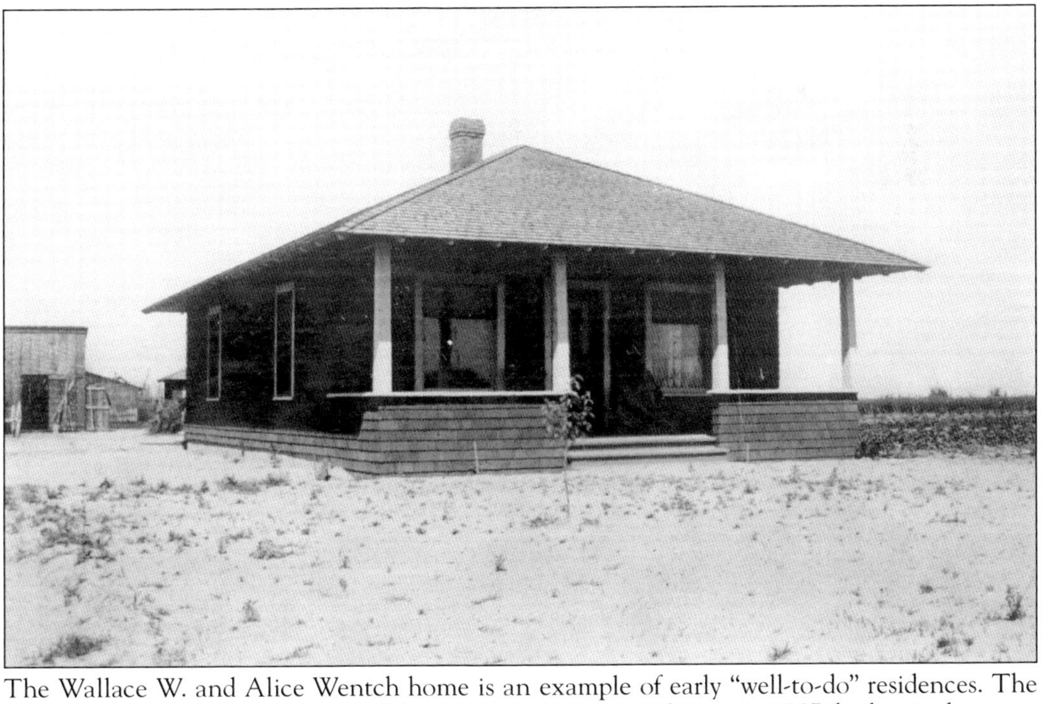

The Wallace W. and Alice Wentch home is an example of early "well-to-do" residences. The newly completed house and outbuildings, shown here east of town in 1907, had a single young tree planted in what appears to be an otherwise unimproved front yard.

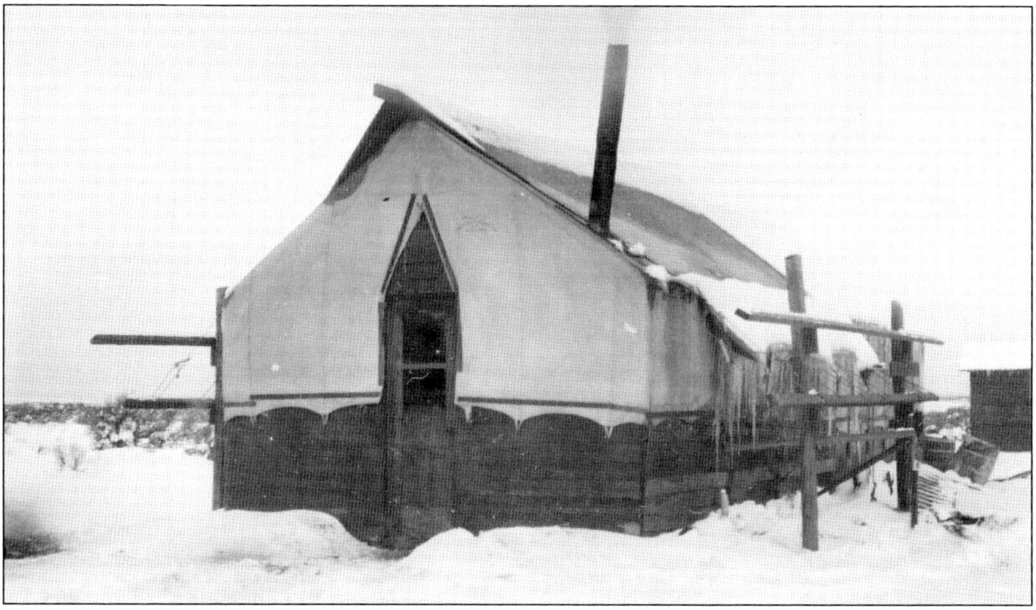

Snow covers the ground in this 1907 photograph of the George Emmert home on Main Street. The fire burning in the woodstove probably did very little to ward off the chill in this typical early Grandview home made of wood and canvas. The canvas covered the upper walls and helped keep out dampness.

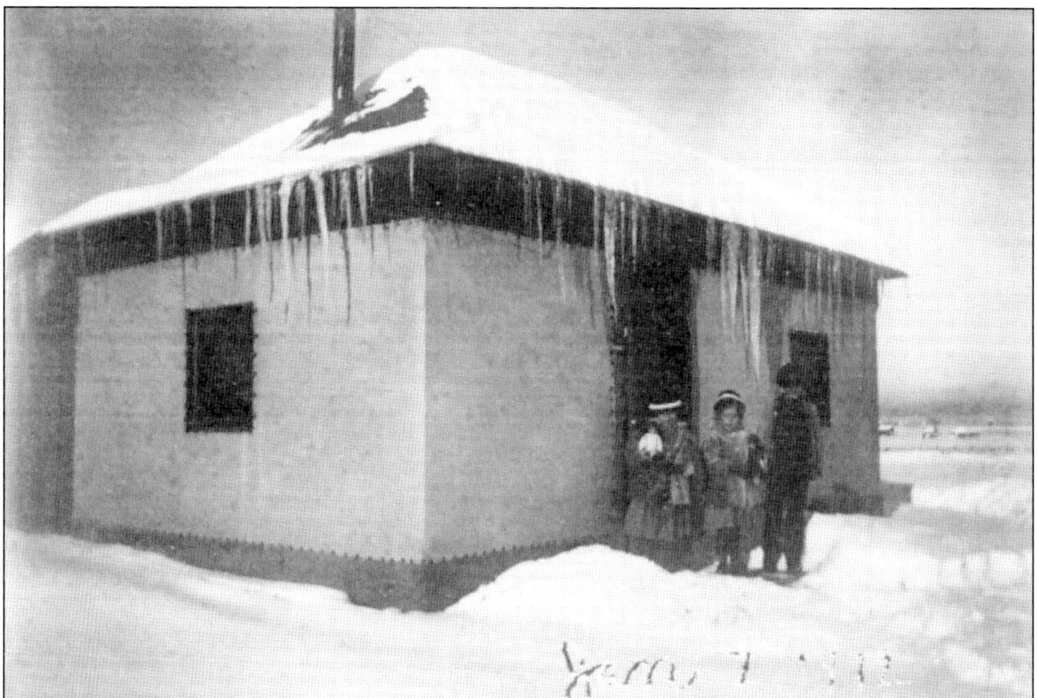

The W.L. Roberts home, shown here in 1912, was a little more substantial than the house shown above. Tightly stretched canvas still served as insulation against the cold, wet weather. Here, three children, with the one on the left carrying a doll, are bundled up against a cold January day.

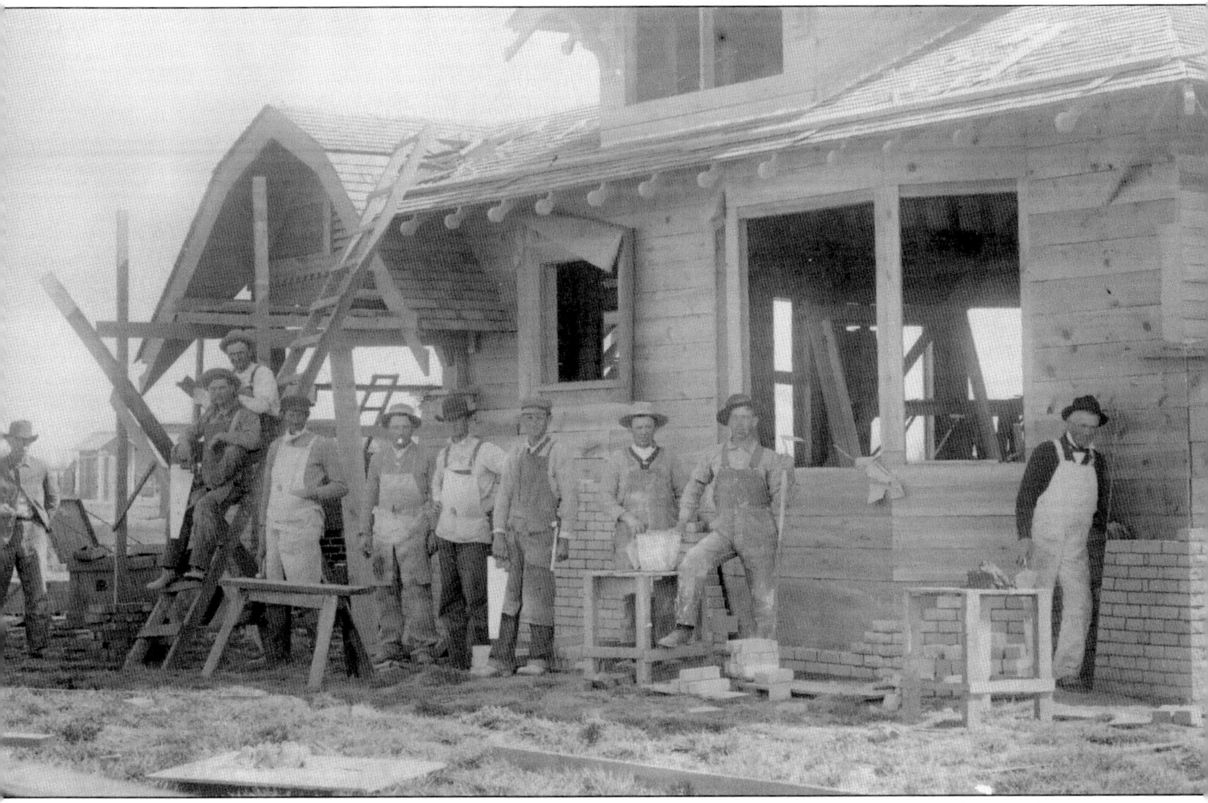

This postcard shows several men building the Chauncey O. Morse home in 1911. The Craftsman-style bungalow, still standing at 404 East Wine Country Road, was very different from its neighbors. The residence was the first in Grandview to receive city water, electricity, and telephone service. In 1929, the Morse family was also the first to install gas heating. Frank Davidson, at center wearing the dark hat, is the only positively identified man in the photograph.

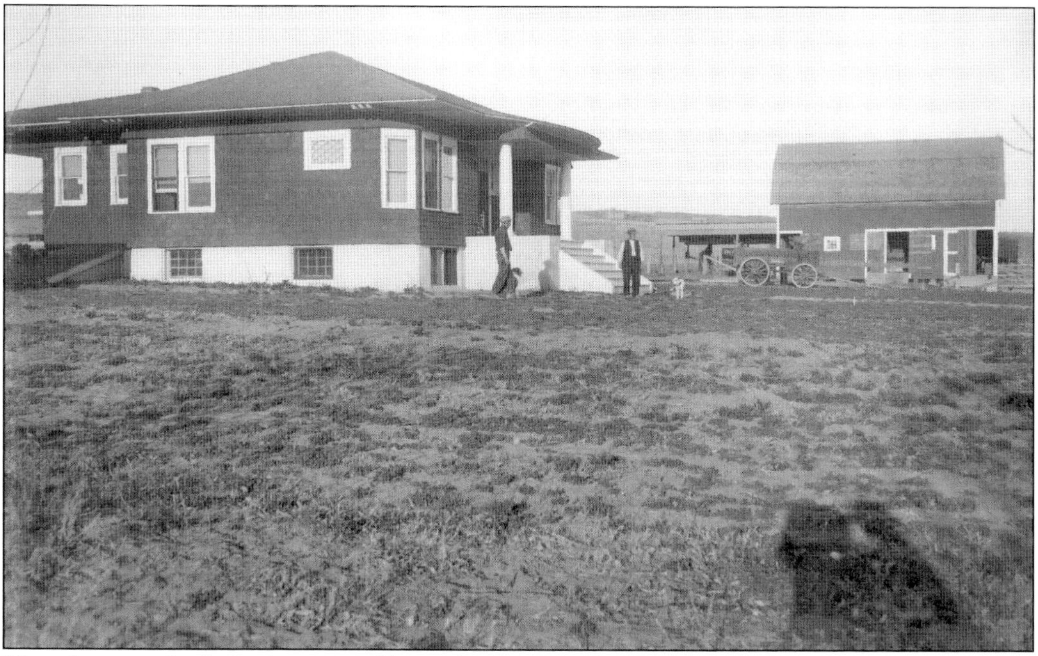

The photographer's shadow is visible in this image of a shingle-sided family home and small barn. Two unidentified men, both with dogs, are standing in the front yard. A Whitewater Farm Wagon, which sold for $86.45 in the 1929 Montgomery Ward catalog, sits beside the barn, and a horse and buggy is in the connecting corral.

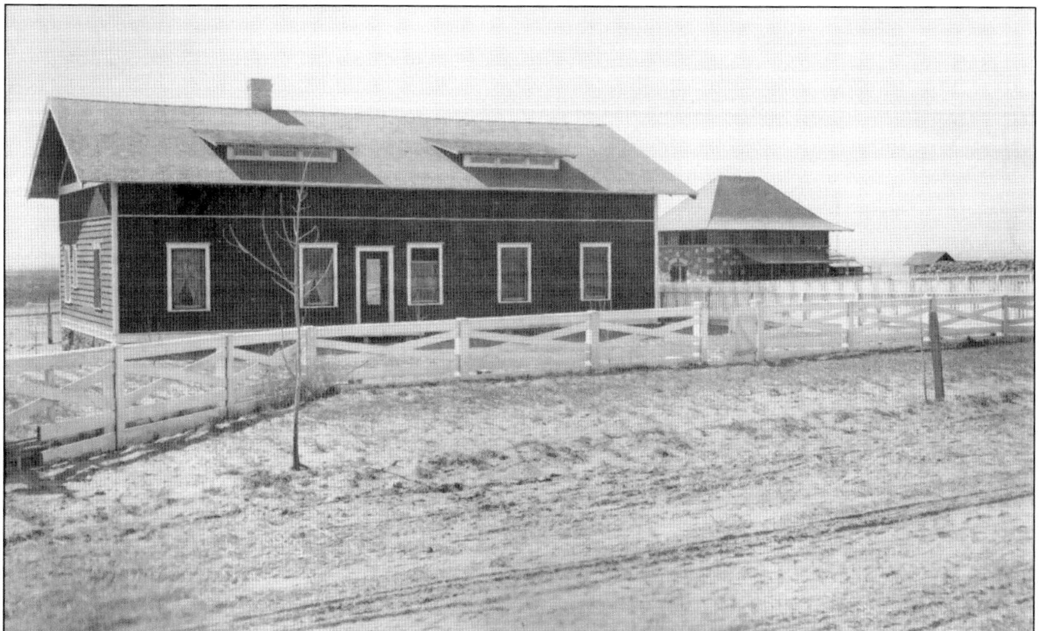

The Alex Parke/H.C. Boelke house on Walnut Lane had an upstairs dormitory for farm workers. Over the years, the Parke house had various owners, including Robert Smith, O.C. Gill, and Jim Conklin. E.F. Blaine, general manager of the Washington Irrigation Company, built the stone barn visible to the right and slightly behind the Parke house.

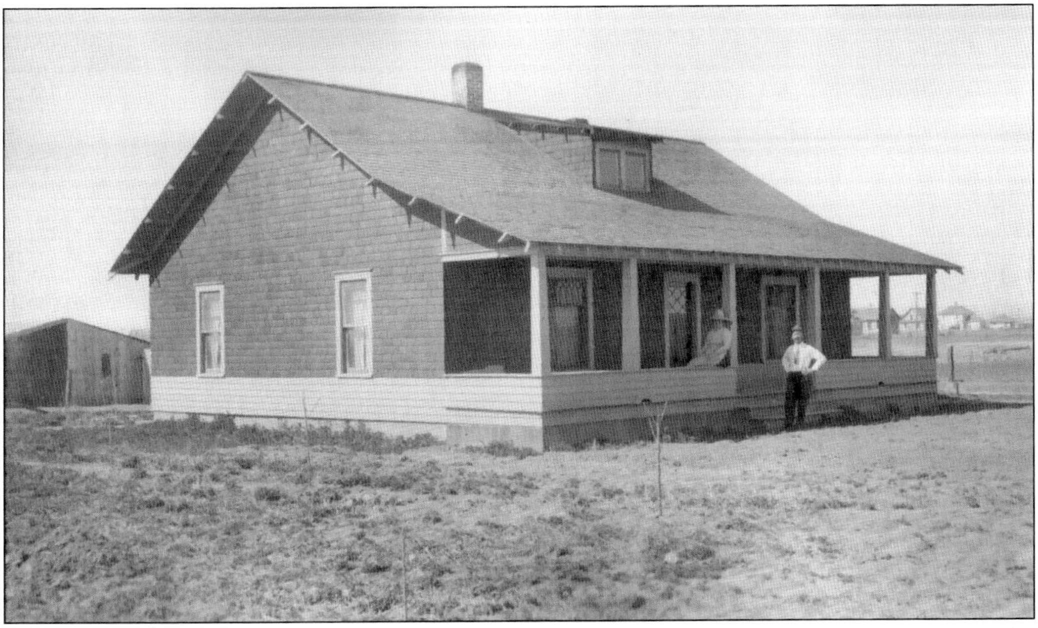

This shake-sided house belonged to Mr. and Mrs. Barendt. Mr. Barendt was a part owner of the Barendt & Snowden Warehouse. Four newly planted trees, perhaps the start of an orchard, are on the south (left) side of the house. At the time of this photograph, Pete Madson owned this house, on the corner of East Fifth and Elm Streets.

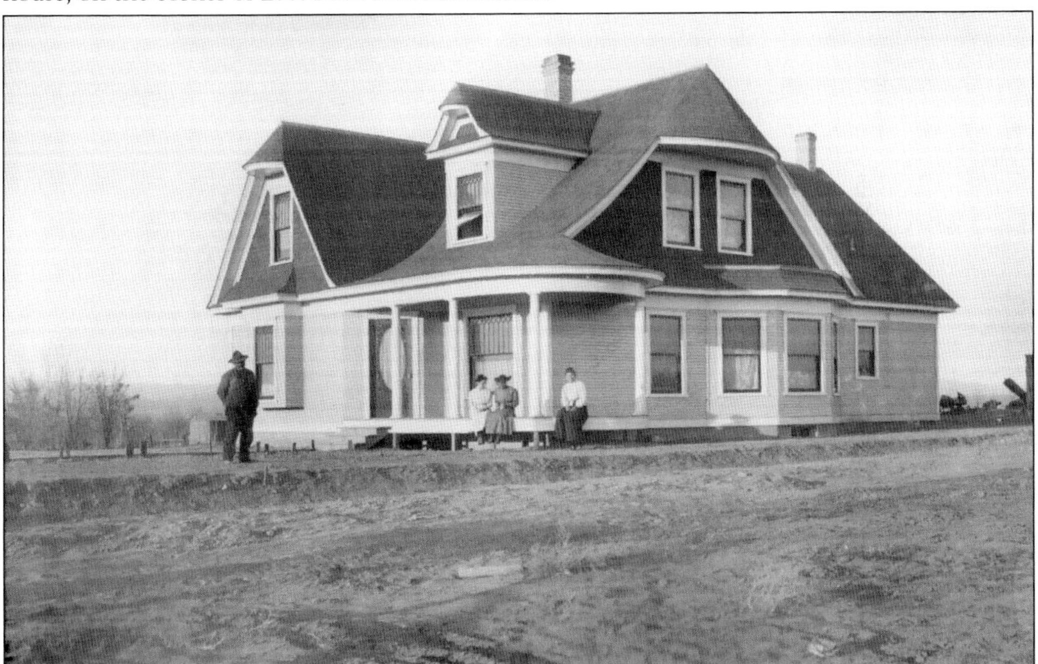

The William P. and Martha L. (Twidwell) Fisher house was built in 1910. A shed is visible behind and to the left of the house, while assorted machinery is on the right. Yet another fruit orchard is noticeable behind the big house. In 1946, Lester B. Judd bought the house, located on Judd Hill, also known as Euclid Hill, and remodeled it for his family, who still own it today.

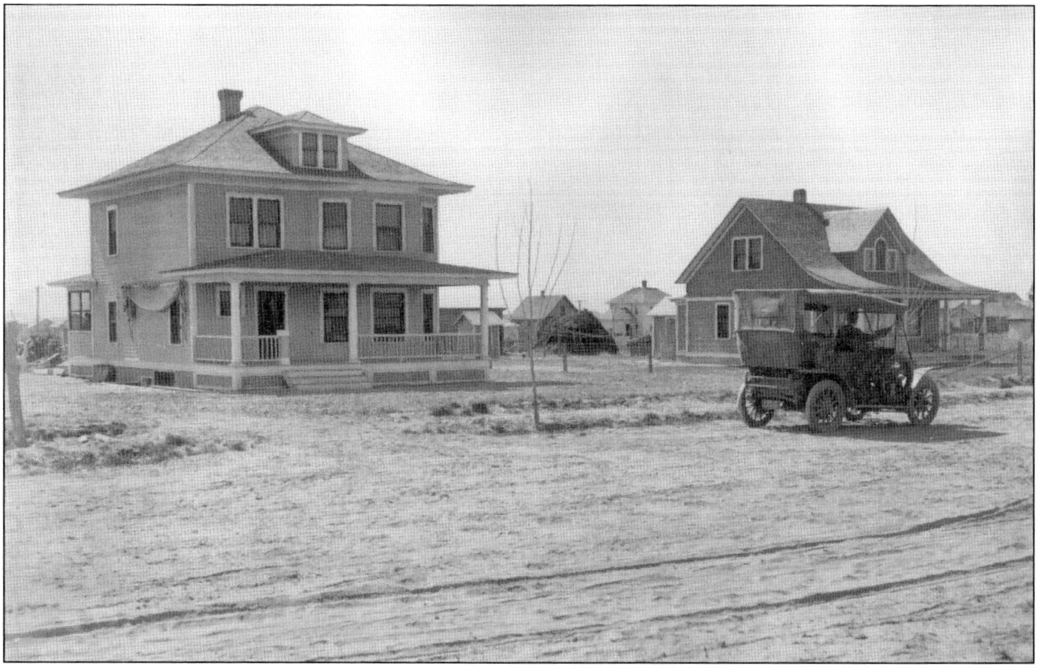

The Gillette and Baker homes are seen here in 1912. W.C. Baker came to Grandview from Wisconsin in 1902. Having very little money and knowing nothing of farming, he bought 20 acres west of town for $40 an acre. When he sold the farm in 1911, at $550 per acre, it had acreage in apples, peaches, strawberries, and grapes.

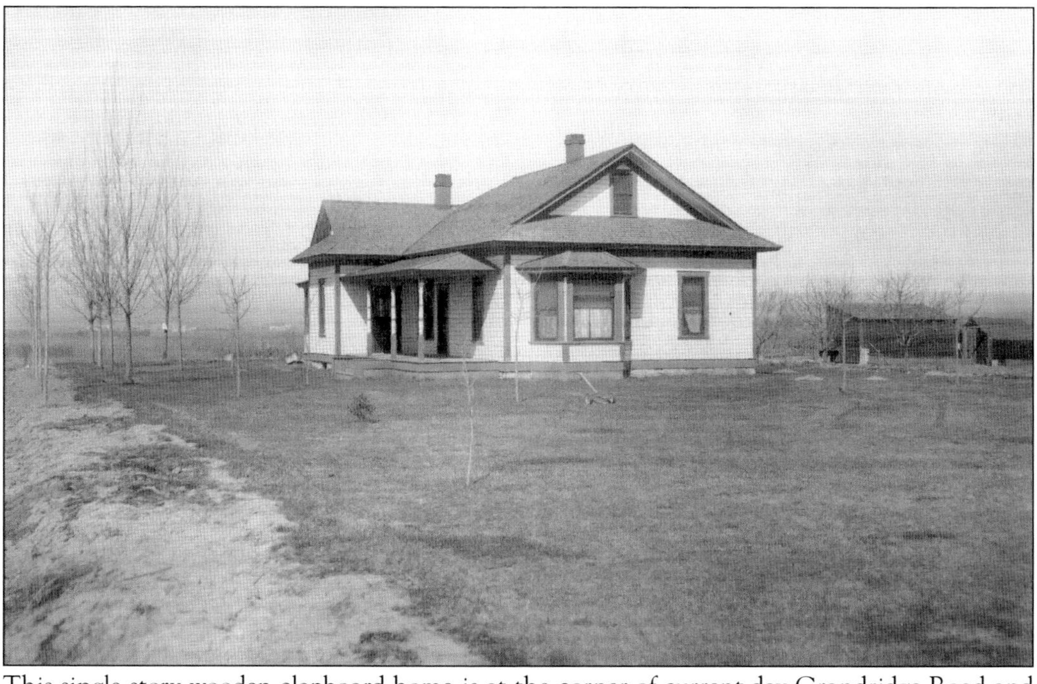

This single-story wooden clapboard home is at the corner of current-day Grandridge Road and Pleasant Avenue. The date of the photograph is unknown, as are the names of the original owners, but later owners included Mr. and Mrs. Lee Miller and Mr. and Mrs. Gary Devoe.

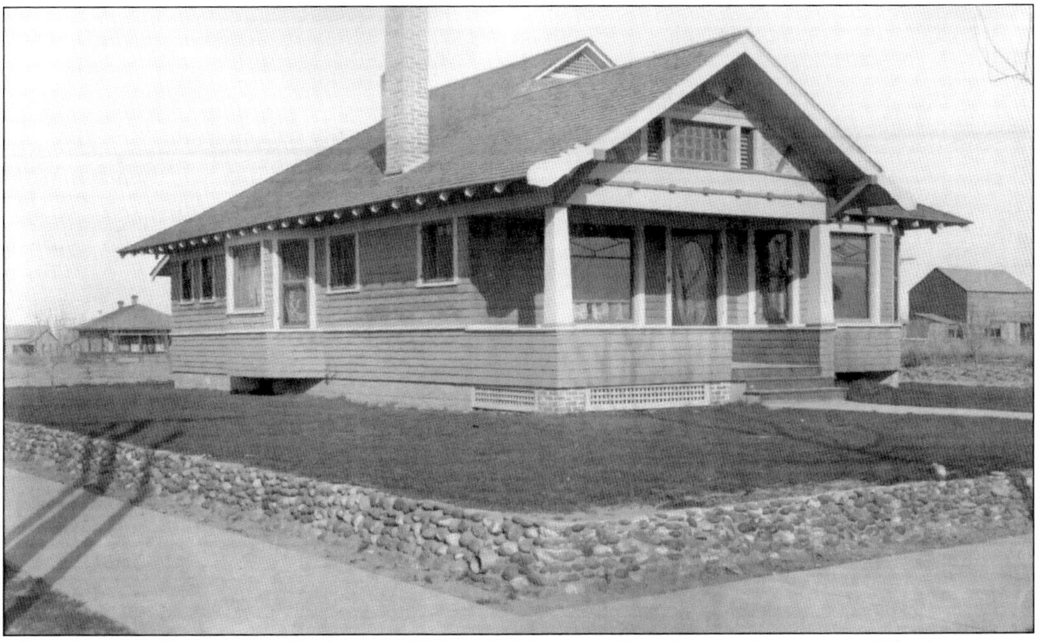

This clapboard house was the home of John G. Monroe, Grandview's first mayor. The house was on a corner lot at Second and Cedar Streets. Surrounded on two sides by a cement sidewalk, the leveled yard has a stone retaining wall. The bare limbs of a lone tree are visible just past the sidewalk in front of the house.

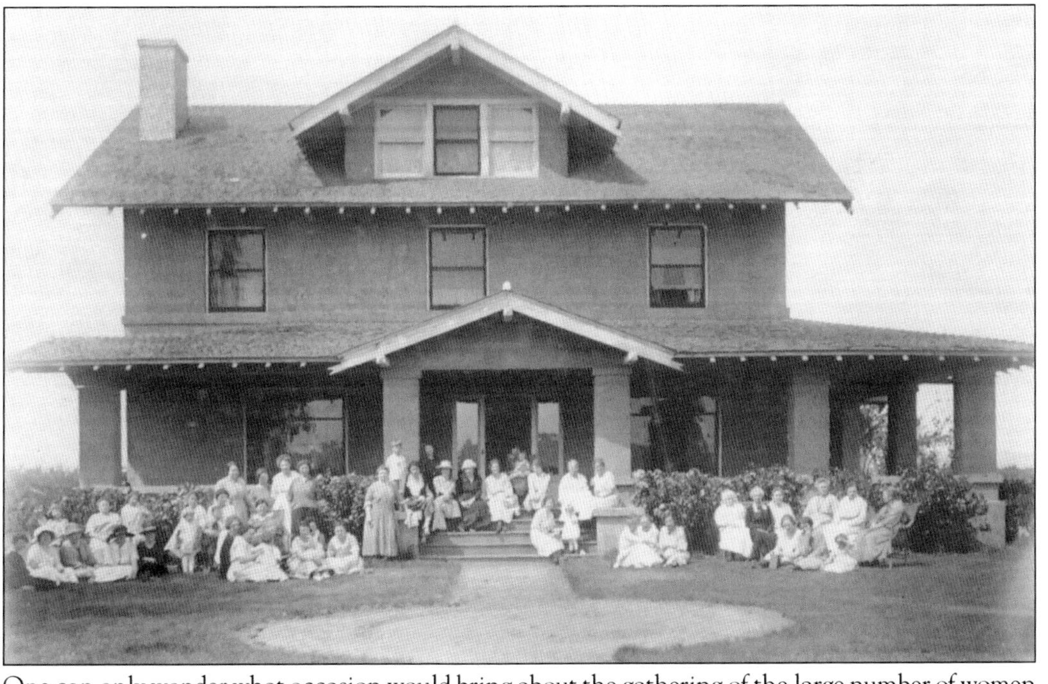

One can only wonder what occasion would bring about the gathering of the large number of women seen here. This large, three-story home on Apricot Drive belonged to the Hogland family. From the group of white-haired ladies on the right to the younger women, many with small children, the group includes a broad range of ages.

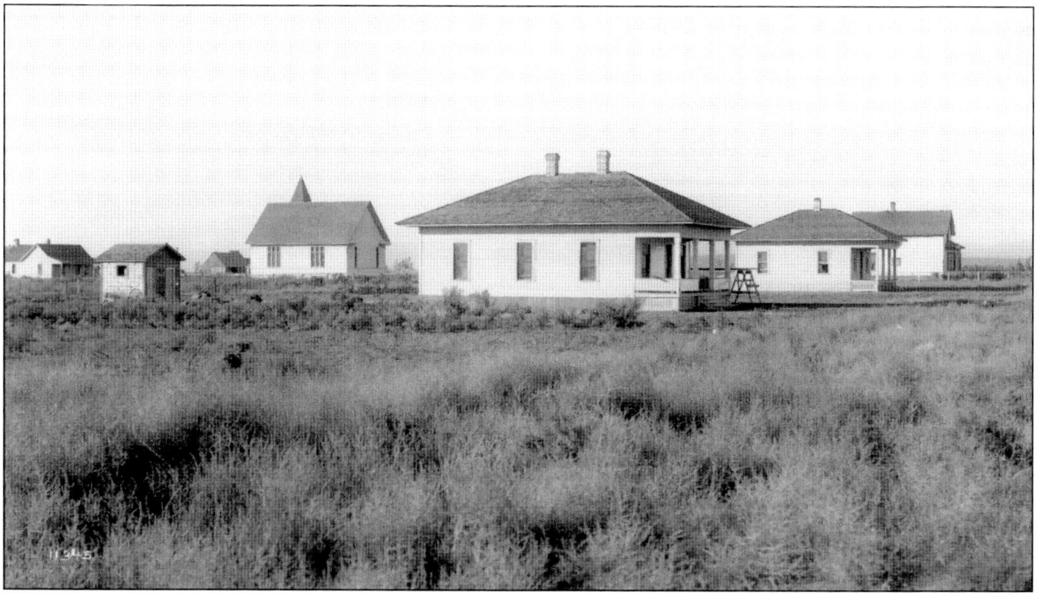

Homes were beginning to fill the area by October 1908, when Asahel Curtis, along with five other photographers, took on the task of developing advertising brochures to entice new landowners. Curtis eventually built a home and planted an apple orchard on what is now the corner of Walnut Lane and Asahel Curtis Drive. (Photograph by Asahel Curtis; courtesy of GHC.)

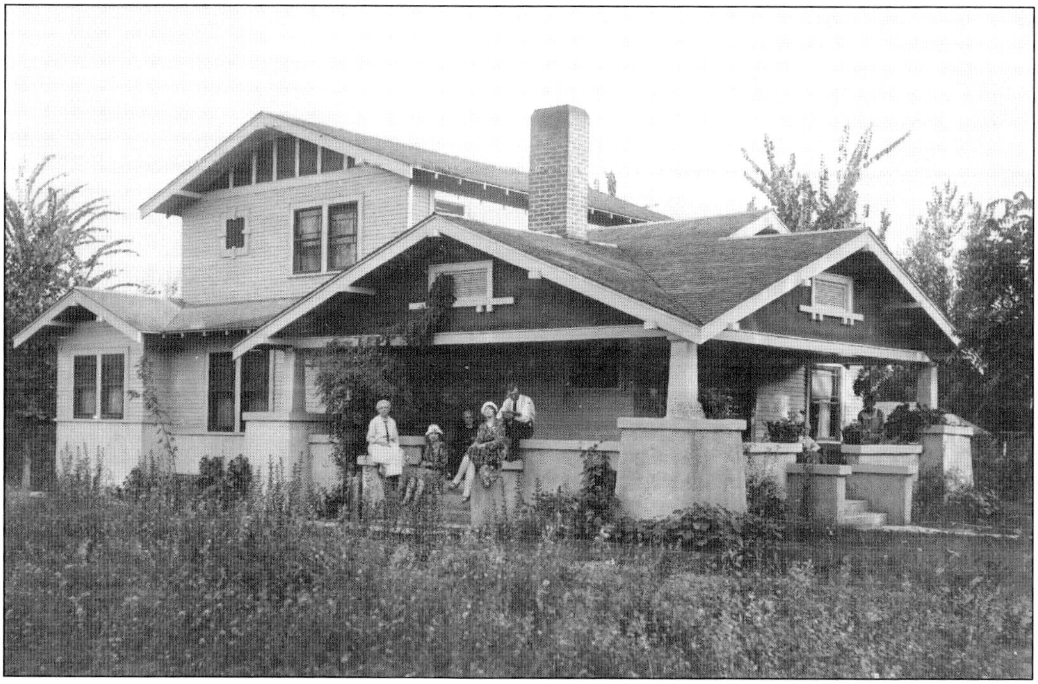

The Holbrook house, which still stands today on Douglas Avenue, has the wraparound porch common to early Grandview homes. A sign leaning on one of the porch pillars reads, "Marcelling Done Here." The Marcel, a popular 1920s ladies' hairstyle similar to the finger wave, was achieved with heated curling tongs. Perhaps one of the unidentified women in the photograph earned a comfortable side income from the enterprise.

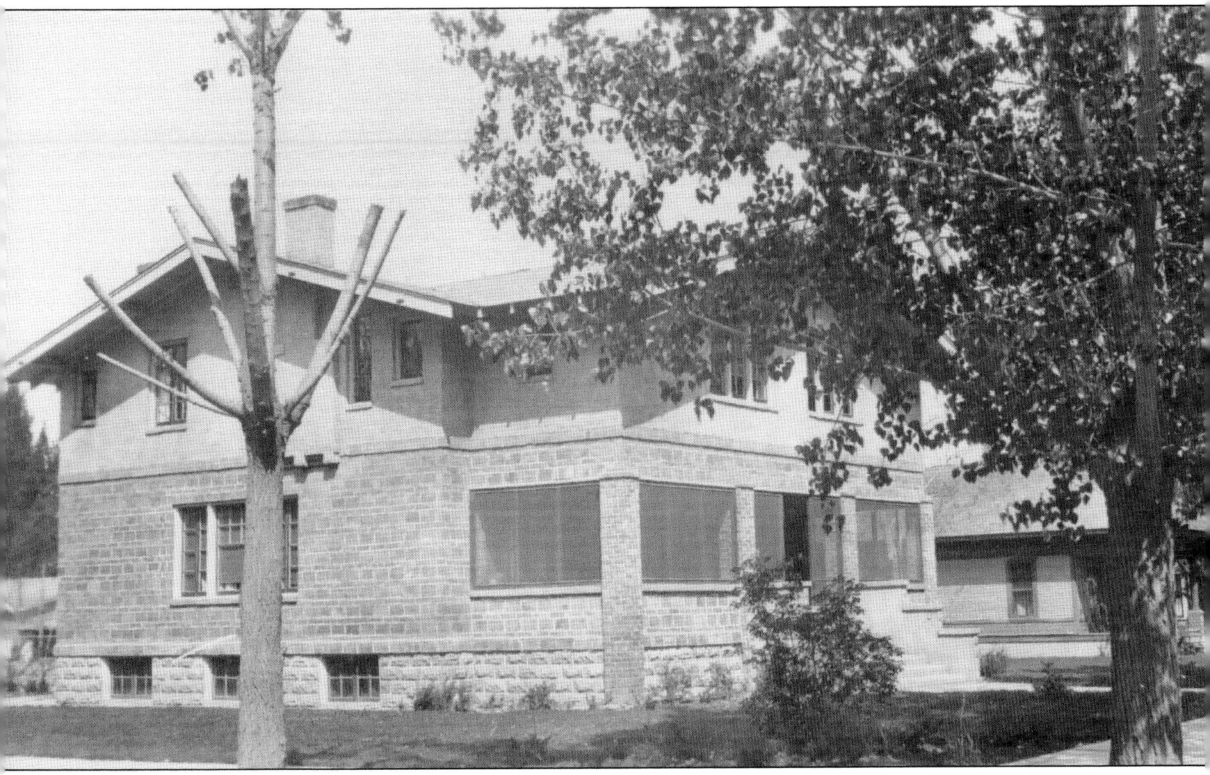

Built between 1920 and 1926, the Howay-Dykstra House, at 114 Birch Street, is listed in the National Register of Historic Places. E.A. Sweet acquired the land from the Granger Land Company in 1907 for $350. In 1910, Sweet sold the property to E.L. Mains, who in turn sold the property to J.W. Howay in 1920. Howay built this eclectic example of an Arts and Crafts–style home. Ownership of the house passed to Frank M. Balcom in 1926 and then to H.C. Dykstra in 1938. Dykstra was very active in the community, serving 15 years on the city council and then 14 years as mayor. During his tenure, Grandview's population tripled and the city itself doubled in size. The current owner, Linda Hartshorn, has carefully preserved the hardwood floors, wooden fireplaces, and original millwork in the larger and more complex home than the Craftsman bungalows built elsewhere in town at the time. Of special note is the fireplace surround in the downstairs parlor, made of Batchelder "Hearthside Dreams" tiles. Ernest Batchelder (1875–1957) was a leading designer of the American Arts and Crafts movement.

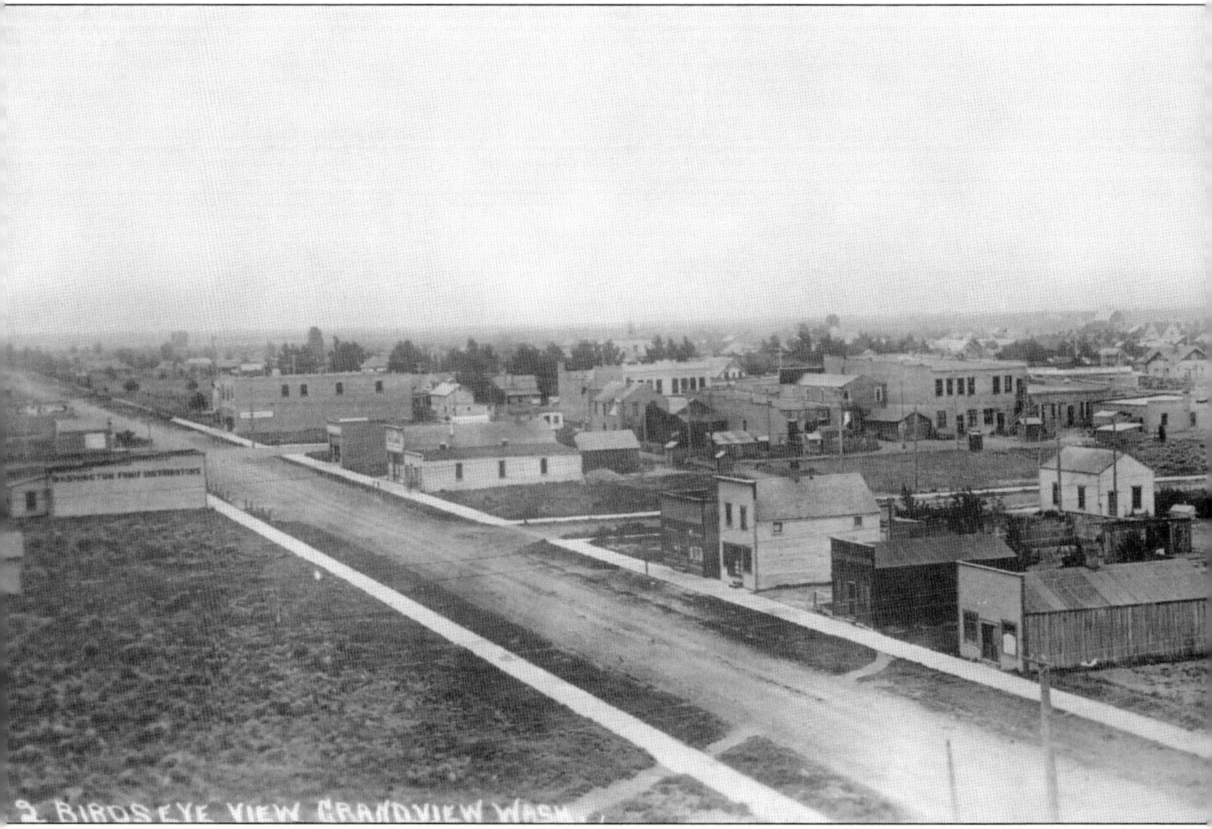

A souvenir copy of the first issue of the *Grandview Herald*, dated March 4, 1909, and housed in the R.E. Powell Museum, contained advertisements for the following businesses: J.M. Fleming, General Merchandise; J.E. Laricheliere, blacksmith; Ray Andrews, groceries and feed, Bruce Lindsey, manager; City Café, C.W. Pace, manager; Cascade Lumber, Robert J. Vennum, manager; Valley Clothing, A.E. Fisk, manager; W.H. Dunbar, civil engineer; C.R. Moulton, real estate; A.H. Robinson, sign painter; Tacoma Lumber, A.W. Brown, manager; The Bargain Store, F.R. Colburn; Central Hotel, Mrs. A. Waugh; Grandview Land and Investment Company, F.C. Tull, manager; Meat Market, A.E. Person; Grandview Hardware, A.G. Hollada; and A.W. Hawn & Company, bank.

Two

Railroad, Agriculture, and Home

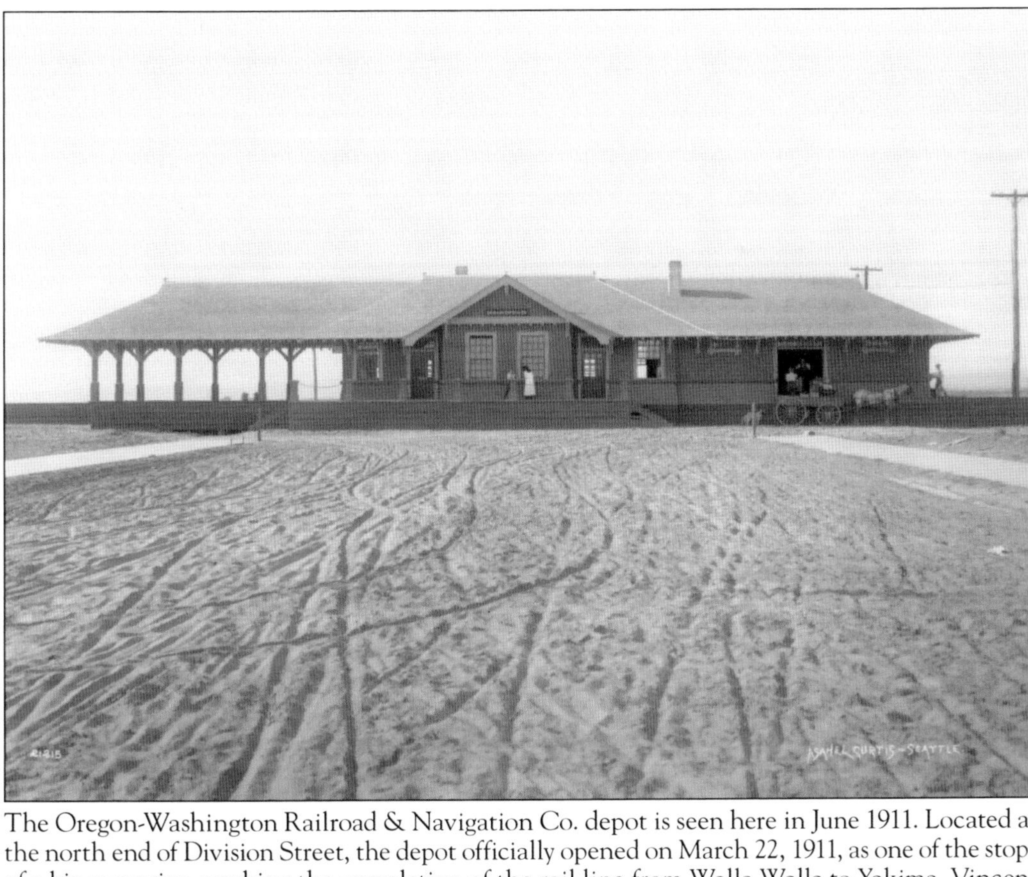

The Oregon-Washington Railroad & Navigation Co. depot is seen here in June 1911. Located at the north end of Division Street, the depot officially opened on March 22, 1911, as one of the stops of a big excursion marking the completion of the rail line from Walla Walla to Yakima. Vincent Walker was the first depot agent. (Photograph by Asahel Curtis; courtesy of GHC.)

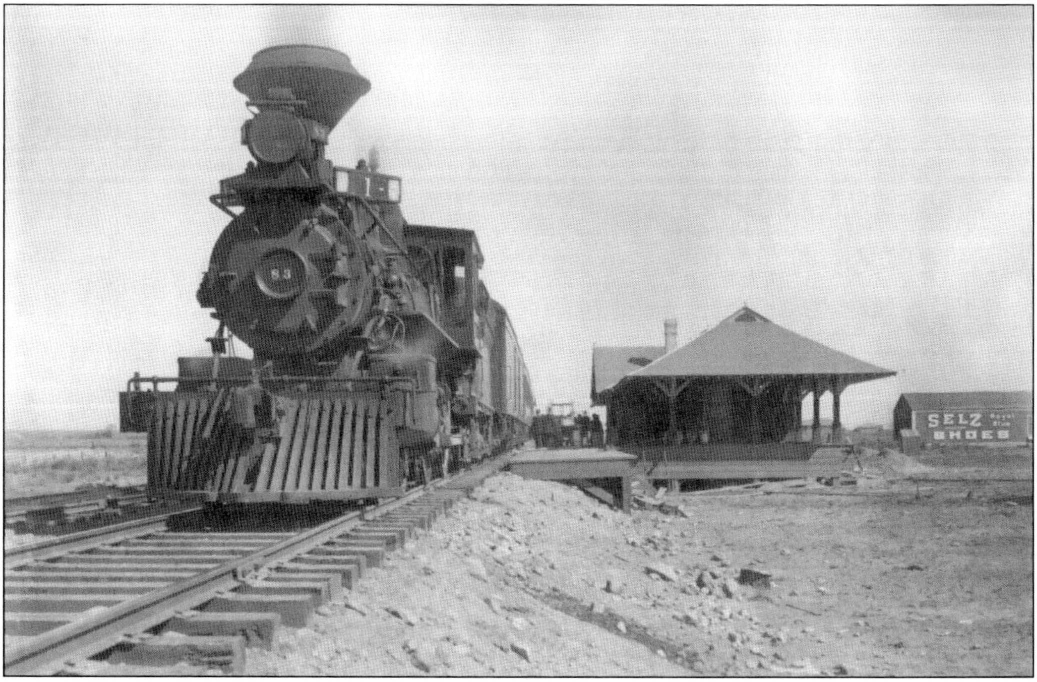

With construction only recently completed, the Oregon-Washington Railroad & Navigation Co. depot, viewed here from the west, does not yet include the roof-mounted Grandview sign. Unused lumber is still piled at the side of the building. Engine No. 83 idles on the track as potential passengers await the "all aboard" call.

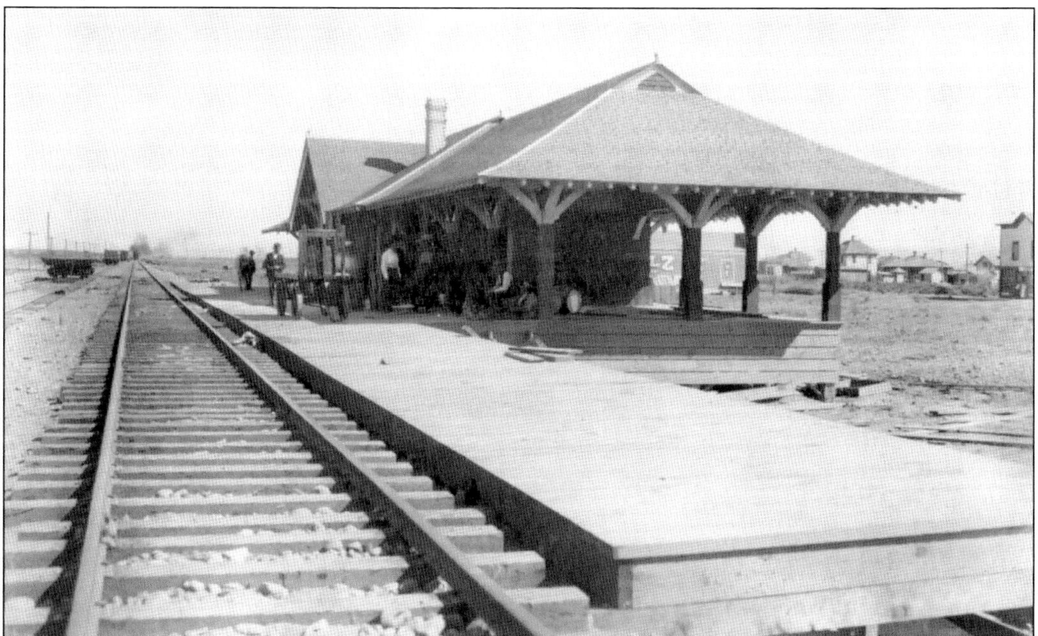

This is the same depot shown above. A train, possibly from the Tri-Cities of Pasco, Kennewick, and Richland, can be seen arriving from the east. To the right, a Royal Blue Selz Shoe advertisement is visible on a building south of the depot.

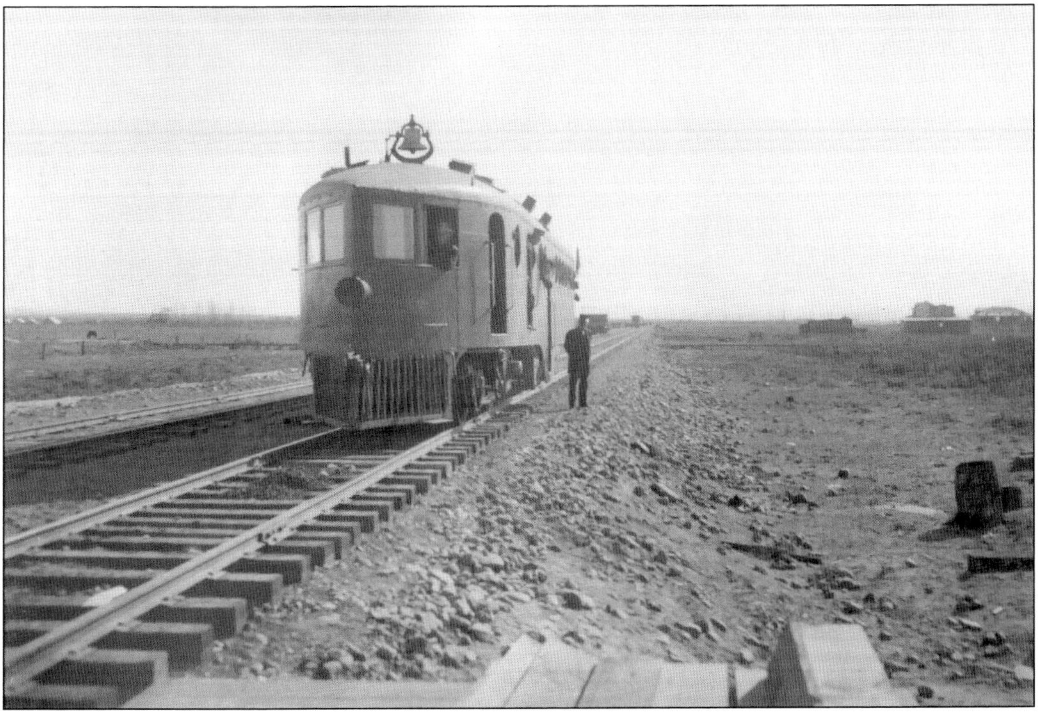

A conductor stands alongside a McKeen gasoline-mechanical passenger railcar owned by the Oregon-Washington Railroad & Navigation Co. "Sage Brush Annie" was the affectionate name given to the train that traveled daily from Yakima, bringing early settlers to Grandview. In the early days, passengers rode in comfort in the parlor car's plush seats and had the use of a full-length dining car.

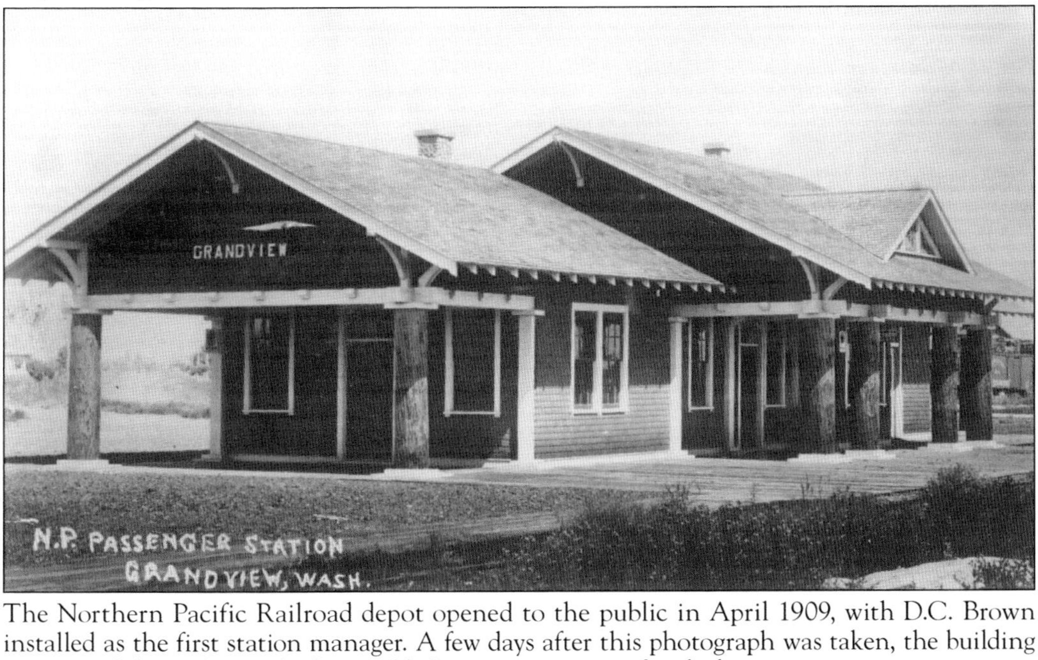

The Northern Pacific Railroad depot opened to the public in April 1909, with D.C. Brown installed as the first station manager. A few days after this photograph was taken, the building was moved down the track along Fifth Street to serve as a freight house.

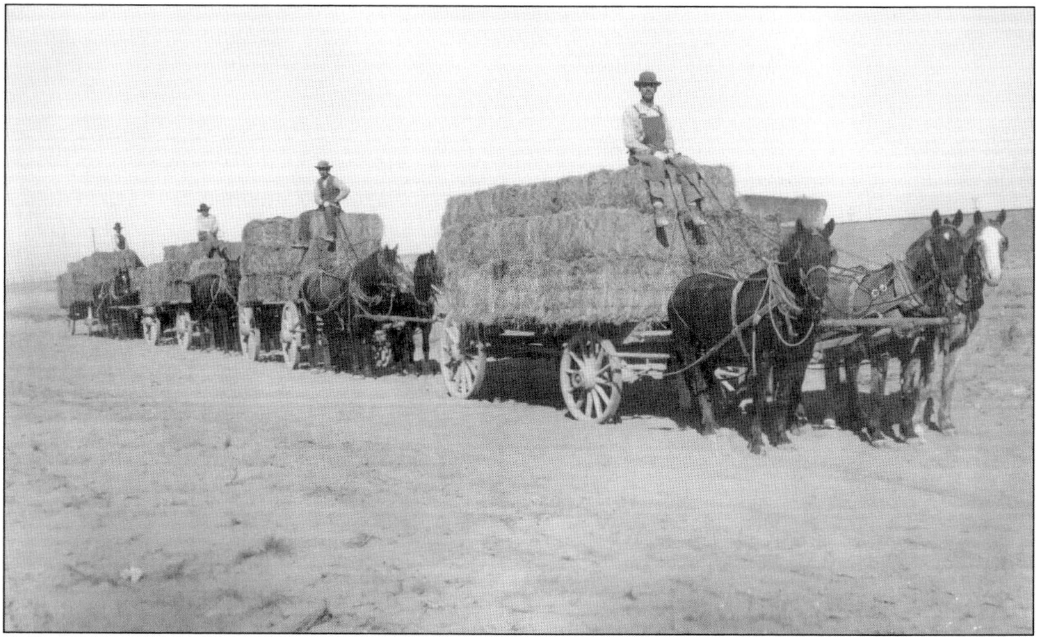

Above, a string of horse-drawn hay wagons are hauling freight on a dirt track north of present-day West Side Park. That dirt track would eventually become part of West Main Street. The last man at left in the line of wagons is John Hartman, and Walter Platt is in front of him. Unfortunately, the identities of the two men on the two wagons in front are unknown. Below, the hay is being loaded onto waiting Northern Pacific railcars. Not a single cultivated acre in the lower Yakima Valley was over four miles from a railroad shipping point, making the transfer of freight an easier chore for local farmers. A total of 500 carloads of fruit, hay, and vegetables were shipped from the Grandview area in 1910.

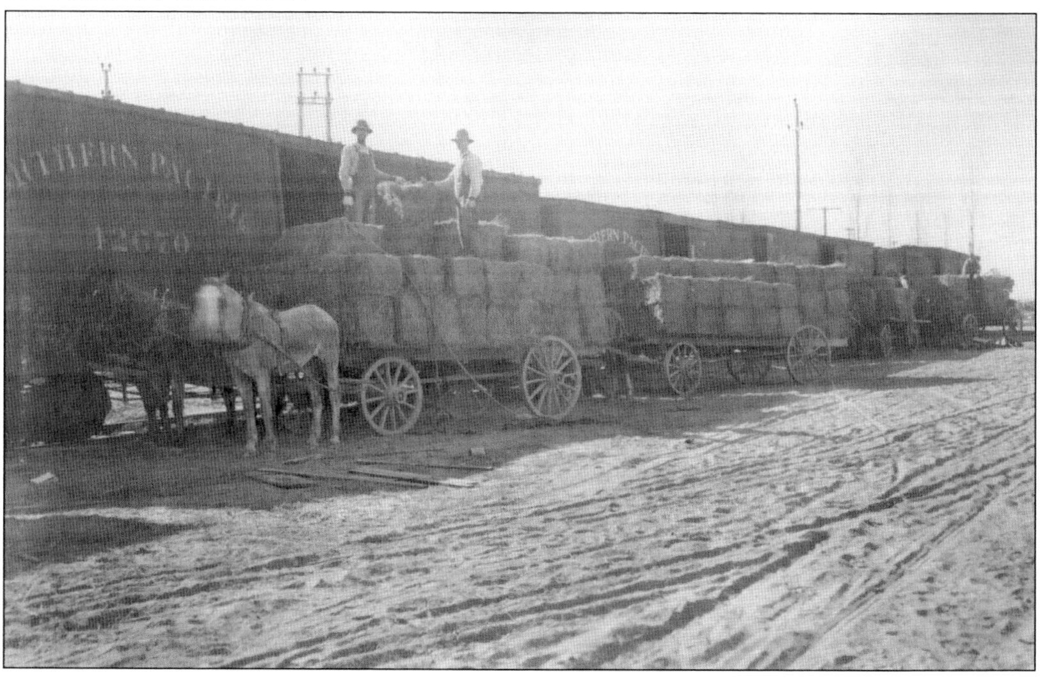

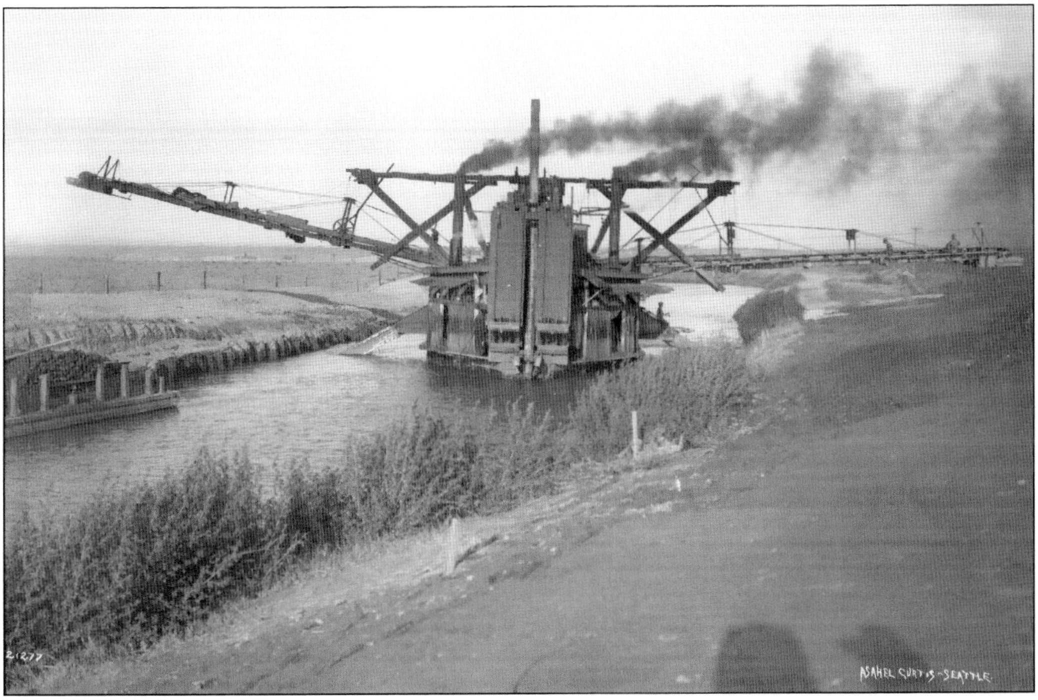

After being widened in June 1911, the Sunnyside Canal, part of the Yakima Irrigation Project (Sunnyside Division, Bureau of Reclamation), was capable of carrying almost twice the amount of water as before. The dredge shown here, one of the largest ever built in the Pacific Northwest, widened the existing canal from 50 to 75 feet. (Photograph by Asahel Curtis; courtesy of GHC.)

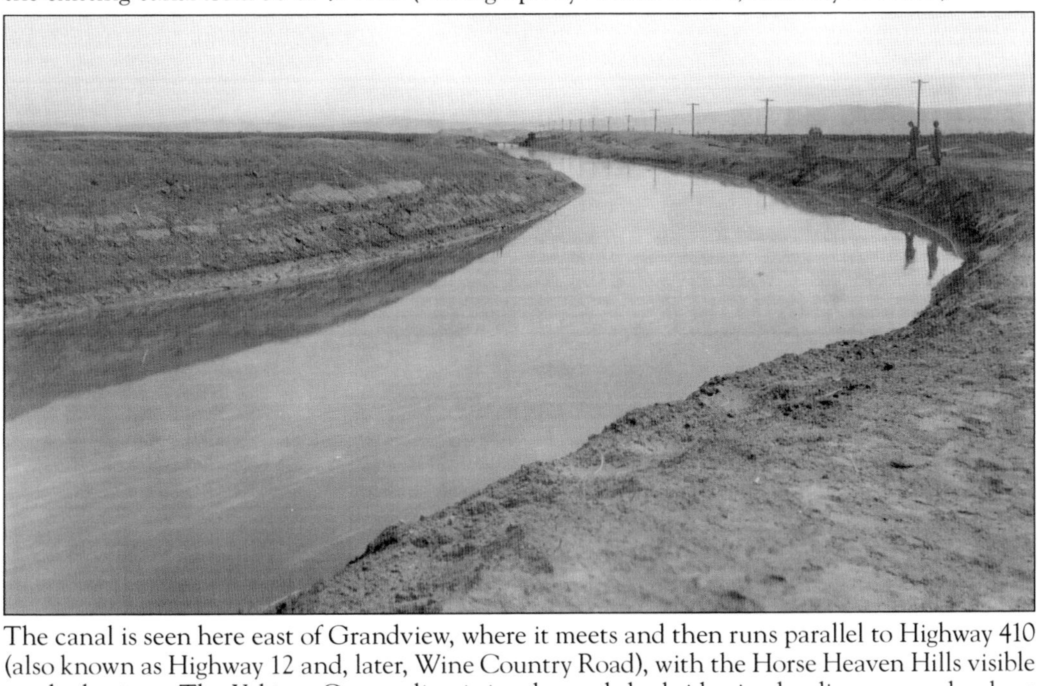
The canal is seen here east of Grandview, where it meets and then runs parallel to Highway 410 (also known as Highway 12 and, later, Wine Country Road), with the Horse Heaven Hills visible on the horizon. The Yakima County line is just beyond the bridge in the distance, and a short distance farther is Prosser (not visible), the southernmost town in the Yakima Valley.

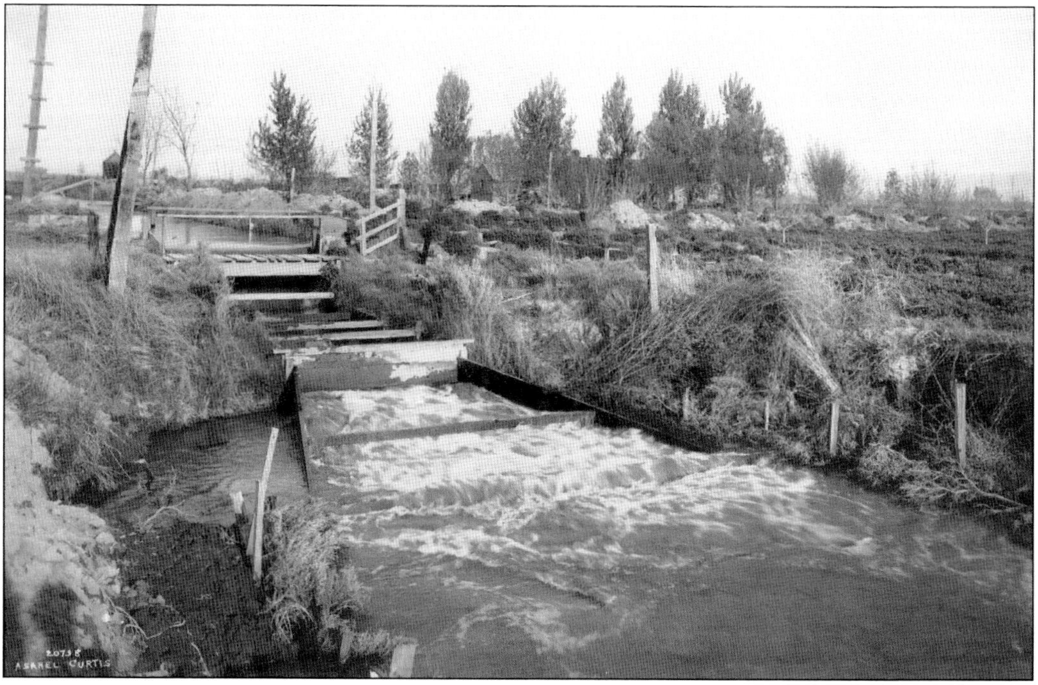

The Rocky Ford Lateral, a side branch of the Sunnyside Canal that ran through the Euclid and Grandview districts, used wooden "checks" to slow the water's flow. In February 1938, improvements to the system included the installation of a turbine at an approximate cost of $4,100. (Photograph by Asahel Curtis; courtesy of GHC.)

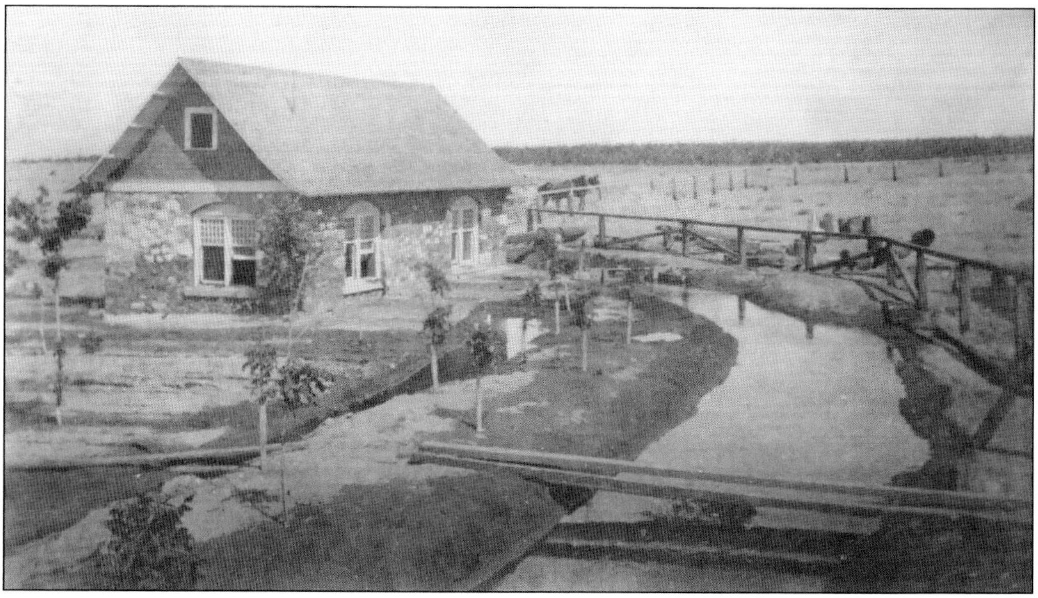

The governor and state land commissioner attended an early sale of parcels in the 1,300-acre Orchard Tracts district. Town planners laid out 40-foot streets and alleys with sites set aside for a public park, a school, and churches. Today, the Orchard Tracts feature early-20th-century farmhouses, antique fruit warehouses, and some of the lower Yakima Valley's oldest orchards. This photograph shows an early irrigation pump house.

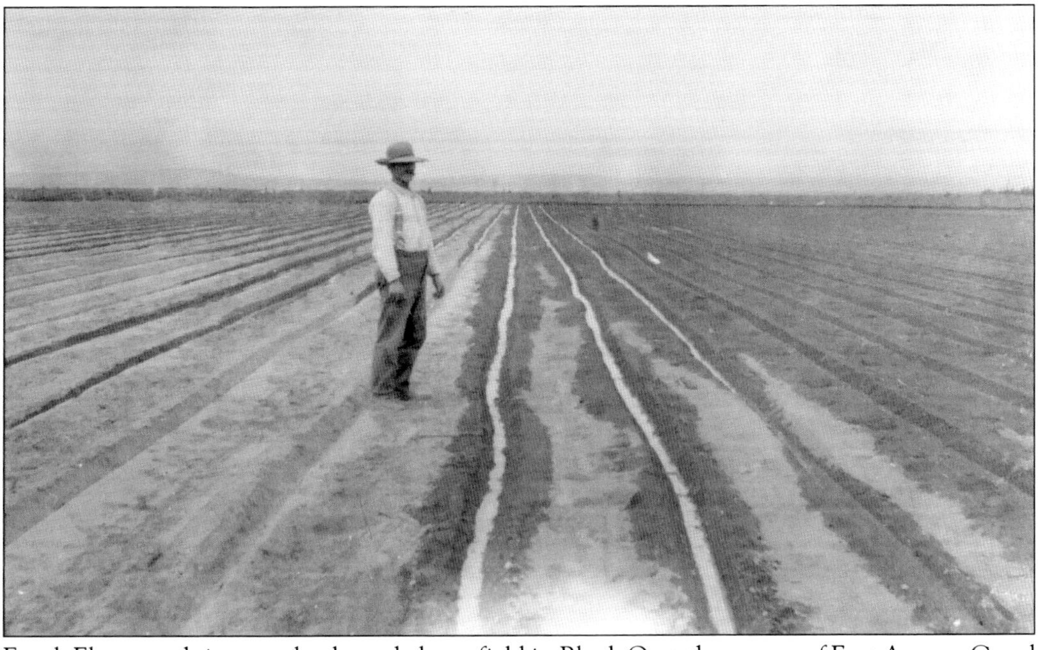

Frank Elser stands in a newly planted clover field in Block Q, at the corner of East Avenue C and Main Street. Vegetables were often planted between the trees in young orchards, enabling the farmers to earn a livelihood until the trees were old enough to bear fruit. This type of "orchard gardening" served a dual purpose. It not only provided a means of making a living; it also required frequent cultivation, which tended to make the land retain moisture, thus requiring less irrigation. Both types of crops were becoming profitable on a commercial scale by 1912, when large areas were planted in apple, peach, pear, apricot, and cherry trees.

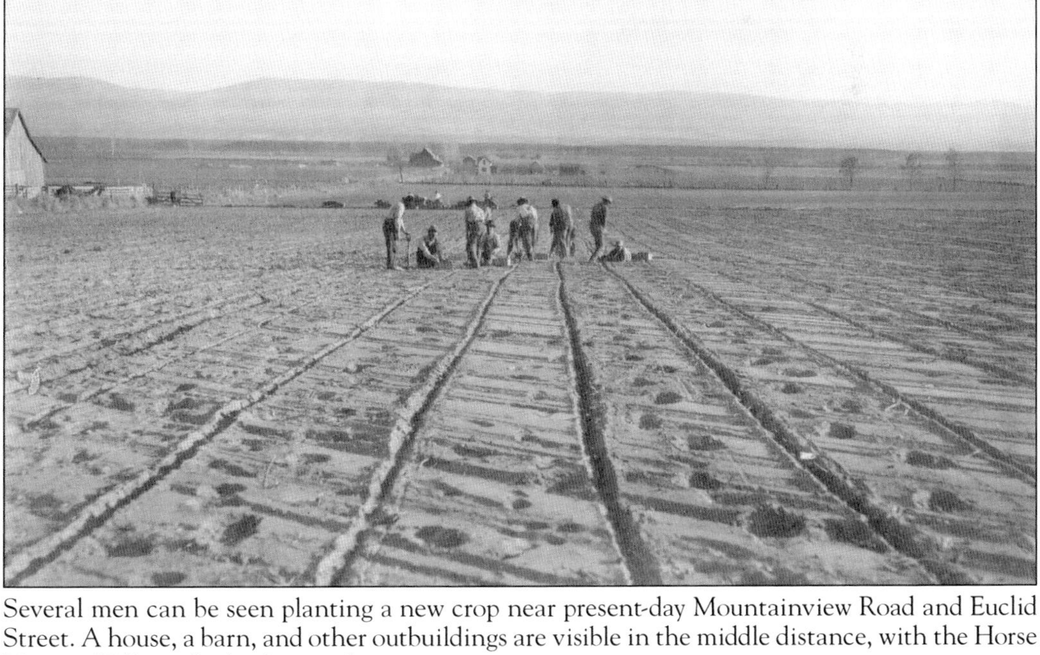

Several men can be seen planting a new crop near present-day Mountainview Road and Euclid Street. A house, a barn, and other outbuildings are visible in the middle distance, with the Horse Heaven Hills in the background.

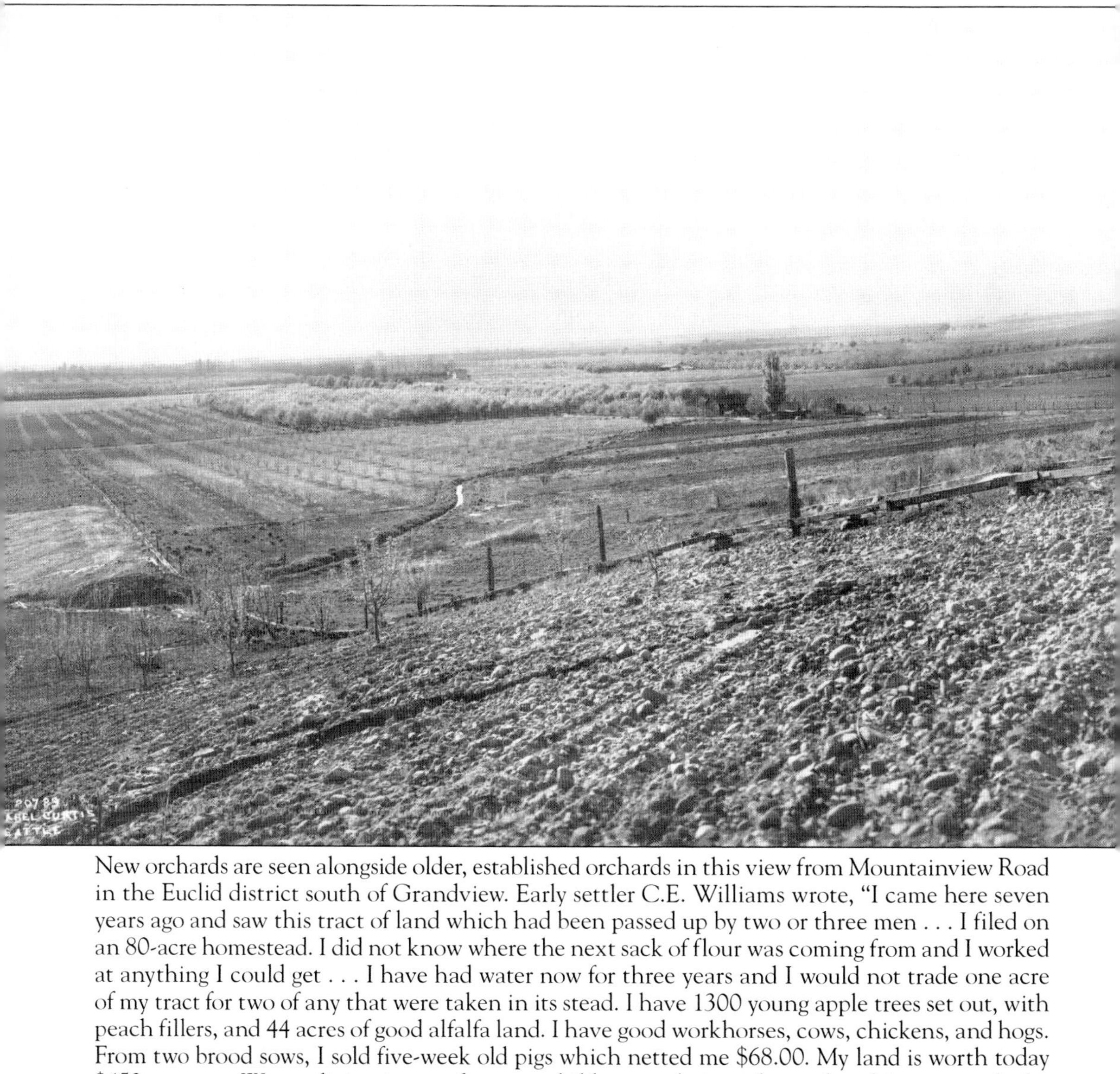

New orchards are seen alongside older, established orchards in this view from Mountainview Road in the Euclid district south of Grandview. Early settler C.E. Williams wrote, "I came here seven years ago and saw this tract of land which had been passed up by two or three men . . . I filed on an 80-acre homestead. I did not know where the next sack of flour was coming from and I worked at anything I could get . . . I have had water now for three years and I would not trade one acre of my tract for two of any that were taken in its stead. I have 1300 young apple trees set out, with peach fillers, and 44 acres of good alfalfa land. I have good workhorses, cows, chickens, and hogs. From two brood sows, I sold five-week old pigs which netted me $68.00. My land is worth today $450 per acre. We are living in comfort, our children are being educated and it was worth the struggle I made to secure this home." (Photograph by Asahel Curtis; courtesy of GHC.)

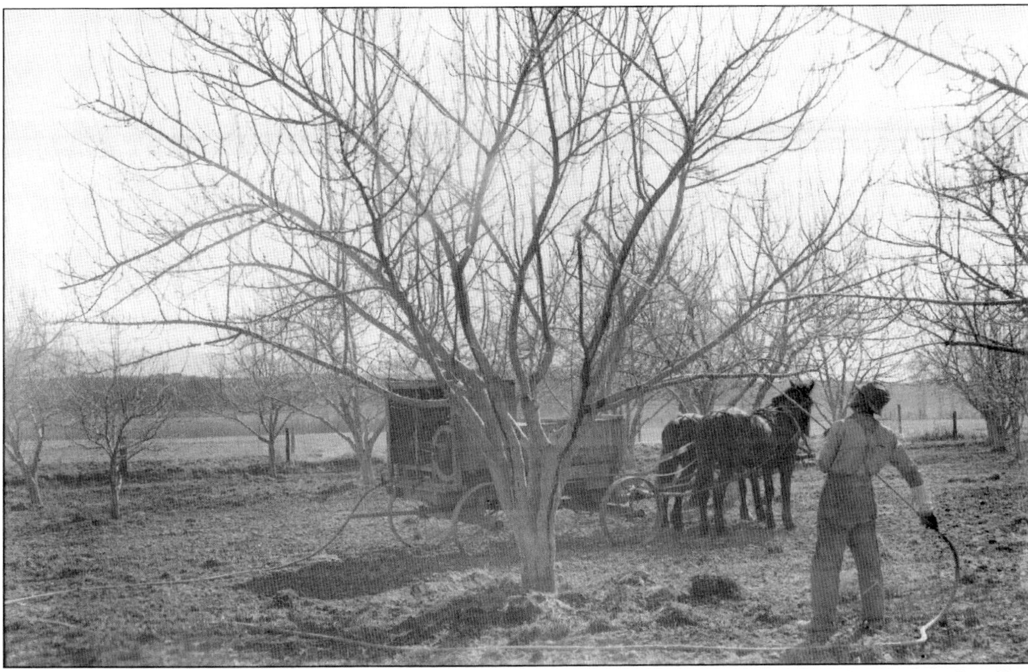

The spraying of bare trees, whether to destroy pests or to encourage fruit growth, was, and still is, an important job that is undertaken each spring by area orchardists. The treatment being applied to the mature orchard in this photograph is unknown, as is the name of the farmer shown with his horse-drawn wagon.

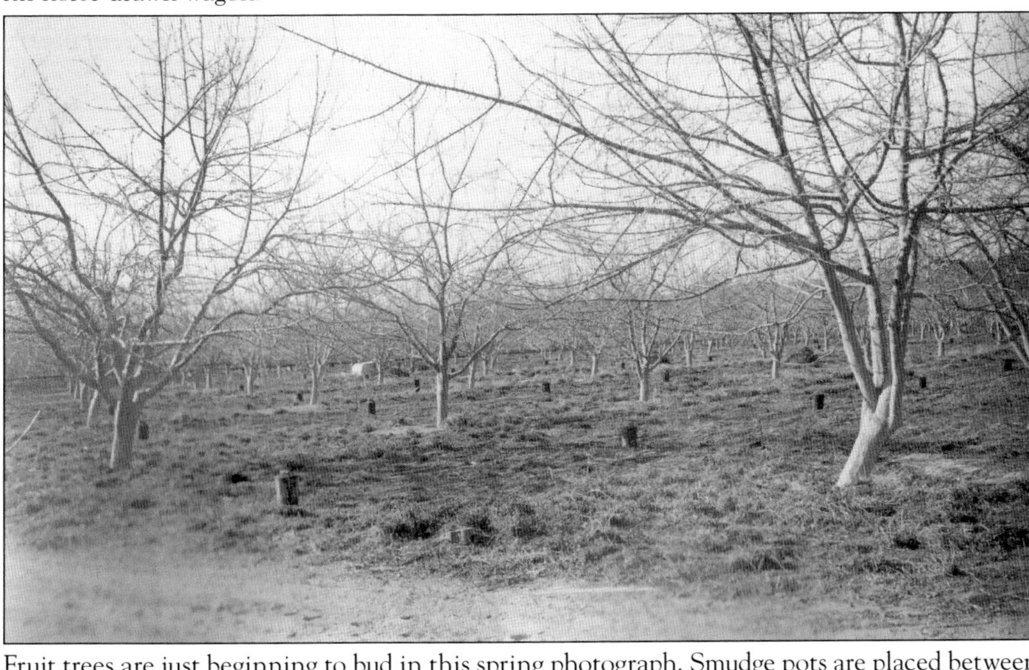

Fruit trees are just beginning to bud in this spring photograph. Smudge pots are placed between the rows of trees in anticipation of a late freeze, which was a constant threat to fruit orchards. Thousands of these pots and other orchard heaters were left in the orchards until all threat of frost had passed; only then was the farmer guaranteed a full night of uninterrupted sleep.

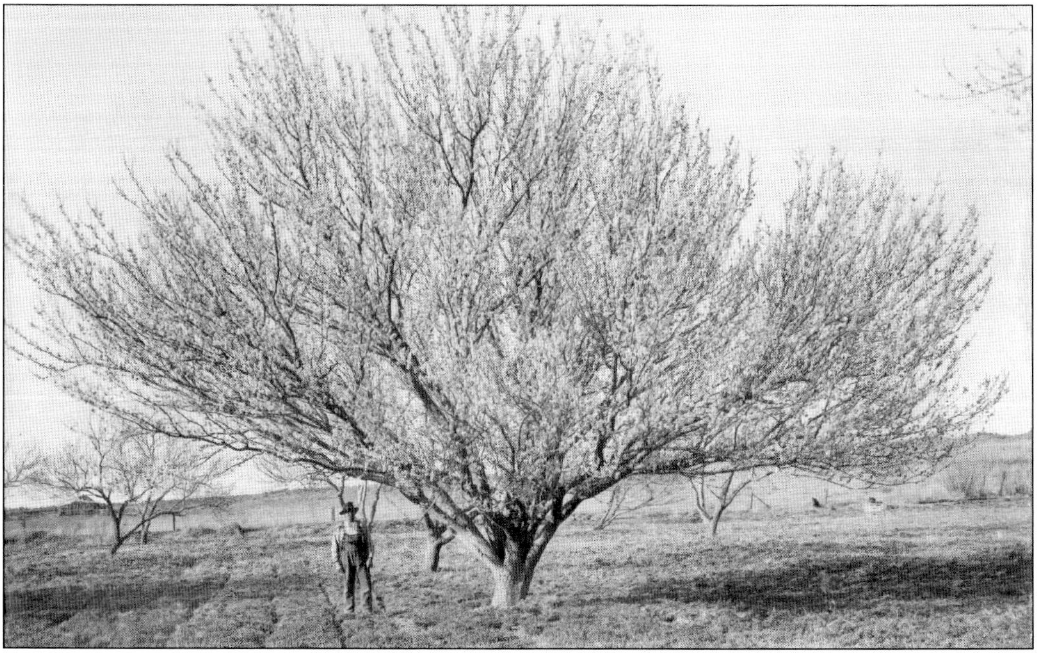

An unidentified farmer proudly stands under his mature, 13-year-old apricot tree in full bloom. The May 7, 1910, issue of the *Bossburg Herald*, a northern Washington newspaper, reported that the officers of state horticultural associations and commercial organizations in the Pacific Northwest were forecasting that the fruit crop would be the largest and most profitable in the history of the four states of Washington, Oregon, Idaho, and Montana.

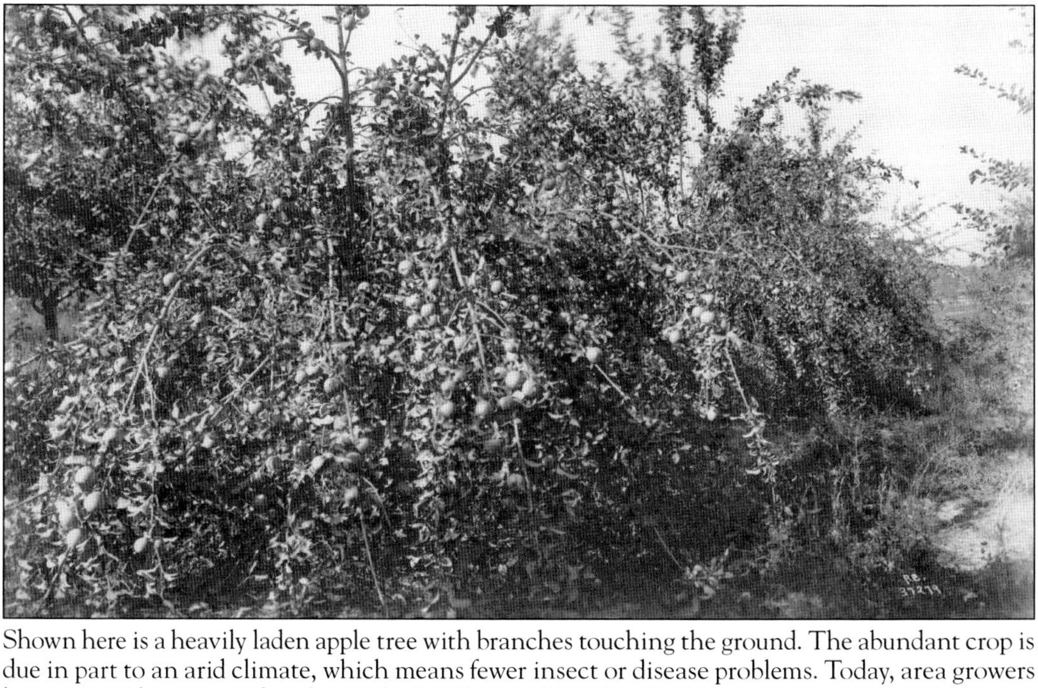

Shown here is a heavily laden apple tree with branches touching the ground. The abundant crop is due in part to an arid climate, which means fewer insect or disease problems. Today, area growers harvest a wide variety of apples, including Red and Golden Delicious, Granny Smith, Braeburn, Jonagold, Fuji, Gala, and many more. (Photograph by Asahel Curtis; courtesy of GHC.)

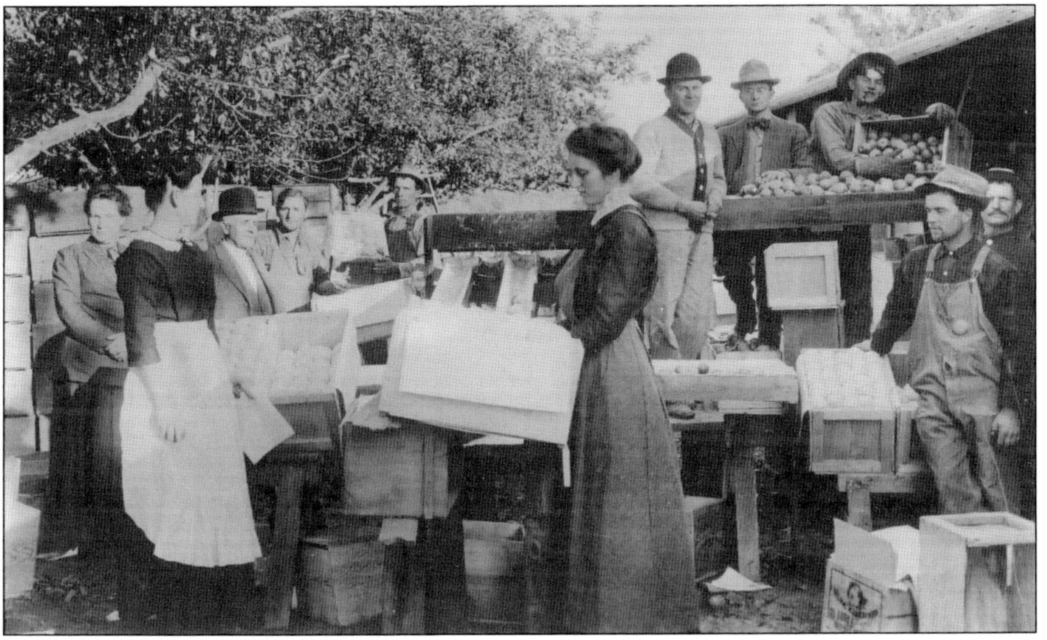

The first fruit-sizer in the Euclid district was used on the Chris Neuenschwander farm in 1911. Here, a group of people including pickers and packers stand around the equipment, which sorted the fruit by size. A woman is wrapping and boxing the sorted fruit. Unfortunately, the identities of the people in the photograph have been lost.

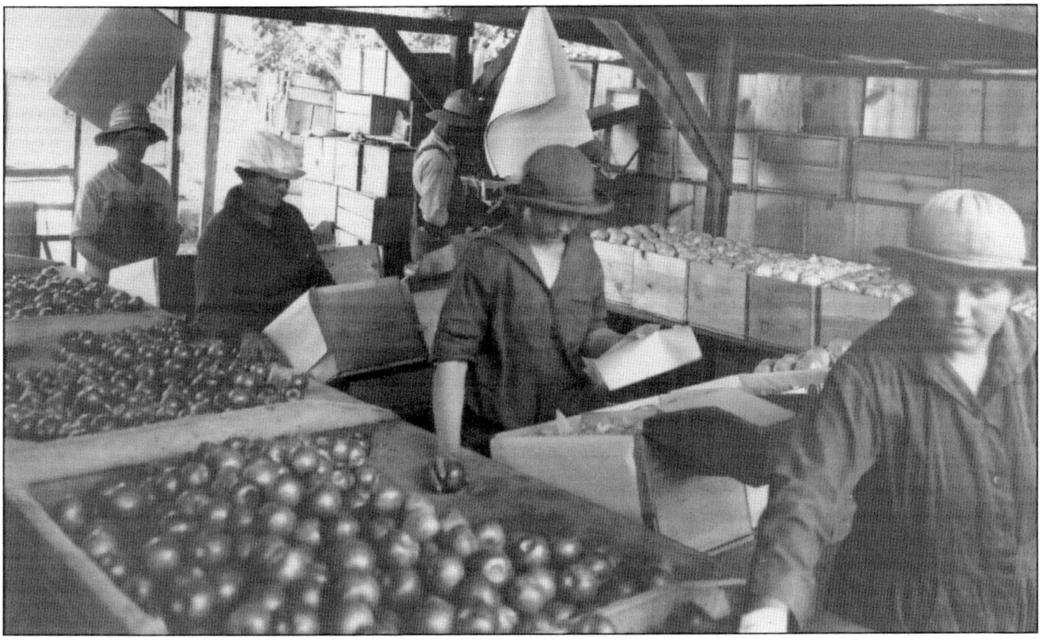

By 1920, apple packing had moved indoors, as this photograph of the Asahel Curtis ranch shows. At a convention of the Fruit Jobbers' Association in Sacramento, California, in February 1911, a display of commercial apples from Grandview orchards received an award of $500 for the best display. The varieties awarded the prize were Arkansas Blacks, Winesaps, Rome Beauties, Yellow Newtowns, and Spitzenbergs. (Photograph by Asahel Curtis; courtesy of GHC.)

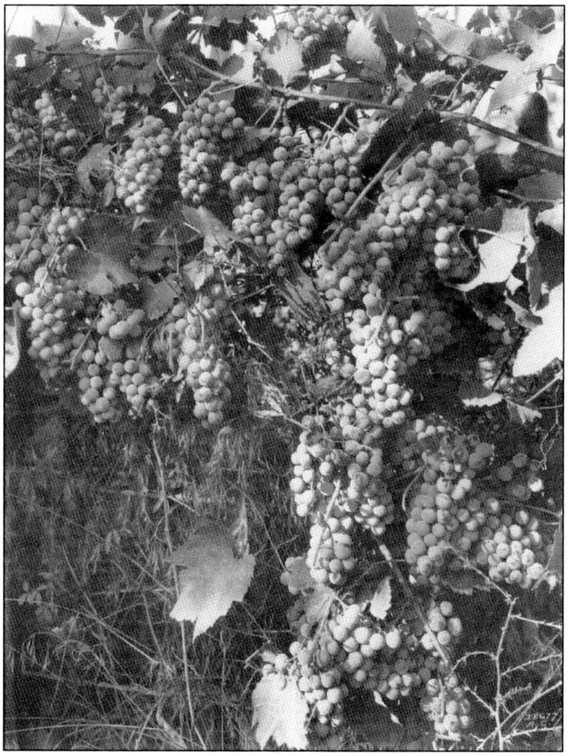

Grapes on the vine are ready for harvest. The Yakima Valley is the oldest and largest wine-producing region in the state. Wine grapes were first planted in the Grandview area in 1917; today, more than one-third of all wine grapes grown in Washington State come from the Yakima Valley, which is known in some circles as the "soul of Washington wine." (Photograph by Asahel Curtis; courtesy of GHC.)

The large vine-covered trellises in the background below sometimes puzzle people unfamiliar with the way hops are grown. The hop vines awaiting harvest in the foreground have been cut from their supporting trellis. In 2012, it was reported by the Hop Growers of America that the United States was second only to Germany in the world production of hops, with the Yakima Valley producing 70–75 percent of the total American crop.

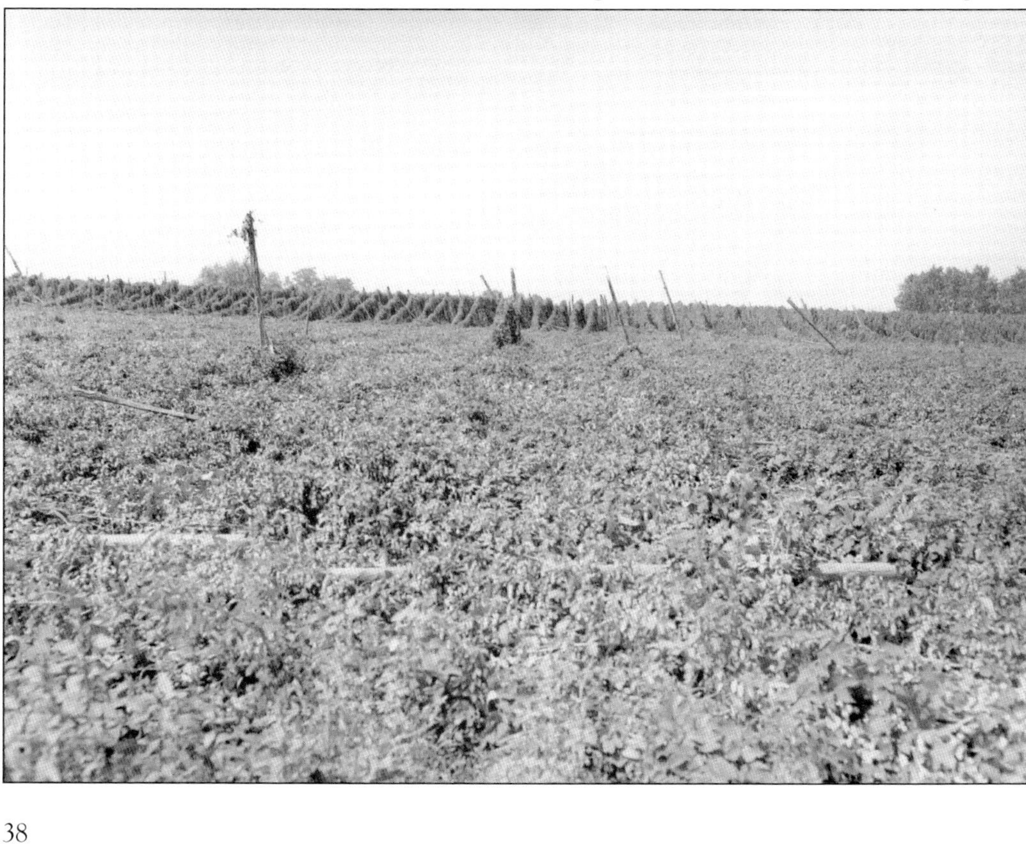

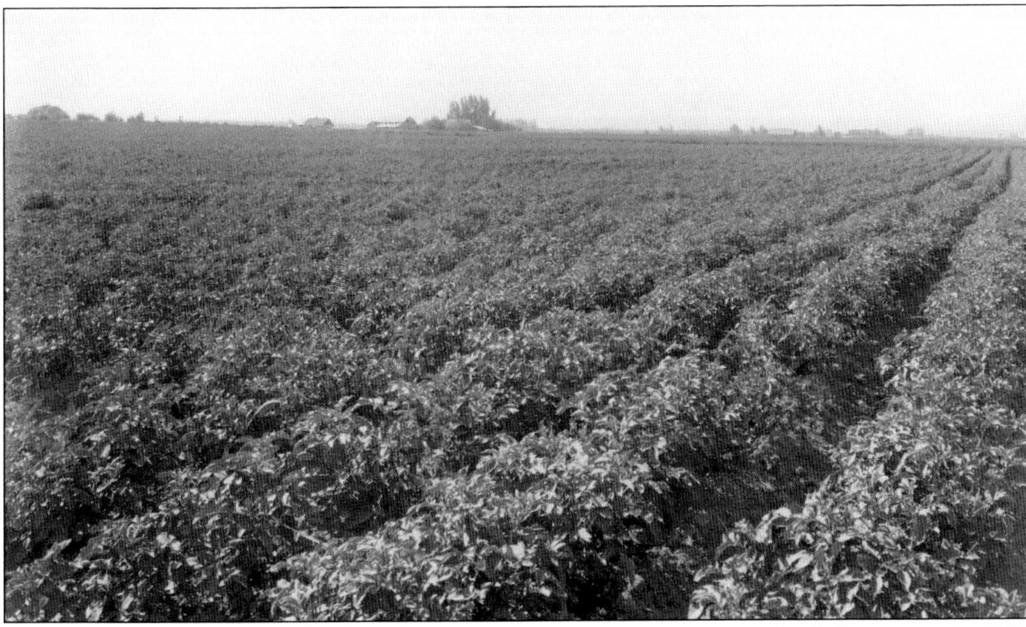

Potatoes were a leading vegetable crop, resulting in yields as high as 600 bushels an acre. In 1909, the Northern Pacific Railroad introduced the "Great Big Baked Potato" in their dining cars after dining car superintendent Hazen J. Titus saw the Yakima Valley's huge two-pounders. Baked up nicely and slathered with butter, the "Great Big Baked Potato" became part of an early Northern Pacific advertising campaign. (Photograph by Asahel Curtis; courtesy of GHC.)

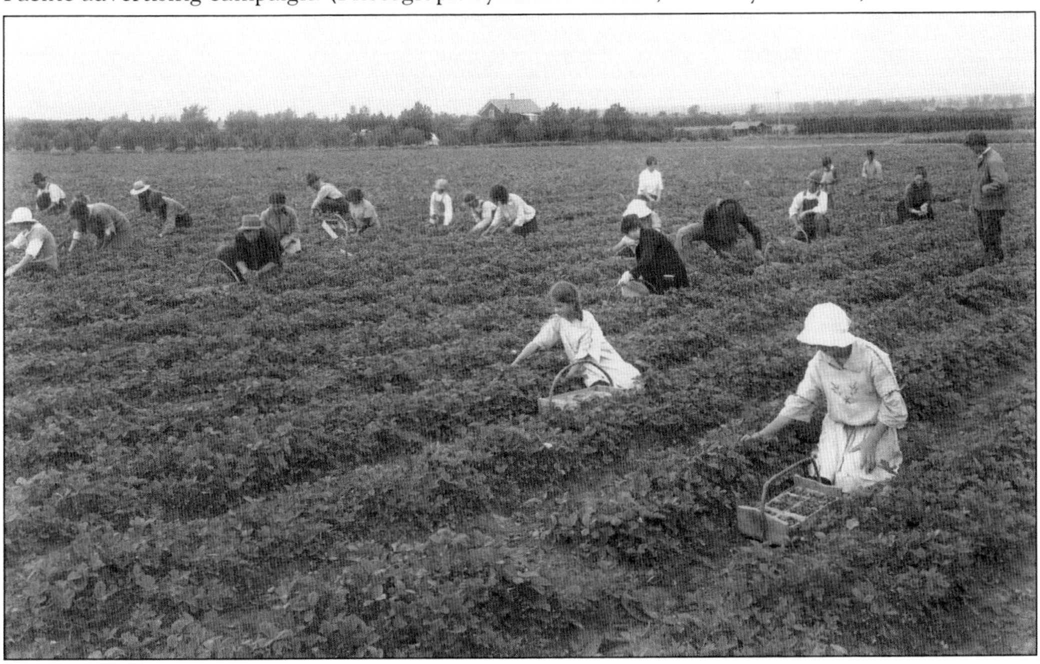

When it came time to harvest strawberries, all hands big and small were welcome. W.J. Bauer wrote, "Strawberries ripened the 18th of May, 1893, and the season was two weeks late at that. I found ready sale for them at $1 per gallon and could have sold many more than I raised, at the same price." (Photograph by Asahel Curtis; courtesy of GHC.)

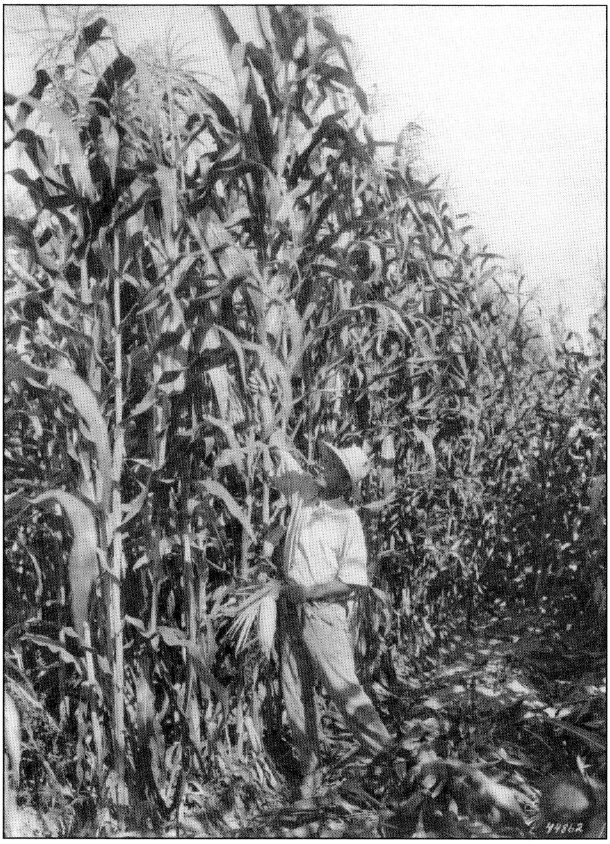

This world champion corn was grown by S.D. Cornell in 1923 only a half mile south of Grandview. A record crop of 57,010 pounds of silage corn per acre was grown that year. Weighing of the corn was done under the direction of A.E. Lovett, county agent. This photograph of a man standing next to the 22-foot cornstalks for scale was used in the November 14, 1935, *Ripley's Believe It or Not!* newspaper column.

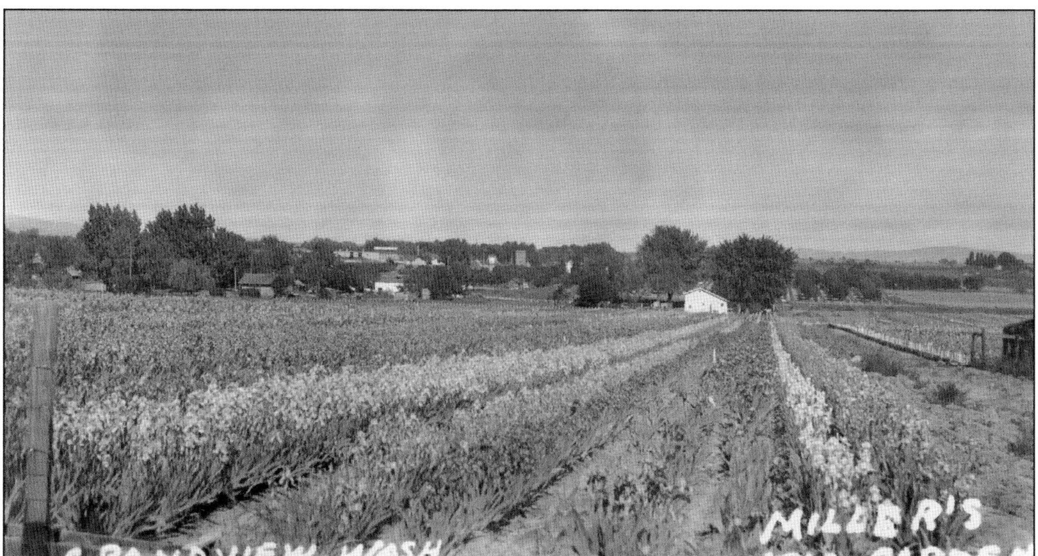

In 1940, Miller's Iris Garden (1924–1945), on land south of present-day West Fifth Street, was the largest single bed of irises in the world. The plants were eventually sold to John Marble, who started a new iris garden on Old Inland Empire Road. In 1964, this new garden was 20 acres and had over 600 varieties of iris, which were shipped all over the world.

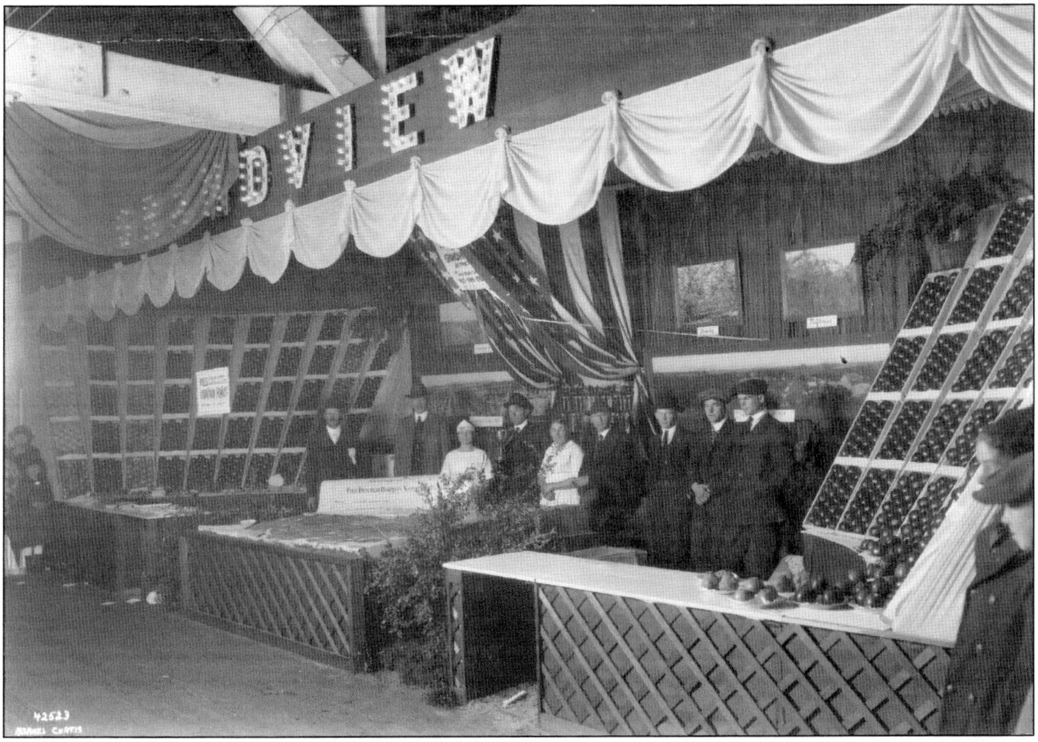

Shown here is the Grandview exhibit at the Northwest Fruit Exposition in Seattle on November 25, 1921. The fruit was excellent, and the advertising was unique, featuring the serving of apple pie accompanied by a folder of recipes. The backdrop contained three photographs taken at the same spot on the Orchard Tracts over a 14-year period. The Grandview exhibit won the grand sweepstakes prize. (Photograph by Asahel Curtis; courtesy of GHC.)

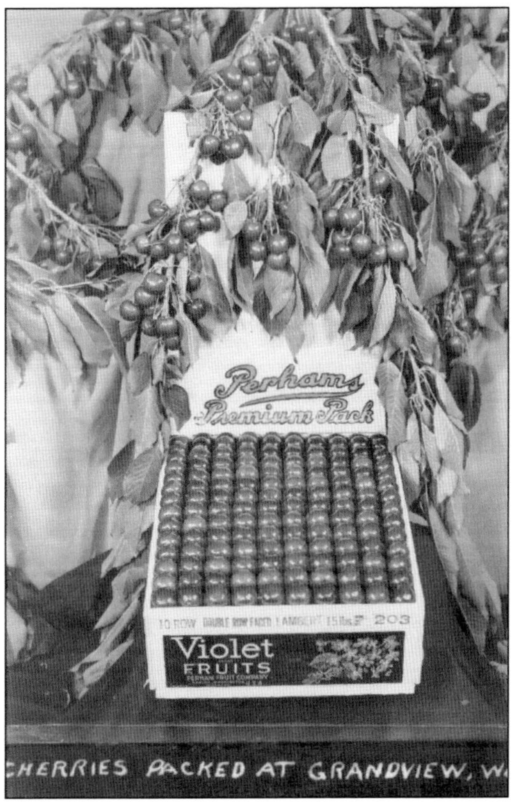

This early postcard shows cherries packed by Perham Fruit Cold Storage in Grandview. Overnight on April 18–19, 1927, a general freeze throughout the Pacific Northwest destroyed practically all of the soft fruit and much of the late fruit in the Yakima Valley. The freeze was a tough blow to area orchardists. To this day, cherry growers go to bed each night in fear of a late frost.

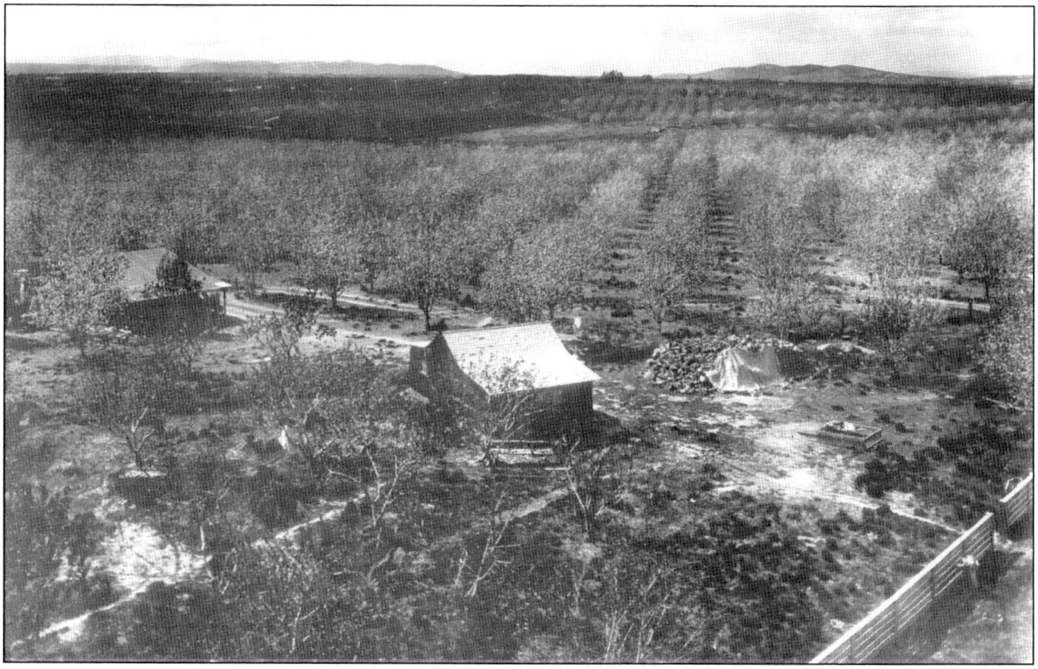

The slightly elevated view above of the Asahel Curtis ranch, bordering Walnut Lane, shows farm buildings surrounded by fruit orchards, some in full bloom. Curtis first came to the Grandview area in 1907 on an assignment by land developers for him to photograph the area in such a way as to display its potential to interested buyers. The unusual pile of rocks to the right of the building at center is destined for his home. Curtis built the house (below) on what is now Asahel Curtis Drive. (Both photographs by Asahel Curtis; courtesy of GHC.)

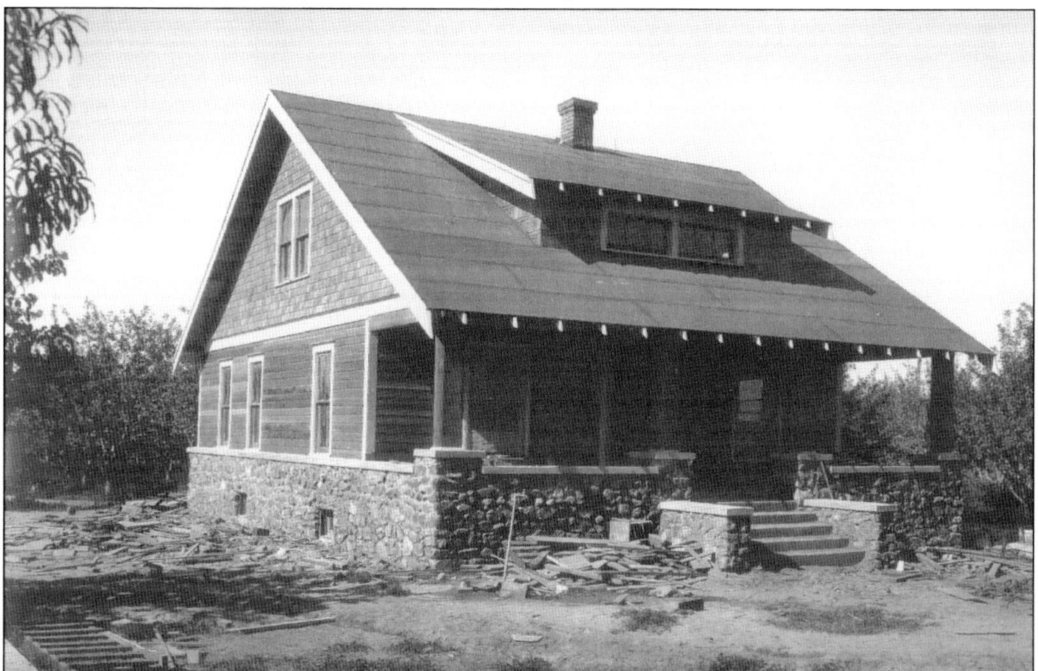

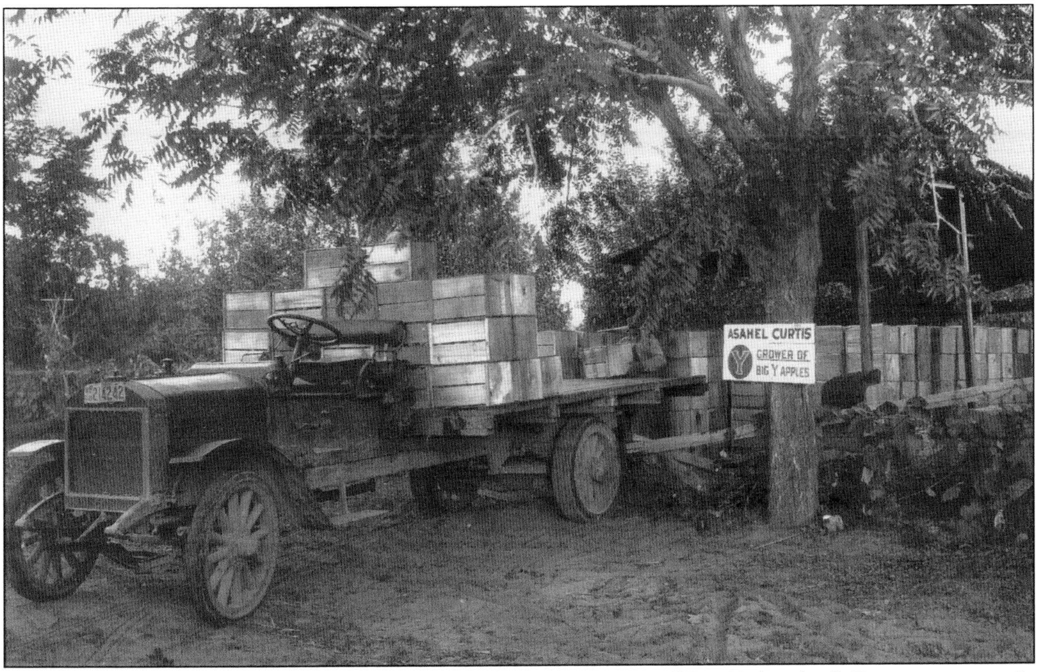

By 1923, Asahel Curtis was marketing himself as a "Grower of Big Y Apples." Curtis apparently also enjoyed working on his ranch, as can be seen in these photographs. Barely visible in the photograph above, he is loading apple boxes onto the back of the truck. Below, the boxes on the loaded truck are tied down and ready for transport to the Yakima Valley Growers Association warehouse in Grandview, where they will receive their distinctive "Big Y Brand Frigid-Pak" labeling. Curtis (left) is seen with an unidentified ranch hand at the wheel of the c. 1915 GMC truck. (Both photographs by Asahel Curtis; courtesy of GHC.)

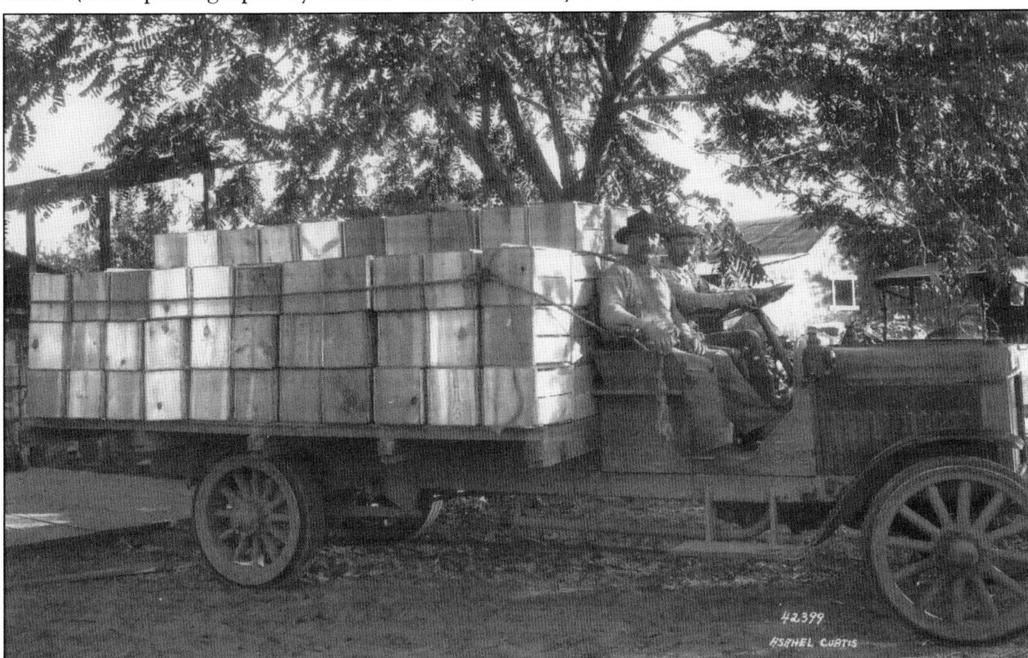

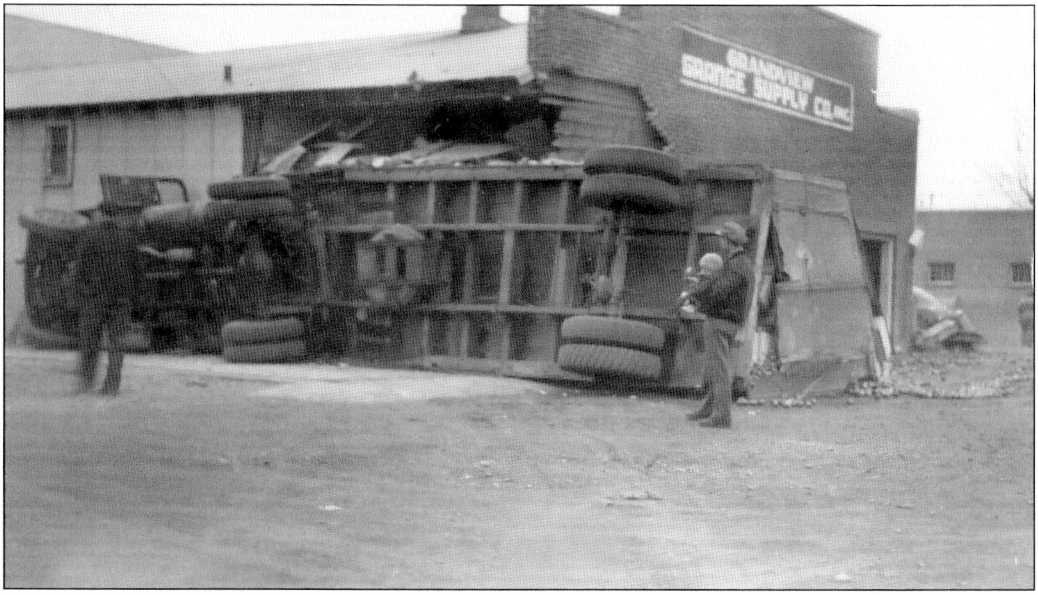

As shown in both these photographs, taken on November 20, 1944, a fully loaded truck does not always stay upright. Whether the driver was turning a corner too fast, his load was unevenly distributed, or a combination of both, his truck flipped on its side and slid into the Grandview Grange Supply building. Considerable damage was done to the truck and the building, as well as the carefully packed apples from the Donelson orchard. The Grange, a fraternal organization, was first organized in 1867 by a group of men to promote the needs of rural America and agriculture. It was not long before members formed supply co-ops, enabling farm families to purchase supplies at the lowest possible cost.

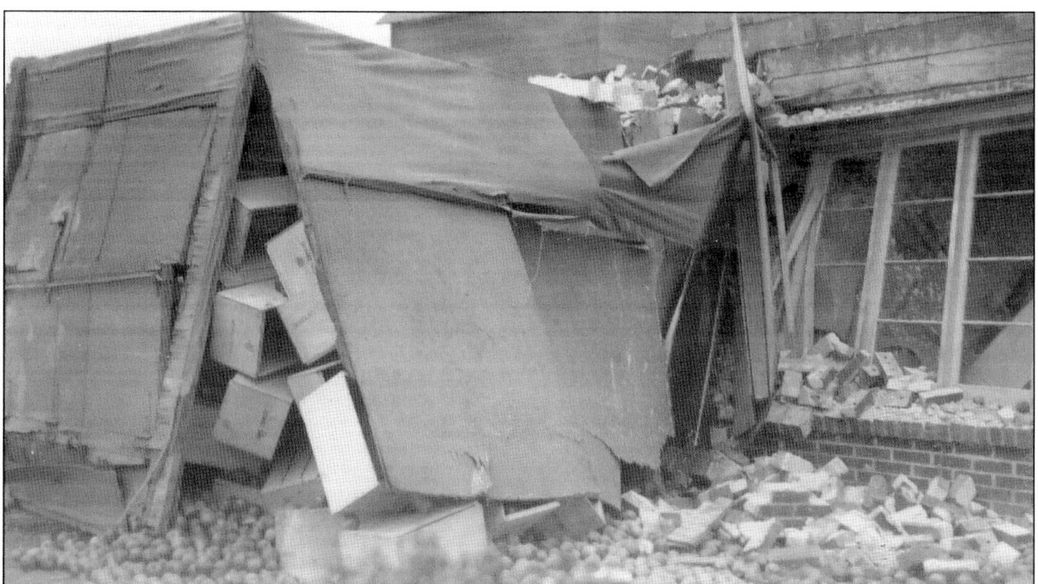

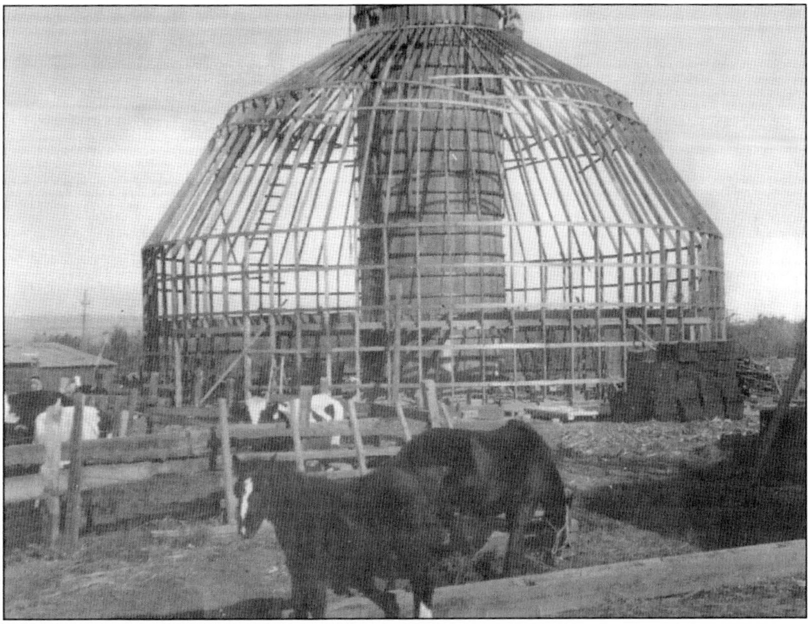

The Marble Barn, as it is known today, was built between 1912 and 1916 by S.D. Cornell, who was also known for his championship corn (see page 40). The round barn form promoted by early-20th-century dairy scientists and "progressive" farmers held several advantages over traditional rectangular barns. It had a central silo, making the feeding stations arranged around it easier to fill, and the single outside alley made for easier cleaning. It was also said that it could be built with a considerable savings in materials and could withstand wind and other stresses better. The disadvantages were its complexity of construction, clearly illustrated above, and its inability to expand. The popularity of the round form was short-lived. In 1986, when the barn and the surrounding farm complex were inventoried for inclusion in the National Register of Historic Places, there were less than a dozen round barns left in Washington. The well-preserved condition of the Marble Barn in 1986 (below) helped it qualify for the National Register in 1987.

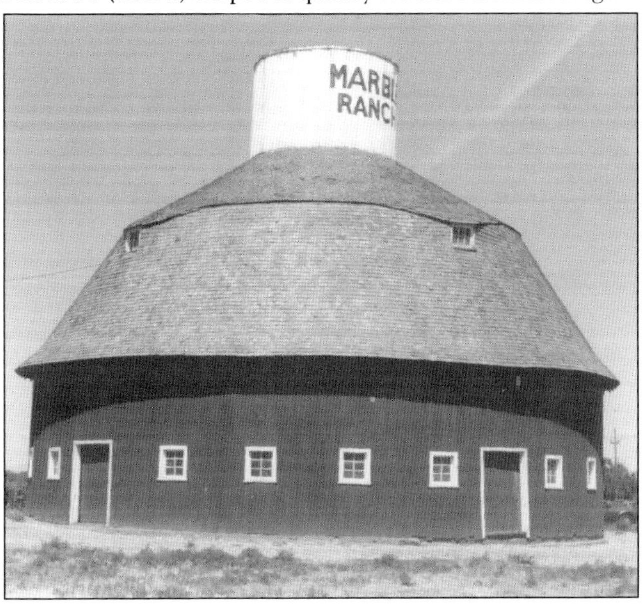

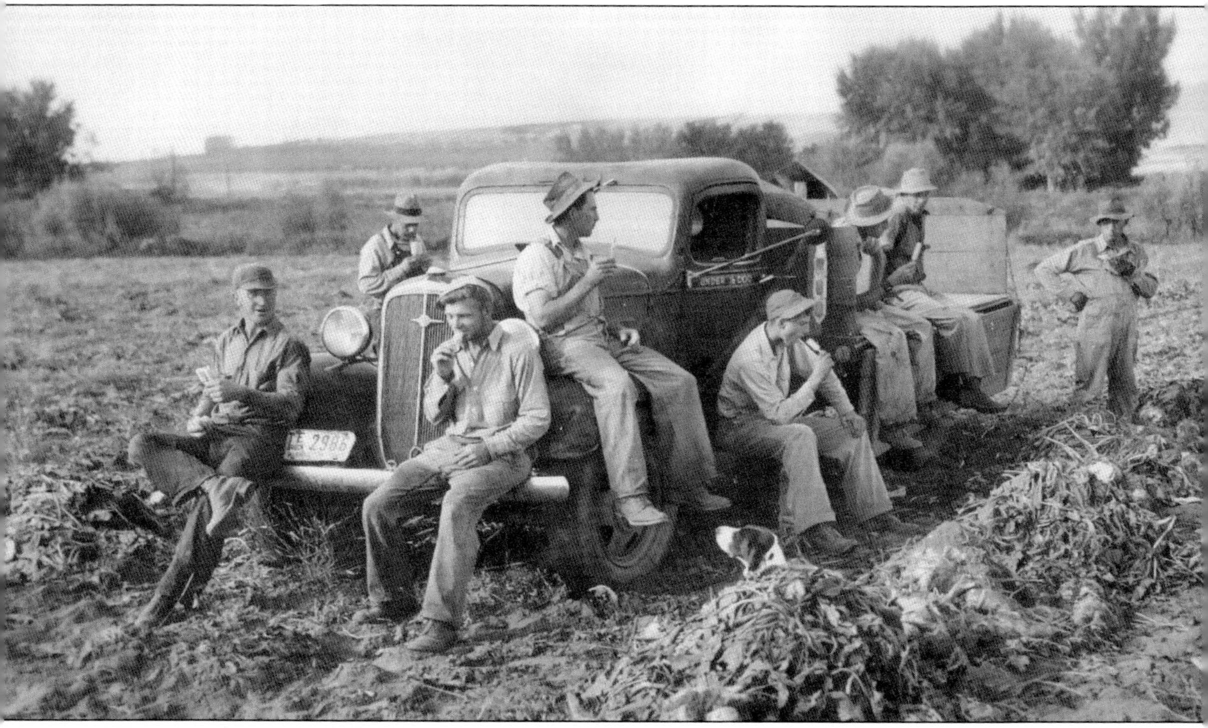

"Time out for pop sickels" is the caption on the back of this photograph, taken on October 20, 1942. The dog at the feet of the man sitting on the fender seems to be wondering where his is. Washington State produced a record-breaking crop of sugar beets in 1942, as the country was forced to lessen its dependence on meat during World War II.

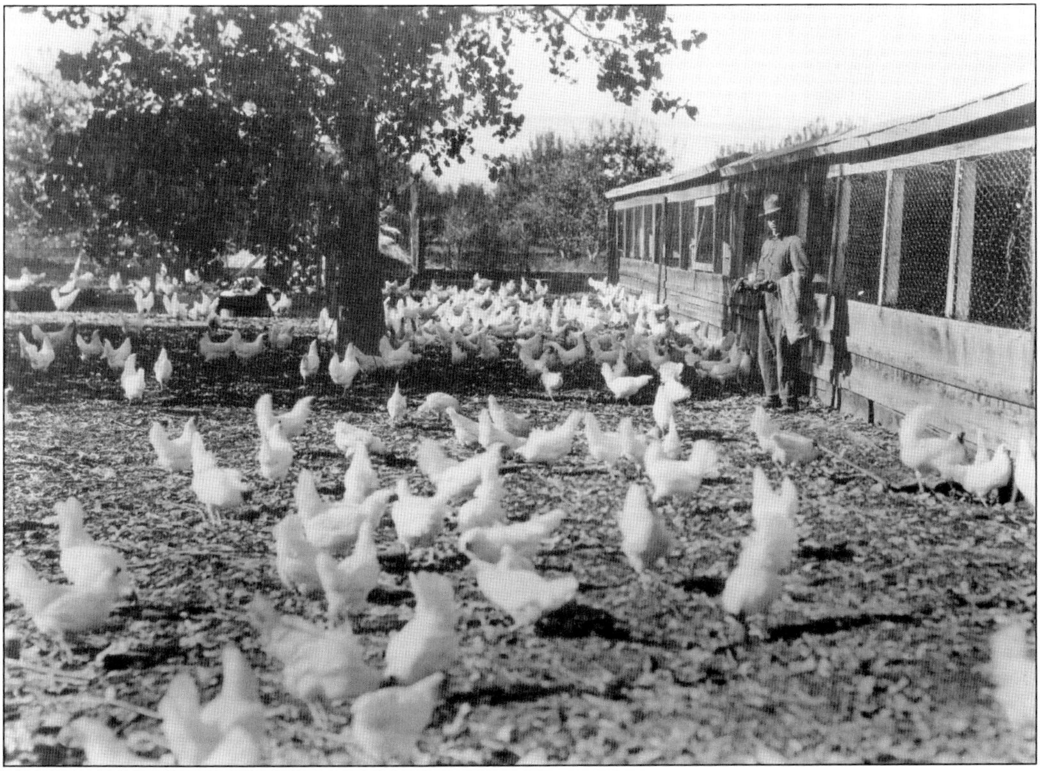

Shown here is the chicken yard at the R.D. Inman ranch. Before 1910, most chickens were raised for their eggs, with chicken served only occasionally at Sunday dinner. Ice-cooled railcars made long-distance shipping possible, and large-scale family chicken farms were profitable by the 1930s.

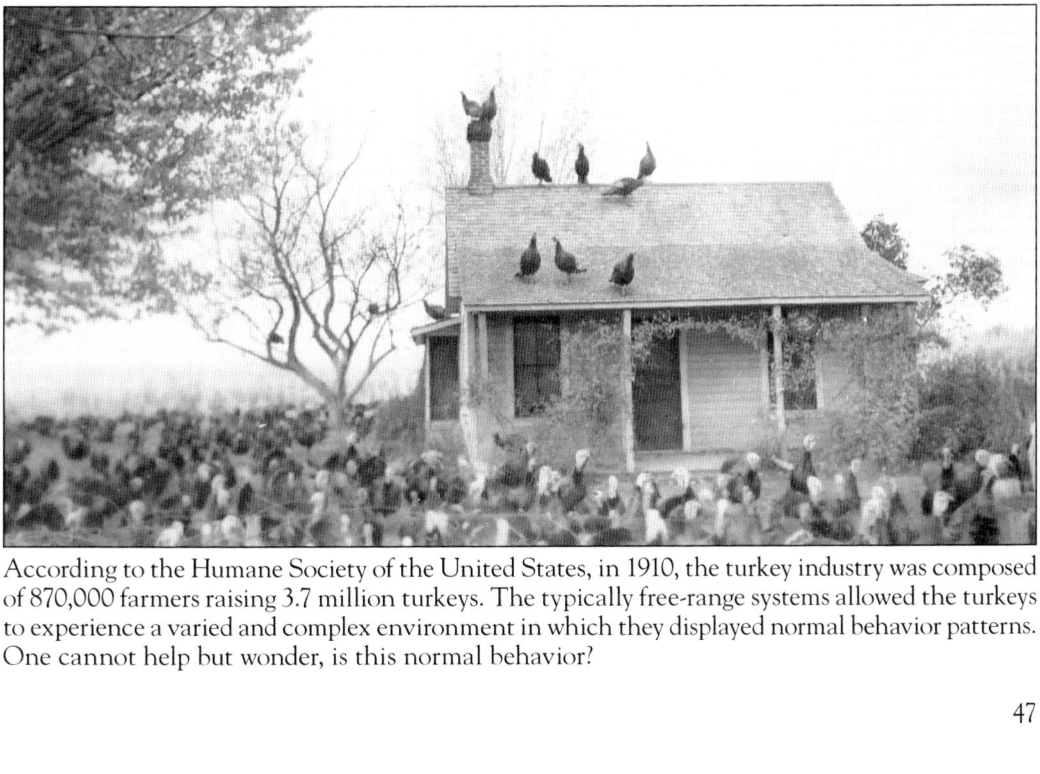

According to the Humane Society of the United States, in 1910, the turkey industry was composed of 870,000 farmers raising 3.7 million turkeys. The typically free-range systems allowed the turkeys to experience a varied and complex environment in which they displayed normal behavior patterns. One cannot help but wonder, is this normal behavior?

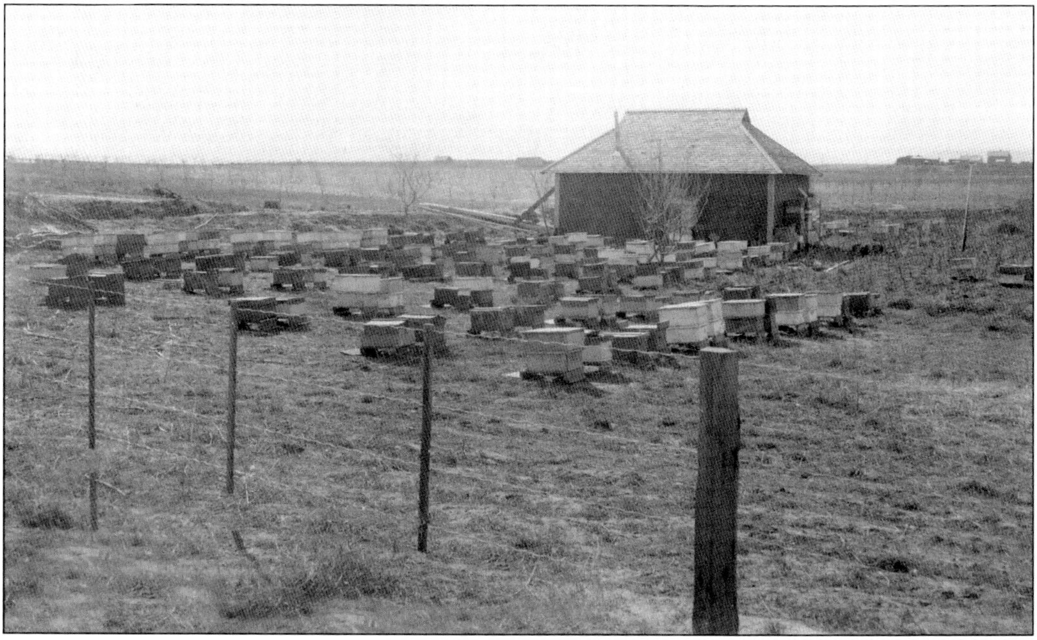

The Alex Kukyenall bee yard, seen here, was located west of Grandview. Another bee yard maintained by C.W. Sager held 125 colonies of bees and produced 25 tons of honey in a seven-year period. A hive took up four square feet of land and required very little labor, which made beekeeping highly profitable in proportion to the farmer's efforts.

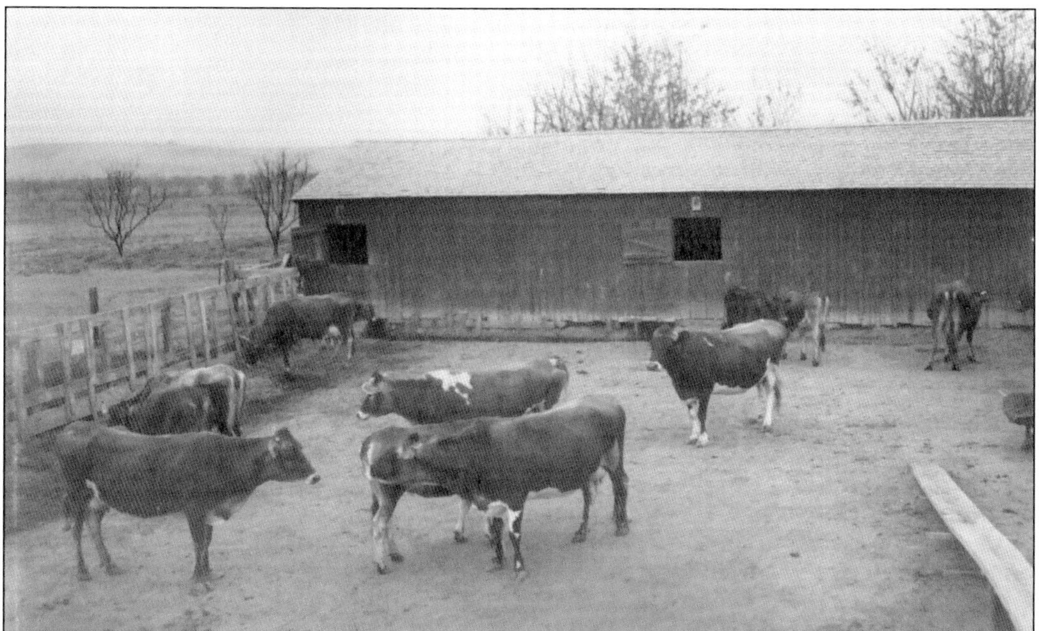

Irrigated country is always good for dairies. Milk cows in the Grandview area netted their owners between $85 and $100 per head each year. Shown here is a typical cow barn. Behind the barn can be seen barren fruit trees. A mature orchard is in the middle distance, and a single building is visible atop the hill on the left horizon.

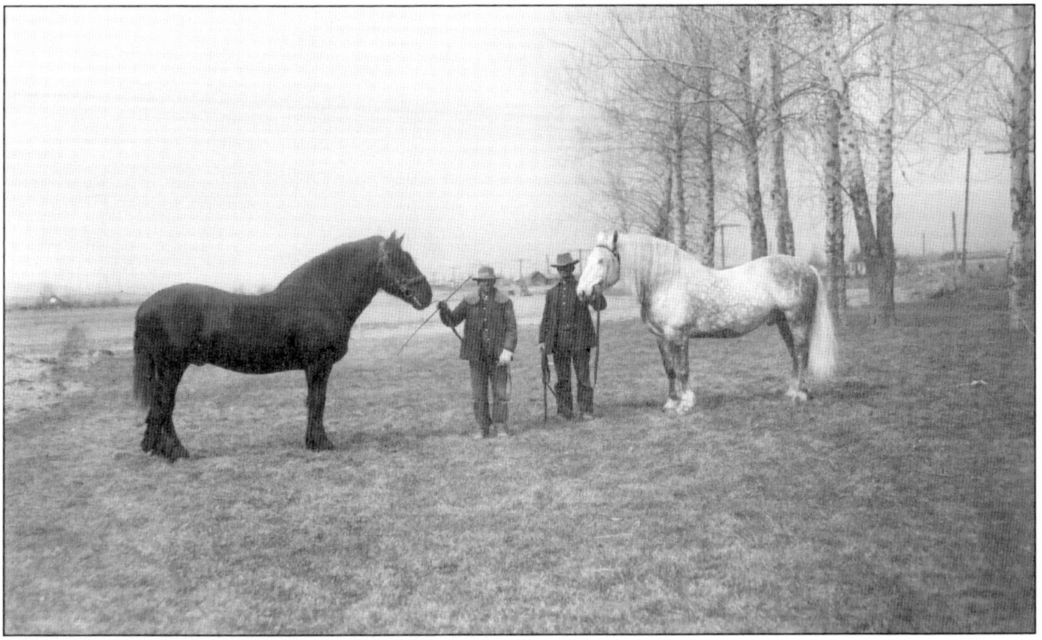

Heavy draft horses like the ones shown here were used by farmers throughout the Grandview area. These tall horses with muscular backs and powerful hindquarters were often raised for sale and were extremely profitable whether sold as two-year-olds or when they were ready to provide "horsepower" to their owners.

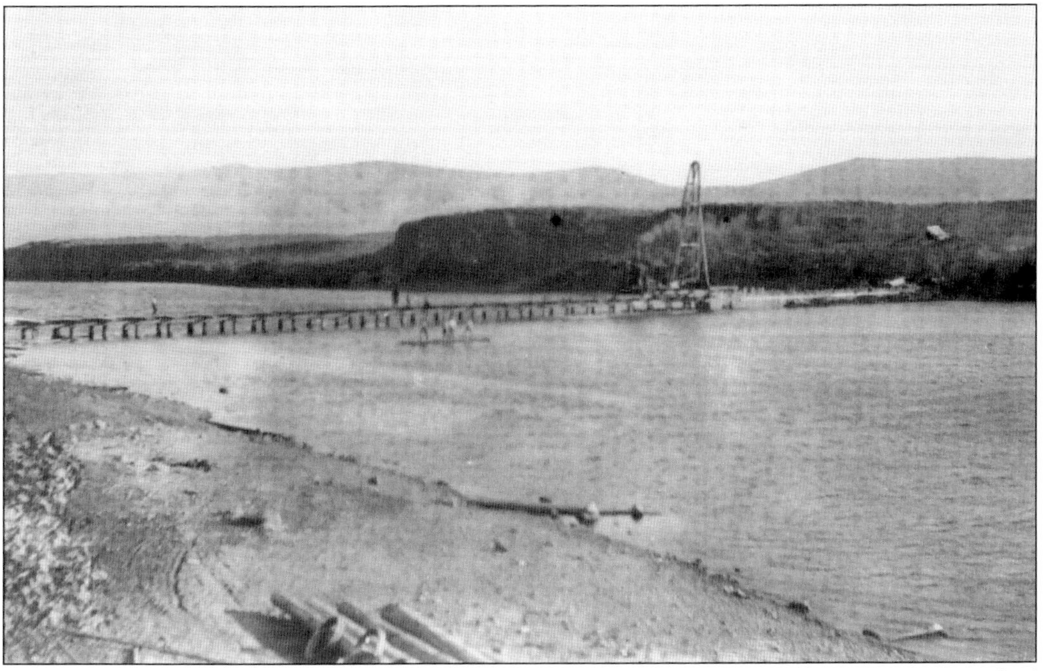

The Mabton Siphon, part of the Bureau of Reclamation's Sunnyside Division project, was laid under the Yakima River between Grandview and Mabton. The siphon is on a platform crossing the river. The south side of the Yakima River is bounded by cliffs made of Columbia River basalt. The Horse Heaven Hills are in the far background.

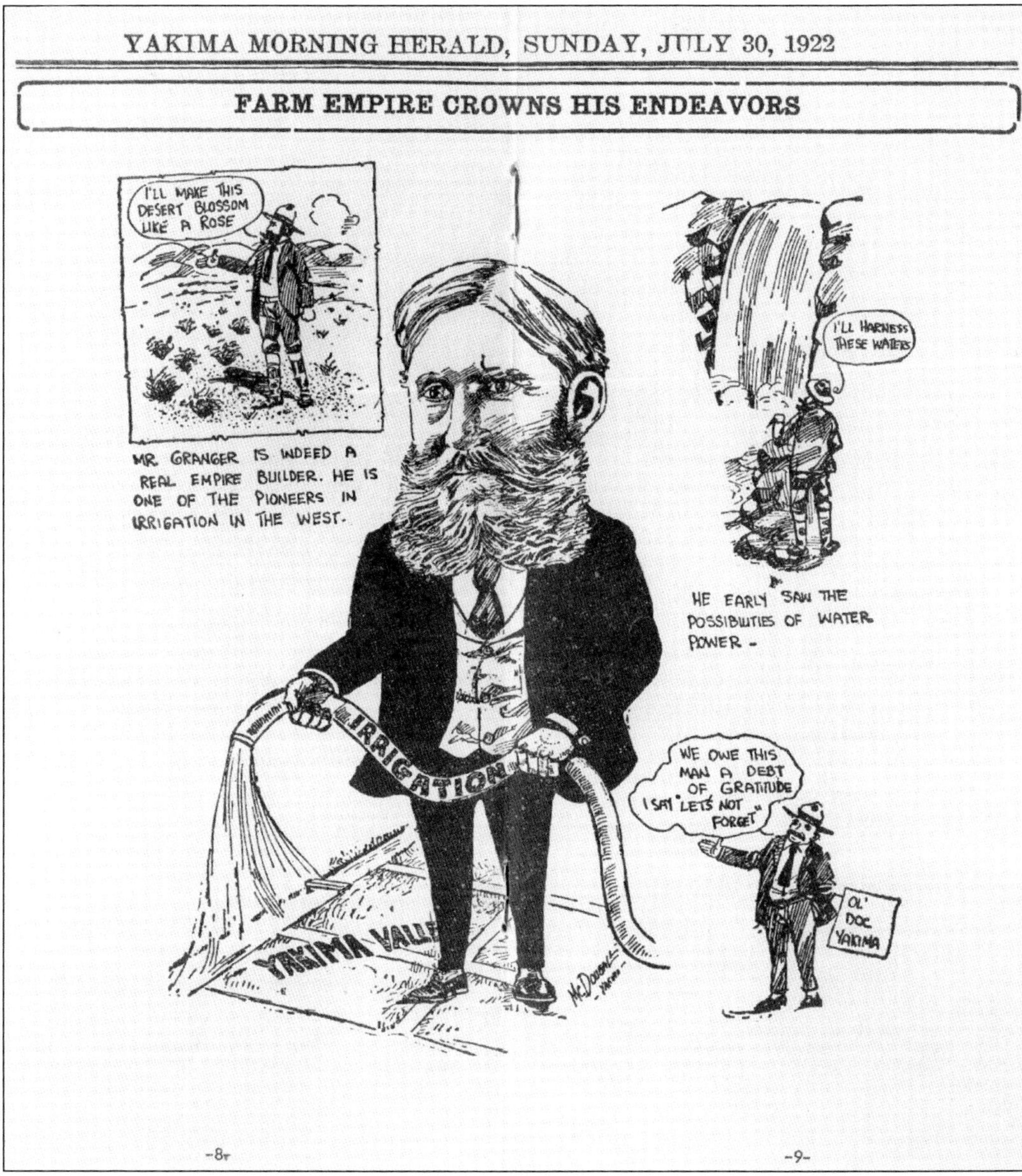

Walter N. Granger and a group of Minnesota investors organized the Yakima Land and Canal Company in late 1889, with Granger named as president. The company purchased land in the Yakima Valley from the Northern Pacific Railroad and created the Sunnyside Project, the valley's first commercial irrigation project. Granger died in Yakima in December 1930. This *Yakima Herald* cartoon was reprinted in the Walter N. Granger and Sunnyside Canal Memorial Fountain dedication brochure, dated June 17, 1961.

Three

Church, School, and Library

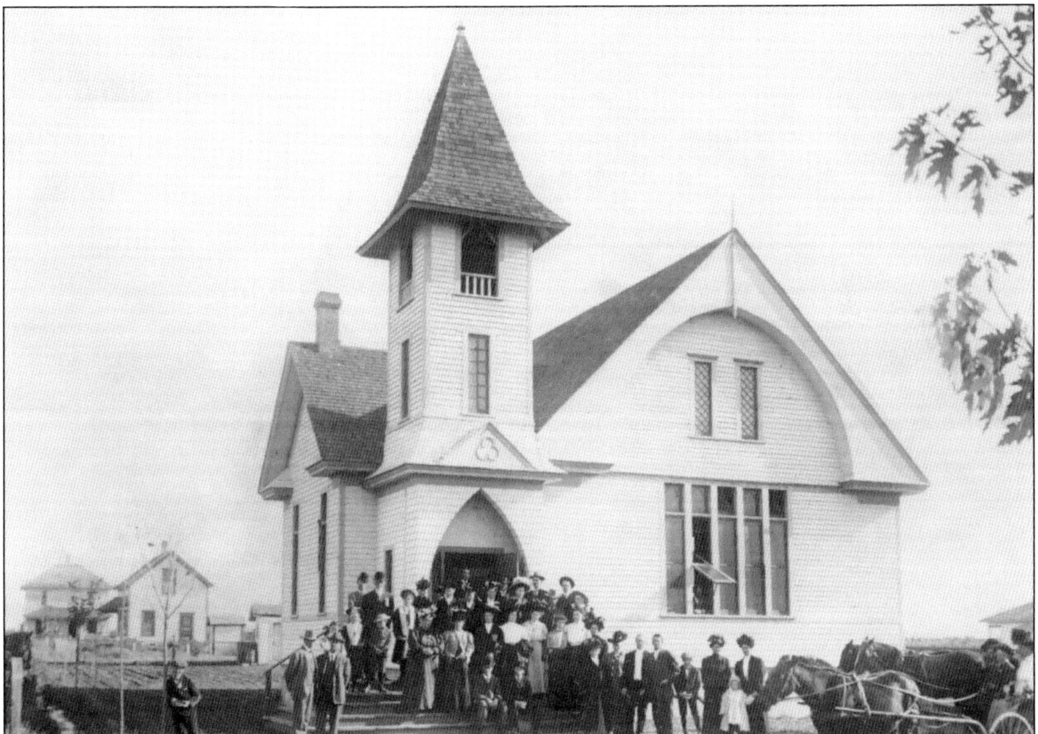

According to Bethany Presbyterian Church's session minute book, "About May 1st, 1903, Rev. Rollin E. Blackman of Sunnyside began to preach regularly every two weeks at the Euclid schoolhouse . . . Upon Sunday, December 20, 1903, a Presbyterian Church was organized at the Euclid schoolhouse by Rev. Thompson and Blackman. This church was afterward named *The Bethany Presbyterian Church.*" The one-room church was built in 1905.

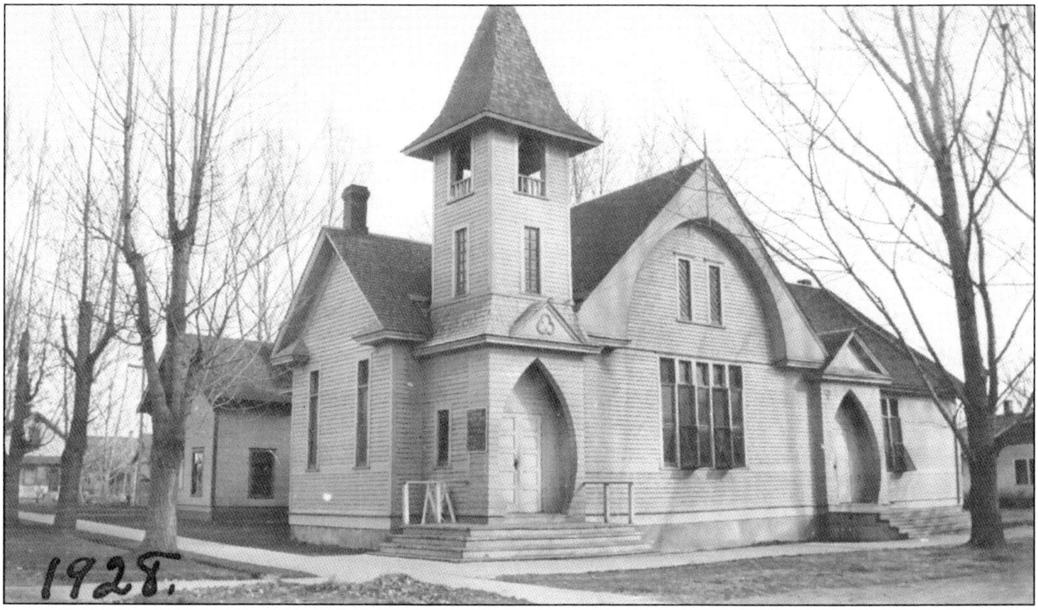

In the spring of 1908, parishioners moved the Bethany Presbyterian Church into town to the corner of what are now Birch and East Second Streets. Using jacks, they lifted the building onto large beams functioning as skids. The skids were lifted onto logrollers, and the building was pulled slowly forward using a one-horse windless winch. The mover and his wife lived in the building during the several months it took to accomplish the move.

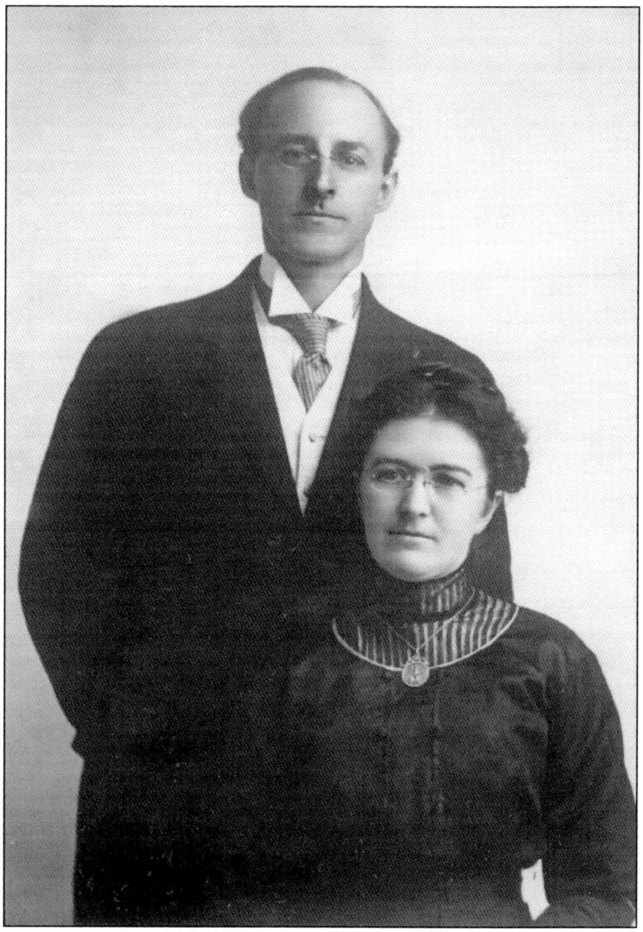

Rev. William Lindsey Killian was the first minister in Grandview. He and his wife, Edith (Depp), of Pennsylvania, were the first couple married in the new Bethany Presbyterian Church. Reverend Killian served the congregation until March 1912. Membership in the church increased from 47 to 183 during his ministry.

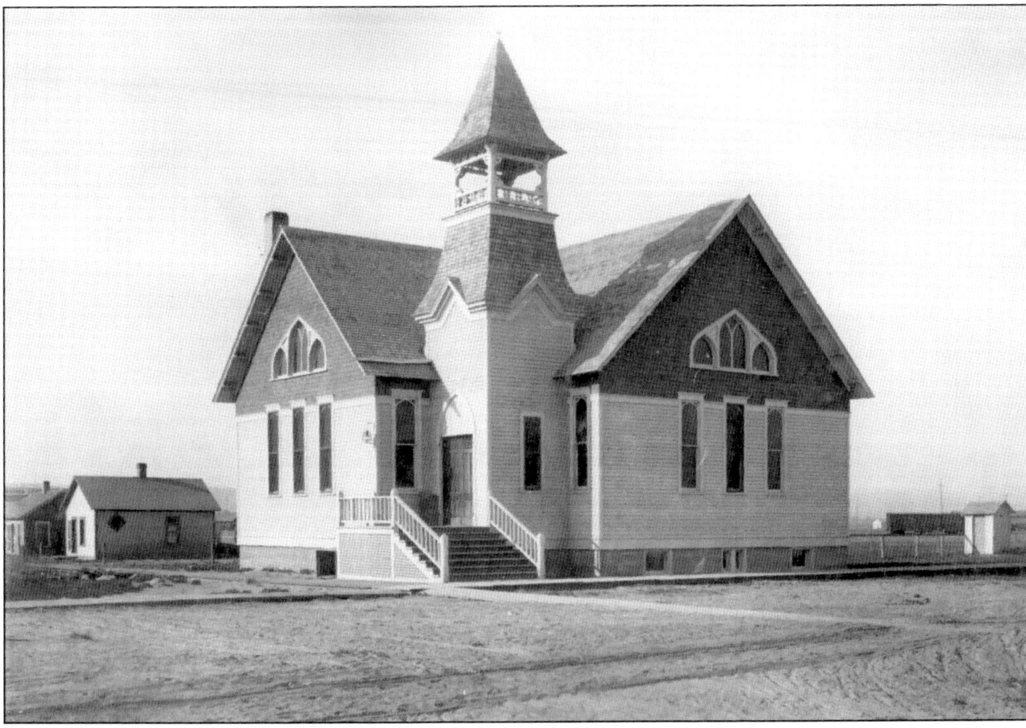

The members of Free Methodist Church held their first regular services in the Euclid schoolhouse with Pastor John E. Williams of Prosser, but the parishioners had to wait until 1908 before they had their own building. By 1909, they built the church shown here at the corner of Avenue A and East Third Street. In the fall of 1920, they added Wesleyan Hall west of the church.

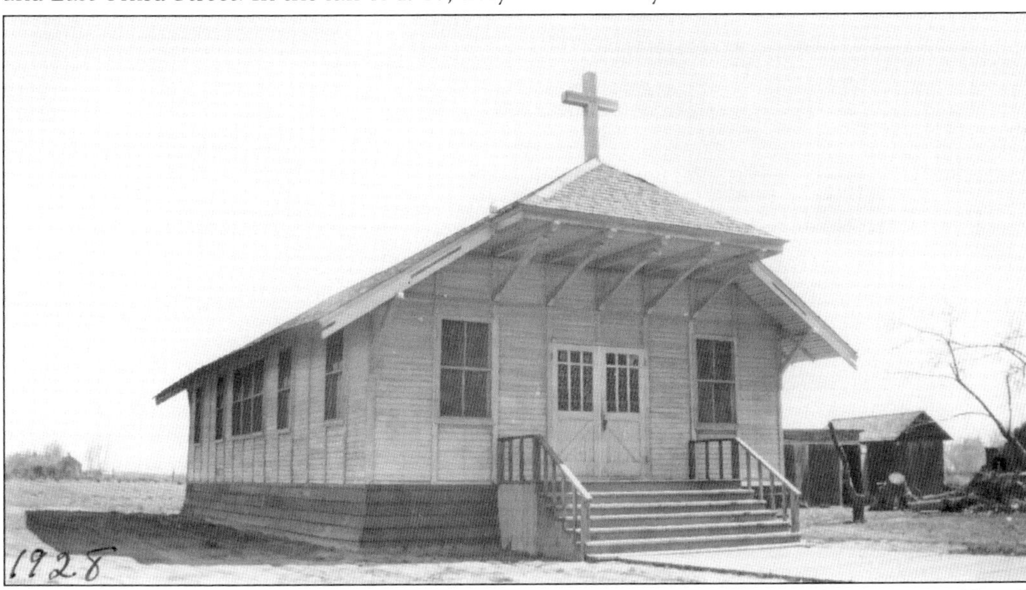

Built in 1918, Grandview's first Catholic church was dedicated as the Blessed Sacrament Church on December 8, 1919. Early in 1927, the building was moved to East Avenue C. Before they had their own church, parishioners celebrated Mass in the E.O. Keck Building on Division Street with Pastor E.T. McCarthy presiding.

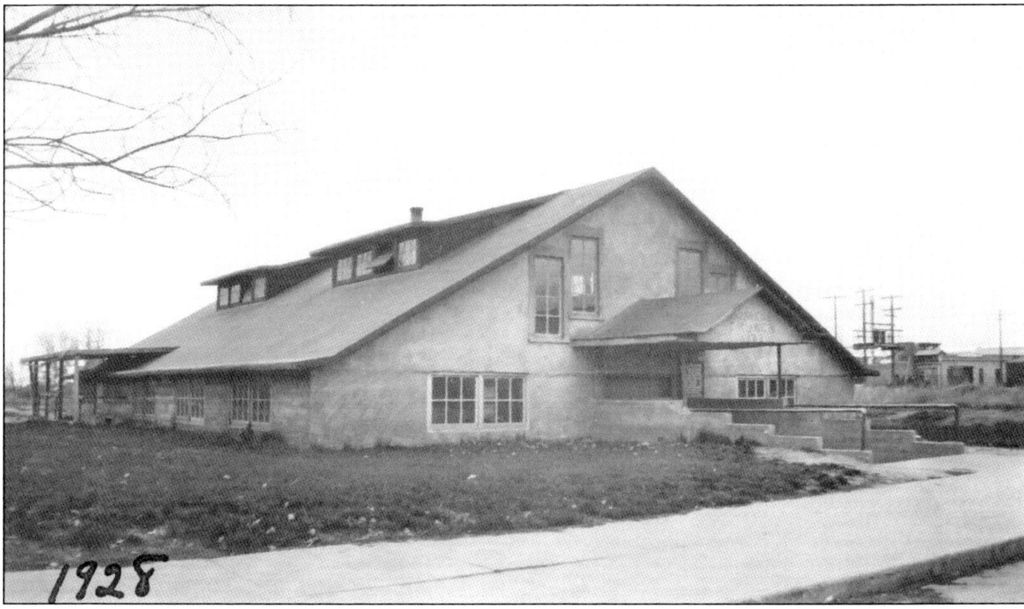

Under the direction of Will H. Neary, the district superintendant from Spokane, the First Nazarene Church welcomed church members for the first time on September 25, 1921, with Rev. John Anglis presiding. In 1923, the congregation moved to a larger building at the northwest corner of Division and East Third Streets.

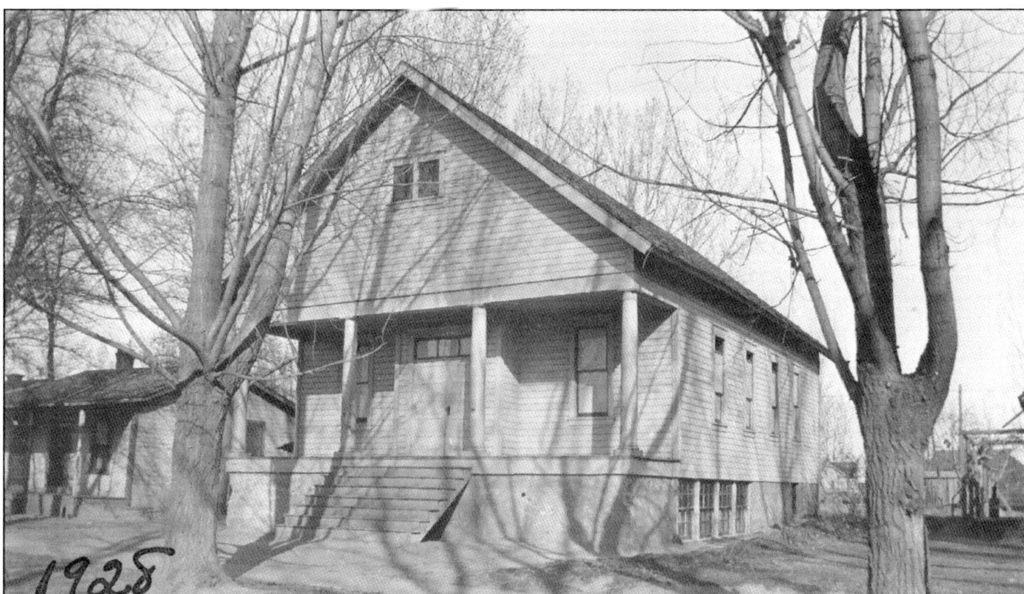

W.H. Thurston organized the first Seventh-day Adventist church in Grandview on May 24, 1919, with Jasper Evans elected as the church's local elder. The members of the Seventh-day Adventist Church purchased this building, located on Avenue A, from the Christian church.

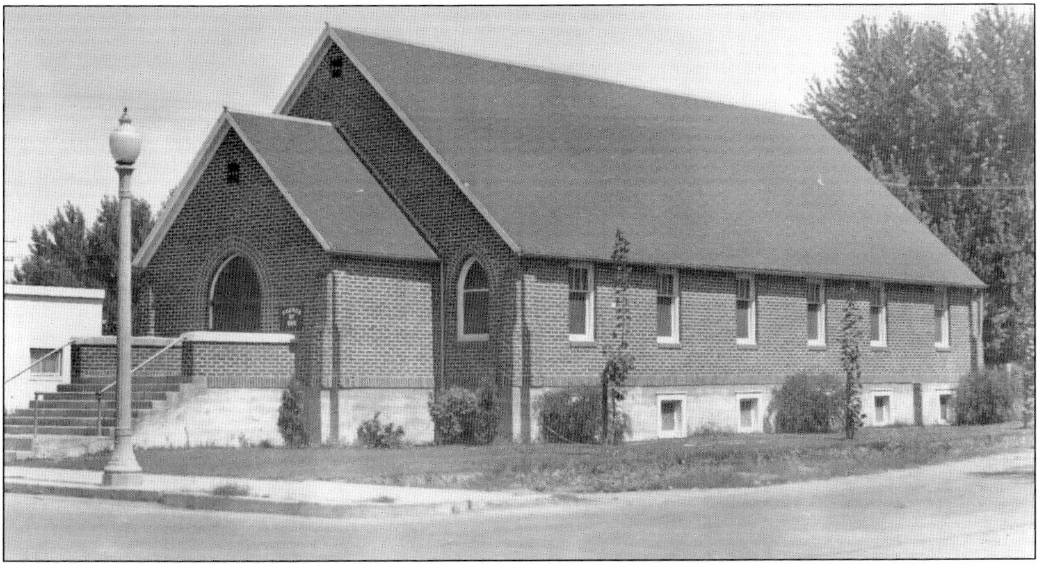

With a congregation of 60, the Grandview Community Church of God organized with superintendent Melvin Bishop on July 4, 1926. In 1927, R.W. May received the calling to serve as pastor. The church building shown here, on the northeast corner of Division and Third Streets, was dedicated in 1938.

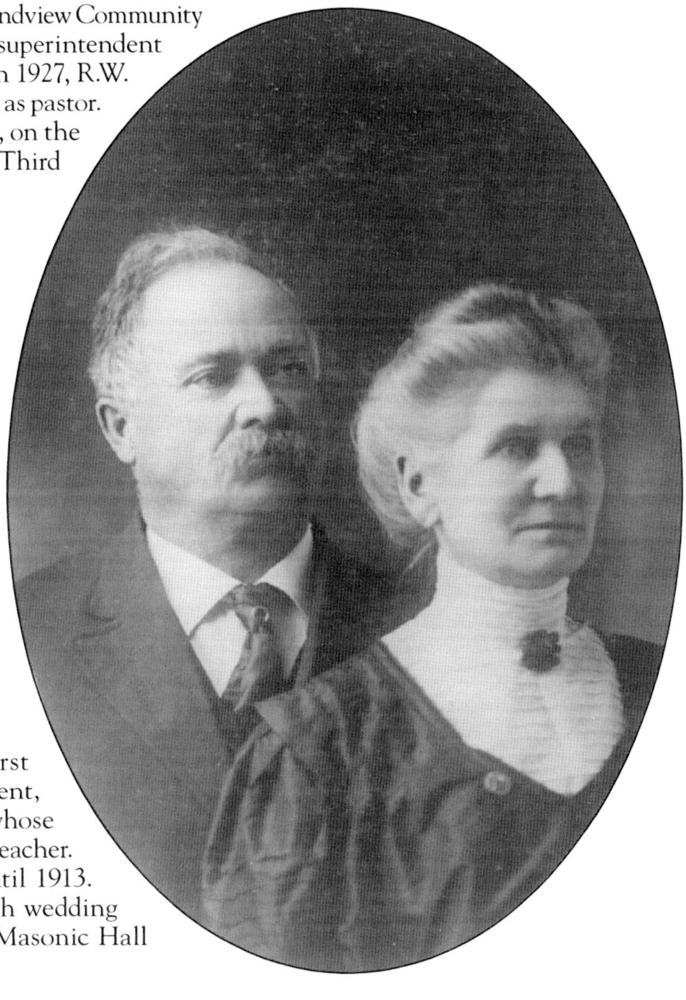

Frank G. Bennett was the first Grandview school superintendent, elected in 1908, and his wife, whose name has been lost, was an early teacher. Bennett was superintendent until 1913. The couple celebrated their 50th wedding anniversary at the Grandview Masonic Hall on December 22, 1931.

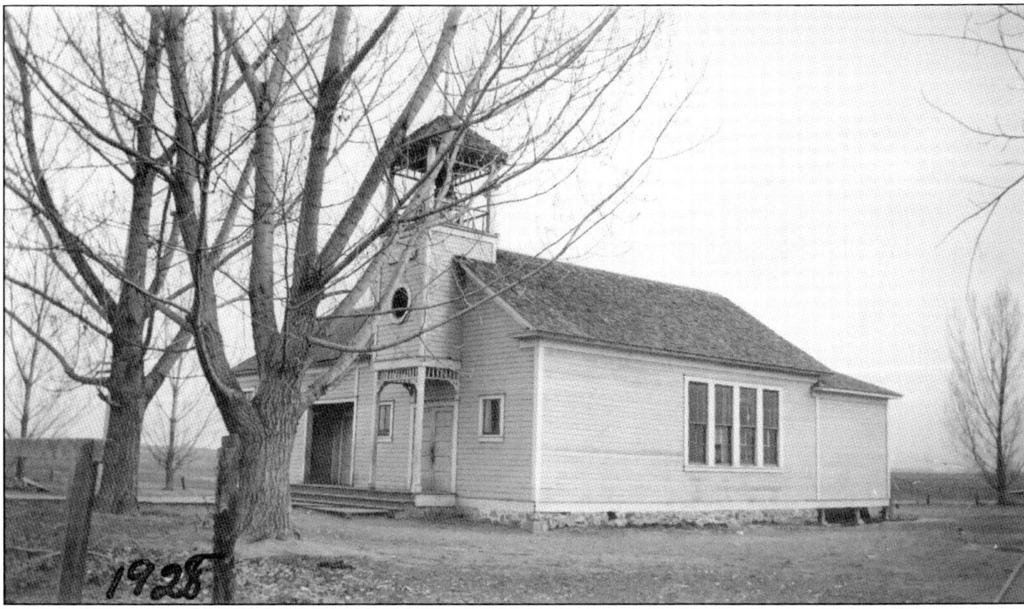

In 1903, the children of the district were called to classes at the Bethany School by the pleasant sounds coming from the bell tower. The new school, built just south of the Robert L. Mains farm, was "midway of the north line of Section 15, near the railway crossing" according to the caption on the original photograph.

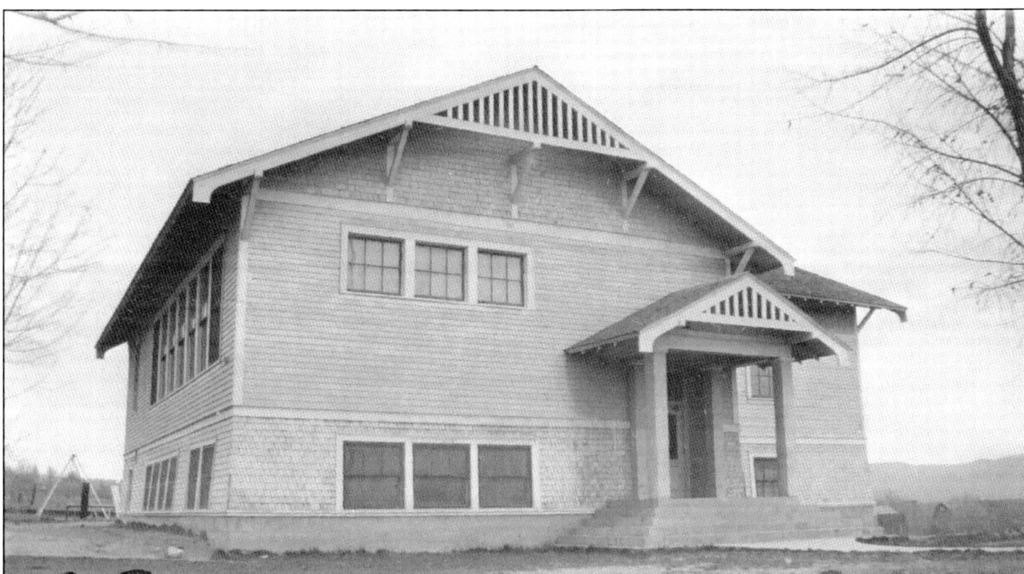

Built at the corner of Euclid Street and Mountainview Road, the second Euclid School began receiving students in 1914. In 1894, a small group of children had held classes in an old deserted shack. A Mr. Plumb had taught classes three months a year at a salary of $50 per month. A list of school supplies included 12 double desks, a 3-foot-by-10-foot cloth blackboard, and a dictionary.

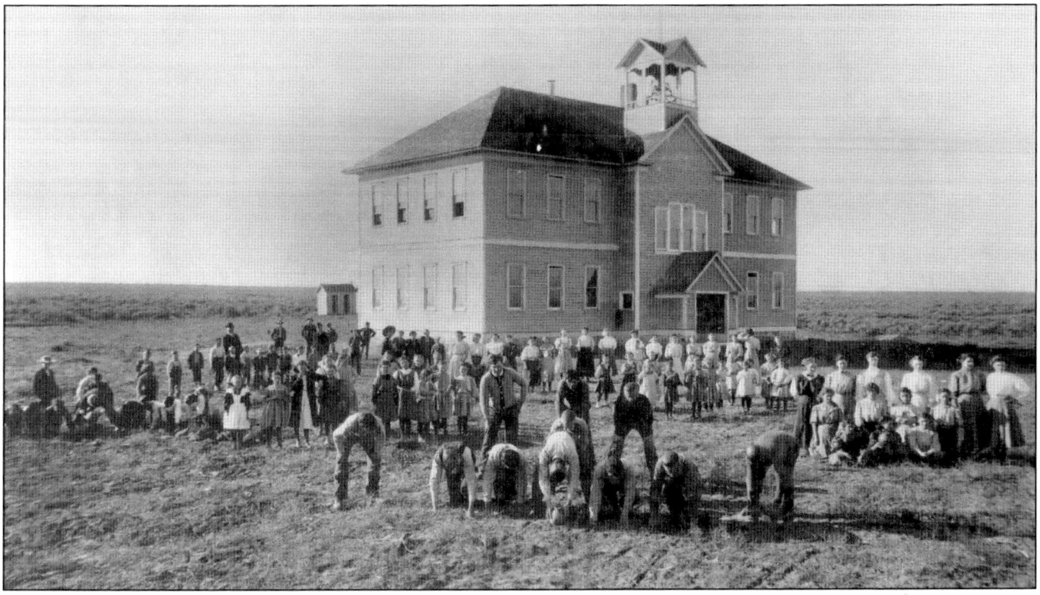

Above, students and staff at the Old Central School gathered for a photograph in the schoolyard, with the football team front and center. Construction of the school, in Block G of West Second Street, began in the fall of 1906 and finished in 1907. Almost immediately, the community realized the building was not large enough to serve the needs of the children of the recently consolidated Bethany and Euclid districts. Additional construction doubled the size of the building by 1909. Originally intended as a high school, the school also held grade-school classes for the younger students. The photograph below shows a Maypole dance during a Community Days celebration. As often happens to wooden structures, the school burned down in August 1924, requiring the students' return to the old Euclid School until the completion of the New Central School in 1925.

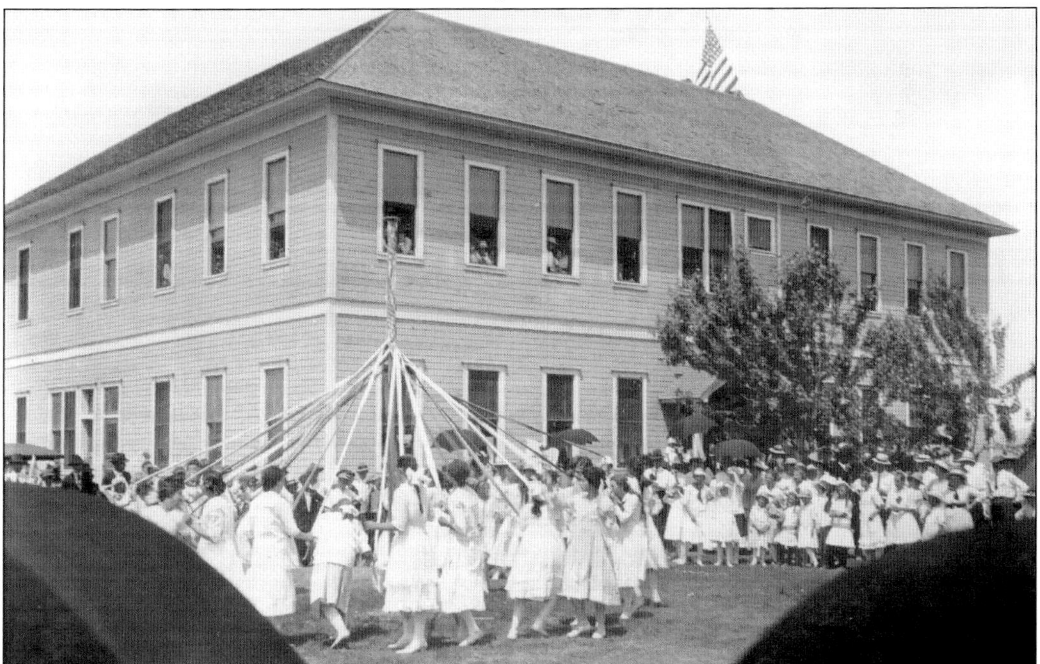

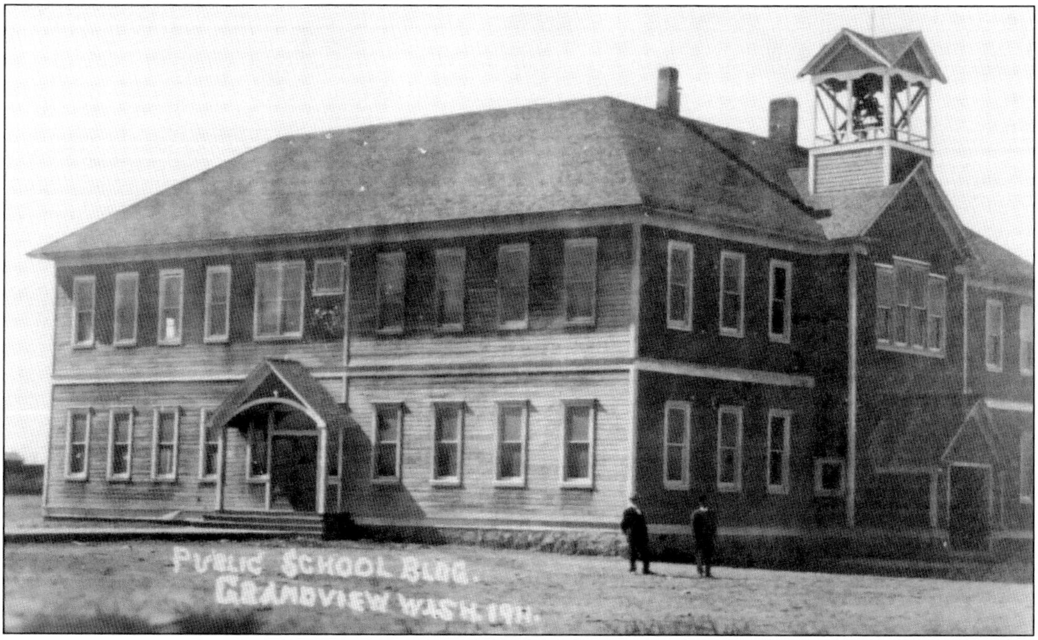

During the 1919–1920 school year, School District No. 81 included Central School, Euclid School, and Bethany School. Superintendent A.C. Kellogg and high school principal D.M. Callaghan led a team of 15 teachers. The teachers at Central School were Harriet Stow, Mildred Robinson, Rosa N. Drow, H. Kenneth Ramnley, William H. Boyd, Anna Corney, Ethel Baker, Helen Davidson, Luella E. Squibb, Nellie Beck, and Mary Grant. Jennie Rose and Jean Ewart were the teachers at Euclid School, and Amelia Johnson and Clara Behnke taught at Bethany School.

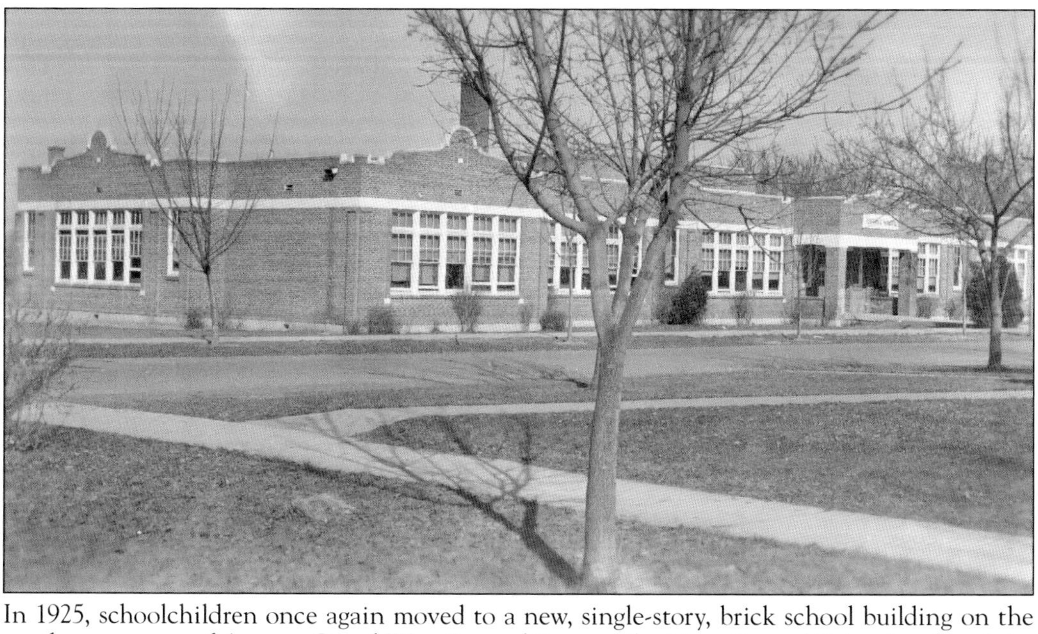

In 1925, schoolchildren once again moved to a new, single-story, brick school building on the northwest corner of Avenue G and West Second Street. The New Central School replaced the Old Central School, which had been lost to fire the year before. Children attended school here until Harriet Thompson Grade School opened in 1949.

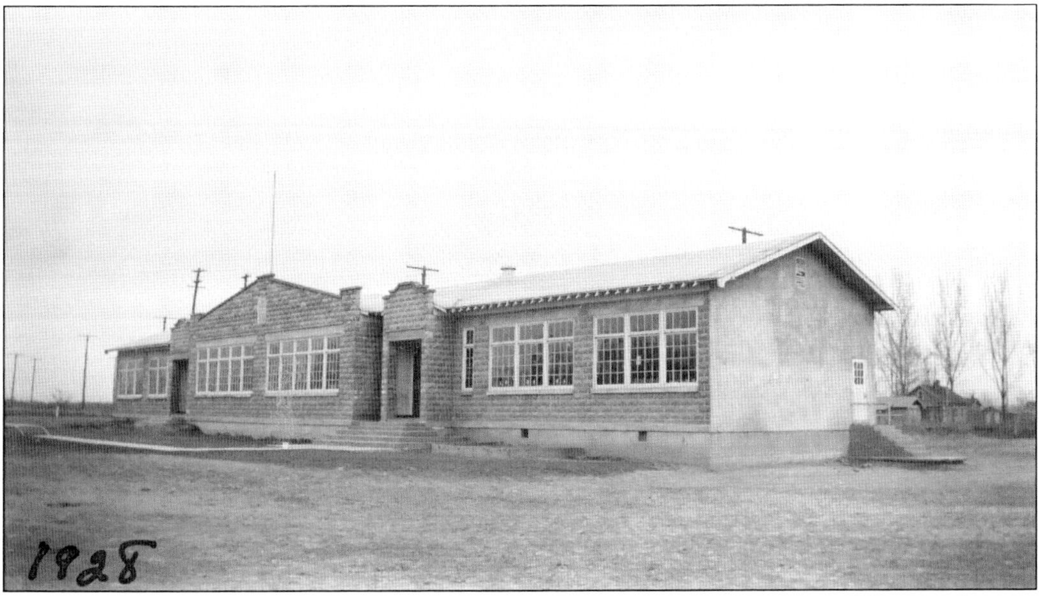

Lincoln Grade School was a cement-block school built in 1920 to serve the children on the east side of town. The school was located just north of the Oregon-Washington Railroad & Navigation Co. tracks on North Elm Street. The Seventh-day Adventist Church bought the building in 1940 for $750.

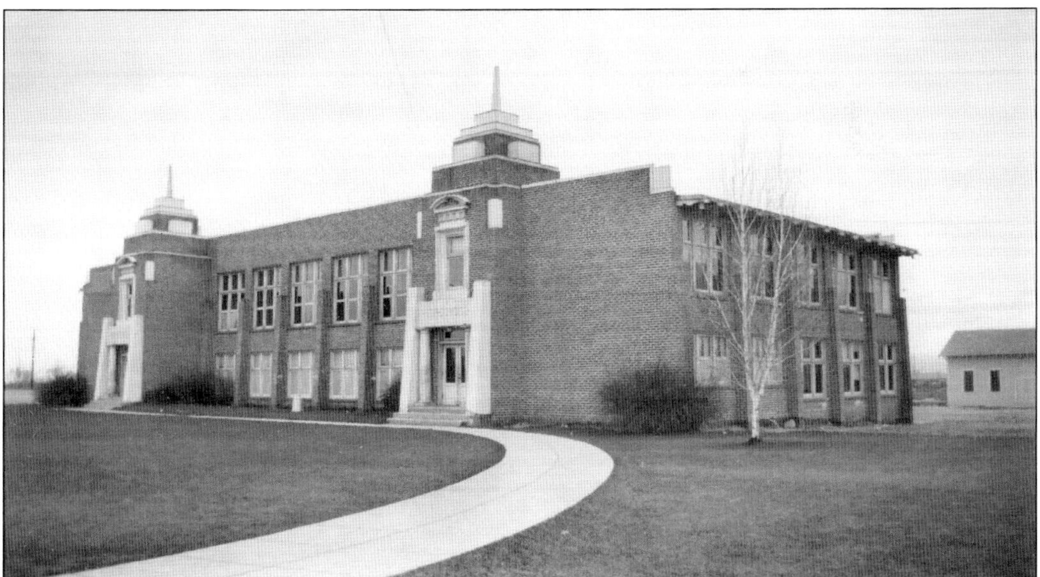

Located in Block G of West Second Street, this two-story brick high school relieved some of the overcrowding at the Old Central School when it opened in 1918. In November 1936, a $36,000 Works Progress Administration grant enabled the construction of yet another high school (following page), at a total cost of $90,000.

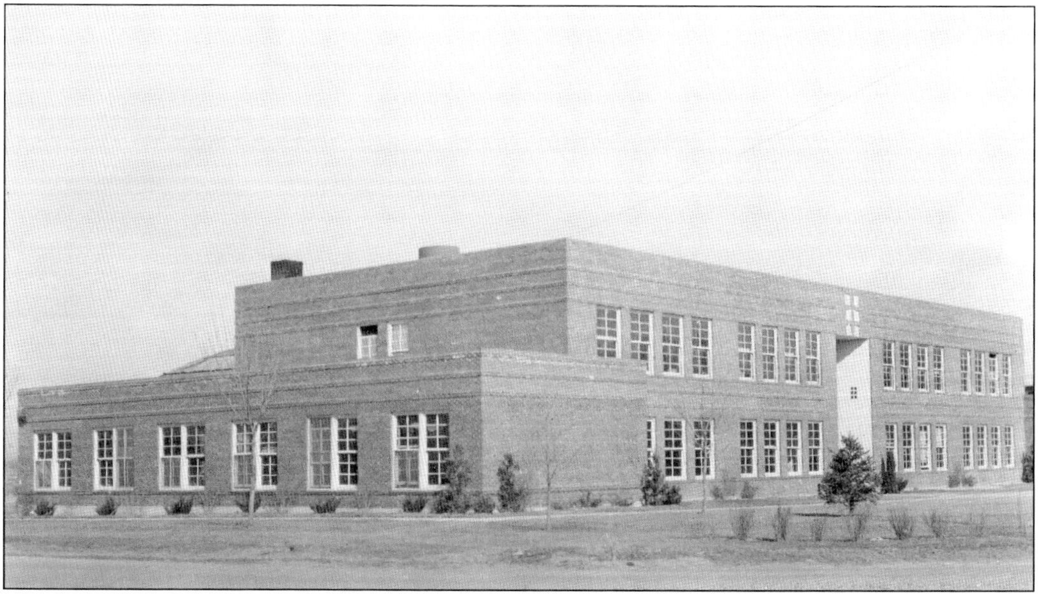

The new high school opened for classes in September 1937. Gov. Clarence D. Martin was the speaker of the evening at the dedication of the building, held on October 29. In 1948, the Atomic Energy Commission donated $56,000 for expansion and the loan of a school bus. Glass blocks and sculptured insets showing scholarly pursuits decorate the building's entry. The building is listed in the National Register of Historic Places.

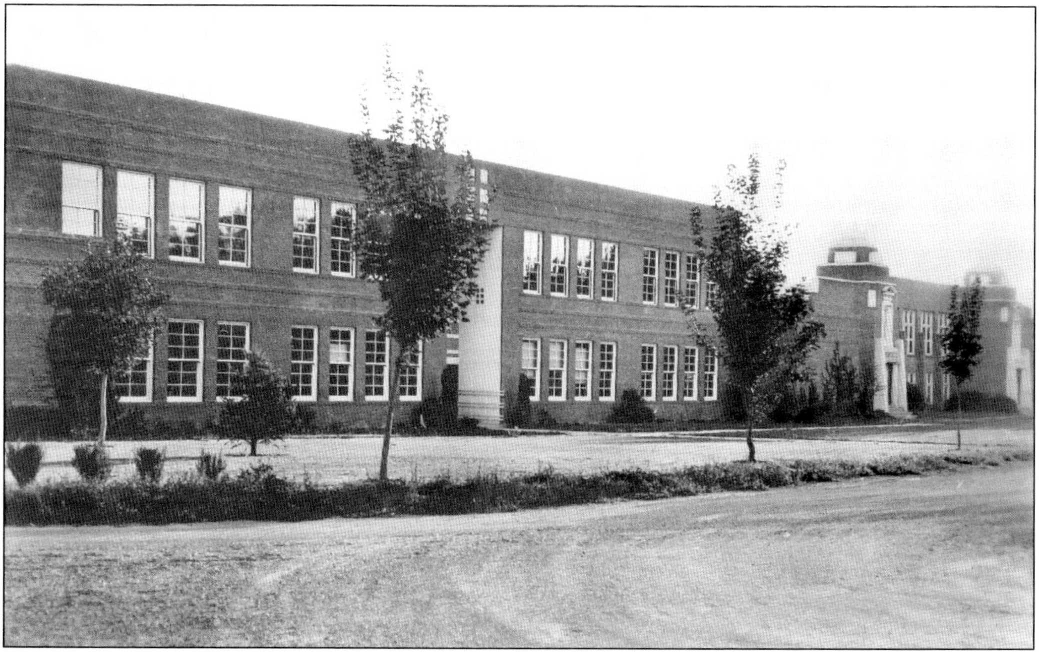

The tradition of recycling school buildings continued in the mid-1970s with the building of yet another new high school on West Second Street. Beginning in 1978 and continuing for over 20 years, McClure Elementary School used some of the space in the 1937 building, seen here, for classrooms. High school students once again roamed the halls in 2002, when the alternative Compass High School moved into the vacated ground-floor classrooms.

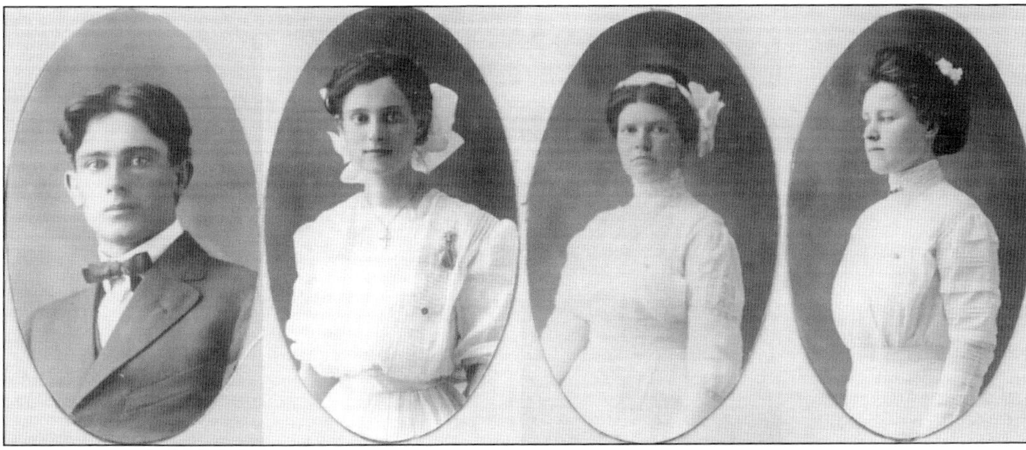

From left to right, Edward Mains, Urba Thomas, Ethel Melton, and Elizabeth Smith made up the first graduating class of Grandview High School in 1910. Mains, born on December 11, 1891, in Roslyn, Washington, was the son of Robert L. and Annie Mains. He became a successful farmer, eventually cultivating 78 acres of hay, corn, and potatoes. In 1916, he married Elizabeth B. Martyn, the daughter of David and Johan Martyn.

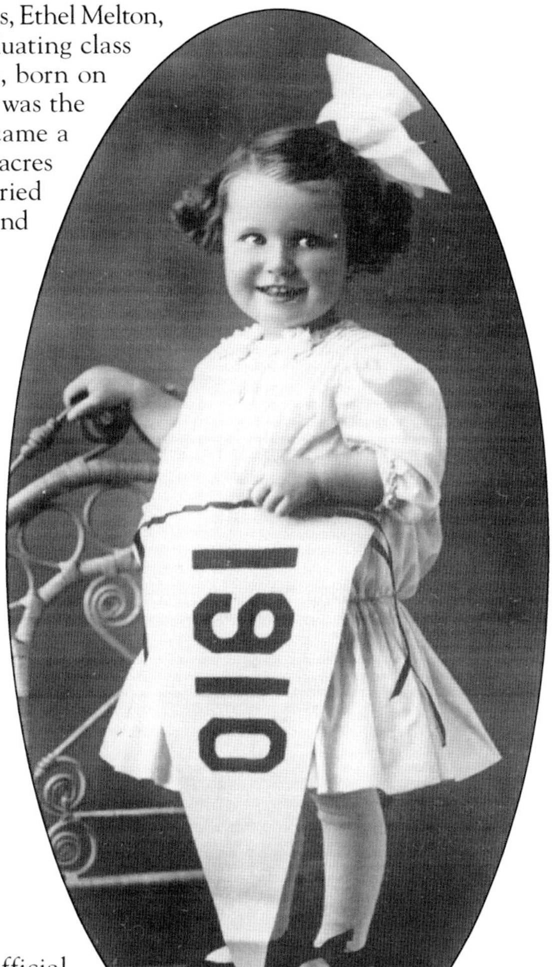

Long before the greyhound became the official Grandview High School mascot, high school classes chose their own mascots. Grandview's first graduating class chose Cornelia Merritt Hawn as the 1910 senior class mascot.

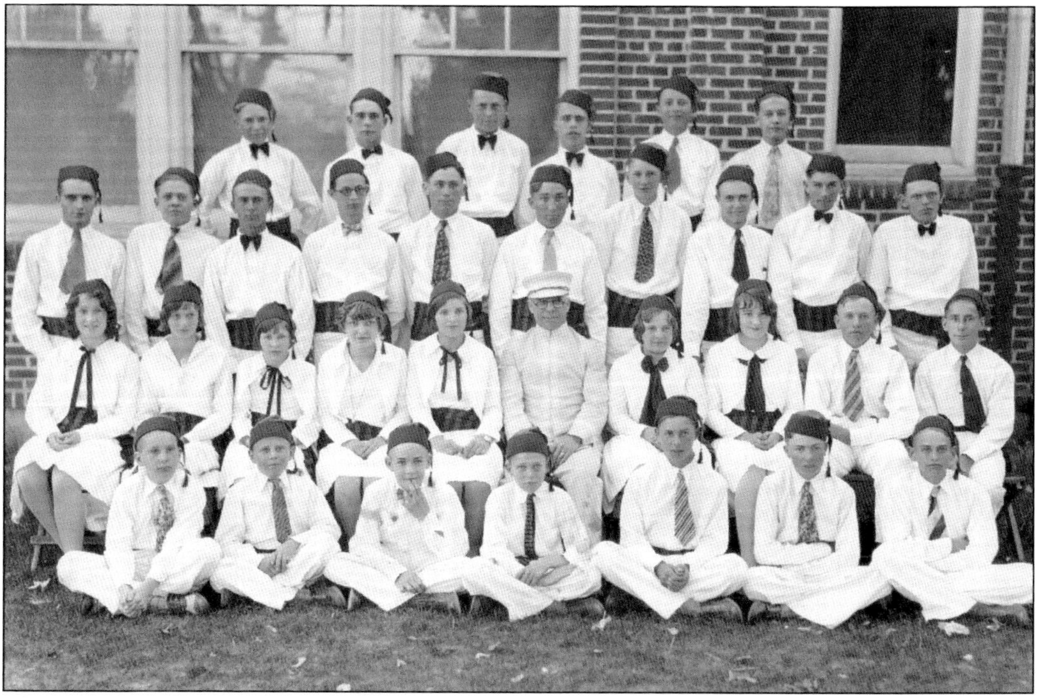

The Grandview Juvenile Band, shown in the 1930 photograph above, had members from Grandview and Mabton. From left to right are (first row) Bob Purdue, Paul Bridges, Glen Hufnail, Lawrence Faxe, Max Soot, Robert Cotter, and Robert Ashley; (second row) Mary Matheson, Ruth King Davis, Betty Soot Olmstead, Pauline Williams, Doris Soot, bandmaster/organizer Henry Hare, Margueryte Hare Mercer, Doris Fisher, Ralph Lyall, and Byron Young; (third row) Kenneth Eakin, Thomas Hare, Paul Neuenschwander, Lowell Rogers, Howard Killian, Pat Bugg, Norman King, Stanley Livingston, Miles Anderson, and Gordon Whiting; (fourth row) John Kiser, Lester Pope, George Ludwig, Lawrence Klock, Gardill Ehmer, and Homer Thiele. The photograph below shows the band during a 1928 parade on Division Street south of Second Street.

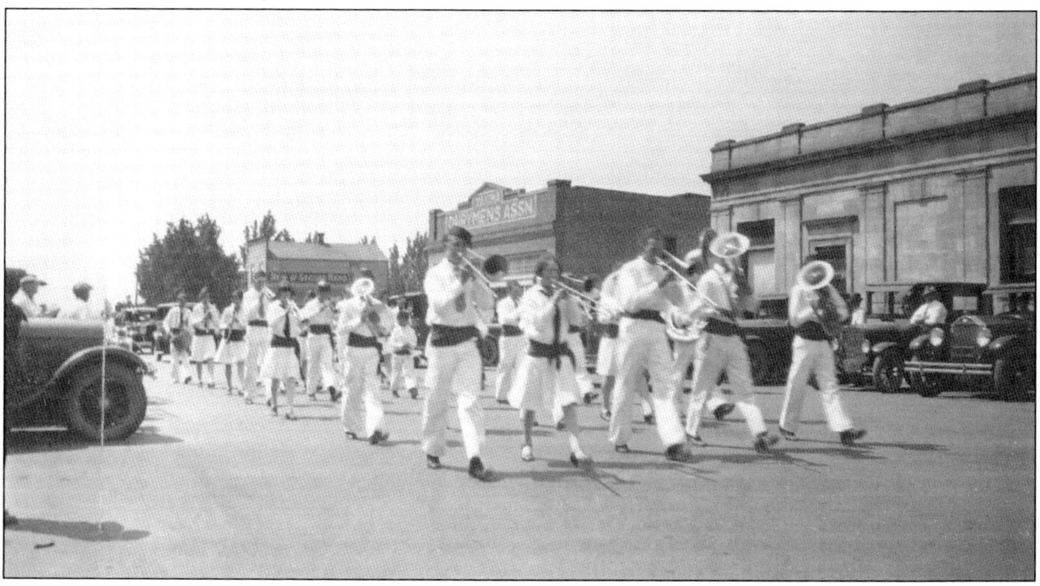

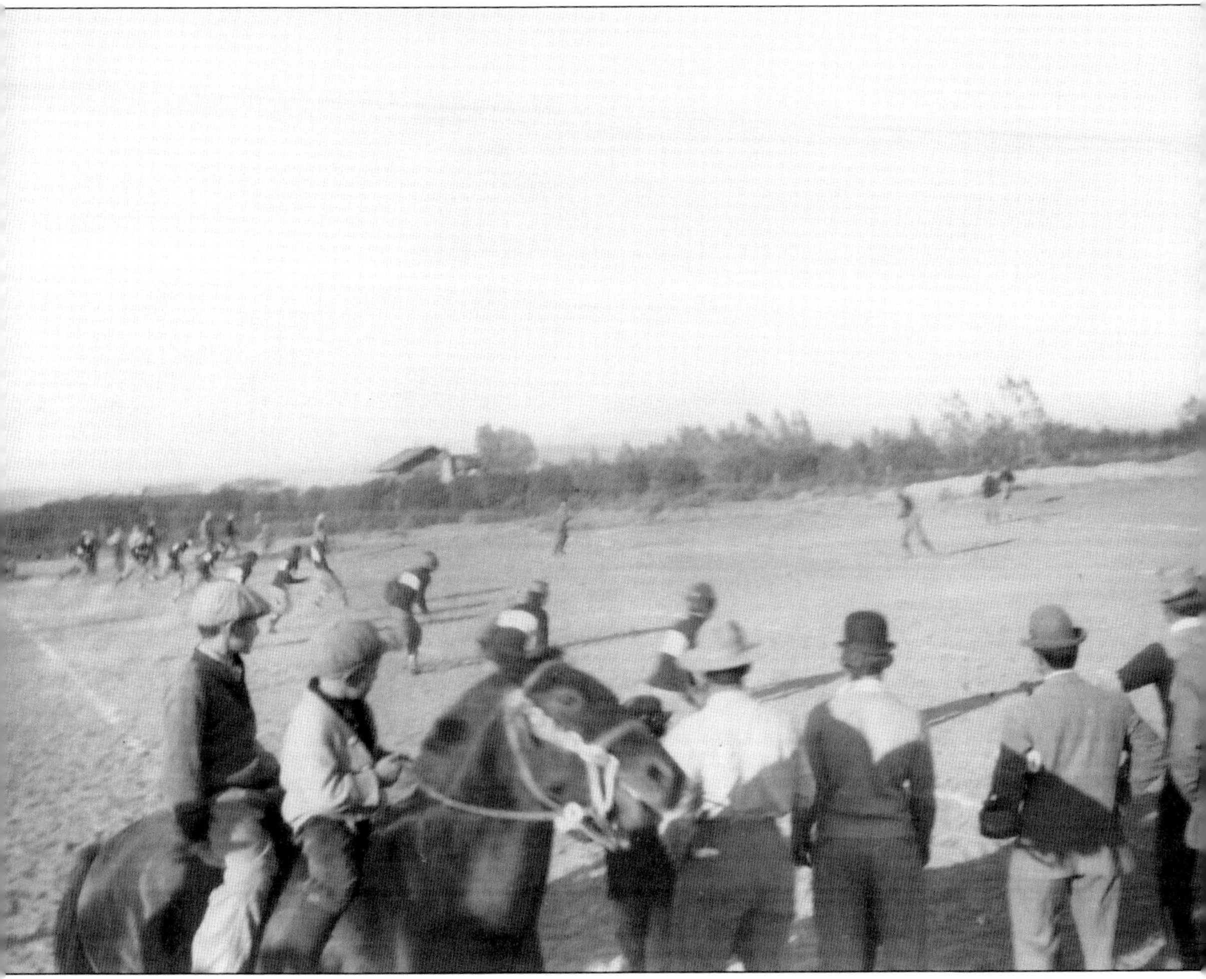

The Grandview High School football team was champion of the lower valley in the fall of 1930. They were defeated only once, in the season's first game, against their traditional rival, Sunnyside, by a score of 7-0. Vindication came during the last game of the season, when Grandview won the Lower Valley Championship with a 7-6 victory over Sunnyside, their first win over their rival in many years. One local player, Floyd Phelps, received acclaim throughout Yakima County for his outstanding play. On October 3, 1958, the 50th anniversary of the school having a football team, the Grandview Greyhounds once again challenged the Sunnyside Grizzlies, winning 13-7. Members of the 1908 team present were Edward Mains, Riley Williams, Roy Pettit, O.C. Gill, and Ben Gill.

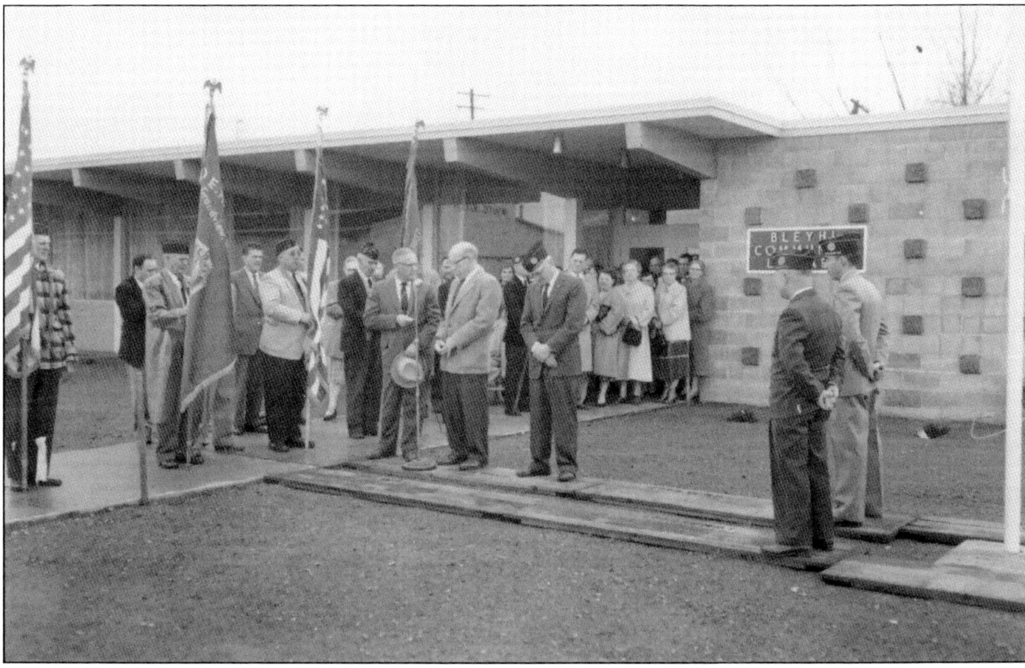

April 2, 1958, saw the dedication of the new Bleyhl Community Library, named for the Bleyhl brothers. Rev. Robert Griffith offered the invocation, and the members of the Grandview High School band provided the music. The Grandview Women's Club, assisted by the Business and Professional Women's Club, served refreshments at an open house held the previous day. Alex and Carl Bleyhl donated the 40-foot-by-80-foot building. Fixtures, furniture, and landscaping were provided by individuals, clubs, and service organizations. The total value of the library on its opening day was $80,000. In the first year, library patrons borrowed a total of 21,981 books and magazines, and the library was open four days a week.

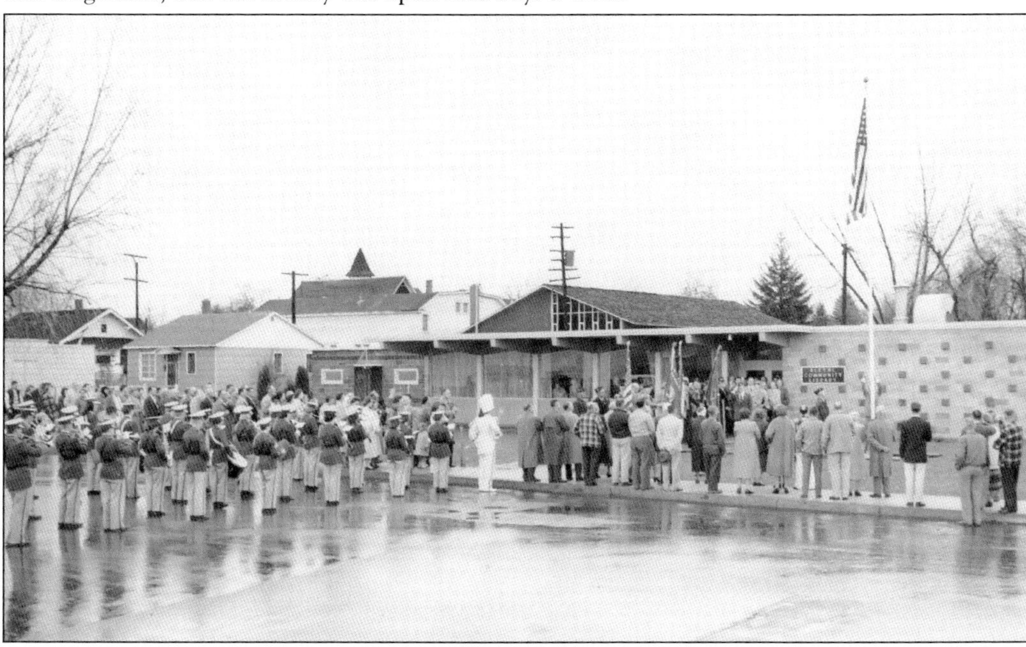

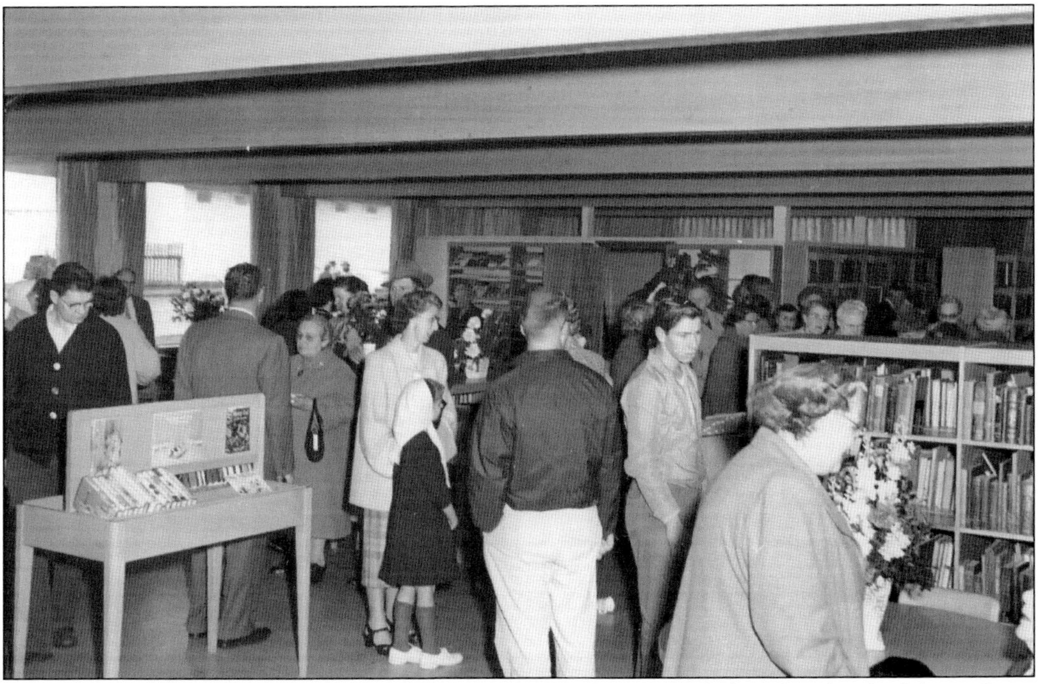

The April 10, 1958, library board minutes show that librarian Ethel Richards asked for and was granted a "well earned vacation of 3 weeks," and Joyce Scott and Betty Krogh, the two high school–aged employees, were "put in charge" during her absence.

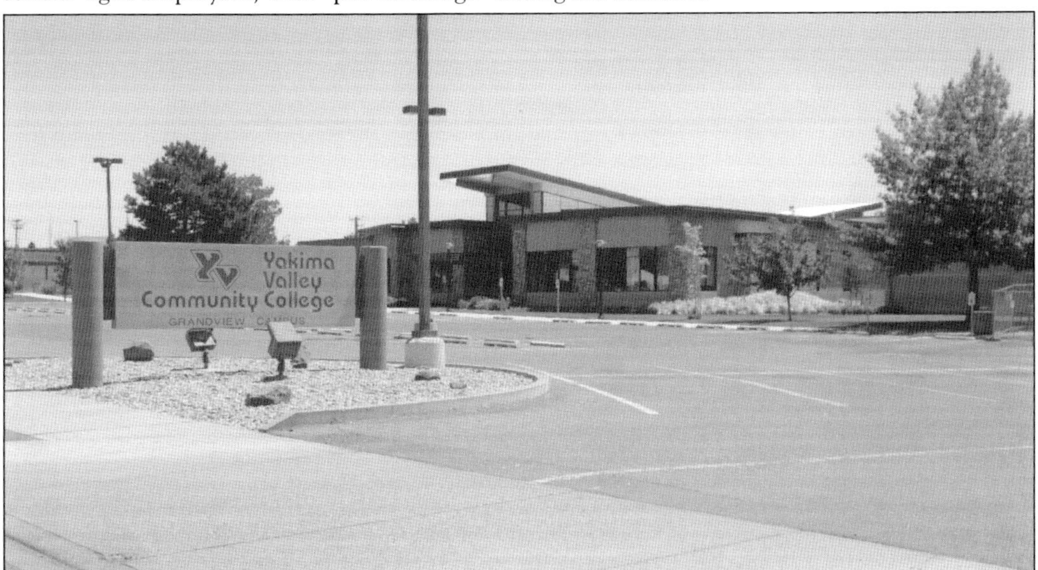

Grandview was one of 11 districts actively campaigning in 1963 to be chosen as a location for a community college. Success came in 1990 when Gov. Booth Gardner dedicated the Yakima Valley Community College (YVCC) Lower Valley Educational Center. In August 1994, the center's name was changed to YVCC Grandview Campus. The Tullar Annex, named in honor of Dr. Phil Tullar, the 14th president of YVCC, was completed in 1994. Another new wing, the Sewell Annex, named for Grandview city administrator Jim Sewell, was added in 2001.

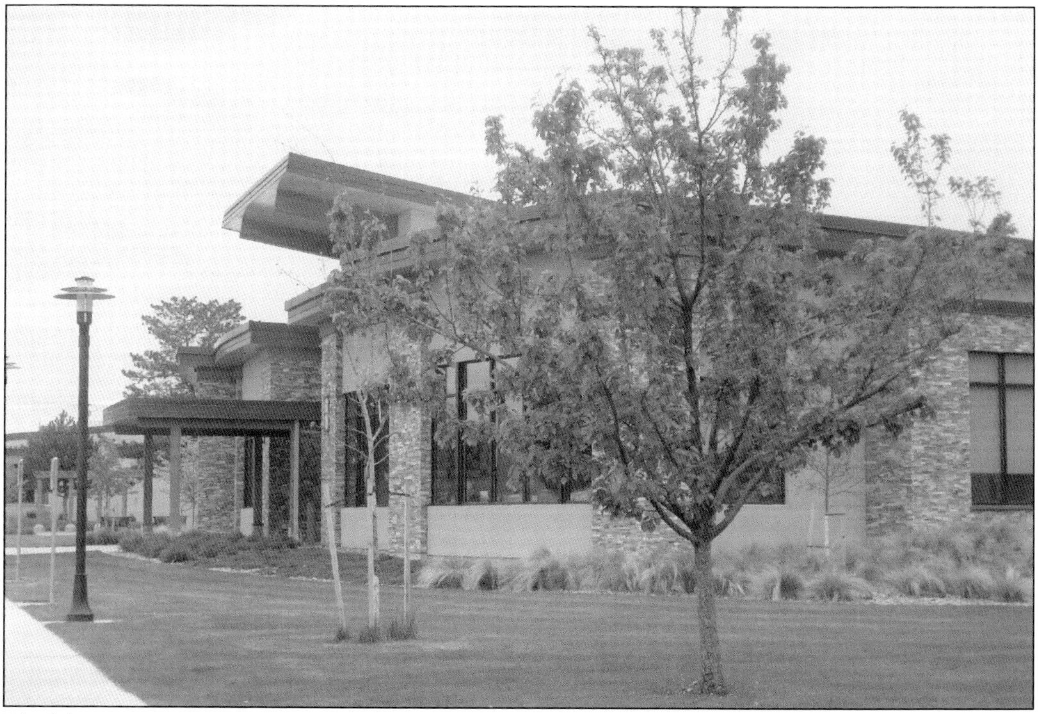

Bleyhl Community Library proudly served its patrons as the only independent library in Yakima County for over 55 years, but it outgrew its space. An idea considered for several years became real when the City of Grandview and Yakima Valley Community College came together once again to build a joint facility. The Grandview Library was dedicated in September 2011. Unusual in design, the library has two entrances, to emphasize its joint purpose. The north entrance (above) welcomes everyone, but its placement gives ready access to college students. The less formal southern entrance (below), on Second Street, offers easier access to families or those with mobility issues.

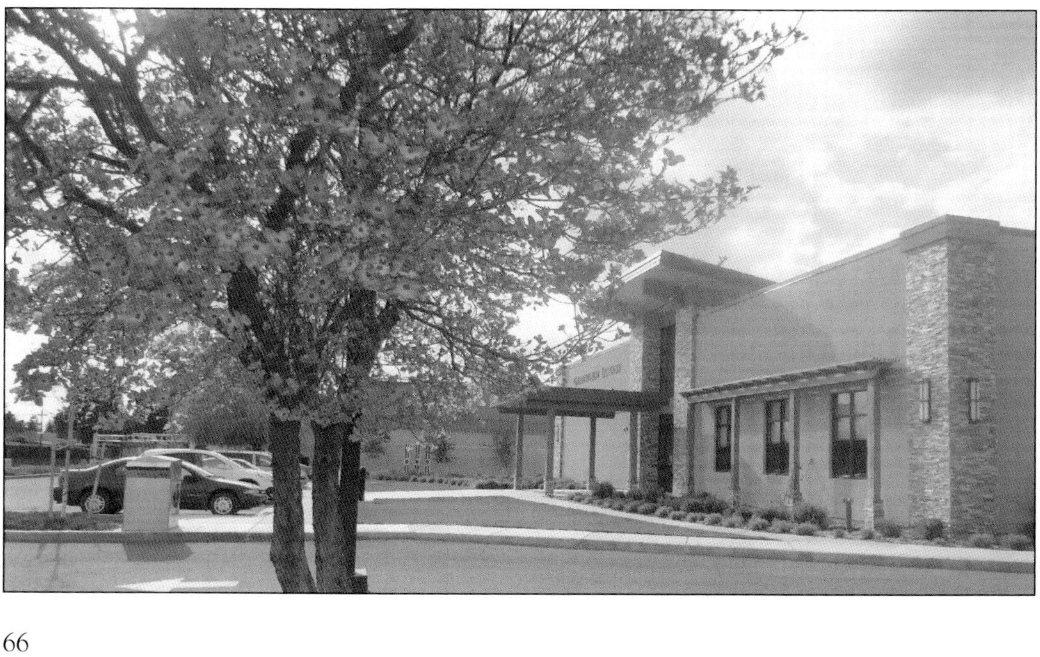

Four

BUSINESS, POLICE, AND FIRE

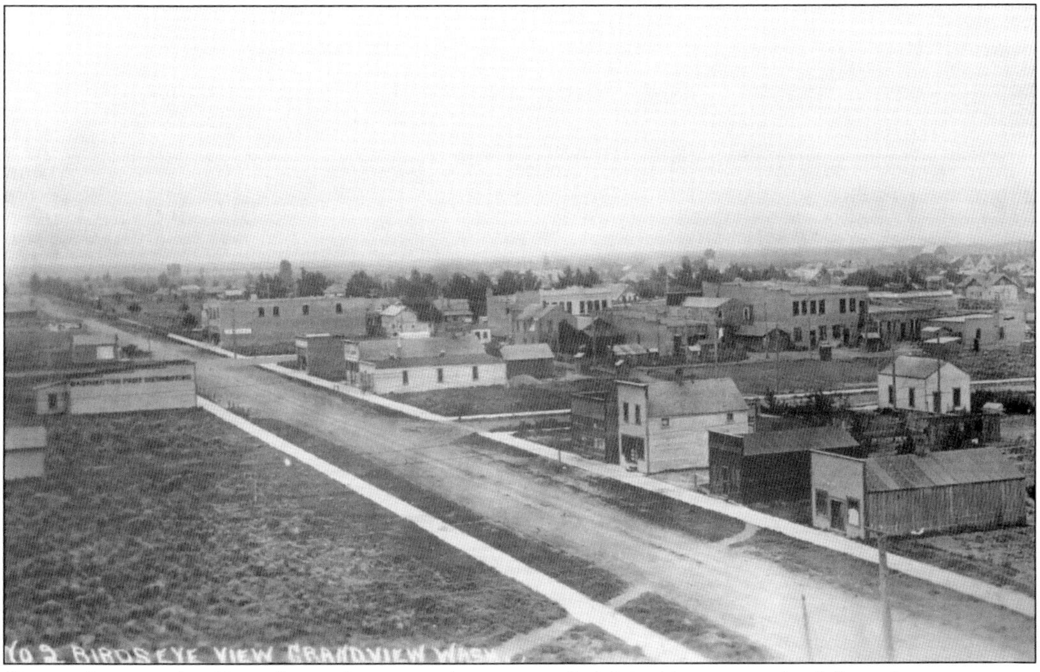

Shown here is the Grandview business district, with Main Street on the left and cross streets Division Street and Avenue A. Identified buildings on Main Street are Washington Fruit Distributors (left), the O.W. Davey Building, and the Fleming & Work store. Identified on Division Street are the post office and home of postmistress Ann E. Sykes (left), the Iowa Building, and the E.O. Keck Building. Grandview First National Bank is on Avenue A.

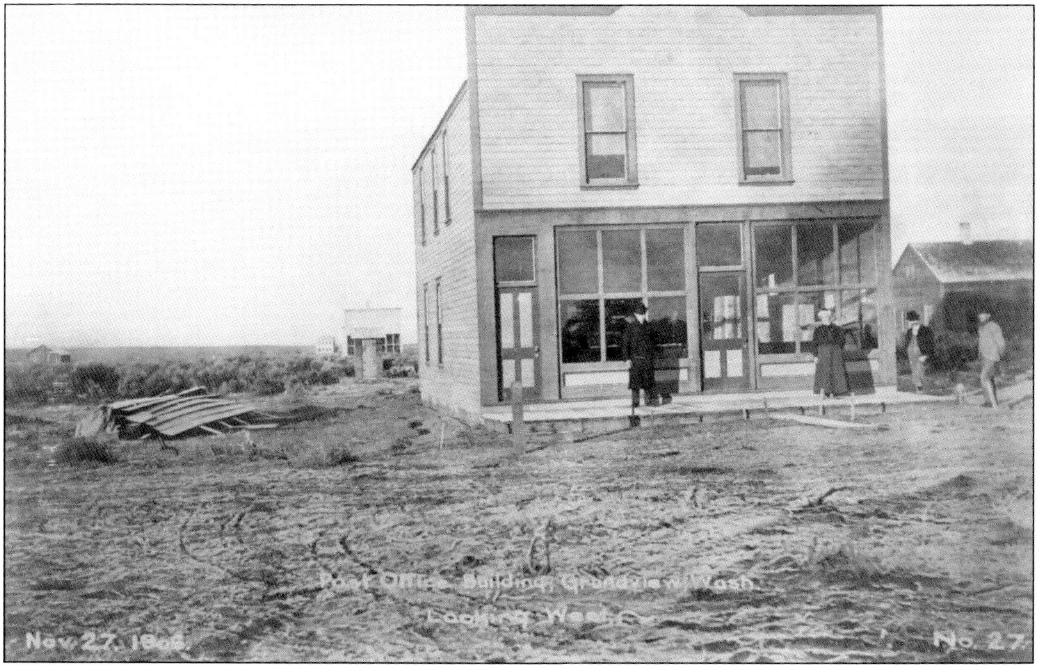

The first building erected in Grandview was the post office, at the direction of postmistress Ann E. Sykes. The structure also served as the home of Sykes and her 98-year-old mother, and the rooms upstairs were available to renters. The postmistress did not receive a salary for the first five years, instead receiving a share of receipts. Her share for the first quarter was $2.42.

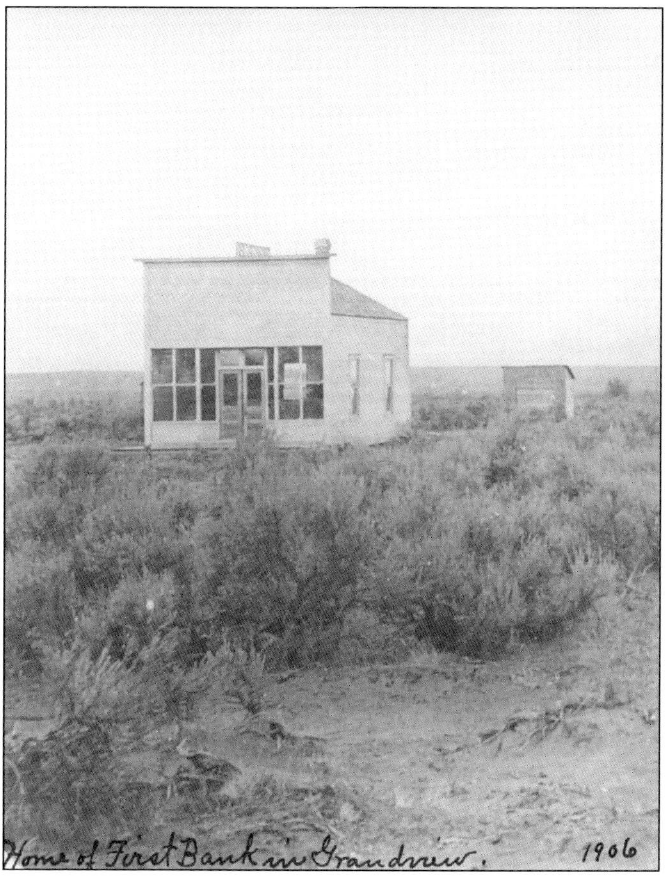

Opening in 1906, Grandview State Bank was the town's first bank. It was located at 106 Avenue A (lot 5, block 16). Carl Harper traveled to Grandview from the main bank in Prosser for two days each week to act as cashier. In 1908, the bank was privatized and purchased by A.W. Hawn & Company.

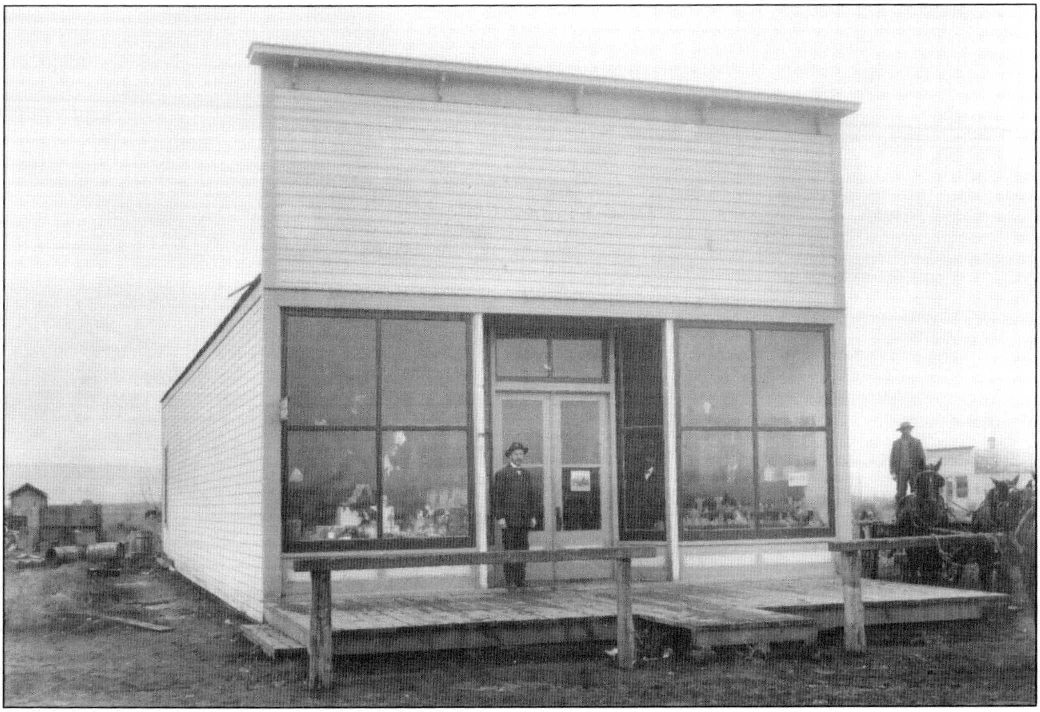

Joseph M. Fleming (below, left) built the first store, and second building, in Grandview, at 116 West Main Street (lot 17, block 17), on September 6, 1906. The business, Fleming & Work (later Pioneer Merchant), was owned by Fleming and J.L. Work (below, right). The store received free telephone service in 1907 for giving space to Grandview's first telephone switchboard, which connected the line with Sunnyside and Prosser. The building visible behind and to the right of the store is the Grandview branch of the Prosser State Bank.

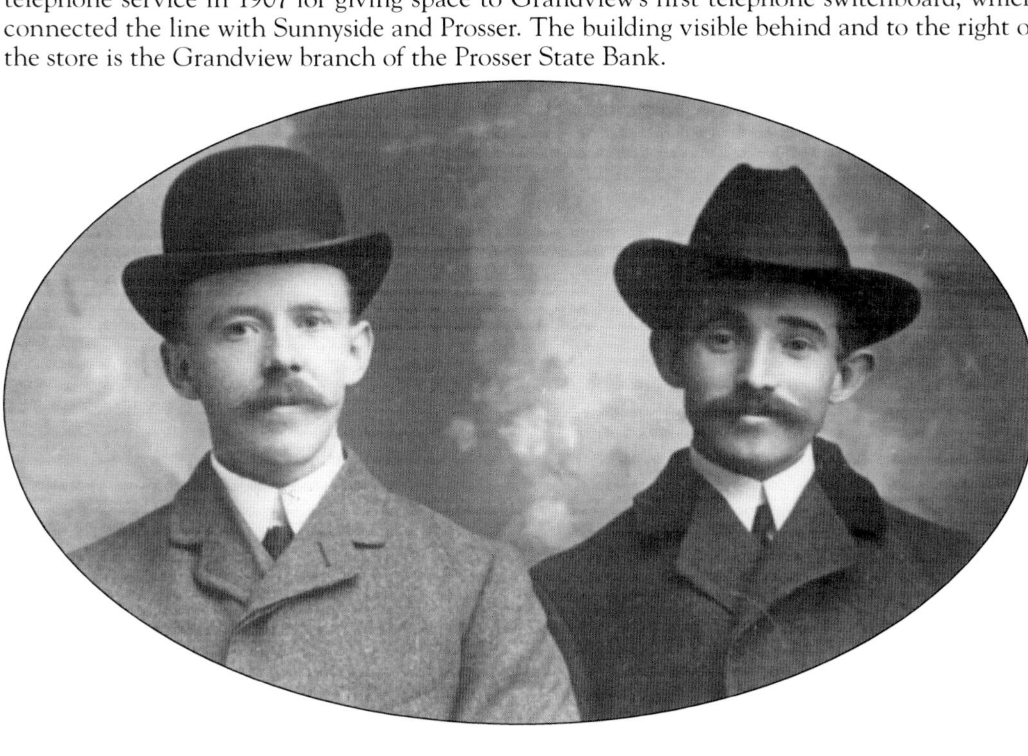

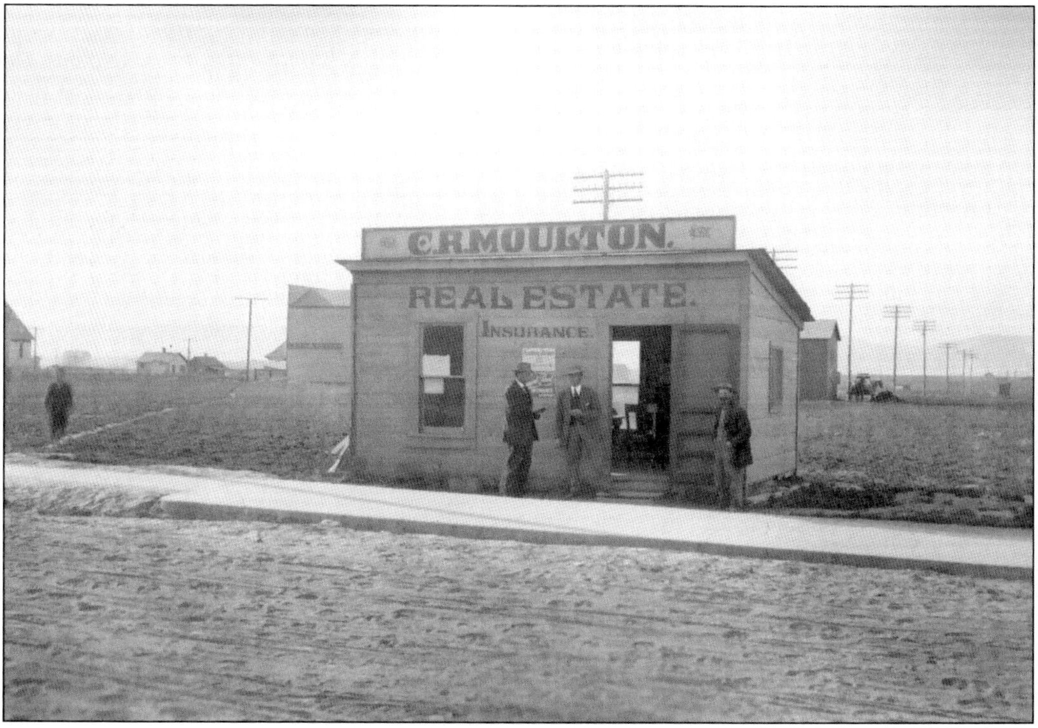

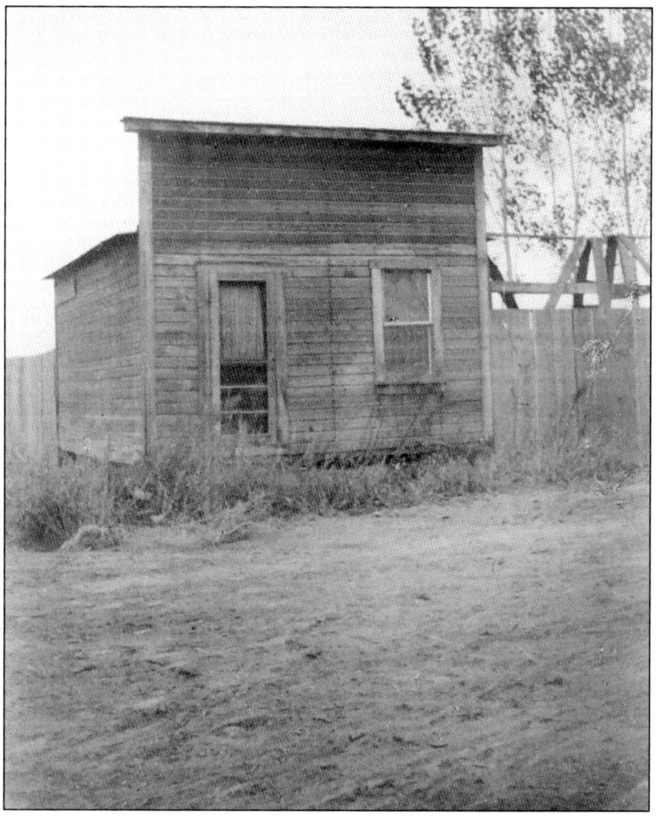

Clarence R. Moulton provided both real estate and insurance services from this small building on Second Street between Division Street and Avenue A. Tacked below the painted signs are two small signs advertising the "Hamburg-Bremen Fire Insurance Company" and the "Saint Paul Insurance Company." Behind the real estate office are several new homes, and visible on the far horizon are the Horse Heaven Hills.

In 1909, this old wooden building was the location of a successful bakery owned by Fannie Bell before her marriage to Emery W. Morse. Fannie, Emery, and their sons Chauncey B. and Charles, as well as other members of the Morse family, are buried in the Grandview Cemetery.

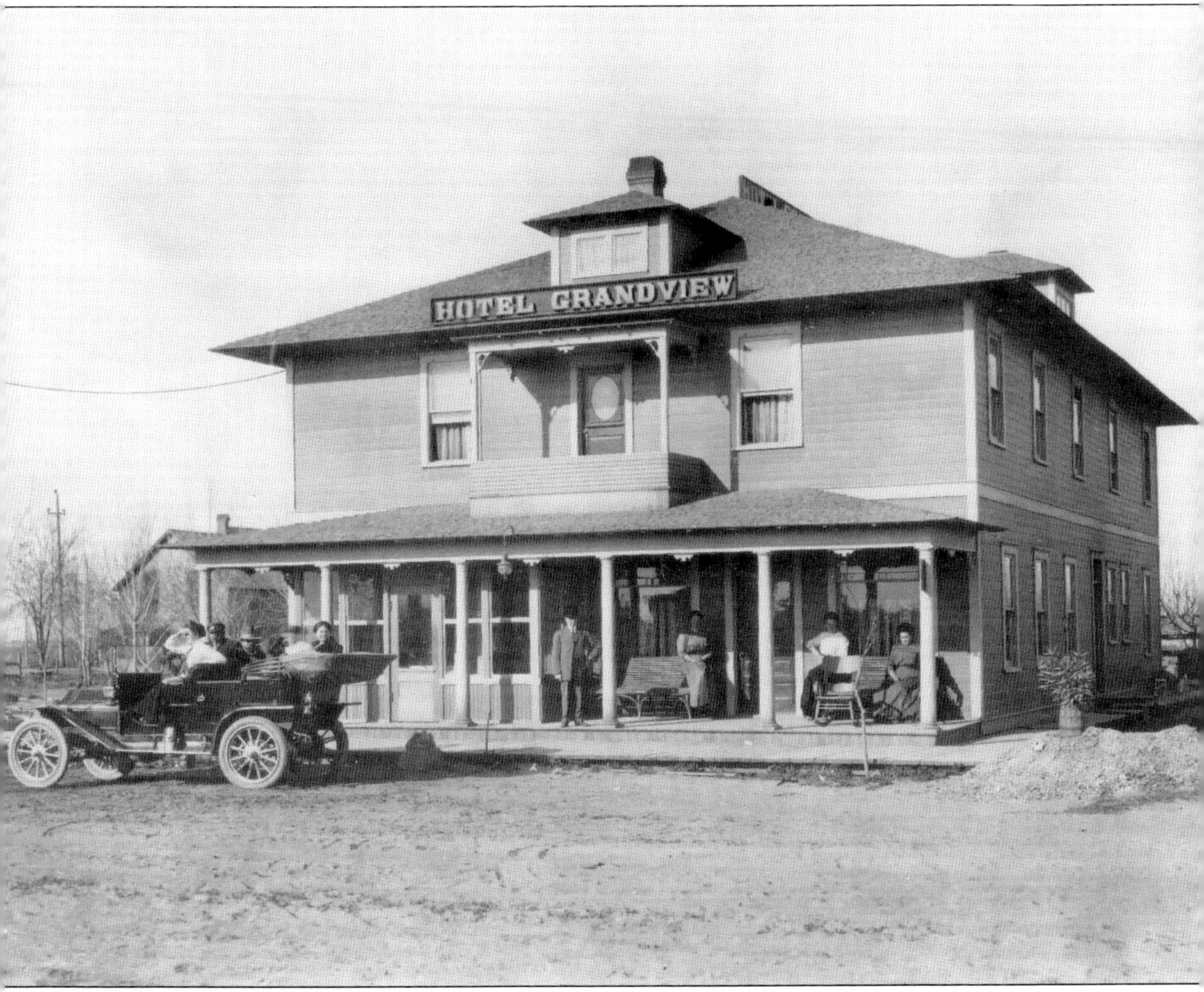

Doctors in Illinois told Minnie Myrtle Dean that she had, at the most, three months to live due to her "coming into consumption." She and her husband, William Frank Elser, moved to the Grandview area in 1905 and settled on a little tract of rented land. Theirs was the only house in the neighborhood. When government surveyors at work on the area's irrigation canals asked to be fed, and eventually for temporary living accommodations in her home, over her husband's protest, she turned their home into a boardinghouse. Soon, the guests outnumbered her ability to provide for them. Over more protests from her husband, Minnie directed the building of the 20-room Grandview Hotel and soon it filled to overflowing. Planning for another hotel was undertaken, and Minnie all but forgot about dying. In addition to Minnie's hotel, William Elser had a 14-acre fruit orchard. They had no money when they arrived in Grandview, but, by 1912, their property was worth $30,000. Minnie Elser finally passed away in the summer of 1925.

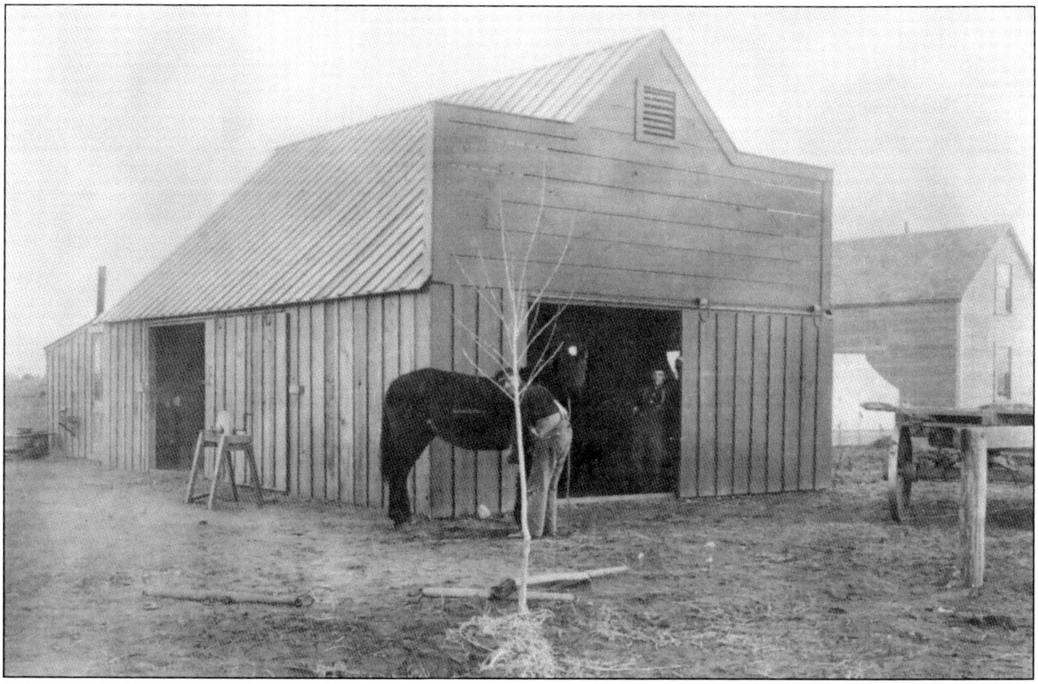

J.E. Laricheliere opened Grandview's first blacksmith shop in 1907. In addition to shoeing horses, Laricheliere probably fashioned and repaired almost anything made of metal. Area farmers would have brought their buggies, sleighs, and wagon wheels to this skilled craftsman for repairs. He was still in business in 1927.

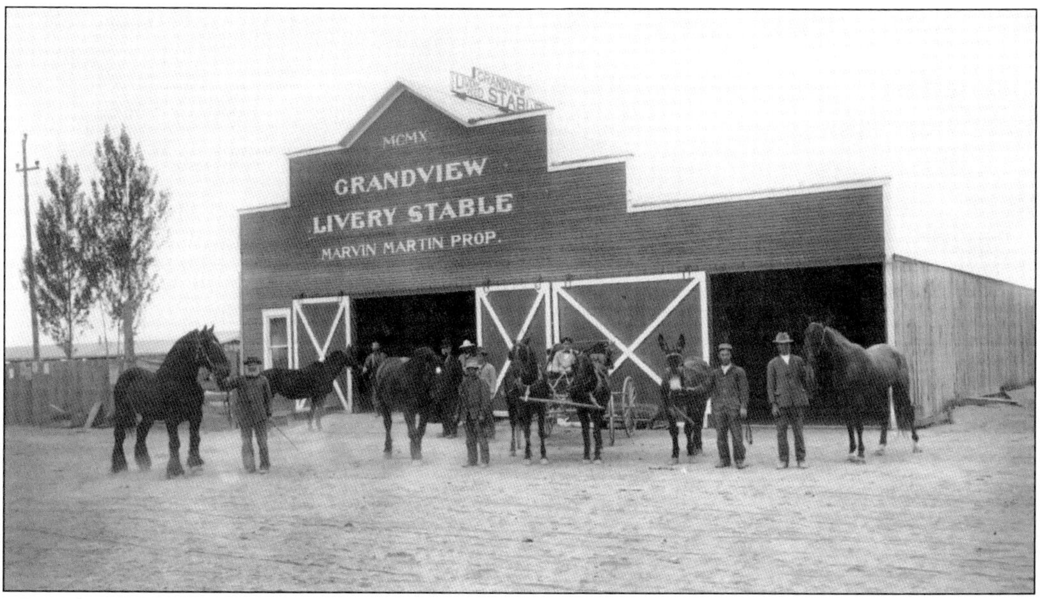

"Grandview Livery Stable, Marvin Martin Prop." reads the identifying sign on this large building in the 200 block of West Second Street. This photograph was taken on April 29, 1911. In August of that year, fire destroyed Martin's livery stable and feed store. Grandview's first large fire destroyed everything east of Division Street between Main and Second Streets. Martin later moved to Ellensburg, where he died on April 29, 1943. (Photograph by Asahel Curtis; courtesy of GHC.)

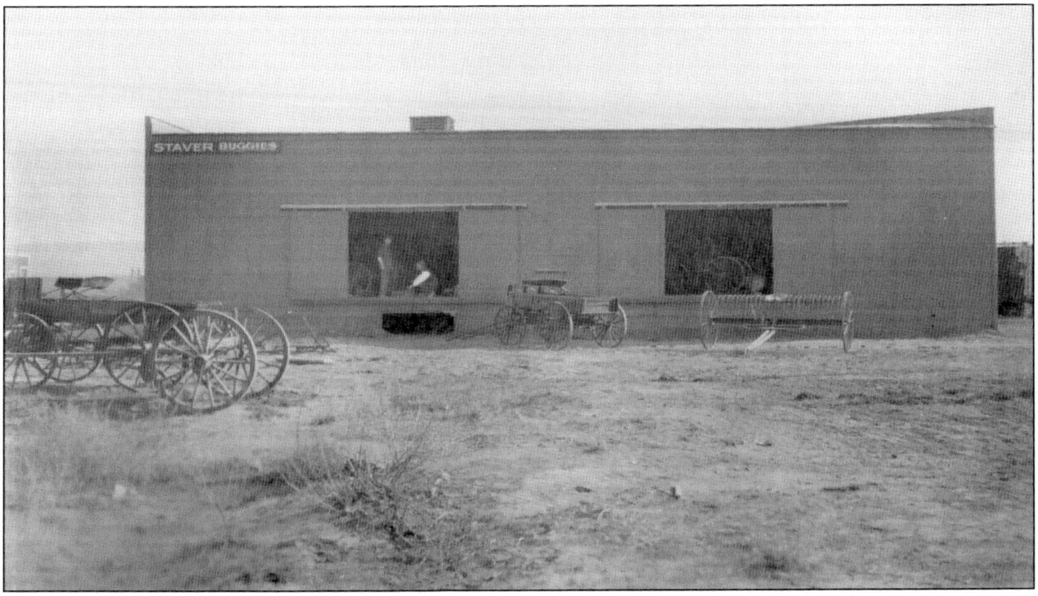

A sign advertising "Staver Buggies" is the only identifier on the front of the Barendt & Snowden Warehouse. The building, on Avenue A, had a triangular footprint in order to fit the lot, which bordered the Northern Pacific Railroad tracks that run diagonally through town. Behind the two men inside the doors on the left, a Staver buggy is barely visible. In front of the building is a Mitchell spring-seat buckboard.

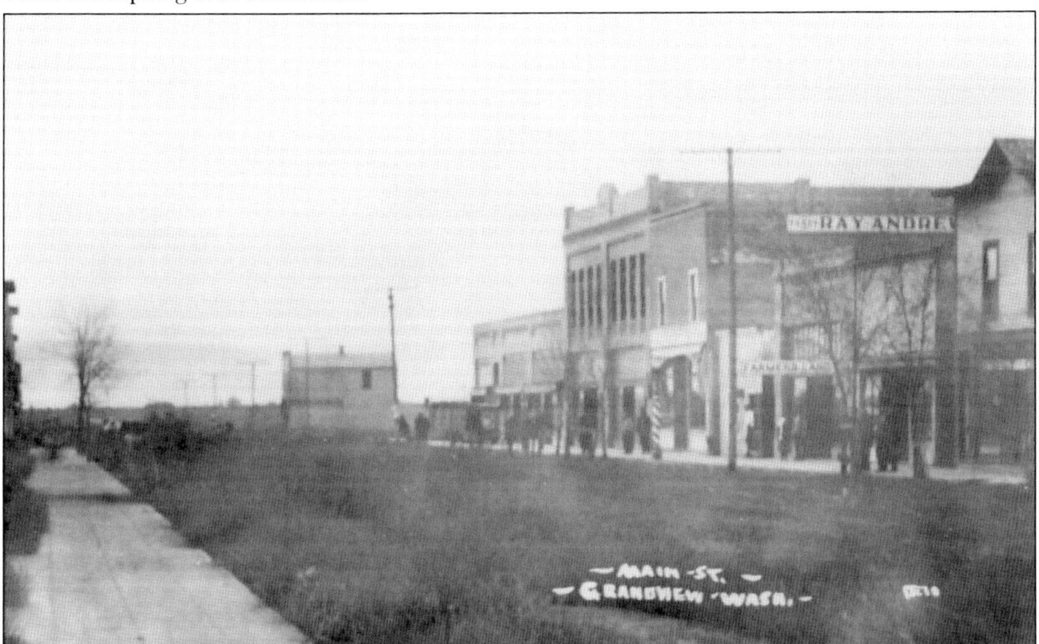

In January 1908, A.G. Fleming of Sunnyside put in a stock of drugs and opened the small Grandview Drug Store on Division Street (lot 9, block 17) with B.N. Coe the pharmacist in charge. The next year, Coe purchased the stock, enlarged the building, and reopened the newly named Grandview Pharmacy. The photograph is misidentified; the street is in fact Division Street, looking south from Main Street. (Photograph by Asahel Curtis; courtesy of GHC.)

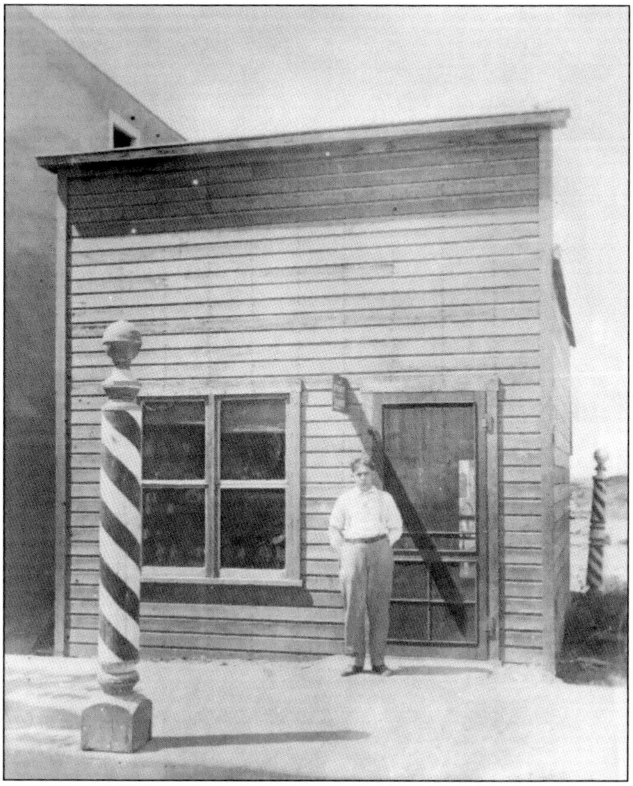

Guy Pope opened Grandview's first barbershop in February 1908. With its opening, Pope made life just a little easier for the men of Grandview; they no longer needed to waste half a day making the drive to Prosser or Sunnyside for a haircut.

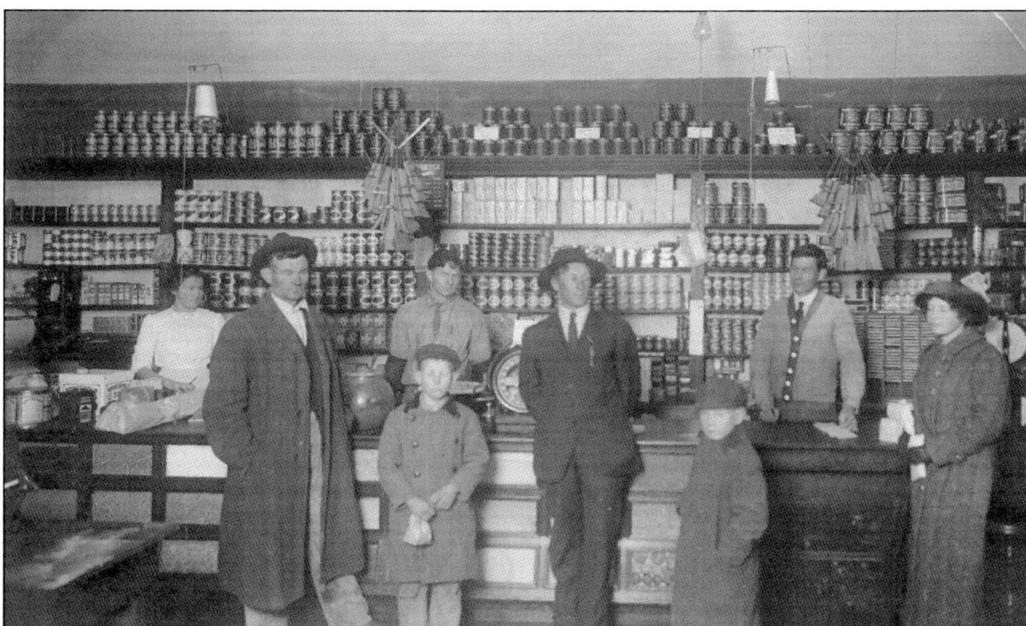

This image is from an advertising postcard for D.W. Brackett Grocery, 1914–1916. In 1912, the store was Bower & Wentch. Pictured from left to right in front of the counter are "Milk Can ?," unidentified, Ray Thompson of Yakima, unidentified, and Blanch Mitchell Thompson; behind the counter are Flossie Caverhill Mitchell of Ellensburg, Homer Gill, and D.W. Brackett.

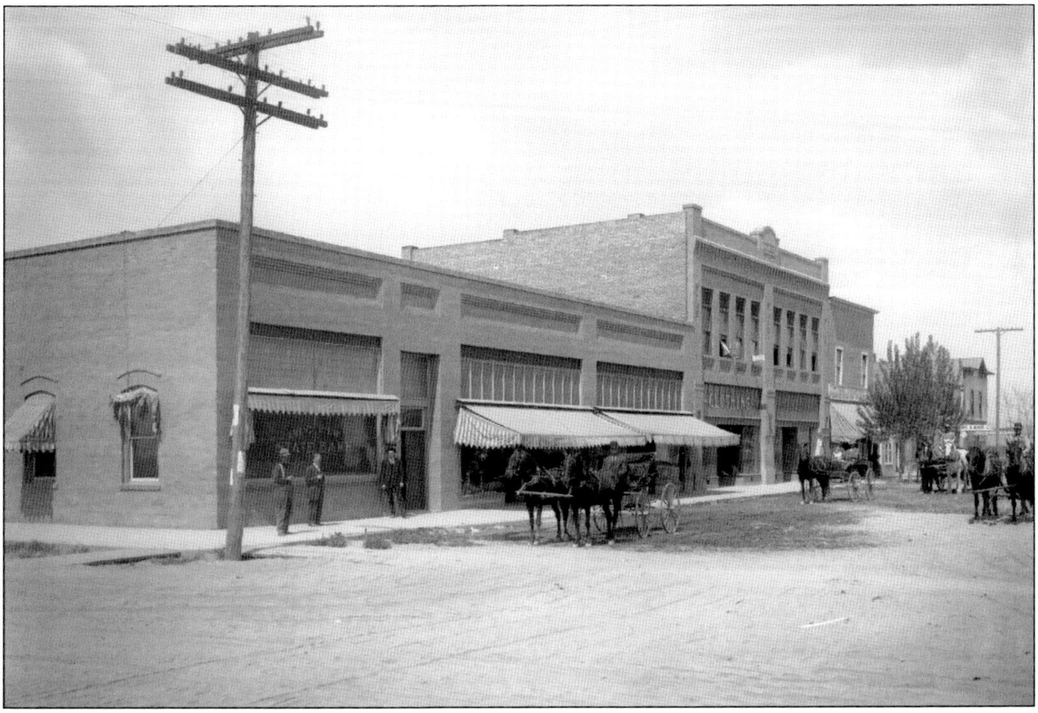

In this photograph from April 1911, the Grandview State Bank is on the northwest corner of Division and South Second Streets. The tallest building, home to the Valley Clothing Company, is the E.O. Keck Building, built in 1910. Listed in the Washington State Register of Historic Places, the Keck Building at times housed both the public library and the post office. (Photograph by Asahel Curtis; courtesy of GHC.)

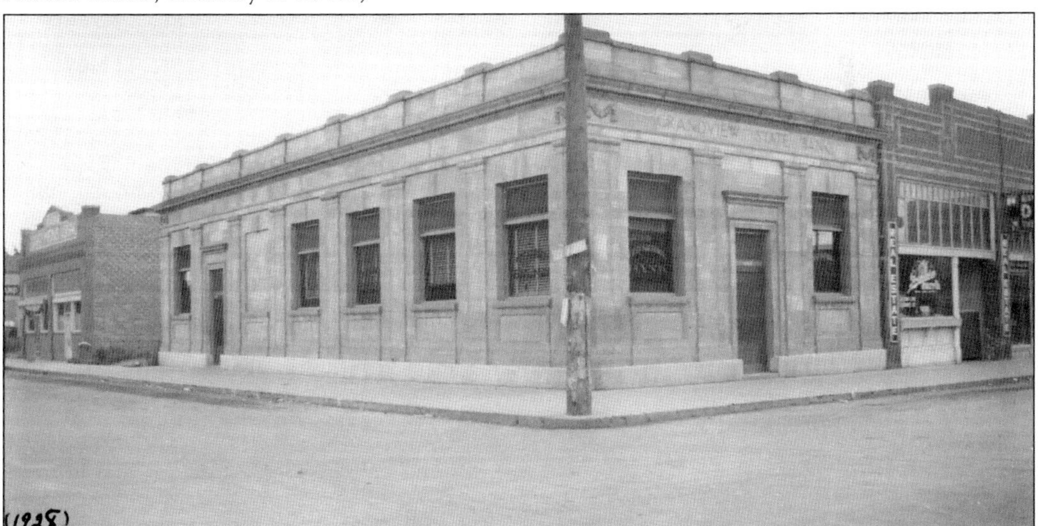

On April 1, 1910, the A.W. Hawn & Company bank reorganized as Grandview State Bank. In December 1919 the name changed again, to First National Bank. Closed by order of Gov. Clarence D. Martin in the middle of the Great Depression, the bank reopened within a week. Built in 1918 across the street from the earlier bank, the building is listed in the National Register of Historic Places.

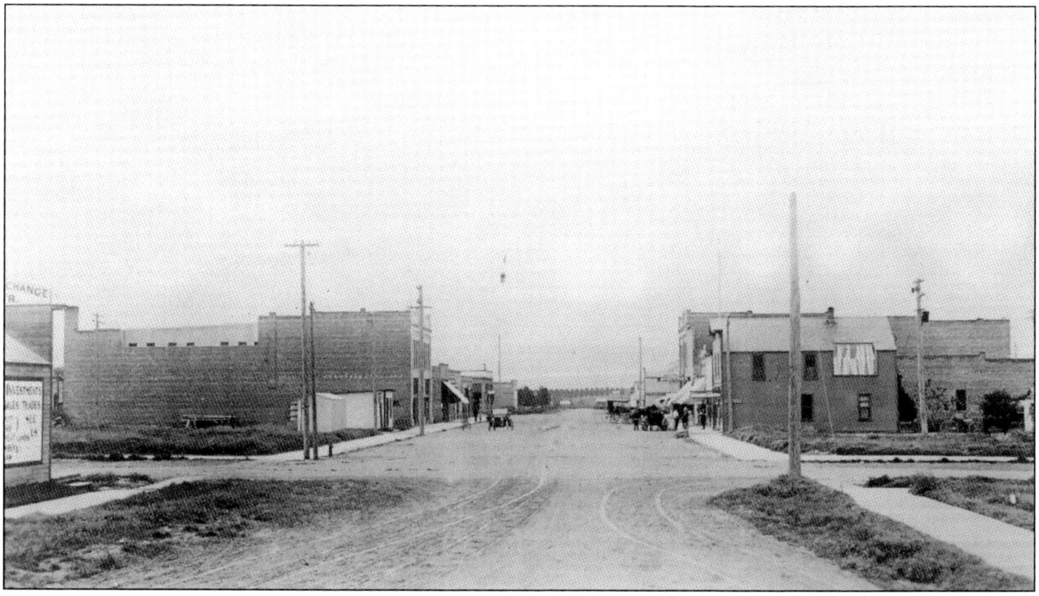

The rare photograph above shows the main business section looking south along Division Street. Main Street is the cross street in the foreground. The Iowa Building, built in 1911, is the large structure on the left side of the street. A little farther south, across the street, is the E.O. Keck Building. The street is more commonly photographed looking north, as it is in the mid-to-late 1930s photograph below. By then, the broad street had been paved and streetlights had been added, but the Oregon-Washington Railroad & Navigation Co. depot still served as a focal point at the north end of the street.

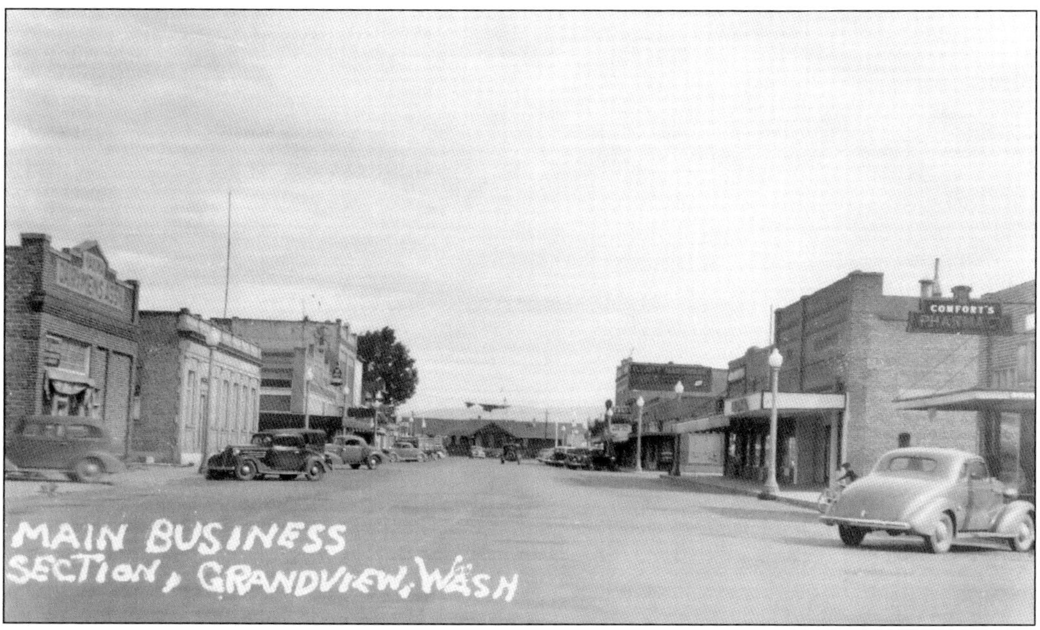

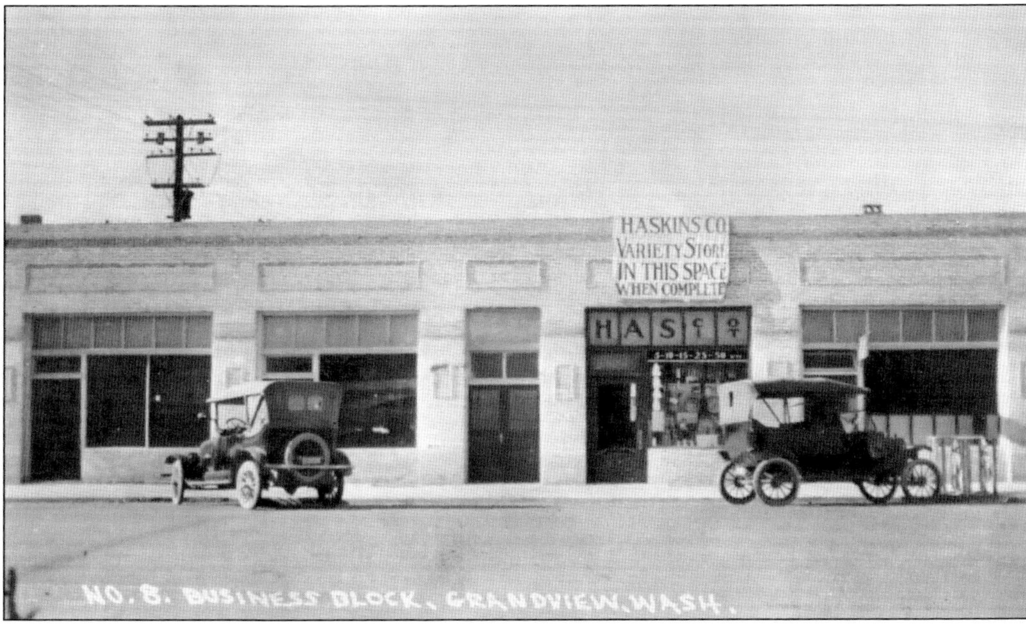

The future home of Haskins Variety Store was in the 100 block of Division Street, seen in this early photograph. It was not long before the store moved down the street to the corner of West Second and Division Streets, the store's more familiar and long-remembered location. Haskins Variety employed many young people and was a one-stop shop for all household needs.

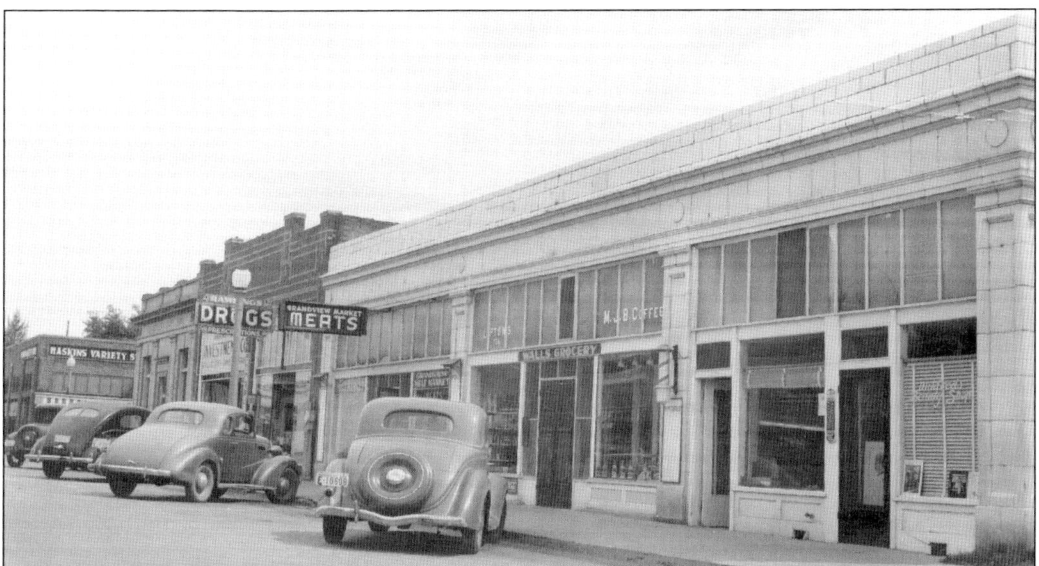

Haskins Variety (far left) had moved to its corner location in this mid-1940s photograph of West Second Street. Across Division Street to the west, Grandview Investment Company is next door to the Grandview State Bank, the building where it eventually moved. Other businesses include Rawlings Drugs, the Grandview Meat Market, Walls Grocery, and Mildred's Beauty Shop.

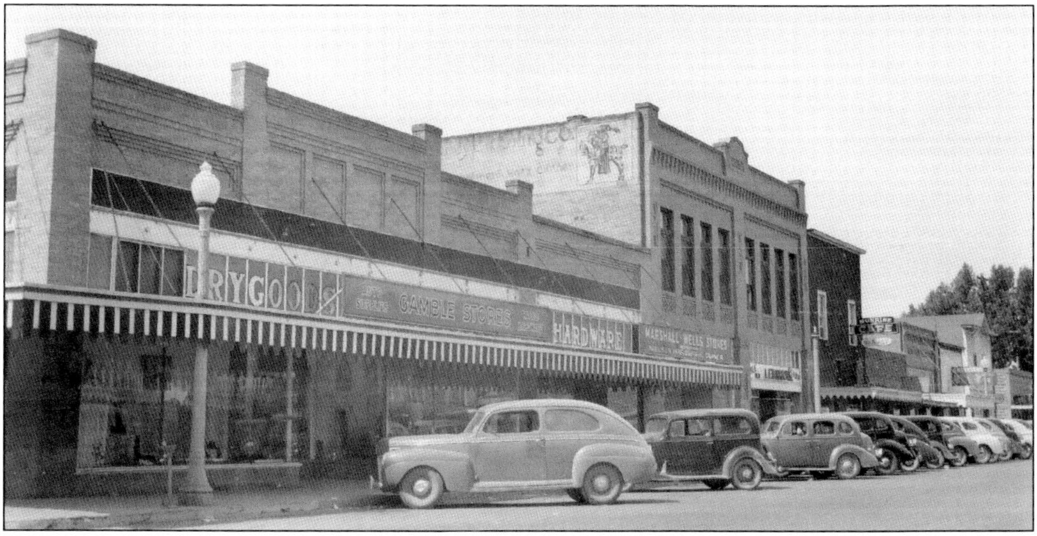

The Grandview Leader, on the corner of West Second and Division Streets, took up almost half of the west side of Division Street, as seen above. The building, an early "mini-mall," has contained several different businesses over the years. The first structure built in Grandview, the white, wooden, two-story building on the north (right) end of the street, once held the original post office (see page 68). Below, across the street in the Iowa Building, was the Elliott Hardware Company, owned by Frank Elliott, where customers could buy a variety of merchandise as well as pay their electric bill at the Pacific Power & Light pay station.

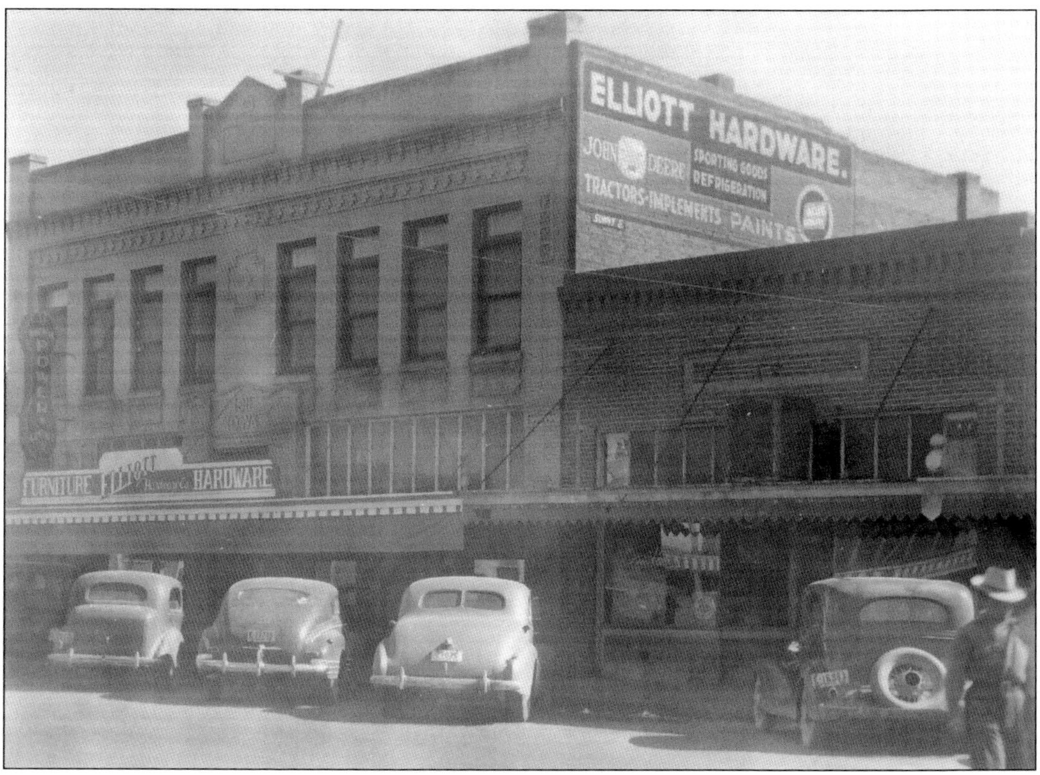

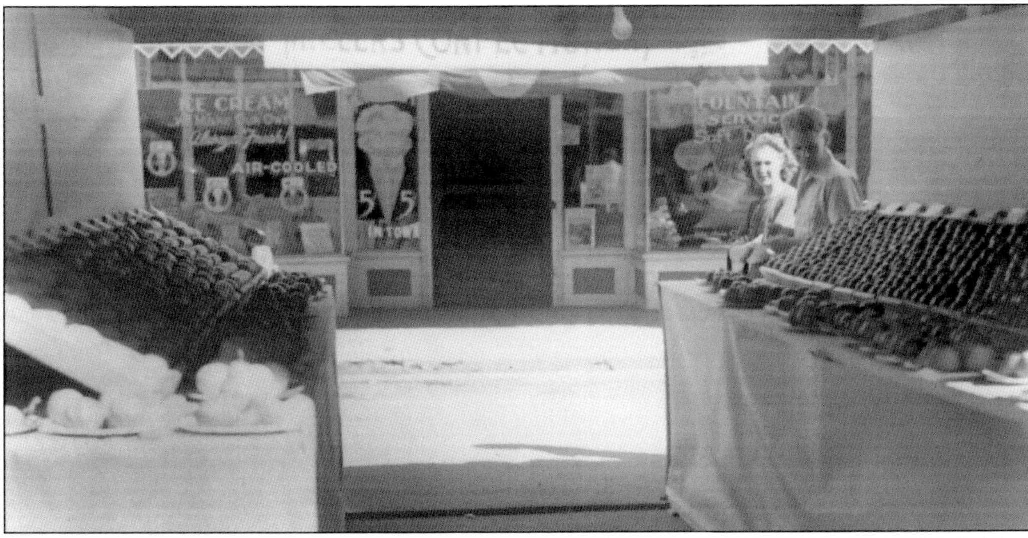

Roy Miller's Candy Kitchen, also known as Miller's Confectionery, was a favorite stop for children of all ages. On warm days, like when this photograph was taken in September 1941, the air-cooled atmosphere was probably appreciated as much, if not more, than the ice cream made on-site. The apple display on the street in front of the store was for the annual Grandview Harvest Festival.

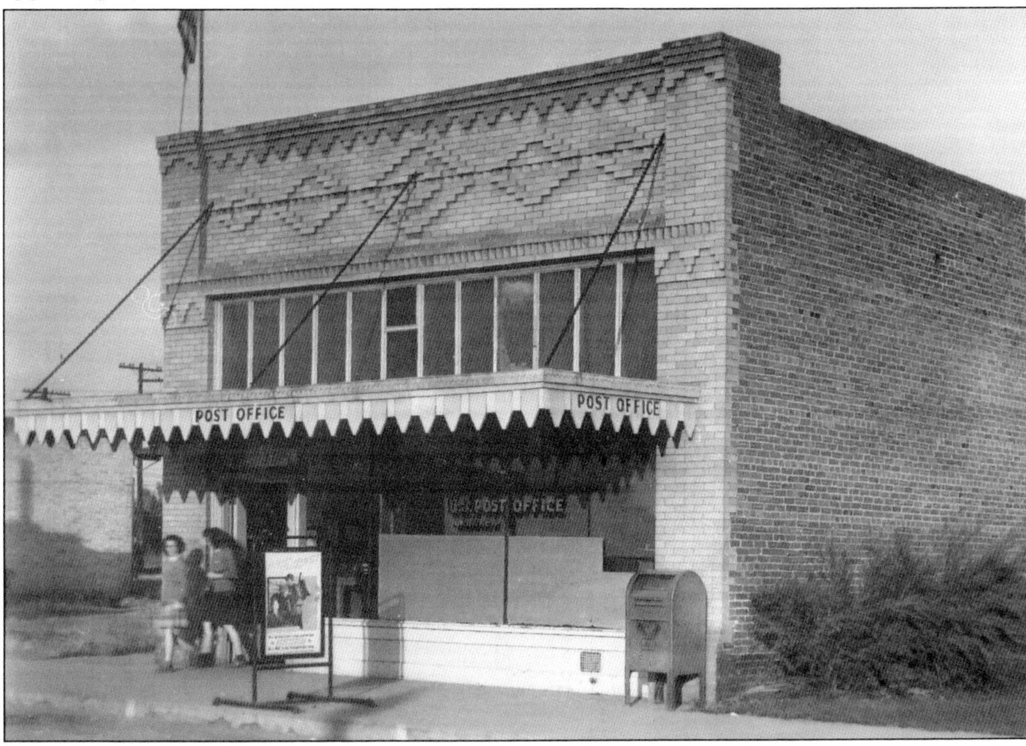

Taken just months before the end of World War II, this October 20, 1944, photograph of the post office shows a recruiting poster prominently displayed on the sidewalk out front. "In His Opinion She's Tops!" the WAC Transportation Corps poster declares. "She's got what it takes to help speed him back." The post office moved to its current location on Grandridge Road in the early 1960s.

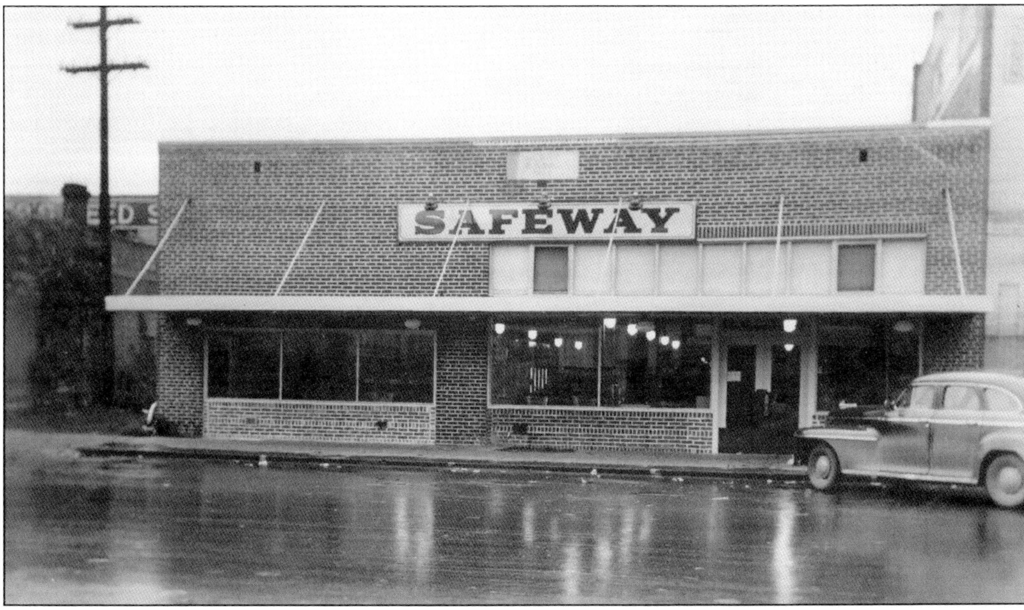

Long before the opening of the current Super Safeway on Wine Country Road, Safeway was located on Division Street in the Henry Building, owned by Alex Parke. The interior of the store (below) shows the typical product displays of the time. Among those easily recognized are Campbell's Soup, Edwards Coffee, and Julia Lee Wright's Enriched White Bread for only 13¢ a loaf. Safeway remained at that address until a new building opened on Grandridge Road on May 31, 1963. That building is now the home of the Yakima Valley Community College. Safeway Stores Inc. operated a processing plant in Grandview for many years, where they processed food items such as fruit juice products, mayonnaise and salad dressings, vanilla flavoring and vinegar, and, most memorably, peanut butter.

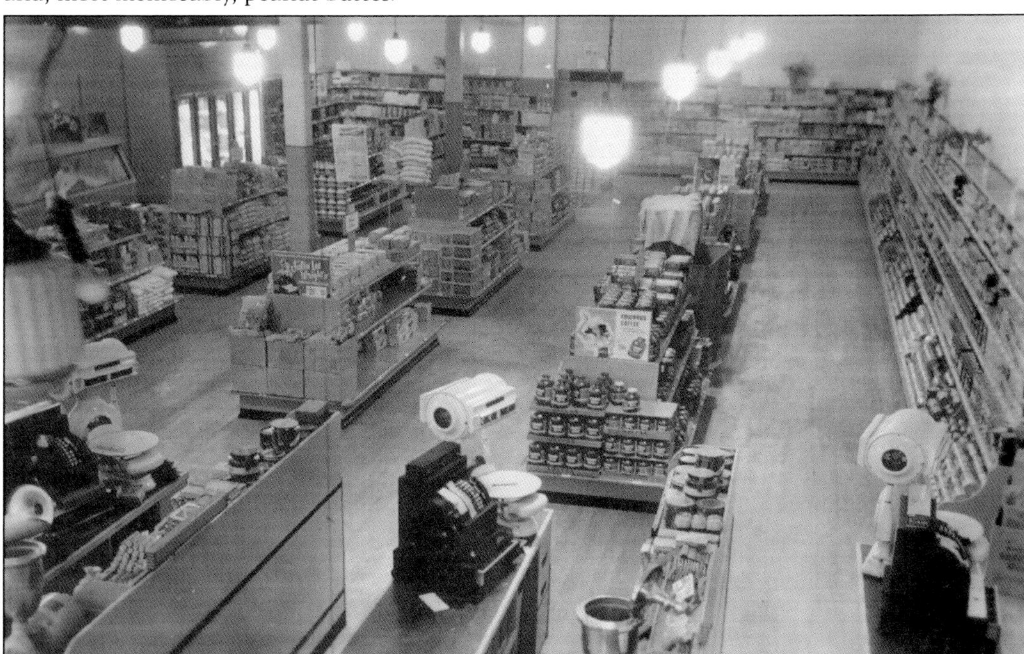

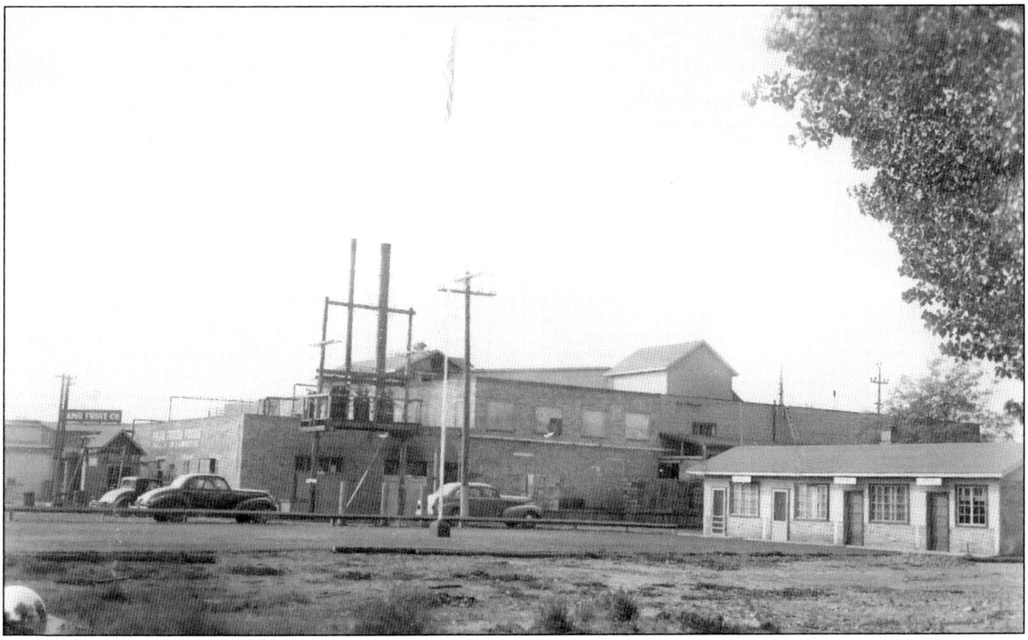

During the Great Depression of the 1930s, the Valley's abundant crops attracted a large workforce. With the increased farm production to aid the war effort in the early 1940s, a commercial building boom hit Grandview. Yakima Valley Frosted Foods, built in 1942 and enlarged in 1944, was one of many commercial businesses built to process the Lower Valley's rich harvest. Shown above as Polar Frozen Foods, the frozen food plant did business under many names over the years, most notably as "the Libby Plant." In 2008, the business—then known as Wild River Foods—was destroyed by fire (see page 102). The Custom Canning Plant (below), built by Vern Parr in 1944, took a different approach by providing space for individuals to process their own produce. During the first season, the plant canned 202,000 cans of produce for over 3,000 different patrons.

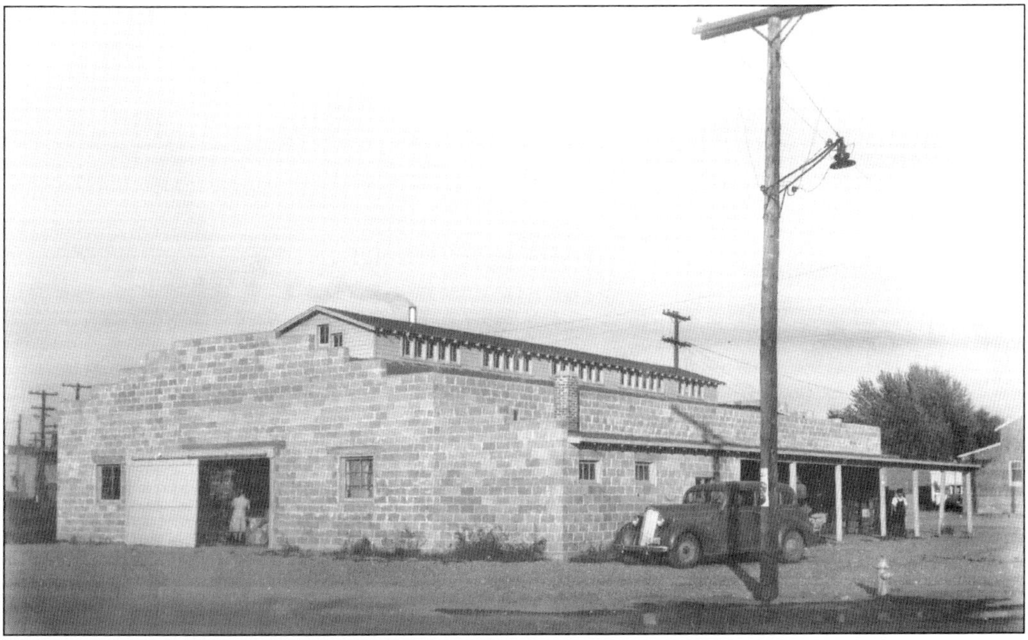

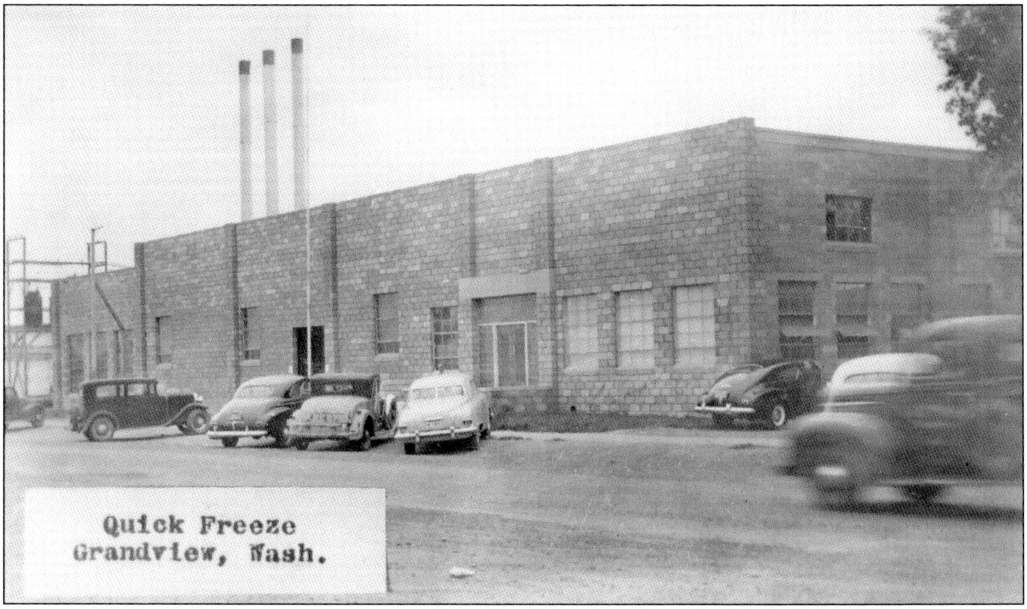

In 1943, the Quick Freeze plant tripled its capacity, at a cost of $50,000. In that year alone, the output of the plant was 400 tons of apples, 300 tons of lima beans, 100 tons of prunes, 1,000 tons of peas, 400 tons of asparagus, 600 tons of peaches, 100 tons of apricots, 500 tons of corn, and 200 tons of cherries.

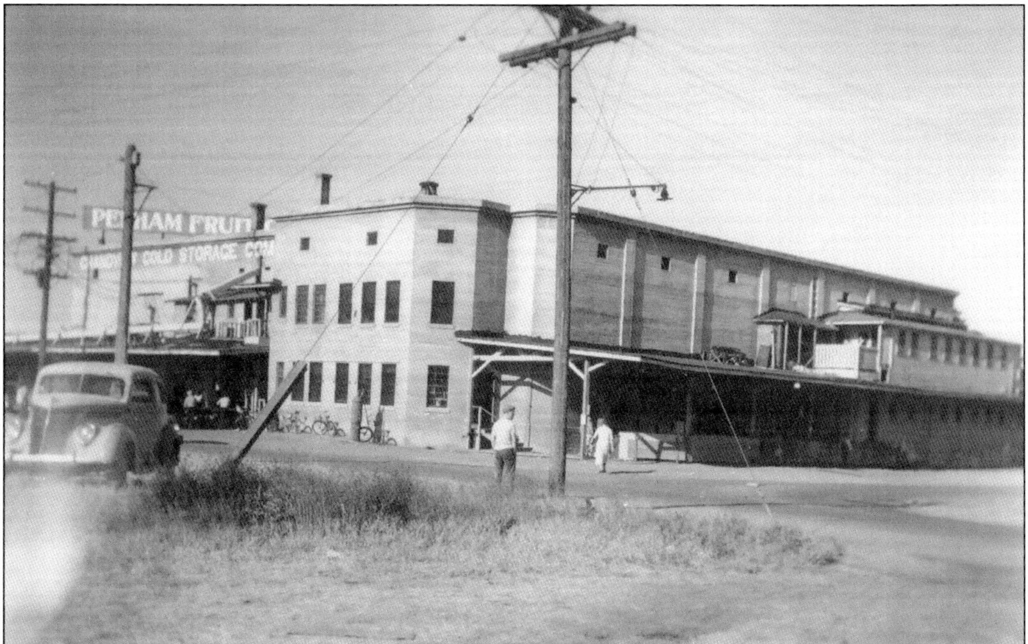

Still in use today, Perham Fruit Cold Storage No. 1 opened in time for the 1920 fruit season. By 1952, the canning and processing of fruit and vegetables was second only to the lumber industry in Washington State. Approximately 88 percent of produce processing was done locally, with a large share in Grandview.

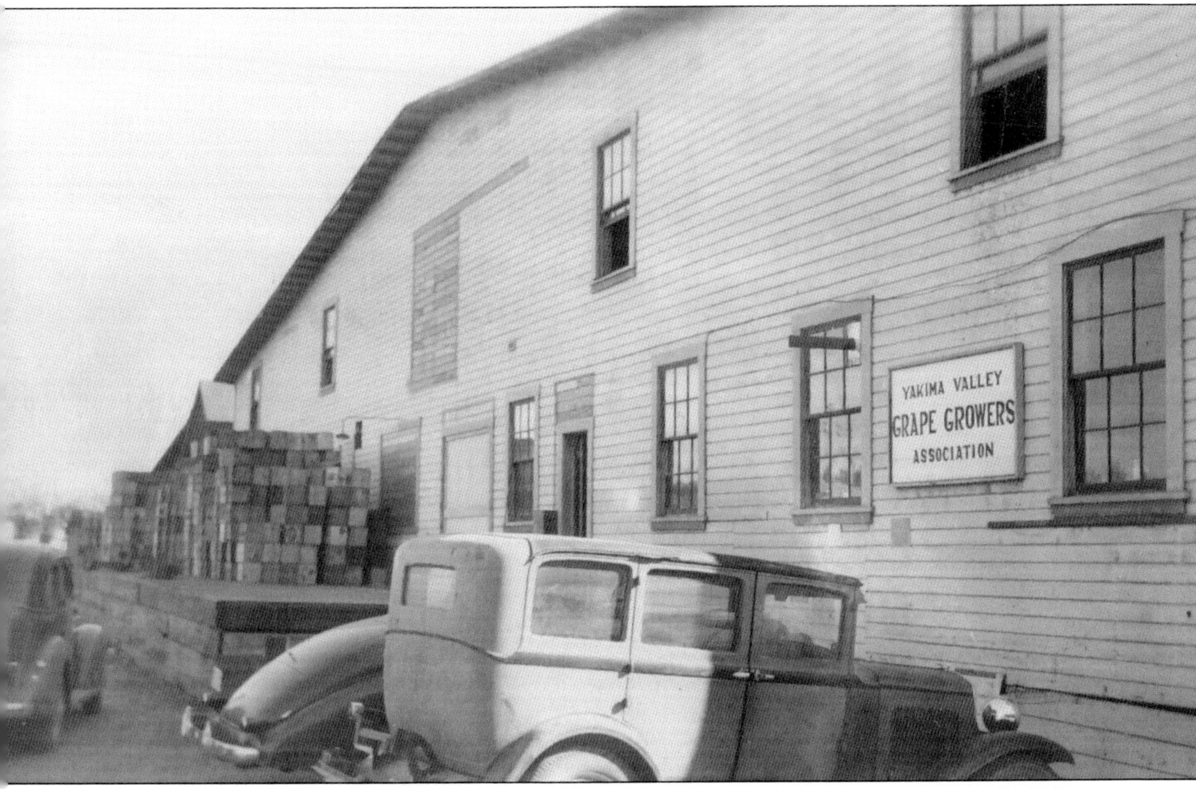

The intent of Yakima Valley Grape Producers, established in 1934 as the nonprofit Yakima Valley Grape Growers Association, was to collectively sell the members' products under a single manager. In 1949, the group reorganized in order to issue stock as a new nonprofit corporation. Growers of 15 tons or more of grapes per year were required to own one share of voting stock, which gave them one vote, regardless of the amount of stock they owned. Non-growers could hold stock, but they did not have voting privileges. In 1959, the Yakima Valley Grape Growers Association was legally dissolved, leaving only the Valley Grape Growers Association, which in 1960 was renamed Yakima Valley Grape Producers. On May 4, 1983, the US Bureau of Alcohol, Tobacco, and Firearms officially designated the Yakima Valley as the first American Viticultural Area in Washington State.

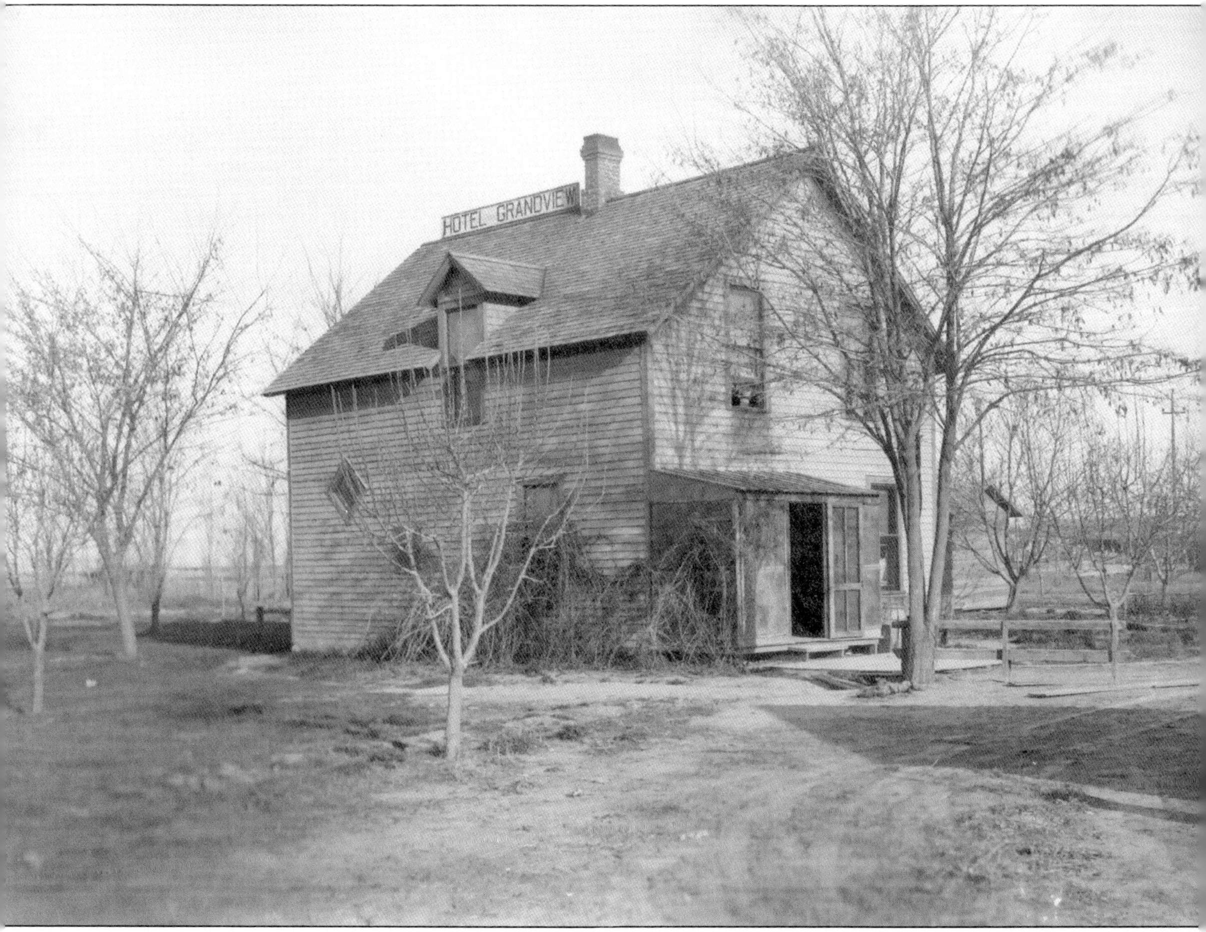

At its original location on Avenue B, the Hotel Grandview, shown here in 1912, was no longer used by permanent lodgers and had fallen into disrepair. The owners moved it to the south side of the highway to serve tourists. Peach Drive and Locust Avenue were names given to portions of the road in the Orchard Tracts. In 1913, the state renamed the road Inland Empire Highway. The route extended south from Ellensburg, Yakima, and Grandview, and then east to Walla Walla before turning north to Spokane and the Canadian border. In 1915, the highway was designated the Yellowstone Trail and became one of the earliest transcontinental highways. It was advertised as "From Plymouth Rock to Puget Sound." In 1926, it was renumbered as US Highway 10. Still known by various names, including Grandview Pavement, to the west, and OIE (Old Inland Empire), to the east, this portion of the Yellowstone Trail is listed in the National Register of Historic Places.

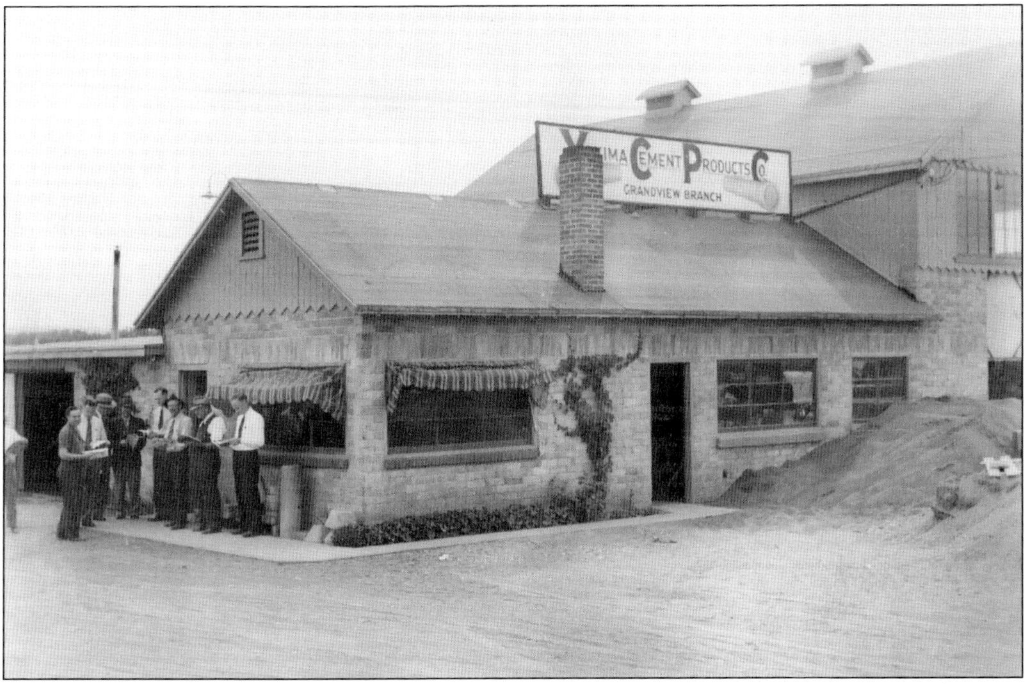

With the addition of irrigation, the area took on the look of an "old and prosperous farming community," according to the Saturday, July 25, 1908, issue of *The Commercial West*, a business trade journal not unlike today's *Business Week*. The Yakima Cement Products Company opened for business in 1941 on Main Street east of Euclid Street, for the purpose of offering farmers an inexpensive solution for the delivery of water to their thirsty crops. The priority of the Grandview location was irrigation supplies, while the Yakima location offered a more diversified product line. The Yakima plant went on to become Western Materials.

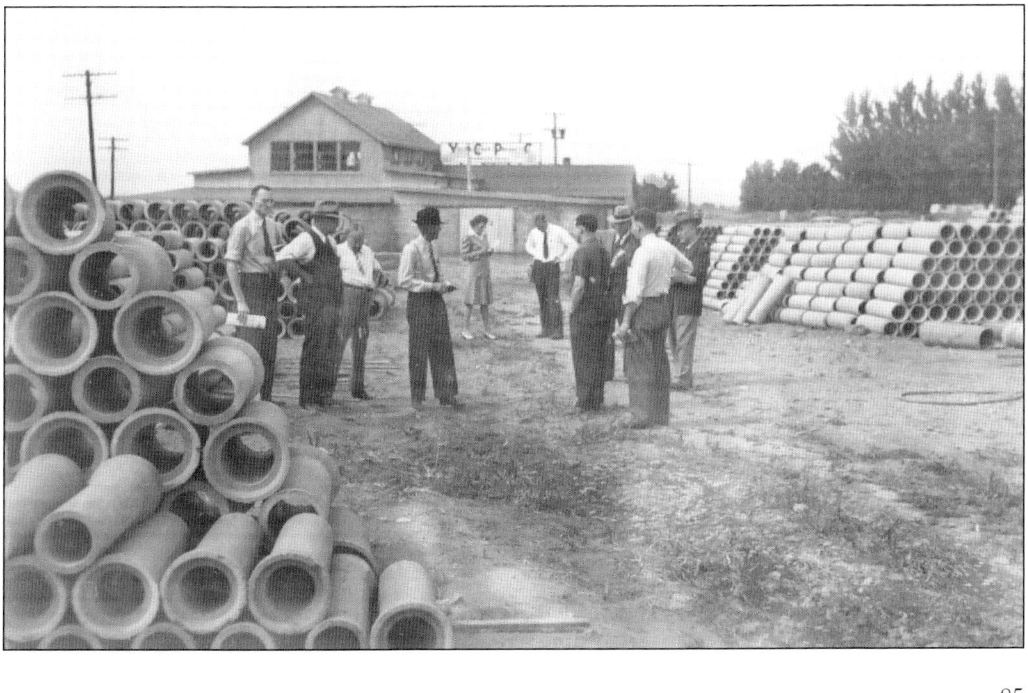

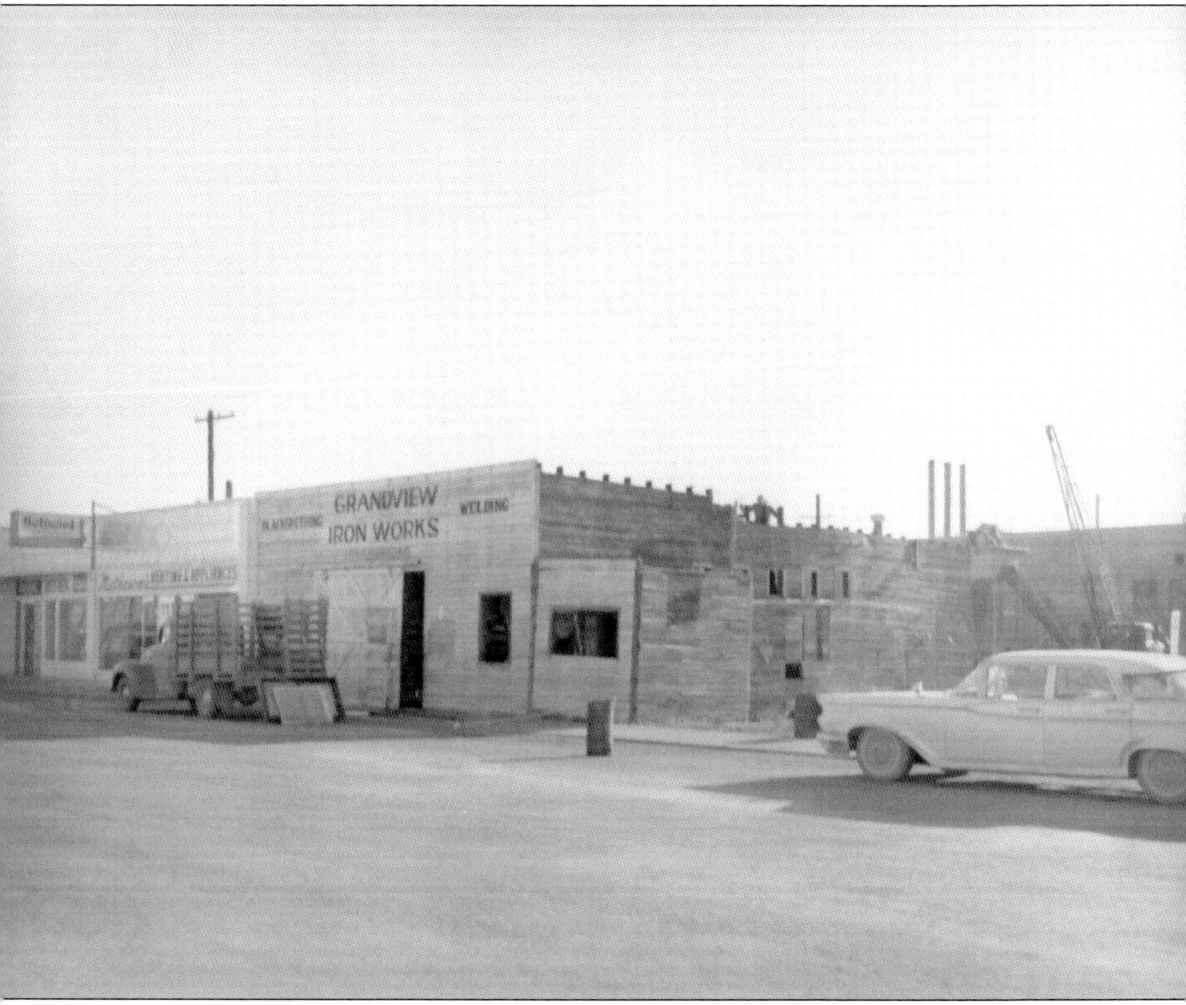

By the late 1950s and early 1960s, some of Grandview's early businesses had outlived their usefulness. Shown here is the dismantling of Grandview Iron Works, across from present-day city hall on West Second Street. In its day, the Iron Works offered horseshoeing, as well as blacksmithing and welding services for the farm wagons those horses pulled.

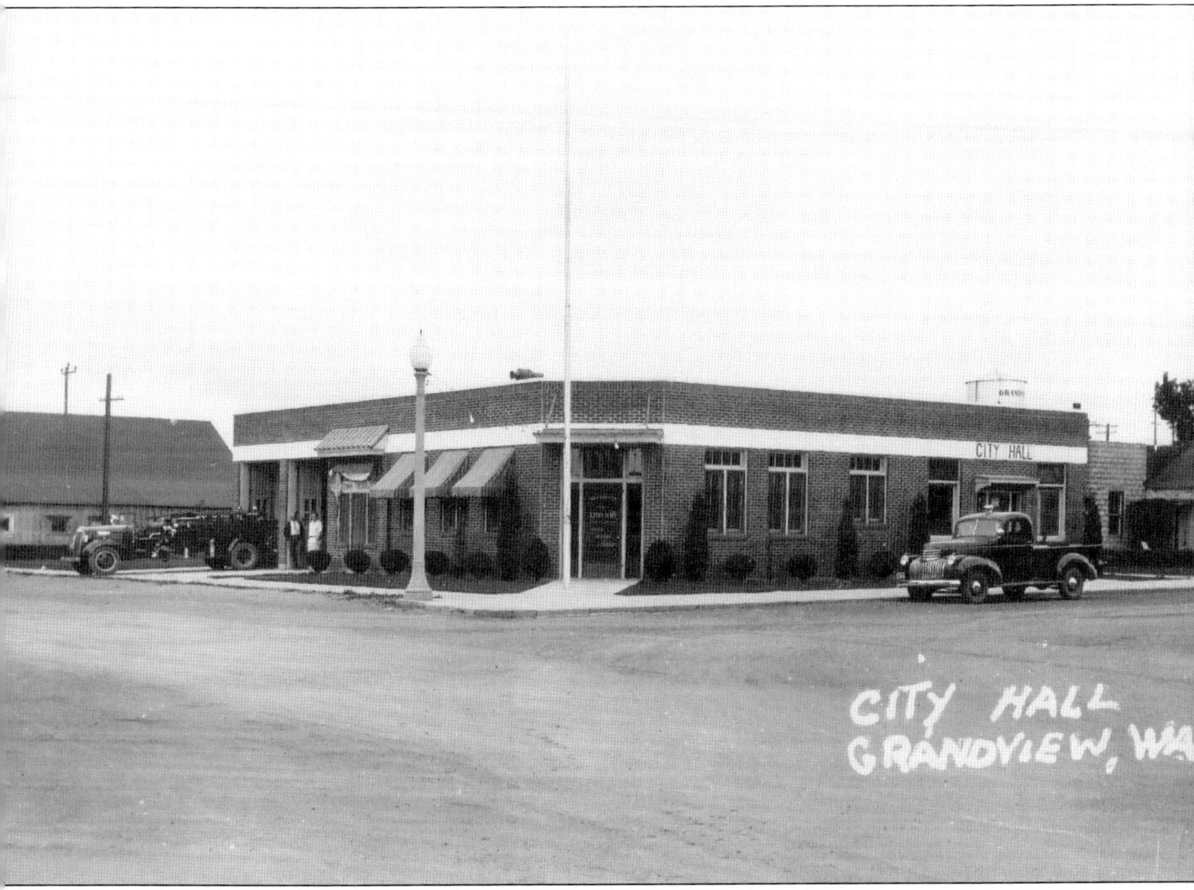

"Grandview's $11,800.00 City Hall and New Fire Truck" was the headline for a July 29, 1937, *Grandview Herald* article. The article read, in part, "Dedication of Grandview's new city hall will take place Saturday evening of this week . . . There will be no speaking program but Mayor A.M. Garrison and the members of the council, R.W. Duncan, Milo Case, W.A. Townsend, A.H. Waugh, and Ralph Solberg with other city officials, Earl Bugg, fire chief and water superintendant; Mrs. Susan Stuckrath, city treasurer; Pete Boye, assistant street commissioner; H.F. Ehmer, city clerk; W.B. Tow, police officer; Mrs. A.H. Smith, librarian, and J. Arnold Cobley, city attorney will be on hand to show visitors around so that they may thoroughly inspect the new building of which Grandview people are very proud. The public is cordially invited to attend this formal opening of the new city hall . . . Following the dedication of the hall the members of the volunteer fire department will sponsor a pavement dance."

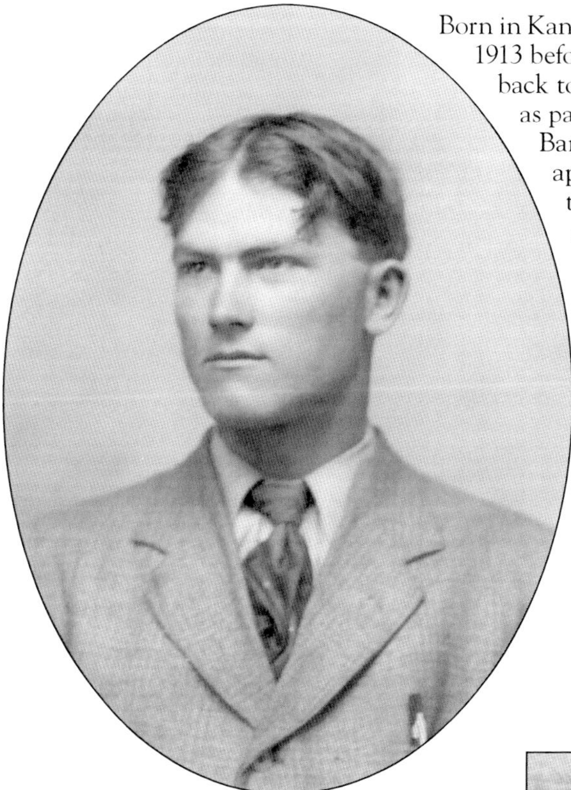

Born in Kansas, Earl Bugg lived in Grandview briefly in 1913 before moving to Stanfield, Oregon. He moved back to Grandview in 1917, where he found work as part of the crew that built the First National Bank. In 1919, Grandview mayor A.L. Thiele appointed Bugg street commissioner. He then served as fire chief and waterworks superintendant before becoming a town marshal in 1923. (Courtesy of the Grandview Police Department.)

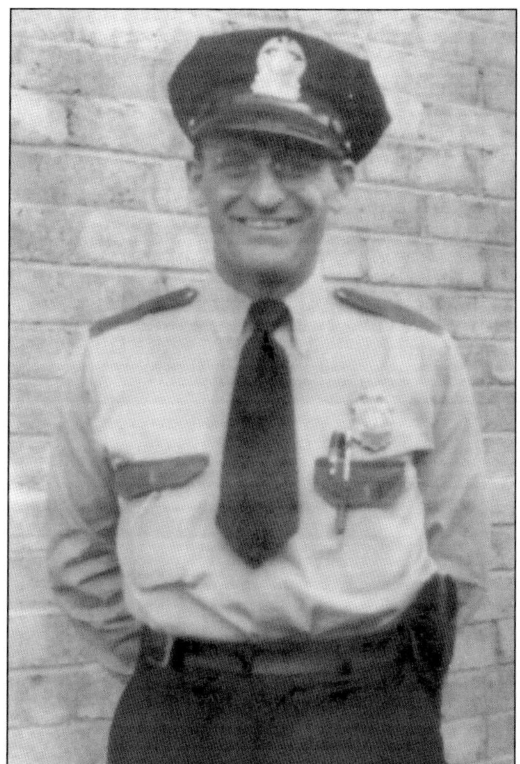

By 1941, when this photograph was taken, Walter M. Krous had served Grandview as night marshal for three years. He had replaced Wallace "Wally" Tow when Tow left to become caretaker of the Grandview Cemetery. Krous held the position until 1943. Krous, who died in 1950 at the age of 42, is buried in the Grandview Cemetery. (Courtesy of the Grandview Police Department.)

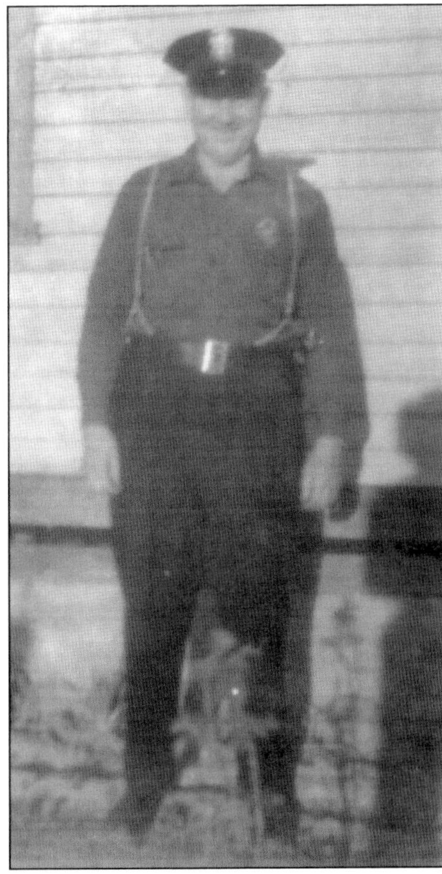

Grandview police chief Clarence W. Ragsdale, shown at right in 1946, replaced Wallace Tow as marshal in 1944. Tow had returned temporarily as marshal in 1943 upon the retirement of Walter Krous. Chief Ragsdale resigned from the police force in 1950 but worked for the street department until his retirement in 1975. Today's SWAT vehicles are very different from Chief Ragsdale's paddy wagon, shown in the photograph below, taken on January 5, 1947. Ragsdale died on October 1, 1979, and is buried in the Grandview Cemetery along with several other members of his family. (Both courtesy of the Grandview Police Department.)

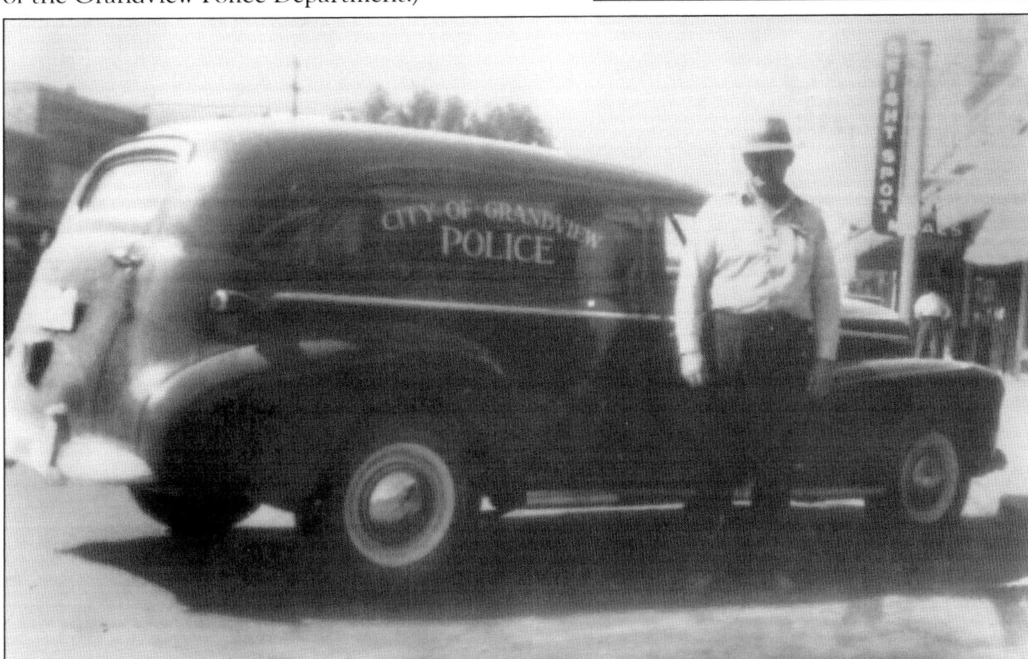

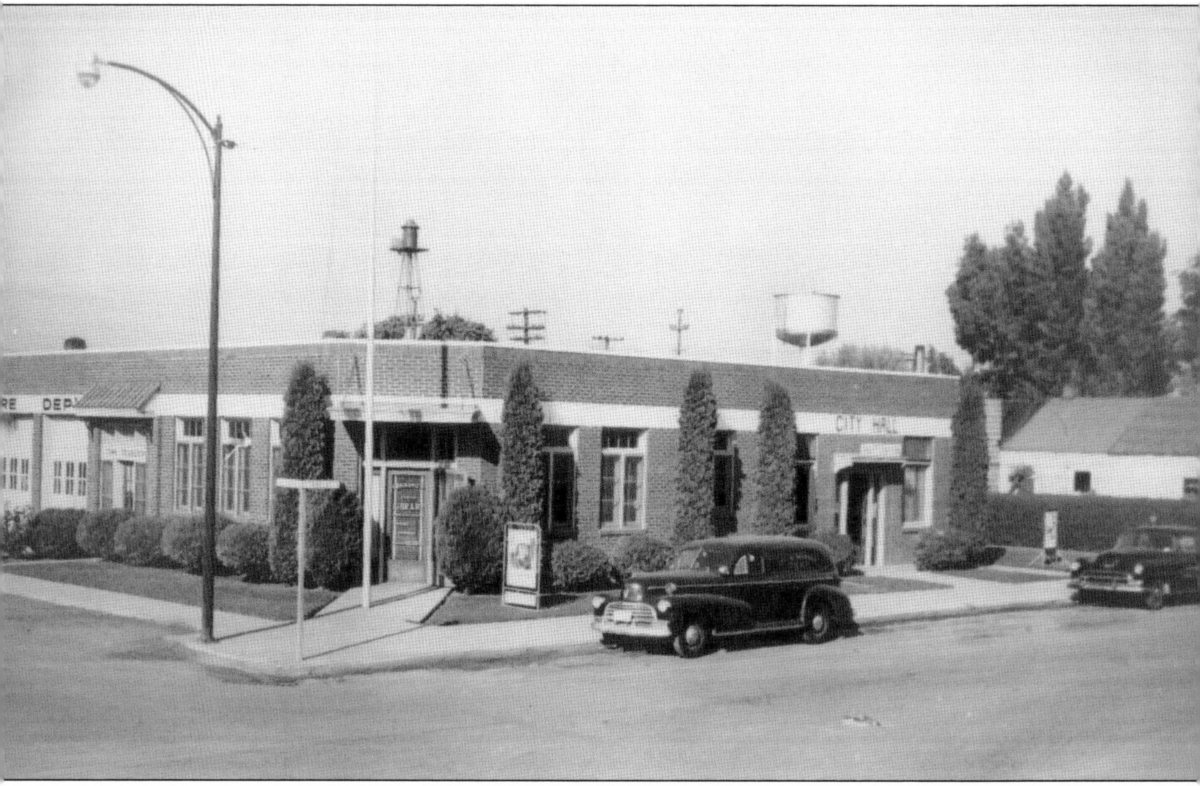

In 1952, townspeople needed to make only one stop to conduct city business. All in this building, they could pay their water bill at city hall, get a fire permit at the fire department, see if their lost dog had been picked up by the police department, and check out the latest bestseller at the public library. The building, listed in the Washington State Register of Historic Places, still serves as the Grandview police station. (Courtesy of the Washington State Historical Society.)

Grandview got a new jail in 1956, when the Lingang Construction Company of Yakima was awarded the construction job with a bid of $19,231.70 for the 20-foot-by-40-foot building. An article in the *Grandview Herald* reported, "The new building will have four separate units . . . for accommodating Grandview's restricted guests." Shown here is the dismantling of the old jail. (Courtesy of the Grandview Police Department.)

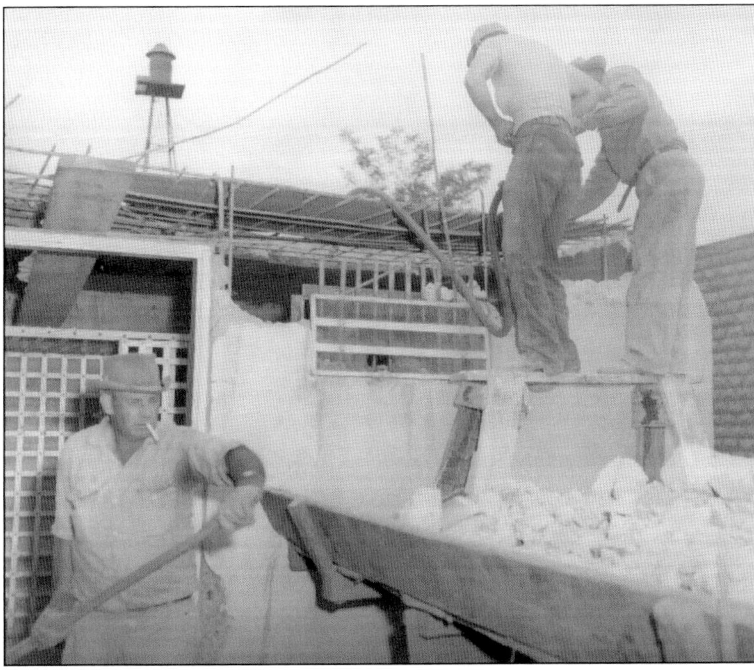

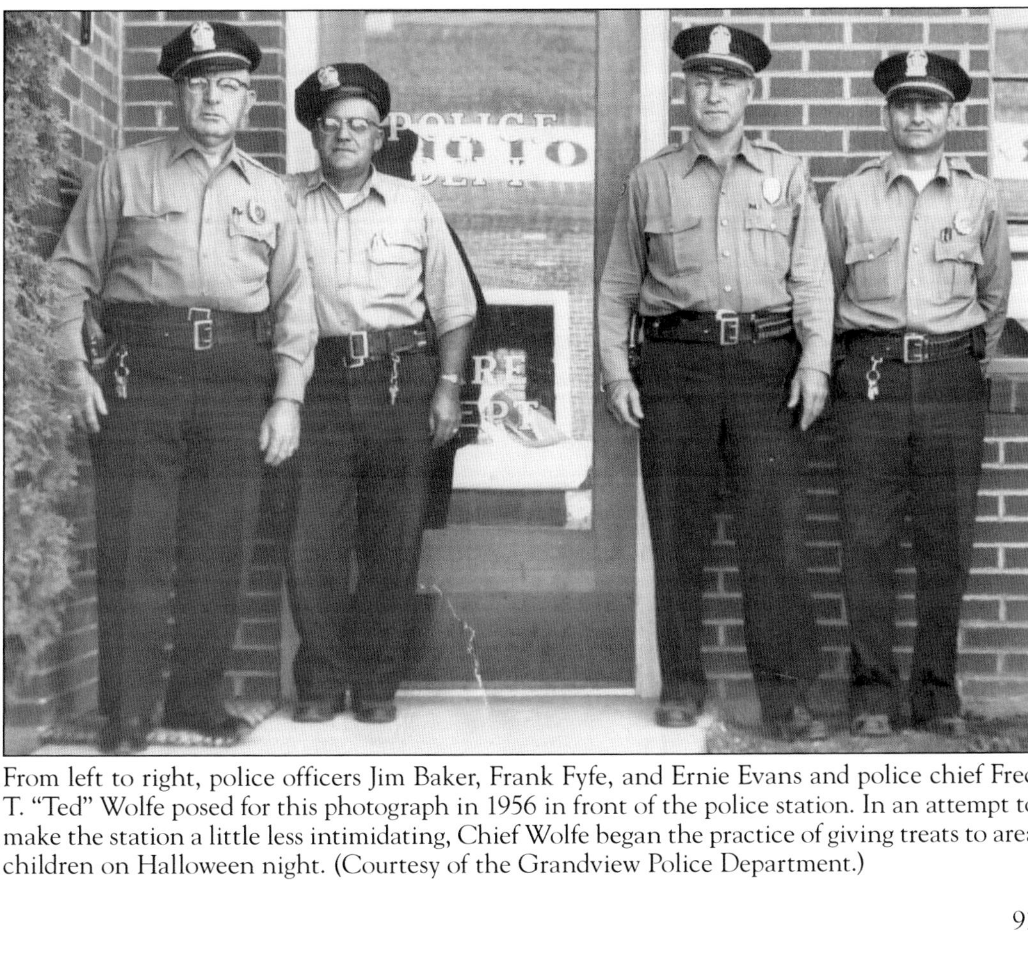

From left to right, police officers Jim Baker, Frank Fyfe, and Ernie Evans and police chief Fred T. "Ted" Wolfe posed for this photograph in 1956 in front of the police station. In an attempt to make the station a little less intimidating, Chief Wolfe began the practice of giving treats to area children on Halloween night. (Courtesy of the Grandview Police Department.)

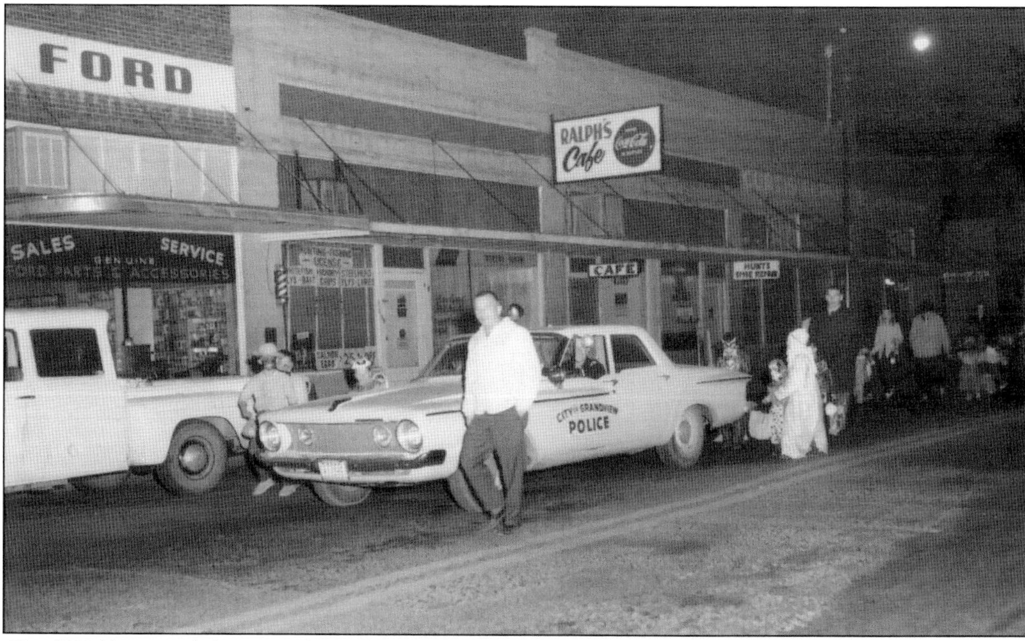

Chief Wolfe started the annual Spook Parade in 1951; by 1963, with the help of the Grandview Kiwanis Club, over 1,000 costumed youngsters paraded around the downtown business area, trick-or-treating at several businesses along the way. Children are following behind and alongside the police car on West Second Street in this 1963 photograph. (Courtesy of the Grandview Police Department.)

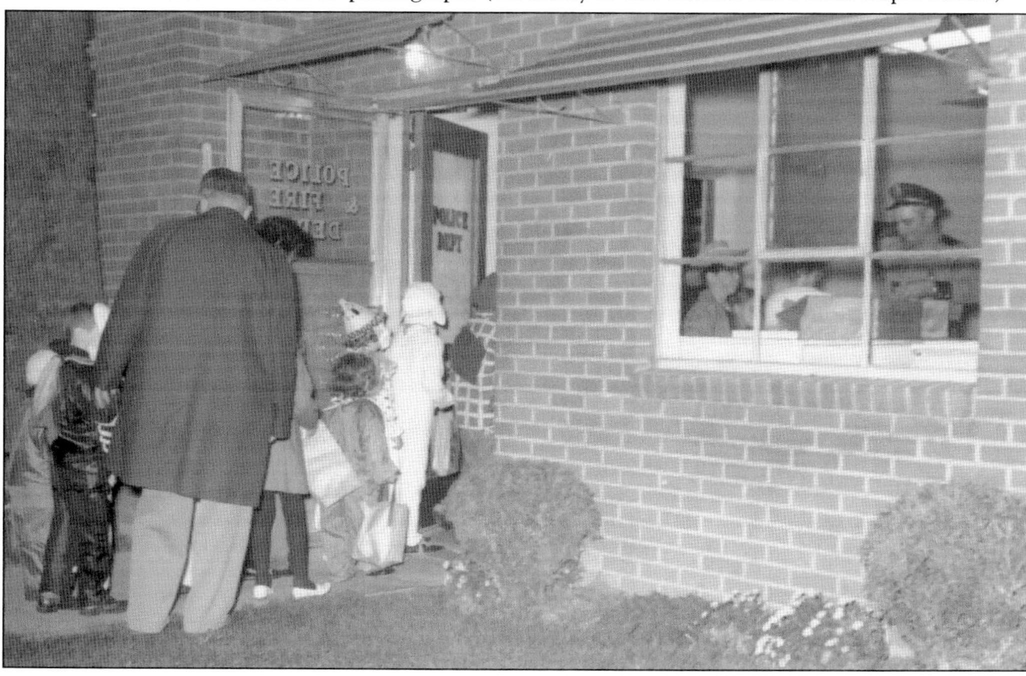

It was the tradition to end the parade at the police station, where the officers provided treats and judged the children's costumes. In this photograph from 1964, Chief Wolfe is seen clearly through the window. The tradition continued well into the 1980s. (Courtesy of the Grandview Police Department.)

Officer Clarence Zahn responds to a break-in at R.H. Smith Distributing on January 18, 1956. In 1947, Robert H. Smith formed the company in Grandview. Over the years, the company has marketed several petroleum brands, such as Signal, Rainbow, Amoco, and Conoco. Today, the business continues to provide fuel and convenience products to customers and travelers from the Cascade Mountains to the Columbia River. (Courtesy of the Grandview Police Department.)

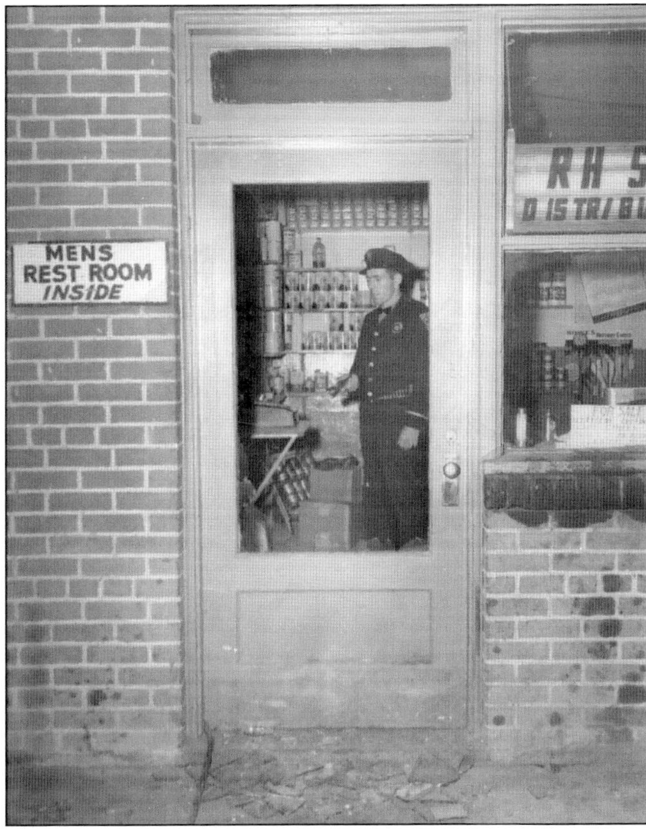

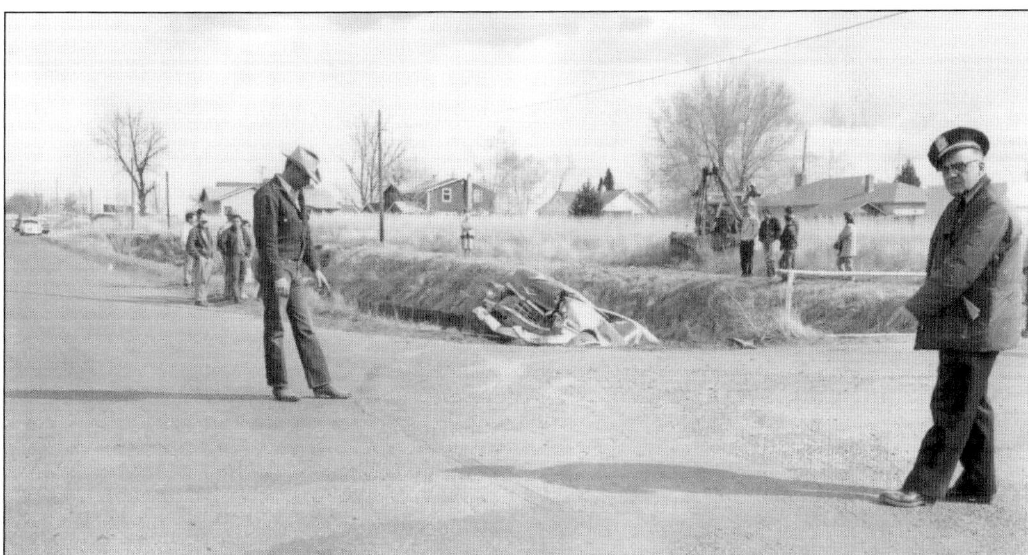

In 1889, the Northern Pacific Railroad hired Walter N. Granger to bring irrigation to the Yakima Valley; by 1892, the Sunnyside Canal project was supplying water to area farms. Unfortunately, the miles of uncovered canals allowed for accidents of the type shown here being investigated by Chief Ted Wolfe (in cowboy hat) and officer Frank Fyfe (far right) in 1956. (Courtesy of the Grandview Police Department.)

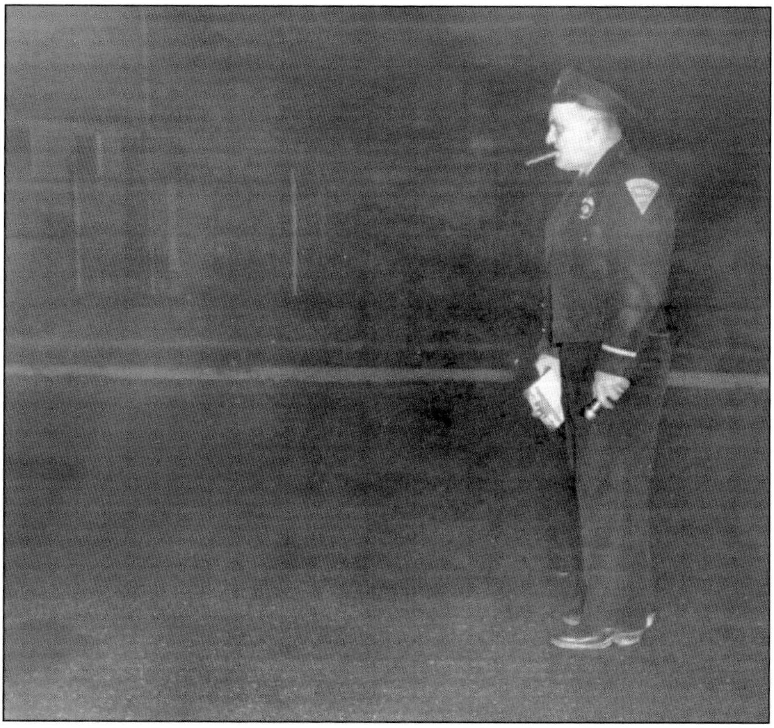

Frank Fyfe, shown here in 1956, lived most of his life in Grandview and was a Grandview police officer from 1953 until his retirement in 1966. Fyfe was instrumental in solving a theft of approximately $2,000 worth of stolen Indian beadwork from John Barney of Goldendale when he spotted a car containing the items during his regular Friday night rounds. (Courtesy of the Grandview Police Department.)

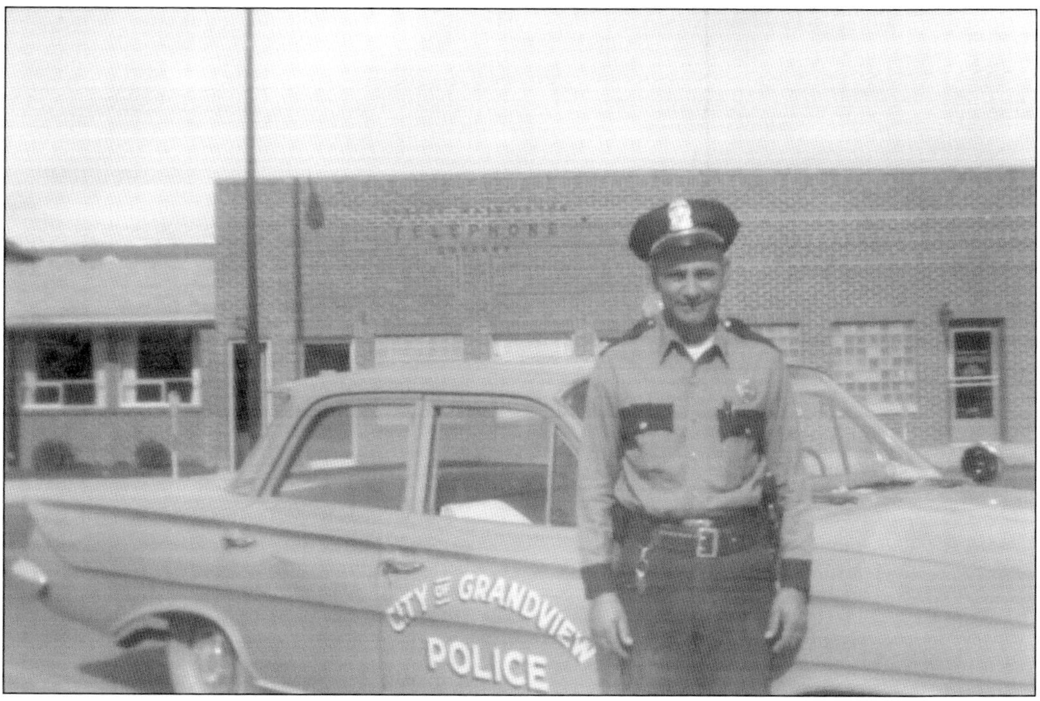

When Ted Wolfe began working for the Grandview Police Department in 1950, Grandview had only two police officers, him and police chief Jack Stock. There were no radios and no uniforms, and "you could wear bib overalls if you wanted," as he told the *Seattle Times* in 1972. Wolfe, shown here in 1962, became police chief in 1951. (Courtesy of the Grandview Police Department.)

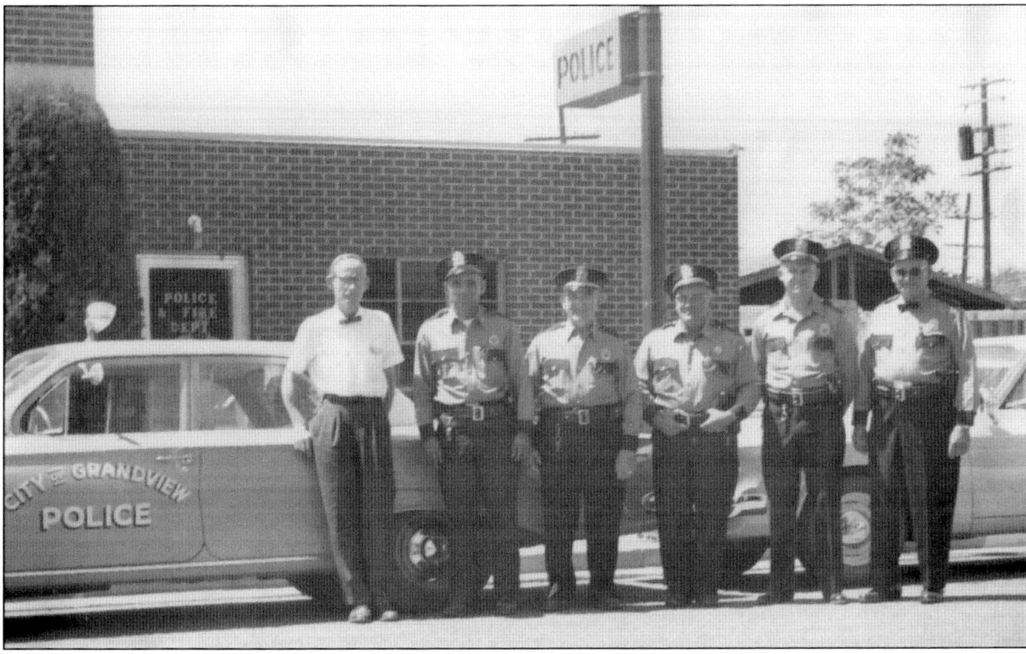

Grandview's law enforcement officers pose outside the police department on Avenue A in July 1962. From left to right, they are Philip M. Noon, Chief Ted Wolfe, Jim Baker, Frank Fyfe, George Miller, and Al Dutcher. Noon, a Grandview Municipal Court judge with 48 years of service, is believed to have been the longest-sitting judge in Washington State. (Courtesy of the Grandview Police Department.)

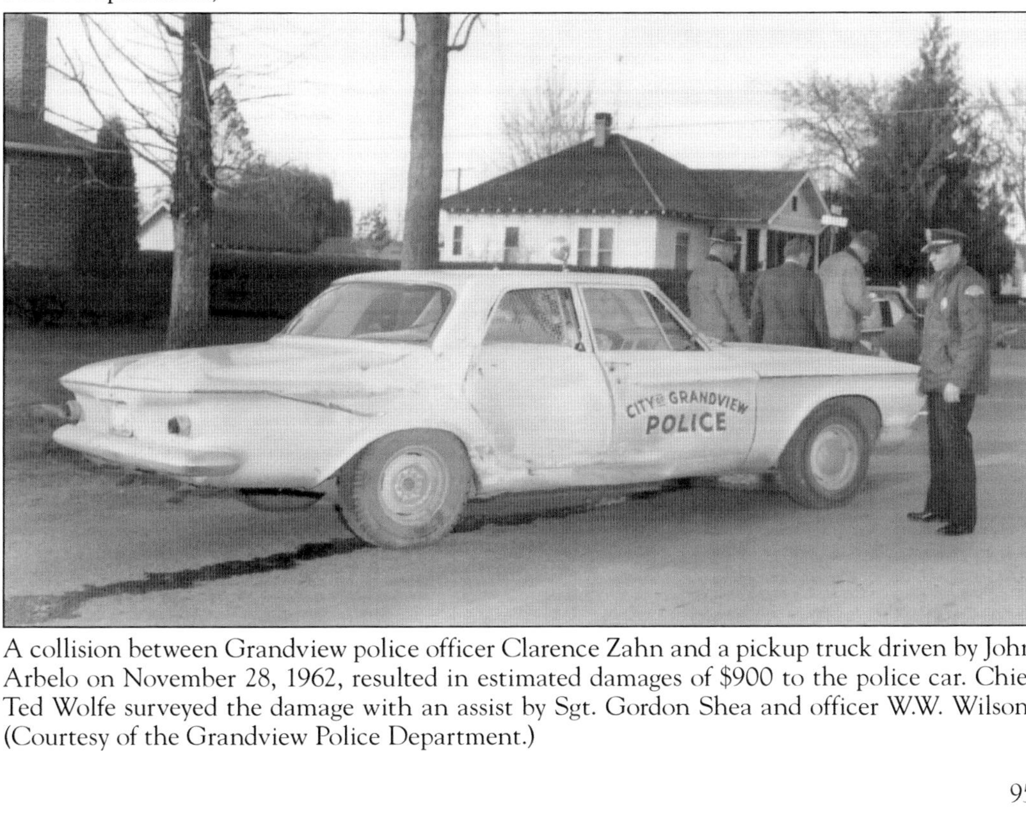

A collision between Grandview police officer Clarence Zahn and a pickup truck driven by John Arbelo on November 28, 1962, resulted in estimated damages of $900 to the police car. Chief Ted Wolfe surveyed the damage with an assist by Sgt. Gordon Shea and officer W.W. Wilson. (Courtesy of the Grandview Police Department.)

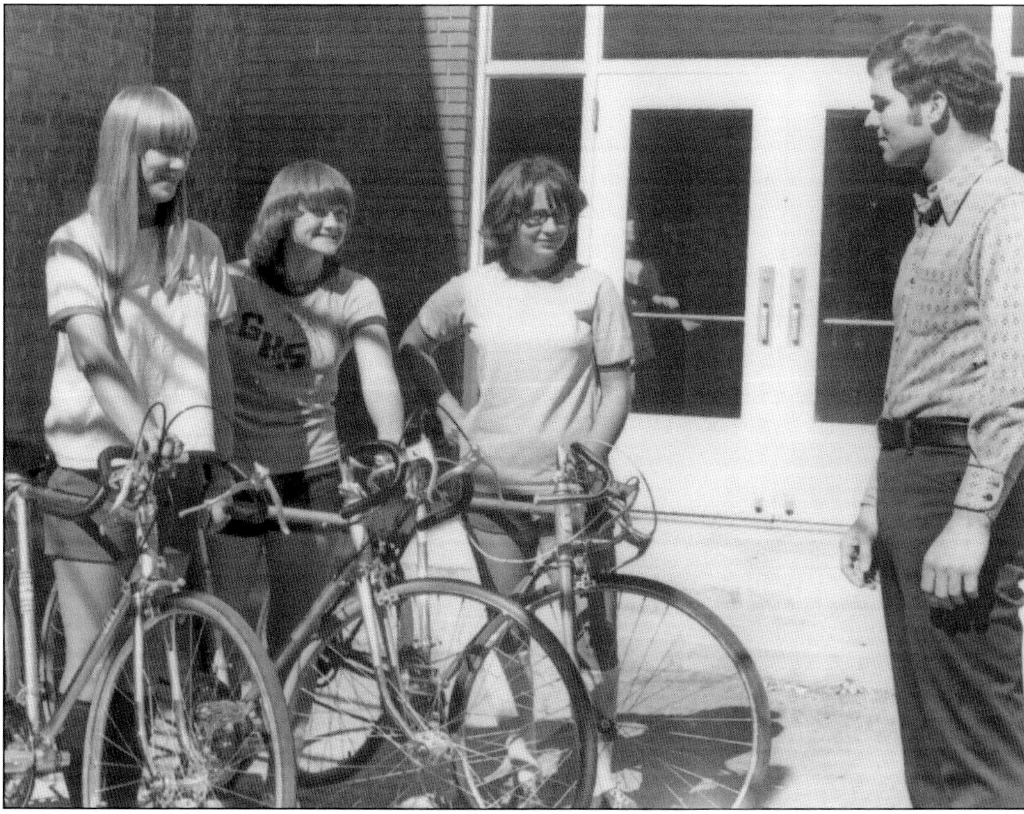

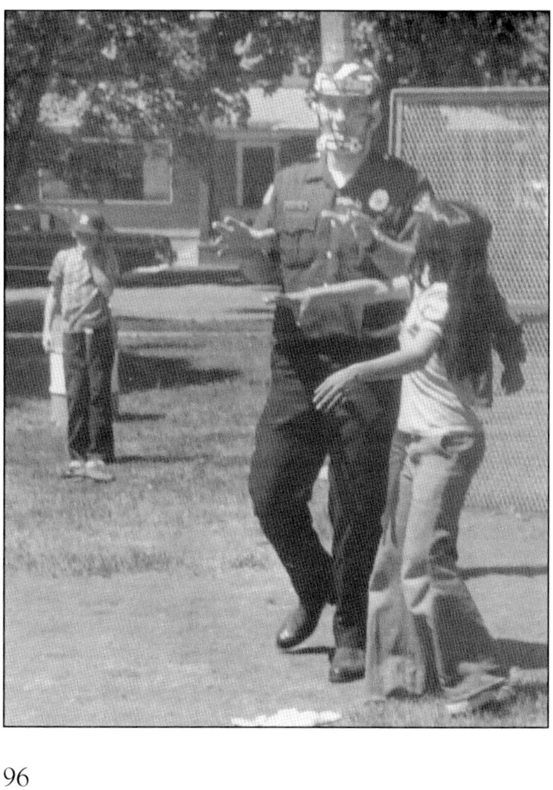

Off-duty police officer Dave Charvet appears to be offering bicycle safety tips to Grandview High School students (from left to right) Judy Sexton, Diane Alderman (Fortune), and Donna Miller in this September 1974 photograph. Donna's father, George, was police chief at the time. (Courtesy of the Grandview Police Department.)

". . . But she was safe!" argues a young girl to umpire and police officer Brian Carey during this May 1975 softball game. Over the years, the members of the Grandview Police Department have volunteered their time to youth sports activities. In January 1977, officer Mark Ware, then 24, said, "It wasn't that long ago I was a kid." Ware, along with Ralph Scott, was an assistant softball coach at Grandview High School for many years. (Courtesy of the Grandview Police Department.)

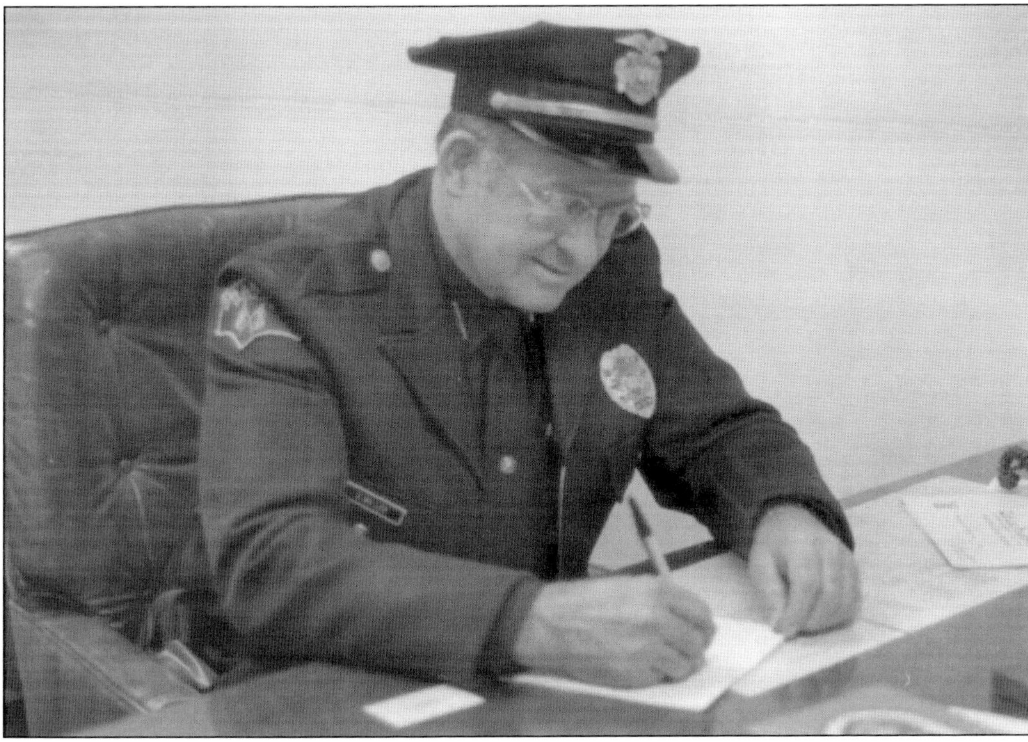

George Miller (above) began his rookie year in the police force in 1958 and was police chief from 1974 until his retirement in 1984. "It's going to be hard to find a place where there are better people to work with," Miller told the *Grandview Herald* in a December 8, 1984, article. Below, police officers gather for a photograph in December 1978. They are, from left to right, Al Schroeder, Bob Reed, John Garcia, Mark Ware, Carl Butler, Armando Martinez, John Dobrauc, Bill Cornwell, Delbert St. George, and police chief George Miller. (Both courtesy of the Grandview Police Department.)

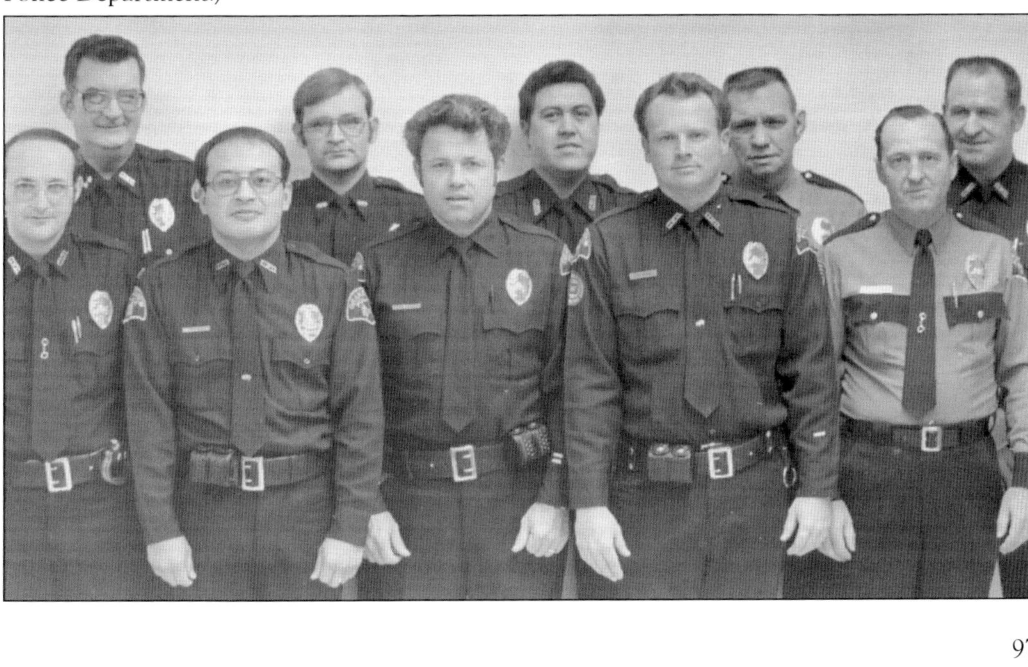

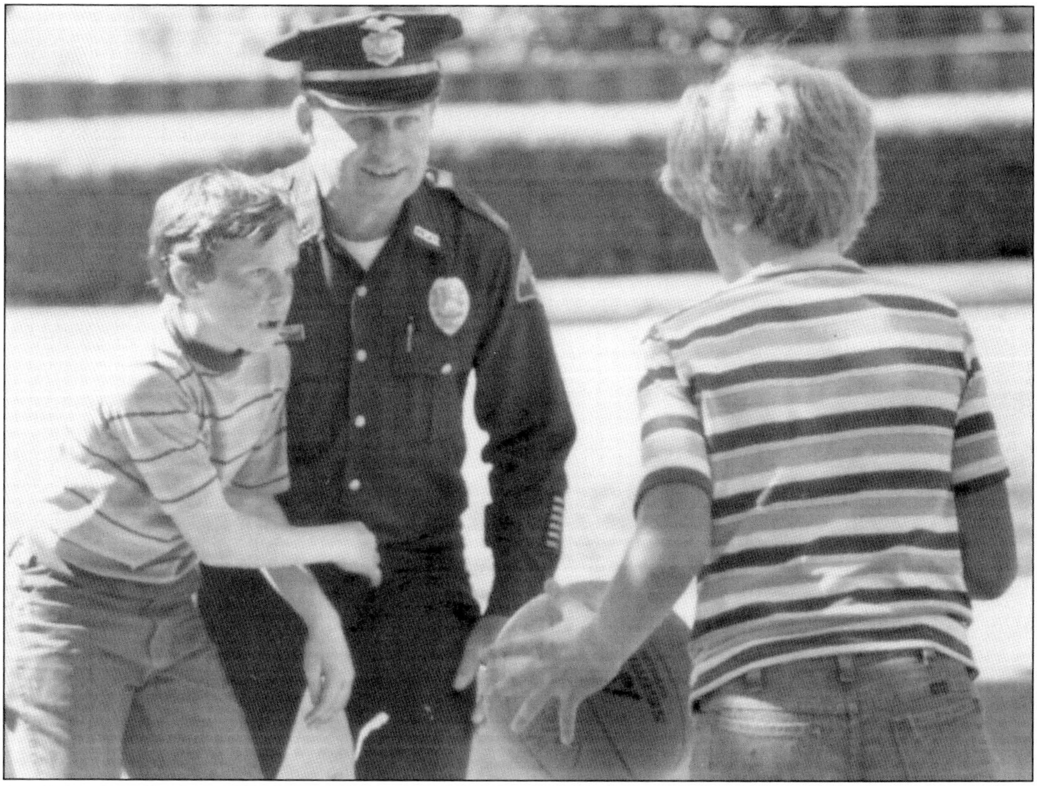

Student patrolman Hal Weisz (left) and police chief George Miller create a tough defense against Gary Anderson during the annual School Patrol picnic on May 25, 1978. "I do it because I really enjoy being with the kids," said Miller. (Courtesy of the Grandview Police Department.)

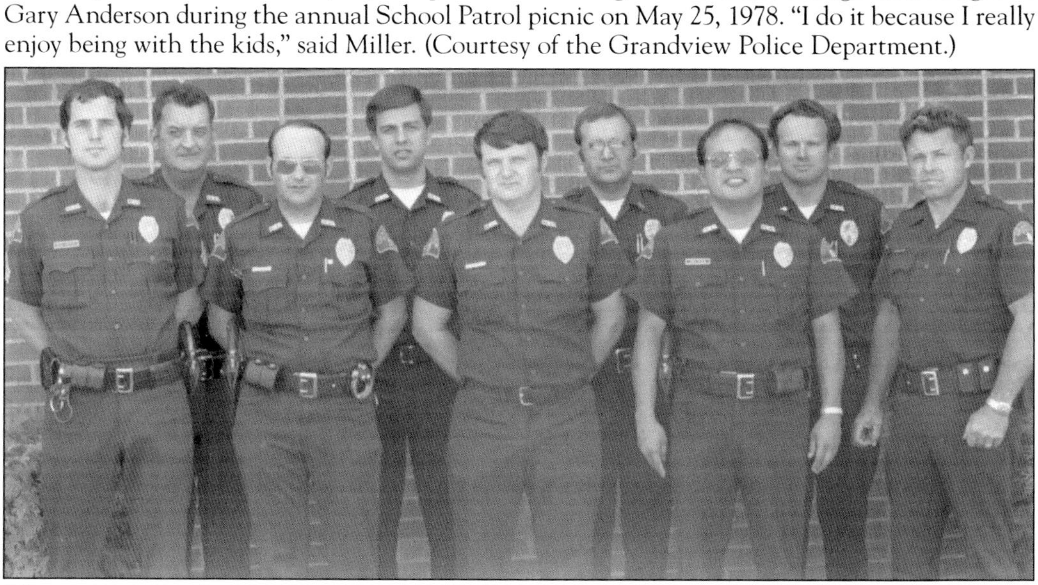

These 1979 Grandview police officers are, from left to right, Dave Charvet, Robert Reed, Al Schroeder, Gary Miller, Steven Coons, Mark Ware, John Garcia, John Dobrauc, and Carl Butler. At his formal police academy graduation earlier that year, Schroeder stated, "A community is as safe as their police officers make it. With the community and the local police working together . . . Grandview can be a town people are proud of." (Courtesy of the Grandview Police Department.)

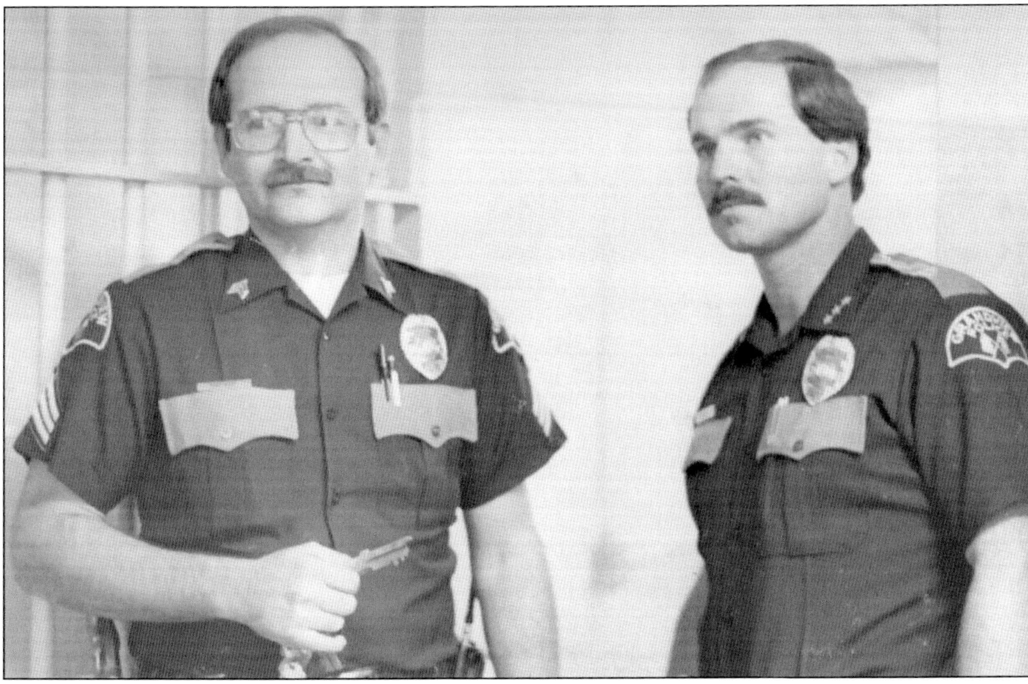

Officer Mark Ware (left), who later became assistant police chief, and police chief Dave Charvet are seen here in October 1985 while filming a public service notice declaring, "If you drink and drive in Yakima County, we'll introduce you to a few new bars." (Courtesy of the Grandview Police Department.)

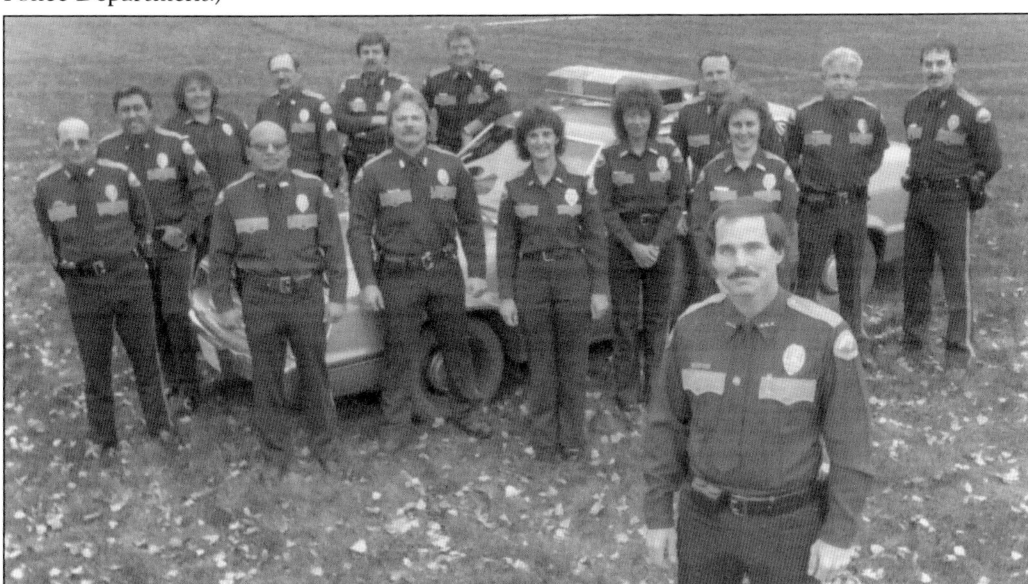

The police force had almost doubled in size by October 31, 1985. Dave Charvet had advanced to police chief the year before, and, in an uncredited *Grandview Herald* interview, he said, "The department is one of the best in the valley," and that the "low turnover rate within the department is a key factor." Chief Charvet retired in January 2014 after 42 years. (Courtesy of the Grandview Police Department.)

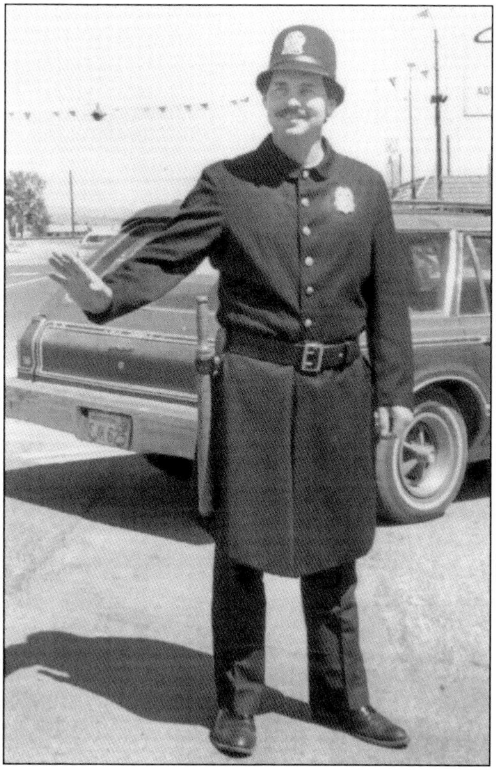

On April 3, 1984, after 12 years on the force, officer Dave Charvet, at the age of 32, was sworn in as chief of the city's 15-man police force. When Charvet joined the force in 1972, there were only five members. On one occasion, he was arresting an armed robbery escapee from Spokane when the man pulled a gun and fired. Charvet grabbed the gun, which had failed to discharge. The chief carried that bullet in his pocket for many years as a reminder of what could have happened. He is seen here in a period uniform for a Community Days celebration on June 5, 1984. (Both courtesy of the Grandview Police Department.)

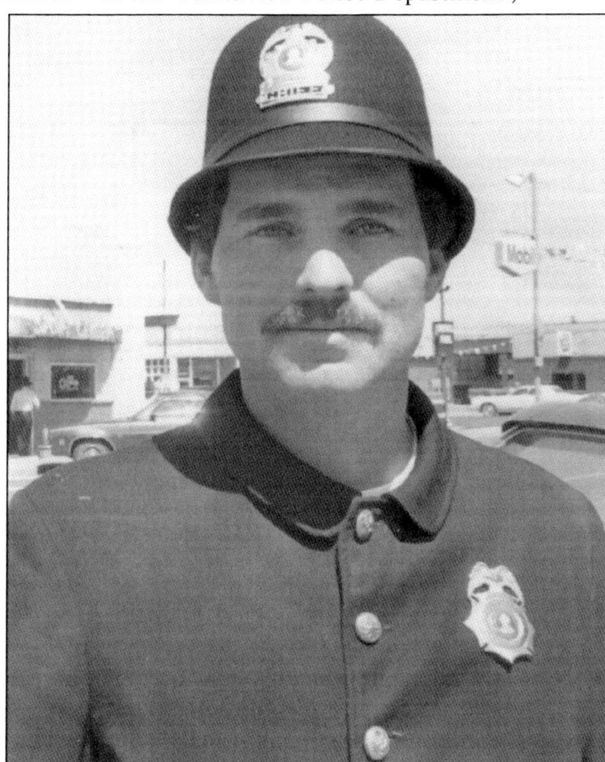

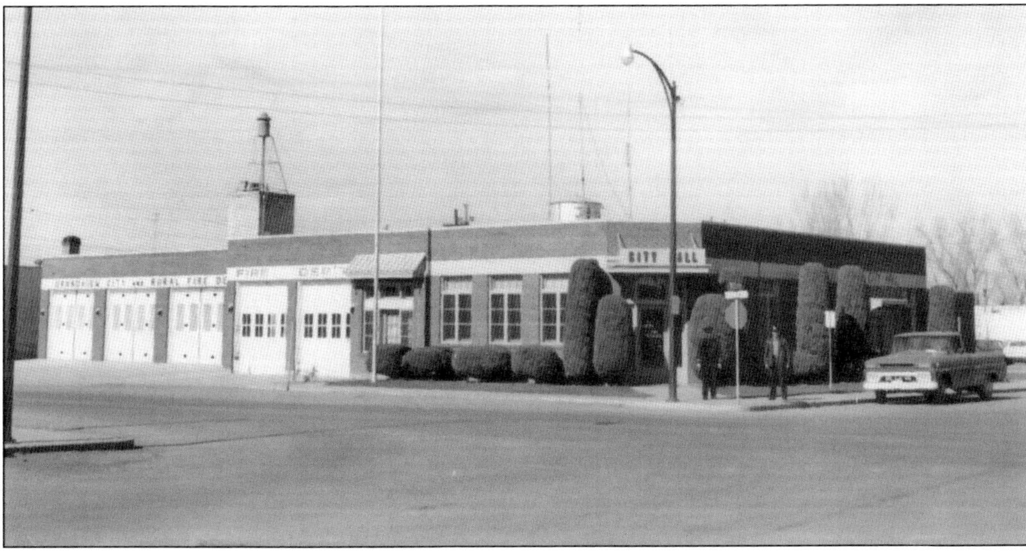

The combined city hall, fire department, and police station continued to enlarge as the needs of the city grew, as can be seen by comparing the photograph above, taken in 1963, with the one on page 87, taken in 1937. Three parking bays have been added to the left of the original building. In the undated photograph below, the fire department proudly displays its equipment. The 1968 American La France (left) is still in use today, while the 1937 Chevrolet (right) has retired to a more genteel existence. The old favorite, purchased new in 1937 from the Howard Cooper Corporation, proudly represents Grandview at area events. (Above, courtesy of the Grandview Police Department; below, courtesy of the Grandview Fire Department.)

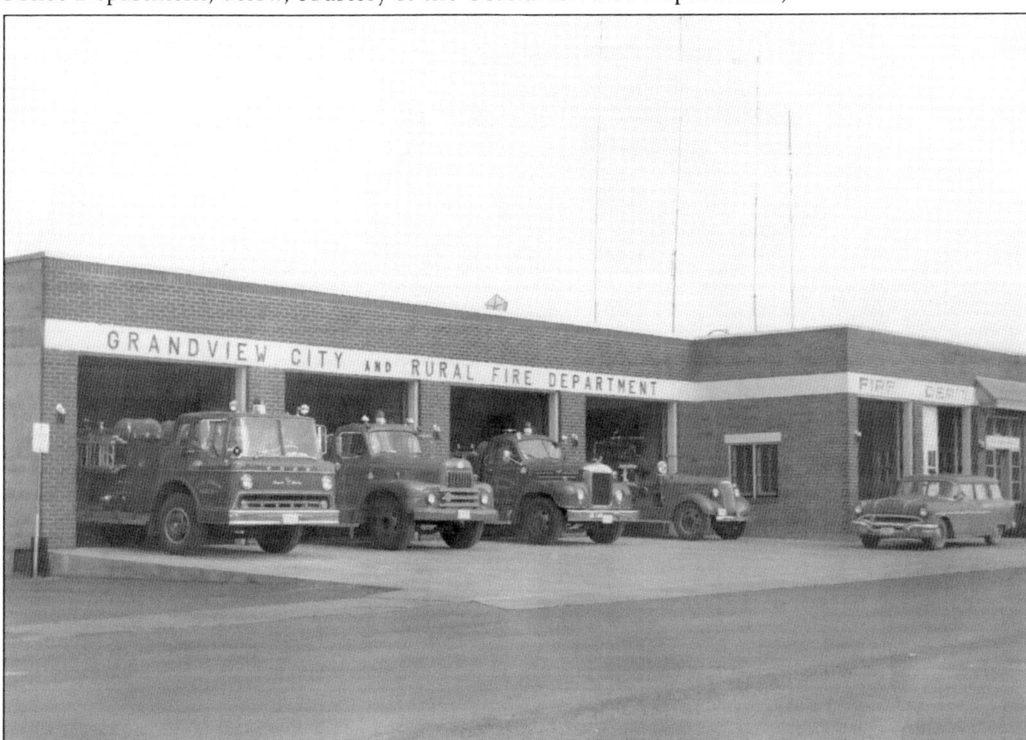

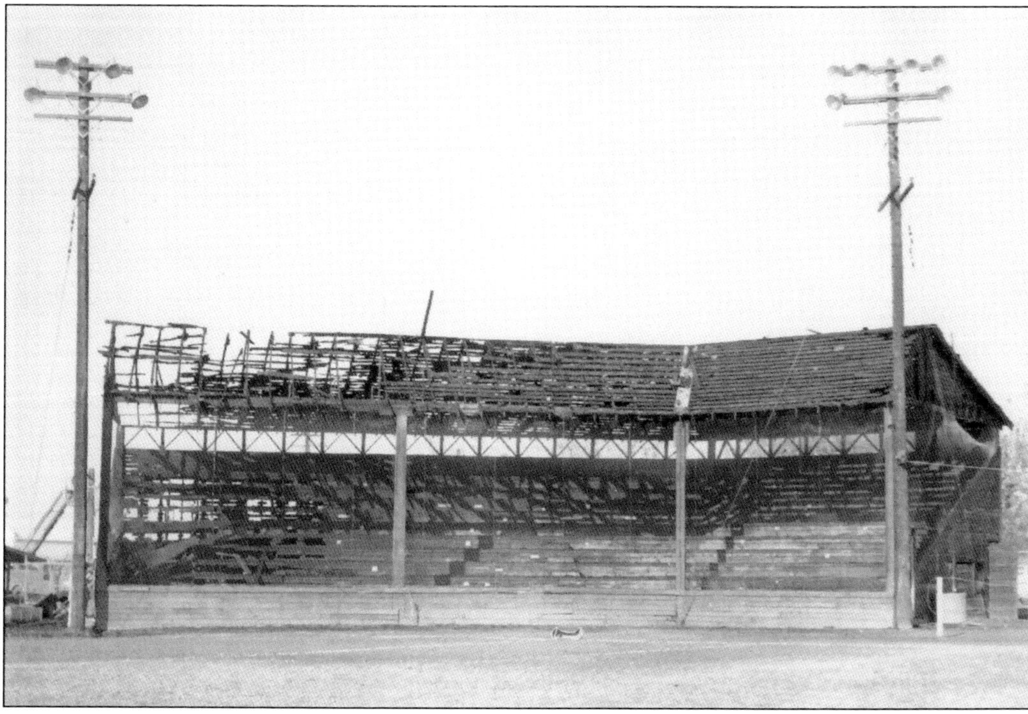

A Grandview landmark was destroyed by fire on November 5, 1964. The ballpark grandstand was located at the fairgrounds between Second and Main Streets, where the Grandview campus of the Yakima Valley Community College stands today, and was used for many community activities (see page 118). (Courtesy of the Grandview Fire Department.)

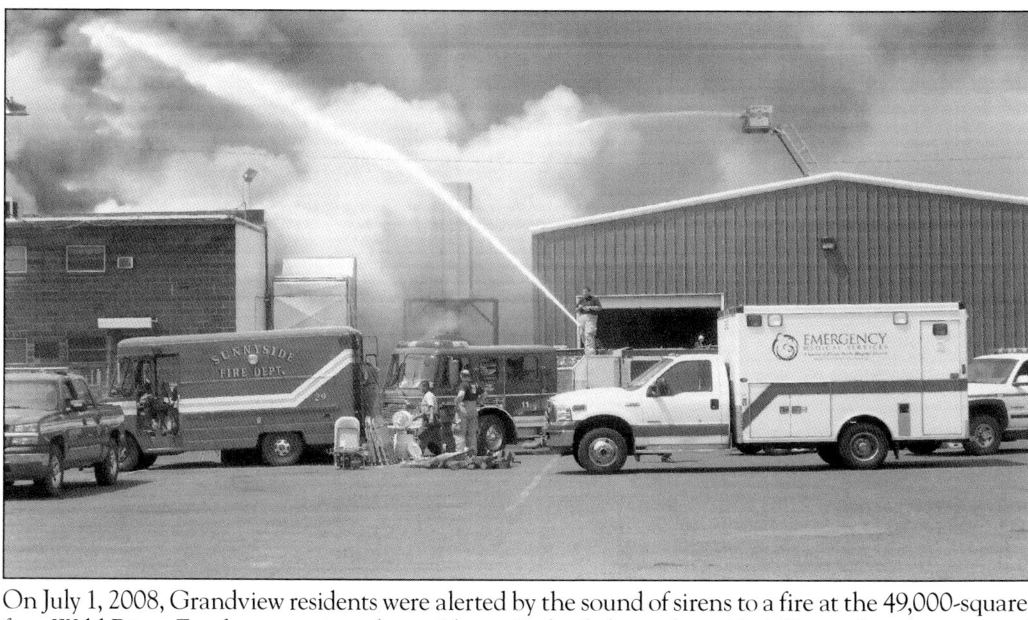

On July 1, 2008, Grandview residents were alerted by the sound of sirens to a fire at the 49,000-square-foot Wild River Foods processing plant. About 60 firefighters from 12 different fire districts and departments united to fight the blaze. At one time, four ladder trucks were shooting water from above the flames. Unfortunately, the plant was a total loss. (Author's collection.)

Five

100 Years in a Grand Place

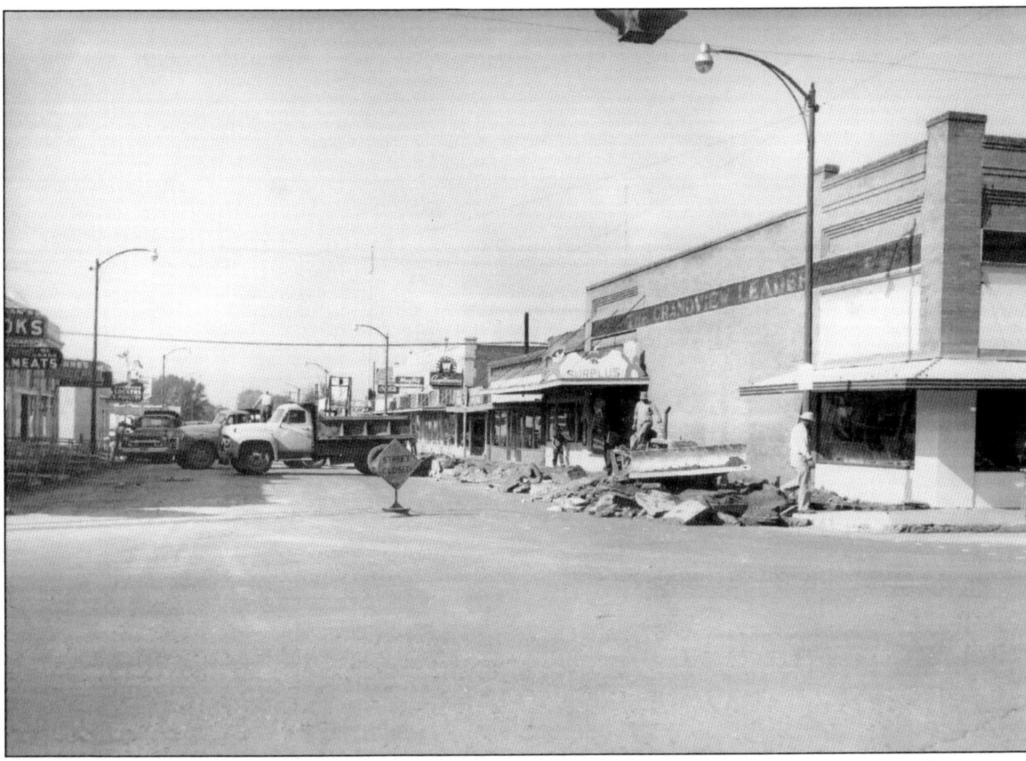

The corner of Second and Division Streets has always been a busy intersection in downtown Grandview. This photograph from around 1960 shows local tax dollars at work on street improvements. The names on the businesses are different, but, with few changes beyond paint and signage, the view towards the west and Mount Adams remains the same to this day. The Grandview Leader building (front right) was an early mini-mall containing several businesses.

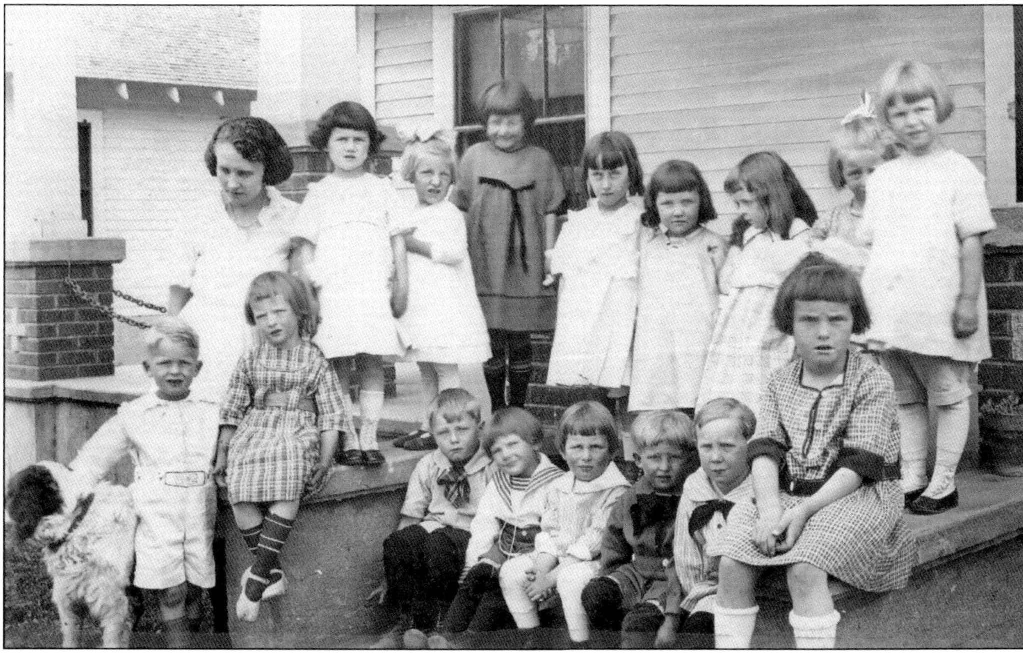

Seen here on the porch are kindergarten teacher Lucretia Matthews and her class from 1921. From left to right are (first row) Brenner Scott, Elizabeth Rogers, Roger Jensen, Charles Eccleston, Bob Purdue, ? Horton, Bob Devoe, and ? Pierce; (second row) Matthews, Peggy Thiele, unidentified, Louise Ehmer, Donna Taylor, Mildred Martin, ? Anderson, unidentified, and Martha Nell Parker. Brenner Scott was the son of Reverend Scott.

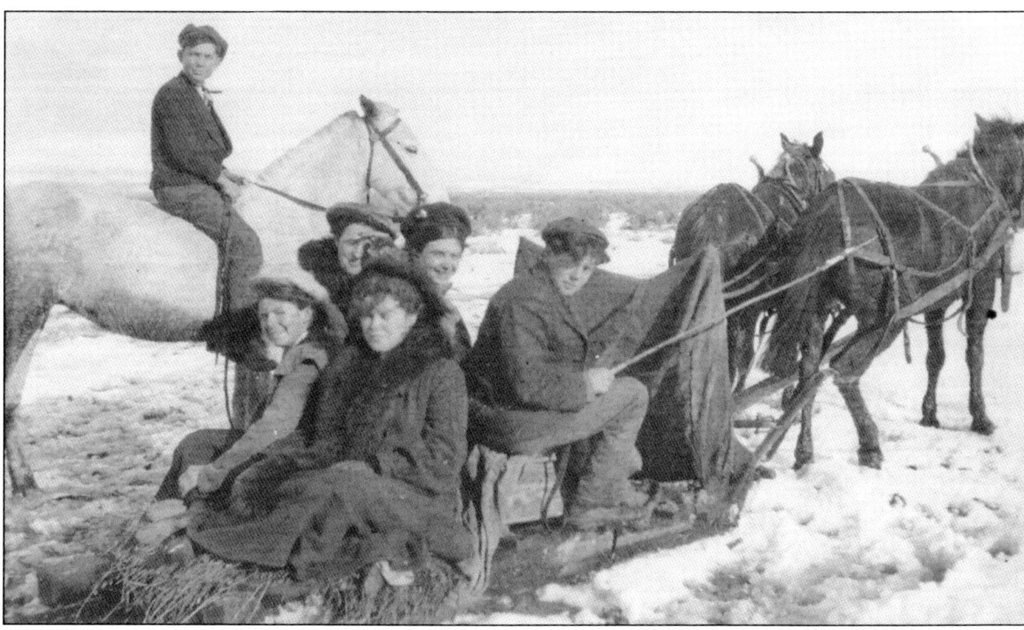

Slushy snow, a sled, and a team of horses provide a sunny afternoon of fun for these unidentified young people in this very early photograph. With the addition of ice and snow, hard and often rutted dirt tracks became nearly useless during the cold months. Removing a cart's wheels and placing the box on flat metal runners created a handy sled both for work and, as seen here, for fun.

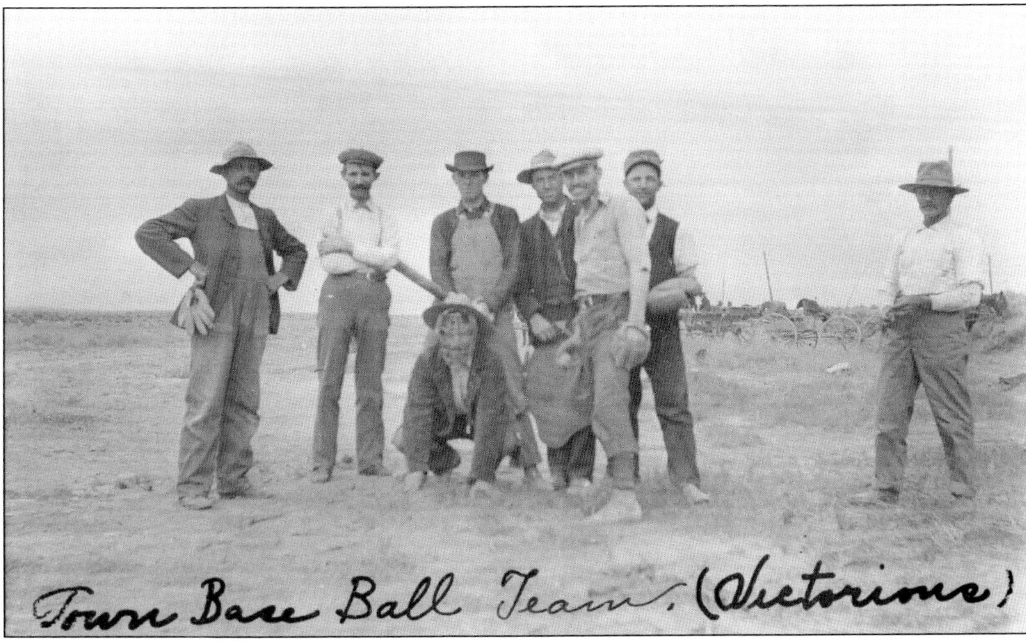

In 1907, Grandview's town team (above) and the Orchard Tract Construction team (below) played in the town's first official baseball game. It can be safely assumed that the Orchard Tract team lost the game because of the handwritten caption of "Victorious" on the town team photograph. A lack of uniforms and equipment—between the two teams, only one bat, one catcher's mask, six gloves, and one baseball can be seen—did nothing to dampen the enthusiasm of the players or fans. The only things needed were an open field and perhaps some conveniently growing sagebrush to serve as bases.

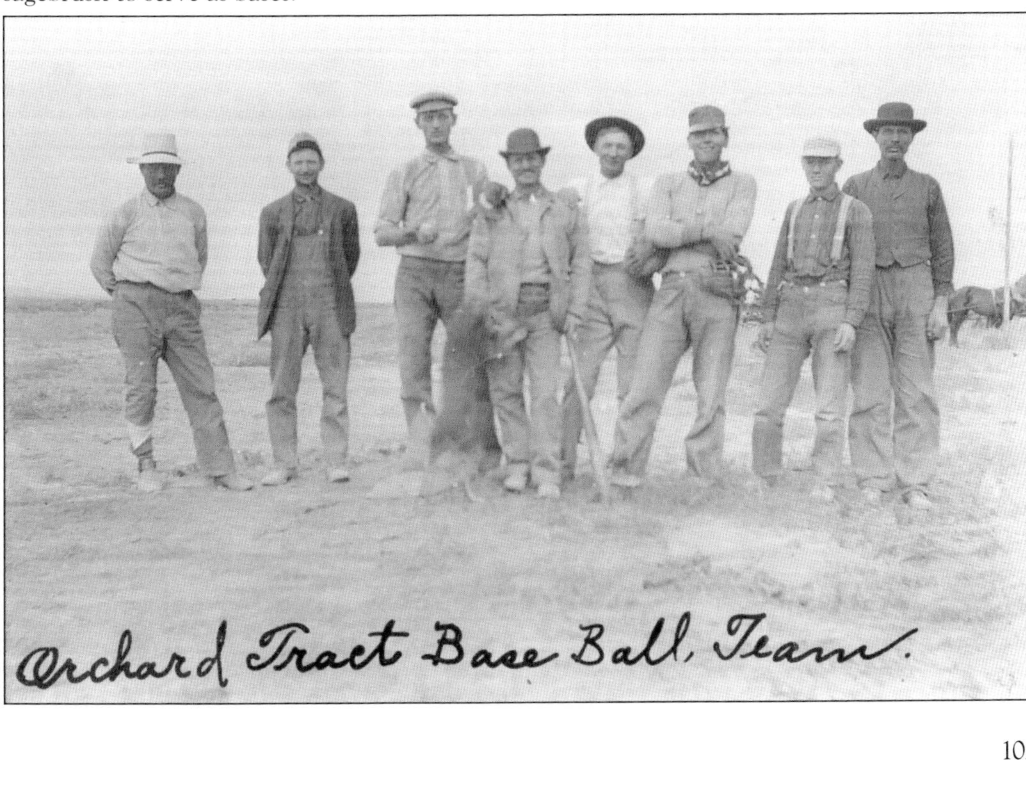

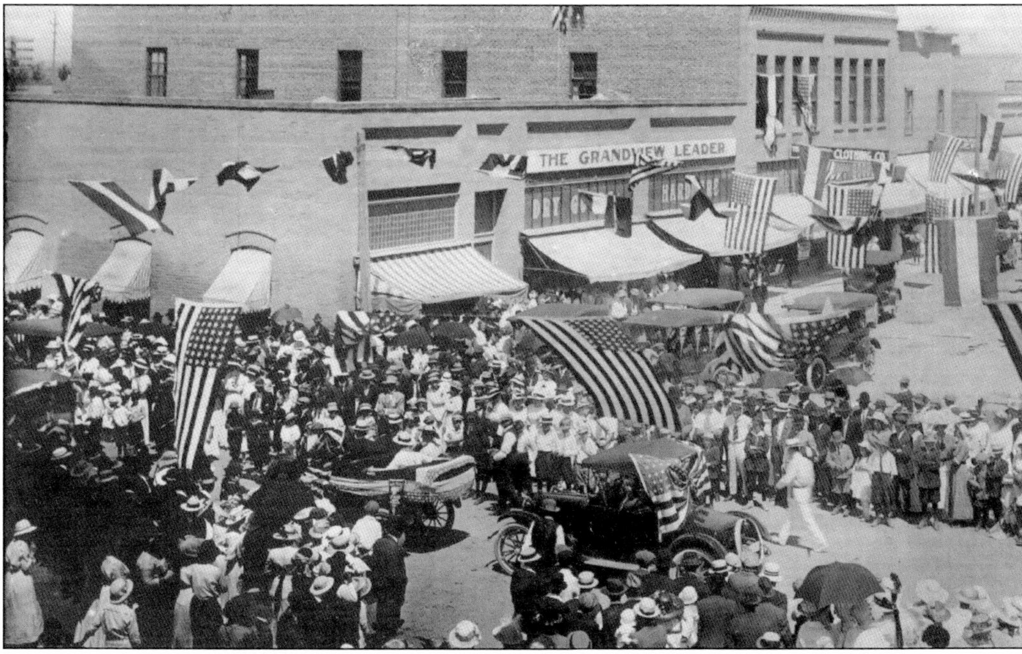

Grandview's first public celebration was held on July 4, 1916. The parade is seen here at the corner of Division Street moving west on Second Street. Today, that same route, although traveling in the opposite direction, is taken in the Yakima Valley Fair parade. Two major buildings visible on the west side of Division Street are the Grandview Leader building (left) and the E.O. Keck Building, housing the Valley Clothing Company.

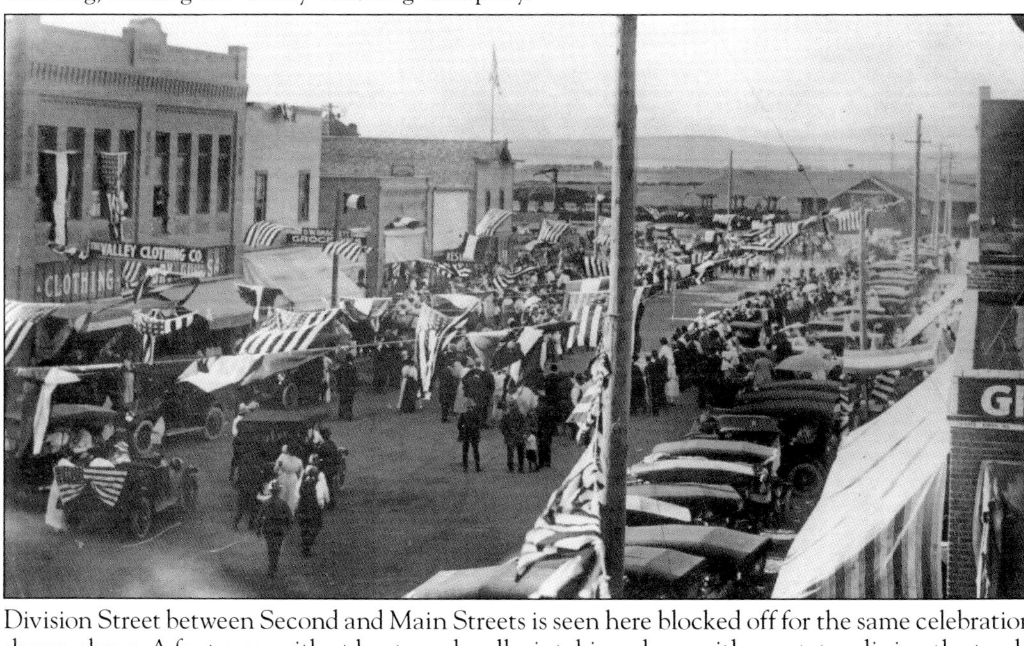

Division Street between Second and Main Streets is seen here blocked off for the same celebration shown above. A foot race, with at least one hurdle, is taking place, with spectators lining the track. To the right of the Grandview Leader building and the E.O. Keck Building are D.W. Brackett Groceries, a restaurant, and the post office. At the north (right) end of the street and across Main Street is the Oregon-Washington Railroad & Navigation Co. depot.

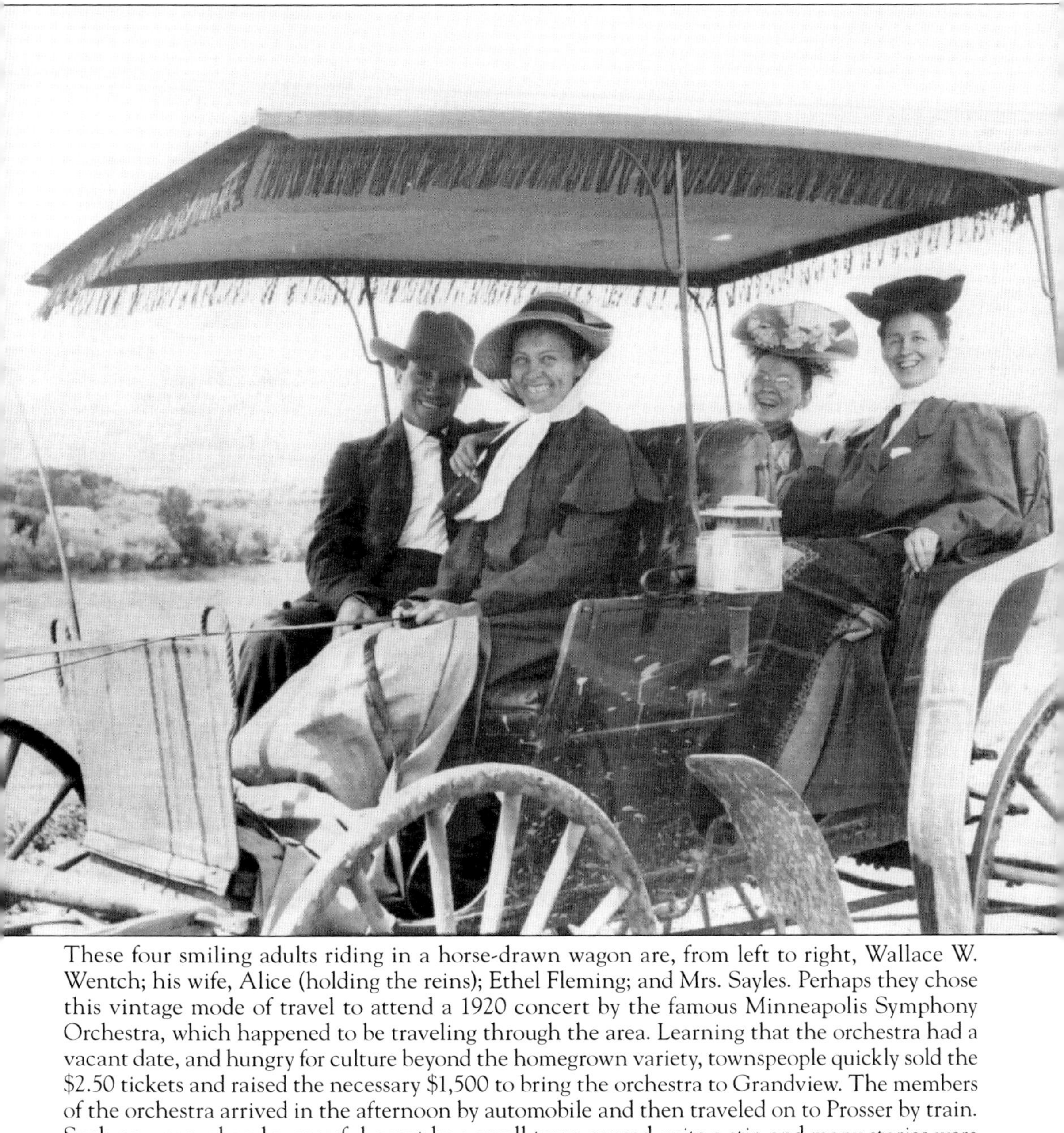

These four smiling adults riding in a horse-drawn wagon are, from left to right, Wallace W. Wentch; his wife, Alice (holding the reins); Ethel Fleming; and Mrs. Sayles. Perhaps they chose this vintage mode of travel to attend a 1920 concert by the famous Minneapolis Symphony Orchestra, which happened to be traveling through the area. Learning that the orchestra had a vacant date, and hungry for culture beyond the homegrown variety, townspeople quickly sold the $2.50 tickets and raised the necessary $1,500 to bring the orchestra to Grandview. The members of the orchestra arrived in the afternoon by automobile and then traveled on to Prosser by train. Such an unusual and successful event by a small town caused quite a stir, and many stories were written about it in Pacific Northwest newspapers.

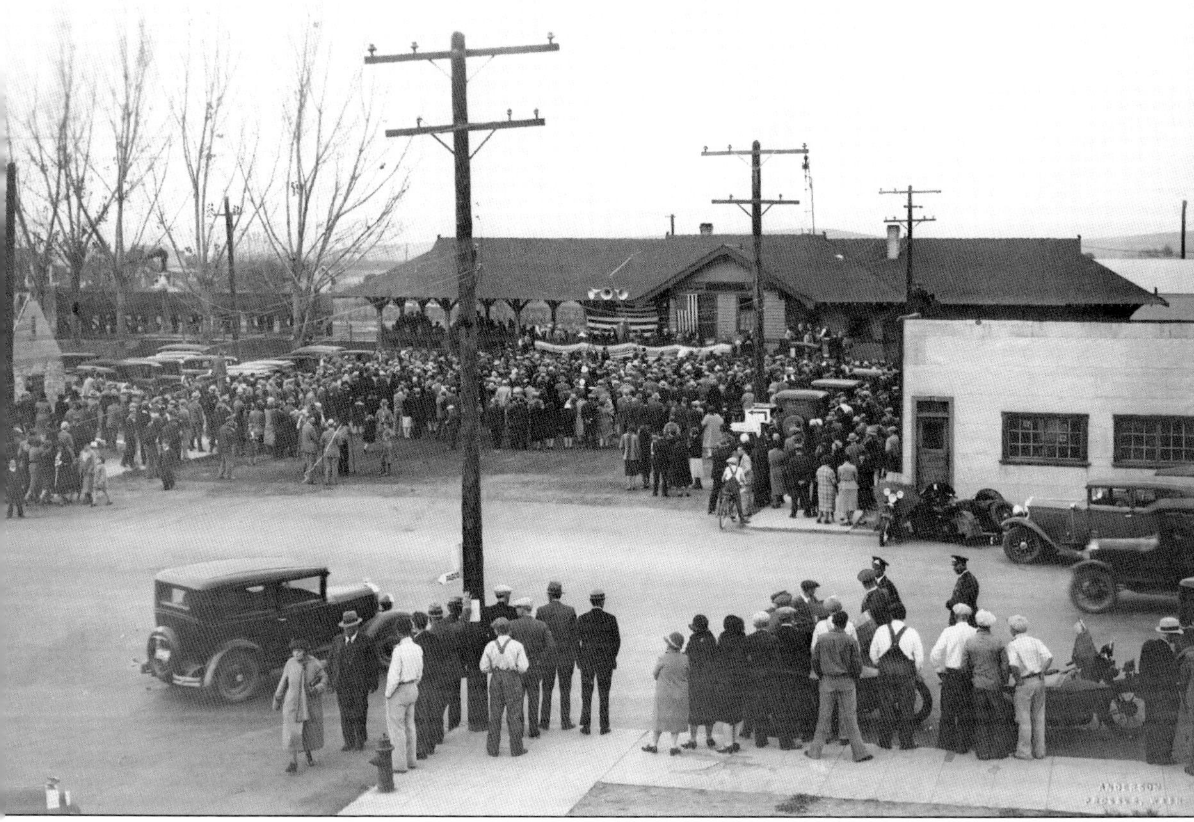

A dedication of the new link in State Route 3 connecting Prosser and Sunnyside took place on November 1, 1931, and attracted an estimated 3,500 people to town. The Union Pacific (originally the Oregon-Washington Railroad & Navigation Co.) depot platform, on the north side of Main Street, served as the dais, and Oscar Boose, a Sunnyside attorney, was master of ceremonies. It was praised in the book *History of Grandview, Washington*: "The new road is a perfect speedway, wide and smooth. It skirts both Sunnyside and Prosser but runs down Main Street in Grandview." The 14-mile stretch of road was built at a cost of $522,000 and has had several names over the years, including Main Street, Highway 12, and Wine Country Road, to name a few. The depot is the same building shown on page 27.

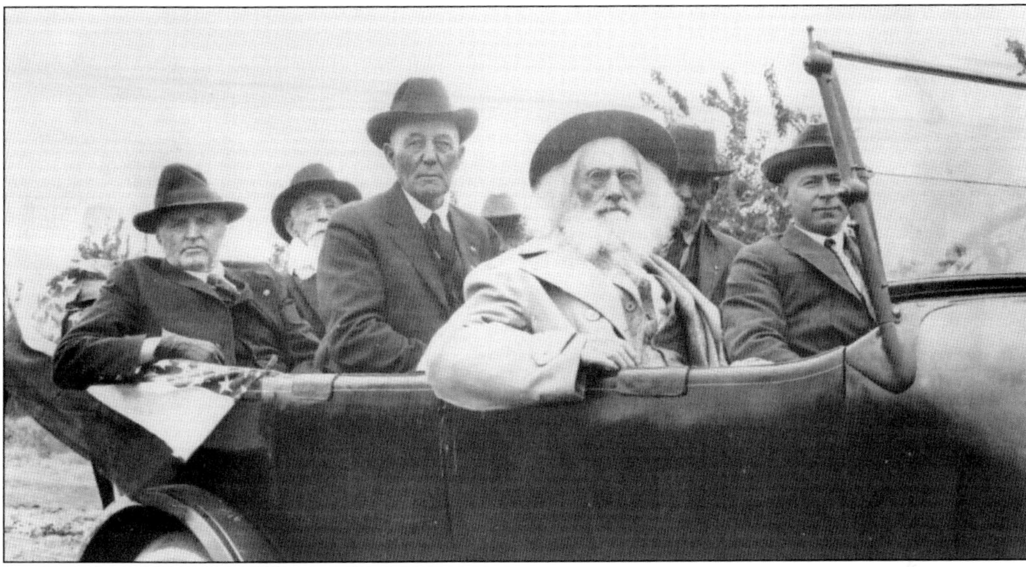

Ezra Meeker (1830–1928), a Washington pioneer, first traveled the Oregon Trail in 1852. Beginning in 1906 and continuing until his death, Meeker devoted his energy to guaranteeing the preservation of the trail for future generations. Specific details about this photograph of the white-haired Meeker have been lost, but it is assumed that it shows him and his traveling companions traveling through Grandview on the Yellowstone Trail (see page 84).

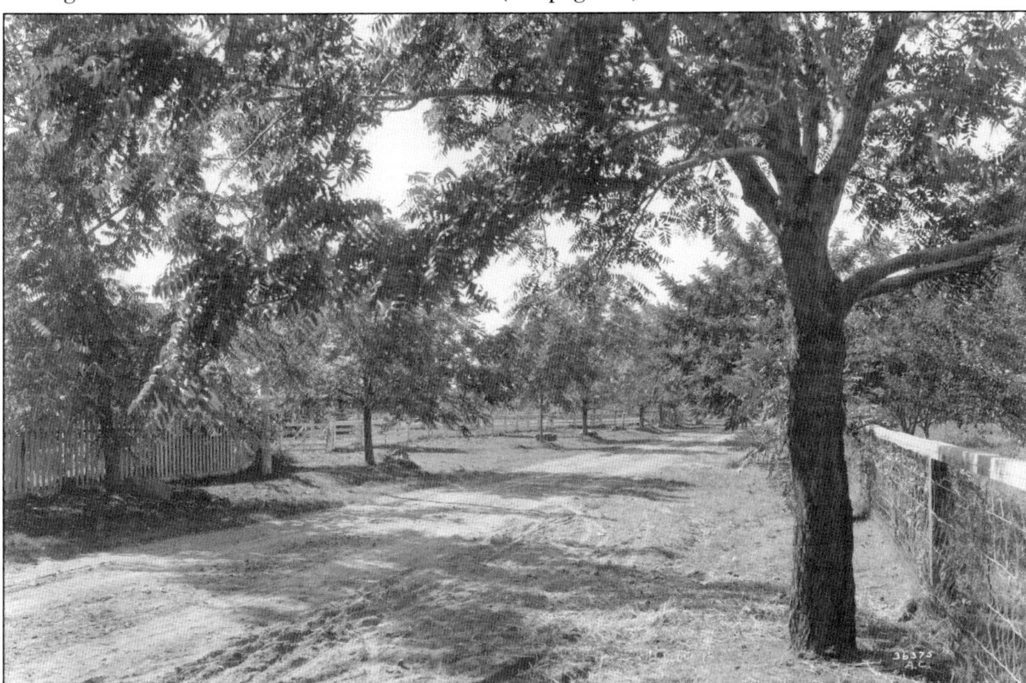

Walnut Drive (now Walnut Lane), a tree-lined road in the Orchard Tracts section of Grandview, bordered the ranch of famed photographer Asahel Curtis in 1918. This and many other original Asahel Curtis photographs are among the treasures to be found in Grandview's R.E. Powell Museum. (Photograph by Asahel Curtis; courtesy of GHC.)

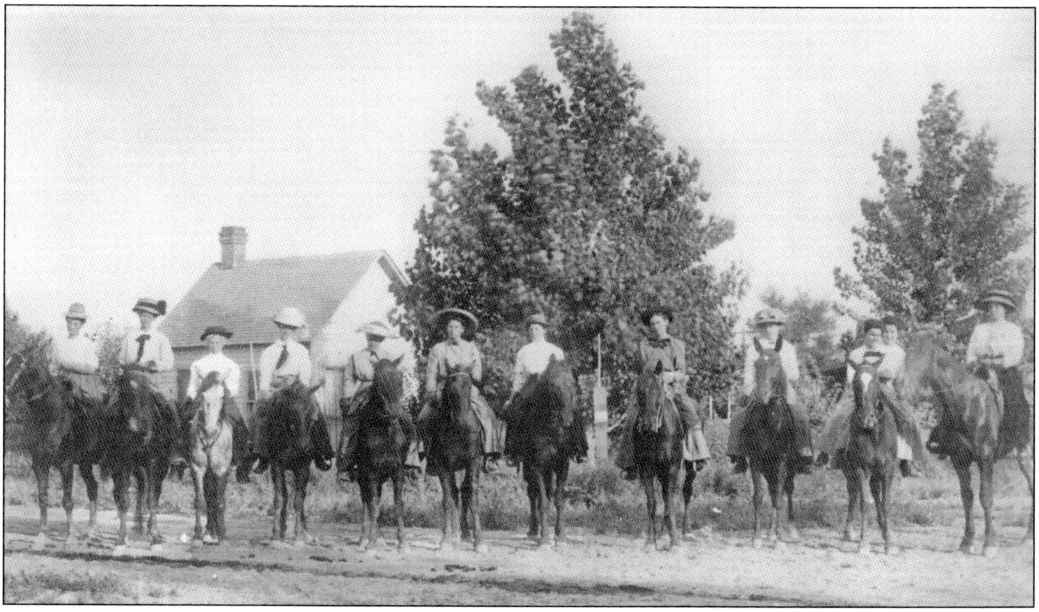

Among the many social groups in early Grandview was the Ladies Riding Club, shown here in 1913. From left to right are Mrs. Skirving, Mrs. Blew, Ann E. Sykes (postmistress), Miss Doyle, Mrs. Balcom, Mrs. Hawn, Mrs. Bower, Alice Wentch, Mrs. Vennum, Mrs. Nelch and Mrs. Butler (on same horse), and Mrs. Bone.

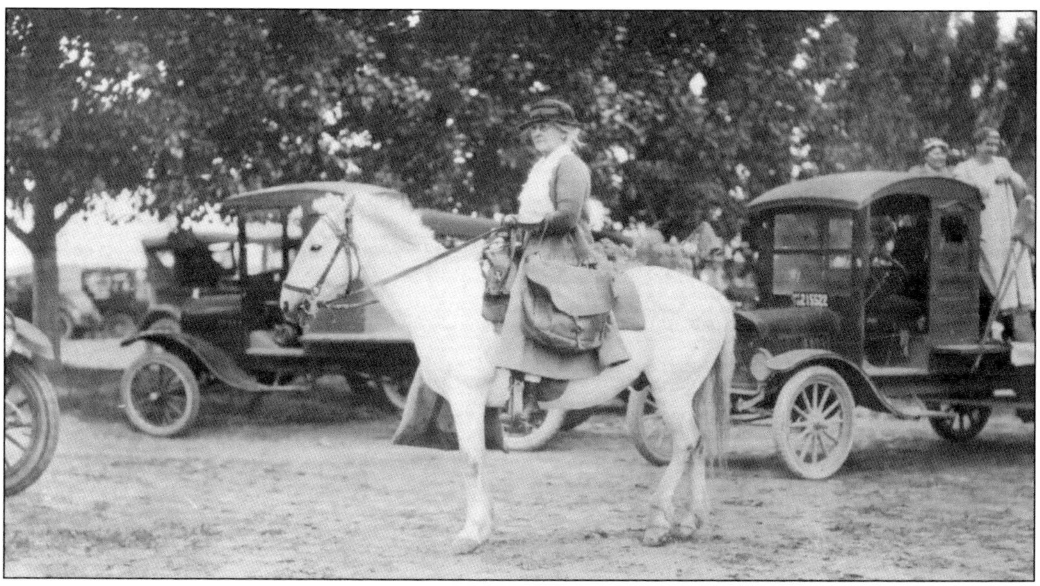

Before coming to Grandview, Ann E. Sykes and her husband ran a country store and post office in Coledale, Illinois. She was appointed postmistress when the town was founded on April 25, 1906. According to W.D. Lyman in *History of the Yakima Valley, Washington*, Sykes was a "brave, self-reliant woman, capable and resourceful, and is very popular among the people of the community."

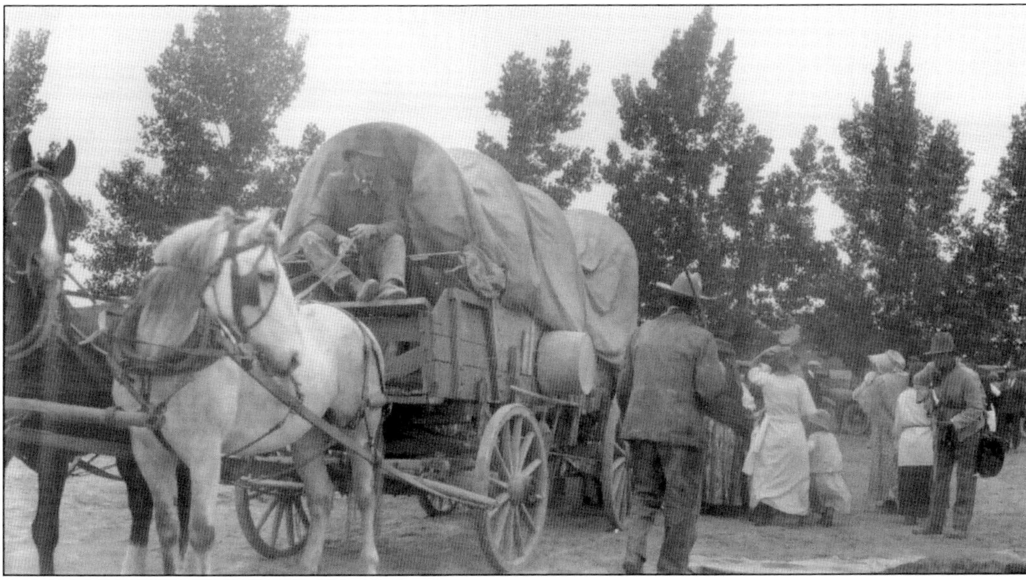

Grandview has held a community celebration each year in the fall for as long as anyone can remember. The celebrations have been known by several names over the years, including the Pioneer Frolic, Community Days, and the Harvest Festival. In 1924, attendees were encouraged to dress in appropriate period costumes for this reenactment of the journey along the Oregon Trail during the Pioneer Frolic. Roy Keller is driving the wagon in the photograph above. The current celebration, the Yakima Valley Fair and Rodeo, takes place each year in August at the Country Fair Park Events Center on Wallace Way.

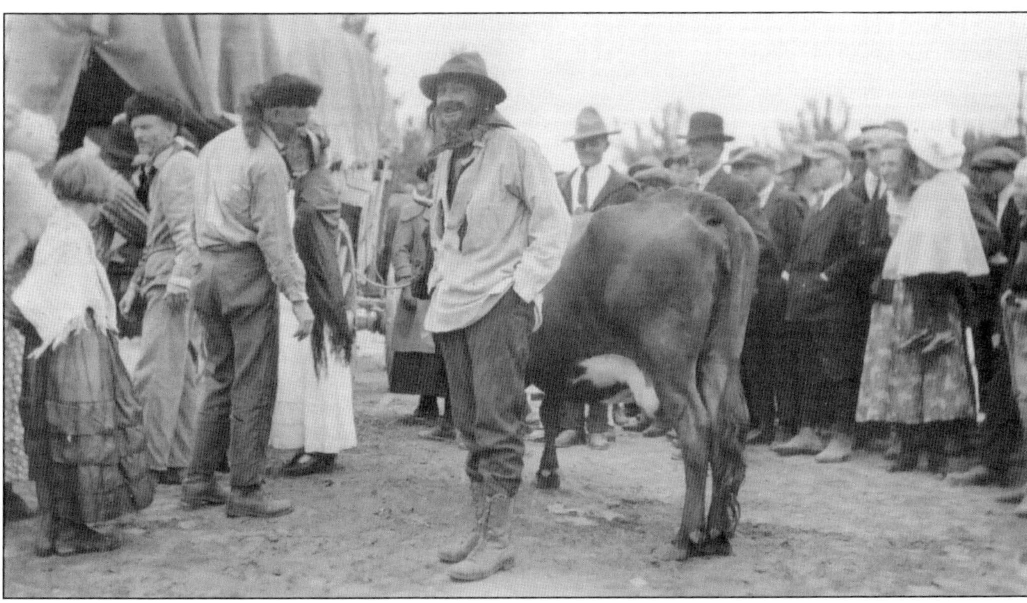

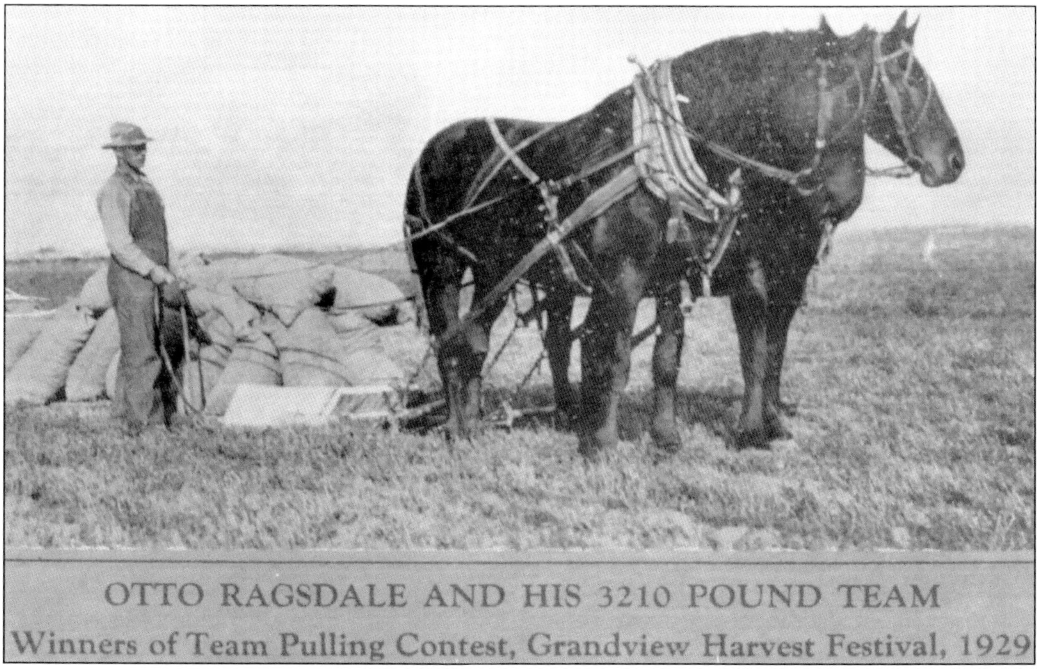

Horse pulling is a competition where harnessed horses pull a weighted sled, and the winning team is the one that pulls the most weight a specific distance. Otto Ragsdale and his 3,210-pound team (above) won the second annual team pull during the Harvest Festival in 1929 by pulling 6,000 pounds. In 1946, Woodrow Cox's team (below) won the lightweight division with a pull of 5,000 pounds. Otto Ragsdale, who was still active in the sport, is the crouching judge to the right. Today, the event is presented by the Washington Draft Horse Pullers Association and sponsored by local businesses and individuals.

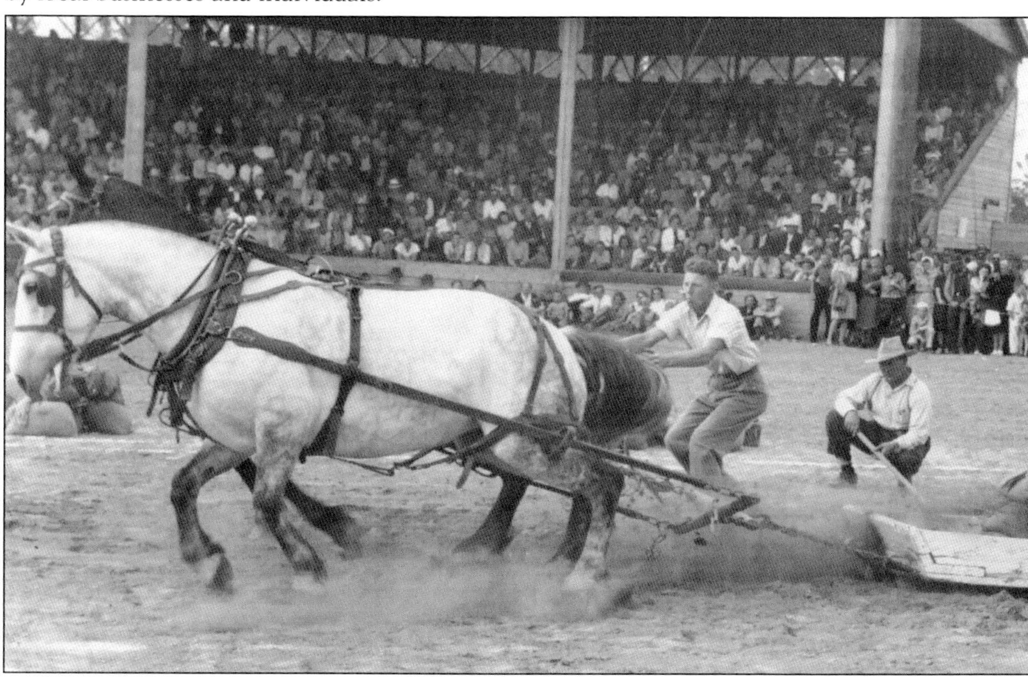

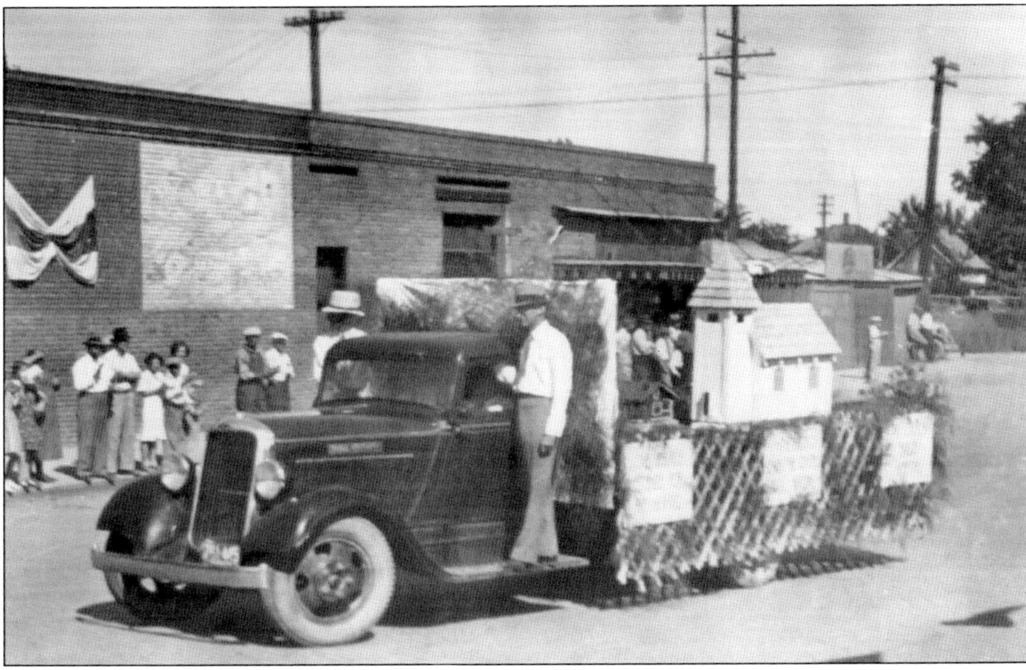

Early each September, Grandview's Harvest Festival featured farm and orchard exhibits, a flower show, a parade, a horse show, 4-H Club contests, and handicraft exhibits. According to *Washington: a Guide to the Evergreen State*, published in 1941 by the Washington State Historical Society, "More than 12,000 persons watched the parade" in 1938. These two photographs show examples of parade entries: the 1935 Methodist church float (above) and an unidentified float from 1941 (below). Both of these images show the parade on Second Street, with the landmark Grandview Leader building prominently labeled below.

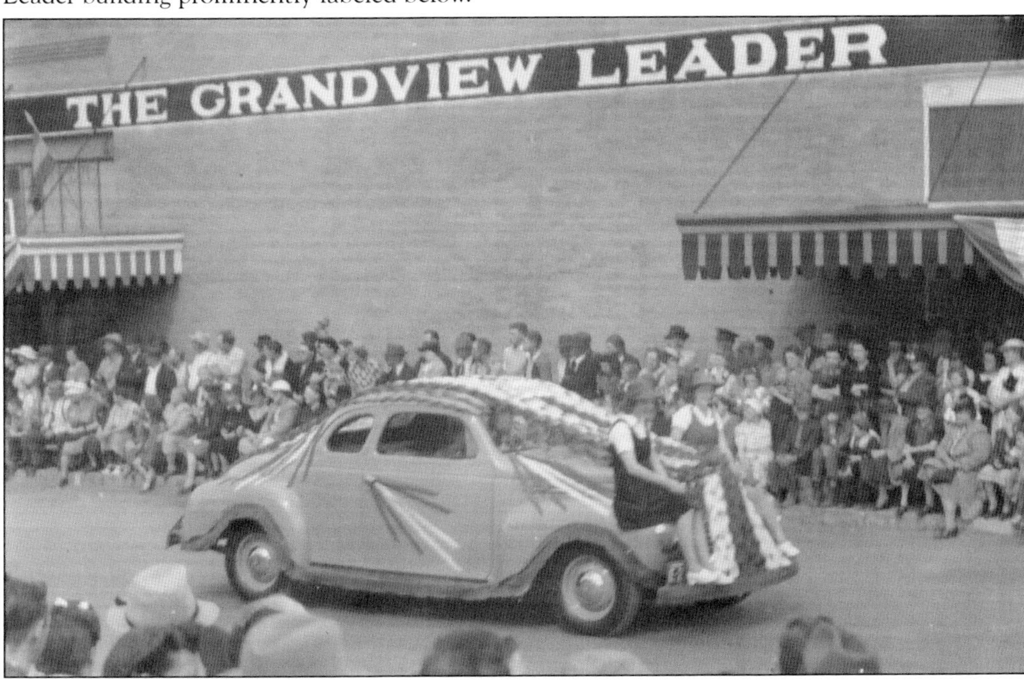

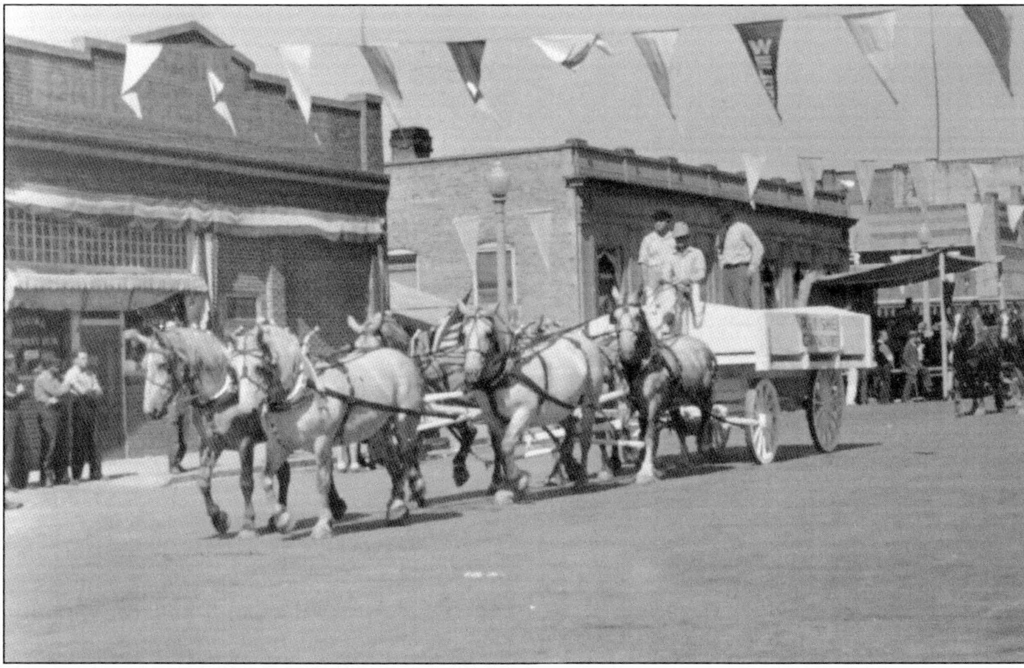

A beautiful matching team of horses pulls a farm wagon in this undated photograph of the Harvest Festival parade traveling south on Division Street. Although horses are a common element of any rural parade, these huge "athletes" were probably on display for the annual horse pulling contests.

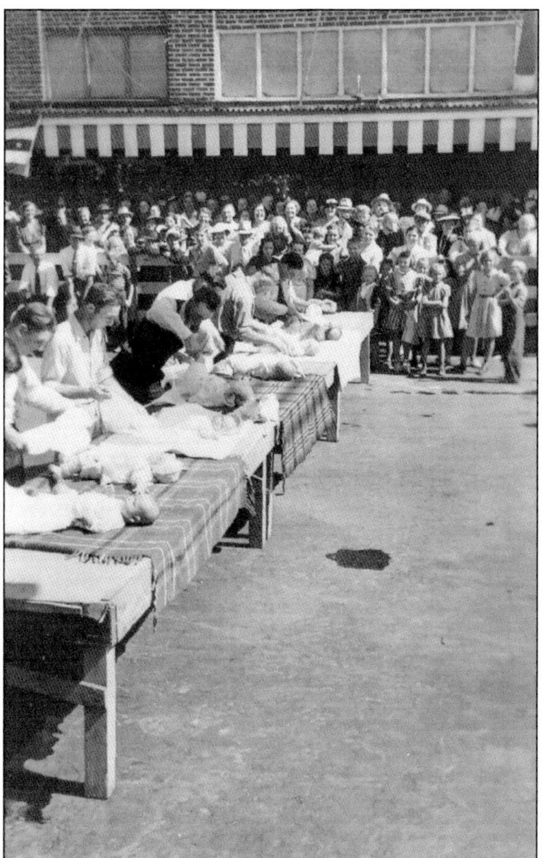

Division Street was blocked off between Main and Second Streets to be the staging area for community events during the Harvest Festival. One well-attended and exciting event was a race for "diapering dads," seen here. The third man from the left is Lester B. Judd, although the year is unknown.

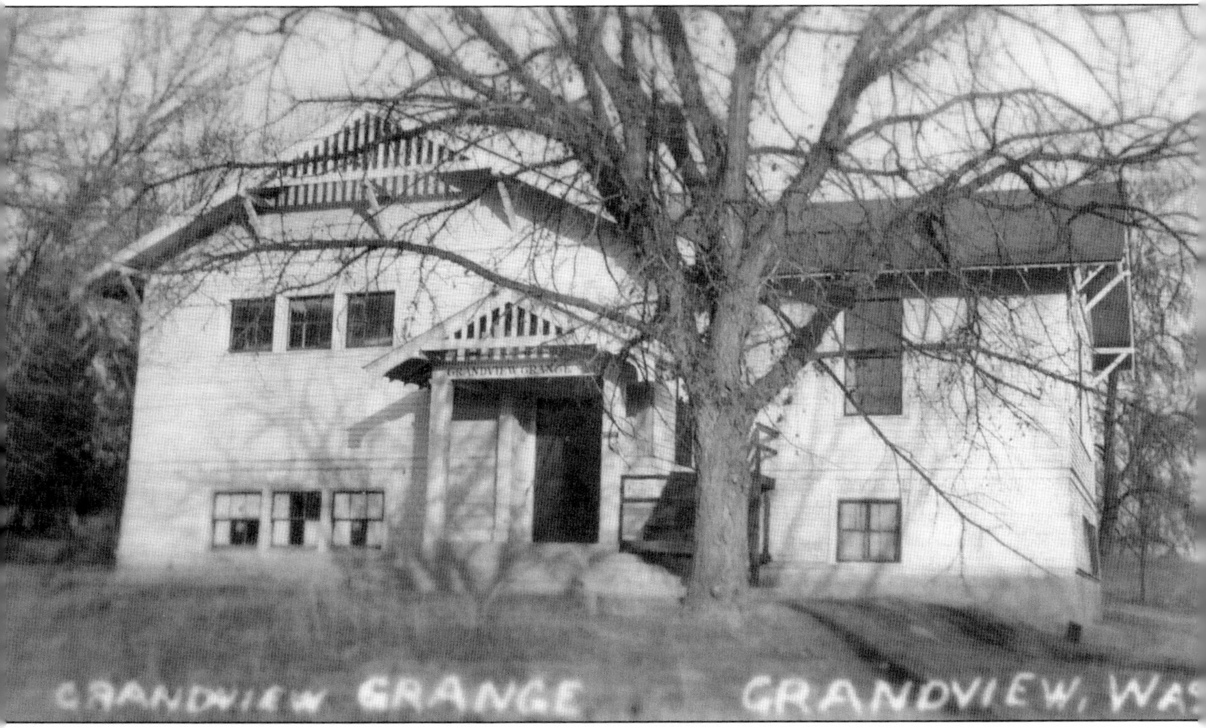

The women of the community organized their own clubs for socializing and community service. *History of Grandview, Washington* mentions the Women's Club, the Neighbor Club, the Home Interest Club, the Euclid Homemaker's Club; the Mothers' Club of Bethany, the Jolly Ranchers' Club, the Pleasant Avenue Club, the Ladies' Golf Club, the Sage Bush Sisters, and Chapter AU, PEO Sisterhood. The latter two organized in 1907 and 1921, respectively, and both continue to this day. Not to be outdone by the ladies, local men began the Outlook Club and the Rotary Club. At the time the Grandview Rotary was created, Grandview held the distinction of being the smallest community in the world to have a Rotary Club. The influential District Club was the most important in town, and, while women were not barred from joining, the membership was made up mostly of men. Seen here is the Grandview Grange, organized in February 1910 with 26 charter members.

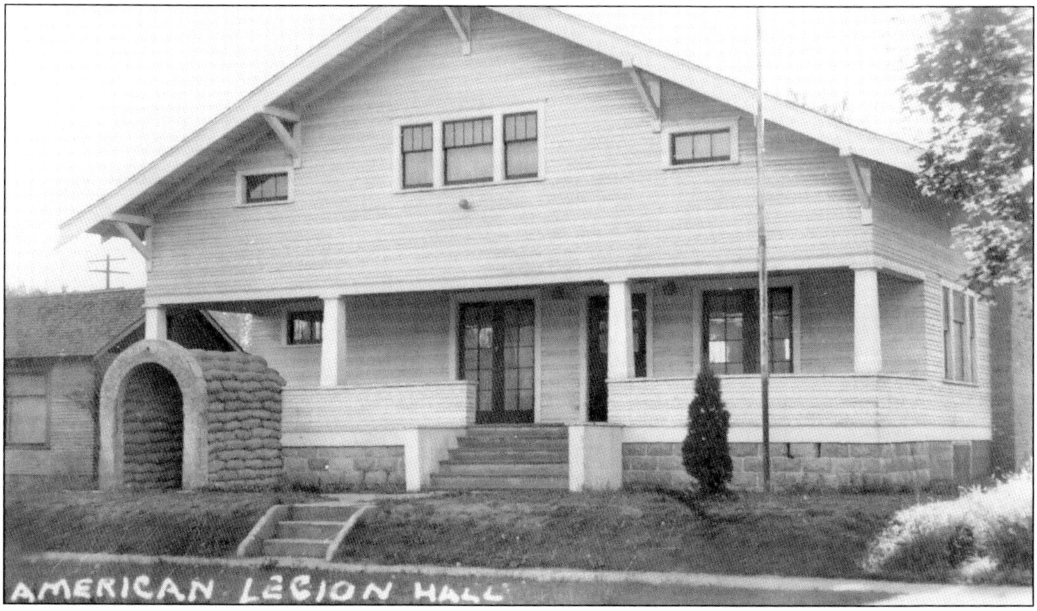

In 1919, a group of returning World War I veterans created an American Legion post named for one of their members. Fred E. Hayes Post 57 of the American Legion received its charter on October 20, 1919, and the ladies auxiliary was formed in May 1920. The legion hall was erected in 1920 on East Avenue B. From 1924 to 1931, the library took over the main floor of the building, and the legion post held its meetings in the basement.

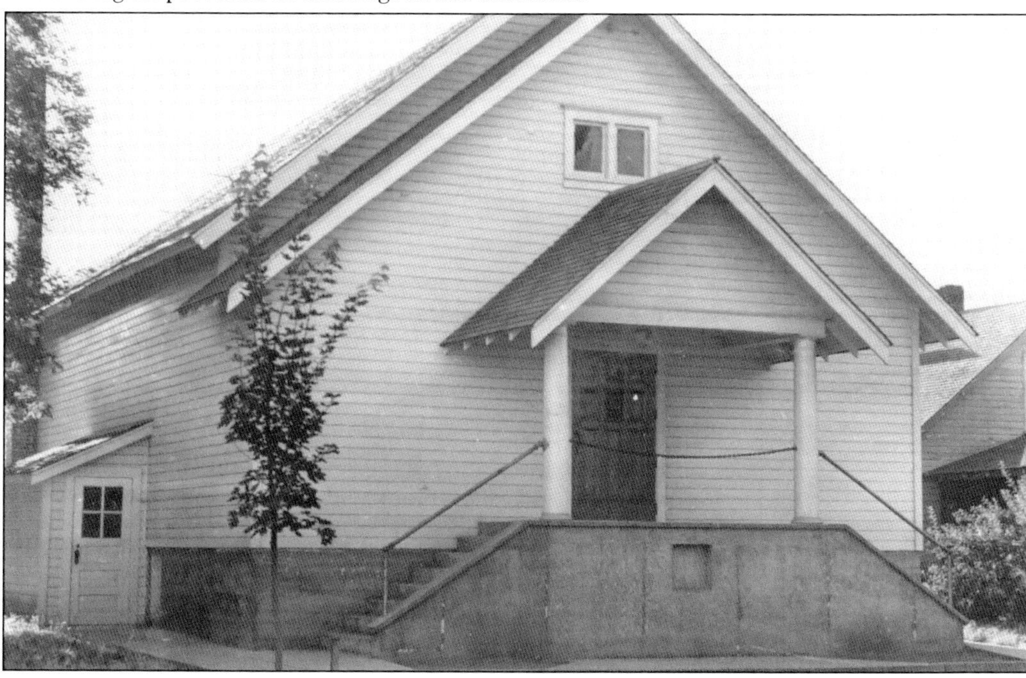

On January 3, 1912, a dispensation was granted by D.S. Prescott, grand master of the Grand Lodge of Washington, to a group of local men to organize a local Masonic lodge. They held their first meeting in the Moody Building. By April 24, their wives and daughters formed a chapter of the Order of the Eastern Star. This building, at 207 Ash Avenue, was dedicated on November 15, 1940.

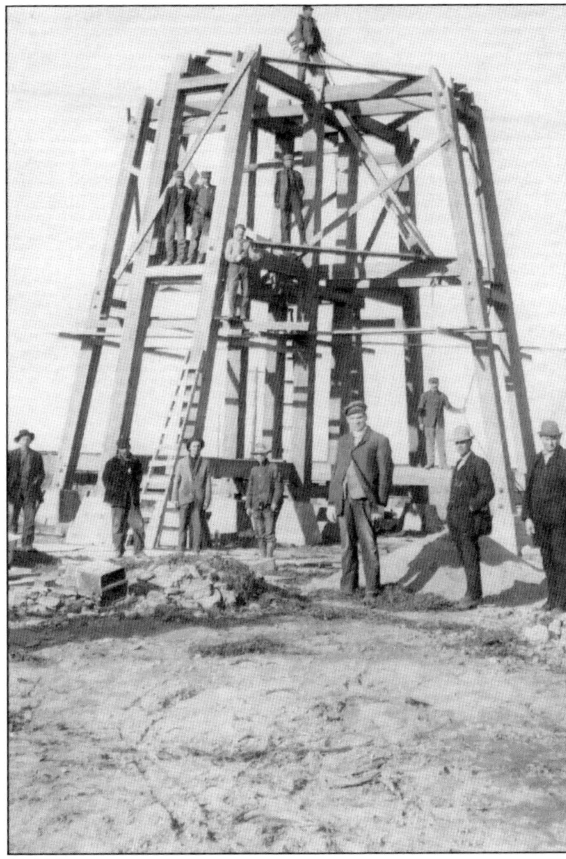

Although it is unknown if both of these photographs are of the same works project, it is evident by the presence of assistant street commissioner Peter J. Boye in both that they are from the same period. Boye, originally from Norway, was also deputy sheriff from 1915 to 1920. In the construction photograph of the city's first water tower (right), Boye is standing at the base of the structure, the second man from left. Below, Boye is the man with the "X" mark above his head. The crew is digging the first water mains along what eventually became Main Street.

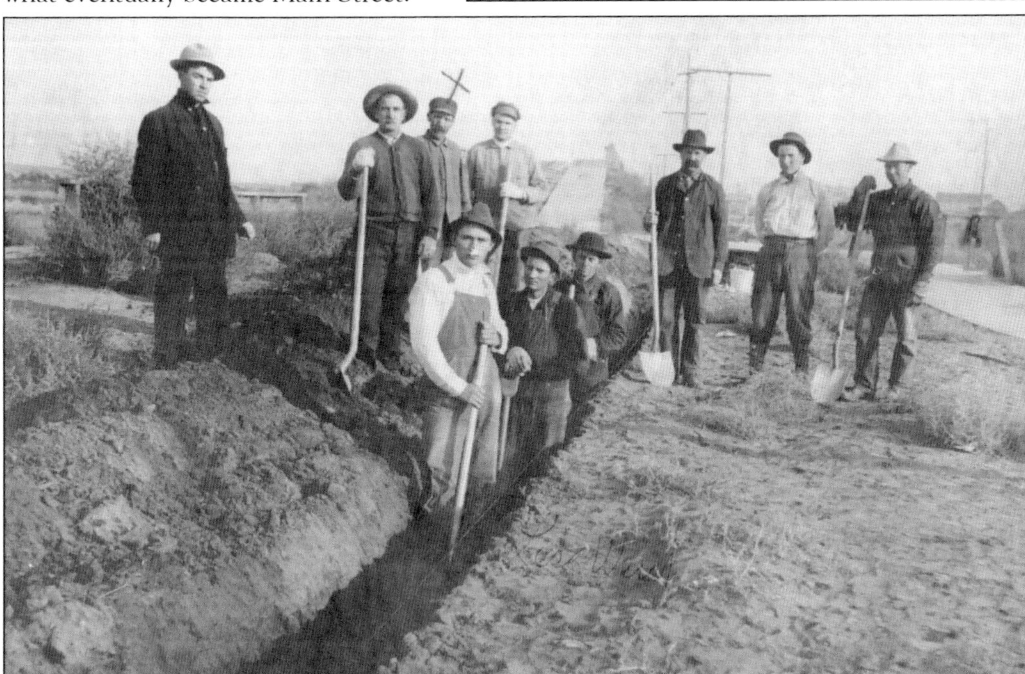

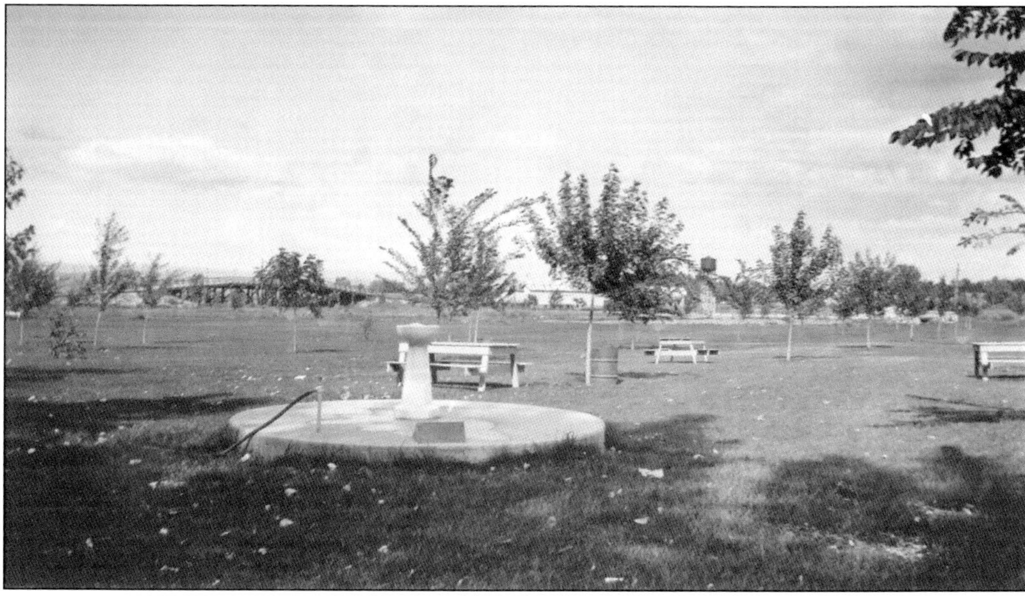

West Side Park, seen in both these photographs, was Grandview's first public park. In 1924, the Women's Club, along with local firefighters, obtained Grandview blocks 11 and 12 and part of block 31, at a cost of $350. The deed was made to the City of Grandview, and Mayor C.E. Haines appointed the first park board, consisting of George W. Parchen, Guy Painter, and James Anderson, on October 7, 1924. A donation drive was held, and local citizens donated $1,178.68, with another $700 pledged, along with 40–50 days of teamwork. On April 2, 1925, local businesses closed so the citizens could gather with shovels to dig ditches and plant trees. Irrigation pipe was laid, much of the area was seeded with grass, and a caretaker was hired. In 1928, the Women's Club installed a beautiful drinking fountain at a cost of $96.

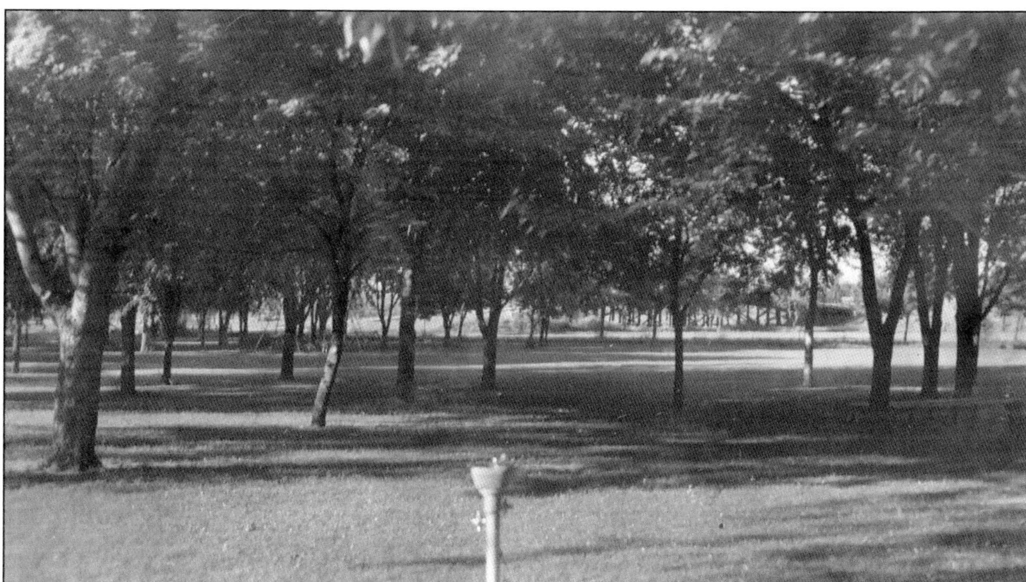

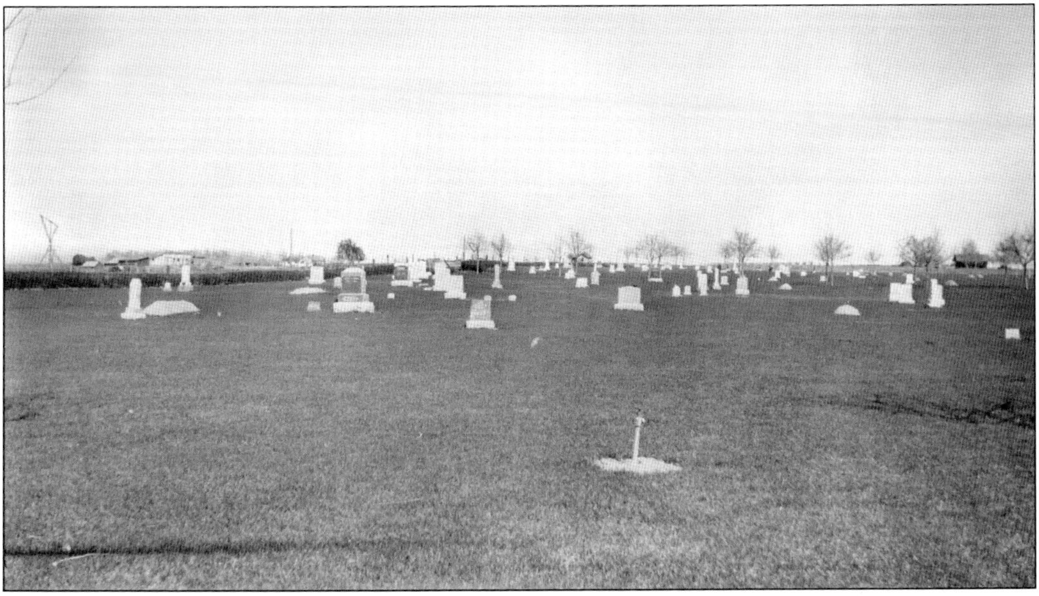

Platted in 1914 on North Elm Street, the Grandview Cemetery is maintained by the Grandview Public Works Department. Records show that many military veterans of World Wars I and II, as well as later conflicts, are buried there. But the burial entry for Claude V. Eliss (1874–1935) is unique. Eliss was a member of the United Spanish War Hospital Corps in 1898. Later, in 1918, at the age of 44, he registered for the World War I draft.

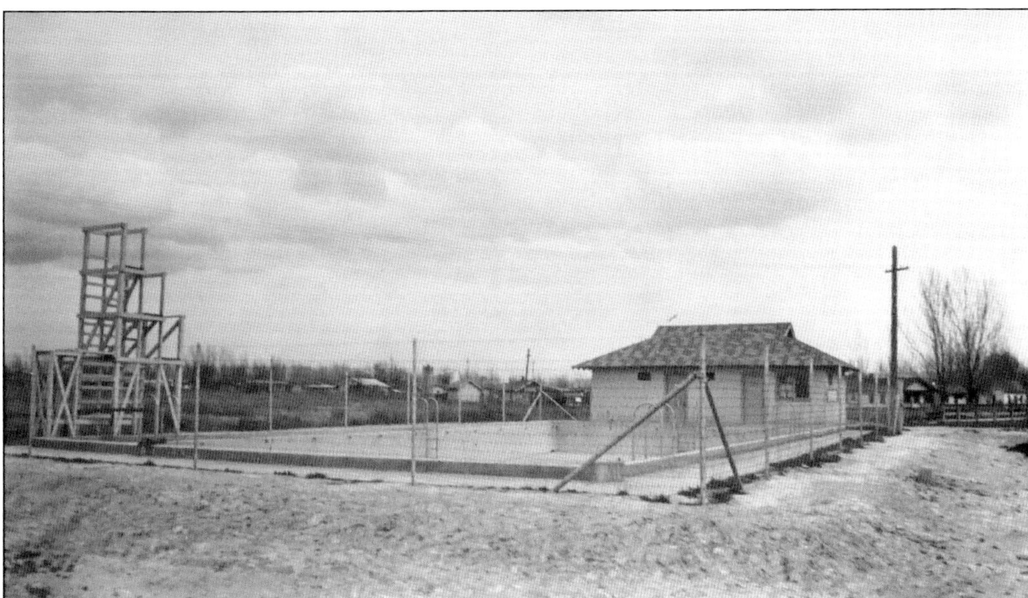

The first municipal swimming pool was funded by public donations and dedicated on July 12, 1927. The $5,000 cost for the swimming pool and the improvements of walks and a bathhouse was funded by contributions from individuals and organizations, with the largest amounts coming from the Grandview Rotary and District Clubs. The pool was located at West Side Park.

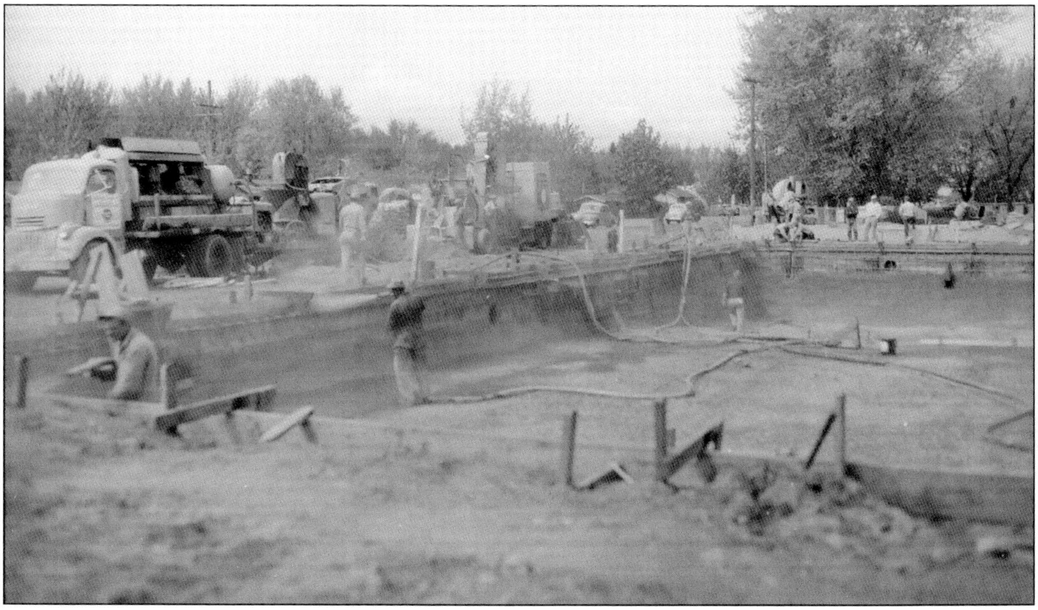

One of the ongoing improvements to West Side Park was the construction of a new swimming pool in 1955. Surrounded by 300 feet of chain-link fence, the pool was built at a cost of $75,000. A total of 24 trees were removed to make way for the pool, and 25 new table and seat combinations were added for picnic facilities. Dedication ceremonies were held on June 15, 1956, with over 400 people enrolling for swimming lessons. To this day, the swimming pool remains a major attraction to the citizens of Grandview during the summer months. It is also home to the Grandview Neptunes Rotary Swim Team.

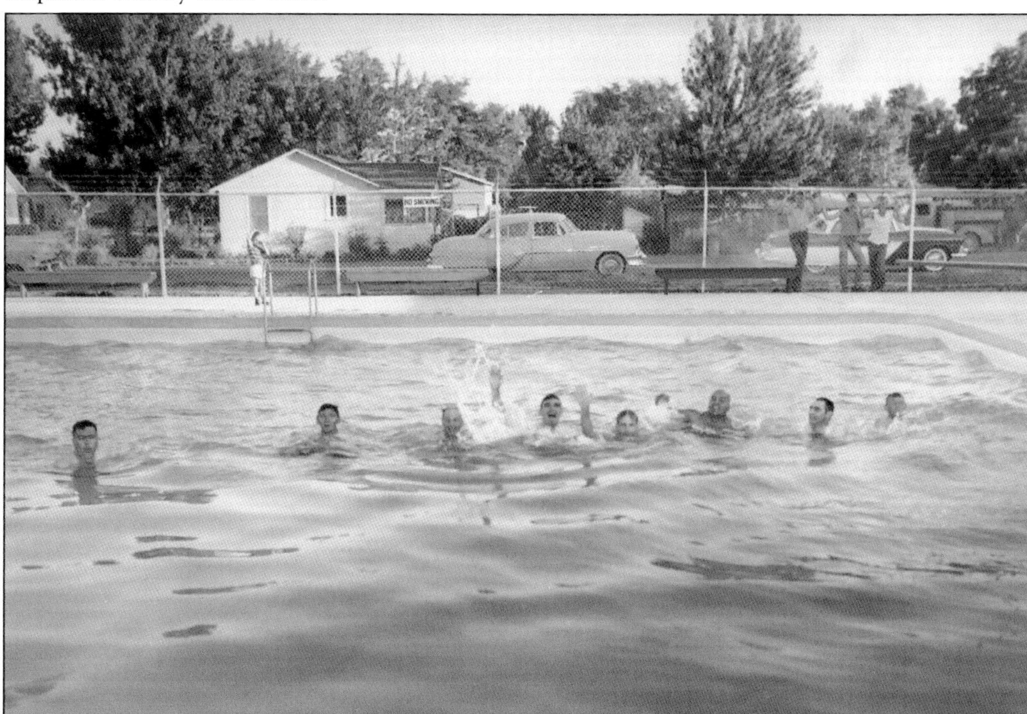

Possibly the only one remaining of its kind, this Kiblinger Horseless Carriage, shown at right with R.E. Powell Museum board members Magdalene Olmstead and Ernest Cowles, is a rare tiller-steered automobile built by the W.H. Kiblinger Company in 1907. The automobile was purchased new that year by a Portland, Oregon, physician who used it for house calls. He in turn sold it to a man in Gresham, Oregon, for $10 and a pocketknife. The automobile was next purchased in 1934 by Earl Shirk of Mabton. In 1935, Shirk was showing it at a parade near an automobile dealership that had a 1903 Oldsmobile. Local firefighters instigated a race between the two, which was easily won by the Kiblinger. Below, Ray E. Powell is shown at the "wheel" of the old vehicle.

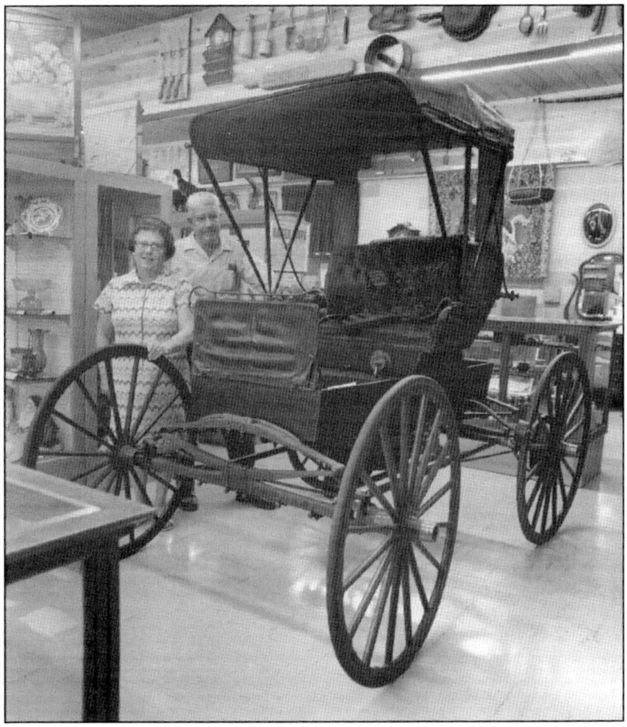

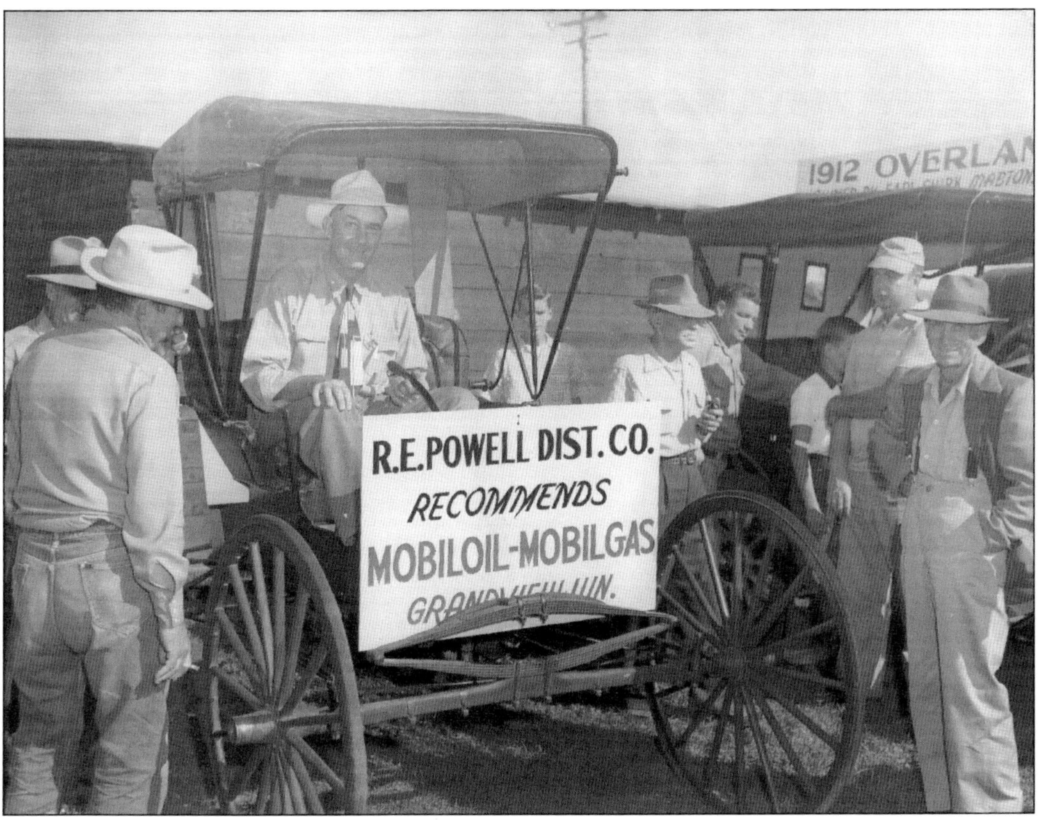

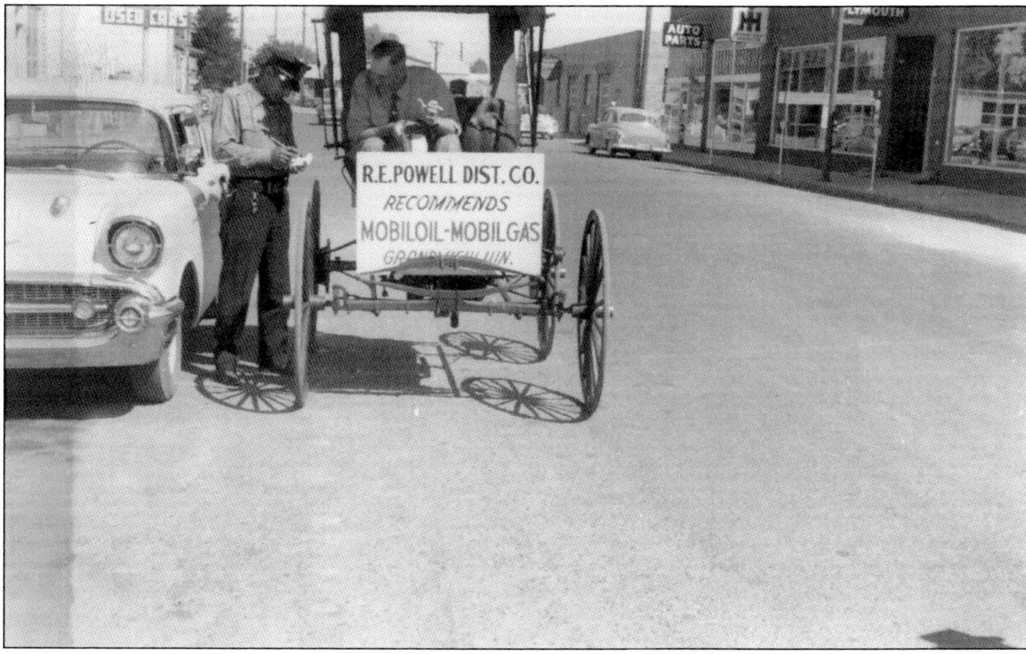

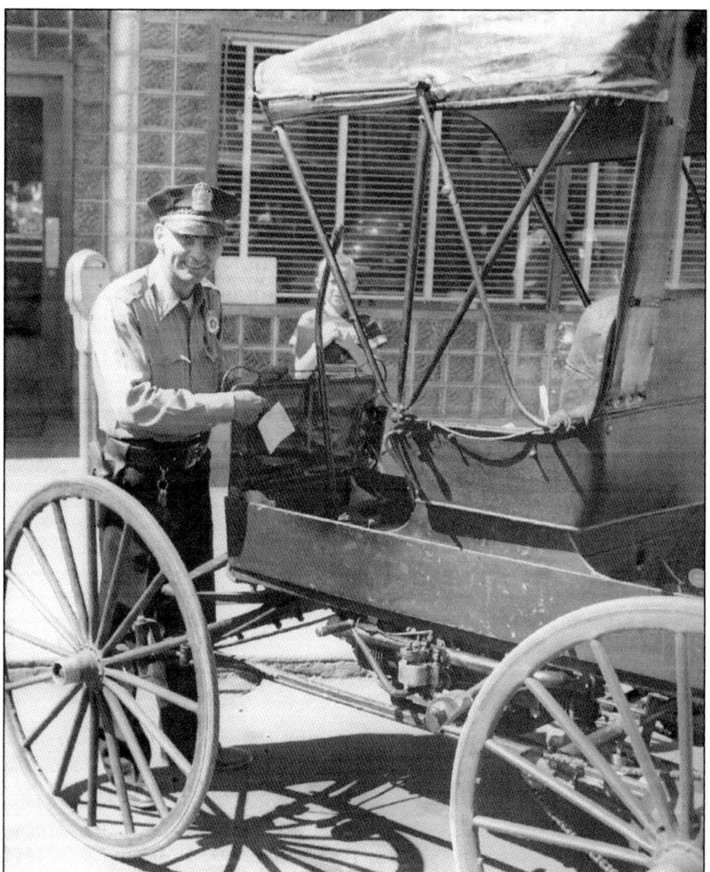

Police chief Ted Wolfe is shown above "ticketing" Ray E. Powell of R.E. Powell Distributing Co. on Avenue A, presumably for the lack of a license plate and other infractions. Powell was the benefactor and namesake of the R.E. Powell Museum. The museum was built mainly to display this rare old Kiblinger Highwheeler. Powell obviously did not get the message, because he forgot to put money in the parking meter and so received yet another ticket from the chief (left). Interestingly, the Kiblinger has lasted longer than the parking meters, which have been gone for quite some time, while the old Model A remains safe behind the museum doors.

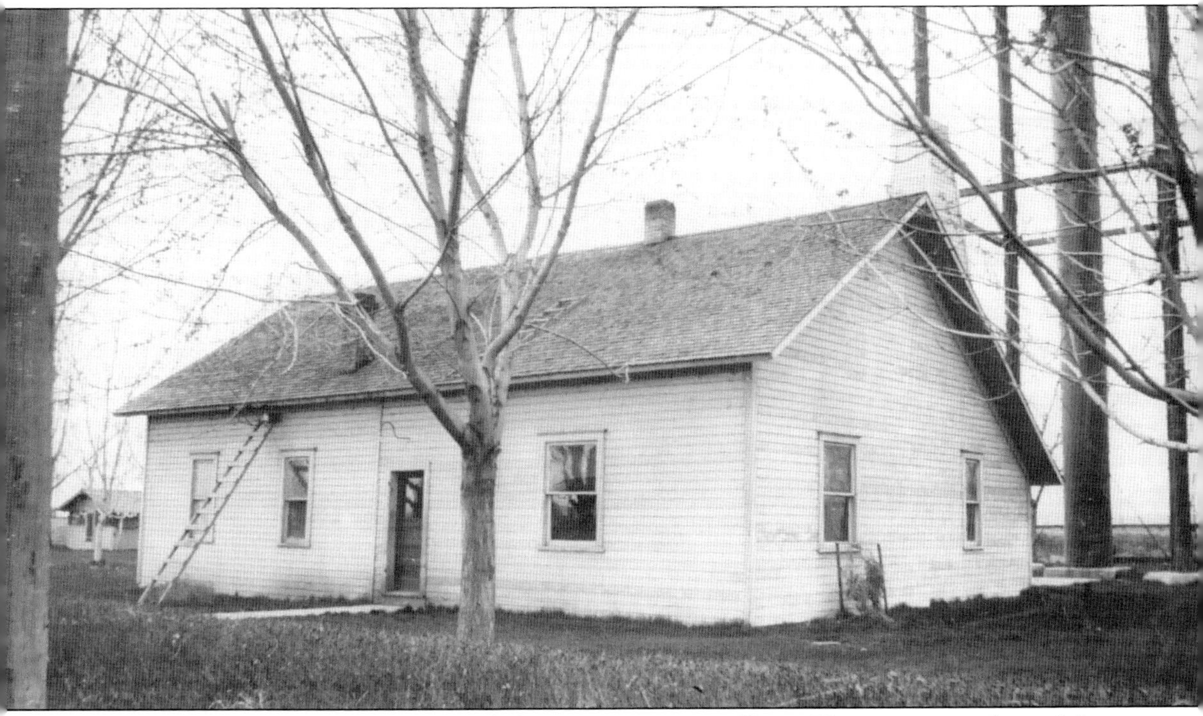

In the summer of 1909, a caucus was called to nominate town officers. Those nominated were John Monroe, mayor; A.W. Hawn, treasurer; and W.R. Elser, D.L. Robertson, A.E. Fisk, C.R. Moulton, and Frank G. Bennett, council members. G.D. Snowden was appointed clerk and Ed Dawson marshal. Ward Wheeler, of the Yakima firm of Holden, Shumate & Wheeler, was chosen as city attorney. The budget for the coming year of 1910 was expected to be $2,215. The building shown here was home to the first city hall. A pump house was added on the right side in 1922.

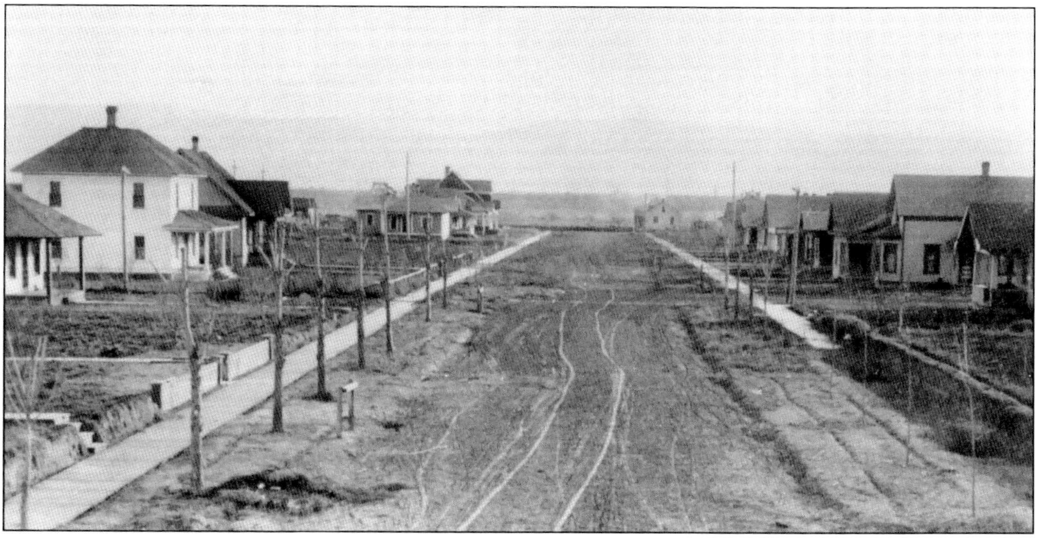

The undated photograph above shows an unidentified residential street in Grandview. The view is to the south, with the faint outline of the Horse Heaven Hills visible on the far horizon. The early springtime view, as evidenced by the recently pruned trees, shows newly built houses along the packed dirt street. Hitching posts can be seen in front of the first houses on the left. In contrast with the photograph above, the view today looking south on Cedar Street (below) is obstructed by large trees. Several homes along the street date from Grandview's early years.

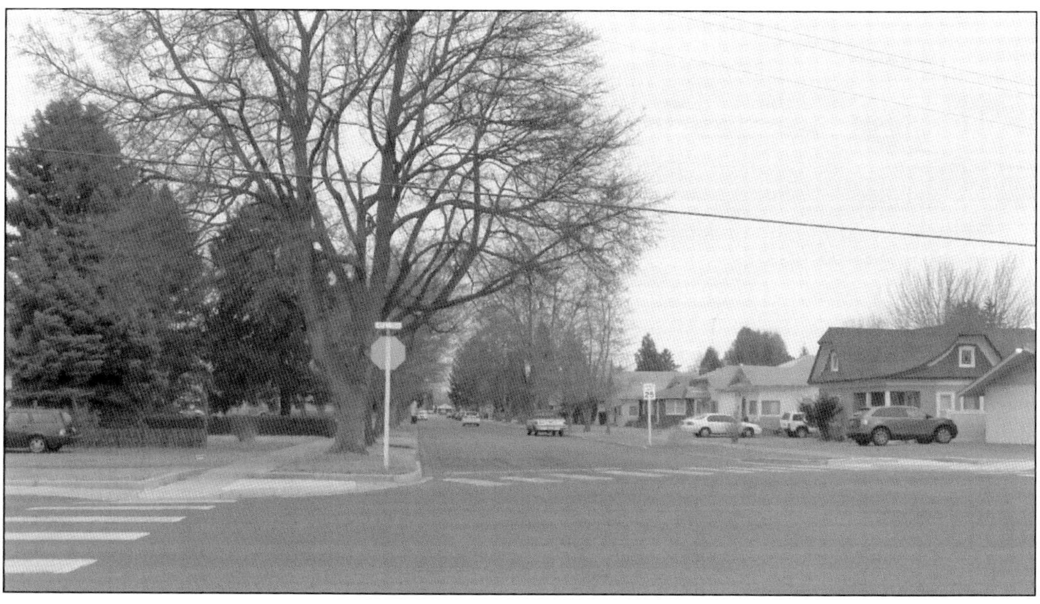

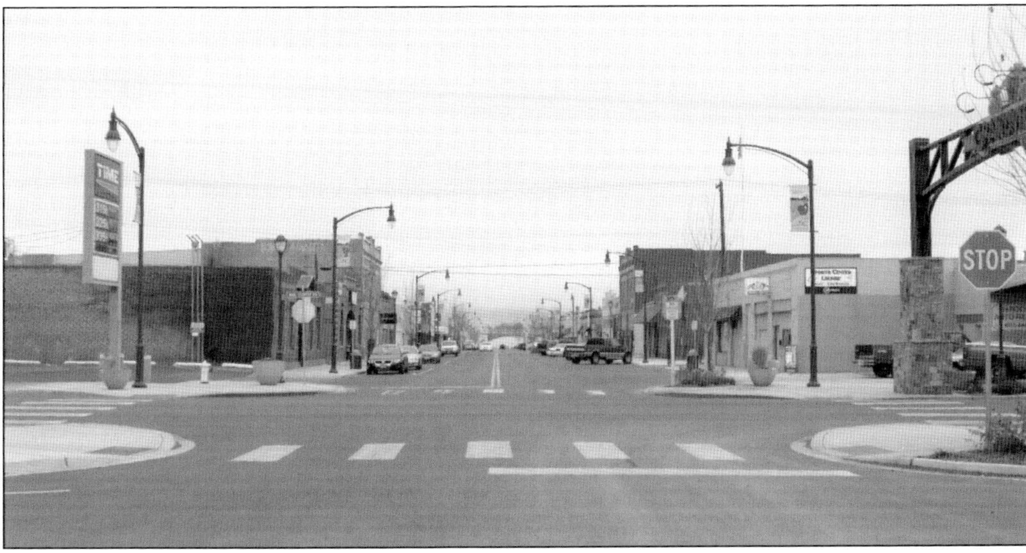

The view looking south on Division Street today (above) is not much different from earlier photographs, with the Iowa Building (left) and the E.O. Keck Building (right) still serving as anchor points. In 2006, a plan to revitalize downtown, called Alive Downtown, was adopted; by 2008, the city had accumulated $3.8 million from several different sources to fund the project. The award-winning effort, completed in 2010, has since influenced other small towns in Washington to take on similar projects. The archway across Main Street (below) welcomes visitors and townspeople alike, while also drawing the eye to the far horizon, where Mount Adams rises in the distance, reminding all that it is, indeed, a "Grand View." (Above, author's collection; below, courtesy of Mike Carpenter.)

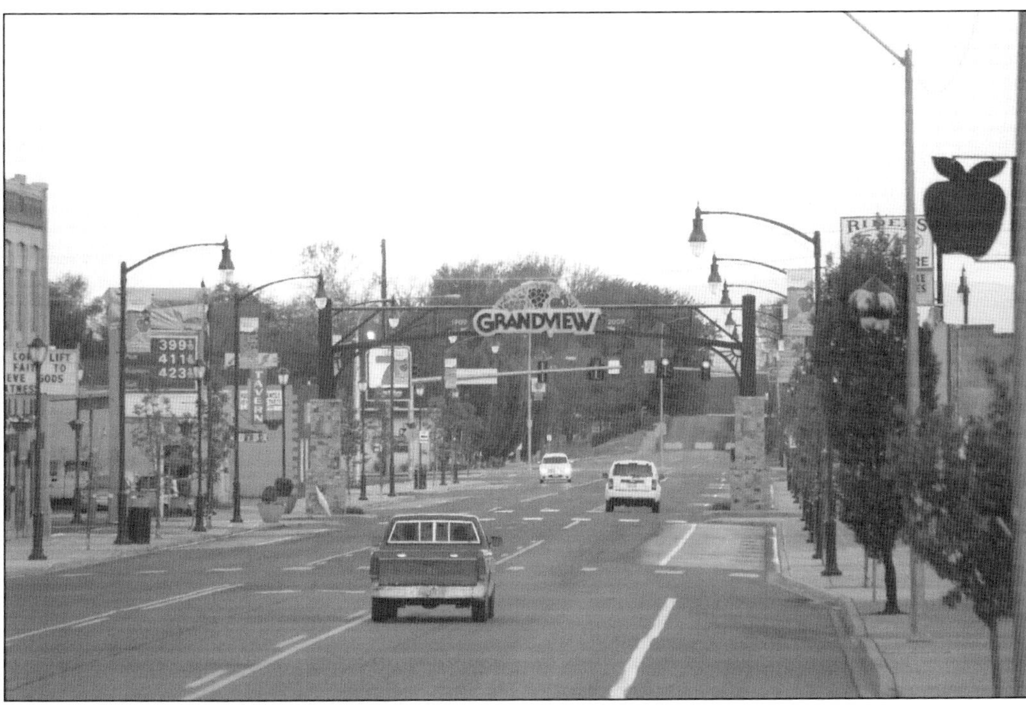

Bibliography

Grandview Pioneer Association. *History of Grandview, Washington*. Grandview, WA: Grandview Pioneer Association, 1927.

Lyman, W.D. *History of the Yakima Valley, Washington: Comprising Yakima, Kittitas and Benton Counties*. Chicago, IL: S.J. Clarke Publishing, 1919.

Oregon-Washington Railroad & Navigation Co. and the Grandview Commercial Club. *Grand View, Yakima Valley, Washington*. Grandview, WA: publicity brochure, 1912.

Washington State Historical Society. *Washington: A Guide to the Evergreen State*. Portland, OR: Metropolitan Press, 1941.

INDEX